CRIMINAL JUSTICE IN TRANSITION

This book represents a critical examination of key aspects of crime and criminal justice in Northern Ireland which will have resonance elsewhere. It considers the core aspects of criminal justice policymaking in Northern Ireland which are central to the process of post-conflict transition, including reform of policing, judicial decision-making and correctional services such as probation and prisons. It examines contemporary trends in criminal justice in Northern Ireland and various dimensions of crime relating to female offenders, young offenders, sexual and violent offenders, community safety and restorative justice. The book also considers the extent to which crime and criminal justice issues in Northern Ireland are being affected by the broader processes of 'policy transfer', globalisation and transnationalism and the extent to which criminal justice in Northern Ireland is divergent from the other jurisdictions in the United Kingdom. Written by leading international authorities in the field, the book offers a snapshot of the cutting edge of critical thinking in criminal justice practice and transitional justice contexts.

Criminal Justice in Transition

The Northern Ireland Context

Edited by
Anne-Marie McAlinden
and
Clare Dwyer

• HART •
PUBLISHING
OXFORD AND PORTLAND, OREGON
2017

Hart Publishing
An imprint of Bloomsbury Publishing Plc

Hart Publishing Ltd
Kemp House
Chawley Park
Cumnor Hill
Oxford OX2 9PH
UK

Bloomsbury Publishing Plc
50 Bedford Square
London
WC1B 3DP
UK

www.hartpub.co.uk
www.bloomsbury.com

Published in North America (US and Canada) by
Hart Publishing
c/o International Specialized Book Services
920 NE 58th Avenue, Suite 300
Portland, OR 97213-3786
USA

www.isbs.com

First published in hardback, 2015
Paperback edition, 2017

British Library Cataloguing-in-Publication Data
A catalogue record for this book is available from the British Library.

ISBN: PB: 978-1-50991-833-1
HB: 978-1-84946-577-9

Typeset by Compuscript Ltd, Shannon
Printed and bound in Great Britain by
Lightning Source UK Ltd

FOREWORD

LEARNING ABOUT JUSTICE IN NORTHERN IRELAND

When I worked at the State University of New York in the 1990s, the policing expert and distinguished professor David Bayley would return from trips to Belfast as part of his work on the Oversight Commission for the Reform of the Police in Northern Ireland perplexed and annoyed—not at the Police Service of Northern Ireland, but rather at academic criminologists. 'Why isn't every criminologist going to Northern Ireland?' he used to lament to anyone who would listen. 'Don't they realise what is going on there and how remarkable this is?'

It is safe to say that most criminologists, internationally, did not then, nor do they now, have a good idea of what goes on in Northern Ireland. Parochialism has notoriously plagued criminology with North American criminologists showing little concern for justice practices or research findings in countries like France, Japan or Scandinavia, let alone in developing countries or in small transitional societies like Northern Ireland. British criminologists are also famously disinterested in reading about Northern Ireland. Cambridge Professor Anthony Bottoms used to joke that using the words 'Northern Ireland' in the title of an article in the *British Journal of Criminology* was the surest way to assure no one would read what you wrote. From my experience, even Irish criminologists find what happens north of the border to be of little relevance to their primary concerns in the south as well, and much of the growing scholarship around Irish criminology excludes mention of Northern Ireland's six counties.

This is a tremendous oversight. I have now lived for a decade in Northern Ireland, observing every aspect of the criminal justice system as the former Director of the Institute of Criminology and Criminal Justice at Queen's University Belfast. These experiences convinced me that Bayley was right: there is an enormous amount to learn from Northern Ireland. Indeed, because of its unique historical, constitutional and cultural context, Northern Ireland may be the ideal laboratory for the understanding of crime and justice in the English speaking world.

For one thing, criminology in Northern Ireland forces us to challenge and confront all of the taken-for-granted assumptions that cloud our thinking around justice issues. In most contexts internationally, thinking around policing, imprisonment and reintegration have become so widely accepted, they risk becoming tedious, *ho-hum* subjects for criminology students and ordinary citizens alike. 'Of course, police should police in the way they do and we should lock people up in the cages we do. It has always been this way and that's just the way it is in every country on earth'. There are debates to be had around the margins of these things, but largely a conservative consensus has emerged around thinking, literally, 'inside the box' on most criminal justice issues. This is far from the case in Northern Ireland's recent history.

Students from outside Northern Ireland are routinely shocked when I tell them that it was only in the past decade that the second largest political party in Northern Ireland voted to recognise the legitimacy of the Police Service of Northern Ireland. How can that be? How can a society function when whole neighbourhoods do not support the police or welcome their presence on the streets to resolve disputes or protect citizens? In Northern Ireland's recent history, this is not a hypothetical thought experiment in a philosophy class; it is a sociological reality on the ground in the streets of West Belfast or Free Derry. Moreover, the results—both legacies of punishment violence and knee-cappings as well as remarkable innovations in community restorative justice projects on all sides of the community—are utterly fascinating and could fill a semester of Durkheimian sociology seminars.

Similar fundamental questions arise when issues like imprisonment, the court system, surveillance, and even probation are addressed in the context of the long-standing constitutional conflict in Northern Ireland and the efforts to build peace there. If probationers need to learn right from wrong or have their cognitive deficits corrected, does this apply to someone who has been convicted on politically motivated charges? What punishment should be given to citizens for rioting when elected political leaders are actively or implicitly encouraging these actions from the safety of their legislative offices? Should the criminal justice system double as a security sector preventing overthrows of the government? What about when the constitutional legitimacy of the state is in dispute? Northern Ireland is *the* place to ask all of these questions in the European context.

The student of crime and justice in Northern Ireland asks not only 'What is probation for?' or 'What is policing for?'; they ask 'What is justice for?' In other words, they start to get to the very heart of the criminological enterprise. The place is simply that fascinating. My recommendation, like that of David Bayley, is to go to Northern Ireland, by all means, and spend as long as you can trying to understand the entrenched and seemingly intractable problems faced by the police and prison services there. While you are at it, get involved in efforts to transform the place through its justice system (and no transformation, no peace, will ever be possible until the criminal justice system can be normalised).

But, if you haven't the time for that, then I strongly recommend instead that you read this important new volume by Anne-Marie McAlinden and Clare Dwyer. Its authors and editors are precisely the sorts of academics I describe above. No one is more immersed in the fascinating histories or day to day administrations of criminal justice in Northern Ireland than this impressive collection of contributors. And, like David Bayley coming back from one of his trips to Belfast, you will put down the book and start to question everything you thought you understood and believed about justice.

Shadd Maruna, Rutgers University Newark

Shadd Maruna is Dean and Professor of the School of Criminal Justice, Rutgers University Newark outside New York City. Prior to this, he was a professor at the School of Law, Queen's University Belfast for nine years. He still spends what passes for summers in Northern Ireland.

CONTENTS

LIST OF ABBREVIATIONS

BAME	Black and Minority Ethnic
CAJ	Committee on the Administration of Justice
CAT	Committee Against Torture
CAVR	Reception, Truth and Reconciliation Commission
CCRC	Criminal Cases Review Commission
CGP	Consultative Group on the Past
CIJ	Centre for Innovative Justice
CIRA	Continuity Irish Republican Army
CJINI	Criminal Justice Inspection Northern Ireland
CJR	Criminal Justice Review
CJRG	Criminal Justice Review Group
CONAPED	Comisión Nacional Sobre la Desaparición de Personas
CPO	Custody Probation Order
CPT	Committee for the Prevention of Torture and Inhuman or Degrading Treatment or Punishment
CRCs	Community Rehabilitation Companies
CRJI	Community Restorative Justice Ireland
CVSNI	Commission for Victims and Survivors Northern Ireland
DCS	Determinate Custodial Sentence
DDR	Disarmament, Demobilisation, and Reintegration
DHSS	Department of Health and Social Services
DHSSPS	Department of Health, Social Services and Public Safety
DoJ	Department of Justice
DoJNI	Department of Justice for Northern Ireland
DPP	Director of Public Prosecutions
DUP	Democratic Unionist Party
ECHR	European Convention on Human Rights
ECS	Extended Custodial Sentence
ECtHR	European Court of Human Rights
EM	Electronic Monitoring
EPAs	Emergency Provisions Acts
EPIC	Ex-Prisoners Interpretive Centre
EWCA	Court of Appeal in England and Wales
EXPAC	Ex-Prisoners Assistance Committee
HET	Historical Enquiries Team
HIU	Historical Investigations Unit
HMCIP	Her Majesty's Chief Inspector of Prisons
HMIC	Her Majesty's Inspectorate of Constabulary
HMP	Her Majesty's Prison

HO	Home Office
HRA	Human Rights Act
ICCJ	Institute of Criminology and Criminal Justice
ICIR	Independent Commission for Information Retrieval
ICPNI	Independent Commission on Policing for Northern Ireland
ICS	Indeterminate Custodial Sentence
IMB	Independent Monitoring Board
INLA	Irish National Liberation Army
IRA	Irish Republican Army
JAC	Judicial Appointments Commission
JARC	Judicial Appointments Review Committee
JJC	Juvenile Justice Centre
JPE	Judicial Performance and Evaluation
LINC	Local Initiatives for Needy Communities
LSRC	Life Sentence Review Commissioners
MAPPA	Multi-Agency Public Protection Arrangements
MASRAM	Multi-Agency Sex Offender Risk Assessment and Management
MoD	Ministry of Defence
MoJ	Ministry of Justice
NCCL	National Council for Civil Liberties
NCM	New Careers Movement
NDPB	Non-Departmental Public Body
NGO	Non-Governmental Organisation
NIA	Northern Ireland Alternatives
NIAC	Northern Ireland Affairs Committee
NIACRO	Northern Ireland Association for the Care and Resettlement of Offenders
NIAO	Northern Ireland Audit Office
NIARLS	Northern Ireland Assembly Research and Library Service
NICA	Northern Ireland Court of Appeal
NICCY	Northern Ireland Commissioner for Children and Young People
NICTS	Northern Ireland Courts and Tribunals Service
NICVA	Northern Ireland Council for Voluntary Action
NIHRC	Northern Ireland Human Rights Commission
NIJAC	Northern Ireland Judicial Appointments Commission
NIO	Northern Ireland Office
NIPB	Northern Ireland Policing Board
NIPS	Northern Ireland Prison Service
NIRPOA	Northern Ireland Retired Police Officers Association
NOMS	National Offender Management Service
NPS	National Probation Service
OAGNI	Office of Attorney General for Northern Ireland
ODCs	Ordinary Decent Criminals
OFMdFM	Office of First Minister and deputy First Minister
OHN	Óglaigh na hÉireann
OIRA	Official Irish Republican Army
ONS	Office for National Statistics
OOC	Office of the Oversight Commissioner
OPONI	Office of the Police Ombudsman for Northern Ireland

PACE	Police and Criminal Evidence (NI) Order 1989
PBNI	Probation Board for Northern Ireland
PFC	Pat Finucane Centre
PFNI	Police Federation for Northern Ireland
PHI	Probation History Interviews
PIRA	Provisional Irish Republican Army
PMFP	Politically Motivated Former Prisoner
POA	Prisoner Officers Association
PPANI	Public Protection Arrangements Northern Ireland
PPS	Public Prosecution Service
PROG	Prison Review Oversight Group
PRT	Prison Review Team
PSNI	Police Service of Northern Ireland
PSOs	Probation Service Officers
PSR	Pre-Sentence Report
REACT	Reconciliation Education and Community Training
RNR	Risk-Need-Responsivity
RSHO	Risk of Sexual Harm Order
RUC	Royal Ulster Constabulary
SACHR	Standing Advisory Commission on Human Rights
SATRC	South African Truth and Reconciliation Commission
SCS	Special Category Status
SEE	Strategic Efficiency and Effectiveness (Programme)
SHSSB	Southern Health and Social Services Board
SOPO	Sexual Offences Prevention Order
SORAM	Sex Offender Risk Assessment and Management
SSI	Social Services Inspectorate
TRC	Truth and Reconciliation Commission
UDA	Ulster Defence Association
UDR	Ulster Defence Regiment
UFF	Ulster Freedom Fighters
UNCRC	United Nations Convention on the Rights of the Child
UUP	Ulster Unionist Party
UVF	Ulster Volunteer Force
ViSOR	Violent and Sexual Offender Register
YCS	Youth Conference Service
YJA	Youth Justice Agency
YJB	Youth Justice Board
YJRT	Youth Justice Review Team
YOC	Young Offenders' Centre

NOTES ON CONTRIBUTORS

Nicola Carr is a Lecturer in the School of Sociology, Social Policy and Social Work, Queen's University Belfast where she teaches social work law and practice in the criminal justice system. She is a qualified probation officer. Her research interests include community justice, youth justice and transitions from the justice system.

Brice Dickson is Professor of International and Comparative Law at the School of Law, Queen's University Belfast. He has been a legal academic since 1977 but has mixed local activism and public service with his academic interests. From 1999 to 2005 he served as the first Chief Commissioner of the Northern Ireland Human Rights Commission, a statutory body established in the wake of the Belfast (Good Friday) Agreement. He is the author of the leading textbook on the legal system of Northern Ireland and has published works on *Introduction to French Law*; *Human Rights and the European Convention*; *The House of Lords: Its Parliamentary and Judicial Roles*; *Civil Liberties in Northern Ireland*; *Judicial Activism in Common Law Supreme Courts*; *The Judicial House of Lords 1876–2009*; and *the European Convention on Human Rights and the Conflict in Northern Ireland*. His book on *Human Rights and the UK Supreme Court* was published by Oxford University Press in 2013.

Clare Dwyer is a Lecturer in Law and Assistant Director of Education in the School of Law at Queen's University Belfast. Her areas of research include criminal justice, transitional justice, penology, former prisoners and children and young people. Her article 'Risk, Politics and the "Scientification" of Political Judgement: Prisoner Release and Conflict Transformation in Northern Ireland' published in the *British Journal of Criminology* (2007) was jointly awarded the Brian Williams Prize 2008 for the best sole-authored article by a 'new' scholar in the previous year. Her current research includes an examination of the experiences of children and young people growing up on an interface, the implications for the social needs, mental health and lifetime opportunities; the experiences of young people with community justice/punishment; young people and the impact of having a criminal record and the flag protests, policing response and community impact. She has acted as a consultant to NIACRO and also serves as an executive board member of the Committee on the Administration of Justice.

Anna Eriksson is a Senior Lecturer in Criminology at Monash University, Melbourne, Australia. In 2009 she was awarded the New Scholar Prize by the Australian and New Zealand Society of Criminology for the best publication, on restorative justice in Northern Ireland. She has also written a book on the topic: *Justice in Transition: Community Restorative Justice in Northern Ireland* (Routledge, 2009). In 2012, she was awarded one of only two of the Australian Research Council's Awards for early career researchers in criminology, funding a three-year study on comparative punishment between Australia and Sweden.

Colin Harvey is Professor of Human Rights Law, and former Head of the School of Law, Queen's University Belfast. In 2011, he was appointed to the Research Excellence Framework 2014 (REF2014) Panel for Law, and to the REF2014 Equality and Diversity Advisory Panel. He has held Visiting Professorships at the London School of Economics, the University of Michigan, and Fordham University. Professor Harvey served on the Northern Ireland Human Rights Commission (2005–11). He is the general editor of *Human Rights Law in Perspective* published by Hart Publishing (a new book series he founded in 2001). He is on the editorial board of *Human Rights Law Review, European Human Rights Law Review, Northern Ireland Legal Quarterly* and is the case editor for the *International Journal of Refugee Law*. He has a record of securing funded research from the Nuffield Foundation, the Joseph Rowntree Trust and the British Academy, among others.

Deena Haydon is a Postgraduate Researcher within the Childhood, Transition, and Social Justice Initiative at Queen's University Belfast. Her research and publications have focused on the issues of socially excluded children and young people, children's rights, family support, and youth justice.

Cheryl Lawther is a Lecturer in Criminology at Queen's University Belfast. She was previously a post-doctoral research fellow in the School of International Relations, University of St Andrews and received her PhD from the School of Law, Queen's University Belfast in 2010. Her article, '"Securing" the Past: Policing and the Contest over Truth in Northern Ireland', published in the *British Journal of Criminology* (2010) was awarded the Brian Williams Article Prize by the British Society of Criminology in 2011. Her monograph 'Truth, Transition and Denial: Northern Ireland and The Contested Past' was published in the Routledge Transitional Justice Series in 2014.

Anne-Marie McAlinden is Reader and Director of Research in the School of Law at Queen's University Belfast. Her first book, *The Shaming of Sexual Offenders: Risk, Retribution and Reintegration* (Hart Publishing, 2007) was awarded the British Society of Criminology Book Prize 2008 for the best first sole-authored monograph published in the discipline in the previous year. Her second sole-authored monograph entitled *'Grooming' and the Sexual Abuse of Children: Institutional, Internet and Familial Dimensions* was published in December 2012 as part of the Clarendon Studies in Criminology series by Oxford University Press. She has acted as a consultant to local government on a number of projects related to sex offending including *Public Attitudes to Sex Offending* and *Employment Opportunities*. She is currently PI (with Professor Shadd Maruna, Rutgers NJ, and Mark Farmer,

NOMs) on a three-year ESRC funded project 'Understanding Desistance from Sexual Offending'.

Siobhán McAlister is a Lecturer in Criminology in the School of Sociology, Social Policy and Social Work at Queen's University Belfast (QUB). Prior to this, she was a Research Fellow with the Childhood, Transition and Social Justice Initiative (QUB), and a researcher with YouthAction Northern Ireland, a voluntary organisation working with marginalised young people. Siobhán has been involved in a range of research projects concentrating on the lives and experiences of children and young people, including: 'Children's Rights in Northern Ireland' (2004); 'Still Waiting: The Stories Behind the Statistics of Young Women Growing up in Northern Ireland' (2007); and 'Childhood in Transition: Experiencing Marginalisation and Conflict in Northern Ireland' (2009). She works closely with NGOs in sharing information and informing research practices, and is a member of Headliners (Foyle) Steering Group.

Kieran McEvoy is Professor of Law and Transitional Justice at the School of Law, Queen's University Belfast. He was previously employed in the NGO sector before entering academia in 1995. He has been a visiting professor at New York University, Berkeley California, Cambridge, and the London School of Economics and spent a year as a Fulbright Distinguished Scholar in the Human Rights Program at Harvard Law School. He has a long history of human rights activism having served as a board member of the Committee on the Administration of Justice for much of the last two decades, as well as on the board of NIACRO and Community Restorative Justice Ireland. He has written or edited six books and over 50 journal articles and book chapters. He has conducted research on transitional justice in Sierra Leone, Rwanda, Uganda, Colombia, South Africa, Argentina, Uruguay, Spain and Italy, as well as Northern Ireland and the Republic. In 2002, his book *Paramilitary Imprisonment in Northern Ireland* was awarded the British Society of Criminology book prize. He has also been awarded the Socio-legal Studies Association article of the year award three times, in 2005 (with H Conway), in 2009 and in 2012.

Linda Moore is Senior Lecturer in Criminology at the School of Criminology, Politics and Social Policy at the University of Ulster. Her research specialisms are imprisonment, youth justice, and children's rights. Before taking up employment at Ulster in September 2007, from 2000–07 Linda was investigations worker at the Northern Ireland Human Rights Commission. Linda is on the Management Board of VOYPIC (Voice of Young People in Care) and has acted as expert consultant to the Children's Law Centre and Include Youth. She has published articles in *Howard Journal of Criminal Justice*, *Northern Ireland Legal Quarterly*, and the *Prison Journal*.

John Morison, LLB, PhD, MRIA is Professor of Jurisprudence at Queen's University Belfast. His books include: *The Barrister's World and the Nature of Law* (with Philip Leith 1992); *Reshaping Public Power: Northern Ireland and the British*

Constitutional Crisis (with Stephen Livingstone 1995); and *Crime Community and Locale: The Northern Ireland Communities Crime Survey* (with David O'Mahony, Ray Geary and Kieran McEvoy 2000) and the co-edited essay collections *Law, Society and Change* (1990); *Tall Stories? Reading Law and Literature* (1996); *Voices, Spaces and Processes in Constitutionalism* (2000); *Judges, Transition, and Human Rights* (2007); and *Values in Global Administrative Law* (2011). In addition, Professor Morison is author of some 30 or so chapters in various books and more than 50 articles in scholarly journals. Current research includes work on an ESRC funded project on 'Important Cases' and a book project on 'the nature of the public'. He was appointed as a lay Commissioner to the Northern Ireland Judicial Appointments Commission at its inception in 2005, and reappointed for a second term which ended in 2012.

Marny Requa is a Lecturer in Law at Queen's University Belfast. Her research is focused on topics at the intersection of criminal justice, international human rights, and transitional justice, with particular emphasis on experience in Chile and Northern Ireland. Marny is currently carrying out research on judicial responses to police brutality in societies undergoing transition, in part through a British Academy grant, intended for publication as a monograph in 2015 (under contract with Routledge), in addition to a project on miscarriages of justice in Northern Ireland. She is also co-investigator on an ESRC-funded project 'Lawyers, Conflict and Transition'. Marny has a *Juris Doctorate* degree (*magna cum laude*) from Fordham University School of Law where she was a Mulderig Scholar and Crowley Scholar in International Human Rights, a Master's degree in Latin American Studies from the University of California, Berkeley, and a BSc degree from Northwestern University. She is a member of the New York Bar and previously worked for US District Judge Denny Chin (SDNY) and as an adjunct professor at Fordham Law School.

Alex Schwartz, PhD, LLM, LLB, BA is Lecturer in Law at Queen's University Belfast. Previously, he was a Banting Fellow and Adjunct Assistant Professor with the Department of Political Studies at Queen's University (Canada). He has also been a visiting academic at the Centre for the Study of Social Justice at the University of Oxford and a post-doctoral fellow with the Canada Research Chair in Quebec and Canadian Studies at l'université du Québec à Montréal. He is co-editor (with Colin Harvey) of *Rights in Divided Societies* (Hart Publishing, 2011).

Phil Scraton is Professor of Criminology at the Institute of Criminology and Criminal Justice, School of Law, Queen's University Belfast and Director of the 'Childhood, Transition and Social Justice Initiative'. His most recent books include: *'Childhood' in 'Crisis?'* (Routledge, 1997); *Hillsborough: The Truth* (Mainstream, 1999); *Beyond September 11: An anthology of dissent* (Pluto, 2002); *Power, Conflict and Criminalisation* (Routledge, 2007); *The Violence of Incarceration* (Routledge, 2012) and *The Incarceration of Women* (Palgrave Macmillan, 2013). He has edited recent special issues of *Social Justice* on deaths in custody and detention and

Current Issues in Criminal Justice on the criminalisation and punishment of children and young people. Recent co-authored research reports are: *The Hurt Inside: The Imprisonment of Women and Girls in Northern Ireland* and *the Prison Within* (both for the Northern Ireland Human Rights Commission); *Children's Rights in Northern Ireland* (Northern Ireland Commissioner for Children and Young People). He was a member of the Hillsborough Independent Panel (2010–12) and primary author of *Hillsborough: The Report of the Independent Panel* (2012). His current research includes the European funded international comparative project 'Children of Imprisoned Parents'.

John Topping is a Lecturer in Criminology and member of the Institute for Research in Social Sciences (IRiSS) at the University of Ulster. His research interests include policing, police reform, community policing and public order/use of force. He has published widely on policing and has also acted as a consultant for the PSNI designing community-policing training, as well as working with the Police Ombudsman for Northern Ireland on informal resolution of police complaints. He currently sits on the board of directors for Community Restorative Justice Ireland.

Azrini Wahidin is Professor in Criminology and Criminal Justice at Nottingham Trent University. She researches on the issues of imprisonment, engendering of punishment and in the experiences of elders in prison in the UK and US. Her previous work focused on older women in prison, managing the needs of elders in prison, abolitionism and women in the criminal justice system. Her latest research focuses on the women of Armagh. She is author of a range of academic articles in international journals and edited collections. Her books include *Ageing, Crime and Society* (with Maureen Cain); *Older Women in the Criminal Justice System: Running out of Time*; *Criminology, Understanding Prison Staff, and Criminal Justice* (with Ben Crew and Jamie Bennett). She is a trustee of the Howard League for Penal Reform, the Irish Penal Reform Trust and is on the executive of the British Society of Criminology. She was an international visiting scholar in the School of Political and Social Sciences at Melbourne University.

TABLE OF CASES

TABLE OF STATUTES

The United Kingdom of Great Britain and Northern Ireland

South Africa

International Instruments

Part I

Conceptualising Crime and Criminal Justice in Northern Ireland

1

Crime and Criminal Justice in Northern Ireland: Conflict, Transition and the Legacy of the Past

CLARE DWYER AND ANNE-MARIE McALINDEN

'Bomb Kills Officer in Northern Ireland'.[1]
'Northern Ireland Prison Officer Shot Dead in Motor Way Ambush'.[2]
'Ulster Flag Protests: Police Injured in Petrol Bomb Attacks'.[3]
'IRA Terror Suspects Lose Right to Immunity'.[4]
'UK Must Pay for Troubles Killings Investigations Says European Official'.[5]
'Bloody Sunday Investigation Faces Judicial Review'.[6]
'Mairia Says Exiled IRA Sex Abusers in "Double Figures" Now'.[7]
'9 Face IRA Charges in Both Parts of Ireland'.[8]
'On the Runs: Record-Keeping of Cases Criticised'.[9]
'Legal Bid over Probe into Alleged Security Forces Collusion in 1992 UVF Murders'.[10]

Introduction

Consider the above selection of recent media headlines from national and international outlets related to crime or justice provision in Northern Ireland. These headlines demonstrate that crime and criminal justice issues stemming from the legacy of violent and political conflict continue to command international media and political attention and dominate legal and public discourses on Northern

[1] The Associated Press, *The New York Times*, 2 April 2011.
[2] H McDonald, *The Guardian*, 1 November 2012.
[3] *The Telegraph*, 12 January 2013.
[4] J Norton, *The Daily Mail*, 3 September 2014.
[5] V Kearney, *BBC News*, 6 November 2014.
[6] *BBC News*, 10 November 2014.
[7] N O'Connor, *Irish Independent*, 11 November 2014.
[8] Associated Press, *The Washington Post*, 17 November 2014.
[9] *BBC News*, 19 November 2014.
[10] *Belfast Telegraph*, 23 November 2014.

Ireland. More pertinently, they also underline how issues related to past abuses, stemming from the 'conflict'[11] or what are euphemistically known as the 'Troubles', are inextricably bound up with issues of national identity—both in terms of how Northern Ireland 'imagines itself' (Anderson 1983) as a society transitioning from conflict as well as how it is perceived on the world stage.

The purpose of this edited volume is to locate the Northern Ireland experience of criminal justice in transition in a broader historical, social, political, cultural and comparative context. The book considers the core aspects of policymaking and justice provision in Northern Ireland which are central to the process of post-conflict transition (McEvoy and Newburn 2003). This includes, inter alia, reform of policing, judicial decision-making, correctional services such as probation and prisons and mechanisms for correcting error. It will also examine contemporary trends in criminal justice in Northern Ireland as related to various dimensions of crime such as female offenders, young offenders, sexual and violent offenders, and restorative justice, and how these relate to or differ from developments elsewhere. Finally, the book seeks to examine the impact of devolution and the transitional context in this regard and the extent to which criminal justice in Northern Ireland continues to be shaped by the legacy of the conflict.

Until relatively recently, academic discourses on criminology and criminal justice pertaining to Northern Ireland could be said to have suffered from two key deficits. The first is the historical and indeed contemporary focus on England and Wales as the dominant paradigm within 'British' criminological discourses with scant mention of the other jurisdictions which constitute the United Kingdom—namely Scotland and Northern Ireland. The second is that whatever Northern Ireland focused scholarship there was, has tended historically towards positivist uncritical accounts. As McEvoy and Ellison (2003) note, these discourses took two distinct forms: those directly engaged in the study of political violence and terrorism (for example, Wilkinson 1986; Wright 1991; Clutterbuck 1994); and those concerned with 'ordinary crime' (for example, Brewer et al 1997; O'Mahony et al 2000). In addressing both of these shortfalls, this collection will mark out new territory in the critical conceptualisation of criminal justice in societies undergoing transition from political violence.

In relation to the first aspect, there has been a general neglect of Northern Ireland within national and international debates on criminology and criminal justice. International comparative criminal justice which makes reference to the United Kingdom is invariably England and Wales focused, with the other jurisdictions in the United Kingdom simply 'tacked on' at best or at worst overlooked completely. As Garland (1999: xiv) notes 'the UK' usually 'really means England and Wales'. Even within British texts, the focus is predominantly on England and Wales, with little or no mention of Scotland and Northern Ireland. Croall et al (2010: 6), who

[11] This is a contested term for the civil/political unrest that occurred from the late 1960s to the mid-1990s. This period has also been referred to locally as the 'Troubles'. Both terms are used interchangeably throughout this volume to refer to this period.

have sought to counter this tendency with respect to Scotland, identify this as 'an unjustifiable and curious omission' given the often marked differences in regional approaches.

In this respect, the book will represent a critical theoretical and empirical examination of key aspects of crime and criminal justice in contemporary Northern Ireland, which are distinct as well as those which have resonance and origins elsewhere. Indeed, the book will also consider the extent to which crime and criminal justice issues in Northern Ireland are being affected by the broader political process of devolution. In particular, human rights and transitional justice frameworks are central to the process of rebuilding the structures and mechanisms of state justice and in moving on from the legacy of an abusive past (Teitel 2000; Elster 2004; Morison et al 2007).

More broadly, a body of work on comparative penal reform (for example, Newburn and Sparks 2004; Nelken 2007; Reichel 2008) has generally highlighted the spread of penal policies which appear to have originated in the United States (for example, Christie 2000; Garland 2001). Within this comparative context, this book will provide an insight into the wider dynamics of 'policy transfer' (Newburn 2002; Jones and Newburn 2006), globalisation, transnationalism and localism. The term 'policy transfer' is generally used to describe the convergence of penal policies between neo-liberal societies such as the United States and the United Kingdom. Such societies are generally characterised by social exclusion of deviants, incapacitation as the dominant penal ideology and high rates of imprisonment (Wacquant 2001). The policy transfer thesis, however, is not 'one-dimensional' but is instead subject to important socio-cultural differences in the way in which policies are reformulated and reconfigured within national and localised cultures (Muncie 2005; Crawford 2006). The chapters also examine whether there is evidence of 'diffusion, differentiation and resistance' (Newburn 2010), within a variety of criminal justice settings in Northern Ireland as one of the jurisdictions which constitute the United Kingdom.

In relation to the second dimension, as McEvoy and Ellison (2003) have pointed out, older criminological scholarship in Northern Ireland has been generally positivist or administrative in nature being centrally concerned with normative uncritical accounts of the functions of the different arms of criminal justice without much upsetting the overall balance of the system. Indeed, historically, there has been a fundamental disconnect between political conflict and critical criminological discourses, with Jamieson (1998: 480) noting that criminology has been 'largely aloof and unmoved' by debates concerning political conflict and its resolution. More recently, however, a growing body of Northern Irish scholars have drawn out the utility and significance of critical criminology as a template for assessing the complex role of the criminal justice process during the conflict. For some such scholars, the study of criminology and criminal justice emerged as a '*political* project'—in effect 'a guide to criminological praxis during the process of conflict resolution' (McEvoy and Ellison 2003: 45).

As these authors have also noted, the establishment of the Institute of Criminology and Criminal Justice (ICCJ) at Queen's University Belfast in 1995 (now located within the School of Law) has facilitated the development of a cohesive criminological and criminal justice research culture and the building of a composite picture about crime and criminal justice issues (McEvoy and Ellison 2003). Prior to this date, while there were a number of academics within Northern Ireland's two universities with an interest in criminological and criminal justice issues and a few more within NGOs, the creation of the ICCJ provided a central disciplinary focus and a resource for local policymaking (McEvoy and Ellison 2003). The emergence of a distinct Northern Irish Criminology, initially related to regional, political and policy developments and the needs of local justice agencies, has simultaneously produced world leading research by some of the most renowned national and international scholars in the field.

The book in this sense also offers an exposition of the breadth of Northern Irish and related scholarship across the key contested domains of criminal justice. The individual chapters offer a snapshot of the cutting edge of critical thinking in criminal justice practice and transitional justice contexts and represent an attempt to theorise change at the micro-level as well as the macro-level. Such a nuanced focus is central to an understanding of the governance of justice and security in general (Crawford 1999; Rose 2000; Garland 2001; Loader and Walker 2007). Using a range of settings and sites of crime from across the criminal justice sphere, collectively the chapters provide a blueprint for new trends and pathways that are beginning to emerge in societies undergoing significant change (McEvoy and McGregor 2008). It offers new ways of thinking about crime and criminal justice in a transitional context, chiefly by relating these issues to broader social and political issues in contemporary Northern Ireland as well as the United Kingdom as a whole. The book draws on comparative experiences in Canada, the United States, England and Wales, Scotland, the Republic of Ireland and elsewhere. It also situates that analysis within supranational and sub-national frameworks.

The remainder of this chapter will provide an overview of the historical, legal and policy contexts to the devolution of policing and justice in Northern Ireland as a society transitioning from political conflict. The structure of the chapter is as follows: the chapter begins with an examination of the Northern Ireland legal and criminal justice system as a constituent part of the United Kingdom and in particular the shared history of policy development with England and Wales. This is followed by the main part of the chapter which considers the core elements of the Northern Ireland conflict and transition in a criminal justice context. These include key themes from the literature on transitional justice and the role of criminal justice reform therein; a brief overview of the history of the conflict; the road to devolution including in particular landmark developments following the Belfast (Good Friday) Agreement (1998)[12] such as the structural and policy reforms following the

[12] This is the name given to the 'peace agreement' reached following multi-party talks on Good Friday, 10 April 1998, in Belfast. It is variously termed the Good Friday Agreement, the Belfast Agreement, or the Peace Agreement, and the terms are used interchangeably by commentators as they are throughout this volume.

Report of the Criminal Justice Review Group (CJRG 2000), and the full devolution of policing and justice in April 2010; and the broader resonance of the conflict for crime and criminal justice more generally. Finally, this opening chapter will provide a brief thematic overview of the constituent chapters within this volume.

An Overview of Legal Systems and Traditions

The constituent legal systems of the United Kingdom—comprised of England and Wales,[13] Scotland and Northern Ireland—have undergone significant change in recent decades. Changing political environments and the advent of recent 'law and order' rhetoric gave rise to a greater willingness to review the system (Garland 2004). In particular, the development of risk-based regulatory policies (Ericson and Haggerty 1997) across the United Kingdom has changed the governance of security and justice wherein criminal justice sanctions have become a regulatory tool (Shearing 2000; Loader and Walker 2007). However, while concerns about 'risk' and 'governance' may have dominated political and policymaking discourses on crime and justice within and across the United Kingdom, for varied reasons criminal justice polices have at times diverged or converged across the Union.

The United Kingdom has three separate legal and criminal justice systems; one each for England and Wales, Scotland, and Northern Ireland. This reflects its historical origins and the fact that both Scotland and Ireland, and later Northern Ireland, retained their own legal systems and traditions under the Acts of Union 1707 and 1801. Scotland had its own system of laws which was in existence before the union with England and Wales in the eighteenth century. The Act of Union of 1707 expressly allowed these to continue, and so Scotland retains many distinctions from the English system (see Gillespie 2013). Since the partition of Ireland in 1921, Northern Ireland's legal system has remained broadly similar to that in England and Wales (Dickson 2013). However, Northern Ireland has some unusual features within the legal system, many of which relate to the political instability and violence which have existed since its establishment.

In brief, Northern Ireland has had a shared legal history and tradition with England and Wales where the legislative relationship between the jurisdictions emerges as a rather intricate one (McLaughlin 2005). The Government of Ireland Act 1920 partitioned Ireland, establishing six of the nine northern counties of Ulster as Northern Ireland within the United Kingdom from May 1921.[14] Although

[13] England and Wales, although two separate countries within the UK (along with Scotland and Northern Ireland), have an integrated legal and criminal justice system. Therefore, both jurisdictions are usually discussed as a single entity in terms of criminal justice provision as they are throughout this book.

[14] The Irish Free State was simultaneously established as a dominion of the British Commonwealth comprised of 26 of the 32 counties. In 1937, the creation of Ireland as a sovereign state replaced the 1922 constitution. In 1949, it secured full independence as the Republic of Ireland (see Tonge 2005).

sovereignty was retained with the UK Parliament, the Government of Ireland Act established a Parliament of Northern Ireland (based on the Stormont estate in Belfast and referred to as 'Stormont'). This new parliament was given power to legislate over almost all aspects of Northern Ireland's internal affairs (with the exception of conducting foreign affairs, armed forces, currency and coinage). The Stormont Parliament sat from 7 June 1921 to 30 March 1972, when it was suspended with the introduction of direct rule from the UK Parliament at Westminster in London (see Carmichael and Knox 2004).

As a result, criminal justice policies enacted for Northern Ireland have had a 'consistent' and 'shared' relationship with those adopted by the British Government but have also been modified to meet Northern Ireland's 'own strategic political needs' (Pinkerton 1994: 29). More broadly, as Pinkerton (1994: 28) has argued, in many areas of social policy the step by step or 'parity principle' has held sway (see also Kelly 1990: 78). Where social policies were not enacted directly for Northern Ireland at the same time as England and Wales, reciprocal legislation was often enacted a short time afterwards. Under the period of direct rule between 1974 and 1999, following the first reintroduction of the Stormont Government in the aftermath of the Belfast (Good Friday) Agreement 1998, this 'process of assimilation between the content of the law in Northern Ireland and that in England was, if anything, fortified' (Dickson 2001: 8). Criminal justice policies, however, were rather different. The criminal justice process was perhaps the state's key armory in the response to political violence and thus the mainstreaming of 'exceptional' aspects of criminal justice (for example, emergency laws, juryless courts, a heavily militarised police force, and a unique prison system) have left a profound impact on the shape and culture of the criminal justice system. At the same time, as noted above and as will be highlighted throughout this volume, Northern Ireland has also been influenced by policy developments elsewhere.

The exceptional aspects of the Northern Ireland criminal justice system as shaped by the legacy of the conflict also have to be considered alongside the complexities of contemporary UK politics, including devolution. As there is no unified criminal justice system, explaining the development of criminal justice policy across the United Kingdom is rather complex. However, what is evident is that in the last 15 years, the three separate criminal justice systems have experienced a series of key legislative and institutional reforms (Matthews and Young 2003; Croall et al 2010). England and Wales, for example, since the years of the 'New Labour' Government, has experienced an overhaul of the criminal justice system. In its eight years in government, New Labour passed over 50 Acts of Parliament relating to crime, disorder, policing, criminal justice and punishment (Emmerson and Frayne 2005: 7). This 'hyper innovation' (Moran 2003) is also evident in Northern Ireland where many of these measures, such as those relating to young offenders or sexual and violent crime, were simultaneously extended to Northern Ireland or subsequently enacted a short time afterwards. Driven by the 'tough on crime' rhetoric and a move to refocus the balance of the justice system towards victims of crime, justice reform remained a priority for the Coalition Government (Fitzgerald and Hale 2013). While political economy and resulting governing strategies are commonly referred to as the underlying drivers of criminal justice developments (Cavadino and Dignan 2006; McAlinden 2012), there is no single narrative of criminal justice developments across the United Kingdom. Indeed, in relation to Northern Ireland, recent developments within criminal justice need to be set against broader debates about the interplay of political process, conflict, the rule of law and the role of transitional justice.

It is often claimed that the criminal justice system is central to the political and constitutional integrity of any state (Walker and Telford 2000: 53–55). While this is the case in most 'settled' societies, this statement has enhanced relevance for a divided society emerging from decades of violent and political conflict. Understanding the criminal justice agenda and policy divergence or convergence between Northern Ireland and the rest of the United Kingdom necessitates consideration of wider political 'post-conflict' objectives. As a divided society emerges from conflict, the transitional process is complex often calling for significant political, social and legal reforms. From the shadows of political violence, Northern Ireland is still undergoing transition some 20 years after the end of the conflict.[15] As discussed throughout this volume, this transitional process has been spearheaded by significant political, institutional and legal reforms where transitional justice frameworks and new governance mechanisms are, for the most part, firmly established across Northern Ireland's criminal justice landscape.

The Northern Ireland Conflict and the Transitional Justice Context

In order to fully understand the transitional framework of criminal justice in Northern Ireland, the devolution of policing and justice, and developments since, it is necessary to provide a brief overview of the core elements concerning the conflict and transition in a criminal justice context. In this vein, the remainder of this chapter deals with a number of key issues: the key elements of transitional justice and how criminal justice and legal reforms feature within this; political conflict in a divided society; landmark events in the road to devolution; and the impact of the conflict on 'ordinary' crime and criminal justice.

Transitional Justice Frameworks

Within previously conflicted societies, the policy and practice of transitional justice has become central to the search for justice in dealing with the legacy of an

[15] Note, although the precise date at which the conflict is thought to have ended is the subject of some contention, this is generally agreed as being the signing of the Belfast (Good Friday) Agreement in April 1998.

abusive past. Broadly understood as making reference to some form of profound political transformation, transitional justice has been defined as 'the conception of justice associated with periods of political change, characterised by legal responses to confront the wrong doings of repressive predecessor regimes' (Teitel 2003: 69). For many transitional justice scholars, transitional justice is a question of a new and more liberal regime, developed and implemented in order to confront past wrongdoings, in the pursuit of justice and political change (see Kritz 1995; Méndez 1997). According to Kritz, for example, the question of transitional justice presents as 'the first test for the establishment of real democracy and the rule of law—the very principles which will hopefully distinguish the new regime from the old' (1995: xxi). The field of transitional justice is, therefore, predisposed to view the past as something 'bad' and the core business lies in consolidating democracy rights and strengthening the rule of law (Teitel 2000: 22).

Transitional justice processes generally involve a range of models which are aimed at helping a society come to terms with previous large-scale human rights abuses, in order to ensure accountability for wrongdoing, and achieve justice and reconciliation for victims (Huyse 1995; Teitel 2000; McEvoy and McGregor 2008). These may include judicial or extrajudicial mechanisms such as prosecution or other forms of reparation (Elster 2004; Grieff 2006), truth commissions (Freeman 2006; Hayner 2001), apology (McMillan 2010), amnesties (Mallinder 2008), and ultimately institutional reform. Within this broader context, a broad programme of legal and criminal justice reform and the introduction of new or improved governance frameworks are usually vital elements of dealing with the legacy of the past. In particular, the development of the state's capacity to deliver justice is viewed as a core element of rebuilding governance structures more broadly in post-conflict societies (Brinkerhoff 2005). In the late twentieth century—from the aftermath of the Second World War, structured transition (from military dictatorship to democracy) in Latin America in the 1980s, transitions in eastern and central Europe in the late 1980s, or the peacemaking process in post-apartheid South Africa from the early 1990s—political and legal reforms have formed an integral part of post-conflict transitions and 'the genealogy of transitional justice' (see generally Teitel 2003).

While several commentators have underlined the importance of law and a programme of legal and institutional reforms as the structuring principles of transition and state reconstruction (see, for example, Huyse 1995; Osiel 1997; Campbell et al 2004: 305–28), the hegemony of legalism in transitional justice discourses more broadly has been the subject of sustained critique (see especially McEvoy 2007). In this respect, a number of underpinning discourses have emerged as being of central importance to transitional justice, 'the policing of the past' (Cohen 1995) and the process of peacemaking. These relate to the use of 'other forms of knowledge' (McEvoy 2007) such as the ongoing development of human rights frameworks to promote institutional accountability, the provision of restorative or reparative justice, local mechanisms for truth recovery and the role of other non-state or non-legal actors at the grass roots level (McEvoy and McGregor 2008).

Such discourses have also emerged at the forefront of transitioning to a new legal and political order in Northern Ireland and the provision of criminal justice in particular as highlighted in many of the chapters throughout this volume.

In the context of Northern Ireland, a number of transitional justice measures have been initiated, implemented, or been 'put on hold' since the Belfast (Good Friday Agreement) 1998. Such initiatives include the creation of a Human Rights Commission tasked with developing a human rights culture (including the potential development of a Bill of Rights); the Independent International Commission on Decommissioning established to oversee the decommissioning of paramilitary weapons; the Commission for Victims and Survivors established to coordinate the delivery of services for victims of political violence; the Sentence Review Commission established to oversee the early release of 'politically motivated' prisoners;[16] several high profile inquiries (including the Bloody Sunday Inquiry[17] and the Cory Inquiries);[18] consultation on dealing with the past (including the Healing Through Remembering project); the setting up of the Historical Enquiries Team, a unit of the police set up to investigate the over 3000 unsolved murders committed during the conflict from 1968 to 1998; and the establishment of a reformed police service (Police Service of Northern Ireland). At the time of writing, the Stormont House Agreement (NIO 2014) was signed in December 2014 to take forward many of the residual issues of dealing with the legacy of the past, including the outstanding aspects of the Belfast (Good Friday) Agreement and subsequent political agreements. In order to understand this transitional process, the chapter will move to briefly consider the historical context to the conflict and the driving forces for both legal and institutional change in Northern Ireland.

[16] Prisoners were deemed as 'politically motivated' if they were serving a 'conflict-related' sentence and were convicted of scheduled offences during the conflict in Northern Ireland. Scheduled offences are those offences listed as an appendix to the various emergency legislation in Northern Ireland (including sch 1 of the Northern Ireland (Emergency Provisions) Acts 1973, 1978, 1996). Scheduled offences are those normally associated with the commission of terrorist acts (eg, murder, manslaughter, explosions, serious offences against the person, rioting, collecting information likely to be of use to terrorists etc). Those convicted of scheduled offences were members of or had connections with various paramilitary organisations including (but not limited to) the Provisional Irish Republican Army (PIRA), Official Irish Republican Army (OIRA), Irish National Liberation Army (INLA) from the republican community, and the Ulster Volunteer Force (UVF) and Ulster Defence Association (UDA) from the loyalist community.

[17] The Bloody Sunday Inquiry, under the chairmanship of Lord Saville, was tasked with examining the events in Derry on Sunday 30 January 1972 which led to the death of 13 unarmed civilians who were shot dead by the British Army following a civil rights march. The report found that the killings were both 'unjustified and unjustifiable'. Following the publication of the Saville Report the British Prime Minister, David Cameron, made a formal apology on behalf of the United Kingdom.

[18] The Cory Inquiries were established to investigate alleged collusion between the security forces and the paramilitaries in relation to a number of high profile murders including that of Pat Finucane, Rosemary Nelson, Robert Hamill and Billy Wright. Prior to the enactment of the Inquiries Act 2005, Mr Justice Cory recommended that inquiries be held in all four cases which occurred in all but the first of these cases.

Political Conflict in a Divided Society

Between the late 1960s and early 1990s, Northern Ireland was locked in an ethno-national conflict, known colloquially as the 'Troubles'. There are many different ways of understanding the beginning and cause of the conflict in Northern Ireland. However, MacGinty and Darby suggest that 'it is a measure of political sensitivities in Northern Ireland that even selection of a date to mark the origin of the conflict is viewed with suspicion' (2002: 14). Many look to the twelfth century with the Norman invasion of Ireland (Darby 1995), while others contend that the roots of the conflict can be traced back to the Plantation of Ulster in the seventeenth century (see O'Leary and McGarry 1996). The plantation of settlers, from Scotland and England, led to three culturally distinctive communities (Irish, Scottish and English) which were divided by language, culture, religion, and political rights and freedoms. These divisions remained up to and following the partitioning of Ireland in 1921 (which for others may have been the date to mark the start of the conflict).

As the new Northern Ireland state was made up of a Protestant majority (with a 65 per cent Protestant and 35 per cent Catholic population at the time of partition), the Stormont Parliament was dominated by the Protestant/unionist community (MacGinty and Darby 2002).[19] In consequence, the underrepresentation of Catholics extended throughout most levels of Northern Ireland government. Since the creation of Northern Ireland, political tensions were constant. The Protestant/unionist community felt threatened by the possibility of a United Ireland being imposed, in which their rights would be curtailed within an overwhelming Catholic country. Catholics in Northern Ireland were alienated, suffered discrimination under the Stormont Parliament, electoral malpractice and ethnic bias in the distribution of housing and welfare services (MacGinty and Darby 2002: 15). While Tonge (2002) notes that there existed disagreement on the occurrence and controversy over the extent of discrimination, the genesis for the most recent conflict can be traced to the late 1960s. The rise of the civil rights movement challenged the political and social system regarding structural discrimination against Catholics (Hewitt 1981; Purdie 1990).

The civil rights demands led to intensifying political tensions and intercommunity violence between the Protestant/unionist and Catholic/nationalist communities. After the deployment of the British Army in response to the violence and street protests, the British forces[20] along with republican paramilitaries[21] and

[19] By the 2011 census, the Protestant population in Northern Ireland had declined—48 per cent of people in Northern Ireland gave their religion as Protestant, 45 per cent of the resident population as Catholic or brought up Catholic, with the remaining 7 per cent belonging to another religion or no religion. See www.nisra.gov.uk/archive/census/2011/results/key-statistics/summary-report.pdf.

[20] The British Army, locally recruited regiment (the Ulster Defence Regiment) and the police—the Royal Ulster Constabulary (RUC) as it then was.

[21] The Provisional Irish Republican Army (PIRA) and the Irish National Liberation army (INLA).

loyalist paramilitaries[22] became embroiled in a 'triangular' conflict comprised of loyalists who sought to retain Northern Ireland's connection to the United Kingdom, republicans who want Irish reunification and the complete withdrawal of the British state (Campbell and Connolly 2012: 3). The Troubles soon became 'a more violent expression of existing animosities and unresolved issues of nationality, religion, power and territorial rivalry' (McKittrick and McVea 2012: 1).

The early 1970s was witness to key political events including internment without trial (1971), Bloody Sunday (1972)[23] and the intensification of political violence. The year 1972 saw the highest death toll in which 467 people were killed, 143 of them in explosions and almost 5000 were injured; there were 10,628 shooting incidents, 1382 explosions and 1932 armed robberies (Wichert 1991: 162). That year, the Stormont Government was suspended and direct rule was imposed from Westminster as a response to the growing political crisis. However, direct rule did not succeed in bringing peace and stability, and for years the British and Irish governments sought to facilitate a political settlement in Northern Ireland. These efforts included the failed attempt at establishing a consociational power-sharing government of Northern Ireland through the Sunningdale Agreement in 1973, and the Anglo-Irish Agreement in 1985 between the United Kingdom and the Republic of Ireland aimed at bringing an end to political violence in Northern Ireland. The Anglo-Irish Agreement was viewed as 'coercive consociationlism' and, similar to the Sunningdale Agreement with regard to intra-community relations, failed due to the lack of necessary intra and inter relations in Northern Ireland society (McGarry and O'Leary 2004: chapters 2–3).

Without political recourse, the Government continued, as it had done before the outset of the conflict, to utilise the legal system to 'manage' the conflict and gain civil control. A criminal justice response and the introduction or reintroduction of numerous emergency legislative measures featured heavily throughout the conflict. In 1971, the British Government reintroduced internment under the Civil Authorities (Special Powers) Act 1922, giving the authorities the power to indefinitely detain terrorist suspects without trial (Spjut 1986; White and White 1995). The introduction of the Northern Ireland (Emergency Provisions) Act 1973 and the Prevention of Terrorism (Temporary Provisions) Act 1974 meant that regulatory tools of the state and ordinary legal process, including due process, were substantially modified to deal with the political situation throughout this period. By way of example, key components of the criminal justice system were altered, including increased policing powers and procedures, which provided the police and army with wider powers of arrest, stop, search and seizure, as well as the introduction of special juryless (Diplock) courts to try people accused of 'conflict-related' offences (Jackson and Doran 1995).

[22] The Ulster Defence Association/Ulster Freedom Fighters (UDA/UFF) and the Ulster Volunteer Force (UVF).

[23] See n 17 above.

Crime and Justice: The Road to Devolution

As noted above, between 1921 and 1972 the Northern Ireland Parliament at Stormont legislated on matters within its own competence as laid down by the Government of Ireland Act 1920. However, when Parliament was prorogued in 1972, the legislative-making powers reverted to Westminster, including most notably 'law and order' powers. Despite law and justice issues remaining at the top of the political agenda throughout the conflict, direct involvement by Westminster in the law and order affairs of Northern Ireland was to last nearly 40 years.

In 1998, the Belfast (Good Friday) Agreement called for a devolved government,[24] with a power-sharing Executive in which unionist and nationalist parties would share power. The Agreement contained provisions on policing, decommissioning and demilitarisation, security normalisation, early release of prisoners and human rights. The Agreement also included the arrangement of a parallel wide-ranging review of criminal justice (*other than policing and those aspects of the system relating to the emergency legislation*), to be carried out by the British Government through a mechanism with an independent element, in consultation with the political parties and others (Belfast (Good Friday) Agreement 1998: paragraph 9.5).[25] The Agreement also set out that the Government '*remains ready in principle* ... to devolve responsibility for policing and justice issues' (Belfast (Good Friday) Agreement 1998: paragraph 9.7).

As noted throughout this volume, the Criminal Justice Review was one of the most important and far-reaching assessments of criminal justice in Northern Ireland. There were nearly 300 recommendations for change (CJRG 2000). Key recommendations included the promotion of a human rights culture within the criminal justice system; a new independent Public Prosecution Service to replace the current Director of Public Prosecutions; the establishment of an independent Judicial Appointments Commission and an independent Criminal Justice Inspectorate. Other issues to be addressed were the needs of victims of crime, an independent Law Commission, improvements to arrangements for young people and the integration of restorative justice into the justice system. Many but not all of its recommendations were implemented through the Justice Act (Northern Ireland) 2002, and the Justice Act (Northern Ireland) 2004. Although the main aims of the subsequent legislation were to 'normalise' and to update the system in line with the rest of the United Kingdom (Walker 2011), as is discussed within this volume, many 'special' provisions remain.

[24] Devolved government by the Northern Ireland Assembly under the Northern Ireland Act 1998 began on 2 December 1999. Devolution was suspended on 14 March 2002. Devolved powers were restored to the Northern Ireland Assembly on 8 May 2007.

[25] During the consultation process the then Secretary of State, Mo Mowlam, stated that the Criminal Justice Review would operate in parallel with, but separately from, an independent review of policing (*Belfast Telegraph*, 'Legal review "offers scope for change"', 27 August 1998). This was undertaken by the Patten Commission (ICP 1999), which eventually led to the formation of the new Police Service of Northern Ireland.

Critics of the Criminal Justice Review have argued that the exclusion of policing and emergency legislation restricted the scope of the Review and meant that it 'was unable to address the very issues which have done more than anything to prevent all sections of Northern Ireland society having confidence in the criminal justice system' (Jackson 2001: 169). Jackson remarked that 'asking the review to address the issue of confidence in the context of future criminal justice arrangements without looking at policing and emergency legislation was therefore rather like asking an architect to design a house without walls and a roof' (2001: 169–70). Notwithstanding the significant changes across the criminal justice system, for over a decade after the Agreement, police and criminal justice matters were looked after by the Secretary of State for Northern Ireland.

During this period tensions remained within the devolved government, but a key juncture came in 2006 with the St Andrews Agreement, which set in place a road map to facilitate key changes, including the operation of the power-sharing institutions, provisions for human rights and called for the devolution of policing and justice powers from Westminster to Stormont by May 2008. However, the two main parties in the Northern Ireland power-sharing Executive, the Democratic Unionist Party and Sinn Féin, remained at odds over the transfer of policing and justice. The 2008 deadline came and went and progress remained slow. In December 2009, the Northern Ireland Assembly passed the Northern Ireland Act 2009, paving the way for the devolution of policing and justice, the establishment of a Department of Justice and the appointment of a Minister of Justice. After a series of further negotiations, the Hillsborough Agreement (2010) set the date for devolution. After nearly 40 years, policing and justice affairs were finally devolved to the Northern Ireland Assembly on 12 April 2010. Since the signing of the Belfast (Good Friday) Agreement and following the devolution of criminal justice in 2010, the Northern Ireland criminal justice system has experienced significant legislative and institutional reforms and more recently has been witness to substantial reviews, including the prison system and youth justice reviews. Many of the chapters in this volume critically examine the implementation of these justice reforms and consider what progress has been made since.

The Impact of the Political Conflict on 'Ordinary' Crime and Criminal Justice

During the Northern Ireland conflict, more than 3700 individuals were killed and 40,000 injured (McKittrick et al, 2007). Although the criminal justice system was dominated by the processing and management of political violence, in parallel it also had to deal with 'ordinary' crime. In this respect, a final interesting dimension is the impact of the political and violent conflict on so-called 'ordinary' crime and criminal justice provision both during and in the aftermath of the conflict.

The impact of the conflict on the ordinary criminal process in Northern Ireland is well documented (see Morison and Geary 2000; McEvoy et al 2002).

Notwithstanding the political unrest, Northern Ireland had one of the lowest levels of recorded crime in Western Europe throughout the duration of the conflict (CJRG 2000: chapter 2). In comparison to England and Wales, the Northern Ireland population experienced a lower incidence of most crimes during the Troubles and this continued up until the 1998 peace agreement. At the time of the Belfast (Good Friday) Agreement Northern Ireland's crime rate represented 6450 per 100,000 population compared with the rate of 9785 per 100,000 in England and Wales (CJRG 2000: 12). Of course figures must be interpreted with a degree of caution and statistics only reflect a portion of crimes that occur in any society, namely those discovered by or reported to the police.

Interestingly, 'post-conflict' Northern Ireland continues to have a much lower level of reported crime compared with England and Wales. In 2013/2014, England and Wales had an overall crime rate of 66 per 1000 population while Northern Ireland has an overall crime rate of 56 per 1000 population (PSNI 2014). Crime levels in Northern Ireland have shown a downward trend for the last 10 years, from the peak of 142,496 in 2002/2003 to 100,389 recorded crimes in 2012/2013 (PSNI 2014). This is reported as the lowest level of recorded crime since the year of the Agreement in 1998. Furthermore, while Northern Ireland had one of the highest prison populations per capita in Western Europe during the conflict (with three-quarters of the prison population convicted of 'conflict-related' offences) (Dwyer 2004), it currently has one of the lowest. At present Northern Ireland has a prison population of 98 per 100,000, this compares with England and Wales which has a prison population of 149 per 100,000 (Prison Statistics 2014/NIPS 2014). Moreover, this figure is also lower than most other European nations apart from Sweden, Finland, Norway and Cyprus (Council of Europe 2014).

Various theories have been developed regarding Northern Ireland's significantly lower 'ordinary' crime rates. Sociological theories of crime focus on a range of social forces which include a sense of community, stability and tradition which may be associated with lower levels of crime. So, for example, Brewer et al (1997) suggest that increased ghettoisation arising from the conflict had the effect of creating more tightknit communities. As a result, informal social controls emerge as a by-product of role relationships, mutual trust, group identities and enmeshed interdependencies. Adler (1983) supports this view and suggests that the crime rate is a product of the strong sense of moral control exerted through religion and family.

Criminological theories of informal social control also extend to an understanding of the role of 'surveillance' by local residents and the 'norms of conduct' by which residents are regulated. Brewer et al (1997) conclude that 'political violence' has ironically protected Northern Ireland from some of the 'worst vagaries of community breakdown and dislocation witnessed in Britain's inner cities. The knock-on effect of this for ordinary crime levels in Northern Ireland are positive irrespective of other effects of political violence' (Brewer et al 1997: 216). According to this view, the low levels of crime in Northern Ireland can in part be explained by the 'informal' or 'alternative' criminal justice system which has evolved since the beginning of the conflict. In opposition to the police, particularly within the republican/nationalist communities, paramilitaries began to fill a vacuum and 'police' their own areas. 'Paramilitary policing' is characterised by the dissemination of a range of punitive measures against individuals 'who violate some community norms, as defined by paramilitary groupings' (which include anti-social behaviour, joyriding, criminal damage, and sex offending behaviour) (see Knox 2002: 172). Knox (2002) further notes that some paramilitary groupings also use this alternative system to 'police their own', to maintain internal discipline within the organisation. Sanctions may include threats, warnings, curfews, public humiliation, exile, punishment beatings or executions (Knox 2002: 164). This 'alternative justice system' is embedded in many local social structures that continue to survive and offer an alternative system of social control to some areas within Northern Ireland. More broadly, as several of the chapters highlight, it also continues to impact in a variety of ways on contemporary criminal justice provision in Northern Ireland including, inter alia, policing and the management of violent and sexual offenders.

An Overview of the Chapters

The first part of the book sets out the conceptual framework for examining crime and criminal justice in transition in the Northern Ireland context. The first substantive chapter in part I, written by Cheryl Lawther, explores truth recovery and dealing with the past in Northern Ireland. In particular, the chapter examines the work of the Historical Enquiries Team (a police led cold case review of all conflict-related deaths), the Office of the Police Ombudsman, the Inquest System, the Criminal Cases Review Commission and litigation by both victims and former combatants. In exploring the capacity and limitations of 'ordinary' criminal justice in a transitional context the chapter argues that the Northern Ireland experience speaks to a range of themes in the transitional justice literature concerning the meaning of accountability, the ways in which hierarchies of victims are created and sustained, the capacity of former prisoners and ex-combatants in seeking redress and the limitations of legalistic variants of truth recovery.

Central to the transition in Northern Ireland is the suggestion that human rights should be at the heart of the new dispensation. In chapter three, Colin Harvey examines how the criminal justice system was and remains a particular target for rights-based reform. In the attempts to ensure institutional transformation, 'rights-talk' began to flow into almost every sphere of the transitional process and the reform of policing and justice in particular. The emergent regimes of accountability and change were plainly intended to 'take rights seriously'. Harvey sketches the human rights transitional context in Northern Ireland and explores how the attempts to mainstream rights have progressed in the sphere of criminal justice, including proposals for a Bill of Rights. He questions where a culture of respect for human rights is emerging in Northern Ireland whether this transformation is evident in the criminal justice system.

The fourth chapter, written by Brice Dickson, explores the key institutional reforms and examines who and what brought about this transformation, seeking to pinpoint the key protagonists and critical junctures which stimulated the reforms, how they were delivered and through what processes they are now being maintained. In his chapter Dickson seeks to identify the key agents of change and considers whether it is possible to generalise from Northern Ireland's experience so that other conflicted societies might benefit from the lessons learned.

Examining what it means to 'govern through risk', Clare Dwyer in chapter five shows that governing criminal justice in a transitional society emerging from decades of political violence, involves a permanent readjustment of the traditional forms of risk management, particularly in light of the possible consequences and incalculability of the risk of the return to conflict. By focusing on the role of risk assessment during and after a political conflict, this chapter draws out the key differences in the evolution of risk strategies and assessment within the criminal justice system in Northern Ireland and highlights the impact this has had on wider penal and social policy development.

Opening the second part of the book, 'The Criminal Justice Process', John Topping explores the issues of policing reforms and policing change in Northern Ireland. Chapter six sets out to demonstrate that in spite of both the political and financial capital invested in the reforms, a number of issues persist which both challenge and limit the extent to which a 'normalised' policing service can be delivered within any 'Peelian' conception of the term. This is particularly the case when set against the broader policing landscape, a continuing, 'severe' terrorist threat, and ongoing paramilitary 'policing', and the potential for mass public disorder associated with ritualistic parades and protests. This chapter charts the development and delivery of policing in Northern Ireland, juxtaposing both the police organisational and societal transitions which underpin the present reality of security and safety in a society transitioning from conflict.

In the seventh chapter, John Morison examines judicial appointments and the Northern Ireland Judicial Appointments Commission. He explores how a non-departmental body (NIJAC), charged by statute with producing a judiciary that is reflective of a changing wider society, has gone about trying to effect widespread, deep-rooted institutional change. Drawing on original empirical data, chapter seven emphasises the relationship between judicial appointments and changes to the wider legal environment, and how the barriers to a more representative judiciary are in large part a product of the legal culture in the local professions. This puts the focus on how ideas of suitability and, particularly, 'merit', are constructed and resonate within the legal profession well beyond the appointment stage, and how they reveal much about the nature of the society in which they operate.

In their chapter, Kieran McEvoy and Alex Schwartz examine the role of judges and judicial culture in Northern Ireland. Drawing on extensive interviews conducted with judges in Northern Ireland and elsewhere, chapter eight considers challenges for the judiciary both during the conflict itself and more recently in coming to terms with the past. Building on that interview data, they focus in particular on the notion of judicial performance arguing that judicial behaviour may be understood as addressing a range of 'imagined' audiences, namely, Parliament, the public and judges themselves. They also argue that in a context wherein discussions are ongoing about whether or not Northern Ireland should have some form of truth recovery process to 'deal with the past' the judiciary itself should be one thematic focus of such a process.

Chapter nine, written by Phil Scraton, examines the complex dynamics of incarceration in contemporary Northern Ireland, within the context of a society undergoing transition from conflict. He demonstrates the impact of the legacy of conflict on the prison estate, operational practices and organisational culture and the challenges and impediments to reform. Reflecting on the range of prison reviews, contextualised by the legacy of conflict, this chapter critically analyses and evaluates current policies, regimes, and staffing and practices within the context of Northern Ireland's three remaining prison establishments: Maghaberry (high security, complex mix of remand/convicted; short-term/long-term; politically affiliated prisoners); Magilligan (low and medium risk prisoners/sex offenders/ foreign nationals); and Hydebank Wood Prison (women only) and Young Offender Centre.

Chapter ten is an analysis of prisoner reintegration in post-conflict Northern Ireland, with particular emphasis on the experience of 'politically motivated' former prisoners. In this chapter Clare Dwyer explores the ways in which organisations who work with and for, the 'politically motivated' ex-prisoner community, were developed through an ethos of 'self-help'. In presenting a critical analysis of the concept of 'self-help' and its application to the experience of the reintegrative process, this chapter illustrates the fundamental importance of the 'self-help' approach to reintegration, particularly for prisoners released following a political conflict. Set within Northern Ireland's unique circumstances as a society transitioning out of conflict, this chapter explores the ethos of ex-prisoner 'self-help' and the potential lessons for those seeking to promote desistance from crime and violence, politically motivated and otherwise. The chapter concludes with discussions on the wider implications of the Northern Irish experience for the reintegration of prisoners more widely, including the role of reintegration in peace-building and conflict transformation more generally.

In chapter eleven, Nicola Carr examines how the conflict has had profound effects on the contours and culture of probation practice within Northern Ireland. The chapter analyses how the passage of the Criminal Justice (Northern Ireland) Order 2008 and the introduction of a range of 'public protection' sentences have intensified probation's focus on assessing and managing risk. Alongside this, and in common with other jurisdictions, the population under the supervision of the service has expanded. By linking the historical context with the present, this chapter explores changes in the nature of probation practice and community sanctions, particularly in the transition from conflict. Through this lens, Carr explores the concept of 'legitimacy' and its relevance for probation practice and the wider criminal justice sphere.

Chapter twelve considers official acknowledgment of miscarriages of justice in post-conflict Northern Ireland, through the quashing of convictions and the provision of compensation. Marny Requa highlights how conflict-related cases continue to dominate proceedings in this area. She argues that as a consequence, the jurisprudence on miscarriages of justice is distinct from elsewhere in the United Kingdom and has strong political resonance in post-conflict Northern Ireland. The high percentage of conflict-related referrals from the Criminal Cases Review Commission involving convictions under counterterrorism legislation is indicative of a continued political focus on the past. The chapter concludes that as a consequence, this perspective overshadows the development of contemporary criminal standards in more routine cases. Recent case law restricts future referrals in conflict-related cases, adding to what is characterised in this chapter as an 'acknowledgement gap' regarding miscarriages of justice in Northern Ireland.

In the opening chapter in part III of the book which explores 'Contemporary Issues in Criminal Justice', Linda Moore and Azrini Wahidin analyse the experience of women within the criminal justice system during the conflict and following political settlement. Chapter thirteen draws on primary research and documents fundamental breaches of women's rights within the criminal justice system. Moore and Wahidin argue that violence and sectarian divisions have shaped penal regimes, both for politically motivated and so-called 'ordinary' women prisoners and discuss women's responses to gendered control and punishment. The chapter explores the historical and current breaches of women prisoners' rights and references contemporary debates on alternatives to custody for women, the provision of gender-specific approaches and abolitionism.

Chapter fourteen written by Deena Haydon and Siobhán McAlister examines children and young people in conflict with the law in Northern Ireland. This chapter outlines the evolution of youth justice policy as Northern Ireland emerged from the imposition of 'direct rule' to devolution. Haydon and McAlister examine three specific forms of state intervention—early intervention targeting those 'at risk' of offending, restorative justice, and imprisonment—while also noting informal, non-state interventions experienced by many children and young people. Drawing out comparisons with England and Wales where relevant, in particular the influence and convergence of risk-based policies, this chapter considers what is unique about policy and practice in Northern Ireland and assesses whether claims made about implementation of human rights standards match the reality of young people's experiences.

Chapter fifteen examines public and policy responses to sexual and violent crime in Northern Ireland within the broader context of national and international trends on crime and justice. Drawing on the theme of 'policy transfer, Anne-Marie McAlinden argues that both before and after devolution Northern Ireland has to a large extent emulated penal policies on sexual and violent crime which have been put in place in England and Wales. Drawing on original empirical data the chapter also suggests that there is a distinct extralegal dimension to policing sexual and violent crime in Northern Ireland stemming from the legacy of the conflict. These factors relate to the presence of paramilitaries, the parochial nature of Northern Irish society and the geographical, land border with the Republic of Ireland. McAlinden concludes that these unique aspects of justice provision in Northern Ireland create additional challenges for offender reintegration, as well as for policing and the criminal justice management of such crimes in a society transitioning from political conflict.

In chapter sixteen, Anna Eriksson explores the development of restorative justice practices in Northern Ireland. The chapter discusses the various challenges of implementing community-based restorative justice in a transitional society and explores how restorative justice has provided tools to aid conflict transformation and reconciliation, including in the field of youth justice. The core strength of restorative justice lies in removing the focus from the *outcome* and placing it where the important interactions take place, during the *process*. The chapter explores the important role of restorative justice in 'building proximity' and resolving conflict at all levels—within and between communities and between communities and the state. In discussing restorative justice practices initiated both within and outside the formal criminal justice system in Northern Ireland, it draws out the key context-specific lessons as well as those that might be generalised to other jurisdictions.

In the fourth and final part of the book the editors pull together the major themes arising from the book. In chapter seventeen, we seek to locate key recent developments within criminal justice in Northern Ireland within the broader transitional context. This final chapter highlights generic themes related to 'doing' criminal justice in Northern Ireland which have broader applicability for discourses on crime and justice. These relate in particular to the significance of the 'policy transfer' thesis within neo-liberal societies, and the impact of the past in the contemporary governance of criminal justice. Finally, the chapter identifies areas for further research and charts the likely future directions of criminal justice policy and criminological scholarship within Northern Ireland and beyond.

References

Adler, F (1983) *Nations Not Obsessed with Crime* (Littleton, CO, Fred B Rothman and Co).

Anderson, B (1983) *Imagined Communities: Reflections on the Origins and Spread of Nationalism* (London, Verso).

Belfast/Good Friday Agreement (1998) *The Agreement Reached in the Multi-Party Negotiations* (Belfast, Northern Ireland Office).

Brewer, J, Lockhart, B and Rodgers, P (1997) *Crime in Ireland 1945–1995—'Here be dragons'* (Oxford, Clarendon Press).

Brinkerhoff, D (2005) 'Rebuilding Governance in Failed States and Post-Conflict Societies: Concepts and Cross-Cutting Themes' 25 *Public Administration and Development* 3.

Campbell, C, Bell, C and Ní Aoláin, F (2004) 'Justice Discourses in Transition' 13 *Social and Legal Studies* 305.
Campbell, C and Connolly, I (2012) 'The Sharp End: Armed Opposition Movements, Transitional Truth Processes and the *Rechtsstaat*' 6 *International Journal of Transitional Justice* 11.
Carmichael, P and Knox, C (2004) 'Devolution, Governance and the Peace Process' 16 *Terrorism and Political Violence* 593.
Cavadino, M and Dignan, J (2006) 'Penal Policy and Political Economy' 6 *Criminology & Criminal Justice* 435.
Christie, N (2000) *Crime Control as Industry*, 3rd edn (London, Routledge).
Clutterbuck, R (1994) *Terrorism in an Unstable World* (London, Routledge).
Cohen, S (1995) 'State Crimes of Previous Regimes: Knowledge, Accountability and the Policing of the Past' 20 *Law & Social Inquiry* 7.
Council of Europe (2014) *Council of Europe Annual Penal Statistics—SPACE I—Survey 2012* (Strasbourg, COE).
Crawford, A (1999) *The Local Governance of Crime: Appeals to Community and Partnerships* (Oxford, Oxford University Press).
—— (2006) 'Networked Governance and the Post-Regulatory State? Steering, Rowing and Anchoring the Provision of Policing and Security' 10 *Theoretical Criminology* 449.
Criminal Justice Review Group (CJRG) (2000) *Review of the Criminal Justice System in Northern Ireland:* The Report of the Criminal Justice Review (Belfast, HMSO).
Croall, H, Mooney, G and Munro, M (2010) *Criminal Justice in Scotland* (Oxford, Willan Publishing).
Darby, J (1995) 'Conflict in Northern Ireland: A Background Essay' in S Dunn (ed), *Facets of the Conflict in Northern Ireland* (London, Macmillan Press Ltd).
Dickson, B (2001) *The Legal System of Northern Ireland*, 4th edn (Belfast, SLS Publications).
—— (2013) *Law in Northern Ireland*, 2nd edn (Oxford, Hart Publishing).
Dwyer, C (2004) 'The Complexity of Imprisonment: The Northern Ireland Experience' 35 *Cambrian Law Review* 97.
Elster, J (2004) *Closing the Books: Transitional Justice in Historical Perspective* (Cambridge, Cambridge University Press).
Emmerson, C and Frayne, C (2005) *Public Spending, Election Briefing 2005* (London, Institute for Fiscal Studies).
Ericson, RV and Haggerty, KD (1997) *Policing the Risk Society* (Oxford, Clarendon Press).
Fitzgerald, M and Hale, C (2013) 'The Politics of Law and Order' in C Hale, K Hayward, A Wahidin and E Wincup (eds), *Criminology* (Oxford, Oxford University Press).
Freeman, M (2006) *Truth Commissions and Procedural Fairness* (Cambridge, Cambridge University Press).
Garland, D (1999) 'Preface' in P Duff and N Hutton (eds), *Criminal Justice in Scotland* (Aldershot, Ashgate).
—— (2001) *The Culture of Control: Crime and Social Order in Contemporary Society* (Oxford, Oxford University Press).
—— (2004) 'Beyond the Culture of Control' 7 *Critical Review of International Social and Political Philosophy* (special issue on Garland's *The Culture of Control*) 160.
Gillespie, A (2013) *The English Legal System* (Oxford, Oxford University Press).
Grieff, P (ed) (2006) *The Handbook on Reparations* (Oxford, Oxford University Press).
Hayner, P (2001) *Unspeakable Truths: Facing the Challenge of Truth Commissions* (London, Routledge).

Hewitt, C (1981) 'Catholic Grievances, Catholic Nationalism and Violence in Northern Ireland during the Civil Rights Period: A Reconsideration' 32 *British Journal of Sociology* 362.

Hillsborough Agreement (2010) *Agreement at Hillsborough Castle* (Belfast, Northern Ireland Office).

Huyse, L (1995) 'Justice after Transition: On the Choices Successor Elites Make in Dealing with the Past' 20 *Law & Social Inquiry* 51.

Independent Commission on Policing for Northern Ireland (ICP) (1999) *A New Beginning: Policing in Northern Ireland* (Belfast, HMSO).

Jackson, J (2001) 'Shaping the Future of Criminal Justice' in C Harvey (ed), *Human Rights, Equality and Democratic Renewal in Northern Ireland* (Oxford, Hart Publishing).

Jackson, J and Doran, S (1995) *Judge Without Jury: Diplock Trials in the Adversary System* (Oxford, Clarendon Press).

Jamieson, J (1998) 'Towards a Criminology of War in Europe' in V Ruggiero, N South and I Taylor (eds), *The New European Criminology: Crime and Social Order in Europe* (London, Routledge).

Jones, T and Newburn, T (2006) 'Three Strikes and You're Out: Exploring Symbol and Substance in American and British Crime Control Politics' 46 *British Journal of Criminology* 781.

Kelly, G (1990) *Pattern of Child-Care Careers and the Decisions that Shape Them* (Belfast, Queen's University, Department of Social Studies).

Knox, C (2002) '"See No Evil, Hear No Evil": Insidious Paramilitary Violence in Northern Ireland' 42 *British Journal of Criminology* 164.

Kritz, N (1995) 'The Dilemmas of Transitional Justice' in J Kritz (ed), *Transitional Justice* (Washington, DC, Institute of Peace Press).

Loader, I and Walker, N (2007) *Civilizing Security* (Cambridge, Cambridge University Press).

MacGinty, R and Darby, J (2002) *Guns and Government: The Management of the Northern Ireland Peace Process* (Basingstoke, Palgrave Macmillan).

Mallinder, L (2008) *Amnesty, Human Rights and Political Transitions: Bridging the Peace and Justice Divide* (Oxford, Hart Publishing).

Matthews, R and Young, J (2003) *The New Politics of Crime and Punishment* (Cullompton, Willan Publishing).

McAlinden, A (2012) 'The Governance of Sexual Offending Across Europe: Penal Policies, Political Economies and the Institutionalization of Risk' 14 *Punishment & Society* 166.

McEvoy, K (2007) 'Beyond Legalism: Towards a Thicker Understanding of Transitional Justice' 34 *Journal of Law and Society* 411.

McEvoy, K and Ellison, G (2003) 'Criminological Discourses in Northern Ireland: Conflict and Conflict Resolution' in K McEvoy and T Newburn (eds), *Criminology, Conflict Resolution and Restorative Justice* (London, Palgrave).

McEvoy, K, Gormally, B and Mika, H (2002) 'Conflict, Crime Control and the "re" Construction of State/Community Relations in Northern Ireland' in G Hughes, E McLaughlin and J Muncie (eds), *Crime Prevention and Community* (London, Sage).

McEvoy, K and McGregor, L (eds) (2008) *Transitional Justice From Below: Grassroots Activism and the Struggle for Change* (Oxford, Hart Publishing).

McEvoy, K and Newburn, T (eds) (2003) *Criminology, Conflict Resolution and Restorative Justice* (London, Palgrave).

McGarry, J and O'Leary, B (eds) (2004) *The Northern Ireland Conflict: Consociational Engagements* (Oxford, Oxford University Press).

McKittrick, D, Kelters, S, Feeney, B, Thornton, C and McVea, D (2007) *Lost Lives: The Stories of the Men, Women and Children who Died as a Result of the Northern Ireland Troubles* (Edinburgh, Mainstream Publishing).

McKittrick D and McVea D (2012) *Making Sense of the Troubles* (Blackstaff Press).

McLaughlin, E (2005) 'Governance and Social Policy in Northern Ireland (1999–2004): The Devolution Years and Postscript' in M Powell, L Bauld and K Clarke (eds), *Social Policy Review 17* (Bristol, Policy Press/Social Policy Association).

McMillan, N (2010) 'Regret, Remorse and the Work of Remembrance: Official Responses to the Rwandan Genocide' 19 *Social & Legal Studies* 85.

Méndez, JE (1997) 'In Defense of Transitional Justice' in AJ McAdams (ed), *Transitional Justice and the Rule of Law in New Democracies* (Notre Dame, IN, University of Notre Dame Press).

Moran, M (2003) *The British Regulatory State: High Modernism and Hyper Innovation* (Oxford, Oxford University Press).

Morison, J and Geary, R (2000) 'Lives Less Ordinary? Key Findings of the Northern Ireland Communities Crime Survey' 10 *Irish Journal of Sociology* 49.

Morison, J, McEvoy, K and Anthony, G (eds) (2007) *Judges, Transition and Human Rights* (Oxford, Oxford University Press).

Muncie, J (2005) 'The Globalization of Crime Control—The Case of Youth and Juvenile Justice: Neo-liberalism, Policy Convergence and International Conventions' 9 *Theoretical Criminology* 35.

Nelken, D (2007) 'Comparing Criminal Justice' in M Maguire, R Morgan and R Reiner (eds), *The Oxford Handbook of Criminology*, 4th edn (Oxford, Oxford University Press).

Newburn, T (2002) 'Atlantic Crossings: "Policy Transfer" and Crime Control in the USA and Britain' 4 *Punishment & Society* 165.

—— (2010) 'Diffusion, Differentiation and Resistance in Comparative Penality' 10 *Criminology & Criminal Justice* 341.

Newburn, T and Sparks, R (eds) (2004) *Criminal Justice and Political Cultures: National and International Dimensions of Crime Control* (Cullompton, Willan Publishing).

Northern Ireland Prison Service (NIPS) (2014) *Analysis of NIPS Prison Population from 01/07/2013 to 30/09/2014* (Belfast, Department of Justice).

O'Leary, B and McGarry, J (1996) *The Politics of Antagonism: Understanding Northern Ireland*, 2nd edn (London, Athlone Press).

O'Mahony, D, Geary, R, McEvoy, K and Morison, J (2000) *Crime, Community and Locale: The Northern Ireland Communities Crime Survey* (Aldershot, Ashgate).

Osiel, M (1997) *Mass Atrocity, Collective Memory and the Law* (New Brunswick, NJ, Transaction Publishers).

Pinkerton, J (1994) *In Care At Home: Parenting, The State and Civil Society* (Aldershot, Avebury).

Police Service of Northern Ireland (PSNI) (2014) 'Police Recorded Crime in Northern Ireland: Monthly Update to 31 August 2014' (Belfast, PSNI).

Purdie, B (1990) *Politics in the Streets: The Origins of the Civil Rights Movement in Northern Ireland* (Belfast, Blackstaff Press).

Reichel, P (2008) *Comparative Criminal Justice Systems: A Topical Approach*, 4th edn (Englewood Cliffs, NJ, Prentice Hall).

Rose, N (2000) 'Government and Control' 40 *British Journal of Criminology* 321.

Shearing, C (2000) 'Punishment and the Changing Face of Governance' 3 *Punishment & Society* 203.
Spjut, RJ (1986) 'Internment and Detention without Trial in Northern Ireland 1971–1975: Ministerial Policy and Practice' 49 *Modern Law Review* 712.
St Andrews Agreement (2006) *The St Andrews Agreement, October 2006* (Belfast, Northern Ireland Office).
Stormont House Agreement (2014) *The Stormont House Agreement* (London/Belfast, Northern Ireland Office).
Teitel, R (2000) *Transitional Justice* (Oxford, Oxford University Press).
—— (2003) 'Transitional Justice Genealogy' 16 *Harvard Human Rights Journal* 69.
Tonge, J (2002) *Northern Ireland: Conflict and Change* (Pearson, London).
—— (2005) *Northern Ireland* (Cambridge, Polity).
Wacquant, L (2001) 'The Penalisation of Poverty and Neo-liberalism' 9 *European European Journal on Criminal Policy and Research* 401.
Walker, C (2011) *Terrorism and the Law* (Oxford, Oxford University Press).
Walker, N and Telford, M (2000) 'Designing Criminal Justice: The System' in *Comparative Perspective, Report 14, Review of the Criminal Justice System in Northern Ireland* (London, HMSO).
White, R and White, T (1995) 'Repression and the Liberal State: The Case of Northern Ireland, 1969–1972' 39 *Journal of Conflict Resolution: A Quarterly for Research related to War and Peace* 330.
Wichert, S (1991) *Northern Ireland Since 1945* (London, Longman).
Wilkinson, P (1986) *Terrorism and the Liberal State* (London, Macmillan).
Wright, J (1991) *Terrorist Propaganda: The Red Army Faction and the Provisional IRA 1968–86* (New York, St Martin's Press).

2

Criminal Justice, Truth Recovery and Dealing with the Past in Northern Ireland

CHERYL LAWTHER

Introduction

During the Northern Ireland conflict more than 3700 individuals were killed and 40,000 injured (McKittrick et al 2007). Reflecting broader international trends, there has been much discussion on how Northern Ireland should deal with its past and, in particular, the recovery of truth about past human rights violations—now considered an axiomatic element of post-conflict reconstruction (see Wiebelhaus-Brahm 2010; Hayner 2011).[1] Setting Northern Ireland apart however, is the absence of a formal truth recovery process. Unlike many other 'post-conflict' societies, truth recovery was not a part of the Belfast Agreement in 1998. Rather, during the negotiations, a premium was placed on avoiding anything as contentious and potentially divisive as a truth commission (Bell 2002; Lundy 2010). Instead, issues that in other circumstances might have fallen under the remit of a truth commission (the reform of the police, a review of the criminal justice system, prisoner releases and so forth), were disaggregated and addressed separately and distinctly (Bell 2002; O'Rawe 2003; Lundy 2010).

That said, legacy issues have loomed large on Northern Ireland's social and political landscape and there have been consistent calls for a full examination of the past. There have been two significant junctures in this debate. First was the establishment of the Consultative Group on the Past (CGP) by the British Government in June 2007. The Group reported in January 2009 and recommended that a Legacy Commission—a bespoke truth mechanism shaped around the themes of 'Review and Investigation', 'Information Recovery' and 'Thematic Examination' be established (CGP 2009).[2] This proposal and the remainder of the CGP's report

[1] Misztal (2003: 147) argues that 'coming to terms with the past has emerged as the grand narrative of our times'.

[2] See the *Report of the Consultative Group on the Past* for full details on these strands (CGP 2009).

subsequently faltered and fell on the recommendation that a £12,000 'Recognition Payment' would be paid to all victims of the conflict—civilians, members of the security forces and former members of paramilitary organisations (CGP 2009).[3] Second and more recently, the former US envoy to Northern Ireland, Dr Richard Haass and Professor Meghan O'Sullivan were appointed in July 2013 to chair an all-party group designed to facilitate discussion on issues relating to flags and emblems, parades and the past.[4] Following six months of meetings and negotiations and over 600 submissions, Haass and O'Sullivan made their final recommendations on 30 December 2013. On the past, they include a Historical Investigations Unit (HIU) which would pull together the Historical Enquiries Team (HET) and the Office of the Police Ombudsman for Northern Ireland (OPONI) and, backed by appropriate powers, would investigate outstanding cases, with a view to prosecution where possible; an Independent Commission for Information Retrieval (ICIR), which would have the power to offer limited immunity from prosecution in return for truth recovery, and would include an internal unit designed to analyse patterns and themes related to the conflict; and other processes to facilitate acknowledgement, storytelling and specialist services for victims and survivors (Haass and O'Sullivan 2013). The process failed to reach agreement on any of the three issues by the deadline of 31 December 2013.[5] In this vacuum, the criminal justice system has become the space wherein victims and survivors have sought 'truth' and contested versions of the past have been examined.[6]

This chapter engages with Northern Ireland's 'piecemeal' approach to the past to critically examine the capacity and limitations of 'ordinary' criminal justice in a 'transitional' context (Bell 2002: 1095). The structure of this chapter is as follows: the first part explores the rationale for 'truth recovery' in the aftermath of violent

[3] This payment was to be awarded on the basis of the inclusive Victims and Survivors (Northern Ireland) Order 2006. It provides the statutory definition of a victim or survivor of the conflict as '(a) someone who is or has been physically or psychologically injured as a result of or in consequence of a conflict-related incident; (b) someone who provides a substantial amount of care on a regular basis for an individual mentioned in paragraph (a); or (c) someone who has been bereaved as a result of or in consequence of a conflict-related event' (art 3(1)).

[4] Northern Ireland Office (NIO), 'Dr Richard Haass to Chair All-Party Talks' press release, 9 July 2013.

[5] *BBC News*, 'Northern Ireland: Richard Haass talks end without deal', 31 December 2013, available at www.bbc.co.uk/news/uk-northern-ireland-25556714.

[6] It should be noted that in the period between writing this chapter and its publication, the Stormont House Agreement was signed in December 2014 and represents a further attempt to break the logjam on dealing with the past. Its key provisions as regards truth recovery and dealing with the past are four fold. One is the creation of a 'Historical Investigations Unit' (HIU), a new independent body, designed to take forward outstanding legacy cases from the Historical Enquiries Team and the Office of the Police Ombudsman for Northern Ireland. Two, a 'Independent Commission on Information Retrieval' (ICIR) which, under a 5 year mandate, will enable victims and survivors to privately seek and receive information about the deaths of their loved ones. Third, it is envisaged that an 'Oral History Archive' will be established by 2016. Fourth, an 'Implementation and Reconciliation Group' will be created 'to oversee themes, archives and information recovery'. At the time of writing, legislation is being drafted to bring these proposals into being. It is anticipated that it will be introduced to Parliament in September 2015 and new institutions may be in place by Easter 2016.

conflict and provides a broad overview of the key truth finding mechanisms at play. These include the police-led HET, the OPONI, public inquiries, the inquest system, the Criminal Cases Review Commission (CCRC) and litigation by victims and former combatants. The remainder and main part of the chapter explores the intersection between these elements of the criminal justice system and dealing with the past. It argues that the Northern Ireland experience speaks to four key themes in the transitional justice literature concerning the limitations of legalistic variants of truth recovery, the meaning of accountability, the ways in which hierarchies of victims are created and sustained and the capacity of victims and former combatants. Each is explored in turn. This chapter concludes by arguing that while the criminal justice system has played an important role in dealing with the legacy of the past in Northern Ireland, it was neither designed to, nor is it capable of, offering a full examination of the causes, context or consequences of the Northern Ireland conflict. Rather, its inherent limitations have resulted in an approach to the past that is piecemeal, incomplete and marked by significant shortcomings.

Truth, Transition and Dealing with the Past

The reasons why a transitional society may choose to 'deal with' its past, typically by seeking truth about past human rights violations, through, for example, a truth commission, a commission of historical clarification or criminal trials, are well established. Lundy and McGovern (2008: 178) argue that 'dealing with the past' is generally taken to refer to three interrelated areas of concern. First, how public memory or commemoration of the past, or processes designed to clarify the historical record, might contribute to positive social change or 'reconciliation' in a violently divided society. Second, how the victims or survivors of the conflict and their relatives can be provided with various forms of support or offered opportunities to come to terms with past experiences. Third, what means (either judicial or non-judicial) might be introduced to deal with outstanding truth and justice issues and provide a record of past human rights abuses. Other cross-cutting objectives include: reaffirming the rule of law; making known the range of forensic, personal and social 'truths' about past conflict; and broadening ownership of the structural causes of violence and conflict transformation (Tutu 1999; Boraine 2000; Smyth 2007; Wiebelhaus-Brahm 2010).

These themes have been well rehearsed in Northern Ireland. As noted above, in the absence of a formal truth process, a patchwork and disaggregated array of measures have been implemented, largely based in the criminal justice system. By way of background, it is helpful to introduce each mechanism at this juncture. The policing approach to the past consists of the HET and the OPONI. The HET was established in 2005 by the former Chief Constable of the Police Service of Northern Ireland (PSNI) Sir Hugh Orde. Its primary objective is to 'assist in bringing a measure of resolution to those families of victims affected by deaths attributed to the troubles in the years 1968–1998' and to chronologically re-examine all 3268 deaths that occurred during this period (HET, undated). Following the investigation, families receive a 'Review Summary Report' which attempts to answer any questions they may have and which details the circumstances of the death and the investigation. Although the unit does gather evidence with a view to prosecution (if deemed viable by the Public Prosecution Service), given the difficulties associated with historical prosecutions, the HET has been careful to manage victims' expectations in this regard (Orde 2009). By mid-2013, the HET had reopened 2068 cases which related to the deaths of 2682 people, and had completed 1713 cases which related to the deaths of 2209 people (Healing Through Remembering 2013). As explored in detail below, the independence and effectiveness of the HET, particularly in respect to its relationship with the PSNI and staffing policies, has been the subject of some critique by academic Patricia Lundy (2009a, 2009b, 2012) and Her Majesty's Inspectorate of Constabulary (HMIC 2013). In late September 2014 it was announced that due to budget cuts, the HET would close at the end of the year.[7]

Completing the policing approach to the past is the OPONI, established in 2000 and with the dual mandate of investigating contemporary allegations of police misconduct and historical conflict-related cases. While historical cases account for 20 per cent of the work conducted by the OPONI, they are the most resource intensive and account for most of the public comment and debate that the Office attracts. At the time of writing, the Office is reviewing over 150 historical cases, comprising complaints from the public and referrals from the PSNI Chief Constable in relation to deaths and other serious matters believed to have involved members of the former police service, the Royal Ulster Constabulary (RUC)[8] between 1969 and 1998 (OPONI 2013). Some of those most controversial cases, particularly under the leadership of Nuala O'Loan, include a highly critical report into the RUC/PSNI investigation of the Omagh bombing and the Operation Ballast report which found evidence of collusion between loyalist paramilitary informers and members of the RUC Special Branch (OPONI 2001, 2007). As with the HET, the OPONI has also faced questions concerning its capacity to deal with historical cases (CAJ 2011; CJINI 2011). Detailed below, the cumulative effect of these reports and a damning BBC1 'Spotlight' investigation was the resignation of the former Ombudsman Al Hutchinson and his replacement by Dr Michael Maguire in July 2012.

At the more 'legal' end of the truth recovery spectrum are public inquiries, a particularly visible form of truth recovery in Northern Ireland. While only those major public inquiries which have occurred during the transitional phase are considered in this chapter, it should be noted that Rolston and Scraton (2005) have documented 23 different types of inquiry into different aspects of state policy during the conflict and, in the main, dealing with the ways in which the criminal

[7] *Belfast Telegraph*, 'PSNI cuts 300 jobs and axes Historical Enquiries Team', 30 September 2014.
[8] See chapter by Topping in this volume for further discussion on the history of the RUC.

justice system, police and military responded to the campaigns of political violence. Post-conflict, the Saville Inquiry into the events of Bloody Sunday 1972 and the Cory collusion inquiries into the allegations of British state/security force collusion with loyalist paramilitaries in the deaths of Rosemary Nelson, Robert Hamill and Pat Finucane, with republican paramilitaries in the death of Billy Wright and collusion between the IRA and members of An Garda Siochána in the deaths of RUC Chief Superintendent Harry Breen and Superintendent Bob Buchanan are highly significant. The Saville Tribunal reported in June 2010, finding that British Army paratroopers were responsible for causing the deaths of 13 people 'none of whom was posing a threat of causing death or serious injury' (Saville et al 2010: 58). Public inquiries into the Nelson, Hamill, Wright and Breen/Buchanan cases were also established, and in all but the Hamill case, have reported (see: Morland et al 2011; MacLean et al 2010; Smithwick 2013). A documentary review of the Finucane case was completed in December 2012 (de Silva 2012). In total, approximately £322 million has been spent on public inquiries (Healing Through Remembering 2010).[9] Calls for further inquiries into the Kingsmills massacre,[10] the Ballymurphy massacre,[11] the Omagh bombing[12] and the Loughinisland murders[13] amongst others are ongoing.[14]

Often described as miniature public inquiries are inquests in the coroners' courts. As in England and Wales, coroners in Northern Ireland are required to hold inquests into deaths in order to identify the deceased and to ascertain 'how, when and where the individual died'.[15] At the time of writing, there are at least 36 conflict-related cases in Northern Ireland awaiting inquests. These cases fall into two broad categories: cases which have never had an inquest ('outstanding legacy cases'), largely comprised of deaths involving state actors/agents or allegations of collusion; and cases in which a previous inquest had been completed, but the Attorney General has directed that a new inquest be held—on the grounds of fresh evidence for example (Amnesty International 2013).[16] There has been persistent criticism of

[9] See also M Hilliard, 'Smithwick Tribunal report: costs incurred run to €15million' *Irish News*, 4 December 2013.

[10] On 5 January 1976, 10 Protestant workmen travelling on a minibus were shot dead by members of the Provisional Irish Republican Army (PIRA).

[11] The Ballymurphy massacre refers to a series of incidents between 9 and 11 August 1971, following the introduction of internment, and during which 11 civilians were killed by members of the Parachute Regiment of the British Army in the Ballymurphy area of west Belfast.

[12] The Real IRA Omagh car bombing of August 1998 killed 29 civilians.

[13] Six men were shot dead by the Ulster Volunteer Force at a bar in Loughinisland, County Down, 18 June 1994.

[14] See, eg, *News Letter*, 'Call for public inquiry into UVF massacre', 25 November 2010; *News Letter*, 'Kingsmills families want killers named', 22 June 2011; *Belfast Telegraph*, 'Rally Calls for Inquiry into Ballymurphy Killings by Soldiers', 13 August 2012; *BBC News*, 'Omagh Bomb Families Make New Call for Inquiry', 8 August 2013, available at www.bbc.co.uk/news/uk-northern-ireland-23607106; *BBC News*, Loughinisland Murders: Police Appeal on 20th Anniversary of UVF Attack, 18 June 2014, available at www.bbc.co.uk/news/uk-northern-ireland-27899485.

[15] Coroners Act (NI) 1959, s 31(1).

[16] ibid, s 14. At the time of writing, the Attorney General has directed over 30 inquests into conflict-related deaths.

the operation of the coronial system in Northern Ireland (see Ní Aoláin 2000). Prior to the Human Rights Act 1998, much critique was levelled at the lack of breadth of investigation and the findings of inquests, in particular given that coroners and juries were prohibited from expressing any opinion 'on questions of criminal or civil liability' (Requa and Anthony 2008; Healing Through Remembering 2013). Latterly, the inquest system has been criticised for falling short of human rights standards (Anthony and Mageean 2007). In the McKerr group of cases, the European Court of Human Rights (ECtHR) criticised the lack of verdicts, the absence of legal aid, the non-disclosure of witness statements, the lack of promptness, the inability to compel witnesses, and the limited scope of some inquests.[17] As a result, the British Government took a number of measures to ensure that future inquests complied with Article 2 of the European Convention on Human Rights (ECHR) (the right to life), including changes to inquest rules so that witnesses could be compelled to attend and the extension of the scope of an inquest (Amnesty International 2013). In 2011, the UK Supreme Court also issued a judgment finding that inquests into conflict-related deaths were required—as a matter of domestic law—to be Article 2 compliant.[18] In the judgment, Lady Hale stated that,

> differences centre on the scope of the available verdict as to 'how' the deceased met his death: in a conventional inquest, 'how' means only 'by what means' whereas in an Article 2 compliant inquest it must also encompass 'in what broad circumstances'.[19]

Despite these rulings, concerns remain over endemic delays within the inquest system and over the scope of some inquests, particularly controversial cases involving the use of lethal force by the state and whether such inquests will establish the broader circumstances of a death (Amnesty International 2013).

The CCRC was created by the Criminal Appeal Act 1995 and began work in April 1997. An independent public body, the CCRC investigates alleged miscarriages of justice occurring in the criminal courts and, where appropriate, can refer cases to the Court of Appeal or, where appropriate, the Northern Ireland Court of Appeal (NICA). It has significant legal powers, including the power to access and review police notes or other documents held by public bodies, as well as commission reports from outside bodies. As the CCRC website makes clear, the test that is applied is not whether or not a person is 'innocent', but rather 'to review the cases of those that feel they have been wrongly convicted of criminal offences or unfairly sentenced. We consider whether there is new evidence or argument that may cast doubt on the safety of an original decision'.[20] Between 1998 and 2011, 33 cases were referred from the CCRC to the NICA, 30 of which were conflict related (Healing Through Remembering 2013). Of these referrals, 26 convictions were quashed and

[17] See *Jordan v UK* (2003) 37 EHRR 2; *Kelly v UK* App no 30054/96 (ECHR, 4 May 2001); *McKerr v UK* (2002) 34 EHRR 20; *Shanaghan v UK* App no 37715/97 (ECHR, 4 May 2001); *Finucane v UK* (2003) 37 EHRR 29.

[18] *In the matter of an application by Brigid McCaughey and another for Judicial Review* (Northern Ireland) [2011] UKSC 20 (18 May 2011).

[19] ibid, paras [82]–[83].

[20] See www.ccrc.gov.uk/about/about_27.htm.

20 of those cases referred to 'problematic' confessional evidence, including allegations of police torture or other abuses and where juveniles or vulnerable persons had been denied access to their lawyers. At the time of writing, over 30 cases are pending before the CCRC. However, as noted by the CGP (2009), there are potentially hundreds of applications which could be brought to the CCRC by individuals, most of whom were convicted under the Diplock system and which relied heavily on confessional evidence for prosecutions (see Jackson and Doran 1995; Dickson 2010).[21] As Quirk (2013) points out, in the absence of a formal truth recovery process, criminal appeals are becoming a proxy for addressing the role of the state during the conflict, as well as remedying individual injustices.

In addition to these mechanisms, the use of litigation to seek redress for past injustices or hurts has long been a feature of the Northern Ireland conflict and transition (McEvoy 2000; Bell and Keenan 2005; Dickson 2010). Legal action by both victims and ex-combatants is ongoing. As regards civil action taken by victims, the case taken by some of the families affected by the 1998 Omagh bombing is well known. The civil action began in 2008, and in 2009, republicans Michael McKevitt, Liam Campbell, Colm Murphy and Seamus Daly were found liable for the bombing and were ordered to pay £1.6 million in damages. In April 2014, Seamus Daly was charged with 29 counts of murder.[22] Legal action by republican and loyalist ex-combatants concerning their internment in the early 1970s is also underway. In August 2011, six former republican detainees served writs on the Ministry of Defence, the Northern Ireland Secretary of State and the police.[23] Charges of trespass of the person, wrongful arrest, unlawful detention and conspiracy to injure are being brought against the British state.[24] Nineteen loyalist ex-combatants are also seeking legal redress for their experiences of internment, again focusing on trauma and human rights violations.[25] Informed by this backdrop, the strengths and weaknesses of utilising a criminal justice approach to the past in a transitional society are explored below.

The Limitations of Legalism

McEvoy (2007) argues that the seductive qualities of legalistic analysis lend themselves to transitional contexts and suggests that claims that the 'rule of law' speaks to values and working practices such as justice, objectivity, certainty, uniformity, rationality and so on are particularly prized in times of profound social and

[21] On the Diplock system see chapter by Requa in this volume.

[22] *BBC News*, 'Omagh Bomb: Seamus Daly Charged with 29 Murders', 10 April 2014, available at www.bbc.co.uk/news/uk-northern-ireland-26976719.

[23] *BBC News*, 'Republicans "To Sue Government" over Northern Ireland Internment', 9 August 2011, available at www.bbc.co.uk/news/uk-northern-ireland-14450327.

[24] *UTV News*, 'Legal Writ Served over Internment', 9 August 2011, available at www.u.tv/articles/article.aspx?cat=news&guid=8b2a9929-fc67-4f06-ac88-5a5b4f58eeee.

[25] *Belfast Telegraph*, 'Kenya Move "Boosts Internment Case"', 5 October 2012.

political transition. In such contexts, law can become an important practical and symbolic break with the past, a part of the effort to publicly demonstrate the legitimacy and accountability of the new regime (Osiel 2000; McEvoy 2007). Yet, as the Northern Ireland case illustrates, there are inherent limits to a legalistic approach to the past in a transitional environment. First, as Campbell and Turner (2008: 376) argue, the 'law "sees" only a limited range of wrongs'. Those typically outside this rubric include issues relating to gender, socio-economic harm, torture and ill-treatment and the experiences of those injured but not necessarily bereaved by the conflict (de Greiff and Duthie 2009; Hayner 2011; CAJ 2009). Moreover, a legalistic approach to the past achieved, for example, through public inquiries—which will by definition only investigate 'top-line' cases, or inquests or appeals to the CCRC, cannot and is not designed to engage in a broader examination of the causes, context or consequences of a period of political violence, or produce a 'social' or 'restorative' truth (Posel 1999). Quirk (2013: 952) is persuasive on this point, arguing that '[i]t is axiomatic that criminal proceedings are not engaged in a quest for truth, rather they test whether or not the prosecution has established legal guilt to the required standard in accordance with the evidential rules in place'. Writing in respect to the CCRC, Quirk (2013) further illustrates this point, stating that the NICA is not an appropriate route to truth recovery, given that it is not its function, the courts are not prone to self-reflection and that the NICA was itself a protagonist during the conflict. In a similar vein, Rolston and Scraton (2005) have argued that public inquiries can become legalistic vehicles for the obfuscation of truth and minimisation of state culpability. The British Government's establishment of the Inquiries Act (2005) that provides for significant ministerial control over the operation of public inquiries and limits the potential for truth telling may be indicative of this point (Requa 2007).

Rather, the narrative that emerges from a criminal justice approach to the past is a 'micro' or 'forensic' construction of truth (Osiel 2000). Amnesty International (2013) has clearly made this point in respect to the inquest system, noting that while it is designed to focus on individual cases, questions concerning patterns of violations and abuses and whether state policy or state-sanctioned practices deliberately or indirectly gave rise to unlawful conduct are not being addressed effectively through this mechanism. The Attorney General John Larkin has been similarly careful not to oversell the truth recovery potential of the inquest system in the absence of other measures—'they cannot, it seems to me, deliver satisfactory outcomes for families whose primary wish is to see successful prosecutions, nor can they offer an effective vehicle for the exploration of broader themes and factors that have shaped our recent past' (Larkin 2012: 15). That the relatives of the 10 individuals killed by members of the British Army in Ballymurphy, west Belfast, August 1971,[26] welcomed the announcement that new inquests would be held into

[26] The British Army has consistently argued that it opened fire in the Ballymurphy area in response to gunfire from republican paramilitaries. The victims' families have continued to protest their innocence. After reviewing the original inquiries, the Attorney General found many weaknesses

the killings, but have publicly stated that they consider them only 'another strand' and continue to demand 'an international independent commission', suggests that at least some victims also recognise these weaknesses.[27] The Northern Ireland Secretary of State has, however, ruled out an independent re-examination of all documents relating to the killings, arguing that such an exercise would not be in the public interest.[28] A focus on individual responsibility may therefore fail to take proper account of the complex collective factors which contributed to violence and may obscure the broader context of patterns of abuse and systemic wrongdoing over time (McEvoy 2007; Campbell and Turner 2008).

Equally, as a matter of practicality, the criminal justice system will only ever be able to look at a limited number of cases. In 2006, for example, Boyd and Doran (2006: 8) raised caution over 'the often harsh realities of proof in context of the criminal trial'. They identified two problems concerning the viability of historical prosecutions—the quality and availability of evidence, and that the range of evidential and procedural protections that are afforded to all suspects of crime may provide difficult barriers for prosecutors to surmount in respect of old cases (Boyd and Doran, 2006). More recently, the Attorney General John Larkin has publicly called to end all conflict-related prosecutions, inquests, inquiries and civil actions.[29] Larkin made a number of interlinked arguments—that prosecution is 'subject to a law of diminishing returns' versus the large number of unsolved cases—only three of 1800 cases examined by the HET have resulted in successful convictions, and that the current inquest system (and also public inquiries and the OPONI) is state centric and imbalanced in its capacity to deliver truth and justice for victims of state and non-state actors.[30] While Larkin's proposal was robustly criticised by victims, political parties and Amnesty International as amounting to an amnesty and denial of justice, that Haass and O'Sullivan (2013) linked the use of limited immunity from prosecution to the proposed ICIR unit arguably represents a pragmatic assessment of the limits of legalism in a transitional setting.

and unanswered questions and in November 2011 ordered that new inquests be held (see *UTV News*, 'New Inquests into Ballymurphy Deaths', 14 November 2011, available at www.u.tv/News/New-inquests-into-Ballymurphy-deaths/6c0fe56b-19fa-42a1-af0d-b39e4903ef5b).

[27] *BBC News*, 'Ballymurphy Families Welcome John Larkin Decision', 15 November 2011, available at www.bbc.co.uk/news/uk-northern-ireland-15731558.

[28] G Moriarty, 'Villiers Rejects Call for Ballymurphy Inquiry' *Irish News*, 29 April 2014.

[29] Larkin argued, 'More than 15 years have passed since the Belfast Agreement, there have been very few prosecutions, and every competent criminal lawyer will tell you the prospects of conviction diminish, perhaps exponentially, with each passing year, so we are in a position now where I think we have to take stock' (see *The Guardian*, 'Northern Ireland Attorney General Calls for End to Troubles Prosecutions', 20 November 2013).

[30] Providing some detail on his controversial statement, Larkin noted, 'the State is responsible for a much, much smaller proportion of the deaths that took place during the Troubles. That means that the larger constituency of victims who sustained loss at the hand of non-State actors don't see any comparable tools available to them. They realize that prosecutions are not going to happen at all or, even if they do, their chances of success are limited and the outcome will be a sentence of at most two years' (see *Belfast Telegraph*, 'Attorney General John Larkin: It's Time to Call Halt to All Troubles Cases', 20 November 2013).

The Meaning of Accountability

Tied into demands to 'deal with' the past is an increasing international expectation that accountability is due after atrocity (Sikkink 2011). Key principles of accountability in transitional settings include the need to uncover the truth, the need to restore the honour and reputation of victims and to identify and deal with those responsible for violent acts (Méndez 1997 cited in Bell 2002; Hayner 2011). Schabas (2009) argues that a key feature of legalistic debates is a narrow deployment of the term accountability as synonymous with the prosecution and punishment of individual perpetrators of human rights abuses. As detailed above, this can be seen in respect to Northern Ireland's piecemeal and legalistic approach to the past, where accountability for past actions and inactions has been atomised. Clear 'accountability gaps' exist in respect to victims of non-state actors, victims of state human rights violations and, more broadly, in respect to the collective and structural factors which contributed to violence (Bell 2002; Ní Aoláin 2000).

Yet, as Amnesty International's (2013) report *Time to Deal with the Past* makes clear, the problems inherent to the piecemeal approach have been exacerbated by serious delays in investigations, concerns about the thoroughness and effectiveness of investigations in some cases, and the independence and impartiality of the HET and OPONI, all of which impacts on the meaning of, and their capacity to deliver, accountability. Criticism of the HET has been well documented. A report by Her Majesty's Inspectorate of Constabulary found, for example, that the HET had not maintained its Article 2 required independence because it failed to ensure that former RUC members now working for the unit were not involved in 'state involvement' cases; that cases involving state actors appeared to be treated less rigorously in a number of ways, including how interviews under caution were conducted and the nature and extent of pre-interview disclosure; and the report expressed concern that the lack of any 'public reporting mechanism or accountability structure' other than reporting to the PSNI Chief Constable meant there was 'a real danger that the HET might be inadequate to meet Article 2 standards on transparency and accountability' (HMIC 2013: 26). Likewise, critical reports into the OPONI by the Committee on the Administration of Justice and Criminal Justice Inspection Northern Ireland (CJINI) raised questions of operational independence between the Office and the PSNI; a lack of any clear definition or consistent application of the term 'collusion', including that different interpretations could be used depending on the circumstances of the case; and that reports into historical cases were altered or rewritten to exclude criticism of the RUC (CAJ 2011; CJINI 2011). While historical investigations have resumed, the current Ombudsman Michael Maguire has acknowledged that the events leading to Al Hutchinson's resignation have seriously damaged public confidence in the Office's capacity to deal with historical cases.

The mechanisms themselves have also been found to have significant weaknesses as regards their capacity to engender truth telling. Lundy (2009a) for example notes that over a period of more than two-and-a-half years, the HET was unable to trace British soldiers through Ministry of Defence channels. The use of limited immunity in a select number of cases has also been less than persuasive. Bell (2002) points to the Saville Inquiry and notes that while the British state, through the Prime Minister, asserted its commitment to being held to account, in practice, it was difficult to hold military actors accountable. More recently, Judge Peter Smithwick who chaired the investigation into the murder of RUC officers Chief Superintendent Harry Breen and Superintendent Robert Buchanan and the allegation of IRA–Garda collusion, reported that evidence given by former IRA members was dishonest and untruthful (Smithwick 2013). The former Police Ombudsman Nuala O'Loan (2010) has also documented several instances where police officers gave evasive, contradictory and on occasion farcical answers to questions and of senior officers who refused to assist historical investigations carried out by her office. The combined effect of these critiques is that existing mechanisms have, or are, falling short of human rights obligations to conduct prompt, thorough and effective investigations in an independent and impartial manner, and that many families of those killed feel their deaths are inadequately investigated or the full truth about the circumstances of their deaths is not being revealed (CAJ 2013). At least in respect to several high profile HET investigations such as those into the 1978 IRA La Mon House Hotel bombing and the 1976 PIRA Kingsmill massacre, the reports made available to victims' families appear to have provoked fresh controversy including calls for prosecutions, more inquiries or state apologies.[31] Their experience alone suggests that demands for accountability and resolution are not being met by current mechanisms.

Truth and Hierarchies of Victimhood

As has been well documented, much of the debate on dealing with the past in Northern Ireland has been marked by discussions over 'innocent' and 'guilty' victims and the creation of a 'hierarchy of victimhood' (Smyth 2007; Brewer 2010; Brewer and Hayes 2011). Referring to how the categorisation or definition of a victim of the conflict is associated with a political value judgement, a number of concerns regarding current methods of truth recovery and the creation of a hierarchy of victims have been raised (Duffy 2010).

On one level, the piecemeal approach to the past, realised through the criminal justice system, is, by its very nature, selective and incomplete. The immediate consequence is competition and resentment over the level and depth of historical

[31] See, eg, *BBC News*, 'Kingsmills Families Demand Full Inquiry into Massacre', 21 June 2011, available at www.bbc.co.uk/news/uk-northern-ireland-13857495; *BBC News*, 'La Mon IRA Bomb Victims Want Public Inquiry After HET Report', 16 February 2012, available at www.bbc.co.uk/news/uk-northern-ireland-17061713.

investigations (CGP 2009; CVSNI 2012). This concern has been particularly acute amongst unionist political elites and representatives of the security forces, specifically those associated with the RUC. There is, for example, a clear rejection of the 'state-centric' nature of truth recovery and opposition to the selective nature of public inquiries and investigations in the coroners' courts, on the grounds that they create a hierarchy of victims, privileging the deaths of those individuals where state involvement is alleged at the expense of the vast majority of those affected by the conflict (Lawther 2010, 2014). The Saville Inquiry and its financial cost of £195 million has been a particular source of critique.[32] The Ulster Unionist Party member, Tom Elliott later re-emphasised this point in light of the announcement that the PSNI is to carry out a murder inquiry into the events of Bloody Sunday:

> Here we see the hierarchy of victims. Those who received a fully funded public inquiry have the Director of Public Prosecutions as part of setting up a murder investigation. Those whose loved ones died at the hands of terrorists and who have been denied such an Inquiry are not being afforded equality.[33]

For representatives of the security forces, a further theme can be identified—that this investigative 'imbalance' is part of a broader attempt to 'blame' the RUC for much of the responsibility for the conflict and to deny their sacrifice (NIRPOA 2008, 2013; PFNI 2008; Lawther 2010). As concluded by the CAJ (2013: 8) in their submission to the Haass talks, 'to apply the same mechanism to all deaths would prevent any sense of their being a hierarchy of cases or victims, or that one group or another was being scapegoated'.

Equally concerning is that within the politics of victimhood, certain victims' voices and their calls for truth may be prioritised because of the heavily politicised message they carry, while leaving others at the margins. Such critiques, concerning essentialism and silencing, are not uncommon elsewhere. The South African Truth and Reconciliation Commission's elevation of the voice of the 'forgiving victim' who directly contributed to the project of national reconciliation is well known (Wilson 2001; Moon 2008; Cole 2010). McEvoy and McConnachie (2013) make the point that voice, or 'the quality of voice' cannot be understood without a keen grasp of how broader political and social narratives are framed (Hamber 2009: 130). This dynamic can be seen in respect to the presence and absence of victims' voices in Northern Ireland. For example, within republicanism, the notion of 'victimhood as resistance' has a particular currency, whereby calls for truth recovery into high profile cases of suspected collusion have dominated the republican narrative. Brown (2011) argues this is part of an implicit narrative of victimhood within republicanism that privileges paramilitary deaths, particularly where they relate to the purported 'oppression' of the British state, over civilians in commemorative space and narrative. Civilian casualties are more likely to be unnamed,

[32] Democratic Unionist Party (DUP), 'Inquiries have Created Hierarchy of Victims—Campbell' press release, 15 June 2010.

[33] Ulster Unionist Party (UUP), 'Elliott Shocked at News of Bloody Sunday Murder Inquiry' press release, 7 May 2012.

even when killed by accident or in premature explosions caused by republicans themselves (Brown 2011). There is also little consideration or calls for truth into the cases of approximately 227 Catholic civilians killed by members of republican paramilitary organisations (Lawther 2014). As regards unionist political elites, the critique has similarly been made that members of the security forces who died during the conflict occupy a higher position in the hierarchy of victimhood than civilians (Lawther 2013, 2014). A concurrent critique, made to the author during a period of fieldwork with victims and survivors organisations, is that individual victims have been forgotten in the call for truth and justice into collective tragedies for the unionist community.[34] Those members of the unionist or loyalist community who are the victims of state collusion also remain missing from this narrative (Dawson 2007). The available mechanisms and the politics of victimhood have therefore both contributed to perpetuating hierarchies of victimhood and hierarchies of truth in Northern Ireland (Lawther 2014).

The Capacity of Victims and Ex-Combatants

The final area this chapter considers is the use of law—namely civil litigation by victims and ex-combatants as a route for seeking redress for past injustices (Teitel 2000). A well-established tradition in Northern Ireland, the resort to law may be viewed as an attempt to 'fix' historical meaning or to shape how events or individuals are remembered (McEvoy 2000; Osiel 2000; Bell and Keenan 2005; McEvoy 2006; Dickson 2010). Moreover, legal processes are often imbued with considerable practical and symbolic importance in broader efforts to uncover and acknowledge unpalatable historical truths (Sarat 1999; McEvoy 2006). As a route to compensation, acknowledgement and/or to uncover or clarify the truth, there is therefore an inevitable 'lure' associated with litigation (Healing Through Remembering 2013). This can be clearly seen in respect of legal action being taken by former republican and loyalist internees. As detailed above, several charges, including wrongful arrest and unlawful detention, are being brought against the British state. However, represented by solicitor Padraig O Muirigh, the former republican detainees have argued that the importance of an official acknowledgement of the discriminatory nature of internment and the subsequent trauma of human rights violations underpins their case—'It's not about money, it's really about acknowledgement, officially, that internment was illegal and discriminatory and the actions of the government at the time were unlawful'.[35] Those involved in this action also regard their cases to be a litmus test on behalf of almost

[34] This project was entitled 'Assessing Support Initiatives for Victims of Terrorism in the UK and Spain: Lessons for the European Context' and was funded by the European Commission—Directorate-General Justice, Freedom and Security (see www.victimsofterrorism.co.uk).

[35] *Irish News*, 'Government Paper Discovery Sparks Internment Test Case', 9 August 2011.

2000 people, the majority of whom were members of the Catholic community who were interned without trial between 1971 and 1975.[36]

However, civil litigation is often lengthy, complex and financially costly, and with no guarantees that those litigating will achieve their objectives. As has been demonstrated in Northern Ireland, claimants will often face a number of barriers, including delays in proceedings, statutory limitations, evidential burdens and the willingness of other actors, including the state, to disclose information (Healing Through Remembering, 2013). The Omagh case well illustrates these difficulties, given that at the time of writing, Michael McKevitt and Liam Campbell who, as detailed above, were found liable for the bombing and ordered to pay a share of £1.6 million in aggravated damages, are in the process of taking their case to the ECtHR in an attempt to avoid paying damages.[37] While speaking clearly to the tenacity and energy of some of the victims, as this case illustrates, there are no guarantees of success even after years of litigation and the emotional, personal and financial investment is often considerable.[38] Doubt has also been cast on the capacity of a lawsuit for damages to serve as a vehicle for truth recovery. British Irish Rights Watch (2012) has picked up on this point in respect of the Omagh case, arguing that it 'might attribute culpability but can establish little more than that in relation to delivering answers which might salve a quest for justice and closure'. Moreover, in practical terms, the Department of Justice for Northern Ireland (DoJNI) has recently closed a consultation on the remuneration of civil legal aid, in which it was proposed that a revised fee structure be introduced, involving standard fees for civil cases (DoJNI 2013). One objective is to make approximately £5 million in savings from the legal aid budget (DoJNI 2013). If implemented, the reforms could potentially restrict the availability of legal aid in civil litigation cases involving the past. Collectively, these barriers are likely to prevent the majority of those affected by the conflict from being able to pursue their objectives of retributive justice, acknowledgement, compensation or truth through the courts alone (Healing Through Remembering 2013).

Conclusion

This chapter has critically engaged with the criminal justice approach to the past in Northern Ireland's transitional setting. As noted above, some notable

[36] *Irish Times*, 'Former Detainees Bring Internment Case', 10 August 2011.

[37] D Barrett and P Sawer, 'Omagh bombing: Real IRA Terrorists Appeal to European Court' *The Telegraph*, 19 April 2014.

[38] Moreover, for those families whose cases do not lend themselves to legal challenge or who do not have the necessary campaigning or political support structures, their need for truth recovery remains unaddressed, leading the former Chief Constable of the PSNI, Sir Hugh Orde (2005: 3) to argue 'It [litigation] lends itself to a survival of the fittest phenomenon since it delivers results for those high profile cases which stay the course or attract the most media or political attention'.

successes have stemmed from, for example, public inquiries, the HET and the CCRC. In such cases, some measure of truth, accountability and resolution has been delivered. Yet, as Quirk (2013: 952) argues in respect of the CCRC, in the transitional context, 'such cases are being dealt with by an institution that was designed to meet the needs of ordinary criminal justice in settled democracy, rather than the exceptionalist institutions, such as truth commissions or amnesty processes, commonly associated with transitional justice'. Borne out by the weaknesses and hurdles faced by victims and ex-combatants who attempt to bring civil actions, the highly selective nature of public inquiries, significant delays in the coronial system and the now tarnished HET and OPONI—both of which inadvertently became 'the' vehicles for truth recovery—Quirk's (2013) comments resonate more broadly. As I have argued above, given the absence of a viable alternative, the criminal justice approach to the past in Northern Ireland has resulted in a process that is piecemeal, overtly legalistic, offers a weak form of accountability and has fed into hierarchal notions of victimhood. It is also crumbling under the weight of historical investigations and contested notions of the past.

A number of significant issues remain outstanding. First, as highlighted in a recent CJINI (2013) publication, the current approach to the past is financially punishing, with particular pressure on the PSNI (Lawther 2010). Second, the available mechanisms cannot deliver a consistent or comprehensive level of truth recovery, with gaps in investigative measures meaning different agencies passing cases to and fro, and resulting in some victims' families falling through the gaps and others having to engage with various processes over a considerable period of time (CAJ 2013). The failure to properly investigate by conducting prompt, thorough and effective investigations in an independent and impartial manner is also a violation of human rights standards (Bell and Keenan 2005). Moreover, as Hayner (2011), Posel (1999) and others have argued, post-conflict, there is a need to move beyond individualised, micro truths to a social and more 'restorative' truth. As yet, the existing mechanisms are neither designed nor equipped to develop a comprehensive understanding of the extent and patterns of violations, or the causes, consequences and context of the conflict. Lacking an overall narrative of the events of the past 40 years, the net effect is that every contest in the peace process becomes a surrogate of the conflict, leading to an endless replay of the meta-conflict (Bell et al 2004). This final point also resonates more broadly. As is the aim of this book, the Northern Ireland case study has much to offer other transitional jurisdictions. The international literature on transitional justice and human rights points to the centrality of rebuilding the structures and mechanisms of state justice and moving on from the legacy of an abusive past (see Teitel 2000; Roht-Arriaza and Mariezcurrena 2006; Olsen et al 2010). The transitional justice 'toolkit'—composed of mechanisms such as truth commissions, inquiries, apologies and reparations programmes—is united by the themes of truth, justice, accountability and acknowledgement. As this chapter has argued, if transitional societies, such as Northern Ireland, are to realise these objectives and deal with their past in a meaningful and effective manner, there is a need for greater creativity beyond a purely criminal justice approach to the past.

References

Amnesty International (2013) *Northern Ireland: Time to Deal with the Past* (London, Amnesty International).

Anthony, G and Mageean, P (2007) 'Habits of Mind and "Truth Telling": Article 2 ECHR in Post-Conflict Northern Ireland' in J Morison, K McEvoy and G Anthony (eds), *Judges, Transition, and Human Rights: Essays in Honour of Stephen Livingstone* (Oxford, Oxford University Press).

Bell, C (2002) 'Dealing with the Past in Northern Ireland' 26 *Fordham International Law Journal* 1095.

Bell, C, Campbell, C and Ní Aoláin, F (2004) 'Justice Discourses in Transition' 13 *Social & Legal Studies* 305.

Bell, C and Keenan, J (2005) 'Lost on the Way Home: The Right to Life in Northern Ireland' 32 *Journal of Law and Society* 68.

Boraine, A (2000) *A Country Unmasked: Inside South Africa's Truth and Reconciliation Commission* (Oxford, Oxford University Press).

Boyd, D and Doran, S (2006) *The Viability of Prosecution Based on Historical Enquiry. Observations of Counsel on Potential Evidential Difficulties* (Belfast, Healing Through Remembering).

Brewer, J (2010) *Peace Processes: A Sociological Approach* (Cambridge, Polity).

Brewer, J and Hayes, B (2011) 'Victims as Moral Beacons: Victims and Perpetrators in Northern Ireland' 6 *Contemporary Social Science* 73.

British Irish Rights Watch (2012) *Consultation: Justice and Security Green Paper* (Cm 8194, 2011) (London, British Irish Rights Watch).

Brown, K (2011) 'Rights and Victims, Martyrs and Memories: The European Court of Human Rights and Political Transition in Northern Ireland' in M Hamilton and A Buyse (eds), *Transitional Jurisprudence and the ECHR. Justice, Politics and Rights* (Cambridge, Cambridge University Press).

Campbell, C and Turner, C (2008) 'Utopia and the Doubters: Truth, Transition and the Law' 28 *Legal Studies* 374.

Cole, C (2010) *Performing South Africa's Truth Commission: Stages of Transition* (Bloomington, IA, Indiana University Press).

Commission for Victims and Survivors Northern Ireland (CVSNI) (2012) *Comprehensive Needs Assessment* (Belfast, CVSNI).

Committee on the Administration of Justice (CAJ) (2009) *Response to the Consultation on the Report of the Consultative Group on the Past* (Belfast, CAJ).

—— (2011) *Human Rights and Dealing with Historic Cases—A Review of the Office of the Police Ombudsman for Northern Ireland* (Belfast, CAJ).

—— (2013) *Dealing with the Past: Investigating Troubles-Related Deaths: Submission to the Multi-party Group Chaired by Richard Haass* (Belfast, CAJ).

Consultative Group on the Past (CGP) (2009) *Report of the Consultative Group on the Past* (Belfast, CGP).

Criminal Justice Inspection Northern Ireland (CJINI) (2011) *An Inspection into the Independence of the Office of the Police Ombudsman for Northern Ireland* (Belfast, CJINI).
—— (2013) *A Review of the Cost and Impact of Dealing with the Past on Criminal Justice Organisations in Northern Ireland* (Belfast, CJINI).
Dawson, G (2007) *Making Peace with the Past? Memory, Trauma and the Irish Troubles* (Manchester, Manchester University Press).
de Greiff, P and Duthie, R (2009) *Transitional Justice and Development: Making Connections* (New York, Social Science Research Council).
Department of Justice Northern Ireland (DoJNI) (2013) *Consultation Document: Civil Legal Aid Remuneration* (Belfast, DoJNI).
Dickson, B (2010) *The European Convention on Human Rights and the Conflict in Northern Ireland* (Oxford, Oxford University Press).
Duffy, A (2010) 'A Truth Commission for Northern Ireland?' 4 *International Journal of Transitional Justice* 26.
Hamber, B (2009) *Transforming Societies after Political Violence. Truth, Reconciliation and Mental Health* (New York, Springer).
Haass, R and O'Sullivan, M (2013) *An Agreement among the Parties of the Northern Ireland Executive on Parades, Select Commemorations, and Related Protests; Flags and Emblems; and Contenting with the Past* (Belfast, OFMdFM).
Hayner, P (2011) *Unspeakable Truths: Transitional Justice* and *the Challenge of Truth Commissions*, 2nd edn (London, Routledge).
Healing Through Remembering (2010) *Paper on Dealing with the Past: Costs to Date and for 2010–2014* (Belfast, Healing Through Remembering).
—— (2013) *Dealing with the Past? An Overview of Legal and Political Approaches Relating to the Conflict in and about Northern Ireland* (Belfast, Healing Through Remembering).
Her Majesty's Inspectorate of Constabulary (HMIC) (2013) *Inspection of the Police Service of Northern Ireland Historical Enquiries Team* (London, HMIC).
Historical Enquiries Team (HET) (undated) *Policing the Past. Introducing the Work of the Historical Enquiries Team* (Belfast, Police Service of Northern Ireland).
Jackson, J and Doran, S (1995) *Judge Without Jury: Diplock Trials in the Adversary System* (Oxford, Oxford University Press).
Larkin, J (2012) *Attorney General for Northern Ireland: Second Annual Report* (Belfast, OAGNI).
Lawther, C (2010) '"Securing" the Past: Policing and the Contest over Truth in Northern Ireland' 50 *British Journal of Criminology* 455.
—— (2013) 'Denial, Silence and the Politics of the Past: Unpicking the Opposition to Truth Recovery in Northern Ireland' 7 *International Journal of Transitional Justice* 157.
—— (2014) *Truth, Denial and Transition: Northern Ireland and the Contested Past* (London, Routledge).
Lundy, P (2009a) 'Can the Past be Policed? Lessons from the Historical Enquiries Team Northern Ireland' 11 *Law and Social Challenges* 109.
—— (2009b) 'Exploring Home-Grown Transitional Justice and its Dilemmas: A Case Study of the Historical Enquiries Team, Northern Ireland' 3 *International Journal of Transitional Justice* 321.
—— (2010) 'Commissioning the Past in Northern Ireland' 1138 *Review of International Affairs* 101.
—— (2012) *Research Brief: Assessment of the Historical Enquiries Team (HET) Review Processes and Procedures in Royal Military Police (RMP) Investigation Cases* (University of Ulster, External Research Report).

Lundy, P and McGovern, M (2008) 'Truth, Justice and Dealing with the Legacy of the Past in Northern Ireland' 7 *Ethnopolitics* 117.

MacLean, R, Coyle, A and Oliver, J (2010) *The Billy Wright Inquiry Report* (London, The Stationery Office).

McEvoy, K (2000) 'Law, Struggle and Political Transformation in Northern Ireland' 27 *Journal of Law and Society* 542.

—— (2006) *Making Peace with the Past: Options for Truth Recovery Regarding the Conflict in and about Northern Ireland* (Belfast, Healing Through Remembering).

—— (2007) 'Beyond Legalism: Towards a Thicker Understanding of Transitional Justice' 34 *Journal of Law and Society* 411.

McEvoy, K and McConnachie, K (2013) 'Victims and Transitional Justice: Voice, Agency and Blame' 22 *Social & Legal Studies* 489.

McKittrick, D, Kelters, S, Feeney, B, Thornton, C and McVea, D (2007) *Lost Lives: The Stories of the Men, Women and Children who Died as a Result of the Northern Ireland Troubles* (Edinburgh, Mainstream Publishing).

Méndez, JE (1997) 'In Defense of Transitional Justice' in AJ McAdams (ed), *Transitional Justice and the Rule of Law in New Democracies* (Notre Dame, IN, University of Notre Dame Press).

Misztal, B (2003) *Theories of Social Remembering* (Maidenhead, Open University Press).

Moon, C (2008) *Narrating Political Reconciliation. South Africa's Truth and Reconciliation Commission* (Plymouth, Lexington Books).

Morland, M, Strachan, V and Burden, A (2011) *The Rosemary Nelson Inquiry Report* (London, The Stationery Office).

Ní Aoláin, F (2000) *The Politics of Force: Conflict Management and State Violence in Northern Ireland* (Belfast, Blackstaff Press).

Northern Ireland Retired Police Officers Association (2008) Submission to the Consultative Group on the Past (Belfast, NIRPOA).

—— (2013) Written submission by the Northern Ireland Retired Police Officers Association to Dr Richard Haass on 'Dealing with the Past' (Belfast, NIRPOA).

O'Loan, N (2010) 'The Police Ombudsman for Northern Ireland: Some Reflections' in J Doyle (ed), *Policing the Narrow Ground: Lessons from the Transformation of Policing in Northern Ireland* (Dublin, Royal Irish Academy).

O'Rawe, M (2003) 'Transitional Policing Arrangements in Northern Ireland: The Can't and Won't of the Change Dialectic' 26 *Fordham International Law Journal* 1015.

Office of the Police Ombudsman for Northern Ireland (OPONI) (2001) *Statement by the Police Ombudsman for Northern Ireland on her investigation of matters relating to the Omagh Bombing on August 15 1998* (Belfast, OPONI).

—— (2007) *Statement by the Police Ombudsman for Northern Ireland on her investigation into the circumstances surrounding the death of Raymond McCord Junior and related matters* (Belfast, OPONI).

—— (2013) *Annual Business Plan 2012–2013* (Belfast, OPONI).

Olsen, T, Payne, L and Reiter, G (2010) *Transitional Justice in Balance: Comparing Processes, Weighing Efficacy* (Washington DC, United States Institute of Peace Press).

Orde, H (2005) 'War is Easy to Declare, Peace is an Elusive Prize' (Telling the Truth in Ireland conference, Trinity College Dublin).

—— (2009) 'War is Easy. Peace is the Difficult Prize' (London, Frank Longford Charitable Trust).

Osiel, M (2000) *Mass Atrocity, Collective Memory and the Law* (London, Transaction Publishers).

Police Federation for Northern Ireland (PFNI) (2008) *Submission by the Police Federation for Northern Ireland to the Consultative Group on the Past* (Belfast, PFNI).

Posel, D (1999) 'The TRC Report: What Kind of History? What Kind of Truth?' in D Posel and G Simpson (eds), *Commissioning the Past. Understanding South Africa's Truth and Reconciliation Commission* (Johannesburg, Witwatersrand University Press).

Quirk, H (2013) 'Don't Mention the War: The Court of Appeal, the Criminal Cases Review Commission and Dealing with the Past in Northern Ireland' 76 *Modern Law Review* 949.

Requa, M (2007) 'Truth, Transition and the Inquiries Act 2005' 4 *European Human Rights Law Review* 404.

Requa, M and Anthony, G (2008) 'Coroners, Controversial Deaths and Northern Ireland's Past Conflict' 62 *Public Law* 443.

Roht-Arriaza, N and Mariezcurrena, J (2006) *Transitional Justice in the Twenty-First Century: Beyond Truth versus Justice* (Cambridge, Cambridge University Press).

Rolston, B and Scraton, P (2005) 'In the Full Glare of English Politics: Ireland, Inquiries and the British State' 45 *British Journal of Criminology* 547.

Sarat, A (1999) 'The Necessity and Challenges of Establishing a Truth and Reconciliation Commission in Rwanda' 21 *Human Rights Quarterly* 761.

Saville, M, Hoyt, W and Toohey, J (2010) *Report of the Bloody Sunday Inquiry* (London, The Stationery Office).

Schabas, W (2009) *Genocide in International Law: The Crime of Crimes* (Cambridge, Cambridge University Press).

Sikkink, K (2011) *The Justice Cascade: How Human Rights Prosecutions are Changing World Politics* (New York, NW Norton & Company Inc).

de Silva, D (2012) *The Report of the Patrick Finucane Review* (London, The Stationery Office).

Smithwick, P (2013) *Report of the Tribunal of Inquiry into Suggestions that Members of An Garda Siochana or other Employees of the State colluded in the Fatal Shootings of RUC Chief Superintendent Harry Breen and RUC Superintendent Robert Buchanan on the 20th March 1989* (Dublin, The Stationery Office).

Smyth, M (2007) *Truth Recovery and Justice after Conflict. Managing Violent Pasts* (London, Routledge).

Stormont House Agreement (2014) *The Stormont House Agreement* (London/Belfast, Northern Ireland Office).

Teitel, R (2000) *Transitional Justice* (Oxford, Oxford University Press).

Tutu, D (1999) *No Future Without Forgiveness* (London, Rider).

Wiebelhaus-Brahm, E (2010) *Truth Commissions and Transitional Societies. The Impact on Human Rights and Democracy* (London, Routledge).

Wilson, R (2001) *The Politics of Truth and Reconciliation in South Africa: Legitimizing the Post-Apartheid State* (Cambridge, Cambridge University Press).

3

Bringing Humanity Home: A Transformational Human Rights Culture for Northern Ireland?

COLIN HARVEY*

Introduction

The discourse of human rights plays a prominent role in Northern Ireland's transitional context. The notion that 'rights-talk'[1] must be deployed is so embedded that critical questions can be legitimately raised about the transformative impact of such a mainstream practice. The pervasive reach of 'rights-talk' can be contrasted with notable absences. An idea endorsed in the Belfast/Good Friday Agreement (1998) (The Agreement), that Northern Ireland might need a Bill of Rights, has not led to a new constitutional instrument. So, there is a public sphere in Northern Ireland where references to human rights are frequent, and a constitutional context where the tools to deliver more inclusive legal protection are still missing. A gap thus opens between expectations, the rhetorical use of rights, and the available formal instruments. Whether this matters is something this chapter will consider but what it does promote is a disparity between grounded normative guarantees and political mobilisation around human rights.

In the wider context of reflection on the transition in the criminal justice system in Northern Ireland, the aim of this chapter is to outline the framework, and then show how human rights function as 'guiding principles'. Criminal justice is where the state and the individual come into sharpest contact; and thus it is (everywhere) a field where tensions and balances are often starkly posed. In post-conflict societies this is even more so, as the justice system can be at the core of conflict, and its reform central to many transitions (see Campbell and Ní Aoláin 2003; McEvoy and Morison 2003; Campbell and Connolly 2006; Campbell et al 2003; McEvoy 2011).

* I would like to thank Dr Anne-Marie McAlinden and Dr Clare Dwyer for their helpful comments on an earlier draft. The research for this chapter was assisted by a BA/Leverhulme Small Research Grant: 'The Belfast/Good Friday Agreement, 15 Years On: Revisiting the Promise of Peace'.

[1] On 'rights-talk' in the US context but with wider implications (see Glendon 1991).

The intention is to indicate how human rights emerged during the transition as a common set of principles, and to reflect on the limitations of legalism in assessing the potential of human rights to make a significant practical difference. The premise is that human rights must be aligned with transformative law and politics if the project is to remain tied to 'real-world' emancipation. Although guarantees will apply in diverse contexts, the global rights regime is not silent on substantive outcomes. To this end, more consideration must be given to the type of human rights agenda being promoted, and the practical impact it is having. There is a politics within 'human rights legality' that must be articulated, acknowledged and discussed as an aid to reflection on why change processes may stall, and the complex ways they are resisted.

The Framework of Rights Protection in Northern Ireland

The legal framework for rights protection in Northern Ireland is governed by its particular constitutional context, and the resulting possibilities and constraints of its legal and political systems (Dickson 2013). It is a legal regime that is informed by the dynamics of British–Irish history and a legacy of violent political conflict, during which human rights were violated and abused, and a society where rights arguments were, and are, regularly adopted (CAJ 2006; Anthony and Mageaan 2007; Dickson 2010). Many of the concerns arising from the conflict remain unresolved, including how Northern Ireland will address all the challenging legacies of its past (Healing Through Remembering 2002; Amnesty International 2013). The human rights conversation and the justice system therefore advance in the shadow of Northern Ireland's history of violence, and the varying and divergent responses to it.

The technical impact of the global rights regime is mediated through the UK's dualist approach (Ireland is also dualist for international law purposes), where the state may have ratified an international human rights instrument but it can have limited domestic impact (particularly when it comes to judicial enforcement). In no sense does this mean that international human rights standards are irrelevant. In addition to the formal ways they enter courtrooms, international norms continue to be regularly used in arguments and debates that flow from civil society (and other) discussions and engagements. The fact that international human rights standards are not incorporated into domestic law does not, for example, mean that they cannot be taught (and awareness of their existence raised) or that they should not be used by anyone who wishes to offer a critique informed by external benchmarks.

The picture is complicated further by the constitutional circumstances of Northern Ireland, with its 'bi-national' forms of political accommodation (McGarry and O'Leary 2004, 2006a, 2006b; Kerr 2005; McCrudden and O'Leary 2013). This results in regular dialogue about the relationship between group and individual rights, and how a focus on 'personhood' interacts with the communal aspects of membership and belonging. 'Humans' have rights but human beings also possess multiple identities. The UK's membership of the European Union adds a further dimension. As the European Union transforms into a constitutionalised entity, with all the attachments to rights that now come with any such process, questions are raised about the potential for rights-based advances (de Búrca 2011). A bare description of the legal architecture does not capture the fluidity of current rights discourse but it gives a sense of the framing environment. The human rights conversation is thus taken forward in a complex constitutional context, where ethno-national conflict remains marked, and where the broad spread of international standards may be asserted but may not be usable for many in practice.

As is now well documented, human rights became intrinsic to the language and politics of the peace process, connected also to wider constitutional conversations about rights reform in the UK (and globally) (Harvey and Livingstone 1999; Bell 2000). Several strands merged in the 1990s, with the result that human rights moved centre stage (Mageaan and O'Brien 1998). The Belfast/Good Friday Agreement 1998 is notable for its extended references to human rights.[2] The 'Declaration of Support' expressly commits participants to 'the protection and vindication of the human rights of all' (Belfast/Good Friday Agreement 1998: paragraph 2); 'Constitutional Issues' elaborates on what the 'right of self-determination' means (Belfast/Good Friday Agreement 1998a: paragraph 1), and notes the obligations of the 'sovereign government' in relation to the 'principles of full respect for, and equality of, civil, political, social and cultural rights' (Belfast/Good Friday Agreement 1998: paragraph 1(v)). This section of the Agreement includes the right of the people of Northern Ireland 'to identify themselves and be accepted as Irish or British, or both, as they may so choose' (Belfast/Good Friday Agreement 1998a: paragraph 1(vi)). Strand One lists safeguards that are intended 'to protect the rights and interests of all sides of the community' (Belfast/Good Friday Agreement 1998: paragraph 1). These safeguards include the European Convention on Human Rights (ECHR), 'and any Bill of Rights for Northern Ireland supplementing it, which neither the Assembly nor any public bodies can infringe, together with a Human Rights Commission' (Belfast/Good Friday Agreement 1998: paragraph 5(b)), as well as 'arrangements to provide that key decisions and legislation are proofed to ensure they do not infringe the ECHR and any Bill of Rights for Northern Ireland' (Belfast/Good Friday Agreement 1998a: paragraph 5(c)).

[2] See the comments by the then UN High Commissioner for Human Rights, Mary Robinson: 'All of this is reflected in the Good Friday Agreement which is conspicuous by the centrality it gives to equality and human rights concerns. Few documents emerging from divisive and difficult political negotiations have so well captured the importance of fairness in creating right relationships'—M Robinson, 'Equality and Human Rights—Their Role in Peace Building: Remarks by Mary Robinson, UN High Commissioner for Human Rights' (Stormont Hotel, 2 December 1998).

The Agreement indicated that the Assembly 'may appoint a special committee to examine and report on whether a measure or proposal for legislation is in conformity with equality requirements, including the ECHR/Bill of Rights' (Belfast/Good Friday Agreement 1998: paragraph 11). On legislation, the Agreement is clear that devolved legislative competence should be subject to the ECHR and 'any Bill of Rights for Northern Ireland supplementing it' (Belfast/Good Friday Agreement 1998: paragraph 26(a)). The textual emphasis on rights is carried further into the document, and into other strands. So, for example, the British–Irish Intergovernmental Conference 'will address, in particular, the areas of rights, justice, prisons and policing … (unless and until responsibility is devolved to a Northern Ireland administration)' (Belfast/Good Friday Agreement 1998, 'British–Irish Intergovernmental Conference': paragraph 6). The section on 'Rights, Safeguards and Equality of Opportunity' is where fullest expression is given to human rights, with affirmation of a specific list, commitments from the British Government, the establishment of new institutions in Northern Ireland, steps to be taken by the Irish Government, as well as a targeted focus on economic, social and cultural issues. Again, in the section on 'Policing and Justice' the Agreement underlines the need for the new arrangements to be 'based on principles of the protection of human rights' and it is plain that the reviews to be subsequently established were to be guided by them (Belfast/Good Friday Agreement 1998, 'Policing and Justice': paragraph 2). What is also evident is that the British and Irish Governments assumed much responsibility too, and that the new arrangements had implications for the two jurisdictions on the island of Ireland; evident in, for example, the notion of 'equivalence' (O'Cinneide 2005).

In the new British–Irish Agreement the governments reaffirmed 'their commitment to the principles of partnership, equality and mutual respect and to the protection of civil, political, social, economic and cultural rights in their respective jurisdictions' (British–Irish Agreement 1998: preamble). In this international agreement, the governments underline the right of self-determination reflected in the Belfast/Good Friday Agreement, and affirmed the view that the 'sovereign government' would be responsible for governing with 'rigorous impartiality' founded on 'full respect' for human rights, among other things (British–Irish Agreement 1998: article 1(5)). The referendums on the island of Ireland that followed give the enterprise a democratic legitimacy that subsequent agreements lack; yet the tendency to view human rights as core persists. For example, the Agreement at St Andrews 2006 (the attempt to revive the political institutions) places 'equality and human rights at the heart of the new dispensation' (St Andrews Agreement 2006: paragraph 3) and the British Government agreed to advance measures to promote a shared future 'in which the culture, rights and aspirations of all are respected and valued, free from sectarianism, racism and intolerance' (St Andrews Agreement 2006: paragraph 8). These measures included the establishment of a forum on a Bill of Rights, and additional powers for the Northern Ireland Human Rights Commission (St Andrews Agreement 2006: annex b).

If further evidence is needed for this trend, it is located in the outcome of the Richard Haass–Meghan O'Sullivan talks in 2013. This was a process instigated by the First Minister and deputy First Minister, following the publication of 'Together: Building a United Community' (OFMdFM 2013). The Panel was established in July 2013, and following lengthy discussions among representatives of the Executive parties, and input from wider society, it failed to reach consensus by the end of the year (but the chairs did issue a final draft of the document) (Panel of the Parties in the NI Executive 2013).

Although the introductory sections do not mention human rights explicitly as 'governing principles'[3] the document is packed with the language of rights. The section on 'parades' starts with references to the ECHR, includes discussion of rights and responsibilities, notes rights from the Belfast/Good Friday Agreement, and cites the advice the Panel received from the Northern Ireland Human Rights Commission (Panel of the Parties in the NI Executive 2013: 4). This spirit is carried into the new arrangements proposed for dealing with parades. The rights focus is less apparent in the sections on 'flags and emblems', though one of the issues for the suggested new 'Commission on Identity, Culture and Tradition' is the Bill of Rights (Panel of the Parties in the NI Executive 2013: 17). The third major element 'Contending with the Past' is also informed by human rights standards, again with specific reference to the ECHR (Panel of the Parties in the NI Executive 2013: 24).

The evidence suggests an established politics of human rights in Northern Ireland, and they are now frequently endorsed as 'guiding principles' of the process. The best documents and models tend also to internationalise the discussion. The formal legal picture remains less impressive. The prominence of human rights discourse is not as fully reflected in law, certainly not to the extent of the wider and more globalised references in civil society. The domestic legal position clings still to the UK's dualist tradition (one grappling with belated acceptance of express declarations of rights). As is well known, the Human Rights Act 1998 gave further effect in UK domestic law to elements of the ECHR, and the Act applies in Northern Ireland. 'Convention rights' are also given effect in the devolved setting as a result of the Northern Ireland Act 1998. The risk thus was, and remains, that the ECHR will mark a finish line that neglects the rich body of international human rights law.

The outcome of this formal legal position is that the ECHR, in particular, is at the core of the new constitutional legal architecture of Northern Ireland. It is equally apparent that this framework embraces the potential for a broader understanding of human rights, includes a conception of the right of self-determination, and does envisage a possible Bill of Rights that will supplement the ECHR (and

[3] 'As this work goes forward, rigorous equality of opportunity and equality before the law, mutual respect, and application of the rule of law must be the governing principles for Northern Ireland, not just now but permanently' (Panel of the Parties in the NI Executive 2013: 3).

even a potential Charter of Rights for the island of Ireland). This spirit was influential in the transitional process, where rights discourse became solidified into its internal discursive logic. Public bodies in the 'policing and justice' worlds are especially attuned to the force of an argument from 'illegality'. In law, however, the framework for domestic rights protection is still firmly tied to the ECHR, and the 'Convention rights' are therefore the practical tools that carry substantial normative weight. The risk is that the full range of international human rights standards will be neglected.

Human Rights as Guiding Principles

Rights and Reform: Policing and Criminal Justice

There are many examples that demonstrate how human rights principles inform the ongoing reform process. The intention is to highlight the more significant examples. The first is policing reform. The 1998 Agreement confirmed that human rights should guide the approach, a fact underlined in the work and the report of the Independent Commission on Policing in Northern Ireland (the 'Patten Commission') (ICP 1999; see the chapter by Topping in this volume for further discussion). The centrality of human rights is plain throughout, and the section on 'Human Rights' starts with a quote from the Universal Declaration of Human Rights (ICP 1999: 18). The report states:

> It is a central proposition of this report that the fundamental purpose of policing should be, in the words of the Agreement, the protection and vindication of the human rights of all. Our consultations showed clear agreement across the communities in Northern Ireland that people want the police to protect their human rights from infringement by others, and to respect their human rights in the exercise of that duty (ICP 1999: 18).

One of the key recommendations is for 'a comprehensive programme of action to focus policing in Northern Ireland on a human rights based approach' (ICP 1999: 20, paragraph 4.6). The specific measures proposed include a new oath, a new Code of Ethics, codes of practice 'on all aspects of policing', human rights training, plus the appointment of a human rights lawyer, with human rights compliance monitored by the Policing Board (ICP 1999: 20, paragraphs 4.7–4.12).The focus of the report is not on mere formal adherence to legal standards; it is quite clear that the ambition is *cultural transformation of policing*:

> The purpose of this programme is that the police should perform functions within the law and be fully respectful of human rights both in the technical sense and in the behavioural sense … Technically, they should know the laws well and master policing skills, for example how to interview suspects, so that they are less likely to be tempted to resort to unethical methods in order to get results. Behaviourally, they should perceive their jobs in terms of the protection of human rights. Respect for the human rights of all, including

> suspects, should be an instinct rather than a procedural point to be remembered (ICP 1999: 21, paragraph 4.13).

Although the Patten Report includes a specific section on 'Human Rights' the whole notion of rights is mainstreamed. In addition to the new monitoring and accountability mechanisms, provision was also made for an Oversight Commissioner, with 'responsibility for supervising the implementation of our recommendations' (ICP 1999: 105, paragraph 19.4).

Following publication, much of the subsequent debate centred on implementation, and putting the sophisticated policing architecture in place.[4] The new regime (informed now by its devolved context), including the Policing Board, the Police Ombudsman, the Police Oversight Commissioner, the Justice Committee in the Assembly, and the Justice Minister, demonstrates an awareness of the human rights context. The final report of the Oversight Commissioner was published in 2007, and while significant progress in implementation was noted, it did highlight problems, including human rights training and the human rights aspects of the appraisal system (OOC 2007: 21–30). On these, recommendations were made on how the Police Service of Northern Ireland (PSNI), Policing Board and the Northern Ireland devolved government could take this work forward. Indicating the continuing nature of the task, the Commissioner noted:

> The creation of a culture of human rights, which was the objective of the Independent Commission, is not something that is achieved once and then endures without further attention. It requires continued monitoring, assessment, adjustment, and reinvigoration. This will be the on-going responsibility of the PSNI, the Policing Board, and the devolved government (OOC 2007: 25).

This sense, that a culture of rights is not a static and one-off achievement, is notable: it indicates that policing will remain a site of contestation between individuals, communities, and the state; that human rights standards evolve; and that improvement in performance will always be possible. It captures the view that, especially for the criminal justice system, a 'culture of respect for human rights' is work in progress, and institutions must therefore strive to go beyond models of simple compliance by thinking about the evolving impact on policy and practice (*cf* Joint Committee on Human Rights 2003: 12).

One practical example (of the emphasis on rights) is the PSNI Code of Ethics, where the extent of the influence is considerable (NIPB 2008). Article 1, dealing with professional duties, underlines that 'police officers shall … protect human dignity and uphold the human rights and fundamental freedoms of all persons as enshrined in the Human Rights Act 1998, the European Convention on Human Rights, and other relevant human rights instruments' (NIPB 2008: 8). This sourcing (from a range of international instruments) is evident across the Code. Other examples include, the Human Rights Monitoring Framework established and

[4] On this, a rights-based challenge (Art 9 ECHR) to the reformed recruitment policy (known as '50:50') was unsuccessful: *Re Parsons* [2003] NICA 20.

applied by the Policing Board, as well as the Human Rights Annual Reports (NIPB 2003; NIPB 2012). This stress on human rights set the tone and structure for much of the subsequent monitoring and compliance work, where *human rights standards* are used to inform analysis of the specific and the general (for example NIPB 2013).

The debates in the 17 years since the adoption of the Belfast/Good Friday Agreement are not on whether 'human rights' are a good thing (or if it is desirable to mainstream human rights) but more often on nuanced questions of interpretation, application, impact, and awareness, and thus whether the hoped for cultural change is happening (see Moore 1998; O'Rawe 2003; Ellison 2007; Ellison 2010; Ellison and O'Rawe 2010; O'Rawe 2010; CAJ 2012). For example, how well is the Policing Board fulfilling its role of monitoring compliance with the Human Rights Act?[5] How effective is the Office of the Police Ombudman? Is the behavioural change, as recommended in the Patten Report, taking place? The evidence suggests that questions remain (and given the critical nature of the human rights agenda *should* remain) over the work of the existing accountability mechanisms, and the ongoing attempts to realise the transformational potential of policing reform. On policing, as in other areas, part of the suggestion here is that the persistent nature of questioning and challenge should be seen as normal and to be expected within a societal culture that should be more open to the democratising impact of human rights discourse. In this sense, getting the human rights culture right assists in encouraging a more ambitious democratic reform project.

The second post-Agreement process to note is criminal justice reform. The 1998 Agreement instigated action on reform of the criminal justice system in Northern Ireland. Phrased in different terms from policing reform, this was a review which would have 'an independent element', and be taken forward by the British Government (Belfast/Good Friday Agreement 1998; CJRG 1998: 6). The Review commenced in June 1998 and issued its report in March 2000 (CJRG 2000). It was apparent that, although limited in comparison with the Patten Commission, the Group was intent—through for example, the extensive commissioning of research—to propose guiding principles for the process (Livingstone and Doak 2000). Human rights were once again mainstreamed throughout, with a chapter on 'Human Rights and Guiding Principles' (CJRG 2000: chapter 3), and rights were embedded securely, with for example, chapters that start with the 'human rights background' to issues such as: lay involvement, the courts, restorative justice, juvenile justice, sentences, prisons and probation, and victims and witnesses (CJRG 2000). The chapter on 'Human Rights and Guiding Principles' commences with a quote from the Universal Declaration of Human Rights (CJRG 2000: chapter 3), and the Review Group makes its starting point evident:

> It was the clear intention of those involved in the talks process, *and one which we fully endorse, that these aims should be achieved within an overarching framework of human rights. The fundamental principle is that people have basic rights by virtue of their common*

[5] The Policing Board produces an annual human rights monitoring report (see NIPB 2012). In addition to this, the Board has also published a number of thematic reviews (see NIPB 2013).

> *humanity*. The principles of freedom and justice which spring from this are central to debate on crime and justice. In protecting the lives and property of citizens, or depriving offenders of their liberty, the state upholds the rights of victims or potential victims of crime, just as it has to ensure that it respects the basic rights of offenders (emphasis added) (CJRG 2000: 25).

The influence of the commissioned research report (on human rights standards) in shaping the conclusions of the Group is noted in several places, for example:

> In the research report which we commissioned, two themes that underlie international human rights standards in the field of criminal justice are identified: the protection of the individual against ill-treatment at the hands of law enforcement authorities; and the protection of individuals against arbitrary arrest, detention, trial or punishment. The report goes on to identify a third emerging theme which puts increasing stress on the need for individuals to be protected against threats to their bodily integrity, liberty and dignity from wherever these may emanate (footnote omitted) (CJRG 2000: 26).

What remains impressive is the emphasis on a broad range of applicable international human rights instruments. The recommendations of the Review Group included making human rights 'a permanent and integral part of training programmes' (CJRG 2000: Recommendation 1) and that 'lawyers should receive appropriate training in human rights principles before starting to practise' (CJRG 2000: Recommendation 11); this awareness of human rights is reflected across the 294 recommendations made by the Group. As with policing, a Justice Oversight Commissioner was also appointed to oversee implementation.

The subsequent impact of human rights discourse on the reform process can be seen in other examples, such as the work of Criminal Justice Inspection Northern Ireland (CJINI). The CJINI is tasked with inspecting listed organisations, including the PSNI, the Public Prosecution Service, the Youth Justice Agency, the Probation Board, and the Police Ombudsman's Office, among others. While the CJINI reports focus on specific institutions and issues, there is evidence, once again, of a human rights perspective informing the analysis.[6] This gains added significance as the CJINI is one of the UK's National Preventive Mechanisms for the purposes of the UN Convention against Torture.[7]

There are many other examples across the existing criminal justice institutions of an *awareness* that human rights discourse, instruments and standards should be at the core of the new arrangements. This does not mean that implementation is effective, consistent or satisfactory. For example, the reform of the Prison Service in Northern Ireland has given rise to ongoing concern. The Prison Review Team that reported in 2011 raised serious questions about the system, and the prospects for reform (Scraton and Moore 2005, 2007; PRT 2011). Again, however, the framework for their review merits comment. In the final report the Review Team

[6] Vision: 'It also means a system that does all these things with absolute fairness, promotes equality and human rights and is responsive to the real concerns of the community' (CJINI 2012: 15).

[7] For details of the UK's National Preventive Mechanism, see www.justice.gov.uk/about/hmi-prisons/preventive-mechanism.

stress the centrality of human rights, reference the legal standards, but also make clear their vision is a *transformative one*:

> But a human rights approach is much more than the negative of preventing abuse—it provides a positive ethical base for the way prisons should be run ... This attention to human rights is not just a question of complying with the law and treaty requirements ... Human rights are not therefore a list of 'don'ts' or a series of legal cases, but a live practical and positive grounding for running a good prison (PRT 2011: 11–12).

The work reflects, yet again, the idea that the human rights culture envisaged for the Prison Service, as elsewhere, is transformational. Further to this, it is worth observing that the Attorney General for Northern Ireland is required, as appropriate, to issue guidance to criminal justice organisations on the exercise of their functions in a 'manner consistent with international human rights standards relevant to the criminal justice system'.[8] Thus far guidance has been issued to Forensic Science Northern Ireland (OAGNI 2013b), the State Pathologist's Department (OAGNI 2013c), the Prison Service (OAGNI 2014b, 2014c), and the Public Prosecution Service (OAGNI 2014a), with general guidance provided on the Protection of the Right to Life (OAGNI 2013a). The general guidance on the right to life, for example, makes reference to the ECHR, the International Covenant on Civil and Political Rights 1966, the International Covenant on Economic, Social and Cultural Rights 1966, as well as customary international law and *ius cogens* (OAGNI 2013a: 1–2).

The evidence noted above—of the spread of a discourse of human rights as part of the transitional process—does not capture the whole picture (see, for example, Access to Justice Review Northern Ireland 2011: 17–20). The ECHR is now routinely applied in the courts in Northern Ireland (Dickson 2007; McQuigg 2010), references can be regularly found in the work of the Northern Ireland Assembly, the Northern Ireland Human Rights Commission (NIHRC 2013a, 2013b), and the Northern Ireland Commissioner for Children and Young People (NICCY 2008). There are many more examples. The purpose here is simply to provide evidence for the argument that 'human rights' are a widely referenced source of guidance across the justice sectors in Northern Ireland. A *version* of 'rights-talk' is now part of the mainstream, but the transformational agenda continues, as those who worked to secure the human rights dimensions of the Belfast/Good Friday Agreement 1998 argued that it would (Mageaan and O'Brien 1998). As one part of this, the 1998 Agreement suggested that the ECHR might be merely the first step, and held out the prospect of a future Bill of Rights.

A Bill of Rights for Northern Ireland?

A Bill of Rights is one way that a post-conflict society can signal a desire for transition and transformation. Bills of Rights are traditional and well used constitutional

[8] Justice Act (Northern Ireland) 2004, s 8.

mechanisms that mark out the 'new' from the 'old'. Their effectiveness in addressing practical violations and abuses of human rights is highly context dependent, and for many they can remain 'paper guarantees'. Nevertheless, transitional societies across the globe intending to embrace a 'new beginning' often find constitutional rights protection to be a convenient device.

It is thus unsurprising that in Northern Ireland one aspect of the post-Agreement agenda, that is relevant here, is the attempt to enhance existing legal protection. This is reflected in the long-standing argument that Northern Ireland needs a Bill of Rights, and the view that there is legal life beyond the ECHR (Livingstone 2001). The enactment of the Human Rights Act 1998, and the direct references in the Belfast/Good Friday Agreement 1998, contribute to an understandable focus on the ECHR (on formal human rights compliance). In the case law, and in law, ECHR rights dominate the reality of legal practice. The 1998 Agreement did, however, give further momentum to the idea that had been around for some time (CAJ 1990, 1993): that Northern Ireland might reflect further on the possible adoption of a new Bill of Rights (Harvey and Schwartz 2009). The Agreement states:

> 4. The new Northern Ireland Human Rights Commission ... will be invited to consult and to advise on the scope for defining, in Westminster legislation, rights supplementary to those in the European Convention on Human Rights, to reflect the particular circumstances of Northern Ireland, drawing as appropriate on international instruments and experience. These additional rights to reflect the principles of mutual respect for the identity and ethos of both communities and parity of esteem, and—taken together with the ECHR—to constitute a Bill of Rights for Northern Ireland. Among the issues for consideration by the Commission will be:
>
> — the formulation of a general obligation on government and public bodies fully to respect, on the basis of equality of treatment, the identity and ethos of both communities in Northern Ireland; and
>
> — a clear formulation of the rights not to be discriminated against and to equality of opportunity in both the public and private sectors.[9]

This 'Agreement mandate' resulted in the launch of a Northern Irish Bill of Rights process in 2000, and would eventually lead to the submission of the Commission's advice to government in 2008[10] (NIHRC 2001, 2003, 2004, 2005, 2008; see also Livingstone 2001; McCrudden 2001, 2007; Dickson 2010: 366–69). The length of time taken is an indication of how extensive the discussions were, and demonstrates the scope for disagreement on even basic principles of human rights and equality. The process saw several significant documents published, which outlined possible approaches, and it encouraged extensive levels of engagement across Northern Ireland, including the establishment of an innovative Bill of

[9] See the reference to this paragraph in Northern Ireland Act 1998, s 69(7). As Stephen Livingstone noted, 'The drafters of the Agreement did not make things easy for the Human Rights Commission' (Livingstone 2001: 278).

[10] The author served as a Northern Ireland Human Rights Commissioner 2005–11, and was one of the Commissioners who endorsed the final advice to government in 2008.

Rights Forum (composed of political parties and members of civil society, with an independent chair).[11] Much of the final advice of the Human Rights Commission was flatly rejected by the British Government (NIO 2009, 2010; Harvey 2011; Commission on a Bill of Rights 2012); however, it remains a document of interest, given the practical reflections on extending rights protection beyond the ECHR. Notable during the Bill of Rights process was the effort undertaken by many organisations and individuals to justify and explain the details of a more inclusive rights framework. It is a body of work, and a broad societal conversation, that remains instructive.

On the right to life, the Commission recommended that a new provision be adopted:

1. Legislation must be enacted to ensure that all violations of the right to life relating to the conflict in Northern Ireland are effectively investigated. Any mechanism established must be fully in compliance with international human rights law (NIHRC 2008: 20).

The Commission argued for Article 5 ECHR (liberty and security of the person) to be extensively supplemented, to underline the importance of specific guarantees, such as the right to consult a lawyer, the right of access to medical assistance, as well as the rights of children and vulnerable adults (NIHRC 2008: 23–24). On Articles 6 and 7 ECHR (fair trial and no punishment without law) the Commission recommended provision for a right to trial by jury 'for serious offences and the right to waive it' (NIHRC 2008: 27), the exclusion of evidence, and rights for children and vulnerable adults, witnesses, jurors and members of the judiciary and legal profession (NIHRC 2008: 27). The equality provisions of the Commission's advice focused on the concept of 'unfair discrimination', with one of the protected grounds being 'irrelevant criminal record' (NIHRC 2008: 33). The provisions on freedom from violence, exploitation and harassment include 'from either public or private sources' and, among other things, note domestic violence or harassment, sexual violence or harassment and sectarian violence or harassment (NIHRC 2008: 40). The rights of victims are also covered in the advice, and the section includes the following:

3. Legislation must be enacted to recognise all the victims of the Northern Ireland conflict and to ensure that their rights are protected. These rights include rights to redress and to appropriate material, medical, psychological and social assistance (NIHRC 2008: 43).

Many other aspects of the Bill of Rights advice have direct implications for the transition in criminal justice in Northern Ireland; however, in the absence of formal enactment reliance still largely rests on the ECHR.

[11] The Agreement at St Andrews states: 'The Government will continue to actively promote the advancement of human rights, equality and mutual respect. In the pursuit of which we commit to the following: We will establish a forum on a Bill of Rights and convene its inaugural meeting in December 2006' (see also NIHRC 2006).

The Bill of Rights process produced extended discussion, and significant contributions to local and global reflections on how rights might be protected in divided societies. As yet, the process has not delivered a Bill of Rights. Although this fact is noteworthy, it is not determinative of how it should be judged. The continuing insistence that the culture of human rights in Northern Ireland is more expansive than the ECHR, and must remain transformative in intent, is in some part due to the participative process around the Bill of Rights. The Bill of Rights discussions shaped conversations about the protection of human rights and equality in Northern Ireland, and informed a wider public sphere about the full range of available international guarantees.

The Limits of Legalism: Bringing Humanity Back

As is evident in the materials documented above, the idea of human rights that filtered into the Northern Ireland transition is not confined to legalistic models of compliance. Law may at times provide the illusion of comforting certainty, but it is precisely that: an illusion. The disagreements of principle remain, the attempts to place law in perspective and in context continue. In this general picture, the contested nature of human rights is well established. Not merely the meaning of particular legal enactments but the 'human rights project' itself. A human rights legal order that primarily legitimised unjust social and political arrangements would rightly attract attention and criticism; and there is evidence that this is how legalism (even of the human rights variety) can function in certain contexts. Boaventura de Sousa Santos thus raises the appropriate questions:

> The quest for a counter-hegemonic politics of human rights amounts to asking if and how it is possible to recuperate the emancipatory potential and the Utopian character of human rights. After such a prolonged and violent period of imperial domination, can human rights still adequately represent human suffering across the world? Are they still part of the conversation of humankind? Is it possible to speak and act progressively in the name of human rights? (de Sousa Santos 2002: 281–82).

His answer is a qualified 'yes' (de Sousa Santos 2002: 282).

Writing in the mid-1970s in *Law and State: The Case of Northern Ireland*, Kevin Boyle, Tom Hadden, and Paddy Hillyard asked why law and lawyers had failed in Northern Ireland, and pointed to several factors, including the lack of constitutional guarantees and mistrust of the legal system (Boyle et al 1975: 6–26).

> When the guarantors of civil rights take refuge in technicalities, aggrieved complainants are more likely to take to the streets … No amount of civil rights litigation or review could of itself have solved the problems created by political bias. Nonetheless the courts and later the ombudsmen failed to bring these issues into the open and in such a way as to assist in the political reform process (Boyle et al, 1975: 23–25).

Their chapter title 'Civil Rights: The Failure of Law and of Lawyers' maps on to a critique of forms of legalism in Northern Ireland, and their argument recognised early on what law can and cannot do in such contexts (Boyle et al 1975: 6–26). As Livingstone suggested,

> ... conceptions of judicial role may be more important than the words of the text, and ... the highest judiciary should be better viewed as potential assistants rather than essential guardians of those rights (Livingstone 1994: 360).

In noting the rise of transitional justice generally as a discipline, Kieran McEvoy observes the 'dominance of legalism' within the emergent field and how this is 'prevalent in the policy and practice of transitional justice' (McEvoy 2008: 16). He charts this also in the domain of human rights, and highlights the problematic approaches it encourages (McEvoy 2008: 21–25). The implication of McEvoy's argument is not the rejection of the notion of legality, but 'a more honest acknowledgement of the limitations of legal thinking and practice that aren't properly grounded in the "real world" in which law operates in places like Rwanda, Colombia, or Sierra Leone (footnote omitted)' (McEvoy 2008: 44). McEvoy's analysis—including his call for 'legal humility'—provides a compelling critique of versions of legalism and the practical impact on transitional justice and human rights (McEvoy 2008: 29–32). A similar concern is voiced by Costas Douzinas and Conor Gearty when they insist that '[t]he "human" in "human rights law" entails openness, fluidity, an earthy resistance to the certain' (Douzinas 2012: chapter 3; Douzinas and Gearty 2012: 2; Gearty 2012, chapter 11). Again, their critical perspective is informed by an understanding of the constraints and flaws of versions of legalism. There is an imperative to interrogate the type of human rights culture, to pose difficult questions, and to nurture a transformative perspective that will assist transitional societies to realise their normative intentions more effectively (McEvoy 2008).

It is plain—even from the limited overview here—that the transitional process in Northern Ireland places human rights discourse at the heart of reform. This does not mean that the original objectives have been realised; the most challenging current discussions centre on problems of implementation, and point to evidence of 'rollback' (CAJ 2013).[12] As O'Rawe (2013: 37) argues:

> The Patten package had its own gaps and weaknesses, but attention has been focussed on simply trying to reclaim Patten—never mind go beyond it. Overall, transformation of policing in Northern Ireland has still a very long way to go.

There is a risk that complacency might weaken the policing and justice mechanisms (a sense that 'the job is done'), that the accountability gaps that do exist

[12] Examples noted include a Bill of Rights, policing accountability and national security, an Irish Language Act, anti-poverty and equality, as well as the treatment of victims and dealing with the past (CAJ 2013: app 1. See, in particular, the contributions of: Monica McWilliams, Daniel Holder, Mary O'Rawe, Maggie Beirne, Patricia Lundy, Niall Murphy, Mick Beyers, Alan McBride, and Mark Thompson).

(such as on national security) might erode rights-based reforms and impede the lesson-learning process, and that the attempts to 'move on' will mean that the legacies of conflict will be forgotten or neglected.

The aspiration behind this critique, however, is evidently not to advance a mechanised culture of narrow legalism. The 'human rights culture' desired in Northern Ireland in the field of criminal justice, and more generally, moves beyond established legal categories and legal formalism. In the debates that followed the Belfast/Good Friday Agreement a tension is revealed between cramped notions of human rights law as limited, confined and accomplished fact, and constructions that view the 'human' in human rights as embracing a larger and more inclusive agenda of transformational change (tied to notions of substantive engagement and commitment). What this latter understanding often means is that achieving legal reform—and even this (as the Bill of Rights process demonstrates) can be challenging—is only a beginning, and a signal for practical and interpretive engagement (and capacity building) to start. The transitional process in Northern Ireland reveals the limitations of narrow forms of legalism—a legalism that promotes an ethos of rigid and mechanical adherence to rules, accompanied by an often punishing view of humanity. The suggestion is that there are rival versions of a culture of respect, and that the 'human rights vision' of the transition goes further. It actively embraces a restorative and transformative perspective that wants to locate 'humanity' in the conversations about human rights law (McEvoy 2011, 2008).

Conclusion

Human rights offer a significant internationalised resource for those writing statements about the 'guiding principles' of the transition in Northern Ireland. Few documents, strategic plans, or review reports in the area of criminal justice (or more generally) fail to include reference to human rights. The risk of being everywhere and nowhere is thus real. Fluency in the language of human rights (particularly the ECHR) is pragmatically and strategically wise for anyone wishing to progress within the institutional contexts of policing and justice. This is not to undervalue the gains achieved in 'mainstreaming human rights' into formal processes; progress at the level of normative commitment is impressive. Who would have predicted the extent to which human rights discourse would become so core to policing, for example? The danger is one of overstating the normative gains and of complacency, that the critical potential of human rights is lost as a process of absorption takes place. The argument is that the Belfast/Good Friday Agreement 1998 reflected and inspired a particular transformative perspective on human rights that is too often neglected in formal legal accounts, and in considering matters of implementation. The repeated stress—markedly evident in the work on justice and policing reform—is on behavioural/cultural/institutional change and transformation, and not solely on models of legal compliance. The advance of human rights is one reason (not the only reason) that this alternative model emerged. The question will remain, in any transitional society, of how to keep this transformational spirit alive during the long pathways of reform.

The final point to retain is that the 'legal compliance' model suffers from another stark problem in Northern Ireland. A Bill of Rights that supplemented the ECHR was not enacted. The proposals for a new human rights agenda—that would, for example, find room for social and economic rights—were not realised. The transition remains then precisely that, and the work continues (as it always will). If this is to be meaningful and sustained, there is an urgency about bringing humanity home in ways that will nourish and inform a critical human rights agenda. If reform of the criminal justice system is to advance further it must be informed by a contextually sensitive and globalised discourse of human rights that will resist closure, and remind participants of the 'human' in all our constructed systems and normative orders.

References

Access to Justice Review Northern Ireland (August 2011) *The Report* (Belfast, DoJNI).

Amnesty International (2013) *Northern Ireland: Time to Deal with the Past* (London, Amnesty International).

Anthony, G and Mageaan, P (2007) 'Habits of Mind and "Truth-Telling": Article 2 ECHR in Post-Conflict Northern Ireland' in J Morison, K McEvoy and G Anthony (eds), *Judges, Transition, and Human Rights: Essays in Honour of Stephen Livingstone* (Oxford, Oxford University Press).

Belfast/Good Friday Agreement (1998) *The Agreement Reached in the Multi-Party Negotiations* (Belfast, Northern Ireland Office).

British–Irish Agreement (1998) *Agreement between the Government of Ireland and the Government of the United Kingdom of Great Britain and Northern Ireland*. Irish Treaty Series 2000 No 18.

Bell, C (2000) *Peace Agreements and Human Rights* (Oxford, Oxford University Press).

Boyle, K, Hadden, T and Hillyard, P (1975) *Law and State: The Case of Northern Ireland* (London, Martin Robertson).

Campbell, C and Connolly, I (2006) 'Making War on Terror? Global Lessons from Northern Ireland' 69 *Modern Law Review* 935.

Campbell, C and Ní Aoláin, F (2003) 'Local Meets Global: Transitional Justice in Northern Ireland' 26 *Fordham International Law Journal* 871.

Campbell, C, Ní Aoláin, F and Harvey, C (2003) 'The Frontiers of Legal Analysis: Reframing the Transition in Northern Ireland' 66 *Modern Law Review* 317.

Commission on a Bill of Rights (2012) *A UK Bill of Rights? The Choice Before Us, Vol 2: Annexes* (London, Ministry of Justice).

Committee on the Administration of Justice (CAJ) (1990) *Making Rights Count* (Belfast, CAJ).

—— (1993) *A Bill of Rights for Northern Ireland* (Belfast, CAJ).

—— (2006) *Human Rights and Peace-Building in Northern Ireland: An International Anthology* (Belfast, CAJ).
—— (2012) *The Policing You Don't See. Covert Policing and the Accountability Gap: Five Years on From the Transfer of 'National Security' Primacy to MI5* (Belfast, CAJ).
—— (2013) *Mapping the Rollback? Human Rights Provisions of the Belfast/Good Friday Agreement 15 years on* (Belfast, CAJ).
Criminal Justice Inspection Northern Ireland (CJINI) (2012) *Corporate Plan 2012–2015* (Belfast, CJINI).
Criminal Justice Review Group (CJRG) (1998) *Review of the Criminal Justice System in Northern Ireland: A Consultation Paper* (Belfast, HMSO).
—— (2000) *Review of the Criminal Justice System in Northern Ireland: The Report of the Criminal Justice Review* (Belfast, HMSO).
de Búrca, G (2011) 'The Road Not Taken: The European Union as a Global Human Rights Actor' 105 *American Journal of International Law* 649.
de Sousa Santos, B (2002) *Toward a New Legal Common Sense*, 2nd edn (Cambridge, Cambridge University Press).
Dickson, B (2007) 'The Impact of the Human Rights Act in Northern Ireland' in J Morison, K McEvoy and G Anthony (eds), *Judges, Transition, and Human Rights* (Oxford, Oxford University Press).
—— (2010) *The European Convention on Human Rights and the Conflict in Northern Ireland* (Oxford, Oxford University Press).
—— (2013) *Law in Northern Ireland*, 2nd edn (Oxford, Hart Publishing).
Douzinas, C (2012) 'The Poverty of (Rights) Jurisprudence' in C Gearty and C Douzinas (eds), *The Cambridge Companion to Human Rights Law* (Cambridge, Cambridge University Press).
Douzinas, C and Gearty, C (2012) 'Introduction' in C Gearty and C Douzinas (eds), *The Cambridge Companion to Human Rights Law* (Cambridge, Cambridge University Press).
Ellison, G (2007) 'A Blueprint for Democratic Policing Anywhere in the World?: Police Reform, Political Transition, and Conflict Resolution in Northern Ireland' 10 *Police Quarterly* 243.
—— (2010) 'Police–community Relations in Northern Ireland in the Post-Patten Era: Towards an Ecological Analysis' in J Doyle (ed), *Policing the Narrow Ground: Lessons from the Transformation of Policing in Northern Ireland* (Dublin, Royal Irish Academy).
Ellison, G and O'Rawe, M (2010) 'Security Governance in Transition: The Compartmentalising, Crowding Out and Corralling of Policing and Security in Northern Ireland' 14 *Theoretical Criminology* 31.
Gearty, C (2012) 'Spoils for which Victor? Human Rights within the Democratic State' in C Gearty and C Douzinas (eds), *The Cambridge Companion to Human Rights Law* (Cambridge, Cambridge University Press).
Glendon, MA (1991) *Rights Talk: The Impoverishment of Political Discourse* (New York, Free Press).
Harvey, C (2011) 'Taking the Next Step? Achieving Another Bill of Rights' 24 *European Human Rights Law Review* 24.
Harvey, C and Livingstone, S (1999) 'Human Rights and the Northern Ireland Peace Process' 162 *European Human Rights Law Review* 168.
Harvey, C and Schwartz, A (2009) 'Designing a Bill of Rights for Northern Ireland' 60 *Northern Ireland Legal Quarterly* 181.

Healing Through Remembering (2002) *The Report of the Healing Through Remembering Project* (Belfast, Healing Through Remembering).

Independent Commission on Policing in Northern Ireland (ICP) (1999) *A New Beginning: Policing in Northern Ireland—Report of the Independent Commission for Policing in Northern Ireland* (Belfast, HMSO).

Joint Committee on Human Rights (2003) *The Case for a Human Rights Commission* (2002–03, HC 489-I) (Parliament of the UK).

Kerr, M (2005) *Imposing Power-Sharing: Conflict and Coexistence in Northern Ireland and Lebanon* (Dublin, Irish Academic Press).

Livingstone, S (1994) 'The House of Lords and the Northern Ireland Conflict' 57 *Modern Law Review* 333.

—— (2001) 'The Need for a Bill of Rights in Northern Ireland' 52 *Northern Ireland Legal Quarterly* 269.

Livingstone, S and Doak, J (2000) *Human Rights Standards and Criminal Justice* (Criminal Justice Review Group, Research Report 14) (Belfast, HMSO).

Mageaan, P and O'Brien, M (1998) 'From the Margins to the Mainstream: Human Rights and the Good Friday Agreement' 22 *Fordham International Law Journal* 1499.

McCrudden, C (2001) 'Not the Way Forward' 52 *Northern Ireland Legal Quarterly* 372.

—— (2007) 'Consociationalism, Equality, and Minorities in the Northern Ireland Bill of Rights Debate: The Role of the OSCE High Commissioner on National Minorities' in J Morrison, K McEvoy and G Anthony (eds), *Judges, Transition, and Human Rights* (Oxford, Oxford University Press).

McCrudden, C and O'Leary, B (2013) *Courts and Consociations: Human Rights Versus Power-Sharing* (Oxford, Oxford University Press).

McEvoy, K (2008) 'Letting Go of Legalism: Developing a "Thicker Version" of Transitional Justice' in K McEvoy and L McGregor (eds), *Transitional Justice From Below: Grassroots Activism and the Struggle for Change* (Oxford, Hart Publishing).

—— (2011) 'What Did the Lawyers Do During the "War"? Neutrality, Conflict and the Culture of Quietism' 74 *Modern Law Review* 350.

McEvoy, K and Morison, J (2003) 'Beyond the "Constitutional Moment": Law, Transition, and Peacemaking in Northern Ireland' 26 *Fordham International Law Journal* 961.

McGarry, J and O'Leary, B (eds) (2004) *The Northern Ireland Conflict: Consociational Engagements* (Oxford, Oxford University Press).

—— (2006a) 'Consociational Theory, Northern Ireland's Conflict and its Agreement: Part 1. What Consociationalists Can Learn from Northern Ireland' 41 *Government and Opposition* 43.

—— (2006b) 'Part 2. What Critics of Consociation Can Learn from Northern Ireland' 41 *Government and Opposition* 249.

McQuigg, R (2010) 'A "Very Limited" Effect or a "Seismic" Impact? A Study of the Impact of the Human Rights Act 1998 on the Courts in Northern Ireland' *Public Law* 551.

Moore, L (1998) 'Policing and Change in Northern Ireland: The Centrality of Human Rights' 22 *Fordham International Law Journal* 1577.

Northern Ireland Human Rights Commission (NIHRC) (2001) *Making a Bill of Rights for Northern Ireland* (Belfast, NIHRC).

—— (2003) *Summary of Submissions on a Bill of Rights* (Belfast, NIHRC).

—— (2004) *Progressing a Bill of Rights: An Update* (Belfast, NIHRC).

—— (2005) *Taking Forward a Bill of Rights for Northern Ireland* (Belfast, NIHRC).

—— (2006) *Submission to the Round Table on a Bill of Rights for Northern Ireland* (Belfast, NIHRC).
—— (2008) *A Bill of Rights for Northern Ireland: Advice to the Secretary of State* (Belfast, NIHRC).
—— (2013a) *The 2013 Annual Statement: Human Rights in Northern Ireland* (Belfast, NIHRC).
—— (2013b) *Racist Hate Crime: Human Rights and the Criminal Justice System in Northern Ireland* (Belfast, NIHRC).
Northern Ireland Commissioner for Children and Young People (NICCY) (2008) *Children's Rights: Rhetoric or Reality—A Review of Children's Rights in Northern Ireland 2007/08* (Belfast, NICCY).
Northern Ireland Office (NIO) (2009) *A Bill of Rights for Northern Ireland: Next Steps* (London, NIO).
—— (2010) *Publication of Responses to Consultation—A Bill of Rights for Northern Ireland: Next Steps* (London, NIO).
Northern Ireland Policing Board (NIPB) (2003) *Monitoring PSNI Compliance* (Belfast, NIPB).
—— (2008) *Police Service of Northern Ireland Code of Ethics 2008* (Belfast, NIPB).
—— (2012) *Human Rights Annual Report 2012: Monitoring the Compliance of the Police Service of Northern Ireland with the Human Rights Act 1998* (Belfast, NIPB).
—— (2013) *Human Rights Thematic Review on the Use of Police Powers to Stop and Search and Stop and Question under the Terrorism Act 2000 and the Justice and Security (NI) Act 2007* (Belfast, NIPB).
O'Cinneide, C (2005) *Equivalence in Promoting Equality: The Implications of the Multi-Party Agreement for the Further Development of Equality Measures for Northern Ireland and Ireland* (Dublin, Equality Commission for Northern Ireland and Equality Authority).
Office of Attorney General for Northern Ireland (OAGNI) (2013a) *Guidance on Human Rights Standards Relevant to the Protection of the Right to Life* (No 1, 22 March 2013) (Belfast, OAGNI).
—— (2013b) *Human Rights Guidance for Forensic Science Northern Ireland* (No 2, 8 May 2013) (Belfast, OAGNI).
—— (2013c) *Human Rights Guidance for the State Pathologist's Department* (No 3, 8 May 2013) (Belfast, OAGNI).
—— (2014a) *Human Rights Guidance for the Public Prosecution Service* (No 4, 21 March 2014) (Belfast, OAGNI).
—— (2014b) *Human Rights Guidance for the Northern Ireland Prison Service: Conditions of Imprisonment* (No 5, 21 March 2014) (Belfast, OAGNI).
—— (2014c) *Human Rights Guidance for the Northern Ireland Prison Service: Prison Order and Discipline* (No 6, 10 April 2014) (Belfast, OAGNI).
Office of First Minister and deputy First Minister (OFMdFM) (2013) 'Together: Building a United Community' (Belfast, OFMdFM).
Office of the Oversight Commissioner (OOC) (2007) *Overseeing the Proposed Revisions for the Policing Services of Northern Ireland Report 19* (Belfast, OOC).
O'Rawe, M (2003) 'Transitional Policing Arrangements in Northern Ireland: The Can't and the Won't of the Change Dialectic' 26 *Fordham International Law Journal* 1015.
—— (2010) 'The Importance of Gender in the Transformation of Policing' in J Doyle (ed), *Policing the Narrow Ground: Lessons from the Transformation of Policing in Northern Ireland* (Dublin, Royal Irish Academy).

—— (2013) *Preventing Ideological Violence: Communities, Police and Case Studies of 'Success'* (New York, Palgrave Macmillan).

Panel of the Parties in the NI Executive (2013) *Proposed Agreement, 31 December 2013: An Agreement Among the Parties of the Northern Ireland Executive* (Haass Talks, Proposed Agreement) (Belfast, OFMdFM).

Prison Review Team (PRT) (2011) *Review of the Northern Ireland Prison Service: Conditions, Management and Oversight of all Prisons* (Belfast, PRT).

Scraton, P and Moore, L (2005) *The Hurt Inside: The Imprisonment of Women and Girls in Northern Ireland* (Belfast, NIHRC).

—— (2007) *The Prison Within: The Imprisonment of Women at Hydebank Wood 2004–2006* (Belfast, NIHRC).

St Andrews Agreement (2006) *The St Andrews Agreement, October 2006* (Belfast, Northern Ireland Office).

4

Criminal Justice Reform in Northern Ireland: The Agents of Change

BRICE DICKSON

Introduction

In 2015 the criminal justice system of Northern Ireland is in a very different place from where it was 21 years earlier. In 1994 it was mired in controversy, still dominated by an approach orientated not just to crime control but to the defeat of terrorism. There was widespread criticism of many of the institutions charged with delivering criminal justice, particularly the police, the prosecution service, the courts and the prisons. Today it is as if a new brush has been swept across the land. Virtually every aspect of the system has undergone root and branch reform, or is well on the way to that position. This chapter examines who and what brought about this transformation, seeking to pinpoint the critical moments which stimulated the reforms, how they were delivered, and through what processes they are now being maintained. It seeks to identify the key agents of change and considers whether it is possible to generalise from Northern Ireland's experience so that other conflicted societies might benefit from the lessons learned.

The Context

Before examining how change occurred it is worth spending a little time assessing more precisely the context in which the defects arose. This is not as straightforward a task as might be supposed, for it is easy to forget that in 1994 there was no consensus on whether any such defects existed at all. The 20:20 vision of hindsight must not be allowed to convey the impression that flaws in the criminal justice system were obvious to all concerned.

What needs to be factored into the picture is the existential threat to the Northern Ireland state during the quarter century leading up to 1994 and the rising fear that the IRA could not be defeated militarily. In the immediately preceding years there had been several high profile atrocities committed by that organisation. Since 1990, amongst many other incidents (detailed in Sutton 1994), it had exploded a bomb at the London Stock Exchange, assassinated a Conservative MP, tied men into vehicles loaded with explosives timed to go off by remote control, fired mortar shells at 10 Downing Street while a Cabinet meeting was in progress, blown up eight Protestant workmen at a junction in County Tyrone, killed three civilians in a bomb at the Baltic Exchange in London also causing £800 million of damage, destroyed the Forensic Science Laboratory in Carrickfergus damaging 700 homes at the same time, killed two children in a country town in England, exploded a bomb at Bishopsgate in London causing £350 million of damage, and blown up nine people at a fish shop in a Protestant area of Belfast. Of course the violence was not all on one side: loyalist paramilitaries committed atrocities too, including the murder of five men in a betting shop, supposedly in revenge for the Tyrone killings, and undercover soldiers killed several alleged terrorists during counter-insurgency operations. Between 1990 and 1993, 339 people were killed in Northern Ireland as a result of the conflict, including 69 police officers and soldiers. Those injured numbered 3758. There were 2038 shooting incidents and 1771 bombing incidents (CAIN 2014).

I supply these figures not to excuse the nature of the criminal justice system at that time but to contextualise it. In a territory as small as Northern Ireland (the population was then about 1.7 million) the level of conflict-related violence was extremely high. Things were as serious as at any time since 1977. Those responsible for operating the criminal justice system were essentially firefighting and had neither the mindset nor the resources for a reform agenda. No one was arguing that defects in the criminal justice system were contributing to the level of violence, so strategies aimed at reducing the violence did not seem to require the remedying of those defects. On the contrary, many in authority believed that remedying the defects would play into the hands of the paramilitaries, giving them a military as well as a political morale boost.[1]

But the defects were definitely there, and several commentators were pointing them out.[2] On the whole, however, these were not elected politicians but rather academics and activists (for example, Walker 1990; Dickson 1992a). Throughout the 'Troubles' in Northern Ireland, between 1968 and 1998, there was essentially a bipartisan consensus between the Conservative and Labour parties in Great Britain concerning Northern Ireland: whichever of them formed the UK government at the time (neither party put forward candidates for election within Northern Ireland itself), they agreed that what was needed first and foremost was a robust response to terrorism. When new measures were put before Parliament there were

[1] Sir Patrick Mayhew, speech during the House of Commons debate on the Northern Ireland (Emergency and Prevention of Terrorism Provisions) (Continuance) Order 1993 (HC Deb 8 June 1993, vol 226, col 153).

[2] Seamus Mallon, MP for Newry and Armagh, speech during the parliamentary debate on the Northern Ireland (Emergency and Prevention of Terrorism Provisions) (Continuance) Order 1993 (HC Deb 8 June 1993, vol 226, col 156).

occasional expressions of dissent from Her Majesty's Opposition, with symbolic votes against motions, but at no stage did the parties fundamentally disagree over basic strategy, and when the opposition became the government it did not make radical changes. Moreover, with no elected Assembly in Northern Ireland (the old Stormont Parliament having been prorogued in 1972), very few local politicians were calling for reforms. Nor, it must be said, were the legal professions terribly exercised about defects in the criminal justice system. Campaigners who spoke out were mainly from small pressure groups such as the Northern Ireland Association of Socialist Lawyers and, from its formation in 1981, the Committee on the Administration of Justice. It was otherwise left to concerned NGOs based in London (NCCL 1993; Amnesty International 1988), together with NGOs and Bar Associations based in the United States (for example, Lawyers Committee 1993; Helsinki Watch 1991) to produce reports criticising the justice system and pointing out that in many respects it was out of line with standards laid down in human rights treaties.

The Defects

What, then, were the defects? On the policing front they were most apparent in five areas. First, there were growing suspicions that the police were using unnecessary force when trying to prevent paramilitaries from carrying out their actions. Second, there were concerns that the police (and army) were improperly colluding with informers within paramilitary organisations; in particular, it seemed that a blind eye was being turned to some attacks by loyalist paramilitaries in situations where the victims were republican activists. Third, there was mounting evidence that the police were inappropriately using their 'emergency' powers to stop and question, search, arrest, and detain; allegations of harassment abounded in particular sectors of the community. Fourth, stories were emerging of the ongoing mistreatment of suspects in police 'holding centres' in Derry, Armagh and Belfast. And fifth, there was widespread disillusionment with the effectiveness of the system for processing complaints against the police, as evidenced in the NGO reports already cited and the annual reports of the Committee on the Administration of Justice (CAJ), the Belfast-based human rights NGO.

The common factor in all of these areas of concern was the lack of proper accountability of the police (Guelke 1992). The Police Authority, an independent body put in place by the Police Act (NI) 1970 to replace the ministerial role in overseeing the Royal Ulster Constabulary (RUC), was proving incapable of guaranteeing that the police adhered to high standards at all times (Weitzer 1995: 182–85; McGarry and O'Leary 1999: 99–104). The Independent Commission for Police Complaints, too, did not have the requisite statutory powers under the Police (NI) Order 1987 to properly investigate allegations against the police (Weitzer 1995: 185–206). The Westminster Parliament, when considering on an annual basis whether to retain or reduce the emergency powers in Northern Ireland, proved remarkably unwilling to amend them, partly because parliamentary procedures did not facilitate piecemeal changes but mainly because no political party wished to be portrayed as being soft on terrorism. This was especially so after the IRA began exploding bombs in England and not just in Northern Ireland. The persons appointed to conduct independent reviews of the emergency powers seemed unduly ready to adopt the government's preferred position and did not undertake fundamental analyses of why emergency laws needed to be used even when ordinary criminal laws could have served just as well (Shackleton 1978; Jellicoe 1983; Baker, 1984; Philips 1984–85; Colville 1986–92; Rowe 1993–2000).

The prosecution service was also criticised by civil libertarians on account of its lack of transparency (PFC 2000) and its failure to hold aberrant police officers to account (Weitzer 1995: 207–10). In a standard case the police would pass evidence it had collected to the Director of Public Prosecutions (DPP), who would then consult a Queen's Counsel on whether there was sufficient material on which to base a prosecution and whether doing so would be in the public interest. Challenging the conclusion on these issues was not legally possible, partly because no reasons for the conclusions had to be supplied, even to victims of the crimes in question (Osborne 1992).[3] To the outside world it seemed curious, to put it mildly, that so few of the deaths caused by members of the security forces resulted in the bringing of criminal charges, despite the dubious circumstances in which many of them occurred (Jennings 1988; Amnesty International 1994: 9–47; Murray 1998; Ní Aoláin 2000). Getting access to evidential material held by the security forces was often made difficult through the use of public interest immunity certificates (Foley 1995: 114–18). For a while the office of the DPP supported the use of 'supergrasses', criminals who were prepared to testify against their former partners in crime in order to win a lighter sentence and perhaps a whole new identity after release (Greer 1995).

To a degree the courts compounded this opacity by dealing with paramilitary defendants in the absence of juries. The government persisted with judge-only courts ('Diplock' courts) partly because it could protect a small number of judges from revenge attacks by paramilitaries but not a large number of jurors dispersed around the country (Baker 1984: paragraphs 107 and 120). Crucially, until the reforms to detainees' rights and admissibility of evidence introduced by the Northern Ireland (Emergency Provisions) Act 1987, it was all too easy for the police to present evidence to the judge that could not be sufficiently undermined by the defence because of the unavailability of objective evidence such as audio and video recordings of interviews, or testimony from an advising solicitor, suggesting that the police had used underhand tactics to compile a case against the accused. It is only now, with the creation of a UK-wide system for revisiting potentially unsafe convictions that we are beginning to learn just how poorly the police behaved on some occasions (Quirk 2013; also see chapter by Requa in this volume). Yes, judges

[3] *R v Director of Public Prosecutions, ex parte Adams* [2001] NI 1.

insisted upon proof beyond reasonable doubt and reaffirmed their discretion to reject evidence that may have been obtained unfairly.[4] Yes, under the Northern Ireland (Emergency Provisions) Act 1973, sections 2(5) and 2(6), as re-enacted, the defendant in a Diplock court trial was entitled to a reasoned judgment (not always available in a jury trial) and had an automatic right of appeal against a conviction. But in practice there was a certain conveyor-belt approach to the processing of cases: judges generally preferred the word of a police officer to that of a member of an illegal paramilitary organisation and they did not have the powers to probe deeply into what was happening in the holding centres (Jackson and Doran 1995). The Court of Appeal did, however, put an end to the supergrass system, so suspicious had it become of the reliability of trial judges' conclusions (Greer 1995: chapter 8).[5] Furthermore, there is no hard evidence that in their sentencing of convicted defendants judges were ever biased in favour of loyalists rather than republicans; for a while, at least, it was the other way round (Walsh 1983: 101–04).

In the prisons there were allegations of brutality by prison officers, especially in the aftermath of the killing of one of their colleagues, 31 of whom were murdered between 1968 and 1998 (Ryder 2000). Paramilitary prisoners resented the removal of the 'special category status' conferred on them between 1972 and 1976 (McEvoy 2001: 216–49). There were allegations of inappropriate strip-searching (Murray 1998: 108–10), and there was a general reluctance to transfer to prisons in Northern Ireland republican prisoners convicted of crimes committed in England (Dickson 2010: 276–92). At the same time, even after the withdrawal of special category status, paramilitary prisoners were given considerable freedom to organise their separate regimes in Northern Ireland's prisons, their educational opportunities were significant (numerous prisoners obtained university degrees, including doctorates) and all conflict-related prisoners benefited from a remission system allowing them to serve just one-half of their sentences.

The Obstacles to Reform

During the tense days of the Troubles change of any kind was stultified by the reality that the UK Government and republican paramilitaries were engaged in a dangerous game of cat and mouse. We now know that contact between the two camps was maintained throughout the entire period (Powell 2008),[6] but as far as the general public was concerned it seemed as if neither side would alter its stance on any issue unless and until it obtained an undertaking from the other side that a corresponding alteration would be made to its position. From the point of view

[4] *R v Corey* [1973] NIJB; *R v Killen* [1974] NI 220.

[5] *R v Donnelly* [1986] 4 *Northern Ireland Judgments Bulletin* 89.

[6] J Powell, Interview with Andrew Marr *BBC Andrew Marr Show*, 16 March 2008, available at www.news.bbc.co.uk/1/hi/programmes/andrew_marr_show/7299374.stm.

of the IRA it was quite convenient that the criminal justice system of Northern Ireland appeared to be unjust, because that bolstered republican propaganda in places such as the United States (Jorgensen 1982: 122). The political wing of the IRA, Sinn Féin, was not very insistent on change, and had no representatives at Westminster who could try to initiate it. No one seems to have suggested that improvements to the justice system could be 'conceded' in exchange for an alteration in the way the IRA was conducting its military campaign. Putting it bluntly, aspects of the justice system were not viewed as bargaining chips in any deal that might be struck between the British and the IRA. *Politically*, the issue had very little currency.

A second reality was that to some extent the injustices evident in the criminal justice system of Northern Ireland were mirrored not just in other parts of the United Kingdom, but also in the Republic of Ireland. While those jurisdictions were not experiencing a putative 'shoot-to-kill' policy,[7] their police forces were still reliant upon informers, they had at their disposal extensive emergency powers, they did not have foolproof systems for ensuring that detainees were not abused while in custody, and they allowed the police to investigate complaints against themselves. The prosecution services were just as unaccountable as in Northern Ireland, and the prison regimes were as harsh if not harsher (Hogan and Walker 1989: chapters 8–13; Thornton 1989: chapters 5–7; Ewing and Gearty 1990; Walsh 1998). True, Great Britain did not have juryless courts, but in several prominent cases, trials in front of jurors did not prevent the police from pulling the wool over their eyes (Conlon and Pallister 1990; Mullin 1997; Maguire and Gebler 2008). In the Republic of Ireland juryless courts *were* used and, although they comprised three judges rather than just one as in Northern Ireland, there was no right to a written statement of reasons for the judgment reached and no automatic right of appeal (Davis 2007). Indeed, the use of juryless trials was expanded to cover non-paramilitary related crimes,[8] in a manner which violated the International Covenant on Civil and Political Rights.[9] The system for regulating the way detainees were treated while in custody was particularly outmoded in the Republic (Martin Report 1990), even if there was a strong rule excluding the admissibility of evidence obtained in breach of a detainee's constitutional rights.[10] All of this made it easier for the UK Government to counter calls for reform in Northern Ireland: if the criminal justice system there was out of step with international standards on human rights then so were the systems throughout the two islands. *Legally*, not much was uniquely askew in Northern Ireland.

The fact that from 1972 Northern Ireland was ruled directly from Westminster and Whitehall was also an obstacle to reform, paradoxical though that may

[7] Ie, a policy whereby elements of the security forces sought to shoot suspected terrorists while they were on active service rather than arrest them at the scene or in a follow-up operation.

[8] *The People v Quilligan (No 1)* [1986] IR 485.

[9] *Kavanagh v Ireland*, CCPR/C/71/D/819/1998, para 10.3.

[10] *People (O'Brien) v Attorney General* [1965] IR 142; *People (DPP) v Kenny* [1990] 2 IR 110.

seem. The law-making system in London was not engineered so as to facilitate amendments to criminal justice legislation in Northern Ireland. Under the terms of the relevant legislation, the emergency powers had to be renewed every six or 12 months, but parliamentary debates on renewal orders were severely time limited and conducted in general terms. It was not until 1986 that they were informed by reports prepared by an independent reviewer of the emergency legislation, and even when those reports recommended reforms these were often not introduced at all or only after the sunset clause in the current legislation had been triggered many years later; for instance, Viscount Colville called for the abolition of exclusion orders and for the complete repeal of the power to reintroduce internment, but he was not listened to. Some reforms could have been introduced voluntarily by the police, the DPP and the Prison Service, but the heads of those bodies lacked the motivation, or perhaps the courage, to do so. The people running them became fixated on an anti-terrorist approach to criminal justice, one that was insufficiently moderated by a modernist approach to due process: as far as the office of the DPP is concerned, the fact that the first Director, Sir Barry Shaw, served for 17 years (1972 to 1989) and the second, Sir Alasdair Fraser, for nearly 21 years (1989 to 2010), may provide some explanation for the apparent conservatism of the institution during those decades. The memoirs of at least one leading figure suggest he was acting—or refusing to act—out of noble motives, namely the detection and punishment of serious crimes (Hermon 1997), but a Nelsonian eye seems to have been turned to aspects of the system that were leading to injustices, in particular the defects in police and army accountability for alleged 'shoot-to-kill' incidents (Ní Aoláin 2000: chapter 3; Jennings 1998: chapter 5).

In the judicial sphere there was from time to time an insistence that fairness must be done as well as seen to be done, and one can easily imagine judges in other conflicted countries not being as supportive of the rule of law as those in Northern Ireland. But in a system in which Parliament, not a written constitution, is sovereign, judges are powerless in the face of legislation which mandates a certain approach. At a time when even the European Court of Human Rights had not yet developed an effective jurisprudence in respect of fair trial rights, and when, if it had done so, domestic judges could not have applied Strasbourg's position in preference to that prescribed by domestic law, one can perhaps excuse the judges in Belfast for not being more interventionist. Senior judges were often accused of being biased against republicans but there is little or no hard evidence to support that view, uncomfortable though it may be for some human rights activists to admit this (Dickson 1992b; McEvoy 2011). If there were judicial failings these are mostly if not entirely attributable to the law and order mindset which judges everywhere are expected to demonstrate and to the lack of a Bill of Rights setting out the rights which those suspected of criminality are expected to enjoy. There was also a prevailing ethos of 'quietism', especially amongst practising lawyers (McEvoy 2011), that is, a willingness to accept the *status quo* and a concomitant reluctance to raise one's head above the parapet to challenge it. In addition, judges in common law countries are not in control of the evidence-gathering processes leading up to a trial, so in a prosecution they can come to decisions only on the material presented to them by lawyers for each side. The prosecutors, in turn, are almost totally dependent on the information discovered as a result of investigations conducted by the police. If the police are overwhelmed, under-resourced, incompetent, prejudiced or corrupt, there is little that the Prosecution Service can do about it in the absence of confirmatory evidence. In the period up to 1994 Her Majesty's Inspectorate of Constabulary does not seem to have had the will, or perhaps the expertise, to get to the bottom of deficiencies of this nature within the RUC.

In summary, the attitudes which had developed within some of the key criminal justice agencies operating in Northern Ireland were the result not so much of anti-republican prejudice as of unreconstructed complacency in the infallibility of traditional ways of doing things in the common law world. Such was the security bubble within which many of the key players worked and lived that they could not raise their eyes above the barriers and seek to emulate reforms that were being suggested in other like-minded jurisdictions.

How the Obstacles were Removed

If one factor is to be singled out as the main reason for the setting aside of obstacles to reform it must be the reduction in levels of violence. During the inter-party talks about ceasefires in the early 1990s there was a growing sense of optimism that a political deal could be struck which would serve the needs of both the unionist and the nationalist communities, but a prerequisite to such a deal was a 'ceasefire'.[11] That is the name given to the announcement by the IRA on 31 August 1994 that it was 'completely ceasing military activities'. It was followed by a similar announcement from the Combined Loyalist Military Command on 13 October 1994 (Rowan 1995). For its part, the state would never have admitted that it was offensively using firepower in the first place, so it did not make any comparable announcement. Whatever way it is portrayed, the cessation of military activities by illegal organisations marked the beginning of the change process. The republican community realised this more than anyone else, which is why it was on their streets that the wildest celebrations took place.[12] Republicans believed they had gained the prospect of a long-term solution to grievances *because of* the violence they had supported. In other people's eyes—those of unionists, nationalists who were not republicans, and 'neutrals'—this position had been reached *in spite of* the violence, and could have been reached a lot earlier if the violence had been halted. In any case, the cessation of hostilities produced time and space for politics to

[11] Statement by Sir Patrick Mayhew in the House of Commons (HC Deb 29 November 1993, vol 233, cols 785–87).

[12] *New York Times*, 'Cease-fire in Northern Ireland: The Overview; IRA Declares Cease-fire, Seeing "New Opportunity" to Negotiate Irish Peace', 1 September 1994.

move front of stage. Reforms to the criminal justice system were not high on the agenda of those who wanted to negotiate a settlement, but progress in that area was made a lot more possible as a result of the huge diminution in the day to day pressures on criminal justice organisations.

The second most important stimulus for change, itself a consequence of the first, was political will. Once the stalemate of the pre-ceasefire situation had been unlocked, the UK Government was free to keep the peace process moving by tabling plans for reform. Accordingly, in order to demonstrate the government's good faith, various confidence-building measures were taken within two months of the IRA ceasefire, including the withdrawal of the broadcasting ban on supporters of terrorism (imposed in 1998), the reopening of border roads and the lifting of some exclusion orders (Dickson 2010: 82–92). In addition, soldiers were taken off the streets, the number of house searches carried out was greatly reduced, and the number of arrests of suspected terrorists fell to a third of what it had been the previous year.[13]

Yet it soon became clear that further steps could not be taken unless and until the IRA moved beyond a mere cessation of military activities and began decommissioning their weapons. In other words, it was not enough that violence had ceased, there had to be as well a removal of the prospect that it could recommence if political negotiations broke down. To incentivise the paramilitaries the British and Irish governments established a body of experienced international statesmen to 'identify and advise on a suitable and acceptable method for full and verifiable decommissioning'.[14] This body was portrayed as a reaffirmation of the governments' willingness 'to continue to take responsive measures, advised by their respective security authorities, as the threat reduces'.[15] Unfortunately, the threat did not significantly reduce, and two weeks after the publication of the report by the International Body on Arms Decommissioning, in February 1996, the IRA exploded a huge bomb in London's docklands, killing two shopworkers and causing £100 million of damage. In March the Prevention of Terrorism (Temporary Provisions) Act was renewed for another year, this time with the full support of the Labour Party. On 2 April the Prevention of Terrorism (Additional Powers) Act was rushed through both Houses of Parliament in a single day, supposedly to allow the police in Great Britain greater powers to thwart any violent commemoration of the eightieth anniversary of the Easter Rising. In elections for a negotiating forum in Northern Ireland later that month, Sinn Féin obtained 15.5 per cent of the votes but the nationalist party which opposed the use of violence, the SDLP, obtained 21.4 per cent. This serves as a reminder that, throughout the Troubles, support for the use of politically motivated violence was a minority position even within the

[13] Statement by Baroness Blatch in the House of Lords Debate on the Prevention of Terrorism (Temporary Provisions) Act 1989 (Continuance) Order 1996 (HL Deb 19 March 1996, vol 570, col 1227).

[14] Joint Communiqué (29 November 1995) para 9. Joint communiqué of the British and Irish governments, available at www.cain.ulst.ac.uk/events/peace/docs/com281195.htm.

[15] ibid.

Catholic population of Northern Ireland, or at any rate within those who voted. Sinn Féin was not to out-poll the SDLP until local government elections in 2001, three years *after* the Belfast (Good Friday) Agreement (when Sinn Féin received 21 per cent of first preference votes and the SDLP received 19 per cent).

Political will to reform the criminal justice system was barely manifested during the negotiations between the IRA's ceasefire in 1994 and the Belfast (Good Friday) Agreement in 1998, but this was because progress on decommissioning had stalled. The IRA's bomb in London was a reminder of the havoc they could wreak. The ceasefire was not reinstated until July 1997, two months after Labour's victory in the British General Election following 17 years of Conservative Party rule. Serious attempts to reform the system had to await the Agreement itself a year later. Even then the parties could agree only to the creation of a Criminal Justice Review (CJR), to be conducted by a group of national and international experts under the chairmanship of Jim Daniell, Director of Criminal Justice at the Northern Ireland Office. This body worked relatively quickly (though not as quickly as the Patten Commission on Policing) and was able to publish its report, along with a series of commissioned research reports, in March 2000 (CJRG 2000). Early in its report the Review Group noted that people in general had 'a high degree of confidence in the fairness of the system as a whole and its component parts' (CJRG 2000: 18). Thus, 77 per cent expressed confidence in the fairness of judges and 74 per cent had confidence in the police. The percentage of Catholics expressing such support was, respectively, 13 per cent and 16 per cent less than that of Protestants, but it was still a majority of that religious grouping.

The report of the CJR is the main reason why a reform agenda in the field of criminal justice was initiated, and credit must go to all the experts involved, and especially to its chairman Jim Daniell, for producing a unanimous report in which the recommendations were well supported by hard evidence. Crucially, as the Patten Commission had done six months earlier, the Review forefronted the need for the criminal justice system to be reformed on the basis of human rights standards:

> Our starting point is the aims which participants to the talks agreed for the criminal justice system. It was the clear intention of those involved in the talks process, and one which we fully endorse, that these aims should be achieved within an overarching framework of human rights. The fundamental principle is that people have basic rights by virtue of their common humanity. The principles of freedom and justice which spring from this are central to debate on crime and justice. In protecting the lives and property of citizens, or depriving offenders of their liberty, the state upholds the rights of victims or potential victims of crime, just as it has to ensure that it respects the basic rights of offenders (CJRG 2000: paragraph 3.2).

We can therefore justifiably pinpoint the concept of human rights as a key agent for change in this context, more even than the concept of equality (which had been at the forefront of change in the 1970s and 1980s through legislation such as the Fair Employment (NI) Acts 1976 and 1989). The concept had been given a prominent place in the Belfast (Good Friday) Agreement partly because, in the year of the fiftieth anniversary of the Universal Declaration of Human Rights, and in the wake of the Labour Party's manifesto pledge to incorporate the European Convention on Human Rights into British law, human rights was a term which could threaten no one in Northern Ireland. In their struggle against unionist domination in the early years of the 1960s, nationalists had pressed their claim for 'civil rights', as blacks had been doing in the US, but by the late 1990s human rights was perceived to be a broader concept with a more universalist appeal. The CAJ, which won the Council of Europe's Human Rights Prize in 1998, played a role behind the scenes in encouraging political negotiators to make use of human rights as a way of settling their differences, though this has not been clearly documented to date. Chris Patten, who as the last British Governor of Hong Kong had overseen the return of that colony to Chinese control the previous year, and Jim Daniell, who had engaged with the CAJ in its work on criminal justice issues earlier in the 1990s, would have been well aware of the utility of human rights as a hook on which to hang change.

The impetus to change also coincided with a more general trend towards greater 'modernisation' within the justice system throughout the United Kingdom. This had begun under John Major's premiership, in 1991, when the government committed to a 'Citizens' Charter'. Labour carried it forward through initiatives such as 'People's Panels' and 'Service First' (Select Committee 2007–08; Shaw 2009). Victims and defendants were becoming 'customers' or 'clients', efficiency and 'value for money' were the new watchwords, and above all, accountability and transparency were now key expectations. People made growing demands that public authorities should operate in ways which genuinely served the needs of all individuals, not the needs of bureaucracy or of some elite. Old shibboleths were being re-examined, traditions were being questioned and a 'continuing improvement' mentality was being instilled. It is hard not to credit Tony Blair for embedding this mindset, which also seems to have infected and to some extent motivated his position on Northern Ireland. Blair's Chief of Staff and main negotiator at the time of the Belfast (Good Friday) Agreement, Jonathan Powell, has written a convincing account of Blair's personal determination to bring about a settlement in Northern Ireland (Powell 2008), and Alastair Campbell, Blair's Director of Communications and Strategy, has provided confirmation of this in his memoirs (Gilfillan 2013). The concept of human rights does not feature much in those accounts, nor do the defects in Northern Ireland's criminal justice system, but Blair's patience and drive, as well as his commitment to equal citizenship broadly defined, certainly do.

Institutions and Leaders

There are many other accounts of the peacemaking process in Northern Ireland but none of them pays much attention to the role played by pressures on the criminal justice system (Hennessey 2000; McKittrick and McVea 2001: chapters 10–12; Morrissey and Smyth 2002; Cox et al 2006; Bew 2008). This indicates that reforms to that system were very much an indirect consequence of the process rather than a direct cause of it. So, following many years of instability and stasis, how have those reforms been delivered in the 15 years that have elapsed since they were first promulgated? Any assessment has to be a positive one, even if in some areas progress has not been as quick or as comprehensive as one might have hoped. A case can be made for attributing the success, first, to the establishment of relevant institutions with significant powers and, second, to the appointment of particular individuals with the requisite leadership skills to drive forward a reform agenda. It must be stressed, however, that these institutions and individuals were only involved because of the primary agents of changes that have already been highlighted—the renunciation of violence, the political will to negotiate, the facilitation of weapons decommissioning, the centrality of a human rights-based approach, and the commitment to a citizen-based model for delivering public services.

Even before the Belfast (Good Friday) Agreement there were small signs that progress could be made in the criminal justice field. In particular, credit must go to Dr Maurice Hayes, an outstanding public servant in Northern Ireland, who in 1995 was asked by the UK Government to conduct a review of the police complaints system in Northern Ireland. This was a topic to which a great deal of attention had already been paid by the CAJ (for example, CAJ 1990), and to some extent by the Standing Advisory Commission on Human Rights (SACHR 1991–92; 1993–94; 1994–95), and Dr Hayes tapped into some of that previous work by consulting the researchers involved in previous studies. In his report published in February 1997 (Hayes 1997), he stressed that the overwhelming message he had received while conducting his enquiries was the need for the investigation of complaints to be conducted by people who were not only completely independent of the police but were also seen to be such. He himself had once served as the Parliamentary Commissioner for Administration in Northern Ireland (ie, the Ombudsman), so it is no surprise that he proposed calling the new complaints body the Office of the Police Ombudsman. The head of the organisation was to be assisted by a team who would have experience of conducting investigations on behalf of say, Customs and Excise, government departments, or other police services outside Northern Ireland. The Conservative Government of the day welcomed the Hayes recommendations,[16] and the Labour Government which took office in May 1997 continued to support their implementation, which culminated in Part VII of the Police (Northern Ireland) Act 1998.

As luck would have it, a relatively unknown academic applied for the post of Police Ombudsman and was successful. Nuala O'Loan has written about her experience in setting up the office and the challenges she faced during her seven years in the role (O'Loan 2010). Her service is best remembered for the robust way in which she stood up to police officers who were reluctant to cooperate with her investigators or who queried the correctness of their findings. Her inquiry into

[16] Statement by Sir Patrick Mayhew to the House of Commons (HC Deb 23 January 1997, vol 288, col 728W).

the way in which the police investigated the bomb in Omagh in 1998, which killed 29 people and two unborn children, led her to conclude that 'the judgment and leadership of the Chief Constable and Assistant Chief Constable for Crime have been seriously flawed. As a result of that, the chances of detaining and convicting the Omagh bombers have been significantly reduced' (O'Loan 2010: 122). The then Chief Constable, Ronnie Flanagan, reacted to this conclusion in a very hostile fashion, saying that he did not think the Ombudsman's investigation was 'fair, thorough or rigorous', that he was considering legal action on a 'personal and organisational basis' and that, if he believed the allegations in the report to be true, 'I would not only resign, I would publicly commit suicide'.[17] In the end, no legal action was taken and the Chief Constable stayed in office. The following year he moved to a position in Her Majesty's Inspectorate of Constabulary, becoming the Chief Inspector in 2005.

Flanagan was succeeded as Chief Constable by Hugh Orde, who continued the work which Flanagan had begun in constituting the Police Service of Northern Ireland (PSNI) and smoothing the transition within the ordinary rank and file of the former RUC. In his own account of this period Orde highlights the critical importance of listening, teamwork and empowerment (Orde 2010: 99–112). The daring use of a positive discrimination measure provided for by the Police (Northern Ireland) Act 2000, section 46, meant that for a 10-year period 50 per cent of new police recruits had to be from a Catholic background. In addition, budgets were devolved to district commanders, a new Crime Operations Department was established with properly regulated intelligence-gathering procedures, national security responsibilities were transferred to the security services in London, a 'policing with the community' approach was adopted, and an effective Policing Board and District Policing Partnerships were created (see also chapter by Topping in this volume). These were all crucial to making the Patten reforms work, even if the total cost, by Orde's calculations, was £647 million by 2009. As an example of organisational change, the process by which the RUC was replaced by the PSNI must be seen as a great success story. It hinged on effective leadership from the top, on close attention being paid to new symbols and emblems, but above all on a commitment to make policing more acceptable to everyone by basing it on international human rights standards. The PSNI Code of Ethics, first agreed in 2003 and revised in 2008, remains one of the world's leading documents on policing. Any breach of the Code is automatically a breach of discipline and can result in severe penalties.

Hugh Orde passed the Chief Constable's baton to Matt Baggott in 2009. For the most part the good work of his predecessors was maintained, though controversies over the re-hiring of former RUC officers who had already benefited from generous severance payments (NIAO 2012), and over the failure of the

[17] *BBC News*, 'Omagh Bomb Report "Grossly Unfair"', 12 December 2001, available at www.news.bbc.co.uk/1/hi/northern_ireland/1707299.stm.

police's Historical Enquiries Team to review killings perpetrated by British soldiers as rigorously as it reviewed killings by members of paramilitary forces (HMIC, 2013), took the shine off other achievements, such as the exemplary planning that went into the policing of the G8 Summit in Fermanagh in June 2013. Matt Baggott was succeeded by George Hamilton at the end of June 2014. The fact that a former member of the RUC was unanimously approved for the role by the Northern Ireland Policing Board, including the three Sinn Féin delegates on the Board, is itself hugely symbolic of the depth of the change process. As regards the PSNI's adherence to human rights standards, the picture is also a very laudable one. Each of the Policing Board's annual reports on this matter, since they began in 2005, have been largely complimentary, while pointing out where further improvements are needed. The exemplary work of the Board's human rights advisers during these years—who include Keir Starmer QC, prior to his service as DPP for England and Wales between 2008 and 2013—should not go unacknowledged. It is another example of the valuable role that independent experts can play in criminal justice reform—and of the utility of a human rights approach to conflict transformation.

Nuala O'Loan completed her term as Police Ombudsman in 2007, shortly after publishing a hard-hitting report on RUC collusion with the Ulster Volunteer Force in a number of murders (OPONI 2007; O'Loan 2010: 122–25), and was succeeded by Al Hutchinson, a former Assistant Commissioner in the Royal Canadian Mounted Police who had spent the previous six years helping to monitor the implementation of the Patten reforms through the office of the Oversight Commissioner (on which see Constantine 2010: 79–98). Despite his great experience in the field Hutchinson ran into trouble over allegations that his office was not maintaining an adequate degree of independence from the PSNI and that investigations into historical allegations of failings by the RUC were somehow not being conducted as thoroughly as they should have been (CJINI 2011; McCusker 2011). Hutchinson stood down early in 2012 and was succeeded later that year by Dr Michael Maguire, who had already served with distinction as the head of the Criminal Justice Inspectorate, another body set up as a result of the CJR. Hutchinson's difficulties illustrate just how important it continues to be in Northern Ireland to demonstrate perceived as well as actual fairness and impartiality.

The Criminal Justice Inspectorate has been hugely significant in delivering change to the criminal justice system. Its great merits are that, first, it applies nationally recognised standards when inspecting a range of criminal justice agencies in Northern Ireland; second, it conducts its inspections quickly and frequently, and produces reports that are evidence-based and focused on what improvements need to be made; and third, it carries out follow-up inspections to see if recommendations made in earlier reports have been fully implemented. Another helpful feature of its work is that it often conducts cross-cutting thematic reviews, such as into the problem of delay throughout the criminal justice system or the ways in which various parts of the system engage with young people. In 2013, the Inspectorate published a revealing report into the resources that are allocated by criminal justice agencies to dealing with the past in Northern Ireland (estimated at

£30 million per year) and tentatively suggested that, in the absence of an agreed way forward proposed by the politicians, the Department of Justice should establish and facilitate (but not lead) a Legacy Executive Group comprising senior representatives from criminal justice agencies. This Group could share information, better coordinate their responses to legacy issues, and 'consider agreeing a criminal justice system wide strategy for prioritising, co-ordinating and progressing legacy cases' (CJINI 2013a: 44). To date the Criminal Justice Inspectorate has been so thorough in its work, and so adept at engaging with agencies in a constructive manner, that it has escaped any significant criticism suggesting it is unrealistic or excessively interventionist. It is something of an unsung hero in the post-conflict period under discussion.

As regards the Public Prosecution Service (PPS) and the courts, here too there have been important drivers for change. After almost four decades during which just two individuals served as DPP, there is now a director in post, Barra McGrory, who is much more willing to engage with stakeholders and to push through reforms. He faces a difficult challenge in restoring public confidence in the PPS after some high profile prosecutorial failures in the post-Agreement era. In 2007, the PPS was criticised for its reliance on 'low copy number DNA' in its failed prosecution of Sean Hoey for his alleged involvement in the Omagh bomb of 1998.[18] In 2008, it was further upbraided for its part in the failed prosecution of a bank worker in connection with a robbery at the Northern Bank in 2004, the largest robbery in British history at the time, at £26.5 million,[19] and also for the way it handled the failed prosecution of Terence Davison for the murder of Robert McCartney in 2005.[20] In 2006 and 2010, the Criminal Justice Inspectorate was critical of the length of time being taken by the PPS to process prosecution files (CJINI 2006, 2010); in 2007 it was even more critical of the exorbitant fees the PPS was paying to barristers and solicitors (CJINI 2007), and in 2013, while praising the PPS for the high quality of its decision-making, the Inspectorate recommended that better assessment and training programmes be put in place for prosecutors (CJINI 2013b: paragraphs 4.54, 4.71 and 4.79).

At the Northern Ireland Courts and Tribunals Service (NICTS) the modernisation programme pursued by the Chief Executive, David Lavery, has been instrumental in creating a leaner and more efficient regime (NICTS 2006). Within the senior judiciary, certainly after Sir Brian Kerr became Lord Chief Justice in 2004 (he was succeeded by Sir Declan Morgan in 2009), there has been a greater preparedness to issue press statements, set sentencing guidelines, give lectures, and appear before Assembly committees. Needless to say, for all prosecutors, senior civil servants and judges, life has been made much easier as a result of the reduced threat level emanating from paramilitary organisations (sadly this remains very

[18] *The Guardian*, 'Police Suspend Use of Discredited DNA Test after Omagh Acquittal', 22 December 2007.

[19] *BBC News*, '£26m Bank Robbery Trial Collapses', 9 October 2008, available at www.news.bbc.co.uk/2/hi/uk_news/northern_ireland/7661017.stm.

[20] *The Guardian*, 'McCartney Sisters Challenge IRA after Man Cleared of Murder', 27 June 2008.

much an issue for police and prison officers, with Constable Stephen Carroll being murdered in 2009 and prison officer David Black murdered in 2012; two British soldiers were also murdered in 2009), and the influence of the Human Rights Act on all actors within the criminal justice system cannot be underestimated either (Dickson 2007; McQuigg 2010). While remnants of the Diplock system remain (Jackson 2009), and the occasional 'supergrass' trial may occur from time to time,[21] the past 21 years have witnessed a sea change in the way individuals are processed through the criminal justice system.

Difficulties have been harder to solve within the Prison Service, largely because of entrenched attitudes on the part of many long-serving officers and the inability of senior governors and officials to change those attitudes. Now that many officers have been incentivised to leave the service by the offer of a generous exit scheme (now ended), and in the wake of an excellent review of the whole organisation led by Anne Owers, a former Chief Inspector of Prisons from Great Britain (PRT 2011), there is hope that reforms will soon manifest themselves within the prisons themselves. On the downside, it has to be admitted that the rate of suicides in Northern Ireland's prisons has remained unacceptably high since the Belfast (Good Friday) Agreement (with reports by the Prisoner Ombudsman into 23 such deaths between 2007 and 2013) and extensive research has also brought to light the particular plight of female prisoners (Moore and Scraton 2013; see also chapter by Scraton and chapter by Moore and Wahidin in this volume).

Conclusion

Northern Ireland's criminal justice system has changed a lot in 20 years, but so has Northern Ireland itself. Perhaps that is the first lesson that can be drawn by societies elsewhere which have experienced conflict and a concomitant dilution of criminal justice standards. It is easier for criminal justice agencies to be reformed if the environment within which those who work for them operate is not life threatening. It also helps if there is political will, not just to propose the required changes but also to implement them. Implementation requires careful planning, stakeholder buy-in, good leadership and sustained oversight (OOC 2003–06). As well as an efficient and effective criminal justice system which provides good value for money, it must be grounded in human rights compliance—whether these are the human rights of victims, witnesses, defendants or the law enforcers themselves. Accountability and transparency must be core values too. This means that no one must be seen to be above the law and that information about the operation of the system must be made public and regularly evaluated. The more the criminal justice system can be 'normalised', without relying on special powers and procedures to deal with a particular category of suspect, the more likely it is that the system will win and retain public confidence. It is in that context that recent

[21] *R v Haddock* [2012] NICC 5.

revelations about the nature and extent of the 'on the runs' scheme in Northern Ireland has caused widespread dismay amongst those who wish to see a transparent and rights-orientated criminal justice system (Hallett 2014).[22]

The degree of fear generated by members of paramilitary organisations in Northern Ireland is much less than it was, although the number of attacks on police officers by dissident republicans is still very worrying and even in the eyes of independent observers seems to justify the retention of special police powers (Whalley 2013: paragraphs 88–119). The need for juryless courts has diminished too, so much so that it no longer seems right to use such courts for the few prosecutions that occur in relation to paramilitary activity which occurred before 1998. They may still be necessary for trials of suspected dissidents, since those groups make no secret of their view that anyone who facilitates the operation of the criminal justice system is a legitimate target.

Key to the success of the transition process over the past 20 years has been the establishment of well-empowered and well-resourced institutions led by effective individuals, but such institutional change was possible only because the political and security contexts were favourable. In a safer environment, and with a devolved Assembly, it has been easier for politicians, civil servants, invited experts and society in general to buy into new ways of delivering criminal justice which are acceptable to all. Perhaps relief from the years of trauma has made the key players all the more determined to implement change. Certainly, no one with any sense wants to return to the bad old days.

References

Amnesty International (1988) *United Kingdom: Killings by Security Forces and 'Supergrass Trials'* (London, Amnesty International).

—— (1994) *Political Killings in Northern Ireland* (London, Amnesty International).

Baker, G (1984) *Review of the Operation of the Northern Ireland (Emergency Provisions) Act 1978* (Cmnd 9222).

Bew, P (2008) *The Making and Remaking of the Good Friday Agreement* (Dublin, Liffey Press).

CAIN (2014) *Background Information on Northern Ireland Society—Security and Defence*, available at www.cain.ulst.ac.uk/ni/security.htm#04.

Colville, Viscount (1986–92) 'Annual Reports on the Operation of the Prevention of Terrorism (Temporary Provisions) Act 1989' (London, Home Office).

Committee on the Administration of Justice (CAJ) (1990) *Cause for Complaint* (Belfast, CAJ).

Conlon, G and Pallister, D (1990) *Proved Innocent: The Story of Gerry Conlon of the Guildford Four* (London, Hamish Hamilton).

Constantine, T (2010) 'The Role of the Oversight Commissioner' in J Doyle (ed), *Policing the Narrow Ground: Lessons from the Transformation of Policing in Northern Ireland* (Dublin, Royal Irish Academy).

[22] *R v Downey*, available at www.judiciary.gov.uk/judgments/r-v-downey. The report of an inquiry into the 'on the runs' scheme conducted by the House of Commons Select Committee on Northern Ireland Affairs is still awaited.

Cox, M, Guelke, A and Stephen, F (2006) *A Farewell to Arms? Beyond the Good Friday Agreement*, 2nd edn (Manchester, Manchester University Press).

Criminal Justice Inspection Northern Ireland (CJINI) (2006) *Avoidable Delay* (Belfast, CJINI).

—— (2007) *An Inspection of the Public Prosecution Service for Northern Ireland* (Belfast, CJINI).

—— (2010) *Avoidable Delay* (Belfast, CJINI).

—— (2011) *An Inspection into the Independence of the Office of the Police Ombudsman for Northern Ireland* (Belfast, CJINI).

—— (2013a) *A Review of the Cost and Impact of Dealing with the Past on Criminal Justice Organisations in Northern Ireland* (Belfast, CJINI).

—— (2013b) *A Report on the Corporate Governance of the Public Prosecution Service* (Belfast, CJINI).

Criminal Justice Review Group (CJRG) (2000) *Review of the Criminal Justice System in Northern Ireland: The Report of the Criminal Justice Review* (Belfast, HMSO).

Davis, F (2007) *The History and Development of the Special Criminal Court, 1922–2005* (Dublin, Four Courts Press).

Dickson, B (1992a) 'Northern Ireland's Emergency Legislation—The Wrong Medicine?' *Public Law* 597.

—— (1992b) 'Northern Ireland's Troubles and the Judges' in B Hadfield (ed), *Northern Ireland: Politics and the Constitution* (Buckingham, Open University Press).

—— (2007) 'The Impact of the Human Rights Act in Northern Ireland' in J Morison, K McEvoy and G Anthony (eds), *Judges, Transition and Human Rights* (Oxford, Oxford University Press).

—— (2010) *The European Convention on Human Rights and the Conflict in Northern Ireland* (Oxford, Oxford University Press).

Ewing, K and Gearty, C (1990) *Freedom Under Thatcher: Civil Liberties in Modern Britain* (Oxford, Clarendon Press).

Foley, C (1995) *Human Rights, Human Wrongs: The Alternative Report to the United Nations Human Rights Committee* (London, Rivers Oram Press).

Gilfillan, K (ed) (2013) *The Irish Diaries (1994–2003) by Alastair Campbell* (Dublin, Lilliput Press).

Greer, S (1995) *Supergrasses: A Study in Anti-Terrorist Enforcement in Northern Ireland* (Oxford, Clarendon Press).

Guelke, A (1992) 'Policing in Northern Ireland' in B Hadfield (ed), *Northern Ireland: Politics and the Constitution* (Buckingham, Open University Press).

Hallett, Lady Justice (2014) *The Report of the Hallett Review: An Independent Review into the On The Runs Administrative Scheme* (House of Commons, HC 380).

Hayes, M (1997) *A Police Ombudsman for Northern Ireland? A Review of the Police Complaints System in Northern Ireland* (Belfast, The Stationery Office).

Helsinki Watch (1991) *Human Rights in Northern Ireland* (New York, Helsinki Watch).

Hennessey, T (2000) *The Northern Ireland Peace Process: Ending the Troubles?* (Dublin, Gill and Macmillan).

Her Majesty's Inspectorate of Constabulary (HMIC) (2013) *Inspection of the Police Service of Northern Ireland Historical Enquiries Team* (London, HMIC).

Hermon, J (1997) *Holding the Line: An Autobiography* (Dublin, Gill and Macmillan).

Hogan, G and Walker, C (1989) *Political Violence and the Law in Ireland* (Manchester, Manchester University Press).

Jackson, J (2009) 'Many Years On in Northern Ireland: The Diplock Legacy' 60 *Northern Ireland Legal Quarterly* 213.
Jackson, J and Doran, S (1995) *Judge Without Jury: Diplock Trials in the Adversary System* (Oxford, Clarendon Press).
Jellicoe, Earl (1983) *Review of the Operation of the Prevention of Terrorism (Temporary Provisions) Act 1976* (Cmnd 8803).
Jennings, A (1988) 'Shoot to Kill: The Final Courts of Justice' in A Jennings (ed), *Justice Under Fire: The Abuse of Civil Liberties in Northern Ireland* (London, Pluto Press).
Jorgensen, B (1982) 'Defending the Terrorists: Queen's Counsel before the Courts of Northern Ireland' 9 *Journal of Law and Society* 115.
Lawyers Committee (1993) *Human Rights and Legal Defense in Northern Ireland* (New York, Lawyers Committee for Human Rights).
Maguire, P and Gebler, C (2008) *My Father's Watch* (London, Fourth Estate).
Martin Report (1990) *Report of the Committee to Inquire into Certain Aspects of Criminal Procedure* (Dublin, Government Publications).
McCusker, T (2011) *Police Ombudsman Investigation Report* (Belfast, DoJ).
McEvoy, K (2001) *Paramilitary Imprisonment in Northern Ireland: Resistance, Management, and Release* (Oxford, Oxford University Press).
—— (2011) 'What Did the Lawyers Do During the "War"? Neutrality, Conflict and the Culture of Quietism' 74 *Modern Law Review* 350.
McGarry, J and O'Leary, B (1999) *Policing Northern Ireland: Proposals for a New Start* (Belfast, Blackstaff Press).
McKittrick, D and McVea, D (2001) *Making Sense of the Troubles* (London, Penguin Books).
McQuigg, R (2010) 'A "Very Limited" Effect or a "Seismic" Impact: A Study of the Impact of the Human Rights Act 1998 on the Courts of Northern Ireland' *Public Law* 551.
Moore, L and Scraton, P (2013) *The Incarceration of Women: Punishing Bodies, Breaking Spirits* (London, Palgrave Macmillan).
Morrissey, M and Smith, M (2002) *Northern Ireland After the Good Friday Agreement: Victims, Grievance and Blame* (London, Pluto Press).
Mullin, C (1997) *Error of Judgement: Truth About the Birmingham Bombings* (Dublin, Poolbeg Press).
Murray, R (1998) *State Violence: Northern Ireland 1969–1997* (Cork, Mercier Press).
National Council for Civil Liberties (NCCL) (1993) *Broken Covenants: Violations of International Law in Northern Ireland* (London, NCCL).
Ní Aoláin, F (2000) *The Politics of Force: Conflict Management and State Violence in Northern Ireland* (Belfast, Blackstaff Press).
Northern Ireland Audit Office (NIAO) (2012) *Police Service of Northern Ireland: Use of Agency Staff* (Belfast, NIAO).
Northern Ireland Courts and Tribunals Service (NICTS) (2006) *Implementing the Northern Ireland Criminal Justice Review* (Belfast, NICTS).
Office of the Oversight Commissioner (OOC) (2003–06) *Six-monthly reports of the Justice Oversight Commissioner for Northern Ireland* (Belfast, OOC).
Office of the Police Ombudsman for Northern Ireland (OPONI) (2007) *Statement by the Police Ombudsman of Northern Ireland on her investigation into the circumstances surrounding the death of Raymond McCord Junior and related matters* (Belfast, OPONI).
O'Loan, N (2010) 'The Police Ombudsman for Northern Ireland—Some Reflections' in J Doyle (ed), *Policing the Narrow Ground: Lessons from the Transformation of Policing in Northern Ireland* (Dublin, Royal Irish Academy).

Orde, H (2010) 'Leading the Process of Reform' in J Doyle (ed), *Policing the Narrow Ground: Lessons from the Transformation of Policing in Northern Ireland* (Dublin, Royal Irish Academy).

Osborne, P (1992) 'Judicial Review of Prosecutors' Discretion: The Ascent to Full Reviewability' 43 *Northern Ireland Legal Quarterly* 178.

Pat Finucane Centre (PFC) (2000) *Briefing Paper on the Public Prosecution Service* (Derry/Londonderry, Pat Finucane Centre).

Philips, C (1984–85) *Review of the Prevention of Terrorism (Temporary Provisions) Act 1976 in 1984 and 1985* (London, Home Office).

Powell, J (2008) *Great Hatred, Little Room: Making Peace in Northern Ireland* (London, Bodley Head).

Prison Review Team (PRT) (2011) *Review of the Northern Ireland Prison Service: Conditions, Management and Oversight of all Prisons* (Belfast, PRT).

Quirk, H (2013) 'Don't Mention the War: The Court of Appeal, the Criminal Cases Review Commission and Dealing with the Past in Northern Ireland' 76 *Modern Law Review* 949.

Rowan, B (1995) *Behind the Lines: The Story of the IRA and Loyalist Ceasefires* (Belfast, Blackstaff Press).

Rowe, J (1993–2000) *Annual Reviews on the Operation of the Prevention of Terrorism (Temporary Provisions) Act 1989 and the Northern Ireland (Emergency Provisions) Act 1996* (London, HMSO).

Ryder, C (2000) *Inside the Maze: The Untold Story of the Northern Ireland Prison Service* (London, Methuen).

Select Committee (2007–08) House of Commons Select Committee on Public Administration, *From Citizen's Charter to Public Service Guarantees: Entitlement to Public Services 12th Report of 2007–08* (HC 2007–08, 411).

Shackleton, Lord (1978) *Review of the Operation of the Prevention of Terrorism (Temporary Provisions) Acts 1974 and 1976* (Cmnd 7324) (London, Home Office).

Shaw, E (2009) 'The Meaning of Modernisation: New Labour and Public Sector Reform' in J Callaghan, N Fishman, B Jackson and M McIvor (eds), *In Search of Social Democracy: Responses to Crisis and Modernisation* (Manchester, Manchester University Press).

Standing Advisory Commission on Human Rights (SACHR) *Annual Reports of the Standing Advisory Commission on Human Rights in Northern Ireland for 1991–92* (HC 54); *1993–94* (HC 495); and *1994–95* (HC 506) (London, HMSO).

Sutton, M (1994) *An Index of Deaths from the Conflict in Ireland 1969–1993* (Belfast, Beyond the Pale Publications).

Thornton, P (1989) *Decade of Decline: Civil Liberties in the Thatcher Years* (London, NCCL).

Walker, C (1990) 'New Developments in the Prevention of Terrorism' in J Hayes and P O'Higgins (eds), *Lessons from Northern Ireland* (Belfast, SLS Legal Publications).

Walsh, D (1983) *The Use and Abuse of Emergency Legislation in Northern Ireland* (London, The Cobden Trust).

—— (1998) *The Irish Police: A Legal and Constitutional Perspective* (Dublin, Round Hall).

Weitzer, R (1995) *Policing Under Fire: Ethnic Conflict and Police–Community Relations in Northern Ireland* (Albany, NY, State University of New York Press).

Whalley, R (2013) *Sixth Report of the Independent Reviewer of the Justice and Security (NI) Act 2007 for August 2012–July 2013* (Belfast, NIO).

5

Governing Justice Through Risk: The Development of Penal and Social Policies in a Transitional Context

CLARE DWYER

Introduction

In recent years there has been an increased focus on the role of law and criminal justice in securing peace and facilitating the transition from conflict to a peaceful society (Campbell et al 2004; McEvoy 2007). In fragile times of transition, process is therefore critical as legislation and institutional reforms are fraught with various challenges and obstacles in the everlasting attempt to reduce the risk of conflict occurring. This chapter will take as its vantage point the role of risk and the ways in which the discourse on risk and uncertainty has affected legal rationalities and the criminal justice structures in post-conflict Northern Ireland. Examining what it means to 'govern through risk', this chapter shows that governing criminal justice in a transitional society emerging from decades of political violence, involves a permanent adjustment of traditional forms of risk management, particularly in light of the possible consequences and incalculability of the risk of the return to conflict.

Risk has had a continuous role within the development of penal policy decision-making and the past few decades in particular have witnessed the dominance of risk as a fundamental organising principle of contemporary penal practices and social policy development. International scholars have documented the significance and the effects of risk as central to law and order policies and the large impact it has had on recent developments in penality and social policy (Feeley and Simon 1992, 1994; O'Malley 2002; Kemshall 2003; Crawford 2006; Ericson 2007; Zedner 2009). However, where scholars have documented this evolution and shift in risk and risk technologies, less commentary is given on the concept of risk during a political conflict and how crime risks change in transitional societies. By focusing on the role of risk assessment during and after a political conflict, this chapter draws out the key differences in the evolution of risk strategies and assessment within the criminal justice system in Northern Ireland and highlights the impact this has had on wider criminal justice development. This chapter argues that the legacy of the conflict and the complex geopolitics of Northern Ireland have led to the development of a particular crime risk paradigm which is dominated by concerns about 'emergency' risks. In consequence, this has not only led to a blockade on the potential opportunity for policy transfer from other jurisdictions, but has also resulted in an overtly precautionary response to 'political' crime risks.

The Role of Risk in Changing Societies

Although absent from discussion on criminal justice reform in transitional societies, one of the most renowned attempts to explain recent societal transformations can be found in various conceptualisations of the notion of risk. Societal discourses on risk have changed significantly over the centuries. In early pre-modern and pre-industrial society, risk was associated with the possibility of objective danger, incalculable threats, attributed to external sources (Lupton 1999). In the seventeenth century risk then became open to scientific scrutiny, where probabilities were adapted to measure and predict risk and threats, and so became transformed into calculable risks (Daston 1987; Lupton 1999). Risk was therefore seen as a way to 'tame chance' (Hacking 1990). Currently, as is reflected by the proliferation of 'risk orientated' concerns, the term 'risk' is used in relation to any situation that may occur in the future which provokes a sense of anxiety and uncertainty among individuals or within the population as a whole (Giddens 2003).

Over the last few decades, the concept of risk has been subject to much theorising within a range of disciplines, with many theorists continually searching for new ways to explain emerging social configurations. Early risk theorists were interested in the changes ushered in by risk rationalities, as characteristics of governance in our late modern and neo-liberal society (Douglas and Wildavsky 1982; Douglas 1990; Ewald 1991; Giddens 1991; Luhmann 1991; Beck 1992; Foucault 2007). Beck's (1992) 'risk society' is one of several prominent theories of late modernity which attempts to address the consequences of increasing reflexivity and the corresponding legitimation crisis within Western liberal democracies. Beck focuses his work on how risk is generated and dealt with at the macro structural level of society, the political implications of this and the social conflicts that arise.

The 'risk society' contends that we have moved from society with a perception of risks as calculable and manageable, to a society based on uncontrollable and incalculable dangers that are direct effects of human action and technology (Beck 1999). Beck's understanding of risks pertains to a specific understanding that contemporary Western societies have undergone a transition where the central issue is 'how to feign control over the uncontrollable—in politics, law, science, technology, economy and everyday life' (Beck 2002: 41). Modernisation has, therefore, become reflective, 'focusing on what in itself could endanger it. Risks as opposed to older dangers are consequences which relate to the threatening force of modernisation and to its globalisation of doubt' (Beck 1992: 21). A particular consequence of this 'reflective modernisation' is that it opens up a wider and more complex scenario, that includes 'non-knowing', as well as the various forms and constructions of knowledge (Beck 2009: 19–20). This scenario of 'non-knowing' can lead to, for example, increased security, which in turn can lead to increased securitisation by the state where there are no objective criteria for evaluating whether a particular issue should be securitised (see Rostoks 2010). The consequence of this quest for increased securitisation is that it seeks to expel and exclude that which is defined as causing risk and security. Dillon (1996: 120–21) notes that

> because security is engendered by … fear … it must also teach us what we fear when the secure is being pursued … Hence, while it teaches us what we are threatened by it also seeks in its turn to proscribe, sanction, punish, overcome—that is to say, in its turn endanger—that which it says threatens us.

This can be particularly relevant to societies experiencing political conflict or where a 'treat of terrorism' against the state exists. In response, the state through its various institutions often implements emergency measures providing legitimacy for breaking pre-existing principles in order to counter what has been deemed as a threat to the state (see Buzan 1991).

Inspired by the work of Foucault, theorists have highlighted the role of neo-liberal social institutions through which people come to recognise, interpret and accept risk (see Castel 1991; Dean 1999; O'Malley 2002). Dean (1999: 131) critiques Beck's risk perspective claiming that there is

> no such thing as a risk in reality. Risk is a way or rather a set of different ways of ordering reality, or rendering it into calculable form. It is a way of representing events so they might be made governable, in particular ways, with particular techniques and for particular calls.

Such scholars explicitly reject the notion that late modernity is any more 'risky' than any other historical time and that there exists any 'new' form of hazard that is predictable or unmanageable. Rather they choose to examine the processes or technologies by which risk is created, understood, appropriated and mitigated as a consequence of emerging rationales about individual rights within the neo-liberal political framework. Risk from this perspective is viewed as a 'governmental strategy of regulatory power by which populations and individuals are monitored and managed' (Lupton 1999: 87) and it is through these efforts that particular situations, social groups and populations are identified as 'risky', creating uncertain dangers, which require precautionary intervention (see also Rose 2000). According to Ewald, this precautionary approach 'does not target all risk situations but only those marked by two principles: a context of scientific uncertainty on the one hand and the possibility of serious and irreversible damage on the other' (2002: 282). A precautionary risk approach, therefore could be understood as an attempt to 'tame the limit and govern what [or who] appears to be ungovernable' (Aradau and van Munster 2007: 107). So for example, scholars have shown how the precautionary principle can account for some of the different technologies used in the 'war on terror' (Ignatieff 2004; Zedner 2005; Aradau and van Munster 2007), whilst others have demonstrated how 'precautionary logic' has also recently had a significant role in both social and penal policy development (Crawford 2006; Ericson 2007; Zedner 2009). This different conceptualisation of risk as 'precautionary risk' sheds light on the contradictory and complex developments of criminal justice in a society in transition from political conflict. Potentially high-security risk scenarios may create a precautionary environment, leading to the deployment of 'precautionary risk' to manage an array of legal, political and social problems.

The Role of Risk in Transforming Criminal Justice Policy

As a predominant concern in this new modernity, it is not surprising that the concept of 'risk' is well situated in postmodern social and penal ideologies and policies. In particular, society's preoccupation with avoiding and managing risk has paralleled various philosophical changes that have taken place in the criminal justice system (Kemshall 2003). Paralleling the growth of the 'risk society', the criminal justice system began to be plagued by a growing sense that 'nothing works'. As a result of an overall proliferation of risk-orientated concerns, there was a shift from the rehabilitative ideal to a preoccupation with the need to manage the threats and dangers posed by those in conflict with the law (Kemshall 2003).

This emergence of a risk management approach to criminal justice was described as the 'new master plan' (Cohen 1985). Yet, O'Malley (2000: 458) argues that although there is 'nothing novel about risk', the last 30 to 40 years have witnessed a resurgence of the notion of risk, where the technology of risk has become more diverse and complex and risk today is more open to interpretation and more disputed (Wilkinson 2001). O'Malley contends that risk societies are never simply societies determined by risk and the trajectory of policy development signalled 'not merely a redirection of particular policies but rather a shift away from disciplinary technology of power itself' (1996: 189). However, for Douglas (1992), it is the attempt to disguise the disciplinary modes of power and governing that contributes to the categorisation of risk, which results in a culture of blame and the notion of the 'criminological other'.

Theoretical enquiries into strategies employed to manage risk imposed 'by others' marginalised within society, began with Feeley and Simon (1992), who proposed an emerging penal agenda. This approach has been described as the 'New Penology' and it embraces both a theory and practice of punishment. This 'New Penology' with risk as its 'key theme', is concerned with the classification and management of groupings, sorted by dangerousness (Feeley and Simon 1992: 452). It is 'neither about punishing nor about rehabilitating individuals. It is about identifying and managing unruly groups' (Feeley and Simon 1992: 455). Feeley and Simon argue that current penal practices exemplify a transition to incapacitation, preventative detention and profiling (Kemshall 2003: 21) and the protection of society as a whole. Alongside, and in response to Feeley and Simon several theorists have concluded their own interpretation of the impact of risk thinking in the criminal justice system (Simon 1998; O'Malley 1992, 2000; Garland 1996, 2000; Shearing 2000; Hannah-Moffat 2004). In particular, social control theorists have responded to the need to characterise the contemporary penal landscape as a complex mix of strategies (Pratt 1996; Brown and Pratt 2000; Rose 2000; Garland 2001).

The last four decades have been witness to a 'punitive turn', away from 'penal welfarism' to a rise of the penal state (O'Malley 1999; Wacquant 2009) and a 'culture of control' (Garland 2001). Emerging from these cultural changes are reactive policies designed to demonstrate persisting control, a phenomenon which commentators have called 'governing through crime' (Simon 1997). This led to the introduction of a 'justice paradigm' emphasising the 'responsibilisation of individuals' (Garland 1996; O'Malley 1999; Rose 2000). Located in a climate of growing crime rates, increased public concern and a growing disenchantment with the 'welfare paradigm', there now exists a culture of blame, focused on punishment rather than rehabilitation, characterised by a 'tough on crime' philosophy in the pursuit of law and order (Kemshall 2003: 39; see also James and Raine 1998). This in turn has led to both a 'punitive' and 'public protectionist' stance on the part of the government in policymaking. With the ascendancy of neo-liberalism (Cavadino and Dignan 2006; Newburn and Jones 2007), there followed the 'death of the social, the demise of the welfare state' (Kemshall 2003: 38), which in turn played a significant role in the 'criminalisation of social policy' (Crawford 1999). Garland (2000: 349–50) argues that current risk strategies which stress intensive and expressive modes of policing legislation and punishment[1] are reflective of the state's need to demonstrate its sovereignty and willingness to control.

Similar analysis has also been used in relation to the criminalisation of social policy in the United Kingdom (Rodger 2008). The United Kingdom's 'tough on crime' rhetoric from the 1980s onwards, was heavily influenced by the importation of policies and strategies from the United States, including the 'prison works' mantra, risk-based interventions such as zero-tolerance, three state strikes sentencing policy, curfews (Newburn 2002; Jones and Newburn 2005, 2006; Simon 2007), electronic monitoring, boot camps, pre-trial 'shock incarceration', plea bargaining, mandatory minimum sentences, sex offender registration and diversion of juveniles into adult justice (Wacquant 2009: 173). Newburn (2002: 184, 166) notes the 'alacrity with which British politicians took to the US for inspiration' and acknowledges that 'the US has been either a direct source or at least the inspiration for, a number of policy developments in Britain over the past 20 years'. Garland (2001) argues that it is the result of the largely shared culture of control which has helped shape penal policies responses to look increasingly alike. Jones and

[1] In his list of sovereign states strategies Garland (2000) also includes mandatory minimum sentencing laws, parole release restrictions, no-frills prisons, imprisonment of children, revival of chain gangs and corporal punishment, boot camps, and sex offender registration systems.

Newburn (2005: 75) similarly acknowledge that there are 'clearly "globalising" elements, in the way the policy ideas emerge, travel and are implemented in different jurisdictions when the political conditions are right'. Such conditions may include 'ideological proximity, the language of politics and government, symbolic politics, the penal industrial complex and the neo-liberal penal policy complex' (Newburn 2002: 172–84).

The conditions of ontological insecurity and the perceived increase of crime risk across the United Kingdom in the last 40 years has translated into a 'preventative', public protectionist stance with justice reforms heavily influenced by US policy, and justified on the basis of risk posed to society by those in conflict with the law. There have been numerous key reforms and legislative changes in the government's 'protectionist' and 'preventative' response when dealing with those who come into conflict with the law, particularly with regard to sexual and violent offenders (see the chapter by McAlinden in this volume). Significant legislative changes can be found in the Crime and Disorder Act 1998, Sexual Offences Act 2003, Criminal Justice Act 2003, Serious Organised Crime and Police Act 2005, Violent Crime Reduction Act 2006 and the Serious Crime Act 2007, to name but a few. Since 1997, the government has introduced 3600 new criminal offences.[2] There has been a 4 per cent increase in the use of custodial sentences (Centre for Social Justice 2009). Sentences have been getting longer and the prison population in England and Wales has increased from 61,000 in 1997 to over 86,000.[3]

The extent to which these reforms have translated across the United Kingdom jurisdiction have varied (McVie 2011; Muncie 2011). However, the complex geopolitics of Northern Ireland has not only presented various barriers to the policy transfer of 'traditional' risk-based criminal justice policy, it has developed its own particular crime risk paradigm over the last 40 years, including a 'preventative' response to 'political' crime risks.

The Role of Risk in 'Law and Order' During Times of Conflict

Where scholars have documented an evolution and shift in risk and risk strategies and their role in criminal justice policy, less commentary is given on the concept of risk during a political conflict and how crime risks not only differ from 'traditional' crime risks, but also how they can change throughout the course of the conflict and also in times of transition. The impact of such differences has led to significant and differential changes in the criminal justice system in Northern

[2] *The Telegraph*, 'Labour Has Created 3,600 New Offences Since 1997', 4 September 2014.

[3] MoJ, 'Prison Population Figures: 2014', available at www.gov.uk/government/publications/prison-population-figures-2014.

Ireland over the past 40 years. As noted in the introduction to the volume, Northern Ireland shares the same legal system as England and Wales and until the signing of the Belfast (Good Friday) Agreement (the Agreement) had in many areas been shaped by the same legislative and policy development. However, as a result of the ethno-national conflict the landscape of the criminal justice system differed significantly and the government's 'preventative' justice policies moved in a different direction from that witnessed in England and Wales.

The conflict in Northern Ireland began in the late 1960s and formally ended in the mid-1990s. The main participants in this ethno-national conflict (referred to locally as the 'Troubles'), included republican and loyalist paramilitary groups and state agencies, including the local police force and the British Army. During this period, over 3600 people lost their lives and over 40,000 more were injured (McKittrick et al 2007). The non-state actors (for example, republican and loyalist paramilitary organisations), claiming to 'fight' on behalf of their constituent communities, were responsible for almost 90 per cent of these deaths and the majority of their victims were civilians (see McEvoy et al 2006). Over the three decades of the conflict, Northern Ireland went from having the lowest to the highest per capita prison population and became the most heavily policed and militarised society in Western Europe (see O'Leary and McGarry 1993).

In response to the rise of political violence, Northern Ireland developed a 'parallel' criminal justice system, creating a 'dual track' system of justice. This system, in essence was designed to accommodate individuals suspected of terrorist or 'politically motivated' offences as well as those suspected of 'ordinary decent crime'.[4] Risk has had a continuous role within the development of this 'distinct' and 'unique' criminal justice system, and since the beginning of the conflict has played a crucial role in the wider conflict management. Although a military approach was initially taken in response to the increase in political violence, with the deployment of the British Army, the state quickly moved to an approach which utilised the 'ordinary' responses of the criminal justice system. In order to deal with the risk of conflict, the justice system was radically transformed and soon the key objectives of the criminal justice system were dominated by 'countering a violent political conflict' (see Tomlinson 2012). The counterterrorism rhetoric throughout the earlier history of the conflict made it clear that the government's emphasis was on risk management, 'containment' and the need to maintain 'law and order' (O'Duffy 1999: 532).

In particular, counterterrorism measures were adopted which were primarily directed at achieving a short-term cessation of hostilities and violence, with little attempt to address the larger causes of the conflict. Various 'emergency' measures, from the Civil Authorities Special Powers Act 1922, the Emergency Provisions Act 1973 and the first Prevention of Terrorism Act 1974 (as amended) were utilised,

[4] 'Ordinary decent criminals' or 'ODCs' is a colloquialism from Northern Ireland for individuals convicted of a crime not related to the conflict and who are not 'politically motivated' (see Guelke 2006; McEvoy 2001).

along with a range of counter-insurgency strategies. Many of these measures and strategies allowed for the creation of a new non-jury court system (Diplock courts),[5] there were significant changes to powers and procedures, including changes to the rules over the admissibility of evidence, the length of detention under anti-terrorist legislation and limitations on the right to silence (see the chapter by Requa in this volume).

As well as the radically different role and powers of the local police service and the courts, penal policy underwent significant changes throughout the course of the conflict. The prison system was to change dramatically, witnessing both a massive influx in the prisoner population and a radical regime change in the treatment and management of those detained (see McEvoy 2001; Dwyer 2008). The increase in prisoner numbers brought with it a change in the background and characteristics of those incarcerated; in particular, it found itself dealing with two distinct prisoner types. First, 'traditional' prisoners, 'ordinaries' or 'ordinary decent criminals' who, once convicted, were processed through the courts, sentenced and served their sentence in a 'traditional' prison setting. Second, there were those charged with a suspected terrorist offence (a 'scheduled offence')[6] and subsequently served their sentence in a very distinct prison regime (usually in Long Kesh/HMP Maze) (see McEvoy 2001). The recognition of 'political motivation' and the 'political' status of prisoners in Northern Ireland was first introduced in 1972 with the initiation of 'Special Category' status (SCS).[7] SCS was granted to prisoners who were convicted of 'scheduled' offences related to the political conflict and who were associated with paramilitary organisations.[8] When SCS was introduced it was conceded as an 'emergency' measure in circumstances of wide-scale social conflict. However, in response to the Diplock Report in 1972, which emphasised that ordinary criminal status should be conferred on prisoners receiving SCS, various changes began to happen in areas of policing, criminal justice and judicial systems. As such, in 1975, the Gardiner Report recommended the phasing out of the use of internment and 'special category' status. This action was seen as not just a piece of prison administration, but 'a major item of government policy

[5] In his report into 'Legal Procedures to Deal with Terrorist Activities in Northern Ireland' in 1972, Lord Diplock recommended the establishment of trials without juries due to possible juror intimidation and difficulties in securing a fair trial for the accused (see further Jackson and Doran 1995).

[6] 'Scheduled offences' are those offences listed as an appendix to the various emergency legislation in Northern Ireland (including Sch 1 of the Northern Ireland (Emergency Provisions) Acts 1973, 1978, 1996). As well as a number of offences specifically concerned with terrorism, they include general offences such as murder, manslaughter, riot, kidnapping, false imprisonment, theft, robbery, blackmail and obtaining property by deception, offences involving criminal damage and arson, and crimes of violence such as assault occasioning actual bodily harm, causing grievous bodily harm and wounding with intent to cause grievous bodily harm. Prisoners convicted of scheduled offences had allegiances to particular paramilitary organisations on both sides of the conflicting factions (republican and loyalist).

[7] The government introduced the 'special category status' through the Civil Authorities (Special Powers) Acts 1922–43.

[8] Prisoners with 'special category' status were allowed to wear their own clothes, were exempt from prison work, and were detained in Nissan huts in similar conditions to, but separate from, internees. The conditions were likened to a 'prisoner of war' style camp (see McEvoy 2001).

in Northern Ireland' (see the Gardiner Report 1975: memorandum 5) and the first step in modifying the criminal justice system towards 'criminalisation'.[9]

The removal of internment, SCS and the introduction of the Diplock courts worked towards changes in the government's approach to the political situation, with wider emphasis on the use of criminal justice structures and judicial process. There was a 'rhetorical abandonment of the symbols of instability—the army, internment, special status for political prisoners—and their replacement with the ordinary tools of the state; the police and the courts' (Ní Aoláin 2000: 28). Individuals involved in 'conflict-related' violence were no longer dealt with through the 'arm of the military' but were afforded due process of the law, and 'no longer was the situation to be viewed as a political conflict, but a criminal aberration' (Rogan 2003: 41). The main principles of this 'normalisation' approach derived from a number of political decisions including an acceptance that 'the structures that have been adapted to contain political violence ... are ... just one specialised part of the "normal" criminal justice system' (Gormally et al 1993: 57). From the mid-1970s until the 1990s, policy development was grounded in the management of risk of political violence, and the use of counterterrorism, and 'emergency' provisions, through the apparatus of the criminal justice system. During this time the government moved to 'normalise' and de-politicise the justice system in Northern Ireland to parallel other Western liberal democracies, where the use of counterterrorism proceedings and emergency measures was seen as 'one additional specialism of a broader *crime control* strategy' (McEvoy et al 2002: 5, emphasis added).

However, it is often claimed that the strategy to utilise the legal process to manage the risk to political violence did little other than undermine the basis of the rule of law but helped exacerbate the conflict (Hillyard 2005; McGovern and Tobin 2010). Hillyard (2005: 3) suggests that using the justice system to deal with political violence, in effect 'corrupted' the ordinary criminal justice process, claiming that, 'anti-terrorism legislation was constantly used to deal with ordinary criminal behaviour ... the whole criminal justice system became discredited as the rule of law was replaced by political expediency'. It is claimed therefore, that counterterrorism and emergency measures not only undermined public confidence in the justice system, but the utilisation of these counter-insurgency strategies, justified on the assessment of 'political' crime risks, became normalised in the operation and processing of justice in Northern Ireland (CAJ 2008). The development of a 'security centred' criminal justice system, dealing with counterterrorism and 'ordinary crime' has not only impacted on the relationship between crime and the political conflict, but has also blurred the role and understanding of the

[9] All those serving sentences related to the conflict were to be redesignated as 'criminal' and the existing criminal prisoner population were to be designated as 'ordinary decent criminals'. This policy was viewed as high risk because, essentially, it was concerned with managing, rather than resolving the conflict and led to a number of high profile prisoner protests, including the 'blanket protest', the 'dirty protest' (Coogan 1980) and the hunger strikes of 1980 and 1981 (see Beresford 1987; O'Malley 1990; McEvoy 2001).

conception of risk in criminal justice policy development throughout the conflict and since. In particular the operation of a 'dual track' system and the transposition of the criminal justice system over political violence in the struggle for both risk and conflict management was a core issue of concern in the development of the Belfast (Good Friday) Agreement.

The Role of Risk During Times of Transition

The overarching political aim of the Belfast (Good Friday) Agreement was to bring an end to the conflict. It included proposals for a Northern Ireland Assembly with a power-sharing Executive, the demilitarisation of both state and non-state parties, in the form of the removal of British Army presence and the reduction of state military installations, the cessation of paramilitary activity and disarmament of paramilitary organisations, as well as the early release and reintegration of paramilitary/'politically motivated' prisoners (see Dwyer 2007). However, reformation of the operation of justice and the criminal justice system was also a central component of the Agreement. As recommended in the Agreement, the complete justice system was subjected to a wide-ranging review and a radical overhaul, conducted with the aim of establishing a structure which would 'deliver a fair and impartial system of justice to the community … to be responsive to the community's concerns … have the confidence of all parts of the community and to deliver justice efficiently and effectively' (Belfast/Good Friday Agreement 1998: paragraph 27). Although this was an opportunity for possible 'policy transfer' and incorporation of 'crime control' policies introduced elsewhere in the United Kingdom, the particular geopolitics of Northern Ireland, give way to a more cautiously driven review process, considering both the risk and management of crime as well as the risk to peace.

A Criminal Justice Review Group was tasked with producing a report of recommendations of reform, within agreed and specified terms of reference. Its proposals were published in March 2000, recommending 294 changes to the operation of criminal justice in Northern Ireland (CJRG 2000). Key recommendations included the promotion of a human rights culture in the criminal justice system; a new independent public prosecution service to replace the current Director of Public Prosecutions; the establishment of an independent judicial appointments commission (see the chapter by Morison in this volume) and an independent criminal justice inspectorate. Other issues to be addressed were the needs of victims of crime, an independent law commission, improvements to arrangements for young people and the integration of restorative justice into the justice system. The review was one of the most important and far-reaching assessments of criminal justice in Northern Ireland and its ensuing recommendations were implemented through the Justice Act (Northern Ireland) 2002, and the Justice Act (Northern Ireland) 2004. Although, the main aims of the subsequent legislation were to 'normalise' and to update the system in line with rest of the United Kingdom (Walker 2011), as is discussed below, many 'special' provisions remain.

In the years following the Agreement the criminal justice landscape underwent some significant changes including the implementation of the Police Act (Northern Ireland) 2000, which abolished the Royal Ulster Constabulary and set up the Police Service of Northern Ireland (see the chapter by Topping in this volume), a new Public Prosecution Service, Judicial Appointments Commission and an Office of the Attorney General, the creation of a Youth Justice Agency (see the chapter by Haydon and McAlister in this volume), and the introduction of Restorative Justice Youth Conferencing under the Justice Act (Northern Ireland) 2002 (see the chapter by Eriksson in this volume). There have also been changes in relation to dealing with violent and sexual offenders under the Criminal Justice (Northern Ireland) Order 2003 (see the chapter by McAlinden). As a result of the prisoner early release scheme under the Agreement, the prison population significantly decreased. The population has shifted from 686 in 1967, to 2946 in 1978 to a low of 910 in 2001. The prison population is currently 1803[10] (see the chapter by Scraton in this volume). However, like many other areas of the criminal justice system, prisons in Northern Ireland remained 'steeped in the legacy of the conflict' (Tomlinson 2012), and continue to be preoccupied by the possibility of the recurrence of political violence.[11]

This future thinking and preoccupation with policy planning has been an emerging theme in contemporary political discourses, particularly in the areas of political violence and terrorism. Rasmussen (2001) has argued that, in consequence, perceived forthcoming events come to direct contemporary policies. The struggle to manage/control the emergence of political violence is cast as a conflict of the present and the future (Rasmussen 2006). Mythen and Walklate (2008: 221) surmise that

> whereas risk assessments have traditionally predicted future outcomes based on past performance ... the new calculus does not assess the future by focusing on the past—'What was?'—nor indeed the present—'What is?' Instead ... assessments are directed by the question 'What if?'

This question of '*What if*' clearly dictates the assessment of risk of political violence in the current operation of the criminal justice system in Northern Ireland. This is evident in key areas across the Northern Ireland justice system, where numerous caveats remain in the delivery of justice and strategies of risk management within the courts, the prisons, policing and in the use of counterterrorism measures. The

[10] This figure includes adult female/male sentenced/non-sentenced, and young people (18–21) male/female sentenced/non-sentenced, available at www.dojni.gov.uk. The imprisonment rate for Northern Ireland is 100 per 100,000 compared with 149 per 100,000 in England and Wales.

[11] There is a growing paramilitary/'politically motivated' prisoner population. Republican and loyalist prisoners are housed separately from 'ordinary' prisoners in HMP Maghaberry (see Dwyer 2008 for further discussion).

next section of the chapter will move to explore these various caveats, including policing powers to stop and search, the existence of a non-jury trial system and the particular approaches to counter-insurgency policing.

Governing Justice Through Risk?

In attempting to move towards a more normalised society, the Belfast (Good Friday) Agreement sought to bring an end to emergency legislation by the 'removal of emergency powers in Northern Ireland' (Belfast (Good Friday) Agreement 1998: paragraph 25). In 2003, a joint declaration by the British and Irish Governments set out a two-year programme of 'normalisation' which envisaged that 'counter terrorism legislation particular to Northern Ireland would be repealed' (British and Irish Governments 2003: annex 1.9). However, over a decade on from this, it is evident that anti-terrorism legislation 'particular' to Northern Ireland remains. Although a lot of 'temporary' anti-terrorism legislation has had its place in the operation of the justice system since the early 1970s, in 2000 the government placed similar laws on a permanent footing. The Terrorism Act 2000 provides a range of measures designed to prevent terrorism and support the investigation of terrorist crime, with the intention of combating all forms of terrorism, not just terrorism connected with the affairs of Northern Ireland, and extends across *all* of the United Kingdom. One controversial section of the legislation was in regard to the powers of 'stop and search' without reasonable suspicion (section 43 and section 44 of the Terrorism Act 2000). This was the focus of a legal challenge in the courts[12] and was subsequently abandoned in July 2010.

In Northern Ireland, however, the Justice and Security Act (Northern Ireland) 2007 has retained the power to stop and search (section 24) and stop and question (section 21) *without reasonable suspicion*. Section 21 of the Act empowers police officers to stop and question without any suspicion whatsoever, in order to ascertain the person's identity and movements including where a person has been and intends to go. Any failure to answer questions posed by the officer in the section is a criminal offence. The power to stop and search was used 1163 times in 2009/10 and 16,023 times in 2010/11, an increase of more than twelve-fold (Anderson 2012). Some of the provisions of this legislation were challenged in July 2012 by way of judicial review, questioning the lawfulness and necessity of such powers and their compatibility with the European Convention on Human Rights.[13]

[12] *Gillan and Quinton v The UK* App no 4158/05 (ECHR, 12 January 2010) 4th section. The applicants alleged that the powers of stop and search used against them by the policed breached their rights under Arts 5, 8, 10 and 11 of the Convention.

[13] Including their compatibility with Arts 5 and 8 of the Convention. *In the matter of an application by Fox and McNulty for judicial review and in the matter of an application by Canning for judicial review* [2013] NICA 19.

Notwithstanding challenges to the operation of this provision, the government's position clearly indicates that additional 'safeguards' are needed and the assessment of risk continues to be driven by the 'particular' circumstances of Northern Ireland. This approach is also evident in the continued use of non-jury trials in Northern Ireland.

As noted above, juryless 'emergency' Diplock courts were introduced in 1973. Throughout the conflict 'approximately one in three serious criminal cases' was tried in Diplock courts, 'with a conviction rate greatly exceeding that of "ordinary" (non-Diplock) criminal courts' (Jackson and Doran 1995: 322). Such convictions resulted from 'confessions and from excessive use of uncorroborated testimony by government informants or "supergrasses"' (Jackson and Doran 1995: 322). Although the Northern Ireland Office (NIO) announced in August 2005 that the Diplock courts were to be phased out and eventually abolished by July 2007, remnants remain with provisions for their use legislated into statute. Sections 1–9 of the Justice and Security Act (Northern Ireland) 2007 includes provisions for the Director of Public Prosecutions (DPP) to certify a case for non-jury trial if the DPP is 'satisfied' that there is a risk that the administration of justice might be impaired if the trial were to be conducted *with* a jury (section 1, Justice and Security Act (Northern Ireland) 2007). The DDP is also not required to give reasons for such decisions. In 2007 the UN Human Rights Committee raised concerns on the continued use of non-jury trials, specifically in regards to the right to a fair trial (UNHRC 2007). In 2008, the Human Rights Committee, reaffirmed their concerns with the continued use of non-jury trials and expressed concern that 'some elements of criminal procedure continue to differ between Northern Ireland and the remainder of the State party's jurisdiction', stating that the government should carefully monitor the situation, 'with a view to abolishing' these intrinsically different judicial procedures (UNHRC 2008: 5).

Although, the NIO gave a commitment in 2010 to undertake a 'comprehensive review of the non-jury trial system' (NIO 2010), this has yet to happen. The government's position remains that 'political' crime risks are an important justification for a 'parallel' apparatus of justice to exist and Northern Ireland is not yet in the position to introduce jury trials 'for all'. The Committee on the Administration of Justice (CAJ), in their submission to the NIO stated that

> jury trial for all cases would be a way to acknowledge and commend the enormous political and social progress which Northern Ireland has made in the past decade … maintaining echoes of the legal regime from the conflict undermines such progress (CAJ 2013: 8).

However, echoes of legal regimes from the conflict continue to be present, including in the delivery of policing.

Within the St Andrews Agreement 2006 the government set out the 'future of national security arrangements in Northern Ireland' (St Andrews Agreement 2006: paragraph 5) and in 2007 provided for the transfer of national security covert policing in Northern Ireland to the Security Service MI5. In 2012, the CAJ highlighted their concerns on this policy, scrutinising covert policing accountability, particularly regarding running undercover operations and the use of paramilitary informants. The report concluded that there were no external oversight mechanisms to ensure that international standards were followed and that rules were abided by (CAJ 2012). It is claimed that the state is

> operating outside of the rule of law—as set out in human rights standards relating to impunity, effective investigation and remedy—fuelled, prolonged and exacerbated the conflict ... the present situation is that primacy for 'national security' covert policing has been transferred to MI5 where it remains impossible to tell the extent the secret agency is operating within or outside of the law (Holder 2013: 1).

Further to concerns of accountability and human rights standards, it is argued that this has not only created a 'two-tier' policing service, but it has also led to a significant regression to policing strategies witnessed during times of conflict. Policing reform was intended to move policing away from 'counter-insurgency' approaches set out in various emergency legislation and policy frameworks (see chapter by Topping in this volume). However, since this transfer of policing powers, the 'most sensitive area of policing is in fact being run by a parallel police force' (CAJ 2012: 15). 'The practical impact of this would be that two different covert policing regimes, in terms of operational techniques ... are potentially now in place' (CAJ 2012: 103), one dealing with 'ordinary' crime risks and one dealing with 'politically motivated' crime risks.

The current resurgence of security-based policing to meet the increasing risk posed by 'political' crime risks has gone from policing community imperatives and returned it to criminal investigation, covert intelligence gathering and technology focused state policing. This risk laden area of policing not only presents significant challenges in attempting to 'normalise' the processing of criminal justice in Northern Ireland, but also has significant impact in regard to how counter-insurgency may become normalised within the processing of criminal justice more generally.

Conclusion

Beck (1992) contends we live in a 'Risk Society'. Is this the case? Is society any more 'risky' than times past? Or is it how we interpret and negotiate risks which matters in a 'post-conflict' transitional society? O'Malley (2004) has referred to the 'uncertain promise of risk'. Is this a much sharper reservation when transferred to 'political' crime risks in a transitional society? The Northern Ireland experience demonstrates how the readjustment of the understanding and interpretation of risk in a society emerging from political violence can create a distinct criminal justice system. Twenty years after the paramilitary ceasefires, 15 years after the signing of the Belfast (Good Friday) Agreement and four years since devolution of criminal justice and policing powers, the landscape of the criminal justice system continues to be significantly impacted by 'political' crime risks. This leads one to question the utility of risk, risk management, and risk assessment more generally. Is there a bigger 'What if?' in a transitional society and should crime risk be measured differently in such societies?

Risk prediction in crime and justice always has been, and always will be problematic. If we consider literature surrounding genetic predisposition and its influence on criminal behaviour (Lombroso 1911), through to prediction of delinquency through academic ability (Hirschi 1969), connections between crime, risk and sanctioning practice have been far from scientifically convincing. Similarly, cornerstone causation themes such as the impact prison has on reoffending and how policing influences crime rates cannot be convincingly or consistently established. If this is the case, then what hope is there for risk-based science of assessing political violence?

Like many forms of crime risks, 'political' crime risk is difficult to evaluate and predict. O'Malley (2007: 2) suggested political risks such as terrorism are not statistically predictable. So, for example, because terrorist events are often 'non-re-occurring events or events that unfold so quickly or invisibly that we cannot gather data on them beforehand, they cannot be predicted using statistical risk techniques'. However, problems with predicting crime risk and justice security outcomes have not stopped expansion of behaviour prediction as a justice policy motivator. We hear so much about 'evidence-based' policy development in regard to 'political' crimes risks, and the extent to which expectations of justice can be validated, particularly in Northern Ireland. However, a number of key questions remain, insofar as, whilst harsh crime control measures should always be justified, can they ever be justified on the basis of the possibility of risk? Should the operation of justice differ within Northern Ireland because of the 'particular' circumstances? What is the wider impact on the rights of the individual because of politicised risk assessment?

With risk prediction and security evaluation more reliant on political and cultural context than on comprehensive and comparative harm measures, many individual rights have given way to political imperatives. The legacy of the political conflict continues to drive the perception of politicised crime risk. As a result of the emergence of 'crime control' and 'peace control', there has been a permanent readjustment of many of the 'traditional' key features of criminal justice, with stricter regulation and securitisation in many areas of the criminal justice system. A cautionary note on this practice, however, as with risk management in social and penal policies more generally, is that there will always be limitations, not least in 'predicting the future'. Added to this, particularly in regard to a transitional society emerging from conflict, is the danger that by continually undertaking a future-orientated approach of 'What if'?, policymakers may be forever tempted to look back, look forward, but never to stop and ask 'What is?'

References

Anderson, C (2012) *The Terrorism Acts in 2011, Report of the Independent Reviewer* (London, HMSO).

Aradau, C and van Munster, R (2007) 'Governing Terrorism through Risk: Taking Precautions, (un)Knowing the Future' 13 *European Journal of International Relations* 89.

Beck, U (1992) *Risk Society: Towards a New Modernity* (London, Sage).

—— (1999) *World Risk Society* (Cambridge, Polity).

—— (2002) 'The Terrorist Threat: World Risk Society Revisited' 19 *Theory, Culture & Society* 39.

—— (2009) *World at Risk* (Cambridge, Polity).

Belfast/Good Friday Agreement (1998) *The Agreement Reached in the Multi-Party Negotiations* (Belfast, NIO).

Beresford, D (1987) *Ten Men Dead: The Story of the 1981 Irish Hunger Strike* (London, Grafton).

British and Irish Governments (2003) *Joint Declaration by the British and Irish Governments* (London, Northern Ireland Office).

Brown, M and Pratt, J (2000) 'Dangerousness and Modern Society' in M Brown and J Pratt (eds), *Dangerous Offenders* (London, Routledge).

Buzan, B (1991) 'New Patterns of Global Security in the Twenty-First Century' 67 *International Affairs* 431.

Campbell, C, Bell, C and Ní Aoláin, F (2004) 'Justice Discourses in Transition' 13 *Social & Legal Studies* 305.

Castel, R (1991) 'From Dangerousness to Risk' in G Burchell, C Gordon and P Miller (eds), *The Foucault Effect: Studies in Governmentality* (Chicago, Chicago University Press).

Cavadino, M and Dignan, J (2006) 'Penal Policy and Political Economy' 6 *Criminology & Criminal Justice* 435.

Centre for Social Justice (2009) *Locked Up Potential: A Strategy for Reforming Prisons and Rehabilitating Prisoners* (London, Centre for Social Justice).

Cohen, S (1985) *Visions of Social Control* (Cambridge, Polity).

Committee on the Administration of Justice (CAJ) (2008) *War on Terror: Lessons from Northern Ireland* (Belfast, CAJ).

—— (2012) *The Policing You Don't See. Covert Policing and the Accountability Gap: Five Years on From the Transfer of 'National Security' Primacy to MI5* (Belfast, CAJ).

—— (2013) *CAJ's Commentary to the Northern Ireland Office on 'Non-Jury Arrangements in Northern Ireland'* (Belfast, CAJ).

Coogan, TP (1980) *On the Blanket: The H Block Story* (Dublin, Ward River Press).

Crawford, A (1999) *The Local Governance of Crime: Appeals to Community and Partnerships* (Oxford, Oxford University Press).

—— (2006) 'Networked Governance and the Post-Regulatory State? Steering, Rowing and Anchoring the Provision of Policing and Security' 10 *Theoretical Criminology* 449.

Criminal Justice Review Group (CJRG) (2000) *Review of the Criminal Justice System in Northern Ireland:* The Report of the Criminal Justice Review (Belfast, HMSO).

Daston, L (1987) 'The Domestication of Risk: Mathematical Probability and Insurance 1650–1830' in L Kruger, L Daston and M Heidelberger (eds), *The Probabilistic Revolution Volume 1: Ideas in History* (Cambridge, MA, MIT Press).

Dean, M (1999) *Governmentality: Power and Rule in Modern Society* (London, Sage).

Dillon, M (1996) *Politics of Security: Towards a Political Philosophy of Continental Thought* (London, Routledge).
Douglas, M (1990) 'Risk as a Forensic Resource' 119 *DAEDALUS* 1.
—— (1992) *Risk and Blame: Essays in Cultural Theory* (London, Routledge).
Douglas, M and Wildavsky, A (1982) *Risk and Blame: Essays in Cultural Theory* (New York, Kegan Paul).
Dwyer, CD (2007) 'Risk, Politics and the "Scientification" of Political Judgement: Prisoner Release and Conflict Transformation in Northern Ireland' 47 *British Journal of Criminology* 779.
—— (2008) 'Dealing with the Leftovers: Post-Conflict Imprisonment in Northern Ireland' 175 *Prison Service Journal* 3.
Ewald, F (1991) 'Insurance and Risk' in G Burchell, C Gordon and P Miller (eds), *The Foucault Effect: Studies in Governmentality* (Chicago, IL, University of Chicago Press).
—— (2002) 'The Return of Descartes' Malicious Demon: An Outline of a Philosophy of Pre-caution' in T Baker and J Simon (eds), *Embracing Risk: The Changing Culture of Insurance and Responsibility* (Chicago, IL, University of Chicago Press).
Ericson, R (2007) *Crime in an Insecure World* (Cambridge, Polity Press).
Feeley, M and Simon, J (1992) 'The New Penology: Notes on the Emerging Strategy of Corrections and its Implications' 30 *Criminology* 449.
—— (1994) 'Actuarial Justice: The Emerging New Criminal Law' in D Nelken (ed), *The Futures of Criminology* (London, Sage).
Foucault, M (2007) *Security, Territory, Population: Lectures at the Collège de France 1977–1978* (Basingstoke, Palgrave Macmillan).
Garland, D (1996) 'The Limits of the Sovereign State: Strategies of Crime Control in Contemporary Society' 36 *British Journal of Criminology* 445.
—— (2000) 'The Culture of High Crime Societies: Some Preconditions of Recent "Law and Order" Policies' 40 *British Journal of Criminology* 347.
—— (2001) *The Culture of Control: Crime and Social Order in Contemporary Society* (Chicago, IL, University of Chicago Press).
Giddens, A (1991) *Modernity and Self-identity: Self and Society in the Late Modern Age* (Stanford, CA, Stanford University Press).
—— (2003) *Runaway World: How Globalization is Reshaping Our Lives* (New York, Routledge).
Gormally, B, McEvoy, K and Wall, D (1993) 'Criminal Justice in a Divided Society: Northern Ireland Prisons' 17 *Crime and Justice* 51.
Great Britain Parliament (1972) *Report of the Commission to Consider Legal Procedures to Deal with Terrorist Activities in Northern Ireland* [Diplock Report] (Cmnd 5185) (London, HMSO).
Great Britain Parliament (1975) *Report of a Committee to Consider, in the Context, of Civil Liberties and Human Rights, Measures to Deal with Terrorism in Northern Ireland* [Gardiner Report] (Cmnd 5847) (London, HMSO).
Guelke, A (2006) *Terrorism and Global Disorder: Political Violence in the Contemporary World* (London, New York, Tauris Academic Studies, IB Tauris Publishers).
Hacking, I (1990) *The Taming of Chance* (Cambridge, Cambridge University Press).
Hannah-Moffat, K (2004) 'Criminogenic Need and the Transformative Risk Subject: Hybridizations of Risk/Need in Penality' 7 *Punishment & Society* 29.
Hillyard, P (2005) 'The "War on Terror"—Lessons from Northern Ireland' (European Civil Liberty Network).

Hirschi, T (1969) *Causes of Delinquency* (Berkeley, CA, University of California Press).
Holder, D (2013) 'Don't Legislate for Collusion?' *The Detail* 5 April 2013.
Ignatieff, M (2004) *The Lesser Evil: Political Ethics in an Age of Terror* (Edinburgh, Edinburgh University Press).
Jackson, J and Doran, S (1995) *Judge Without Jury: Diplock Trials in the Adversary System* (Oxford, Oxford University Press).
James, A and Raine, J (1998) *The New Politics of Criminal Justice* (London, Longman).
Jones, T and Newburn, T (2005) 'Comparative Criminal Justice Policy Making in the United States and the United Kingdom: The Case of Private Prisons' 45 *British Journal of Criminology* 58.
—— (2006) 'Three Strikes and You're Out: Exploring Symbol and Substance in American and British Crime Control Politics' 46 *British Journal of Criminology* 781.
Kemshall, H (2003) *Understanding Risk in Criminal Justice* (Philadelphia, PA, Open University Press).
Lombroso, C (1911) *Criminal Man* (Montclair, NJ, Patterson Smith)
Luhmann, N (1991) *Sociology of Risk/Soziologie des Risikos* (New York, W de Gruyter).
Lupton, D (1999) *Risk* (London, Routledge).
McEvoy, K (2001) *Paramilitary Imprisonment in Northern Ireland: Resistance, Management, and Release* (Oxford, Oxford University Press).
—— (2007) 'Beyond Legalism: Towards a Thicker Understanding of Transitional Justice' 34 *Journal of Law and Society* 411.
McEvoy, K, Gormally, B and Mika, H (2002) 'Conflict, Crime Control and the "re" Construction of State/Community Relations in Northern Ireland' in G Hughes, E McLaughlin and J Muncie (eds), *Crime Prevention and Community Safety: New Directions* (London, Sage).
McEvoy, L, McEvoy, K and McConnachie, K (2006) 'Reconciliation as a Dirty Word: Conflict, Community Relations and Education in Northern Ireland' 60 *Journal of International Affairs* 81.
McGovern, M and Tobin, A (2010) 'Countering Terror or Counter-Productive?: Comparing Irish and British Muslim Experiences of Counter-insurgency Law and Policy' (Ormskirk, Edge Hill University).
McKittrick, D, Kelters, S, Feeney, B, Thornton, C and McVea, D (2007) *Lost Lives: The Stories of the Men, Women and Children who Died as a Result of the Northern Ireland Troubles* (Edinburgh, Mainstream Publishing).
McVie, S (2011) 'Alterative Models of Youth Justice: Lessons from Scotland and Northern Ireland' 6 *Journal of Children's Services* 106.
Muncie, J (2011) 'Illusions of Difference: Comparative Youth Justice in the Devolved United Kingdom' 51 *British Journal of Criminology* 40.
Mythen, G and Walklate, S (2008) 'Terrorism, Risk and International Security: The Perils of Asking "What if?"' 39 *Security Dialogue* 221.
Newburn, T (2002) 'Atlantic Crossings: "Policy Transfer" and Crime Control in the USA and Britain' 4 *Punishment & Society* 165.
Newburn, T and Jones, T (2007) *Policy Transfer and Criminal Justice: Exploring US Influence over British Crime Control Policy* (Maidenhead, Open University Press).
Ní Aoláin, F (2000) *The Politics of Force: Conflict Management and State Violence in Northern Ireland* (Belfast, Blackstaff Press).
Northern Ireland Office (NIO) (2010) 'Non-jury Trials Remain Essential for Justice System' (Belfast, NIO).

O'Duffy, B (1999) 'British and Irish Conflict Regulation from Sunningdale to Belfast, Part I: Tracing the Status of Contesting Sovereigns, 1968–1974' 5 *Nations and Nationalism* 4.
O'Leary, B and McGarry, J (1993) *The Politics of Antagonism: Understanding Northern Ireland* (Belfast, Athlone Press).
O'Malley, P (1990) *Biting at the Grave: The Irish Hunger Strikes and the Politics of Despair* (Belfast, Blackstaff Press).
O'Malley, P (1992) 'Risk, Power and Crime Prevention' 21 *Economy and Society* 252.
—— (1996) 'Risk and Responsibility' in A Barry, T Osborne and N Rose (eds), *Foucault and Political Reason. Liberalism, Neo-Liberalism and Rationalities of Government* (London, UCL Press).
—— (1999) 'Governmentality and the Risk Society' 28 *Economy and Society* 138.
—— (2000) 'Configurations of Risk' 29 *Economy and Society* 457.
—— (2002) 'Criminologies of Catastrophe?: Understanding Criminal Justice on the Edge of the New Millennium' 33 *Australian & New Zealand Journal of Criminology* 153.
—— (2004) *Risk, Uncertainty and Government* (London, Cavendish Press).
—— (2007) 'Experiments in Risk and Criminal Justice' 12 *Theoretical Criminology* 451.
Pratt, J (1996) 'Governing the Dangerous: An Historical Overview of Dangerous Offender Legislation' 5 *Social & Legal Studies* 21.
Rasmussen, MV (2001) 'Reflexive Security: NATO and International Risk Society' 30 *Millennium: Journal of International Studies* 285.
—— (2006) *The Risk Society at War* (Cambridge, Cambridge University Press).
Rodger, JJ (2008) *Criminalising Social Policy: Anti-social Behaviour and Welfare in a Decivilised Society* (Cullompton, Willan Publishing).
Rogan, M (2003) 'Legitimacy in the Criminal Justice System of Northern Ireland: A Criminological Analysis' 6 *Trinity College Law Review* 34.
Rose, N (2000) 'Government and Control' 40 *British Journal of Criminology* 321.
Rostoks, T (2010) 'Securitization and Insecure Societies' in Ž Ozoliņa (ed), *Rethinking Security* (Zinātne).
Shearing, C (2000) 'Punishment and the Changing Face of Governance' 3 *Punishment & Society* 203.
Simon, J (1997) 'Governing Through Crime' in L Friedman and G Fisher (eds), *The Crime Conundrum* (Boulder, CO, Westview).
—— (1998) 'Managing the Monstrous: Sex Offenders and the New Penology' 4 *Psychology, Public Policy, and Law* 452.
—— (2007) *Governing Through Crime: How the War on Crime Transformed American Democracy and Created a Culture of Fear* (Oxford, Oxford University Press).
St Andrews Agreement (2006) *The St Andrews Agreement, October 2006* (Belfast, Northern Ireland Office).
Tomlinson, M (2012) 'From Counter-terrorism to Criminal Justice: Transformation or Business as Usual?' 51 *The Howard Journal* 442.
United Nations Human Rights Committee (UNHRC) (2007) *UN Human Rights Committee: Sixth Periodic Report, United Kingdom of Great Britain and Northern Ireland* (CCPR/C/GBR/6).
—— (2008) *Consideration of Reports submitted by States Parties under Article 40 of the Covenant: International Covenant on Civil and Political Rights: concluding observations of the Human Rights Committee: United Kingdom of Great Britain and Northern Ireland* (CCPR/C/GBR/CO/6).

Wacquant, L (2009) *Punishing the Poor: The Neoliberal Government of Social Insecurity* (Durham, NC, Duke University Press).
Walker, C (2011) *Terrorism and the Law* (Oxford, Oxford University Press).
Wilkinson, I (2001) *Anxiety in a Risk Society* (London, Routledge).
Zedner, L (2005) 'Securing Liberty in the Face of Terror: Reflections from Criminal Justice' 32 *Journal of Law and Society* 507.
—— (2009) 'Fixing the Future? The Pre-emptive Turn in Criminal Justice' in B McSherry, A Norrie and S Bronitt (eds), *Regulating Deviance: The Redirection of Criminalisation and the Futures of Criminal Law* (Oxford, Hart Publishing).

Part II

The Criminal Justice Process

6

Policing in Transition

JOHN TOPPING

Introduction

On an international scale, Northern Ireland's policing of security affairs have long occupied a distinct and 'elevated' position over the past four decades. Indeed, the political, economic and research attention devoted to both understanding and framing the polity's emergent transitional character have far outstripped that afforded to other jurisdictions in the United Kingdom and beyond in the Western world (Topping and Byrne 2012c). So too on a variety of political and policing plains, the journey out of a protracted, internal armed conflict towards a (relatively) peaceful and democratic society has presented global 'lessons' on conflict transformation, police reform, and not least 'hope' for other countries ravaged by violent, internal strife (Campbell et al 2003; Brogden 2005; Mulcahy 2006; Ellison and O'Reilly 2008).

But most significantly, the issue of policing has always been (and remains) central to the wider political progress and *status quo* of the country's transitional landscape (Dickson 2000; Topping 2008a). With policing and its delivery having become entwined with the socio-political discourse of the country's conflict, it may be observed that 'implicitly, bargaining about policing became meta-bargaining as to the very nature of the conflict' (Campbell et al 2003: 342). To this extent, the 'direction' of the transition has been intimately tied to a consensus that 'if policing can somehow be "got right" many of the other pieces of the jigsaw will slot into place' (O'Rawe and Moore 2001: 181). Furthermore, it must also be understood that the task of 'getting policing right' was (and still is) symptomatic of the complex interaction between the social, cultural and political interfaces of the traditionally divided communities which comprise the jurisdiction (Shirlow and Murtagh 2006).

In specific reference to police reform, conflict and the wider 'peace process' in Northern Ireland, the Belfast Agreement was reached on 10 April 1998, as a significant milestone in the history of the region's troubled affairs (Bew 2007). Consolidating the progress made from the republican and loyalist ceasefires of 1994, this all-party political settlement sought to establish the foundations for resolving the intractable social and political divisions of the country (McGarry and O'Leary 2004). Out of the 1998 Agreement, a watershed development came in the form of the Independent Commission on Policing for Northern Ireland (ICP)—as an independent, international body tasked with reforming not just the incumbent Royal Ulster Constabulary (RUC) as a police organisation, but constructing an entirely new policing *architecture* designed to provide a new beginning for policing; to reconnect the police with those whom they were meant to serve; and deliver an effective, efficient, impartial and accountable police service for an entire population (Ryder 1997; ICP 1999; Tomlinson 2000; O'Rawe 2003; Topping 2008b). Chaired by the former Governor of Hong Kong, Chris Patten, the eventual ICP recommendations (otherwise known as the 'Patten Report') published in 1999 were 'viewed as symptomatic of a perceived need for an end to incremental and politically nuanced "tinkering" with policing, and the beginning of a substantial, inclusive and permanently acceptable change process' (Topping 2008b: 778–79).

On a broad level, the ICP has generally been hailed as the most 'significant' and 'complex blueprint' for police reform ever attempted in the world through 175 recommendations for policing change—resulting in the creation of the Police Service of Northern Ireland (PSNI) on 4 November 2001 (OOC 2006; Bayley 2007). On the one hand, narratives as to the success of the ICP reform process cannot ignore evidence that the 'spirit' of a 'new beginning' to policing was ultimately 'gutted' and 'diluted' in terms of how the wide-ranging recommendations were translated into legislative form under the Police (Northern Ireland) Act 2000 (Hillyard and Tomlinson 2000; McEvoy et al 2002).[1] There was significant resistance in unionist quarters to such wholesale change of the RUC as a *de facto* partisan police force (mainly) serving Protestant communities (Mulcahy 2006). Such dilution may be considered a function of unionist sentiment towards the ICP, described by the former Ulster Unionist leader and Nobel Peace Prize winner, David Trimble, as 'a gratuitous insult and [the] most shoddy piece of work seen in his entire life' (Anderson 2007: 14).

Yet on the other hand, neither can evidence related to the scale of change and reform to the policing institutions be underestimated on a practical level. As confirmed by the Office of the Oversight Commissioner (OOC)—established out of the ICP to ensure a 'faithful and comprehensive' implementation of the 175 recommendations across 772 performance indicators (ICP 1999: paragraph 19.2)—the vast majority have now been completed (OOC 2007). Notwithstanding the *additional* 1070 subsequent recommendations directed at the PSNI from the new policing structures (including the Northern Ireland Policing Board (NIPB) and Office of the Police Ombudsman for Northern Ireland (OPONI)), it is impossible to argue against the weight of change momentum, epitomised through

[1] See also, C Shearing, 'Patten Has Been Gutted: Clifford Shearing An Independent Member of the Patten Commission on the RUC Speaks Out' *The Guardian*, 14 November 2000.

the PSNI and all they have come to stand for in the post-ICP period (Topping 2008a).

But aside from the practicalities of such significant and permanent change to the policing landscape, it is also important to note that since 2007, the police institutions have had cross-party support for the first time in history, as an inclusive political endorsement of the wider reform process.[2] Similarly, autonomous policing and justice powers have been devolved to the Northern Ireland Executive for the first time since 1972, cementing the contention that policing still remains wedded to wider political progress.[3]

As part of the broad policing narrative associated with the transition from conflict to peace, at a superficial level it would appear that policing in Northern Ireland, as the last piece of the peace process 'jigsaw' has indeed been slotted into place (O'Rawe 2003). Yet at the same time, it may be claimed the policing and security dynamics underpinning transitional democracies tend neither to be static nor linear in their progression, especially where the source of conflict in the first place is a function of deep-rooted history, culture, political tradition—as well as societal receptiveness to change (Teitel 2000). Indeed, this may be observed through the constant 'tension' and fragility surrounding political progress and community support for the policing institutions according to wider events and developments—themselves grounded in the legacy of the conflict.[4]

In this respect, the remainder of the chapter seeks to engage with the various factors underpinning the contemporary policing environment in Northern Ireland as part of the more 'normalised' security landscape in 2014. Beyond the outwardly positive picture of the country's progress towards peace at an international level, it is of note that little academic attention is generally paid to the parameters of police reform as an *evolving*, transitional democracy; and where the issue of policing remains a 'work in progress' (Topping and Byrne 2012c). Indeed, it was one of the former Oversight Commissioners, David Bayley, who observed that 'Northern Ireland fatigue' has obscured both international and academic interest into the polity's affairs, with the ideals of police reform and change tenuously tied to the empirical realities of their outworking (Bayley 2007). Capturing this position in relation to the contemporary 'state' of policing and security affairs, it is thus apt to note Mulcahy (1999: 278), who identifies that precisely because of such change around policing, 'in the aftermath of a … conflict, peace itself can constitute a crisis to the extent that it undermines the policies, practices and assumptions ingrained and institutionalized over the years'.

[2] See *Belfast Telegraph*, 'Blair Hails Historic Decision by Sinn Féin Leadership', 29 January 2007; *Belfast Telegraph*, 'The Miracle of Belfast', 4 May 2007; *Belfast Telegraph*, 'Sinn Féin to Take its Seats on the Northern Ireland Policing Board', 14 May 2007.

[3] H McDonald and N Watt, 'Stormont Votes to Take Over Northern Ireland Policing Powers' *The Guardian*, 9 March 2010.

[4] T Whitehead, 'Northern Ireland Tensions at Boling Point Over Gerry Adams Arrest' *The Telegraph*, 3 May 2014.

The Nature of Policing Change

To examine the nature of the policing 'change' in Northern Ireland, it is important to set that task, bestowed upon the ICP, in more specific context. As noted by Moxon-Browne (1983: 28), 'to seek a solution to the Northern Ireland problem is to pursue a mirage in the desert: a better ploy would be to irrigate the desert until the landscape looks more interesting'. The ICP reform process, as the 'irrigating' mechanism, was therefore about a 'commitment to a fresh start … the opportunity to take best practice from elsewhere and lead the way in overcoming some of the toughest challenges in modern policing' (ICP 1999: paragraph 1.5). As part of this 'change dialectic' (O'Rawe 2003), the ICP was *generally* about engendering a paradigmatic shift within the RUC—creating a movement away from their status as a 'reactive, hierarchical, militaristic and counter-insurgency *force* into a proactive … *service* working with the grain of the communities it policed' (Topping and Byrne 2012c: 160). However, central to understanding the *specific* nature of these reforms is a need to move beyond the ICP recommendations as a homogeneous 'block' of change 'forced' upon the RUC; and consider the reform process in two interrelated, but distinct 'streams' (Kempa and Shearing 2005).

This first stream, which has largely reached the end of its natural life cycle, is that related to the 'system' of policing, or that which could more broadly be attributed to the physical manifestations of police change. These reforms included, for example, the name of the PSNI, badges, uniform, recruitment processes and human rights training which were espoused in the publication of the nineteenth and final report of the OOC back in 2007, demarcating an end to this phase of reform (Ellison 2007; OOC 2007). But it is the second 'stream', 'concerned with broader questions around the governance of security, or policing more broadly conceived' (Kempa and Shearing 2005: 5) which resonates closely with the social and political vagaries of police reform grounded in the transitional, community context of Northern Ireland. Underlying this second stream was the central focus for the ICP—namely recommendation 44—which states 'Policing with the Community should be the core function of the entire police service' (ICP 1999: paragraph 7.9).

Indeed, community policing, or 'policing with the community' under the rubric of the ICP may be understood as central to many police organisations across the globe (Oliver and Bartgis 1998; Brogden 2005; Brogden and Nijhar 2005). At a cursory level, community policing simultaneously represents a plethora of divergent police organisational practices, styles, philosophies—concerned primarily with the provision of a local, tailored and community-anchored policing service (Loader 2000; Dixon 2004). Yet beyond theoretical contentions, the ICP's core recommendation acquires additional, distinct meanings as part of the transitional landscape within which policing is situated. On the one hand, the delivery of community policing in Northern Ireland is symbolic of a movement away from the police merely enforcing the rule of law *upon* particular populations, towards engendering more legitimate, consensual styles of policing and working *with* communities previously distanced from the state police apparatus during the conflict (Hillyard 1988; Ellison 2000, 2007; Topping 2008a).

But on the other hand, the practical delivery (and success or otherwise) of community policing as a primary goal of the PSNI additionally allows an extraction of meaning from underlying social and political trends impacting upon this style of policing delivery (Kempa et al 1999; Topping and Byrne 2012a). As shall be observed, through the lens of the ICP's core policing approach, policing delivery is also linked to the fact 'the police have … the capacity to tell us something about the normative ordering of society' (Ellison and Martin 2000: 694).

It must also be noted from the outset that in spite of the significant police organisational and political progress related to policing witnessed since 1999, current research indicates that beyond pockets of good practice, much of the post-ICP policing landscape has been characterised by an indeterminate 'drift' with regard to the full implementation of a community policing ethos within the PSNI (Byrne and Monaghan 2008; Topping 2008b; Topping and Byrne 2012a). While the PSNI has changed 'vertically' in the sense of its movement away from counter-insurgency to community policing; and 'horizontally' in terms of downsizing and 'normalising', research continues to contradict the 'official' picture of full community support and police–community relations in the country (NIPB 2013).

Across the country, alienation of republican/nationalist (and to a lesser extent loyalist/unionist) communities from any normal conception of policing remains apparent. With a sizeable minority of the population distanced from, or ambivalent towards, engagement with the PSNI, and deriving 'satisfaction' with the PSNI through its absence at a local level, contemporary research points towards the significant limitations associated with the community policing project on behalf of the PSNI (Ellison and Mulcahy 2001; Mulcahy 2006; Topping 2009). As succinctly captured by Topping (2008b: 791–92):

> It is clear the PSNI's 'policing with the community' philosophy has struggled beneath the sheer weight of division and diversity within Northern Ireland's transitional landscape … while the PSNI have been radically transformed in line with [the ICP's] first 'stream' of reforms, the changes to policing on the ground through his second 'stream' have largely been negligible … in many areas of Northern Ireland, policing largely mirrors the reactive style of policing characteristic of the conflict, albeit in a peace-time context.

More specifically, and related to policing as a function of the normative ordering of the country's post-conflict space, it is critical to consider that republican/nationalist *and* loyalist/unionist communities too, have had the very basis of their policing experiences and expectations drastically altered. Within loyalist areas traditionally supportive of the police (and formerly the RUC), there exists a perception of a 'diminished' policing service, primarily due to the significantly reduced numbers of PSNI officers (circa 6900) available to deliver community-oriented policing in comparison with the RUC 'heyday' which peaked at 13,500 officers (Mulcahy 2000; Topping 2008b). Similarly, the RUC, as a police service once 'theirs' has been removed and replaced, and in many cases 'vilified'—raising issues of legitimacy and affinity with the rule of law as exercised through the PSNI (Lundy 2011; Cadwallader 2013).

Within republican communities, it is also evident that the PSNI is perceived to have 'missed the mark' in regard to the delivering of a more 'normalised', community-oriented policing service—as was promised politically and expected locally—following the political negotiations of 2007 when Sinn Féin (as the largest republican/nationalist party in the country), supported the policing institutions for the first time in their history (Topping 2008b).

Yet in taking a step away from such broad critiques levelled at the PSNI as to its ability (or otherwise) to deliver the ICP's central tenet of reform and change, or indeed the altered community experiences of a police service in transition at the community level, it must be remembered that dynamics which comprise the country's conflicted democracy cannot easily be separated from policing, nor viewed without reference to the other (Teitel 2000). In this respect—and exploring issues which impact upon policing and the rule of law—it is vital to consider the wider operating environment within which policing is situated, both to qualify and calibrate the nature of policing against ongoing tensions and contradictions within the polity. Similarly, such an approach also assists with understandings that beyond the 'change dialectic' are many factors which continue to remain outside the control of the PSNI, but which laterally influence the police–community nexus set within a highly segregated society currently under a 'severe' terrorist threat (Shirlow and Murtagh 2006; Frampton 2010).[5]

The Contested Environment and Parameters of Transitional Policing

In terms of considering the operational parameters of current policing arrangements in the country, the majority of academic and policy attention over the past 15 years has concentrated either upon the reform of the policing institutions, or their interaction with (mainly) urban, working class loyalist and republican communities (Byrne and Monaghan 2008). Yet comparatively little attention has been directed at the transitional 'climate' in which policing is actually delivered. Thus, the following sections will 'map' the parameters of the environment which in turn defines the limits to policing delivery—and especially so where it may be observed that those conditions are by no means conducive to the delivery of

[5] See also H McDonald and M Townsend, 'For Ireland's Hardcore Dissidents 'The Queen is a Legitimate Target' *The Observer*, 24 April 2011; *BBC News*, 'Union Flag Protests: Police Attacked and Traffic Disrupted', 12 January 2013, available at www.bbc.co.uk/news/uk-northern-ireland-20985521.

'normal' policing within any 'Peelian' conception of the term as part of the post-conflict setting (Kelling 2005; Frampton 2010).[6]

Furthermore, the contemporary, transitional landscape of Northern Ireland may be observed as presenting not just difficulties for the PSNI and communities *per se*, but also evidences a number of counterfactual narratives around the idea that the 'policing project' has been completed. This is turn helps to provide both understanding of, and insight into, the complex dynamics underpinning the 'positive peace' in the country—or merely the removal of everyday cultural and structural violence—as it emerges from conflict (Holen and Eide 2000; Ellison and Mulcahy 2001; Topping 2009).

The Criminological Landscape

An initial enquiry would suggest that in spite of Northern Ireland's transition from conflict to (relative) peace it suffers from comparatively low levels of crime. Unlike the often compared transitional democracy of South Africa (Shaw and Shearing 1998; Altebeker 2005), the 'official' low crime projection of the country has endured and been bolstered by the significant political progress which has facilitated the historical devolution of policing and justice powers to Stormont, as noted above (Van Dijk et al 1990). Such low crime levels within this 'criminological netherworld' (Ellison and Mulcahy 2001) have tended to be explicated through a Durkheimian school of 'solidarity in conflict', in conjunction with the detailed sociological accounts of close-knit communities and 'grapevines' prevalent across the country (Brewer 2001). Furthermore, the 'official' (and compelling) state-based narratives of crime, policing and security add further weight to the conception of a low crime, safe society (PSNI 2013).

From the first International Victim Survey in 1989 reporting Northern Ireland as Europe's low crime comparator (Van Dijk et al 1990; Brogden 2000), contemporary evidence points to the lowest levels of conflict-related violence on record; the lowest levels of recorded crime in the past 12 years; along with victimisation rates at 13.8 per cent—the lowest since records began in 1998, comparing favourably to England and Wales (Toner and Freel 2010). Furthermore, the NIPB continues to claim that satisfaction levels with the PSNI remain at record highs (Lyness et al 2004; NIPB, 2013). Although by the same token, research by the NIPB indicates that crime rates in terms of what can be defined as predominantly Protestant or Catholic areas vary significantly—with higher crime rates generally within Catholic wards in comparison to Protestant wards and the national average (NIPB 2007). Similarly, official statistics by the PSNI indicate that the general trend towards

[6] See also H McDonald, 'One in Seven Northern Ireland Nationalists Sympathise with Dissident Terrorists' *The Guardian*, 6 October 2010; H McDonald, 'Northern Ireland Terror Threat At "Severe" Level' *The Guardian*, 4 February 2011; H McDonald, 'Police Say 1200 Officers Have Been Hurt in Northern Ireland Riots in Seven Years' *The Guardian*, 4 September 2012.

decreases in crime must be tempered with the fact that violent crime has risen by approximately 59 per cent since 1998/99 (Topping and Byrne 2012b). However, it is important to note that beyond criminological projections underpinning policing 'success', a number of additional, underlying factors must also be considered as part of the debate and which contest narratives as to how far Northern Ireland's transition has really come within a policing and security framework.

Normal Policing, Exceptional Environment?

In regard to understanding the PSNI's ability and capacity to deliver policing within a contested environment, they may be viewed as a relatively 'young' organisation. While the changes wrought by the reform process were certainly short of full 'lustration' (Teitel 2000), the ICP's attempts at rebalancing the Protestant/Catholic composition of the service to more closely reflect society, along with the generous severance packages totalling over £500m to remove the RUC 'old guard', has simultaneously transformed and depleted the PSNI's experiential base—and specifically that related to counterterrorism expertise.[7] As argued by Topping and Byrne (2012a), the overall impact of this process has been to reduce the PSNI's strategic and operational abilities to deal with the counterterrorism environment in which they operate (Frampton 2010).[8]

Looking in more detail at this environment, it must be acknowledged that violent dissident republicanism is still an everyday feature of the security landscape in the country.[9] While such a threat is in no way comparable to that posed by mainstream republicans during the height of the conflict, it is within this tenebrous landscape that viable explosive devices and attempts to kill members of the PSNI and security forces remain an unpalatable fact of the post-conflict environment.[10] Indeed, the main perpetrators of such activities are the so-called 'dissident' republican factions, including: the Continuity Irish Republican Army (CIRA), first formed in 1986 as the paramilitary wing of the splinter political party Republican Sinn Féin; the Real IRA, first formed in 1997 through a split with the mainstream Provisional IRA over the Belfast Agreement of 1998; and Óglaigh na hÉireann (OHN), considered an umbrella group for disaffected republicans since 2005 (Tonge 2004; IMC 2006).

The contemporary efforts of these groups as part of the ongoing terrorist threat have resulted in the recent deaths of British soldiers in March 2009; the murder of

[7] *BBC News*, 'Number of PSNI Officers Fell Too Quickly—Matt Baggott', 4 December 2010, available at www.bbc.co.uk/news/uk-northern-ireland-11919158; *BBC News*, '50:50 Police Recruitment "Achieved a Lot"'—Baggott', 18 April 2011, available at www.bbc.co.uk/news/uk-northern-ireland-13112723.

[8] See also *Belfast Telegraph*, 'Fears for Police Officers' Health', 21 August 2013.

[9] *Belfast Telegraph*, 'Mortar Bomb Found at Derry PSNI Station', 11 October 2013.

[10] *BBC News*, 'Timeline of Dissident Republican Activity', 1 December 2014, available at www.bbc.com/news/uk-northern-ireland-10866072.

PSNI constables Carol and Kerr in April 2012; and prison officer Black in 2012).[11] It is thus a feature of the 'exceptional' policing landscape that, at the time of writing, the terrorist threat remains at 'severe' as classified by MI5 (IMC 2010). [12] It must also be noted that such terrorist activity emanates not only from republican paramilitaries, but also from loyalist groupings where paramilitary structures remain in place and command the capacity both to control local communities and orchestrate mass public disorder.[13]

Yet as part of aligning the PSNI's community policing goals with such counter-terrorism realities, one of the most contested terrains lies with both the 'framing' and acceptance as to the state of this 'conflicted peace'. In spite of the officially graded 'severe' terrorist threat, the nature of this paradox has been captured by Her Majesty's Inspectorate of Constabulary (HMIC), detailing that:

> There is a source of contention amongst some officers and the Police Federation ... when information is provided to the media (and other government departments) by PSNI on bombings and shootings. If asked by the media how many 'terrorist attacks' (bombings or shootings) have taken place in Northern Ireland, or when presenting figures connected to terrorism, PSNI responds with a figure around 25% of the absolute total (HMIC 2011: 26).

In this respect, the *actual* state of 'peace' and the security situation has thus become a matter of interpretation, which itself politicises transitional security affairs beyond their technical definition (Topping and Byrne 2012a). In addition to attempts by the PSNI to move away from their counter-insurgency 'roots' (Ryder 1997), the exigencies of dealing with an ongoing terrorist threat has necessarily stifled community-led policing approaches. At a cursory level, this paradox has been further evidenced by the former Chief Constable of the PSNI, Sir Hugh Orde, who stated:

> The threat of domestic terrorism is always present in Northern Ireland ... because officers are now more visible in communities where historically they would have not patrolled on foot or on bicycle, they are more vulnerable to attack (cited in Marchant 2007: 5).

Thus, a significant increase in allocations to the terrorist security budget in 2011 to £245 million[14] has not been matched by equivalent funding directed at bolstering

[11] *Belfast Telegraph*, 'Civilians Targeted by Dissident Republicans', 27 October 2008; *Belfast Telegraph*, 'Dissident Republicans Blamed for Gun Attack on Police', 27 August 2008; *Belfast Telegraph*, 'Dissident Vowed to Kill Catholic Officer After McGuinness Visit', 26 November 2008; *Belfast Telegraph*, 'Dissident Threat Severe After MI5 Attack', 13 April 2010; *Irish News*, 'Bombers Trying To Kill Officers: Detective', 11 September 2008; *Belfast Telegraph*, 'Real IRA Determined to Murder PSNI Officers', 5 January 2009; H McDonald and M Townsend, 'For Ireland's Hardcore Dissidents "The Queen is a Legitimate Target"' *The Observer*, 24 April 2011; *Belfast Telegraph*, 'Ambush Killers Denounced at Funeral of Prison Officer David Black', 7 November 2012.

[12] See also V Kearney, 'Dissident Threat Level Increases' *BBC News*, 22 April 2010, available at news.bbc.co.uk/2/hi/uk_news/northern_ireland/8638255.stm; J Owen and K Dutta, 'More People Go Armed as Ulster Dissident Threat Grows' *The Independent*, 5 June 2011.

[13] H McDonald, 'The Truth About Belfast's Riots' *The Guardian*, 27 June 2011.

[14] *BBC News*, 'Matt Baggott Welcomes Extra £245m for Police', 18 February 2011, available at www.bbc.co.uk/news/uk-northern-ireland-12500020.

community policing strategies and operations beyond sweeping policy promises by the former Chief Constable Matt Baggott (PSNI 2011); although the direction of community policing and its development within the PSNI may change under the new Chief Constable, George Hamilton, appointed in June 2014.

This position in which the PSNI finds itself has also been confirmed in a physical, sense insofar as HMIC have additionally posed questions about the PSNI's organisational 'shape' when juxtaposed with its outward 'policing with the community' ethos. It is therefore interesting to observe that HMIC have confirmed that the PSNI actually retains a relatively militaristic, hierarchical structure oriented towards public order and counter-insurgency capabilities compared with what are described as 'most similar forces' in England and Wales (HMIC 2007). With six times as many officers dedicated to public order policing roles, and four times the number of officers allocated to intelligence-type duties compared with 'most similar forces', it is indicative that during the same period, only 35 per cent of District Commanders in Northern Ireland have claimed to be carrying out policing under what may be conceived as 'normal' community conditions (HMIC 2007). With the country's police-to-population ratio also one of the highest in the Western world (approximately 1:250), PSNI capacity remains a critical issue as part of dealing with the current terrorist threat, especially where 'mutual aid' from police forces in England and Wales remains an exception rather than the norm (Bullock 2008).[15] At the same time, however, such facts actually predate the now heightened, 'severe' terrorist threat as noted, notwithstanding the return of mass public disorder to the streets of the country and daily, disruptive bomb alerts.[16]

In this regard, the post-conflict environment remains challenging for the delivery of policing by the PSNI not only in and of itself, but also in terms of the competing narratives about the state of policing affairs in the country. In spite of the dominant political narrative of reformed, 'normalised' policing, the evidence points to the *exceptional* nature of the security landscape (in terms of both the police and the policed) as the empirical reality. With an obvious disjuncture between community policing and counterterrorism agendas, it is Topping and Byrne who summarise the current *status quo* insofar as:

> Once in place, counter-terrorism structures cannot suddenly be removed where a terrorist threat remains in place … This is especially so when: i) recent data suggests that only 10 per cent of PSNI's organisation capacity is actually dedicated to what might be defined as neighbourhood policing duties … and ii) holistic, community-level contact between the PSNI and many working-class Loyalist and Republican communities in Northern Ireland has yet to move beyond 'critical engagement' where contact with police remains at best an option of last resort (2012c: 164–65).

[15] See also C Cromie, 'Hundreds of G8 Police to Return to Northern Ireland for Twelfth Parades' *Belfast Telegraph*, 9 July 2013.

[16] *UTV News*, 'Stolen Car Sparked '14th Alert in Month', 14 October 24 2013, available at www.u.tv/News/Stolen-car-sparked-14th-alert-in-month/d6fb5706-6b32-41a1-a236-00be4acb3963.

Paramilitary Policing: The Security Interlopers

Below the level of national counterterrorism concerns in Northern Ireland, no account of post-conflict policing affairs would be complete without reference to the ongoing delivery of paramilitary 'policing' or 'justice'. As Brewer (2001) contends, the legitimacy of the state police and alternatives to state policing provision have a long pedigree within the context of the polity—as a blunt capacity for communities to simply 'sort things out'. This is especially so within republican (and to a lesser extent loyalist) communities during the conflict and post-conflict periods of history, where ideological and political opposition to the formal criminal justice apparatus have acted as the 'justification' for extra-juridical, violent and brutal punishment attacks and shootings as a form of localised social control (Morrissey and Pease 1982; Hillyard 1985; Brewer et al 1998; Silke 1999; Feenan 2002; Knox 2002; Monaghan 2008). However, aside from descriptive accounts of such grim, 'back-alley' justice, further complexities to the post-ICP policing environment may be observed as part of identifying the 'place' of these paramilitary interlopers beyond simple ascriptions of terrorist labels.

An initial enquiry into the levels of combined paramilitary shootings and assaults in Northern Ireland would point to what has been a general decline in their use as a form of 'policing' at a community level—having reduced from a peak of 298 in 2003/04 to 63 in 2012/13—although tempered by a rise between 2005 and 2010 (PSNI 2013). While difficult to explain empirically, these recent rises may in part be due to the PSNI failing to meet community expectations around the delivery of 'new' policing promised at the political table (see further below). But on the one hand, the wider downward trends may be linked to political progress, with all-party political and community support for the PSNI as the fulcrum upon which the 'new beginning' to policing has turned (Topping 2008a). To an extent, it may be argued that new-found state police legitimacy effected through the reform process has manifested itself through communities 'distancing' themselves from such 'policing' regimes of the past. But on the other hand, as argued by Topping and Byrne (2012b: 51):

> A difficulty with this over-simplistic political frame of assessment is that localized paramilitary policing tends to be conflated with the national terrorist threat ... and packaged as an isolated aberration of the peace-time landscape ... by 'othering' the actual levels and effects of paramilitary violence ... the PSNI and Government have effectively ignored the cries of communities that 'people still go to the paramilitaries in regard to certain crime issues rather than going to the police'.

Set against perceived and actual deficits of a 'normal' policing service at a community level, an enduring and overlapping legacy of the conflict relates to a 'blurring' of the boundaries in regard to social control and 'police primacy' as to who could or should deliver policing within the contested transitional space (Minnaar 2002). In large part, this ambiguity and ambivalence in many republican and loyalist communities relates to the uneven *spread* and *effects* of the wider police reform in those localities—a fact seldom acknowledged in a sophisticated, empirical fashion beyond government recourse to blunt measures set forth by the NIPB (Topping 2012). In spite of NIPB and PSNI stoic adherence to 'record' accounts of confidence in the policing institutions, localised studies continue to question both the veracity and validity of such claims (Byrne and Monaghan 2008; Ellison and Shirlow 2008; Topping 2008b, 2009; NIPB 2013). Thus, at the 'edges' of competing policing narratives there exists what may be called: '"a relationship crisis" between PSNI and urban, working-class [areas] … which in turn has manifested itself in terms of renewed support, and increased levels of, paramilitary policing in those areas' (Topping and Byrne 2012b: 46).

In terms of framing the continuing presence of these 'security interlopers', it might be expected that significant police reform and political progress made over the past 15 years would have removed a substantial pillar of community self-justification for turning to paramilitary actors as a policing resource (Topping and Byrne 2012c). Yet it is precisely because of the lack of uniform perception that policing on the ground has changed beyond the first 'stream' of reforms, that questions have been raised, in both republican and loyalist communities, as to whether the political 'hard-sell' of the police reform process has been matched by improvements locally (Kempa and Shearing 2005). It is thus possible to observe that nestled within these policing fissures are 'security vacuums' across the country 'in which paramilitarism still survives … "selling" the legitimacy of their activity through filling the perceived "deficit" of state policing provision—as policing entrepreneurs seeking to reinvigorate the credentials of the security "business" of the conflict' (Topping and Byrne 2012b: 47).

While in one respect the PSNI is undoubtedly constrained in the delivery of a 'normalised' policing service due to the omnipresent terrorist threat in the country, it would also appear that both the PSNI and government, as part of the transition, have *undervalued* the importance of providing an effective community policing service. Indeed, research associated with paramilitary policing across both communities during the conflict would point to the fact that it is viewed as a swift and visible form of policing and justice at the local level (McGarry and Morrissey 1989; Feenan 2002; Monaghan 2008). Yet in the post-conflict period of the country's history, so too research continues to point to the fact that paramilitary policing is used as a 'benchmark' with which to compare the speed and utility of the PSNI's response to local criminality—itself often deemed to be lacking (Byrne and Monaghan 2008; Topping 2009). This is especially so where communities being promised a new start to policing at a political level face a very different reality.

Significantly, any such calculations about current levels of paramilitary policing in the country cannot be viewed without reference to the bitterly divided nature of the region, with a variety of physical, social and cultural barriers still demarcating 'the other' religion (Shirlow and Murtagh 2006). Substantive barometers of such ethno-national segregation are evidenced through social housing provision—over 98 per cent in Belfast and 71 per cent nationally is allocated on a religious basis (Byrne et al 2006). Here, it may be argued that in addition to the operational comparisons made between paramilitary policing and the service delivered by the PSNI, many of these segregated communities are still alive as homogeneous, Weberian 'political communities'—necessary for the support of paramilitary actors (Cavanaugh 1997). In this regard, generating change at a local, rather than political level, around the paramilitary policing 'option' is a more complex and deep-rooted calculation than simply seeing more PSNI officers on the streets.

In essence, the continuing nature of paramilitary policing—which is distinct from the broader terrorist threat—may also be viewed as a battleground where the PSNI has not so much credibility to 'lose' as a new organisation, but has legitimacy to gain. As outlined above, gaining police operational legitimacy is clearly a more complex proposition than that presupposed by the 'tick box' success of change outlined by the OOC (OOC 2007). As contended by Ellison (2007), it was the very 'externalised' nature of the police reform process in Northern Ireland which divorced measures of success from such contested and conflicted policing realities on the ground. But significantly, it remains a fact that the paramilitary interlopers play a part in the country's low crime narrative as constructed by the very policing institutions attempting to supplant them. Therefore, communities emerging from the shadow of conflict and who are attempting to move away from paramilitary policing have not just become desensitised to the use of violence as a means of policing (Monaghan 2008). But rather, within the post-conflict space such communities have become more sensitive to the need for someone at a local level to enforce social order and control (PSNI or otherwise), as a means of maintaining the low levels of crime which they are being told exist (Brewer et al 1998; Shaw and Shearing 1998; Topping and Byrne 2012a).

Shadow Policing: Legitimate Security from Below

In addition to the dynamics impacting upon the PSNI's delivery of policing as outlined, a third key element of the transitional policing 'jigsaw' relates to the generation of security 'from below' by legitimate, non-state actors located within Northern Ireland's civil society. Traditionally, attention focused on the production of security has tended to centre upon the polemics of security provision—either examining that delivered under the auspices of the PSNI, or that of our paramilitary actors. Beyond the 'official' criminological picture of Northern Ireland as a low crime society, the available evidence would suggest that a significant 'blind spot' exists in this regard—related to an insufficient interrogation of the operational reality underpinning the etiology of policing and security 'production'. This is especially so with the presumption of causal security relations having remained firmly with the PSNI (Topping and Byrne 2012a). Thus, chances to conceive policing in language (or by actors) *other* than that set by the policing institutions as part of the reform process have remained limited—especially where non-traditional policing discourse challenges the orthodoxy of the PSNI's organisational 'expertise' on crime control (Topping and Byrne 2012c). Yet as pointed to by the ICP, and substantiated by one of the ICP commissioners, Clifford Shearing:

> Here in Northern Ireland—and in many other unsettled political contexts—another form of 'non-state' agent is particularly important in challenging the monopoly over the business of policing of the public police: civic bodies of various forms, including, but certainly not limited to, agencies that deploy violence as part of their practices of control (Kempa and Shearing 2005: 7).

On a practical level (and outside the paramilitary paradigm), a substantial 'reservoir' of non-state 'policing' in Northern Ireland developed out of the security exigencies associated with the conflict (Brogden 1998), often as 'alternatives' to the provision of policing by the state—either because of legitimacy issues, or due to the constraining nature of the security environment within republican and loyalist areas (Hamilton et al 1995; Topping and Byrne 2012a). More specifically, and developing out of what may be termed a policing and security 'vacuum', the historical separation of mainly working class republican and nationalist communities from state police intervention has further generated a sense of 'security liminality' in which the normal processes of 'Peelian' policing simply do not work (Mulcahy 2006; Byrne and Monaghan 2008). Thus, it is within these liminal 'spaces' in which a variety of actors beyond the state have existed (and continue to deliver policing as broadly conceived) within the complex policing environment. As considered by Morrow (2006: 73):

> Where the state could not provide protection, which was the starting point for many Catholics and Nationalists and could easily emerge for less well protected working class Protestant communities ... there was an enormous reservoir of understanding for extra state [policing].

On a more philosophical and policy plain, 'alternative' layers of security production within a transition such as Northern Ireland also raise,

> important normative and policy issues about what attitudes democracies should take ... does it [non-state policing] constitute a vital assistance to weak states faced with under-resourced police, or does it constitute a threat to the state by allowing a function to be conducted by private elements over which the state should have monopoly (Baker 2002: 30).

As reflected in the study by Acheson et al (2004), with a myriad of voluntary and community sector groups in the country involved in a variety of roles, the social 'presence' of civil society is an undeniable 'fact' of life (NICVA 2005; CJINI 2006). Although with approximately 5000 voluntary and community sector organisations in the country (with the majority not concerned with policing issues *per se*—see below) it must be noted that the 'extent and nature of community action is neither self-evident nor securely defined within clear boundaries (Acheson et al 2006: 19).

Specifically in regard to non-state policing and security production, little empirical attention (government or otherwise), has been paid to outlining, mapping or detailing the actual contributions of this tranche of civil society to the policing landscape, or indeed to the country's 'low crime' status. Within government and PSNI circles, reticence to engage with this latent 'soft power' (Vaughan 2007) has been indicative of an attitude which has dismissed conceptions of community involvement and ownership in the process of policing and justice (McEvoy et al 2002: 197). A key example may be observed through returning to the ICP and recommendation 32, which stated that:

> District Councils should have the power to contribute an amount initially up to the equivalent of 3p in the pound towards the improved policing of the district, which could enable the District Policing Partnership Board to purchase additional services from the policing or other statutory agencies, or from the private sector (ICP 1999: paragraph 6.33).

Yet under a barrage of (unfounded political) criticism that such community-level taxation powers would provide an 'open door' for paramilitary entry into publicly funded security arrangements, recommendation 32 was the only provision of the 175 never to have been enacted in legislative form (Mulcahy 2006; Bayley 2007; Topping 2009). Indeed, such 'dampening' of holistic community partnership potential was also foreshadowed by the parallel Review of the Criminal Justice System in 2000. Here, the prospect for a 'fascinating experiment' in bringing together community energies as part of community-centred policing initiatives was ignored in favour of the bureaucratic metrics of reform, indicative of the ICP's much lauded first 'stream' of change (McEvoy et al 2002; Gormally 2004; Ellison and O'Rawe 2010).

In terms of a more detailed exploration of civil society contributions to the policing landscape, 'security vacuums' related to PSNI legitimacy, capacity and the rule of law—as well as terrorist and paramilitary dynamics—have further limited the PSNI's ability to engage in holistic approaches to social problems at a local level (Topping 2008b). It is thus within these 'vacuums' in which civil society organising around policing is most highly visible. As two of the only empirical studies specifically examining non-state policing provision in Northern Ireland, Topping (2009) and Topping and Byrne (2012a) have detailed that beyond the impact of any one organisation or grouping which contributes to policing in the country, it is the collective ability of civil society to mediate the 'gaps' of policing need which is of significance.

Across eight key operational domains which comprise: community advocacy; education and intervention; emergency response; interface violence; partnership working; crime prevention; mediation; and restorative justice—not only are such efforts at 'policing from below' highly focused, but so too the communities themselves may be viewed as highly organised in terms of community infrastructure underpinned by trust, social capital and normative shared values (Acheson et al 2004; Morrow 2006). It must be cautioned, nonetheless, that much of this organising is based upon insular, sectarian lines—perpetuating the divided, often self-serving delivery of security provision between republican and loyalist communities respectively (Shirlow and Murtagh 2006; Topping and Byrne 2012a).

Outside the parameters of security in a police-centric concept, for many urban, working class republican and loyalist communities who bore the brunt of the conflict (Shirlow and Murtagh 2006), security may thus be imagined on a more human level insofar as many of the deep-rooted social, economic and sectarian issues—for so long hidden under the veil of 'bigger' conflict-related issues—are now starting to emerge within post-conflict space. In this respect, and evidencing the holistic, rather than police organisational approaches, many of those bodies involved in non-state forms of social control do not readily associate their work within the context of a formal police framework. Indeed, evidence points to such efforts being charaterised as 'community development', 'good relations' or 'social justice' (CJINI 2007; Topping and Byrne 2012a). Capturing this approach, as summarily detailed by those at the coalface of such work,

> people are phoning us to deal with stuff rather than phoning the police … because we'll find a way of dealing with it. Sometimes people don't *see* the situation a child is in—they just see the crime and the consequences of it … it's trying to find ways of dealing with it without punishment beatings, or dragging them through the courts … it's local knowledge again (Topping 2009: 284).

Related to the complex dynamics which inform the relationship between the country's transition and community engagement with policing is the primacy of such non-state policing within many communities to the exclusion of the PSNI. Grounded in histories, politics and culture—along with continuing issues of PSNI legitimacy and capacity—many areas of civil society see the PSNI as an option of *last* rather than *first* resort on policing matters (Topping and Byrne 2012a). But additionally, and because of the delicate and sensitive nature of local social problems, such non-state bodies are often the only ones 'qualified' to deal with the problem in terms of community knowledge, capacity and respect (Topping and Byrne 2012a). As articulated in Topping (2009: 249) by an organisation dealing with interface violence in Belfast, such non-state policing primacy is seldom to do with the *politics* of policing, but rather the *necessity* of simply making communities safer:

> I think we'd [as a society] be a lot worse off without that. We're careful about making overstated claims about the community sector holding this place together for 30 years … but the cutting edge work on policing and security and parading and interfaces and all that … Frankly, no one else would have been *able* to do it.

Therefore, in taking a step away from the relations between the PSNI and civil society policing within the post-conflict space, it is somewhat ironic that 'forcing' the PSNI into such local non-state policing environments could actually destabilise community relations through the removal of local 'ownership' on local policing matters (Tonkiss and Passey 1999). Thus, precisely *how* to quantify or render (in a political and operational sense) non-state contributions more accessible to the police and *vice versa* without damaging the vitality of local policing efforts is another dilemma yet to be resolved as part of the transition from conflict to peace (Topping and Byrne 2012a).

Conclusion: The Complexity of 'Doing Policing' in Transition

In attempting to reconcile the variegated picture of policing in Northern Ireland, it is evident the reforms brought under the ICP were only the beginning of a change to the *police organisational* aspects of what is a complex *policing system* in the country—itself tied to political, social and historical dynamics informed by over 30 years of conflict. As part of the ICP process, by Western policing standards both the necessity for, and scale of, this 'blueprint' for reform has created one of the most overseen, accountable and human rights compliant police services anywhere in the world (O'Rawe 2003; Ellison 2007). Yet in reference to the issues of a continuing terrorist threat; of paramilitary 'policing', and of civil society contributions to the criminological landscape, it is undeniable that 'doing' policing in a transitional context, at least from a state perspective, is a task greater than the sum of the ICP's individual parts.

Beyond the first 'stream' of physical reforms embodied through the PSNI, the second 'stream' of delivering 'policing more broadly conceived' has become the new site of contest within the current phase of post-conflict history. With the PSNI's service simultaneously constrained and cajoled, on the one hand the majority of Northern Irish society peers down through a 'glass floor' of policing, gladly accepting that the conflict is over and that affairs are not as bad as they once were in the past. As if through a process of socio-political osmosis, this unproblematic majority, as those removed from the sharp edges of the criminological 'netherworld', almost expect that the outstanding issues of policing and security will somehow 'fix' themselves through the natural wastage of time.

On the other hand, however, this 'floor' also acts as a ceiling through which many republican and loyalist communities gaze upwardly, unable to reach that which has been promised as part of a new beginning to policing under the ICP. Thus, for communities at the sharp end of policing, terrorism and paramilitary activity, time moves more slowly, where the ripples of their problems still continue to be felt across Northern Ireland. With such sections of society absorbing the reality of more 'colourful' accounts of the conflicted peace set forth by government and the policing institutions, it is at such societal junctures where terrorism, paramilitiarism and alternatives sources of policing will continue to ferment—as part of the 'long shadow' cast by the 'unfinished business' of the conflict.

In terms of the harsh reality of policing within Northern Ireland's post-conflict space, successful claims as to the normalisation of policing cannot therefore be made where politics, terrorism and community resistances continue to dictate the police agenda. This is especially so when in 2014, nearly 15 years after the ICP, the 'new' vision of policing,

> may be supported by one community, yet across a peace divide in another, it must be conducted from the back of an armoured Land Rover where lethal force remains the ultimate (and necessary) expression of police power and legitimacy (Topping 2008a: 392).

As part of a more circumspect view of 'doing' policing in transition, it must also be remembered that while international attention continues to focus on the 'lessons' to emerge from a country, the optimism of the broad peace should also be tempered with caution. As Bayley (2008) contends, a degree of realism (if not pessimism) needs to accompany that which has been achieved. Both situated within, and funded by, an advanced Western industrial nation, Northern Ireland,

> is relevant to post-conflict reconstruction in what it has faced; it may be irrelevant in terms of what can be achieved. To put the point another way, if police reform requires what Northern Ireland has, then the prospects for it are bleak in all one or two of the world's other trouble spots (Bayley 2008: 240).

Additionally, policing is but one element of a wider criminal justice system which must collectively deal with a unique set of legacy and historical issues associated with the conflict. Thus, beyond the germane issues of 'everyday' crime, security and safety, the criminal justice system is simultaneously being 'stretched'—financially, socially, procedurally and politically—beyond the parameters of that which it was designed for as part of UK legal structures. But ultimately, it is the police who remain as the 'face' of security developments in the polity—both locally and globally.

Furthermore, until wider political gains can be made in relation to a shared society and dealing with the past, violence will undoubtedly remain as the lowest common denominator in the country as part of an ever thinning, but indelible 'green line' to be policed—as used to describe the 'space' in which PSNI has to operate. In this regard, if there is a key lesson for other countries emerging from conflict, it remains that an absence of violence is no guarantee of peace. And even with the best training, financing and oversight in the world, police responses to political problems will only every achieve so much.

References

Acheson, N, Harvey, B, Kearney, J and Williamson, A (2004) *Two Paths, One Purpose: Voluntary Action in Northern Ireland, North and South* (Dublin, Institute of Public Administration).

Acheson, N, Williamson, A, Cairns, E and Stringer, M (2006) *Voluntary Action and Community Relations in Northern Ireland. A Report of a Research Project funded by the Community Relations Council and the Office of the First Minister and Deputy First Minister* (Belfast, NICVA).

Altebeker, A (2005) *The Dirty Work of Democracy* (Johannesburg, Jonathon Bell).

Anderson, MJ (2007) 'Why is Policing a Persistently Contentious Issue in the Politics of Northern Ireland?' (Northern Ireland Political Studies Graduate conference, Jordanstown, University of Ulster, June 2007).

Baker, B (2002) 'Living with Non-State Policing in South Africa: The Issues and Dilemmas' 40 *Journal of Modern African Studies* 29.

Bayley, DH (2007) *Police Reform on Your Doorstep: Northern Ireland* (World Seminar, Transitional Justice Institute, Jordanstown, University of Ulster, February 2007).
—— (2008) 'Post-conflict Police Reform: Is Northern Ireland a Model?' 2 *Policing* 233.
Bew, P (2007) *The Making and Remaking of the Good Friday* Agreement (Dublin, Liffey Press).
Brewer, J (2001) 'The Growth, Extent and Causes of Crime: Northern Ireland' in M Shaw (ed), *Crime and Policing in Transitional Societies Seminar Report* (Johannesburg, KAS).
Brewer, J, Lockhart, B and Rodgers, P (1998) 'Informal Social Controls and Crime Management in Belfast' 49 *British Journal of Sociology* 570.
Brogden, M (1998) *Two-Tiered Policing—A Middle Way for Northern Ireland?* (Belfast, Democratic Dialogue).
—— (2000) 'Burning Churches and Victim Surveys: The Myth of Northern Ireland as Low-Crime Society' 10 *Irish Journal of Sociology* 27.
—— (2005) '"Horses for Courses" and "Thin Blue Lines": Community Policing in Transitional Societies' 8 *Police Quarterly* 64.
Brogden, M and Nijhar, P (2005) *Community Policing: National and International Approaches* (Cullompton, Willan Publishing).
Bullock, S (2008) *Police Service Strength England and Wales Home Office Statistical Bulletin* 31 March 2008 (London, Home Office Statistical Bulletin).
Byrne, J, Hanson, U and Bell, J (2006) *Shared Living: Mixed Residential Communities in Northern Ireland* (Belfast, Institute for Conflict Research).
Byrne, J and Monaghan, L (2008) *Policing Loyalist and Republican Communities* (Belfast, Institute for Conflict Research).
Cadwallader, A (2013) *Lethal Allies: British Collusion in Ireland* (Dublin, Mercier Press).
Campbell, C, Ní Aoláin, F and Harvey, C (2003) 'The Frontiers of Legal Analysis: Reframing the Transition in Northern Ireland' 66 *Modern Law Review* 317.
Cavanaugh, K (1997) 'Interpretations of Political Violence in Ethnically Divided Societies' 9 *Terrorism and Political Violence* 33.
Criminal Justice Inspection Northern Ireland (CJINI) (2006) *Added Value? A Review of the Voluntary and Community Sectors' Contribution to the Northern Ireland Criminal Justice System* (Belfast, CJINI).
—— (2007) *Community Restorative Justice Ireland: Report of a Pre-inspection of Schemes in Belfast and in the North West with View to Accreditation under the Government's Protocol for Community Based Restorative Justice* (Belfast, CJINI).
Dickson, B (2000) 'The Protection of Human Rights: Lessons from Northern Ireland' 3 *European Human Rights Law Review* 213.
Dixon, B (2004) 'Community Policing: "Cherry Pie" or Melktert?' 35 *Society in Transition* 251.
Ellison, G (2000) '"Reflecting all Shades of Opinion" Public Attitudinal Surveys and the Construction of Police Legitimacy in Northern Ireland' 40 *British Journal of Criminology* 88.
—— (2007) 'A Blueprint for Democratic Policing Anywhere in the World?: Police Reform, Political Transition, and Conflict Resolution in Northern Ireland' 10 *Police Quarterly* 243.
Ellison, G and Martin, G (2000) 'Policing, Collective Action and Social Movement Theory: The Case of the Northern Ireland Civil Rights Campaign' 51 *British Journal of Sociology* 681.
Ellison, G and Mulcahy, A (2001) 'Policing and Social Conflict in Northern Ireland' 11 *Policing and Society* 243.

Ellison, G and O'Rawe, M (2010) 'Security Governance in Transition: The Compartmentalising, Crowding Out and Corralling of Policing and Security in Northern Ireland' 14 *Theoretical Criminology* 31.

Ellison, G and O'Reilly, C (2008) 'From Empire to Iraq and the "War on Terror": The Transplantation and Commodification of the (Northern) Irish Policing Experience' 11 *Police Quarterly* 395.

Ellison, G and Shirlow, P (2008) 'Community Attitudes to Crime, Anti-social Behaviour and Policing in the Greater New Lodge' (unpublished report).

Feenan, D (2002) Community Justice in Conflict: Paramilitary Punishment in Northern Ireland in D Feenan (ed), *Informal Criminal Justice* (Aldershot, Ashgate Publishing.

Frampton, M (2010) *The Return of the Militants: Violent Dissident Republicanism* (London, ICSR).

Gormally, B (2004) 'Tough Questions on Community Policing from Northern Ireland' 3 *Community Safety Journal* 23.

Hamilton, A, Moore, L and Trimble, T (1995) *Policing a Divided Society: Issues and Perceptions in Northern Ireland* (Coleraine, Centre for the Study of Conflict).

Her Majesty's Inspectorate of Constabulary (2007) *Baseline Assessment Police Service of Northern Ireland, October 2006* (London, HMIC).

—— (2011) *Police Service of Northern Ireland, Inspection Findings* (London, HMIC).

Hillyard, P (1985) 'Popular Justice in Northern Ireland: Continuities and Change' 7 *Research in Law, Deviance and Social Control* 247.

—— (1988) 'Political and Social Dimensions of Emergency Law in Northern Ireland' in A Jennings (ed), *Justice Under Fire: The Abuse of Civil Liberties in Northern Ireland* (London, Pluto Press).

Hillyard, P and Tomlinson, M (2000) 'Patterns of Policing and Policing Patten' 27 *Journal of Law and Society* 394.

Holen, T and Eide, E (2000) *Peace Building and Police Reform* (London, Frank Cass).

Independent Commission on Policing (ICP) (1999) *A New Beginning: Policing in Northern Ireland* (Belfast, HMSO).

Independent Monitoring Commission (IMC) (2006) *Twelfth Report of the Independent Monitoring Commission* (London, The Stationery Office).

—— (2010) *Twenty-third Report of the Independent Monitoring Commission* (London, The Stationery Office).

Kelling, G (2005) 'Community Crime Reduction: Activating Formal and Informal Control' in N Tilley (ed), *Handbook of Crime Prevention and Community Safety* (Cullompton, Willan Publishing).

Kempa, M, Carrier, R, Wood, J and Shearing, C (1999) 'Reflections on the Evolving Concept of "Private Policing"' 7 *European Journal on Criminal Policy and Research* 197.

Kempa, M and Shearing, C (2005) 'Post-Patten Reflections on Patten' (public lecture, Queen's University of Belfast, 8 June).

Knox, C (2002) '"See No Evil, Hear No Evil" Insidious Paramilitary Violence in Northern Ireland' 42 *British Journal of Criminology* 164.

Loader, I (2000) 'Plural Policing and Democratic Governance' 9 *Social & Legal Studies* 323.

Lundy, P (2011) 'Paradoxes and Challenges of Transitional Justice at the "Local" Level: Historical Enquiries in Northern Ireland' 6 *Contemporary Social Science* 89.

Lyness, D, McEnarney, R and Carmichael, M (2004) *Digest of Information on the Northern Ireland Criminal Justice System* (Belfast, NIO).

Marchant, C (2007) 'Threat Level to Visible PSNI Officers is High, says its Chief' 22 *Police Review* 5.

McEvoy, K, Gormally, B and Mika, H (2002) 'Conflict, Crime Control and the "re" Construction of State/Community Relations in Northern Ireland' G Hughes, E McLaughlin and J Muncie (eds), *Crime Prevention and Community Safety: New Directions* (London, Sage).

McGarry, J and Morrissey, M (1989) 'Community, Crime and Punishment in West Belfast' 28 *The Howard Journal* 282.

McGarry, J and O'Leary, B (eds) (2004) *The Northern Ireland Conflict: Consociational Engagements* (Oxford, Oxford University Press).

Minnaar, A (2002) 'The New Vigilantism in Post-April 1994 South Africa: Searching for Explanations' in D Feenan (ed), *Informal Criminal Justice* (Aldershot, Ashgate Publishing).

Monaghan, R (2008) 'Community-based Justice in Northern Ireland and South Africa' 18 *International Criminal Justice Review* 83.

Morrissey, M and Pease, K (1982) 'The Black Criminal Justice System in West Belfast' 21 *The Howard Journal* 159.

Morrow, D (2006) 'Sustainability in a Divided Society: Applying Social Capital Theory to Northern Ireland' 2 *Shared Space: A Research Journal on Peace, Conflict and Community Relations in Northern Ireland* 63.

Moxon-Browne, E (1983) *Nation, Class and Creed in Northern Ireland* (Aldershot, Gower).

Mulcahy, A (1999) 'Visions of Normality: Peace and the Reconstruction of Policing in Northern Ireland' 8 *Social & Legal Studies* 277.

—— (2000) 'Policing History and the Official Discourse and Organisational Memory of the Royal Ulster Constabulary' 40 *British Journal of Criminology* 68.

—— (2006) *Policing in Northern Ireland: Conflict, Legitimacy and Reform* (Cullompton, Willan Publishing).

Northern Ireland Council for Voluntary Action (NICVA) (2005) *State of the Sector IV* (Belfast, NICVA).

Northern Ireland Policing Board (NIPB) (2007) *Research into Recent Crime Trends in Northern Ireland* (Belfast, NIPB/Ipsos MORI).

—— (2013) *Public Perceptions of the Police, PCSPs and the Northern Ireland Policing Board* (Belfast, NIPB).

Office of the Oversight Commissioner (OOC) (2006) *Overseeing the Proposed Revisions for the Policing Services in Northern Ireland Report 18* (Belfast, OCC).

—— (2007) *Overseeing the Proposed Revisions for the Policing Services of Northern Ireland Report 19* (Belfast, OCC).

Oliver, WM and Bartgis, E (1998) 'Community Policing: A Conceptual Framework' 21 *Policing: An International Journal of Police Strategy and Management* 490.

O'Rawe, M (2003) 'Transitional Policing Arrangements in Northern Ireland: The Can't and Won't of the Change Dialect' 26 *Fordham International Law Journal* 1015.

O'Rawe, M and Moore, L (2001) 'A New Beginning for Policing in Northern Ireland?' in C Harvey (ed), *Human Rights, Equality and Democratic Renewal in Northern Ireland* (Oxford, Hart Publishing).

Police Service of Northern Ireland (PSNI) (2011) *Personal, Protective, Professional Policing—What Do You Want From Your Police Service?* (Belfast, PSNI).

—— (2013) *Recorded Crime and Clearances 1st April 2011–31st March 2012 Annual Statistical Report* (Belfast, PSNI).

Ryder, C (1997) *The RUC 1922–1997 A Force Under Fire* (London, Mandarin Paperbacks).

Shaw, M and Shearing, C (1998) 'Reshaping Security: An Examination of the Governance of Security in South Africa' 7 *African Security Review* 3.

Shirlow, P and Murtagh, B (2006) *Belfast: Segregation, Violence and the City* (London, Pluto Press).

Silke, A (1999) 'Ragged Justice: Loyalist Vigilantism in Northern Ireland' 11 *Terrorism and Political Violence* 1.

Teitel, R (2000) *Transitional Justice* (Oxford, Oxford University Press).

Tomlinson, M (2000) 'Frustrating Patten: Commentary on the Patten Report' 10 *Irish Journal of Sociology* 103.

Toner, S and Freel, R (2010) *Experience of Crime: Findings from the 2009/10 Northern Ireland Crime Survey* (Belfast, DOJNI).

Tonge, J (2004) 'They Haven't Gone Away, You Know: Irish Republican "Dissidents" and "Armed Struggle"' 16 *Terrorism and Political Violence* 671.

Tonkiss, F and Passey, A (1999) 'Trust, Confidence and Voluntary Organisations: Between Values and Institutions' 33 *Sociology* 257.

Topping, JR (2008a) 'Community Policing in Northern Ireland: A Resistance Narrative' 18 *Policing and Society* 377.

—— (2008b) 'Diversifying From Within: Community Policing and the Governance of Security in Northern Ireland' 48 *British Journal of Criminology* 778.

—— (2009) 'Beyond the Patten Report: The Governance of Security in Policing with the Community' (PhD thesis, University of Ulster).

—— (2012) 'Policing and the Process of Confidence in Northern Ireland: More than Community Metrics' (invited speaker at Northern Ireland Policing Board, Belfast, 27 February).

Topping, JR and Byrne, J (2012a) *Community Safety: A Decade of Development, Delivery, Challenge and Change in Northern Ireland* (Belfast, Belfast Conflict Resolution Consortium).

—— (2012b) 'Paramilitary Punishments in Belfast: Policing Beneath the Peace' 4 *Behavioral Sciences of Terrorism and Political Aggression* 41.

—— (2012c) 'Policing, Terrorism and the Conundrum of "Community": A Northern Ireland Perspective' in B Spalek (ed), *Counter-Terrorism: Community-based Approaches to Preventing Terror Crime* (Basingstoke, Palgrave Macmillan).

Van Dijk, JJM, Mayhew, P and Killias, M (1990) *Experiences of Crime across the World: Key Findings from the 1989 International Crime Survey* (Denenter, Kluwer Law and Taxation).

Vaughan, B (2007) 'The Provision of Policing and the Problem of Pluralism' 11 *Theoretical Criminology* 347.

7

Finding 'Merit' in Judicial Appointments: The Northern Ireland Judicial Appointments Commission (NIJAC) and the Search for a New Judiciary for Northern Ireland

JOHN MORISON

Introduction

The post-Agreement constitutional architecture has produced a new legal space in Northern Ireland. While the court structure has largely endured in a recognisable format there are perhaps now new expectations of how it will function in the next stage of Northern Ireland's transition from a society in conflict. These expectations come into focus around the nature and role of the judiciary that is to oversee this new legal space. At the same time there are other, wider forces pressing upon the judiciary across the United Kingdom and these are being acted out in the various appointment commissions and regimes that have been created to modernise the judiciary. This all contributes to establishing a dynamic context for considering whether and/or how the judiciary in Northern Ireland is changing, and the forces that may be conditioning any change.

This chapter looks at some of the expectations that might arise for the judiciary. It focuses both on some ideas about what might be the role of a judge in a transitional context, and the debate about how judges generally should be appointed across the United Kingdom where the idea of 'merit' emerges as the governing concept. Next, consideration is given to how this idea of merit plays out in the Northern Ireland context and, in particular, how it impacts on the appointment of women to senior judicial roles which has emerged as the central concern in the new dispensation. Here the chapter draws on two pieces of research: the first looking at the issues surrounding judicial appointments and attitudes towards seeking such posts in the Northern Ireland context, and a second project where the idea of 'merit' as a governing factor in judicial appointment was further explored (Leith et al 2008; Leith and Morison 2013).[1] Finally the chapter looks ahead at the challenges around judicial appointment that remain and suggests that notion of 'merit' has not provided the robust foundation which its proponents imagined it would.

Post-Agreement Northern Ireland: A New Legal Space

Here the view is taken that the wider constitutional changes consequent on the Belfast Agreement have produced such significant changes and opened up such possibilities in the legal system generally that it is possible to consider this as a new legal space (Morison 2013: 120–44). In part this new space has been created by a number of formal changes around devolution, and in particular the further devolution of justice functions (Anthony 2011: 197–212). This has built upon existing structures and relationships which now, in a new context and with additional revisions, results not only in the continuation of the separate formal jurisdiction but also a degree of 'apartness' and exceptionality. The other sense in which a new legal space has been created is less formal and depends on a sense that the peace process here as elsewhere has brought an opportunity for a new start. Both of these must be considered in turn.

Prior to the major engineering works on the constitution in Great Britain, that is the Constitutional Reform Act 2005, the judiciary in Northern Ireland operated with a strong degree of independence. This was true for the 50-year period of devolution and during the time of direct rule.[2] It has remained the case even after the peace process. The Northern Ireland Courts Service existed as a local

[1] The first report was titled *Propensity to Apply for Judicial Office under the New Northern Ireland Judicial Appointments System: A Qualitative Study for the Northern Ireland Judicial Appointments Commission (2008)* and the second *Rewarding Merit in Judicial Appointments?* (2013). Both research reports can be accessed at www.nijac.gov.uk/index/what-we-do/publications/research.htm. The projects were funded by the NI Judicial Appointments Commission (NIJAC). The author is grateful to all those involved in both research projects. This includes the members of the legal profession and judiciary who contributed to the surveys and interviews. It also encompasses the wider research team composed of Professor Sally Wheeler and Professor Brice Dickson, Dr Lisa Glennon, and also Dr Marie Lynch and Ben Christman who provided research assistance, as well as the Project Steering Groups from NIJAC which included Commissioners and NIJAC's Head of Diversity, Ms Adeline Frew. Particular acknowledgement must be given to Professor Philip Leith who led the research teams in both projects and carried out an online survey in the second study. I am grateful also to Professor Leith for his involvement in the early stages of drafting this chapter, although he does not wish to be a co-author on this output from the project. (The author served as a commissioner with NIJAC from its inception in June 2003 until June 2012, was involved in this capacity with the first study and joined the research team for the second project to undertake the interview element which forms the basis of this chapter. However, all the views presented here are made in a purely private capacity and should not be attributed to the Commission).

[2] See the contribution in this book by McEvoy and Schwartz.

branch of the Lord Chancellor's Department, and although the Lord Chancellor was the formal head of the judiciary in Northern Ireland, a concordat negotiated in 1979 gave the Lord Chief Justice of Northern Ireland and his extensive office operational control over the court system locally. The Constitutional Reform Act formally made the Lord Chief Justice head of the judiciary in Northern Ireland and settled this idea of the Northern Ireland jurisdiction being not only formally separate, but also a place apart in the sense that it is organised and controlled locally (Gee et al forthcoming 2015).

The devolution of justice, made by the Department of Justice Act (Northern Ireland) 2010 and the Northern Ireland Act 1998 (Devolution of Policing and Justice Functions) Order 2010, led to the establishment of the Northern Ireland Courts and Tribunals Service as an agency of the new Department of Justice within the Northern Ireland Executive (NICTS 2010, 2013). This devolution of the machinery of justice into the care of the local political structures was not only the last piece in the puzzle of the peace process, and the final stage in the formal process of devolution, but a further recognition perhaps of a new chapter in the story of the legal system (Blackbourn 2014). Although the framework has changed, arguably the separateness and independence continues—albeit now in very different circumstances of post-ceasefire and economic retrenchment.

Other changes to the judiciary and the courts are more qualitative. They are less clear-cut and relate less to formal constitutional change. They impact perhaps more significantly on the fundamental nature and role of the judiciary in the new circumstances of a devolved Northern Ireland. Such change is perhaps of a political or cultural nature, and it mirrors much else in the wider peace process whereby a degree of 'creative ambiguity' allows opposing political perspectives to interpret change in their own way. For some there is a new legal system: an oath of allegiance to the Queen is no longer a requirement of appointment as QC, there is a new law officer in the shape of the Attorney General, and some of the existing senior appointments are distributed more widely across the political/ethnic spectrum than in the past. For others there remains a degree of continuity that confirms an idea that the legal system served Northern Ireland well in the difficult circumstances of the past and is well placed to do so in the future, with only a few modifications.

However these changes are interpreted, their origins lie with the Criminal Justice Review (CJR) launched on the foot of the Belfast Agreement (CJRG 1998, 2000). Much of the impact of the CJR certainly is focused on the judiciary. The CJR recognised that 'an effective and impartial judiciary is crucial to the well-being of any society, especially one where there have been divisions and conflict such as have been experienced in Northern Ireland' (CJRG 2000: paragraph 6.3). Throughout the history of Northern Ireland the administration of justice at whatever level and in almost any context—like many other issues—has been capable of being seen and interpreted as a political or even constitutional issue (Morison and Livingstone 1995: chapters 3 and 4). The CJR acknowledged the need for manifest openness and fairness at every level if the court system was not to be seen as 'owned' and staffed by one community rather than the other. For those who saw the judges and the court system as inherently unionist it was vital that it be depoliticised, while for those who did not accept this characterisation it was equally important that the new regime continued to establish this clearly.

The CJR anticipated also that judges in Northern Ireland increasingly would be called upon to interact with executive and legislative decisions. The Review predicted that in the new rights regime of the Agreement and the Human Rights Act 1998, judges would be not only weighing the merits of competing rights, but also considering arguments about their economic and social impact (CJRG 2000: paragraphs 6.3–6.5). While the Review Group did not use language that specifically suggested that judges in the new Northern Ireland would be performing a different constitutional role, they did acknowledge a new constitutional reality whereby judges are

> empowered to declare primary Westminster legislation incompatible … [and] set aside lesser legislation, including Acts of a Northern Ireland Assembly … [as well as] determin[ing] whether individuals have been treated in accordance with Convention rights and whether acts of public authorities are in contravention of such rights (2000: paragraph 6.6).[3]

While this constitutional role would not necessarily fall to all judges, at every level, it was something that was new and important.

Academic writers have developed more theoretical understandings of this new role, and assessed how this fits in with experience elsewhere. The present author undertook an ESRC funded project exploring how 'constitutional litigation' developed in the early days of the settlement and how this measured up to various new understandings of constitutional practice and theory internationally, particularly in what might be regarded as a transitional context (Morison and Lynch 2007: 105–46; see also Anthony 2009). This study considered how the Northern Ireland transition could be seen in terms of a range of theoretical understandings. For example, it may be considered as an outworking of a notion of a constitutional revolution occurring through the agency of a particular coalition of forces taking control (Balkin and Levinson 2001), or gradual processes of change and consolidation across dominant sets of institutions or ideology (Tushnet 2004). Ideas of transitional constitutionalism too are often directly invoked. Whereas traditionally constitutionalism is viewed as foundational and forward looking, transitional constitutionalism looks back to undoing problems of the past as well as laying foundations for the future (Teitel 2000; McEvoy and Morison 2003). It is also provisional, subject to revision, and contested, where the boundary between 'ordinary' and 'constitutional' politics becomes blurred. Such a description may

[3] In addition to 'the Agreement cases' discussed below, the emergence of a number of cases from the other devolved administrations (including *Imperial Tobacco v Lord Advocate* [2012] UKSC 61 [15] and *Local Government Byelaw (Wales) Bill* [2012] UKSC 53, [2012] 3 WLR 1294 [80]) suggesting the possibility of fundamentally new understandings of the sovereignty of Parliament in relation to devolution indicate the prescience of the CJR's view.

seem to have purchase in Northern Ireland and require both a new constitutional practice and theory, particularly among the judiciary. It may require judges to use their power creatively 'not to "block" democracy but to make it more deliberative', as Sunstein describes it (2001). It may involve what Klare in the South African context describes as a 'transformative constitutionalism' (1998: 156). Dorf and Sabel have an idea of 'democratic experimentalism' which involves an idea of judges working with other constitutional actors to develop the future (1998).

All of these understandings of the Northern Ireland constitution, and the new society it is still in the process of creating, urge a new and very particular view of what it is that judges should be doing, and who they should be. The rights basis of what is fundamentally an agonistic settlement undoubtedly creates a new sort of legal space where decisions that are fundamental to *constituting* the post-Agreement society are possible at any time and from almost any source.[4] These ideas come in addition to wider debates about the changing nature of the judicial role generally in the context of a changing and globalising society (Robertson 2010; Mak 2013). They also join with the increasingly pressing concern about diversity on the bench and the need for modern judges to be drawn from as wide a background as possible. Arguments here encompass, broadly, equal opportunities, including accessing all available talent; democratic legitimacy; and the potential benefits of including different perspectives in the process of judging (Hale 2001; Feenan 2008: 490–519; Rackley 2013: 501–19; Hunter 2015; Cahill-O'Callaghan 2015).[5] This is a general concern in the United Kingdom and beyond but it has particular resonance perhaps in Northern Ireland where a new legal culture is being formed in the post-conflict context. Here all talents are necessary and welcome to ensure a legal space that is led by the widest pool of judges as possible. It is this issue of diversity that must now be addressed.

Judicial Appointments: The Search for Diversity Across the United Kingdom

Interest in the character and background of judges in general is as intense now as at any time since JAG Griffith began to publish successive editions of *The Politics*

[4] It is characteristic of transitional societies in general that a whole range of matters are seen as central to how new societies are 'constituted' (see further Hart (2001) and the list of issues that the International Center for Transitional Justice takes within its remit, available at www.ictj.org). It is particularly the case in Northern Ireland that almost any issue from housing to marching, flag flying to the siting of leisure centres is capable of being construed as a 'constitutional' one.

[5] The arguments for a diverse judiciary, including more women, are extensively discussed, and put in a Northern Ireland context, by Feenan (2008: 490–519). Feenan concludes correctly that 'seeing the issue only in terms of equality denies a much more complex field that requires understanding of the social construction of the judge, judging, and judicial authority, and the associated exclusion of outsider groups' (2008: 518).

of the Judiciary in 1977.[6] It is possible to speculate about all sorts of reasons for this, even beyond Northern Ireland and its new legal space. Some of the attention may be due to the enhanced role of judges generally in the United Kingdom and in public law issues in particular. In the United Kingdom generally there is now increased debate over the future of the Human Rights Act 1998 and the role that should be given to judges (Commission on a Bill of Rights 2012a, 2012b; Braver 2014). The new Supreme Court too has alerted a wider public to the constitutional importance of judges and the prospect of a US-style third branch of government emerging to determine significant aspects of public and private life. Interest in the process by which judges are appointed has become intense—whether as a symptom of the wider interest in judges or another cause of it.

The challenges facing each of the Judicial Appointments bodies that were founded first in Scotland in 2002, and then in Northern Ireland in 2005, and in England and Wales in 2006, have much in common.[7] However, different emphasises exist in each jurisdiction, and within the particular legal cultures that pertain there. The devolution context provides a momentum for development in Scotland (and, as has been seen, to a degree, Northern Ireland). In England and Wales (and to some extent in Scotland) the initial objective was to ensure an appropriate representation from women and from black and ethnic minorities, and there this theme has remained important.[8] In Northern Ireland the focus historically was on recruiting a judiciary that would have the support of all sections of the community (which here means particularly Catholic or nationalists since it was from this section of the population that support was historically missing).

Of course imperatives evolve and change. In Northern Ireland, the results of NIJAC's annual equity monitoring reports which began in 2007,[9] and the conclusions of NIJAC's first research report (Leith et al 2008) show, perhaps surprisingly, that the religion theme was not generally seen as particularly problematic. In fact, the appointment of women has emerged as the most significant feature. Despite relatively good representation of women in the tribunal system and in the lower courts, the absence of a single woman in the High Court in Northern Ireland (at the time of writing) has proved a point of particular contention. In all jurisdictions

[6] The final, fifth edition of *The Politics of the Judiciary* (London, Fontana) was published in 2010.

[7] See the comparison of the various research projects undertaken by all three bodies provided by the Judicial Appointments Board for Scotland (2009). See also some further possible challenges as identified by the House of Commons Political and Constitutional Reform Committee (2014) *Constitutional Role of the Judiciary if there were a Codified Constitution*, Fourteenth Report of Session 2013–14 (2014), available at www.publications.parliament.uk/pa/cm201314/cmselect/cmpolcon/802/802.pdf.

[8] The most recent Judicial Appointments Commission, *Statistics Bulletin* (JAC 2013) shows that while there has been a steady rise in the number of successful female applicants in England and Wales, the statistics for candidates from Black and Minority Ethnic (BAME) backgrounds have not shown any significant improvement on previous periods. Although the Scottish Judicial Appointments Board does not publish statistics about the background of applicants, it does have a diversity remit and continues to monitor applications. It has conducted research on diversity issues, although this does not seem to be ongoing (see the perhaps rather worryingly titled *Diversity Group Final Report* (2010)).

[9] Eight years of reports can be found at www.nijac.gov.uk/index/what-we-do/publications/research.htm.

there are also issues remaining about social class—although it is generally difficult to collect data that can reinforce a general perception that senior judges in particular are drawn from within a narrow social compass. The relatively well-worn complaint about the lack of appointments from the ranks of solicitors to the higher courts remains and is now joined by criticisms that lawyers working in the public sector are overlooked.

All of these concerns are contained within appointment systems that have avoided the more obvious forms of social engineering such as quotas, tiebreaks or schemes of positive discrimination. 'Appointment on merit' has been the supreme governing principle and the pole around which all processes have circulated.[10] This reflects international best practice and a whole series of international declarations.[11] Every jurisdiction within the United Kingdom has enshrined this in legislation.[12] In the Republic of Ireland a high-level review of judicial appointments, led by the Chief Justice, has recommended that the merit principle be placed on a legal footing there too (JARC 2014).

It is interesting however that the initial near universal support for new processes, and for the merit principle, is now beginning to fracture. Even among the legal profession (where merit was initially thought to be essential to ensure their support) and with others who might be thought to have an interest in the wider policy aims of providing a transparent process, there are some who now take a hostile view of the processes, and the concept of merit has been at the centre of this revolt. Recently the voices of dissent have become louder and divisions have appeared within the senior legal profession and judiciary itself.

Lord Sumption, a former England and Wales Judicial Appointments Commissioner, on his appointment to the Supreme Court, gave a lecture to the Law Society

[10] See, eg, Lord Falconer's foreword to the initial consultation paper 'Constitutional Reform: A New Way of Appointing Judges' (Department for Constitutional Affairs 2003) where he insists that 'of course the fundamental principle in appointing judges is and must remain selection on merit' (p 5). See also the response to the consultation by the Judges' Council (available at.www.webarchive.nationalarchives.gov.uk). Here the Judges' Council maintains that 'The reputation of our judiciary rests on the fact that it has predominantly been recruited from practising members of the legal profession … and the fact that all appointments have been based purely on merit' (para 69) and 'the overriding requirement for any appointment body that the best candidates be appointed on merit' (para 80).

[11] See, eg, Basic Principles on the Independence of the Judiciary adopted by the Seventh United Nations Congress on the Prevention of Crime and the Treatment of Offenders held at Milan from 26 August to 6 September 1985 and endorsed by General Assembly resolutions 40/32 of 29 November 1985 and 40/146 of 13 December 1985; Recommendation No R (94) 12 of the Council of Europe's Committee of Ministers on the Independence, Efficiency and Role of Judges (see www.wcd.coe.int/ViewDoc.jsp?id=524871&Site=CM; and the Venice Commission (2010).

[12] In England and Wales s 63(2) of the Constitutional Reform Act 2005 provides that 'selection must be solely on merit'. In Northern Ireland, s 5(8) of the Justice Act (Northern Ireland) 2002, as amended by the Justice Act (Northern Ireland) 2004 provides that 'the selection of a person to be appointed, or recommended for appointment, to a listed judicial office (whether initially or after reconsideration) must be made solely on the basis of merit'. In Scotland, s 12 of the Judiciary and Courts (Scotland) Act 2008 provides that 'selection must be solely on merit'. See also G Gee and K Malleson, 'Judicial Appointments, Diversity and the Equal Merit Provision' U.K. Const. L. Blog (6 May 2014), available at www. ukconstitutionallaw.org/2014/05/06/graham-gee-and-kate-malleson-judicial-appointments-diversity-and-the-equal-merit-provision.

in which he argued that the pool for appointment of judges is 'dominated by white males'.[13] For Sumption an important part of the problem is the issue of merit. Although appointment on merit is essential to retain the quality and attractiveness of the bench to the best candidates, it does not, in his view, allow selection with a view to altering the make-up of the judiciary as a whole. The result of this, he argues, is that in the absence of positive discrimination (to which he is opposed) it will take at least 50 years to achieve even 'a reasonably diverse judiciary'. It appears that 'merit' in Sumption's view currently lies—for whatever reason—with white males.

Lord Hacking, a leading practitioner, has taken issue with how merit is measured by the Judicial Appointments Commission (JAC), particularly through its lay membership. He claims that the lay commissioners cannot have the benefit of knowing each candidate closely from years of working together in legal practice. Hacking maintains that he is reflecting the dismay of the wider legal profession as he complains about the JAC's approach to merit and the 'humiliating' role of 'rigorous essay writing, formal presentations and two lengthy formal interviews' in finding a new Lord Chief Justice of England and Wales.[14] This insider perspective offers an interesting viewpoint and it is one that sees merit as something that is clear and demonstrable—but only to those in the know.

A counter to these has been Lady Hale who in a recent speech has suggested that 'as some of us have always known, it is not enough to get the appointments process right, though that is hard enough. We have to get the definition and assessment of merit right too and that is much harder'.[15] Unfortunately, Hale does not provide a view of just what any definition of merit should be except to suggest that it should not necessarily include high quality advocacy.

Jack Straw, former Lord Chancellor and Minister of Justice, also sees merit as of central importance. He takes issue directly with Sumption's idea that merit and diversity are in some way to be seen as mutually exclusive and pitted in opposition to each other (2013: 67). Reflecting on the introduction of the current appointments system, Straw maintains that it may have been naive to believe that if the system were changed then outcomes would be different. Importantly, however, he does not see the problem as being about how merit is created and operationalised. Straw recognises that 'merit is an empty vessel which needs careful filling: merit can too easily mean "people like us"' (2013: 71) (which follows perhaps the Hacking view). Straw continues, 'appointing "on merit" does not necessarily result in the most meritorious, or best, candidates being appointed' (2013: 72). There are, he argues, several possible reasons for this: it may be because the best candidates are not applying; or because something is going wrong in the process. Alternatively, it may be 'because merit has been wrongly defined' (Straw 2013: 72). Straw derides

[13] 'Bar Council Law Reform Lecture, Home Truths about Judicial Diversity', available at www.barcouncil.org.uk/media-centre/news-and-press-releases/2012/november/home-truths-about-judicial-diversity-speech-by-the-rt-hon-lord-sumption.

[14] D Hacking, 'Letter to the Times' *The Times*, 18 July 2013, 27.

[15] 'Kuttan Menon Memorial Lecture, Equality in the Judiciary', available at www.supremecourt.uk/docs/speech-130221.pdf.

the idea of an unrealistic, illusory concept of merit—a league table of brilliance—which is always perfectly distinct and measurable. This is a view with which it is possible to concur enthusiastically. However, Straw then goes on to develop an argument for increasing diversity that rather undermines this important insight and demonstrates perhaps the limits of a 'solely on merit' approach. He suggests that faced with two equally meritorious candidates in a tiebreak situation it may sometimes be necessary to achieve a balanced judiciary to favour a candidate from an under-represented group. This is all very well but it hardly offers a route to a more balanced judiciary. More importantly, however, it begs the question of what is actually meant by 'equally meritorious'? That in itself suggests that there is some way in which merit can be scored in an absolute manner, and certainly does not provide an alternative view of what might constitute merit.

The diverse views on merit from a range of 'insiders' reveals the centrality of the concept to judicial appointments and how it acts as a lightning rod for a wide variety of other concerns. It is, however, Lady Hale and Jack Straw's initial insight about the very nature of merit that resonates most with the views that the research uncovered in Northern Ireland. Here the problem is not only about finer judgements of merit, and the possibilities of bringing in diversity among the equally meritorious, but about how the very idea is created by a case-based system, conditioned by experience at the Bar, determined by seniority and maleness, and policed by a judiciary which may see meritorious candidates looking as much like themselves as possible. As shall be discussed now, there exists very real scepticism about how merit is defined and used in the appointments process. This is particularly widespread within female perspectives inside the legal profession, and it is here that its impact is most obviously marked. This must cause some concern as we move forward towards establishing a judiciary appropriate for the new circumstances in Northern Ireland.

What does 'Merit' Mean in Northern Ireland?

It is known that women do not do well in the higher judicial appointment competitions even though they are often well qualified.[16] It is known also that 'merit' is

[16] It is not just in the UK that the problem whereby the higher levels of judicial office are dominated by male office holders is particularly found. This has been discussed by Cheryl Thomas, where she comments on 'recent research by the European Social Affairs Commission, which showed that women clearly succeed in gaining judicial appointments where competitions are anonymous and the criteria for appointment are knowledge-based, not experience based. The data in Italy (and France) bear this out. Sixty per cent of successful applicants to the Italian judiciary are women for entry-level competitions that are purely knowledge-based and almost completely anonymous. However, after entry women find progression to the senior ranks, where appointment is increasingly experience and seniority based, extremely difficult. Only 7.9 per cent of all senior judicial positions in Italy are held by women' (2005: 67; see also Thornton 2007).

something that most insiders agree is an essential requirement for judicial appointment, although there are some serious concerns about how it is working.[17] In the second of two pieces of research undertaken for the Northern Ireland Judicial Appointments Commission[18] the focus was placed particularly on testing through quantitative and qualitative methods whether 'merit' as presently understood is in fact the cause of these problems. This project was thus designed to elicit views on the nature of 'merit'; how it is perceived and how it might be changing. The project used both an online survey with a variety of vignettes or stories to elicit views from respondents, and a more traditional series of interviews and focus groups. The findings which relate particularly to merit can be enunciated quite briefly:

1. Merit—in the sense of having the qualities needed for being a good judge—was often defined by respondents more widely than meaning simple technical legal expertise combined with court experience at the higher level. Frequent mention was made of qualities of empathy and judgement, case management, good listening skills and experience as well as problem-solving.
2. There was a general view that merit in this sense could be found in non-traditional candidates and judicial appointments could and should be made from a broad range of individuals where this idea of merit could be found.
3. The current view of merit used in the appointments process was quite widely seen as based on qualities mainly possessed by the Bar, and to be based on seniority and experience of advocacy in court. Judges were thought to reinforce this view of merit and ensure its dominance in the appointments process. Women generally believed themselves less likely to be seen as having this sort of merit or indeed have the opportunities to gain it.
4. There were very considerable differences in attitude between male and female respondents, particularly in regard to the nature of merit required for the High Court. Women respondents were generally much more favourable to non-traditional backgrounds being seen as meritorious.
5. While barristers were most likely to see merit in traditional terms, there was a significant number who acknowledged the wider view of merit.
6. The more encompassing view of what constitutes merit was widespread among solicitors and, particularly, lawyers in public service.
7. While there was some recognition that lower courts and tribunals were beginning to accommodate a wider range of talent, there was generally a considerable amount of scepticism that merit is being rewarded at the High Court appointment level, and this was seen as a particular problem.

Although the project was undertaken in Northern Ireland there is little reason to believe that many of the findings on gender are not relevant to other jurisdictions.[19]

[17] For further discussion on this see the list of senior figures decrying the current situation in the UK provided by Rackley (2013: 501–02).

[18] See n 1 above for full details.

[19] For discussion of international appointments, see Thomas (2005); Mackenzie, Malleson and Sands (2010); and Schultz and Shaw (2013).

The Research Study Findings

The NIJAC study on merit has two elements. The first involved an online survey where six vignettes were created to highlight issues of gender, age, familiarity to senior judges, part-time working, solicitor–barrister division, type of practice, and family responsibility which might be thought relevant to appointment to judicial posts. (See further Leith and Morison 2013 and Leith 2013). Overall those responding to the survey seemed prepared to see merit in a wider sense than often is traditional in the appointments process. Although there were degrees of conservatism from many who answered the survey, particularly over age and status, female respondents were more favourable towards non-traditional candidates than were men. There were, however, many who felt that meritorious candidates may not be recognised within the system as it operates presently but that this is not necessarily the fault of NIJAC processes as such but rather a failing of the wider legal system which sustains the current view of merit.

The second element of the research—and the one on which this account concentrates—relates to a series of interviews and focus groups that was carried out by the author with individual practitioners from both branches of the professions at various levels of seniority. There were some women only focus groups and focus groups drawn from lawyers working in the public sector. In all about 60 individuals took part. Generally the views elicited from the scenarios were confirmed in the focus groups. Merit was seen generally as more than simple technical legal knowledge. As one barrister expressed it, 'knowing the law is just the start … the merit principle needs to be broadly defined to include a wider range of skills, and disentangled from experience in the traditional sense'.

There was, however, considerable variation expressed as to what *exactly* merit might mean and how it could be evidenced. For some, this was clearly related to the sort of work that an individual might have before appointment. Often focus group respondents, particularly from the Bar, took the view that a mixed, high-end practice provided the best basis to demonstrate merit. Criminal law was mentioned frequently as important and so too was judicial review and high value chancery work which was thought to provide an opportunity to demonstrate the requisite attributes. However, this linking of merit to particular kinds of work was not universally held. It was suggested that complexity and difficulty might be found in all sorts of areas of law. As one barrister saw it,

> anyone dealing with children's cases, freeing orders … social security cases are the hardest cases that I read, dealing with really complex law … chancery cases … anyone who can do that has the intellectual ability to do the job [of a judge]—provided they are given the training in evidence and so forth.

If an applicant's caseload was mainly in the High Court with occasional visits to the Court of Appeal or even the Supreme Court or Strasbourg this too was seen as significant. As a barrister pointed out, 'how else do you demonstrate merit except if you can do the more difficult cases?' In part this seems to be because the standard of practice is generally agreed to be higher in the higher courts. As one relatively new QC put it, 'You do learn from higher level courts … everyone gets better, you get better, the questions get harder … and you learn about how to behave in court'.

This view was, however, far from widespread, and respondents not from the Bar, tended to express doubts about the extent to which specific sorts of cases in particular courts demonstrated merit as opposed to some sort of prestige. It was in fact a senior barrister who told us, 'It's about kudos … often high value cases are straightforward, easy, they can be a penalty kick … and murder is not the most complex crime … it is not depth or quality it is about kudos'. This view was supported enthusiastically by a public sector lawyer who expressed the view that 'if you can handle … industrial tribunal cases … equal value … indirect discrimination you can handle anything that is likely to come up in the High Court … you would be very unlucky in the high court to come up against anything as complex'. Similarly social welfare law was mentioned as a complex area where skills developed there would be transferable to a senior court appointment, although generally it was not thought to be seen as such.

Merit and the Bar

The interviewees generally agreed that merit is more likely to be seen as existing within a Bar practice. This view was not unique to barristers but also noted in a more critical way by those not at the Bar. Indeed, a solicitor at partner level expressed the view that 'the solicitors' profession is at the bottom and people want to keep them there'. From the barristers' perspective, however, it was felt that the high profile of court work brought particular value, and showed merit very clearly. As one moderately senior barrister put it, 'our skills are as advocates … if you have cross-examined witnesses on a day and daily basis this is an appropriate skill for a judge'. Another barrister went further in seeing the importance of advocacy for judicial office saying 'you need to have experience with advocacy so you can see when the wool is being pulled over your eyes'. Generally experience of court work over a sustained period of time and at a reasonably high level was felt, particularly by some barristers, to be the most effective—if not indeed the sole—way of demonstrating merit for judicial office. This experience was seen (by some barristers) to be unique to the Bar and it meant that identifying merit was relatively straightforward. As one barrister put it simply, 'the most successful practitioners are the most successful judges. They have demonstrated that they know the law … and get on with colleagues … and if females have got on despite the obstacles [then they too must have merit]'.

However, it would be inaccurate to see this view of merit as being Bar oriented as universal to barristers. The more senior Bar appeared more willing than juniors to find merit beyond their ranks. One senior barrister told us, 'There are two examples of judges … who have come from the solicitors' profession and they are excellent judges'. However, the same respondent went on to say, 'but the Bar think that we have a particular set of skills that make us good judges … our skills are more transferable'. This view was expressed more trenchantly by younger barristers with one in a focus group insisting that 'There is a difference between a barrister and a solicitor … they [solicitors] routinely sit behind the junior and senior counsel … they have all sorts of opinions but they don't have to ask the questions, put themselves on the line'. While it may not be entirely clear how this translates into the judicial role, barristers generally did represent their work as closer to that of the judge than other lawyers.

Of course there are consequences to such a view and those (particularly non-barristers) who did not share the Bar orientation were fully alive to them. One of these is that a Bar-oriented focus on merit meant that other important skills were being overlooked. A solicitor said:

> Some [barristers] are very good at paperwork, at drafting an opinion or the black and white letter of the law but that doesn't necessarily translate to them being good in a court situation, having to weigh up pros and cons, deal with the people in front of you and decide if someone is credible or not.

It was a moderately experienced public sector lawyer who expressed the view that:

> A fairly homogenous group are describing themselves to themselves, and, although you have a fair and transparent appointment process, the way in which a candidate is described will favour someone who has a traditional, mixed private practice … if you go into any public voluntary or public sector [body] you find people are doing things that are very different … and yet you will be exercising very relevant skills.

It may be that not all skills relevant for judicial appointment are developed in a private practice at the Bar, and that to see it in this way misses other important attributes. As a partner in a firm of solicitors remarked: 'A lot of them are good advocates but that doesn't make them a good judge … a good judge is the opposite, not a spin doctor'. Another public sector lawyer pointed out that 'the judicial skill set and the private practice skill set are not necessarily exactly the same. You need things that people from non-traditional backgrounds can bring … case management, managing staff … you need people who have these skills'.

Merit and Seniority

There was a also a view that merit was most likely to be found with senior practitioners—those with many more years of experience than the formal requirement for most judicial posts. This view was fairly widely held but seemed particularly prevalent among barristers. It was a senior barrister who said:

> We need the very best people who have dealt with high value cases, been to the Court of Appeal, Strasbourg, dealt with difficult and complex cases and only if you have done this are you really good enough to demonstrate the sorts of skills [for the High Court].

This view, that experience often far in excess of the minimum required is important, reinforced the idea of a 'pecking order' for judicial appointment that was discovered in the earlier research (Leith et al 2008: 13–14 and 97–98). Here again the idea emerged that the Bar (mainly) but the legal profession in general, would have some idea of who was 'worthy' and who should be next on the bench. For example, an interviewee said, 'there would have been quite a bit of disapproval if [XX] hadn't got it … There are appointments that are seen as surprising because the Bar know how those people perform in court but the judicial appointments commission can't'. Views of this sort also tied into more general criticisms that 'outside' bodies could not be expected to be alive to the pecking order. For example, the view was expressed that 'competence based [appointment] works in England and Wales where there are a lot of people … but we are still a small enough jurisdiction, and people know each other and know their reputation'.[20]

There were of course other views. Many of those interviewed were willing (at least in theory) to look for merit where it could be found. As one barrister said:

> Does experience equate with age? … I know people who have done 12 or 13 years of work at the very highest level and others who have been pottering around for 25 years and more and will never do the same level of work.

Others confirmed that it is the nature and quality of work that is important, and this is not the same as simple length of service: it may be possible to obtain sufficient experience of work at the appropriate quality in a short period. There were several respondents who were very aware of the consequences of equating merit with seniority. As one senior practitioner put it, 'there are no High Court judges who are work shy but there is an expectation that you are going to work harder in your sixties than you did even in your twenties that is unusual'. This was felt to narrow the applicant pool to those who maintained an energy and enthusiasm about continuing the long hours, hard work culture that had put them in the position where they may be seen as meritorious. It was also seen as potentially limiting the pool yet further as it was felt by some that such a decision about extending one's active working life may well be one that men would find easier to take than women for a whole host of reasons relating to caring responsibilities and life patterns. A senior male barrister made the point that:

> If you become a high court judge in your late fifties you are probably thinking about working until you're seventy … if you are a man you would find it easier to make a decision about working on in a high pressure job until you are seventy.

Merit as Male

Of course this view that merit may most often be associated (at least by some people) with practice at the Bar, with a particular sort of caseload and obtainable only with a degree of experience has other consequences too. The view was expressed that women were less likely to be able to offer merit of this sort. Frequently it was mentioned how difficult it is for women to avoid being channelled into family

[20] As the same respondent put it, 'in Northern Ireland, we kind of know who is "right"'.

work. Respondents expressed a divergence of views as to whether the necessary experience could be attained in family law as opposed to other sorts of work. However, many respondents did take the view that this channelling of women into family law, and the uncertain status of the skill sets there, has the consequence that any merit that may be displayed there is likely to be overlooked in favour of other forms of merit that can be observed more easily in more 'mainstream' work. For some respondents this was a result of the nature of the work. As one respondent put it, 'there's not a lot of law in family law' echoing the view found in the earlier research about the status often accorded to 'chick law' (Leith et al 2008: 23, 56 and 61). Other interviewees took the view that there was a rather different skill set, and it was one that was just as valuable in evidencing merit for judicial appointment. For example, a QC who practised only rarely in the family court reported an experience of seeing a female barrister in action:

> I was in court and was blown away by her advocacy skills but judges don't see her … I thought it was a lot more difficult … a very limited number of judges see them … and they are held in private.

The view was expressed quite strongly that this pigeonholing of women combined with the way in which merit is seen may have the effect that it is difficult for women to present themselves as having the same degree of merit. As one interviewee said, 'if you have criminal experience, that is the gold standard … family law experience is not what is wanted … and the vast majority of those barristers and solicitors who practise criminal law are male, and there you are'. Indeed female respondents, as well as some males, were very keen to make the point that generally female merit is something different, and does not seem to be transferable. As a member of one focus group put it, 'the requirement to succeed is that you must think just like a man, you must act like a man … be as good as a man'.

Some of female respondents were anxious to report that it is often particularly difficult for women to emulate this male model of merit. There are wider factors which may make it more difficult for women to progress in the same way. These include not only the diversion of women into family law specialisms and sexist briefing patterns at the Bar, but also some structural factors. There was a view expressed by female respondents—and not generally contradicted by male respondents—that men were better able to pursue the informal networks that can lead to success. For example, one focus group respondent said:

> Men can stay on here [the Bar library] and then go home to a cooked dinner, the kids in bed, and go straight into the study … they can hang around here … do their work in the library … networking in a an informal way … they can run into someone in the servery or on the stairs … and get worked passed on.

In contrast women talked of the difficulties of managing careers and families. As one female barrister put it, 'I have watched my male peers at the Bar advance far beyond me … they have good wives at home'. There was general agreement that a lot more networking goes on among male practitioners, particularly at the Bar: '[I]t's not what you know, it's very much the golf and the rugby'.

There is, however, a view that this may be changing—albeit at a very slow pace. There was some mention of the feminisation of the legal professions at the lower levels but also something about the emergence of a cohort of women lawyers who are more ambitious than their predecessors. It was also thought that the general move to specialism in legal practice may in fact facilitate this development. However, even the most enthusiastic heralds of change of this sort recognised this as both a very uncertain and long-term process, and as a reaction to the continuing male dominance of the legal profession rather than a more fundamental change in its nature. As one interviewee expressed it, 'the women are adopting a male way of succeeding … but the system, the way of succeeding, needs to be changed'.

Merit Policed by Judges

The idea of merit being Bar influenced and in large part male is conditioned and reinforced, according to many of the interviewees, by the role that they see the existing judges playing as gatekeepers to judicial appointment. As one barrister respondent reported:

> Those on the bench see the skill sets they bring as being the ones that are needed … it is an advocacy skill set by and large … Judges have the view that the profile we [barristers] have represents what a good judge is.

From the perspective of some barristers this was not a problem. Indeed, it may be seen as a good thing—particularly if the view of merit being Bar focused is accepted. However, solicitors in particular often expressed the view that their skills were being overlooked because the judges controlled the idea of merit and viewed it in relation to barristers' skills. There may even be wider considerations at play reflecting the perceived status of the two branches of the profession. It was in fact a barrister who made the comment 'how the judiciary address solicitors in courts compared to how they address barristers, particularly QCs … this all helps to perpetuate the hierarchy … a lot of the Bar would feel this'.

Many see the existing judiciary playing an undue role in determining appointments. This is indirect, in terms of validating certain understandings of merit, and even sometimes more direct. It was a solicitor who reflected a fairly common view of the consultee or referee process involving the existing High Court bench that is required for some senior posts when he commented that:

> The High Court still have their black balling, if I can put it like that … all applicants have to be known to people on the High Court either personally or professionally … whenever you have that criteria—that discriminatory criteria—it sends out huge signals that we want to keep it to ourselves or pull up the drawbridge when we have the right people on our side.

The processes and structures of NIJAC, including alternative consultee arrangements and the presence of the lay commissions, were treated with varying degrees of scepticism. One respondent asked, 'do all the commissioners carry equal weight? Do the judicial commissioners have more say? Can they say he appeared in front of me last week and he's no good?' Another expressed a more unequivocal view: 'NIJAC doesn't work: it is a front, there is still a tap on the shoulder approach'.

The High Court—and the Absence of a Woman in the High Court—as a Focus for Concern

Although this research was interested in the range of judicial appointments it was immediately fairly clear that the position in the High Court established the tone for the whole judicial appointments system. When it was mentioned to respondents that the balance of men and women was moderately healthy in proportion to the applicant pool in some of the lower courts and tribunals this was sometimes dismissed. As one respondent said, 'a lot of people don't consider … those to be judicial offices … lower down the judicial ladder it is easier [but] the High Court sets the scene'. Another solicitor respondent put the situation more directly:

> You just have to look at the High Court. They perpetuate themselves, they just want more of them up there. They don't want diversity. You only have to go along to a function with High Court judges and they are all there in their dark grey suits … no women sends out the wrong signals.

Indeed, it was the absence of women in the High Court (at the time of the research) that coloured all conversations about merit at every level in the judiciary. It would be difficult to exaggerate the significance that is attached to the absence of a woman judge in the High Court which remains the case up to the middle of 2015. Unfavourable comparisons were frequently made with the Republic of Ireland with more than one respondent pointing out that Northern Ireland is many years behind its neighbour in this regard.[21] There was, however, a general recognition that this absence of female High Court judges was an intricate issue which required a complex solution. As a senior barrister put it:

> Self-evidently the problem is that there are no women on the High Court bench but if you are just trying to design a process that is going to [appoint a women to the high court] for its own sake, how is this going to be a good process?

Fear of a tokenistic appointment was widespread. Some respondents recognised the problem as far-reaching. It was said:

> Until more women advance in the profession, both branches of the profession, you will not see a woman in the High Court … there is a lack of assistance to women to succeed in the legal profession … we need something more general and systemic … it can't be left to the endeavours of some one individual.

[21] According to the Irish Judicial Appointments Review Committee, over 30 per cent of judges are female which represents the highest percentage of females ever in the Irish judiciary. There are currently nine women judges of the Superior Courts, including a female Chief Justice. This represents over 20 per cent of the 44 serving High Court and Supreme Court judges, and in the Circuit Court the trajectory of female appointments is quite markedly upwards, since 19 judges representing over 43 per cent of the Court's judiciary are female (JARC 2014: para 47).

There was considerable speculation in the conversations about what sort of individual might be the first to take the role. A female barrister made the observation that,

> the last thing any women wants is to lead the charge … because we all know what will be said—'You are only there because of your gender' and that would be a nightmare to work through. We all know it is said of women judges on the bench now.

Indeed, a fairly common theme, particularly among female respondents, was one which stressed the challenges of being the first female in this role. Mention was made of 'the considerable chill factor of going into a club of 14 or 15 men'. Another respondent said that 'the back corridor can be seen as a very special sort of club … and that club atmosphere might very well put off anyone who is not an iconoclast from applying'. One thought from a female barrister was that 'maybe we would need to have two or three appointed at the same time' to overcome the perceived difficulties. However, there was a view strongly expressed particularly among female respondents at the Bar that such a candidate could and would be found. For example, one interviewee said: 'She exists … the High Court bench is not full of dinosaurs. There are many High Court judges who would more than welcome a woman colleague, and would be welcoming and supportive'.

Judicial Pathways—Formal and Informal

The existence of a formal career path that might lead to appointment at the higher level was not something that the research was able to uncover to any great degree.[22] There was mention of a few individuals who, it was reported, seemed to have taken on judicial office at a relatively junior level but who were thought to have further ambitions. However, this was not seen as a universally available career option, although it was suggested that it might be a good thing in that it 'would allow a wider range of people to demonstrate the appropriate competencies … [as] the part-time roles have the potential to do this'. As one focus group member put it, 'If you shine in one tier you should have the opportunity to move up'. It was thought that this possibility might even encourage good applicants who would not otherwise think of a judicial career. A senior lawyer from the public sector made the point that 'a judicial pathway is the *key thing* … I work in a sector where there are some extremely capable women but who have no perception of the possibility to be a part-time judge'. The creation of this possibility was felt to be an important attraction. This was seen by some as the best possibility of securing a female

[22] 'Judicial Career' is a concept which appears as recommendation 44 of the 'Report of the Advisory Panel on Judicial Diversity 2010' in England and Wales: 'The concept of a judicial career is key to achieving progress on a more diverse judiciary … This means identifying clearer career paths so that those considering joining the judiciary understand their options and know how they can develop the skills and experience required to progress from one section of the judiciary to another' (Advisory Panel on Judicial Diversity 2010).

appointment to the High Court. It was said that 'women have taken the route of … coming up through the tiers, from other judicial jobs' and that 'there are a large number of female applicants in the County Court who may well be where the next High Court judge comes [from]'. There was a view expressed widely that a series of appointments, moving up through the tiers of the judiciary to the county court, might be thought to be an appropriate proving ground, and perhaps of at least equal validity to a career in the Bar. As one respondent put it,

> merit has to be real merit … but if someone is a solicitor, a female in family work west of the Bann … they need a place to show that they can do the hard work. It is the County Court that is the place. They can progress from there.

Although the idea of a formal pathway to a judicial career that might take a judge up the rungs of the career ladder remains an uncertain although interesting possibility, there was very little doubt among informants about the existence of an informal pathway to judicial preferment. It was widely reported in all the focus groups that there were a number of important attributes and career choices that were likely to have been made in order for a candidate to appear meritorious. These were widely and easily recognised by informants. As one interviewee remarked, 'it is funny how, irrespective of the existence of NIJAC, there are certain truths that are self-evident … senior crown counsel will become a judge'. When pressed further on what this informal track might involve it was said, 'you have access to the right sort of work … if you're known in the back corridor, if you're Treasury Counsel, if your father was a judge'. Another informant characterised a successful candidate as someone who may well have been 'vocal on the Bar Council or served on it … very high profile, everyone would have heard of them'. Much of this idea of a career pathway was seen to be about networking and making the correct contacts, and much seemed to exclude women for structural reasons.

Various events including dinners and lectures were thought to be important. It was here that the necessary impressions could be made and the important contacts fostered. As one informant put it, 'the person who has played at that level is going to have an advantage … you have access to the right sort of work' and, crucially, 'you know the judges'. This latter element—connections with the senior judiciary—is seen as particularly important, mainly in relation to access to appropriate consultees or referees. This was believed by some respondents to be a feature that impacts particularly on women. Women reported themselves as less likely to network and less willing to ask judges for support.

It was felt that these informal career pathways are taken at a very early stage. As one young practitioner said, 'it would be naive to say there are no pathways … if you look into any year group you can see that for some people the path is laid out before them, the connections are there'. The existence of these pathways was thought to be common knowledge: an interviewee said, 'of course that goes on, there is evidence of that. Everybody knows that'. (Selection to the QC panel was mentioned frequently as being subject to a similar process, and here too a belief in informal pathways as significant was widely and firmly held.) The existence of this informal career path was not seen as providing the most open and accessible route to judicial office and it was felt to miss talent—particularly among women—who may not have chosen or been able to negotiate a way to the glittering prizes. As one informant put it,

> NIJAC has been looking for other experiences, outside of work, so that flies in the face of what they are trying to do ... People who are on the inside track know how to fill in the form, know the buzz words ... but others don't.

There was a feeling that relying on judicial insiders reporting on those that are known to them had the effect that experiences outside the informal career pathway were undervalued.

Conclusion: What Might Scepticism about Merit Mean for New Legal Spaces?

It is clear then that the legal profession as a whole is not entirely at ease with the present system for appointing judges, or perhaps more accurately it is not fully convinced that the appointments process is yet yielding the sort of judiciary that many would like, especially in the new circumstances that pertain in Northern Ireland. In particular there is concern that women are not being appointed to the highest level, and this colours perception of the whole system. This feeling is fed by a notion that 'merit' can and should be seen in a wider context than it has been traditionally. Women—the group which suffers most from the present construction of merit—are, it was found, very much more liable to see the idea of merit in this wider manner than men (and public service lawyers and solicitors more likely to have this view than barristers, irrespective of gender).

These findings in terms of the socially constructed nature of merit are hardly novel. For example, it is a commonplace among researchers into judicial appointments that merit is a social construct and what constitutes merit is defined by relatively small elites. For example, Malleson has explored this where she notes that merit has been constructed around the needs of 'certain preferred groups in a way which has unfairly advantaged them' (2006: 136). In an argument that is very familiar within feminist approaches it can be maintained that this idea of merit, while posing as neutral, is in reality a strongly gendered concept.[23] The argument is that this concept of 'merit', and the method for assessing it, is at the heart of the failure of many women (not only in law but in many sectors of society) to advance to the upper reaches of professional life. This is not of course because women are not meritorious, but simply that merit is identified in a way which emphasises some attributes and minimises the importance of others.

[23] See, eg, Gilligan (1982); Mackinnon (1989); Ruddick (1990); and Fiorenza (2009).

What *is* novel from the findings of this study is the strength of the view suggesting a growing realisation within the profession itself—particularly among women—that 'merit is the problem', and that there is no longer a consensus about how it is defined and the methods used to assess it. This comes through in the high degree of scepticism found in the idea that merit would be rewarded in judicial appointments. As one of the interviewees noted, 'there is a meritocracy but it's *their* meritocracy ... that's a fact of life'.

On one view of the findings all that might be necessary is some relatively minor re-working of the appointments process by the Northern Ireland Judicial Appointments Commission. This could provide a process resulting in a more appropriate and diverse judiciary for the new legal space that may be emerging in post-conflict Northern Ireland, and this might be sufficient to counter criticism. Such a process might involve, for example, a concerted effort to include more women in shortlists; an enhanced judge-shadowing scheme; a promotion process for incumbents in the lower to higher courts; or a drive to see more solicitors or public sector lawyers in the upper courts. However, it is contended that such steps alone are unlikely to be sufficient. There are a large number of challenges to the justice system in Northern Ireland which require a more fundamental rethinking of the kind of judiciary needed, and a radical re-working of the idea of 'appointment on merit'. Further, it is maintained in what may seem initially as a paradoxical position that discussions of merit in appointment need to be moved beyond gender precisely in order to achieve the sort of gender balance that is appropriate for a modern judiciary seeking the most talented judges. If we allow the current idea of 'merit' to remain unchallenged, and see the problem as only about how to move more women into this definition, change will be very slow, if it happens at all. Respondents in the focus groups may have initiated scepticism about merit, but this cannot be the final statement. NIJAC, and indeed the wider system, needs to become more involved in defining the notion of 'merit'. There is a real need to think beyond what might take the 'bad look' off the profile of the present bench, and to realise that any new concept of merit properly considering the needs of the legal system for a changing world will undoubtedly result in more female judges—and much more besides.

As Northern Ireland moves forward to consider how the bench should be composed in the new legal space established in the post-Agreement Northern Ireland, it is important we do not listen only to the voices of those who are closely involved or have a direct interest in the answer. Indeed, the inward looking perspectives of many respondents in the study was striking. They have to a very large extent viewed 'the problem' from their own perspective (that is as individuals building careers) and with little discussion or thought directed towards the needs of users of the legal system or the public at large who finance much of it. Certainly, although most respondents indicated that diversity would be 'a good thing', the diversity proposed from many respondents goes only so far. There seems to be little interest in appointing judges who might meet the current problems of the system directly: problems such as access to justice for the very large sections of the community who are losing or have lost the ability to utilise the court system through cost.[24] A critical reader of the respondents' views presented here might pose the question: what would this more diverse judiciary do to make the system better, fairer, cheaper, and more responsive to public need in Northern Ireland? From the information obtained from respondents it would seem it would do very little indeed. It seems that the judicial appointments system is, in reality, trying to resolve a small problem (that is female representation at the higher judicial levels) when a number of other larger ones which are present or becoming obvious are not being acknowledged. If these wider issues were to be faced up to this may well resolve the problem of diversity anyway.

It is important to be clear here. There is no wish to undermine the aim that women should be found more frequently in judicial roles. The argument rather is that a judicial appointments process which looks at the wider needs of the judicial system could be the most effective way in which to increase diversity, because it could lead to a judiciary where the skill set more closely matches those of all suitable applicants—male and female—possessing a whole range of attributes.[25] That is to say, if merit could be redefined according to external need (rather than conditioned by internal professional structures) then diversity would surely follow and the legal system might better benefit the population which it is designed to serve.

This suggests that it is necessary to start thinking of the judiciary and the wider legal system as a *public resource*, and consider what the public might want or legitimately expect from the judiciary. It is unlikely that diversity will naturally flow from correcting particular under-representations in the system. Instead, in order to achieve a real diversity it is necessary to change the perception of the judiciary and see it as a public resource acting in the wider interest and as delivering access to justice (rather than mainly reflecting the career development ladder within the legal professions). Paterson and Paterson's recent (2012) critique of the Supreme Court appointments system echoes some of this but also makes the point that merit should be seen in a more broadly contextual manner, taking into account the needs of the court as a body acting in the public interest rather than as a group of individual judges chosen as 'best' on the day. It is important to begin to consider more closely several elements of the judicial task:

— What is it that judges actually do (rather than what applicants for these posts do)?
— What is it that users of the court system want from judges (which they might not be currently getting)?

[24] In a way this mirrors the general reaction of much of the profession towards new funding regimes which have focused for the most part on how cutting legal aid will result in poorer quality representation rather than on more general issues of the unmet legal need. For the wider context of legal aid in Northern Ireland and the budgetary pressures pertaining there, see *Access to Justice Review Northern Ireland: The Report* (NICTS 2011) and the second part of the Review promised for the end of 2015 (see further www.dojni.gov.uk/index/access-to-justice-2.htm).

[25] As Joanne Conaghan has suggested, too much of a focus upon gender can not only take one's eye off other factors, but can be just as oppressive (2000).

- How can judges contribute to reducing the expenditure on legal aid in Northern Ireland which currently runs at just under £2 million per week (Northern Ireland Legal Services Commission 2015)?
- What are the skill sets actually required for the judicial task?
- What is the role of the judge in ensuring effective case management and team work to deliver efficient access to justice?
- How exactly does it help the judicial process, or its perception, to have judges who are more 'reflective' of the broader community?

There has been some growing interest in this recently.[26] However, much of this research has not attempted to test some of the basic assumptions that have come to inform the appointments process whereby, for example, judicial skills are equated with High Court advocacy experience in complex cases such as leading barristers may have developed. The appointments process remains too concentrated on what an applicant has done within the career structure of the legal profession rather than on what he or she should be expected to do as a judge serving a wider interest.

This is perhaps the beginning of an exciting period in judicial studies. Researchers want to know much more about the roles which judges perform and how much of this involves the skills of technical substantive law in the traditional sense and how much the resolution of relatively straightforward law and facts but with complex factors surrounding the wider public context. For example, in the new rights regime in Northern Ireland that Harvey discusses in this volume there may well be difficult issues of balancing a range of political (with both a small 'p' and large 'P') factors occurring within relatively straightforward legal contexts. Beyond this, a judiciary that is seen as a public resource would be alive to the whole range of other roles and tasks which might include: case management and ensuring value for money; public relations and making sure that although parties may leave court having lost, they feel they have been heard; assisting litigants in person; and pursuing the various values of justice for everyone in a context of declining legal aid and increasing costs. The list is nearly endless, but is surely worth building our knowledge about its contents. In Northern Ireland in particular, policymakers should be encouraging this enquiry. A most desirable side effect will be a more diverse judiciary as well as perhaps a more effective one.

References

Advisory Panel on Judicial Diversity (2010) 'Report of the Advisory Panel of Judicial Diversity 2010' (London, Ministry of Justice).

[26] Other than early work such as that by Paterson (1982 and more recently in 2013) there has been only very limited research on the judicial role in the UK (see further Rock 1993; Darbyshire 2011; Thomas 2013; and the work of the ULC Judicial Institute, available at www.ucl.ac.uk/laws/judicial-institute).

Anthony, G (2009) 'Judicial Review in Northern Ireland: A Guide to the "Real" Devolution Issues' 14 *Judicial Review* 230.

—— (2011) 'The Devolution of Policing and Criminal Justice' 17 *European Public Law* 197.

Balkin, J and Levinson, J (2001) 'Understanding the Constitutional Revolution' 87 *Virginia Law Review* 1045.

Blackbourn, J (2014) *Anti-Terrorism Law and Normalising Northern Ireland* (London, Routledge).

Braver, J (2014) 'Counter-Interpretation, Constitutional Design, and the Right to Family Life: How the Conservatives Learned to Stop Worrying and Love the HRA (Briefly)', available at www.ukconstitutionallaw.org/2014/01/06/joshua-braver-counter-interpretation-constitutional-design-and-the-right-to family-life-how-the-conservatives-learned-to-stop-worrying-and-love-the-hra-briefly.

Cahill-O'Callaghan, R (2015) Reframing the Judicial Diversity Debate: Personal Values and Tacit Diversity 35 *Legal Studies* 1.

Commission on a Bill of Rights (2012a) *A UK Bill of Rights? The Choice Before Us, Vol 1* (London, Commission on a Bill of Rights).

—— (2012b) *A UK Bill of Rights? The Choice Before Us, Vol 2: Annexes* (London, Commission on a Bill of Rights).

Conaghan, J (2000) 'Reassessing the Feminist Theoretical Project in Law' 27 *Journal of Law and Society* 351.

Criminal Justice Review Group (CJRG) (1998) *Review of the Criminal Justice System in Northern Ireland: A Consultation Paper* (Belfast, HMSO).

—— (2000) *Review of the Criminal Justice System in Northern Ireland: The Report of the Criminal Justice Review* (Belfast, HMSO).

Darbyshire, P (2011) *Sitting in Judgment: The Working Lives of Judges* (Oxford, Hart Publishing).

Department for Constitutional Affairs (2003) 'Constitutional Reform: A New Way of Appointing Judges' CP 10/03 (London, Department for Constitutional Affairs).

Dorf, M and Sabel, C (1998) 'A Constitution of Democratic Experimentalism' 98 *Colombia Law Review* 267.

Feenan, D (2008) 'Women Judges: Gendering Judges, Justifying Diversity' 35 *Journal of Law and Society* 490.

Fiorenza, E (2009) 'Exploring the Intersections of Race, Gender, Status and Ethnicity in Early Christian Studies' in L Nasrallah and E Fiorenza (eds), *Prejudice and Christian Beginnings: Investigating Race, Gender, Status and Ethnicity in Early Christian Studies* (Minneapolis, MN, Fortress Press).

Gee, G, Hazell, R, Malleson, K and O'Brien, P (2015) *The Politics of Judicial Independence in the UK's Changing Constitution* (Cambridge, Cambridge University Press).

Gilligan, C (1982) *In a Different Voice: Psychological Theory and Women's Development* (Cambridge, MA, Harvard University Press).

Griffith, JAG (2010) *The Politics of the Judiciary* (London, Fontana).

Hale, B (2001) 'Equality in the Judiciary: Why Should We Want More Women Judges?' *Public Law* 489.

Hart, V (2001) 'Constitution-Making and the Transformation of Conflict' 26 *Peace & Change* 153.

Hunter, R (2015) 'More than Just a Different Face? Judicial Diversity and Decision-making' *Current Legal Problems* 1.

Judicial Appointments Board for Scotland (2009) 'Three Surveys … Same Answers?' (Edinburgh, Judicial Appointments Board for Scotland).
—— (2010) 'Diversity Working Group: Final Report' (Edinburgh, Judicial Appointments Board for Scotland).
Judicial Appointments Commission (JAC) (2013) 'Judicial Selection and Recommendations for Appointment Statistics, April 2013 to September 2013' (London, JAC).
Judicial Appointments Review Committee (JARC) (2014) 'Preliminary Submission to the Department of Justice and Equality's Public Consultation on the Judicial Appointments Process' (Dublin, JARC).
Klare, K (1998) 'Legal Culture and Transformative Constitutionalism' 14 *South African Journal on Human Rights* 146.
Leith, P (2013) 'A Note on Using Vignettes in Socio-Legal Research' 19 *Web Journal of Current Legal Issues*.
Leith, P, Lynch, M, Glennon, L, Dickson, B and Wheeler, S (2008) *Propensity to Apply for Judicial Office under the New Northern Ireland Judicial Appointments System: A Qualitative Study for the Northern Ireland Judicial Appointments Commission* (Belfast, Queen's University Belfast School of Law).
Leith, P and Morison, J (2013) *Rewarding Merit in Judicial Appointments?* (Belfast, Queen's University Belfast School of Law).
Mackenzie, R, Malleson, K and Sands, P (2010) *Selecting International Judges: Principles, Process, and Politics* (Oxford, Oxford University Press).
MacKinnon, C (1989) *Toward a Feminist Theory of the State* (Cambridge, MA, Harvard University Press).
Mak, E (2013) *Judicial Decision-Making in a Globalised World: A Comparative Analysis of the Changing Practices of Western Highest Courts* (Oxford, Hart Publishing).
Malleson, K (2006) 'Rethinking the Merit Principle in Judicial Selection' 33 *Journal of Law and Society* 126.
McEvoy, K and Morison, J (2003), 'Beyond the "Constitutional Moment": Law, Transition, and Peacemaking in Northern Ireland' 26 *Fordham International Law Review* 961.
Morison, J (2013) '"A Sort of Farewell": Sovereignty, Transition, and Devolution in the UK' in R Rawlings, P Leyland and A Young (eds), *Sovereignty and the Law: Domestic, European and International Perspectives* (Oxford, Oxford University Press).
Morison, J and Livingstone, S (1995) *Reshaping Public Power: Northern Ireland and the British Constitutional Crisis* (London, Sweet & Maxwell).
Morison, J and Lynch, M (2007) 'Litigating the Agreement: Towards a New Judicial Constitutionalism for the UK from Northern Ireland' in J Morison, K McEvoy and G Anthony (eds), *Judges, Transition, and Human Rights* (Oxford, Oxford University Press).
Northern Ireland Courts and Tribunals Service (NICTS) (2010) 'Northern Ireland Courts and Tribunals Service Framework Document' (Belfast, NICTS).
Northern Ireland Legal Services Commission (2011) *Access to Justice Review Northern Ireland: The Report* (Belfast, NICTS).
—— (2013) 'Business Plan 2013–14' (Belfast, NICTS).
—— (2015) *Annual Report and Accounts for the Year Ended 31 March 2015*.
Paterson, A (1982) *The Law Lords* (London, Macmillan).
—— (2013) *Final Judgment: The Last Law Lords and the Supreme Court* (Oxford, Hart Publishing).

Paterson, A and Paterson, C (2012) 'Guarding the Guardians: Towards an Independent, Accountable and Diverse Senior Judiciary' (London, CentreForum).
Rackley, E (2013) 'Rethinking Judicial Diversity' in U Schultz and G Shaw (eds), *Gender and Judging* (Oxford, Hart Publishing).
Robertson, D (2010) *The Judge as Political Theorist: Contemporary Judicial Review* (Princeton, NJ, Princeton University Press).
Rock, P (1993) *The Social World of an English Crown Court: Witnesses and Professionals in the Crown Court Centre at Wood Green* (Oxford, Clarendon Press).
Ruddick, S (1990) *Maternal Thinking: Towards a Politics of Peace* (London, Women's Press).
Schultz, U and Shaw, G (eds) (2013) *Gender and Judging* (Oxford, Hart Publishing).
Straw, J (2013) *Aspects of Law Reform: An Insider's Perspective* (Cambridge, Cambridge University Press).
Sunstein, C (2001) *Designing Democracy: What Constitutions Do* (New York, Oxford University Press).
Teitel, R (2000) *Transitional Justice* (Oxford, Oxford University Press).
Thomas, C (2005) 'Judicial Diversity in the United Kingdom and Other Jurisdictions: A Review of Research, Policies and Practices' (London, Commission for Judicial Appointments).
—— (2013) *Decision-Making by the United Kingdom Supreme Court and the Judicial Committee of the Privy Council 2009–13* (London, UCL Judicial Institute).
Thornton, M (2007) '"Otherness" on the Bench: How Merit is Gendered' 29 *Sydney Law Review* 391.
Tushnet, M (2004) *The New Constitutional Order* (Princeton, NJ, Princeton University Press).
Venice Commission (2010) 'Report on the Independence of the Judicial System Part I: The Independence of Judges' (Venice, Venice Commission).

8

Judging and Conflict: Audience, Performance and the Judicial Past[1]

KIERAN McEVOY AND ALEX SCHWARTZ

> Neither I nor my brethren, much as I admire them all, are the heroes of this story. I am confident that our judicial brethren in England and Wales and in Scotland would cope equally well with our unusual problem if called upon. My object is simply to follow how the Courts have reacted to an extraordinary situation. For nearly eighteen years the Queen's Peace itself has had to meet in a part of her Kingdom a vigorous and continuous challenge, and the Queen's Justice had to be administered during that time without fear or favour.
>
> (Lord Lowry CJ 1986: 109)

> The Northern judiciary are seen by nationalists as being subservient to the needs of the Unionist parties. The large number of judges who owe their present positions to previous Unionist patronage confirms this view … the judiciary cannot now escape that increasing numbers of loyalists are now coming to share the view long held by nationalists that the judiciary are merely the legal arm of political power that lies outside these shores.
>
> (McDonough 1985: 10)

Introduction

In recent decades, the role of judges in periods of authoritarianism, conflict and political transition has attracted much scholarly interest (see, for example, Ginsburg and Moustafa 2008; Helmke and Rios-Figueroa 2011; Kapiszewski et al 2013). The waxing and waning of judicial autonomy, the complex contours of judicial acquiescence in human rights abuses, as well as sometimes courageous

[1] We are very grateful to the editors and Dr Hannah Quirk for invaluable comments on previous drafts of this chapter. We would also like to thank Rachel Rebouche and Louise Mallinder for their previous research assistance on the original project. This chapter is dedicated to the memory of Stephen Livingstone who remains much missed.

defences of the rule of law, are well discussed in the literature on judges in authoritarian, post-authoritarian or transitional regimes in Latin America (for example, Helmke 2005; Hilbink 2007), across sub-Saharan Africa (for example, Dyzenhaus 1998; Yusuf 2010; Ellet 2013), in Asia (for example, Ginsburg 2003), and throughout central and eastern Europe and the former Soviet Union (for example, Epstein et al, 2001; Sadurski 2005; Trochev 2008). Hard questions have also been asked about the role of the judiciary in established democracies (such as the United States, Israel and the United Kingdom) where significant human rights abuses have been perpetrated as part of broader counterterrorist strategies (for example, Pohman 2008; Mautner 2011; de Londras 2011, especially chapter 6). Although there are myriad differences between these different contexts, common and often overlapping themes emerge from this literature that resonate strongly with the Northern Ireland experience.

While our focus in this chapter is primarily historical, we would contend that decades of political violence in Northern Ireland are likely to have had an enduring effect on attitudes within the judiciary and patterns of judicial behaviour. By way of analogy, no one would suggest that one can hope to understand contemporary policing or imprisonment in Northern Ireland without a keen grasp of the history of the Royal Ulster Constabulary or the events in the Maze prison during the conflict.[2] In a similar vein, we would argue that one cannot properly 'judge the judges' (Dyzenhaus 1998) in the transition in Northern Ireland without a keen grasp of how they were shaped as legal actors by the previous years of violence and how they in turn helped shape understandings of the rule of law which have outlasted the violence.

Although commentators do not always agree in their appraisal of the record of Northern Ireland's judiciary during the conflict, much of the academic literature argues that the judiciary was often overly deferential to the state's counter-insurgency agenda, acquiescing to altered evidentiary standards in criminal prosecutions, detentions on the grounds of subjective suspicion (for example, Boyle et al 1980; Walsh 1983; Finn 1991; Dickson 1992; Morison and Livingstone 1995; Livingstone 2001; McColgan 2011) and, at least initially, the use of uncorroborated accomplice evidence in a series of controversial 'supergrass' trials (see Greer 1995). In particular, Korff (1984), Walker (1999) and others were highly critical of the willingness of 'Diplock' judges to accept evidence that had been extracted through the mistreatment of paramilitary suspects, with the judges often appearing to take the word of the police over the defendants that such injuries either had not occurred or, where there was medical evidence, that they had been self-inflicted. Nevertheless, Northern Ireland's judges were not unwaveringly pliant servants of the State (see Livingstone 2001). The judiciary was occasionally willing to impose significant common law constraints on the interpretation and application of emergency powers (see Dickson 1992; and Livingstone 2001). Furthermore, Northern

[2] See the respective chapters by Scraton and Topping on prisons and policing elsewhere in this collection.

Ireland's judges eventually rejected the tactic of supergrass prosecutions, both at the trial level and at the Court of Appeal, where all convictions based solely or primarily on supergrass evidence were eventually quashed (see Greer 1995). Accordingly, a more rounded account of judicial behaviour during the conflict should explain *both* the judiciary's deference to security imperatives *as well as* instances of judicial resistance to those imperatives.

The existing literature on the role of the judiciary during the Northern Ireland conflict has been based on a close reading of its published judgments. Given that Northern Ireland's judges were notoriously difficult for researchers to access during the conflict, scholars had little realistic alternative. While much of that literature is discussed below, given that we had access to primary interviews with Northern Ireland judges and judicial colleagues elsewhere, we chose not to replicate the close doctrinal reading of the case law which has been done well by others. Rather, building on the doctrinal work of previous scholars, our approach has been to draw on the local and comparative data and to try to make sense of it using the broader socio-legal literature on judicial performance, judicial audience and the judiciary as a focus of enquiry in transitional justice. The rationale for utilising these frameworks is outlined below.

Our arguments are informed in particular by interviews that McEvoy conducted (in collaboration with Livingstone and Rebouche) with a range of senior judicial and legal figures in Northern Ireland during 2002–03. The results of that research into the judiciary have never been published due to the untimely death of Professor Livingstone in 2004.[3] Despite the passage of time since Stephen Livingstone's death, in part as a way of marking his continued powerful influence on ourselves and legal scholarship more generally, we have been encouraged by colleagues to draw upon that fieldwork for this chapter.[4]

Although some elements of the fieldwork are over a decade old, given that the judiciary was being asked to 'reflect backwards' on conflict-related human rights (then 8–9 years after the first ceasefires), their comments arguably remain as relevant today and indeed may have been fresher then than they would be today. A total of 37 interviews were conducted with lawyers in Northern Ireland during that period, including 12 with senior judicial figures of the day. A number of the then lawyers interviewed have subsequently gone on to become judges.[5] All (with the exception of the then Director of Public Prosecutions, Sir Alistair Fraser and a number of his senior staff) were interviewed on condition of confidentiality and anonymity. Interviews were semi-structured, framed around key human rights and historical themes and usually lasted 1–2 hours. In common

[3] McEvoy and Rebouche (2007) and McEvoy (2011) have drawn upon some of that fieldwork in previous published work on lawyers in the jurisdiction.

[4] Although Stephen had begun to draft some of his preliminary views on the fieldwork, and he had published previously on the judiciary in Northern Ireland, we of course make no claims that he would have agreed with our findings in this chapter.

[5] McEvoy conducted a further 14 interviews with lawyers in Northern Ireland between 2008 and 2010, but none with judges during that period.

with much research into the judiciary and legal profession, a 'purposeful sampling' methodology (Creswell 2013) was deployed where interviewees were chosen using a range of criteria including professional seniority, experience of working on conflict or human rights related cases or knowledge and experience of debates within the legal community. An initial 'wish list' of key interviewees was drawn up, these were written to, and after some negotiation almost all agreed to be interviewed. Once fieldwork was commenced, others were recruited using 'snowball' referrals to professional friends and colleagues. All of the judges interviewed were senior, ie, members of the High Court and above.

The original Northern Ireland component of the research was also supplemented by comparative fieldwork involving interviews with senior judicial figures and legal figures in the United States, Canada, South Africa, Britain and the Republic of Ireland in 2002–03. A total of 57 interviews were conducted in the comparative fieldwork including with judges of the Supreme Courts of the United States, Canada, South Africa, the Republic of Ireland, Scotland and the then House of Lords in England some of which are referred to below.[6] Finally in 2014, as part of another comparative project on lawyers, McEvoy conducted a total of 22 interviews with senior legal and judicial figures in South Africa. Given the prominence of South Africa as a site wherein a truth recovery body has attempted to engage with the past performance of the judiciary, and the close mutual interest in both jurisdictions by leading jurists, some of that data is also referred to below.[7]

Audience and Performance

Judges are not like Darwin's Galapagos finches (Darwin 1859); they are aware that they are being observed, perhaps even studied, and they are likely to have strong preferences about how their behaviour is interpreted, preferences which may motivate them to 'perform' for the benefit of certain key 'audiences' (see generally Baum 2006). Given the 'performativity' of judicial decision-making, both in how trials are conducted and in how judicial reasoning is recorded and disseminated, it is not surprising then that scholars have been interested in the themes of judicial audience and performance. Summarising for the sake of brevity, much of this literature speaks to the various audiences judges perform *to* or *for* and how a concern for reputation or esteem among these audiences, both at the individual level and on a corporate-institutional basis, may influence judicial behaviour (see Miceli and Cosgel 1994; Schauer 1999; Baum 2006; Garoupa and Ginsburg 2008). Although this literature is often sociological, or 'socio-psychological' in

[6] Grant Reference, *Judges, Human Rights and Political Change*, Atlantic Philanthropies, 2002–04.

[7] Grant Reference, *Lawyers Conflict and Transition*, Economic and Social Research Council, 2013–16, ES/J009849/1.

style (for example, Baum 2006), some of it also adopts the lens of 'rational choice' more familiar in political science and economics (for example, Posner 1993; and Garoupa and Ginsburg 2008).[8] As Garoupa and Ginsburg explain:

> Whatever it is that judges seek to maximize, their ability to do so depends on certain audiences that react to their decisions: the media, politicians, lawyers and law professors, and the public itself ... Through their decisions and actions, judges acquire a reputation with different audiences. A judge with a good reputation will enjoy the esteem of his friends and colleagues, and may be able to advance to a higher court; a judge with a bad reputation with colleagues is less likely to have significant career advancements. A judge with a good reputation with the media will have more opportunities for exposure ... Individual reputation with different audiences goes side by side with group or collective reputation (2008: 452–53).

In addition to these instrumental or strategic 'pay-offs', the pursuit of judicial esteem and reputation is also bound up with social relations and social status. Constructing and maintaining professional and personal esteem and a sense of professional legitimacy is a fundamentally social process which requires validation from others (Johnson et al 2006). Dating at least to Goffman's classic *The Presentation of Self in Everyday Life*, much of the literature on such matters inevitably focuses on what Goffman (1959: xi) referred to as the 'theatrical' and the 'dramaturgical' (1959: xi) which, as was noted above, lends itself well to an analysis of the judiciary. However, there is more to this notion of performance than simply the more obvious dramatic aspects of the judicial function.

Borrowing insights from this social psychology literature, Baum observes that judges, like people in general, presumably want to be liked by other people, especially by those with whom they share salient social identities (Baum 2006: chapter 2). He argues then that judges, like all of us, engage in acts of 'self-presentation' (or 'impression management') in the attempt to project a desirable image of themselves (Baum 2006: 32–39; see also Posner 1993). Such acts might range from stylistic flourishes in a written decision, to deciding the final outcome of a case one way or the other for the benefit of one audience or another.

Naturally, the broadest possible audience for acts of judicial self-presentation is the public at large. Of course judges are acutely aware that sometimes the job

[8] There is a more evaluative and managerial sense of judicial 'performance', referred to in the literature on Judicial Performance and Evaluation (JPE). This (largely US) literature originally emerged in States where judges are directly elected by the public and is used to inform the public on a particular judge's record in office when seeking re-election. JPE programmes vary but in general they are process rather than outcome-focused and tend to concentrate on issues such as: case management and efficiency; whether cases were decided on the basis of established facts and applicable law; clarity of explanations and exhibiting proper courtroom demeanour. Judges are typically evaluated by an independent commission consisting both of lawyers and non-lawyers, and such commissions survey lawyers, jurors and others who have interacted with the judge in a professional setting (see Kourlis and Singer 2008 for an overview). While such an evaluative approach is interesting, needless to say, no such regular surveys were conducted amongst the legal community or public concerning the Northern Ireland judiciary during the period under review, and thus our notion of performance is sociological, socio-psychological and political.

requires them to take unpopular decisions with the public, so beyond a general desire for public approval, judges may have special regard to certain 'reference groups' whose esteem is particularly important to them. By way of illustration, in some contexts, such reference groups might include politicians, important media outlets, legal professionals, legal academics, and other influence formers (see Baum 2006: chapter 4).

The themes of judicial audience and performance are especially relevant in the case of Northern Ireland. For example, the judges who presided over high profile Diplock trials for the most serious of offences were involved in the performance of what Lawrence Douglas (2001: 114) has termed a dual spectacle of legality and self-legitimation. As McEvoy (2000) has previously explored, these trials (and related legal actions such as civil suits or conflict-related judicial reviews) were intense and high stakes legal dramas where, in cases involving republicans at least, the legitimacy of the state itself was being challenged by the defendants or litigants. Despite the ritual judicial insistence that such events were simply proof positive that law was running its course (for further detailed discussion see Boyle et al 1980; Jackson and Doran 1995), these were intense sites of both legal and political drama with the judges inevitably given a starring role. More broadly, as we have argued above, the ways in which judges performed their role beyond the court—shaped as these were by the realities of the security situation and other factors—created powerful norms and values about what it meant to be a judge and how judges imagined certain audiences which continue to have relevance in the transition.

In what follows, we consider several possible audiences for acts of judicial performance during the conflict with a view to setting an agenda for future research. Having reviewed the secondary literature and our own interview data, we argue that Northern Ireland judges were, for a mix of socio-psychological and rational-strategic reasons, performing to at least three key audiences during the Northern Ireland conflict. These were: (i) *Parliament*—or as it was often expressed to us, the 'Will of Parliament'; (ii) *the public*—broadly understood as those who supported the rule of law and did not endorse political violence; and (iii) *other judges*—both in Britain and on the bench in Northern Ireland.

Performing for Parliament

Broadly speaking, the comparative literature on courts and judicial behaviour identifies several possible threats to the judiciary from the 'political' branches of government (see Ginsburg 2003). The first is non-compliance: unwelcome judicial decisions may simply be ignored. The second is override: branches of government can attempt to annul or reverse an unwelcome decision by passing new legislation, making fresh appointments to 'pack' the court with more docile judges, or, in more extreme cases, actually amending the constitution. The third is retaliation: the judiciary can be 'punished' by freezing salaries and funding, by suspending the court, or by impeaching individual judges. It should be obvious that judges will generally wish to avoid any of these consequences; non-compliance and override undermine the relative authority of judges (perhaps even making a mockery of them) while retaliation may directly impact a judge's resources and job security (Ginsburg 2003).

Scholars have marshalled compelling evidence to suggest that such threats sometimes induce strategic judicial behaviour, whereby judges moderate or adjust their decision-making in *anticipation* of the expected responses of other actors or institutions. Strategic decision-making may help account for patterns of judicial behaviour in contexts as diverse as Argentina (Helmke 2005), Germany (Vanberg 2005), Russia (Epstein et al, 2011), Taiwan (Ginsburg 2003), the United States (Epstein and Knight 1998) and even at the European Court of Justice (Carrubba et al 2008). Naturally, the immediacy or plausibility of any of the above noted threats varies by context. Political and institutional differences make legislative override more feasible in some systems than others (see Ferejohn et al 2007; and Cooter and Ginsburg 1996) and diffuse popular support for the courts may, in some contexts, rule out the possibility of direct retaliation against the courts (see Vanberg 2005).

Clearly, not every possible threat to the judiciary would have been equally credible in the case of Northern Ireland during the conflict. First, unlike in most jurisdictions, Northern Ireland's judges did not have to be conscious of locally elected politicians as a particularly significant judicial audience, at least not for much of the conflict. Bearing in mind the facts of 'direct rule' from Westminster from 1972 until December 1999 and that local councillors had only minimal responsibilities for 'drains, bins, graves and sports centres' (Morison and Livingstone 1995: 160), in reality Westminster served as the locus of political power to which judges would have addressed themselves. Thus, instead of having to 'perform' for the discordant and divided audience of locally elected politicians, judges could focus their attention on heeding a more abstract (and relatively remote) 'Will of Parliament'.

Second, unlike in other conflicted societies, judges in Northern Ireland would have had little fear of direct retaliation by political branches for unwelcome decisions. Much like their counterparts in Great Britain, Northern Ireland's judges have historically enjoyed a great deal of formal independence. Although, the process of appointment to the bench was (until recently) more 'political', judges in Northern Ireland have no fear of being impeached or seeing their salaries reduced or frozen in response to their decisions (see Dickson 2013: 79–92). Furthermore, neither Stormont nor Westminster has tried (at least not to our knowledge) to 'pack' the courts with more reliably pliant judges. In short, the threat of 'court curbing' that hangs over the heads of the judiciary in many other parts of the world is virtually unknown in Northern Ireland, leaving the judges comparatively free from the usual pressures that might induce strategic deference to other branches of government (on 'court curbing' and judicial independence, see Epstein et al 2001; Ginsburg 2003; Helmke 2005; Chavez et al 2011).

Although threats of non-compliance and retaliation were substantially mitigated by the political context, the threat of 'override' from Parliament was arguably more tangible. The doctrine of parliamentary sovereignty and the absence of an entrenched Bill of Rights allowed Parliament to reverse or revise unwelcome judicial decisions with relative ease. Indeed, we know of at least one example of such a reaction. In passing the Northern Ireland (Emergency Provisions) Act 1973, Parliament overruled the Northern Ireland courts' more demanding approach to confession evidence, attempting to limit judicial discretion by legislating for the admission of confession evidence, unless the evidence in question was shown to be obtained by torture or inhuman or degrading treatment. Later, when the Court of Appeal attempted to preserve its discretion to exclude confessions which were strictly permissible under the revised statutory guidance, judicial nervousness at 'subverting the will of Parliament' was palpable in a number of high profile cases.[9] As John Jackson (2009: 22) has detailed, while they recognised that they retained such a discretion to exclude such confessions, the judges were 'consistently reluctant to give this much scope in view of the need to adhere to the will of Parliament'.

Our data chimes with the analysis of the relevant Northern Ireland case law by Jackson (2009), Dickson (2006), Livingstone (1994) and others. Notwithstanding their relative *power* with regard to the state, it is clear from the interviews conducted that where the state had legislated clearly and explicitly to abrogate established rule of law protections, the judges by and large appeared unwilling to go against the perceived 'Will of Parliament'. As one judge discussed in speaking about the relationship with Parliament more generally:

> I think we were all concerned both in our training and in our judicial viewpoints, always concerned about not trespassing into political fields in areas where there is democratic mechanism for determining matters of policy … judges were reluctant to take on the role of the policy makers in areas where Parliament has seen fit to enact legislation or pursue policies.[10]

Performing for 'the Public'

With regard to 'the public' as an audience for judicial performance, the nuances in Northern Ireland during the conflict are potentially even more intriguing. Research from elsewhere suggests that judges may have narrow instrumental reasons for bearing the views of the public in mind (for example, elected judges whose sentencing patterns may be featured in re-election campaigns) but also, at a broader strategic level, maintaining diffuse public support for the judiciary is often viewed by judges themselves as vital to retaining the legitimacy and independence of the judiciary as an institution (see Gibson et al 2003; Bingham 2010; see also Vanberg 2005; Staton 2010). Furthermore, a key feature of the 'judges and the public'

[9] See, eg, *R v Tohill* [1974] NIJB (Mar); *R v McCormick* [1977] NI 105.

[10] Interview senior Northern Ireland judge, 5 December 2002.

literature is its focus on the fact that judges work and live in the communities which they serve as a way of keeping judges 'grounded'. For example, even in the more well-heeled communities in which judges inevitably live, Peltason (1971) has provided fascinating detail about the social and political pressures faced by Southern judges in the United States as they ruled on controversial civil rights matters.[11] In the case of Northern Ireland, the political context of the conflict had (at least) two important consequences for the judiciary's relationship with its public audience. First, the realities of the security context had a direct effect on the material relations between judges and the community and (we would argue), on the ways in which the judicial notion of the public was conceived. Thus, the ways in which Northern Ireland's judges could practically engage with the public were heavily circumscribed. Second, the importance that judges typically ascribe to projecting a neutral or apolitical image to the public was undoubtedly heightened by the divided and often sectarian nature of society in Northern Ireland.

The personal consequences for serving as a judge during the Northern Ireland conflict should not be underestimated. At least 18 republican paramilitary attacks were carried out against the judiciary during the conflict, resulting in the murders of two magistrates, two county court judges, and Gibson LJ and his wife (discussed further below, see Blair 2000: 29). Judges were (and indeed some still are) assigned 24-hour security protection by the police, restrictions were necessarily placed upon their movements and social habits, and their families were inevitably affected by the realities of being constantly under threat. The attendant anxieties came out in the interviews:

> I think it is very hard on families. Since we are all men, well on the High Court I mean, I would say wives are the people who have the hardest time because they have security all day.[12]

> It is particularly difficult for my wife I think because of the restrictions that there are on your movements. She finds that she can't go out and about as she would like without someone being around. There are restrictions of course on you going to regular places at particular times and so on—that is quite a strain.[13]

[11] As noted above, McEvoy (with Rebouche) also conducted interviews with senior judges in South Africa, Canada, Britain, the Republic of Ireland and the United States. In one instructive US interview, with legendary Federal Judge William Wayne Justice (who implemented some of the key civil rights changes introduced by the Kennedy and Johnson Administrations in Texas), Judge Justice described the social consequence of his decision-making thus: 'Well, my troubles weren't nearly as severe as some … it affected my family. The women in beauty parlours would not take care of my wife's hair, she ended up with long hair down to her waist [laughs] and she had to go back to our little hometown 35 miles away to get her hair done. I was having some work done on my new home that I'd bought, when the carpenters and bricklayers found out who they were working for they left. I also got many hateful calls on the phone and threats and so on but I ignored them. I'm not trying to be brave, that wasn't what my purpose was, I just didn't want to have a life where I had to have guards all the time. My view was if somebody wants to give you a lickin', it doesn't make any difference how many guards you got around you' (interview, 13 May 2003). Judge Justice agreed to have his anonymity waived.

[12] Interview senior Northern Ireland judge, 13 December 2002.

[13] Interview senior Northern Ireland judge, 23 April 2003.

> It hasn't perhaps borne in on me as much as it has on some of my colleagues … we have people [police officers] who live in the house, not in the house but in the garden all the time. I don't find it obtrusive because I've sort of got used to, although other colleagues find it absolutely suffocating.[14]

> One can't just decide to drop down into town and meet somebody outside the Opera House, and go and have a drink, and go to the performance, and maybe go and have supper afterwards with half a dozen of your old friends, it's not as easy as that.[15]

While no one would dispute the inevitable personal and familial challenges of the security context, the key issues for current purposes is what impact (if any) the enforced isolation from aspects of normal community life had upon the judges' performance of their duties on the bench. One senior lawyer, himself now a judge, suggested a number of subtle ways in which the security context may have influenced some judges at the height of the conflict. His detailed reasoning is worth including in full:

> Well there were indirect threats, there were direct threats and people had their families, judges' families, relatives and friends getting murdered. So firstly it was a very real threat. Now the effect, I think there were direct effects and there were indirect effects and the indirect effects were probably the more dangerous of the two. The direct effects obviously were the surrounding the judges in cotton wool, policemen appearing everywhere with them, on social occasions, at golf clubs etc … I would not like to think that these would have a direct impact on the judge except obviously he was being kept out of an ordinary normal culture. They just were not mixing with normal people and they weren't living a normal everyday life. The indirect effects I would say is that certain judges started to show degrees of paranoia. It began to affect them I think. I think there are some judgments, particularly away back in the supergrass days, at the height of the terrorist threat, in which you can say judges were clearly being influenced. I am not saying that judges were being got at in the popular sense that people were being influenced by nameless people rushing in and out of their rooms but I think mentally many of them and many of their judgments paid the penalty.[16]

Certainly some judges themselves expressed concern about precisely the dangers of their enforced social isolation because of the security threat:

> [W]hat worries me about it is getting isolated, so when I am out of here I always travel on buses and trains. I like it when you can go round talking to people. And I think that is the danger, that judges will be in this sort of a cocoon.[17]

> I've always taken the view, I don't want to know about any security threats to me, I don't want to know if I've been identified in documents or anything like that, unless I have to. I've also recognised right from the start that there's a real danger of becoming institutionalised in this security.[18]

[14] Interview senior Northern Ireland judge, 9 December 2002.
[15] Interview senior Northern Ireland judge, 8 October 2002.
[16] Interview senior Northern Ireland lawyer, now a judge, 25 November 2002.
[17] Interview senior Northern Ireland judge, 13 December 2002.
[18] Interview senior Northern Ireland judge, 9 December 2002.

Judicial sensitivity to the perceived dangers of social isolation and proximity to (and reliance upon) the security forces for protection were of course allied in the Northern Ireland context to the importance of the community background of the judiciary. While to this day the community backgrounds of judges are still not published, in practice in a place where the skills of what Shirlow (2001: 72) has termed 'ethnic cognition' are well honed, discerning such information is fairly straightforward. In the early 1970s the Protestant and unionist background of the majority of the judiciary was an issue of long-standing concern (Boyle et al 1975).[19] In reviewing the research conducted from the 1970s, 1980s, 1990s (for example, Boyle et al 1980; Walsh 1983; Greer 1995; Jackson and Doran 1995), broadly, there is no compelling evidence of systematic unionist bias on the part of the judges in the Diplock system (for example, of pro-loyalist/anti-republican sentencing patterns), notwithstanding that such bias was a staple of republican discourses throughout the period.[20] By the late 1980s and early 1990s, as Jackson and Doran note, 'in recent years the composition of the bench has been brought more into line with the balance of religious persuasion in society' (1995: 30). Nevertheless, regardless of the actual religious make-up of the judiciary, community background was an issue about which the judges were sensitive. Thus, according to one judge, judges in Northern Ireland should take special care to explain and emphasise the ostensibly legal basis for their decisions, so as to prevent any accusation of political bias:

> Because there's so many things in this society, somebody would be bound to say, 'oh he would say that, wouldn't he, look where he comes from', and if you're going for good judicial reasons the way that people say, 'well that's his background, he's bound to say that', you want to make sure that you have expressed the proper reasons, the judicial reasons, and sometimes it's quite hard to get it across.[21]

[19] As Boyle et al note, of 20 High Court judges appointed since the formation of the state, 15 had been openly associated with the Unionist Party, two of the three judges in the Northern Ireland Court of Appeal were ex-Attorneys General in Unionist Governments, one of the four High Court judges was likewise an ex-Attorney General and another the son of a unionist Attorney General (1975: 11). Hadden and Hillyard further note that while a convention had emerged to ensure that at least one senior judge was Catholic, such judges were widely seen by nationalists as 'Castle Catholics, more likely than not to support the government which had promoted them' (1973: 11). This was a view echoed by one lawyer interviewed, himself now a judge: 'At the start of the Troubles the bench was predominantly Protestant. This changed and all levels of the judiciary now seem to reflect a religious balance comparable to the population. The reality was, though, that appointments were establishment Catholics who turned out to be more right wing than the Protestant judges. Protestant judges didn't have anything to prove' (interview, 20 November 2002). 'Castle Catholics' is a derogatory term for Catholic unionists who are deemed 'loyal' to the unionist political cause.

[20] McEvoy (2001) and with Shirlow (2008) has conducted over 200 interviews with former republican and loyalist activists and almost universally republicans assert this belief. Boyle et al (1980) and Walsh (1983) both point to some evidence of disparities in charging by the Director of Public Prosecutions at the lower end of the spectrum of offences (ie, Protestants being charged with lesser offences than Catholics) but provide no detailed findings on discriminatory sentencing patterns by judges. As with this chapter, only a large and detailed study of cases over a lengthy period of the conflict could actually provide definitive information as to whether such bias was in fact a feature of the conflict with regard to republicans and loyalists.

[21] Interview senior Northern Ireland judge, 8 October 2002.

In a similar vein, another judge expressed the view that judicial decisions should be purposively tailored for the benefit of audiences in the public and the media, so that 'the public listening and the press noting can see as clearly as possible where your reasons are without having to go away and dig for it and they don't always'.[22] He went on to confess that he sometimes included a special paragraph at the end of his judgments—particularly in 'political' cases—in which he took care to explain how the case was decided within what he termed the four corners of the proper judicial role.[23] In a similar vein, another judge echoed the need to be conscious of how the press would report judicial decisions to the public. Thus, to his mind, judges should write clear and careful reasons that discourage the press from reducing complex legal issues to simplified 'banner headlines'.[24]

For some judges, the cumulative effect of the security situation and the politically charged nature of many of the conflict-related cases appeared to encourage a very cautious view of the judicial role beyond the courtroom. Taken as read, the fact that judges cannot comment on cases which may come before them, senior judges interviewed for the comparative part of this project were clear that measured engagement in public debates about human rights and the rule of law was actually a key part of the judicial educative function.[25] However, the opposite was the case in the Northern Ireland context. While judges did of course give public lectures in both Northern Ireland and Britain, there was a discernible aversion to judicial engagement during the conflict with the public through lectures, media and the usual ways in which judges seek to 'reach' the public other than through their judgments. One judge was adamant that the judiciary ought to avoid being seen to pursue 'a particular political agenda', that they should be 'very, very careful' to avoid being identified with any particular political view and, consequently, should refrain from expressing their views in public.[26] The same judge even cautioned against judges participating in consultation processes in which they would be required to voice opinions on matters of legal reform.[27] Another judge said the judiciary should largely refrain from participating in public debates less it

[22] ibid.

[23] ibid.

[24] Interview senior Northern Ireland judge, 9 December 2002. These views are echoed by Lord Lowry, former Chief Justice, when he wrote that Northern Ireland judges need to be aware that their judgments would be scrutinised not only by the appellate courts, but also potentially by 'well-informed and possibly hostile critics' (Lowry 1992: 131).

[25] eg, interviews with US Supreme Court Justice Ruth Ginsberg, 19 December 2002; US Supreme Court Justice Sandra Day O'Connor, 7 November 2012; Chief Justice of the Supreme Court of Canada, Beverly McLachlin, 20 June 2002; Justice Claire L'Heureux-Dubé of the Supreme Court of Canada, 19 June 2002. As the then Lord Chief Justice of England and Wales Lord Woolf CJ summed up: 'the judgment has got to be the explanation and I don't believe that you should start and discuss those. However, discussing issues generally and explaining the law, it's really important on human rights issues to get across that the difficult decisions are really important ones and they're usually very unpopular ones and these are the things that I think, we've got to explain, it's part of the job' (interview, 30 October 2002). Lord Woolf and the other judges mentioned in this footnote all waived their right to anonymity.

[26] Interview senior Northern Ireland judge, 5 December 2002.

[27] ibid.

impugn judicial independence.[28] In a similar vein, another judge explicitly identified public appearances and statements as presenting a danger to the judiciary's esteem among the public.[29] In light of what he called the 'undemocratic position' of judges, he reasoned that the judiciary is 'probably not very highly regarded at all but … would be less so if [they] exposed [themselves] too much'.[30]

In short, the version of the public which appears to have been imagined by the Northern Ireland judiciary was one which was, perhaps inevitably, socially and politically shaped by the contours of the conflict and the divided society in which they lived and worked. Although references to 'right thinking' people in Northern Ireland are replete in judgments throughout the conflict[31]—a term apparently deployed as being synonymous with an opposition to political violence and support for the rule of law—in reality significant elements of the public did not fit into such palatable categories. Once Sinn Féin began to contest elections in the early 1980s, its electoral support was to remain steady at approximately one-third of the nationalist community (Feeney 2003). While loyalist paramilitary organisations or their political counterparts never enjoyed such support in the unionist community, attitudes towards state violence were much more ambiguous with the two main unionist parties (the Ulster Unionist Party and the Democratic Unionist Party) constantly calling for ever more vigorous security policies including the use of the supergrass system and 'shooting to kill' republican paramilitary suspects (Graham 1983; Robinson et al 1984). Mindful of the security risks posed by normal social interaction and consequently isolated for their own protection, conscious that their public pronouncements would inevitably be read through the competing narratives of the conflict, the realities of relations with the public for judges during the Northern Ireland conflict and their performance for same often appeared to be one shaped by wariness, distrust and suspicion.

Performing for Peers

Finally, the third key audience to whom judges appeared to be performing during the Northern Ireland conflict was the judiciary itself. As Baum (2006: 103–04) points out, over and above esteem among regular lawyers, judges are likely to ascribe special value to the opinions of other judges. Judges will have similar educational backgrounds and similar professional experiences and, perhaps most importantly, share in the prestige of occupying a special position within an already

[28] Interview senior Northern Ireland judge, 9 December 2002.

[29] Interview senior Northern Ireland judge, 13 December 2002.

[30] ibid.

[31] See, eg, *R v Shaw and Another* [1989] unreported (Hart J) The case involved a petrol bomb attack on the home of a police officer. 'The police are in the front line in the struggle against terrorism in Northern Ireland and like members of the Regular Army and the Ulster Defence Regiment they are constantly exposed by virtue of their duties to the risk of grave injury and death. They are entitled when this kind of offence occurs to look to the courts to show the disgust which right thinking members of the community must show for this type of cowardly and despicable behaviour'.

high status profession. In short, being a judge is a conspicuous part of social identity and so the approval of other judges is of course important to the individual judge's sense of self-worth.

In a small jurisdiction, particularly during the conflict, the decision to become a judge inevitably involved some degree of personal and professional isolation. A number of the judges interviewed spoke explicitly about the realities of the isolation of being on the bench, how this was so markedly different from being at the Bar, and how in effect the judges themselves became a small community within the broader legal system:

> Yes, it's very different. It took about a year actually to get accustomed to it because if you've been in the Bar Library, there's such a buzz in the Bar Library, there's 500 people working in there, scampering round every day and coming out in the hall and trying to get everything organised and you are plucked out of that *torrent*. So it's a very quiet and solitary life by comparison, it's quite a transformation ... Certainly one's judicial colleagues become an important source of support.[32]

> There's a dramatic change in lifestyle, I mean you go from ordinary daily practice in the Bar Library to the rare upright atmosphere of the back corridor which is physically quite different and emotionally quite different from practice at the Bar and then you've got changes in lifestyle, the security situation and all of us [judges] are in the same boat.[33]

> It was very lonely at first, after the gregarious life at the Bar and when I came first we used to sit in our own rooms having lunch on our own ... Now if we can we [the judges] will have lunch or a coffee together, have a chat and so forth—and its actually really quite good ... and you hear ... 'I've got a case like that', sure I did that last week and so on.[34]

The understandable urge towards the human collegiality amongst one's peers is common amongst judges everywhere. This impulse is both social and professional—a desire to be respected and esteemed by other judges with whom one works on a frequent or daily basis (see Baum 2006: 53–57; and Edwards 2003). Being seen as technically and legally skilled by one's peers—what Posner (1993) has termed 'professional pride' within the prevailing standards of their profession—is a key part of the judicial socialisation process. Because of their professional proximity and the degree of specialism involved in their job, judges are particularly well positioned to evaluate one another's performance (Baum 2006). Of course these motivators—collegiality and professional pride—will not always be in harmony. While a judge might be motivated by professional pride to write clever and creative decisions, he or she might also jeopardise collegiality amongst colleagues if those opinions stray too far from established doctrine or if, at the appellate level, he or she dissents too frequently (see Epstein et al 2011). Thus, especially when one considers the relatively small size of the Northern Ireland bench, one might broadly expect acts of

[32] Interview senior Northern Ireland judge, 23 April 2003.
[33] Interview senior Northern Ireland judge, 5 December 2002.
[34] Interview senior Northern Ireland judge, 13 December 2002.

judicial self-presentation intended for an intra-court audience to have a generally conservative flavour, eschewing radical new interpretations in favour of consensus and well worn doctrinal tropes.

At one level, this notion of judges in a small community which was undergoing a prolonged and brutal period of political violence, performing the judicial function in a way which resonated with the mores and values of their colleagues is perhaps unsurprising. However, judges were also of course aware that their judicial performance was open to scrutiny by judicial colleagues elsewhere, particularly in Britain. Throughout the conflict, the House of Lords remained the final appellate court in the United Kingdom for decisions made in Northern Ireland courts. As Livingstone notes writing in 1994 (the year of the ceasefire declarations), at that time only 13 conflict-related cases had actually been appealed to the House of Lords from Northern Ireland. Indeed, in reviewing those cases, Livingstone concludes that they point to a lack of judicial willingness (on the part of the House of Lords) to engage with the human rights aspects of the Northern Ireland conflict and that in fact the Northern Ireland Court of Appeal had been more effective in upholding human rights standards.[35] In sum, therefore, any notion that the 'fear' of the highest appellate court looking over the shoulder of the Northern Ireland judges could have shaped judicial performance would appear largely misplaced. Still, the relevance of such a judicial audience should not be rejected entirely. As noted above, the notion of judicial performance is broader than simply focusing on the formal mechanisms for review by an appellate court. The example of changing judicial attitudes to the use of supergrass evidence in Northern Ireland is instructive.

During the early 1980s, over 500 paramilitary suspects were charged on the basis of evidence from 27 so-called 'supergrasses' (Bonner 1988). Often the charges laid were based exclusively on the evidence provided by these 'cooperating witnesses'—in practice, usually paramilitary suspects or in some cases state agents who were giving evidence in return for promised immunity and resettlement by the state (Hillyard and Percy-Smith 1984; Jackson 1985). Despite their initial acceptance of the tactic, the courts in Northern Ireland, at both trial and appellate levels, began

[35] 'The members of the House of Lords have seen Northern Ireland over the past twenty-five years as essentially a dangerous place where a fragile social order is maintained by security forces stretched to the limit. In order to maintain that order, these security forces are to be accorded wide powers and should be largely relieved from the burden of judicial supervision ... In an emergency situation the role of the judiciary is to scrutinise more closely both the nature and operation of such powers, in order to ensure that citizens' rights are only derogated from to the extent clearly mandated by Parliament ... [this is] A perspective grasped by some of Northern Ireland's judges who live closer to the conflict and are themselves under constant threat from that dangerous society the decisions of the House of Lords portray' (Livingstone 1994: 351). In his follow-up article reviewing post-1994 Northern Ireland cases at the House of Lords, Dickson largely agrees with Livingstone's conclusions although he does argue that in the cases since the ceasefires, the House of Lords has 'begun to demonstrate that they appreciate the historical and political background to the conflict-related cases brought to them from Northern Ireland' and have shown a 'freshness and sophistication' that was not apparent during the conflict (Dickson 2006: 414).

to subject uncorroborated accomplice evidence to much more exacting standards, so that by the mid-1980s, achieving a conviction in such cases became virtually impossible. As noted above, ultimately, all convictions based on the uncorroborated evidence of supergrass informants were overturned on appeal and no new supergrass trials were initiated between 1986 and the ceasefires in 1994 (Greer 1995).[36]

In his extensive study of the rise and fall of the supergrass trials in Northern Ireland, Stephen Greer examines the factors which ultimately appeared to prod the judicial conscience sufficiently to reject the evidence of the supergrasses. Greer accepts the argument, presented by many judges themselves, that the judges became increasingly uneasy that they were in effect becoming complicit in the efforts by the government and the police to take large numbers of individuals off the streets without having sufficient robust evidence to properly convict them—a shift from guilt beyond a reasonable doubt to 'probable guilt' (Greer 1995: 111).[37] Significantly for our current purposes, Greer suggests that the growing judicial unease at the use of supergrasses in Northern Ireland was probably influenced by a highly critical report on the phenomenon authored by Labour peer Lord Anthony Gifford QC (Gifford 1985). Gifford's report was launched in a press conference in the House of Lords. Unlike many of the critical human rights reports on the supergrass system which had been aimed largely, although not exclusively, at an international audience, this report by a prominent British lawyer outlined a series of trenchant and largely legalistic criticisms in a carefully measured and neutral tone, and in particular, invited lawyers and judges 'on the mainland' to conclude that in handling the supergrass issue, the Diplock courts had behaved in a way that could not be justified by reference to traditional common law standards of fairness and due process (Greer 1995: 114). As Greer notes, this central argument was eventually subtly endorsed by the Northern Ireland Court of Appeal by judges who had themselves previously convicted on similar uncorroborated supergrass evidence (Greer 1995: 174). Several of the prominent lawyers interviewed for this research concurred. As one veteran human rights lawyer summed up:

> Gifford's report was crucial in changing the mood music. He is a respectable peer and a prominent human rights lawyer. He wasn't just some mad lefty or some Irish American that could be easily dismissed as a Brit basher … I know for a fact because I was there that the report started getting discussed at conferences in England at which our judges were

[36] In 2012 a new so-called 'supergrass trial' of 12 suspected Ulster Volunteer Force (UVF) members also collapsed when Mr Justice Gillen described the evidence from the two principle witnesses as 'so flawed and unreliable' that it could not be safely relied upon to convict the accused in the murder of Ulster Defence Association (UDA) member Thomas Little. See *R v Haddock* [2012] NICC 5.

[37] As one QC, now a senior judge, described to one of the authors: 'the supergrass cases may not have created a great deal of public confidence. However, the judges showed that they weren't there just to be messed about and do the Executive's business, that they were going to apply it [the rule of law] as they saw it and that they weren't going to be party to a type of judicial internment' (interview, 28 February 2003).

> also attending and in sensible and well-reasoned way, taking apart all that was wrong with the supergrass system. It made them very uncomfortable, looking bad in front of judges across the water, they simply couldn't ignore it.[38]

To recapitulate, we have argued here that it is useful to consider the notions of performance and audience in order to better understand the behaviour of judges during the conflict. In particular, we believe that the judges were 'performing' to at least three audiences—*Parliament*, *the public* and *fellow judges*. In the case of both Parliament and the public, these audiences were socially and politically constructed or 'imagined' by the judiciary. When allied to the notion of the judicial performance for fellow judges, the cumulative effect was, in our view, to contribute to a conservative judicial culture—what Dickson (1992: 142) has described as a 'pro-establishment attitude'—a world view which, as Dickson rightly points out, hardly distinguishes them from judges in other jurisdictions.

As we have made clear throughout, we do not take the view that judges in Northern Ireland were slavishly subservient to the desires of the Executive, or that they never 'did the right thing' in terms of protecting human rights or upholding the rule of law. We have also explicitly recognised the very real dangers faced by judges and the price paid by some of them and their families as a result of their decision to serve on the bench. That said, as with other aspects of civic and political life in Northern Ireland, we believe that there is a strong case to explore in a more structured fashion the role played by the judiciary during the conflict with a view to extracting what lessons may be learned both for the future of this jurisdiction and also more broadly for judges facing similar pressures and dilemmas in other justice systems 'under pressure'. This is the theme that we address in our concluding section below.

Conclusion: Judging and the Past?

The final part of this chapter explores the complex issue of whether and how the role of judges during the Northern Ireland conflict might be addressed as part of broader efforts to deal with the past. In particular, we are interested in the potential to examine the role of judges not simply as arbiters of the past who are deemed axiomatically to be 'above the fray' (for example, in chairing judge-led inquiries or commissions), but also as actors in an institution which was itself an important part of the conflict and transition. In addressing this question, two comments from the fieldwork for this project are instructive. The first anonymous quote is from one of Northern Ireland's most distinguished judges when asked if he would be in favour of a truth commission; the second is from the man he cites, Judge Albi Sachs.

[38] Interview Northern Ireland solicitor, 11 October 2004.

> I would talk to Albi Sachs about that because he could persuade me to do anything. He is pretty persuasive! ... If you had your wife or husband killed, you don't know who did it or why they did it or what is the explanation for it. Surely it is helpful to actually know ... However, on balance, I am probably slightly against it because I think where would we then go? Where would you begin? Where would you end? ... Inquiries do not always provide universal satisfaction no matter how hard you try.[39]

> The criticism of our truth process was it was dominated by the Church, by Desmond Tutu with a strong emphasis on forgiveness rather than lawyers. Another criticism from the conservative side is that it wasn't lawyerly enough, in terms of deposits, interventions when people who were going to be denounced in terms of the statements coming up and that has a right to be represented and to question the witnesses and so on ... however, one of the questions I ask is why did so much truth come out of the truth commission and so little truth comes out of due process of law.[40]

The relationship between law and truth recovery is a complex one and well beyond the available space here. On a political level, as is discussed elsewhere in this collection,[41] dealing with the legacy of the past remains one of the most challenging aspects of the Northern Ireland transition. In the absence of an overarching mechanism established as part of the negotiations which led to the Good Friday Agreement, the transition has seen a piecemeal approach to examining the legacy of the conflict (Bell 2002). This has included a range of measures—including judge-led pubic inquiries into controversial events, civil actions and referrals from the Criminal Cases Review Commission into alleged miscarriages of justice, inquests into controversial killings—all of which have placed judges front and centre in the effort to 'deal with the past' (Healing Through Remembering 2006; 2013; Lawther 2014; Quirk 2013).[42] In recognition of the limitations of this fragmented way of dealing with the past, there have also been a number of initiatives that attempted to devise more holistic approaches. These have included a major civil society initiative (Healing Through Remembering 2006) as well as important 'top-down' efforts—a British government appointed Consultative Group on the Past (CGP 2009) and lengthy political negotiations between the five political parties on the Northern Ireland Executive chaired by two external US facilitators (Haass and

[39] Interview Northern Ireland judge, 13 December 2002.

[40] Interview Justice Albi Sachs, 11 August 2014. Albi Sachs is a former South African political prisoner, exile and judge on the post-apartheid Constitutional Court—South Africa's Supreme Court. Justice Sachs waived his right to anonymity.

[41] See in particular the chapter by Lawther in this volume.

[42] In November 2014, in Court of Appeal judgment on a legacy inquest, the Lord Chief Justice Sir Declan Morgan himself suggested that a judge-led inquiry might provide a mechanism to deal more holistically with inquests into controversial deaths. He commented that while it was not for the judiciary to determine how the Executive and legislature should deal with the government's investigative obligations regarding the past under Article 2 of the European Convention on Human Rights, 'it is abundantly clear that the present arrangements are not working'. The Lord Chief Justice went on to suggest that perhaps an ongoing inquiry into historical abuse (which is chaired by a judge) might provide a template for examining legacy-based inquests rather than the current piecemeal system: *Re Jordan's Applications* [2014] NICA 42.

O'Sullivan 2013). Further negotiations completed in December 2014 culminated in the signing of the Stormont House Agreement, the legislative implementation of which is slated for autumn 2015. Across all of these truth recovery initiatives, the potential for the role of the judiciary becoming a subject for review and discussion is obvious.

Healing Through Remembering (2006: 27) proposed a range of mechanisms for dealing with the past which included the judiciary and legal profession as institutions which could be asked to account for their conduct during the past. The CGP envisaged a thematic unit, part of a broader Legacy Commission, which 'would examine themes arising from the conflict which remain of public concern' (CGP 2009: 125).[43] In a similar vein, the Haass–O'Sullivan document also contained provisions for examining 'overarching patterns and themes about the conflict' (Haass and O'Sullivan 2013: 32). This document envisaged a number of mechanisms to deal with the past, including an Independent Commission for Information Retrieval (ICIR), a body with the power to investigate themes, in order 'to understand context and contribute to public awareness of history, both now and for subsequent generations' (Haass and O'Sullivan 2013: 32).[44] The Haass–O'Sullivan document also provided a non-exhaustive list of examples of themes which might be explored, including the alleged UK 'shoot-to-kill' policy, the use of lethal force in public order situations, detention without trial and mistreatment of detainees and prisoners. While the Stormont House Agreement (2014) takes the responsibility for thematic analysis away from the ICIR to academics working for a politically appointed 'Implementation and Reconciliation Group', the same logic applies that it would be hard to imagine any serious systematic review of such themes which did not explore the role of the judiciary.

Similar questions relating to judicial performance during a period of conflict or authoritarian rule have been addressed by truth recovery bodies in a number of contexts. For example, both the Argentinian Comisión Nacional Sobre la Desaparición de Personas (CONAPED) and the Rettig Truth and Reconciliation Commission in Chile explored and were explicitly critical of the failure of the judiciary to protect human rights and the rule of law during the military dictatorships in those countries (CONADEP 1984; Rettig 1991; Barros 2002).[45] Similarly, the Reception, Truth and Reconciliation Commission (CAVR) in East Timor criticised judges for, amongst other things, failing in their duties to provide an independent

[43] The CGP report produced a non-exhaustive list of the exemplar themes. While judges were not explicitly mentioned, several of the CGP have assured one of the authors that they had envisaged that the role of the criminal justice system (including the prosecuting authorities and judiciary) would inevitably become the subject of such thematic examinations.

[44] The report continues that suggested themes should 'offer meaningful insight into the political and strategic context of events during the conflict; involve serious human rights violations; or have left a legacy that is particularly important for the work of reconciliation' (Haass and O'Sullivan 2013: 33).

[45] The CONADEP (1984: 392) report concluded, 'The Judicial Power, which should have set itself as a brake on the prevailing absolutism, became in fact a simulacra of the jurisdictional function to protect its external image ... the reticence, and even the complacency of a good part of the judiciary, completed the picture of abandonment of human rights'.

and objective adjudication in political trials and handing down sentences which were disproportionate to the offences (CAVR 2005: chapter 7.6).[46] More recently, the Truth and Reconciliation Commission in South Korea criticised the role of the judiciary during periods of emergency which in turn led to an official apology from the Korean Chief Justice in which he acknowledged that there had been times when the judiciary had previously failed to maintain judicial independence, protect citizens' rights and uphold the rule of law (Hanley 2014).

However, it is the debates concerning the institutional hearings on the judiciary and legal profession by the South African Truth and Reconciliation Commission (TRC) which are probably most germane to the Northern Ireland context. As evidenced in the quote above, the Northern Ireland judiciary was and is very well aware of the issues raised by the South African TRC—indeed the TRC was a constant reference point during the fieldwork for this chapter when the issue arose and thus their experience with regard to the judiciary and the past is worth examining in some detail for its read-across value.

Section 3(1)(a) of the Promotion of National Unity and Reconciliation Act 1995, which set out the remit of the TRC, states that the key objective of the TRC was 'to establish as complete a picture as possible of the causes, nature and extent of the gross violations of human rights which were committed during the period from 1st of March 1960 to the cut-off date'. The TRC's Committee for Human Rights Violations organised a number of 'institutional hearings' towards that end and invited participants from the legal community to address a number of themes.[47] The letters of invitation made clear that the purpose of the hearings was to understand the broader role of the legal system during apartheid and specifically not to 'establish guilt' or hold individuals responsible. Despite the best efforts of the TRC chair Archbishop Tutu, and other commissioners, no judge gave evidence in person to the TRC. While the TRC did have the power to subpoena witnesses, this power was not utilised to compel judges to attend. A number of written submissions were received, including from the new Chief Justice Ismail Mahomed, Arthur Chaskelson President of the Constitutional Court and several others (Rombouts 2002).

[46] However, as Linton, one of the legal advisers to the Commission acknowledges, the CAVR did not interview any Indonesian judges to explore their views on the judicial function during the occupation (Linton and Tiba 2013: 219).

[47] These included the relationship between law and justice; principles and standards by which to evaluate the legal system; what informed judicial policy? What, if any, attempts were made by the Executive to undermine judicial independence? The relationship between the judiciary and the state, political parties or organisations; judicial appointments; the role of the judiciary in applying security legislation; the exercise of judicial discretion; the role of other players (eg, Bar associations, law societies; recommendations on how to transform to a human rights culture). The report went on, 'It is not the purpose of the hearing to establish guilt or hold individuals responsible; the hearing will not be of a judicial or quasi-judicial nature. The hearing is an attempt to understand the role the legal system played in contributing to the violation and/or protection of human rights and to identify institutional changes required to prevent those abuses which occurred from happening again. We urge all judges both serving and retired to present their views as part of the process of moving forward' (TRC Institutional Hearing Report 1998: 94–95).

In replying to the original invitation from the TRC, outgoing Chief Justice Michael Corbert (an apartheid-era judge) argued that while it would be 'foolish' to claim that the courts did all they could have done under apartheid, 'the broad picture is, in my estimation, a favourable one' (Chapman 2008: 176). He defended the 'bad spots' on the judiciary's apartheid record on the grounds of the fact that Parliament was supreme, and hence judges were bound to interpret the law as they found it. He also objected to the judges attending on two grounds—'unfeasibility' (ie, that the TRC would have to review every judicial decision without counsels' arguments to determine if justice was done—'a mind-boggling undertaking') and second, that judicial attendance would encroach upon judicial independence, 'a key element of the constitutional separation of powers' (Dyzenhaus 1998: 37). To this day in South Africa, the decision by the judiciary not to attend the TRC remains a highly controversial issue. Some commentators view it as a pragmatic decision by a judiciary struggling to hold together a mixture of 'new' judges, some of whom (such as Sachs) had been very prominent in the anti-apartheid struggle as well as judges from the old order. As one South African academic lawyer involved in the institutional hearings on the judiciary and legal profession summed up: 'I understand why the judges did what they did here. It would have torn apart a very fragile group had they gone any other route'. For others, the absence of the judges is an object of significant criticism. As another former law professor and ANC minister Kadar Asmal (1998: x) summed up, it represented 'a calculated refusal to take on board the full extent of their culpability in the policies of the past' by apartheid-era judges. Another subsequent Chief Justice, now retired, Pius Langa and his Constitutional Court colleague Edwin Cameron have talked about the '*agonising debate and much controversy*' amongst the judges before the decision was taken not to attend. They concluded that:

> We think the judiciary's decision to stay out of the TRC was wrong. Judges should have attended the hearings voluntarily, and submitted to questioning. Their participation would have legitimated the TRC and the judiciary itself. It would have countered the perception that judges viewed themselves as somehow separate from and above the politics of the rest of the country (Langa and Cameron 2008: 28).

Some South African judges interviewed by one of the authors have taken a similar view. As one High Court judge summed up:

A. *It was an absolutely right thing for lawyers and the Law Society and the Bar Councils and the judiciary to be called to the TRC ... Some of the judges said 'they want us to come and justify our judgments in the TRC, we're not going to do that'. But they missed the point. The issue was accountability of the judiciary [speaker's emphasis], not on particular judgments, sentences or decisions but rather how they allowed the judiciary to be part of the edifice of apartheid.*

Q. Do you think it would have been possible to maintain judicial independence as well as collegiality amongst the old apartheid judges and new post transition judges?

A. *Yes, we had to do it and it could have been managed. The judges of old ought to have accounted, not individually but as the collective, as the institution. And that, if anything, would have strengthened the ethical position of the judiciary around independence.*

Of course one cannot make simplistic comparisons between Northern Ireland and apartheid-era South Africa in general or indeed about the role of the judiciary in the two jurisdictions. That said, the broad themes at stake are similar, and indeed the debate in South Africa encapsulates perfectly the issues which would be raised by a truth or information recovery process involving an examination of the past role of the judiciary. How does one protect the independence of the judiciary if judges are asked to account for past behaviour to a body which will inevitably be established by the Executive? What would be the consequences for current public confidence in the judiciary if there were to be a very public conversation about how well (or not) judges performed their role during the conflict? How would the judiciary avoid becoming overtly politicised by competing political or communal narratives on the past? What would be the consequences amongst the judges themselves with perhaps some judges being willing to participate in such a process and others not? These and other questions underline that the issues involved are both complex and sensitive.

Having invested significant time and energy in talking to judges themselves, as well as reviewing a broad range of their legal judgments and relevant academic literature, we have come to the conclusion that including the judiciary as an element of dealing with the past in Northern Ireland is both manageable and necessary. The themes identified above are illustrative of the broader design challenges that are inherent in any attempt at systemic truth recovery (Freeman 2006; Hayner 2011). Of course, the judiciary would have to be satisfied that these and other concerns could be addressed. It would also have to be persuaded of the legal and political bona fides of the structure as well as the operating rules of any such truth recovery mechanism. Provided that appropriate mechanisms were devised to ensure that such challenges could be met, it seems counter-intuitive that the judiciary should somehow be exempt from any broader process for dealing with the past.

A central tenet of what Mayer-Rieckh and Duthie (2009) refer to as a 'justice sensitive approach to institutional reform' is that an honest appraisal of the past is required in order to underpin and strengthen contemporary and future public confidence in that institution. One of the charges most often levelled by politicians against the judiciary in Northern Ireland is that it is too sensitive to any sort of criticism.[48] Engagement in some form of truth recovery process would underline the capacity of the institution of the judiciary in Northern Ireland to engage in a mature, reflexive and where appropriate self-critical fashion in a process about

[48] eg, in 2014 the DUP's Paul Given (then chair of the Northern Ireland Assembly Justice Committee) accused the judiciary of being 'too precious about their status'. Mr Given's comments came in support of his party colleague the former Health Minister Edwin Poots. The Minister had been upbraided by the Lord Chief Justice after the former had indicated in an Assembly debate that he was not minded to consider appealing a High Court judgment recently lost by his department because he would not get fair a hearing at the Court of Appeal. In a strongly worded response, the Lord Chief Justice Sir Declan Morgan accused the Minister of undermining confidence in the rule of law and respect for the independence of the judiciary; see *UTV News*, 'Minister's comments "Damaged Rule of Law"', 5 September 2014.

the good and bad of its own history. As Lord Bingham (2010: 25) puts it 'a truly independent judiciary is one of the strongest safeguards against Executive lawlessness'. However, achieving what Tarr (2012) has termed in the United States the 'institutionalisation' of judicial independence requires more than the legislative and policy framework which protects judges from undue pressure or influence; it also requires a historical and contemporary public understanding of why it really matters.

In the pre-conflict era, judges came largely from the unionist establishment and, rightly or wrongly, their background and proximity to unionist politics meant that for some nationalists at least, they were viewed as an integral part of the 'Orange State' (Boyle et al 1975; Farrell 1980). During the conflict, judges were at the apex of a transformed criminal justice system which included internment without trial, emergency laws, supergrass trials and other developments which undoubtedly led to human rights abuses (Amnesty International 1978, 1988, 1991). Moreover, the judiciary itself was never completely 'above the fray', simply interpreting the rule of law as detached, scientific legal technicians. Real people were involved. Being on the bench had very direct human consequences. Judges and their family members were murdered. Their daily lives, the performance of their judicial function and their understanding of the community which they served were all shaped by the conflict. A balanced, fair and objective exploration of the complex contours of judicial history should be part of the broader mosaic of dealing with the past in Northern Ireland. Michael Ignatieff (1996) has famously offered a rationale for engagement with truth recovery that, while one may never get the complete truth about any conflict, such a process does reduce the opportunity for what he termed 'permissible lies' about the past. By including the role of the judiciary in such a process it would no longer be politically or intellectually tenable to describe the judges in monochromatic terms, as either 'heroes' who were beyond reproach or the supine lackeys of either unionism or the British state referred to in our opening accounts of this chapter. Narrowing the space for such versions of history about such a centrally important institution should be a key element of coming to terms with our collective past.

References

Amnesty International (1978) *Report of an Amnesty International Mission to Northern Ireland (28 November 1977–6 December 1977)* (London, Amnesty International).

—— (1988) *United Kingdom: Killings by Security Forces and 'Supergrass Trials'* (London, Amnesty International).

—— (1991) *United Kingdom: Allegations of Ill-treatment in Northern Ireland* (London, Amnesty International).

Asmal, K (1998) 'Foreword' in D Dyzenhaus (ed), *Judging the Judges, Judging Ourselves: Truth Reconciliation and the Apartheid Legal Order* (Oxford, Hart Publishing).

Barros, R (2002) *Constitutionalism and Dictatorship: Pinochet, the Junta and the 1980 Constitution* (New York, Cambridge University Press).

Baum, L (2006) *Judges and Their Audiences: A Perspective on Judicial Behavior* (Princeton, NJ, Princeton University Press).

Bell, C (2002) 'Dealing with the Past in Northern Ireland' 26 *Fordham International Law Journal* 1095.

Bingham, T (2010) *The Rule of Law* (London, Allen and Lane).

Blair, C (2000) *Judicial Appointments: Research Report 5, Criminal Justice Review of Northern Ireland* (Belfast, HMSO).

Bonner, D (1988) 'Combating Terrorism: Supergrass Trials in Northern Ireland' 51 *Modern Law* Review 23.

Boyle, K, Hadden, T and Hillyard, P (1975)*Law and State: The Case of Northern Ireland.* (Amherst, MA, University of Massachusetts Press).

—— (1980) *Ten Years on in Northern Ireland: The Legal Control of Political Violence* (London, Cobden Trust).

Carrubba, CJ, Gabel, M and Hankla, C (2008) 'Judicial Behavior under Political Constraints: Evidence from the European Court of Justice' 102 *American Political Science Review* 435.

CAVR (2005) *Report of the Timor–Leste Commission for Reception, Truth and Reconciliation, CHEGA!* (Dili, CAVR).

Chapman, A (2008) 'Truth Recovery through the TRC's Institutional Hearings Process' in AR Chapman and H van der Merwe (eds), *Truth and Reconciliation in South Africa: Did the Truth Deliver* (Philadelphia, PA, University of Pennsylvania Press).

Chavez, RB, Ferejohn, J and Weingast, B (2011) 'A Theory of the Politically Independent Judiciary' in G Helmke and J Rios-Figueroa (eds), *Courts in Latin America* (Cambridge, Cambridge University Press).

CONADEP (1984) *Nunca Más, Report of the National Commission on the Disappeared* (Buenos Aires, CONADEP).

Consultative Group on the Past (CGP) (2009) *Report of the Consultative Group on the Past* (Belfast, CGP).

Cooter, R and Ginsburg, T (1996) 'Comparative Judicial Discretion: An Empirical Test of Economic Models' 16 *International Review of Law and Economics* 295.

Creswell, J (2013) *Research Design: Qualitative, Quantitative, and Mixed Methods Approaches* (London, Sage).

Darwin, C (1859) *On the Origin of the Species* (London, John Murray).

de Londras, F (2011) *Detention in the 'War on Terror': Can Human Rights Fight Back?* (Cambridge, Cambridge University Press).

Dickson, B (1992) 'Northern Ireland's Troubles and the Judges' in B Hadfield (ed), *Northern Ireland: Politics and the Constitution* (Buckingham, Open University Press).

—— (2006) 'The House of Lords and the Northern Ireland Conflict—A Sequel' 69 *Modern Law Review* 383.

—— (2013) *Law in Northern Ireland*, 2nd edn (Oxford, Hart Publishing).

Douglas, L (2001) *The Memory of Judgement. Making Law and History in Trials of the Holocaust* (New Haven, CT, Yale University Press).

Dyzenhaus, D (1998) *Judging the Judges, Judging Ourselves: Truth, Reconciliation and the Apartheid Legal Order* (Oxford, Hart Publishing).

Edwards, H (2003) 'The Effects of Collegiality on Judicial Decision Making' 151 *University of Pennsylvania Law Review* 1639.

Ellett, R (2013) *Pathways to Judicial Power in Transitional States: Perspectives from African Courts* (London, Routledge).

Epstein, L and Knight, J (1998) *The Choices Justices Make* (Washington DC, CQ Press).

Epstein, L, Knight, J and Shvetsova, O (2001) 'The Role of Constitutional Courts in the Establishment and Maintenance of Democratic Systems of Government' 35 *Law & Society Review* 117.

Epstein, L, Landes WL and Posner, RA (2011) 'Why (and When) Judges Dissent: A Theoretical and Empirical Analysis' 3 *Journal of Legal Analysis* 101.

Farrell, M (1980) *The Orange State* (London, Pluto Press).

Feeney, B (2003) *Sinn Féin, A Hundred Turbulent Years* (Dublin, O'Brien Press).

Ferejohn, J, Rosenbluth, F and Shipan, C (2007) 'Comparative Judicial Politics' in C Boix and S Stokes (eds), *The Oxford Handbook of Comparative Politics* (Oxford, Oxford University Press).

Finn, JE (1991) *Constitutions in Crisis: Political Violence and the Rule of Law* (New York, Oxford University Press).

Freeman, M (2006) *Truth Commissions and Procedural Fairness* (Cambridge, Cambridge University Press).

Garoupa, N and Ginsburg, T (2008) 'Judicial Audiences and Reputation: Perspectives from Comparative Law' 47 *Columbia Journal of Transnational Law* 451.

Gibson, JL, Caldeira, GA and Spence, LK (2003) 'Measuring Attitudes Toward the United States Supreme Court' 47 *American Journal of Political Scienc* e 354.

Gifford, A (1985) *Supergrasses in Northern Ireland* (London, Liberty).

Ginsburg, T (2003) *Judicial Review in New Democracies; Constitutional Courts in Asian Cases* (Cambridge, Cambridge University Press).

Ginsburg, T and Moustafa, T (eds) (2008) *Rule by Law: The Politics of Courts in Authoritarian Regimes* (Cambridge, Cambridge University Press).

Goffman, E (1959) *The Presentation of Self in Everyday Life* (Garden City, NY, Anchor).

Graham, E (1983) 'A Vital Weapon in the Anti-terrorist Arsenal' 198 *Fortnight* 10.

Greer, S (1995) *Supergrasses: A Study in Anti-Terrorist Law Enforcement in Northern Ireland* (Oxford, Clarendon Press).

Hadden, T and Hillyard, P (1973) *Justice in Northern Ireland: A Study in Social Confidence* (London, Cobden Trust).

Haass, R and O'Sullivan, M (2013) *An Agreement among the Parties of the Northern Ireland Executive on Parades, Select Commemorations, and Related Protests; Flags and Emblems; and Contending with the Past* (Belfast, OFMdFM).

Hanley, P (2014) 'Transitional Justice in South Korea: One Country's Restless Search for Truth and Reconciliation' 9 *University of Pennsylvania East Asia Law Review* 138.

Harding, A and Nicholson, P (eds) (2011) *New Courts in Asia* (London, Routledge).

Hayner, P (2011), *Unspeakable Truths: Transitional Justice and the Challenge of Truth Commissions*, 2nd edn (London, Routledge).

Healing Through Remembering (2006) *Making Peace with the Past: Options for Truth Recovery Regarding the Conflict in and about Northern Ireland* (Belfast, Healing Through Remembering).

—— (2013) *Dealing with the Past? An Overview of Legal and Political Approaches Relating to the Conflict in and about Northern Ireland* (Belfast, Healing Through Remembering).

Helmke, G (2005) *Courts under Constraints: Judges, Generals, and Presidents in Argentina* (Cambridge, Cambridge University Press).

Helmke, G and Rios-Figueroa, J (eds) (2011) *Courts in Latin America* (Cambridge, Cambridge University Press).
Hilbink, L (2007) *Judges Beyond Politics in Democracy and Dictatorship: Lessons from Chile* (New York, Cambridge University Press).
Hillyard, P and Percy-Smith, J (1984) 'Converting Terrorists: The Use of Supergrasses in Northern Ireland' 13 *Journal of Law and Society* 335.
Ignatieff, M (1996) 'Articles of Faith' 25 *Index on Censorship* 110.
Jackson, J (1985) *The Use of Supergrasses as a Method of Prosecution in Northern Ireland*, Annual Report of the Standing Advisory Commission on Human Rights (Belfast, SACHR).
—— (2009) 'Many Years On in Northern Ireland: The Diplock Legacy' 60 *Northern Ireland Legal Quarterly* 213.
Jackson, J and Doran, S (1995) *Judge Without Jury: Diplock Trials in the Adversary System* (Oxford, Clarendon Press).
Johnson, C, Dowd, T and Ridgeway, C (2006) '*Legitimacy as a Social Process*' 32 *Annual Review of Sociology* 53.
Kapiszewski, D, Silverstein, G and Kagan, RA (eds) (2013) *Consequential Courts: Judicial Roles in Global Perspective* (Cambridge, Cambridge University Press).
Korff, D (1984) *The Diplock Courts In Northern Ireland: A Fair Trial?: An Analysis of the Law, Based on a Study Commissioned by Amnesty International* (Utrecht, Studie- en informatiecentrum Mensenrechten).
Kourlis, RL and Singer, J (2008) 'A Performance Evaluation Program for the Federal Judiciary' 86 *Denver University Law Review* 7.
Langa, P and Cameron, E (2008) 'The Constitutional Court and the Court of Appeal After 1994' *Advocate* April 28.
Lawther, C (2014) *Truth, Denial and Transition: Northern Ireland and the Contested Past* (London, Routledge).
Linton, S and Tiba, F (2013) 'Judges and the Rule of Law in Times of Political Change or Transition' in MC Bassiouini, G Joanna and P Mengozzi (eds), *The Global Community Yearbook of International Law and Jurisprudence* (Oxford, Oxford University Press).
Livingstone, S (1994) 'The House of Lords and the Northern Ireland Conflict' 57 *Modern Law Review* 333.
—— (2001) 'And Justice for All? The Judiciary and the Legal Profession in Transition' in C Harvey (ed), *Human Rights, Equality, and Democratic Renewal in Northern Ireland* (Oxford, Hart Publishing).
Lowry, Lord (1986) 'Civil Proceedings in a Beleaguered Society' 2 *The Denning Law Journal* 109.
—— (1992) 'National Security and the Rule of Law' 26 *Israel Law Review* 117.
Mautner, M (2011) *Law and the Culture of Israel* (Oxford, Oxford University Press).
Mayer-Rieckh, A and Duthie, R (2009) 'Enhancing Justice and Development through Justice-Sensitive Security Sector Reform' in P de Greiff and R Duthie (eds), *Transitional Justice and Development: Making Connections* (New York, Social Science Research Council).
McColgan, A (2011) 'Northern Ireland, Terrorism Now and Then, and the Human Rights Act' in TK Campbell, KD Ewing and A Tomkins (eds), *The Legal Protection of Human Rights: Sceptical Essays* (Oxford, Oxford University Press).
McDonough, R (1985) 'Are the Judges Another Arm of British Policy?' 216 *Fortnight* 10.

McEvoy, K (2000) 'Law, Struggle, and Political Transformation in Northern Ireland' 27 *Journal of Law and Society* 542.

—— (2001) *Paramilitary Imprisonment in Northern Ireland: Resistance, Management, and Release* (Oxford, Oxford University Press).

—— (2011) 'What Did the Lawyers Do During the "War"? Neutrality, Conflict and the Culture Of Quietism' 74 *Modern Law Review* 350.

McEvoy, K and Rebouche, R (2007) 'Mobilising the Professions: Lawyers, Politics and the Collective Legal Conscience' in J Morison, K McEvoy and G Anthony (eds), *Judges, Transition and Human Rights* (Oxford, Oxford University Press).

Miceli, TJ and Cosgel, MM (1994) 'Reputation and Judicial Decision-Making' 23 *Journal of Economic Behavior & Organization* 31.

Morison, J and Livingstone, S (1995) *Reshaping Public Power: Northern Ireland and the British Constitutional Crisis* (London, Sweet & Maxwell)

Peltason, J (1971) *Fifty Eight Lonely Men: Southern Federal Justices and School Desegregation* (Champaine, IS, Illinois University Press).

Pohman, HL (2008) *Terrorism and the Constitution: The Post 9/11 Cases* (Lanham, MD, Rowman and Littlefield).

Posner, RA (1993) 'What Do Judges and Justices Maximize? (The Same Thing Everybody Else Does)' 3 *Supreme Court Economic Review* 1.

Quirk, H (2013) 'Don't Mention the War: The Court of Appeal, the Criminal Cases Review Commission and Dealing with the Past in Northern Ireland' 76 *Modern Law Review* 949.

Rettig (1991) *Report of the National Commission for Truth and Reconciliation in Chile* (Santiago, Rettig).

Robinson, P, McCrea, W, Allister, J and Foster, I (1984) *A War to be Won* (Belfast, Democratic Unionist Party).

Rombouts, H (2002) *The Legal Profession and the TRC: A Study of a Tense Relationship* (Johannesburg, Centre for the Study of Violence).

Sadurski, W (2005) *Rights Before Courts: A Study of Constitutional Courts in Postcommunist States of Central and Eastern Europe* (Dordrecht, Springer).

Schauer, F (1999) 'Incentives, Reputation, and the Inglorious Determinants of Judicial Behavior' 68 *University of Cincinnati Law Review* 615.

Shirlow, P (2001) 'Fear and Ethnic Division' 13 *Peace Review* 67.

Shirlow, P and McEvoy, K (2008) *Beyond the Wire: Former Prisoners and Conflict Transformation in Northern Ireland* (London, Pluto Press).

Staton, JK (2010) *Judicial Power and Strategic Communication in Mexico* (Cambridge, Cambridge University Press).

Stormont House Agreement (2014) *The Stormont House Agreement* (London/Belfast, Northern Ireland Office).

Tarr, G (2012) *Without Fear or Favor: Judicial Independence and Judicial Accountability in the States* (Stanford, CA, Stanford University Press).

Trochev, A (2008) *Judging Russia: The Role of the Constitutional Court in Russian Politics, 1990–2006* (Cambridge, Cambridge University Press).

Truth and Reconciliation Commission of South Africa (TRC) (1998) *Report of the South African Truth and Reconciliation Commission; Volume 4, Chapter 4, Institutional Hearing, The Legal System* (South Africa, Truth and Reconciliation Commission).

Vanberg, G (2005) *The Politics of Constitutional Review in Germany* (Cambridge, Cambridge University Press).

Walker, C (1999) 'The Commodity of Justice in States of Emergency' 50 *Northern Ireland Legal Quarterly* 164.
Walsh, D (1983) *The Use and Abuse of Emergency Legislation in Northern Ireland* (London, Civil Liberties Trust).
Walters, MD (2012) 'Dicey on Writing the Law of the Constitution' 32 *Oxford Journal of Legal Studies* 21.
Yusuf, HO (2010) *Transitional Justice, Judicial Accountability and the Rule of Law* (London, Routledge).

9

Prisons and Imprisonment in Northern Ireland

PHIL SCRATON

Introduction

The social and societal transition from violent conflict to relative peace is a gradual and uneven process. In Northern Ireland, hostilities and tensions across geographical boundaries of segregated communities are most visibly marked by 'peace walls', often portrayed in murals memorialising paramilitary actions and commemorating key historical events (Rolston 2010). They represent powerful, territorial reminders of profound social, political and ideological divisions. At all levels—particularly, but not exclusively, in working class neighbourhoods—segregation remains evident and institutionalised: churches; schools; housing; sports; leisure; policing and criminal justice (Shirlow and Murtagh 2006). It is no surprise, given the significance of internment without trial, sentences without juries and the early release of politically affiliated prisoners[1] as part of negotiated peace agreements, that the contemporary penal process in Northern Ireland is burdened with the legacy of conflict.

Throughout the conflict, Northern Ireland's prisons held two distinct, broad populations: politically affiliated predominantly long-term prisoners held under emergency legislation or 'special powers' and convicted without jury trial; and routine prisoners remanded or sentenced through the due process of regular courts.[2] Inevitably in a jurisdiction policed and regulated by the administration of special powers, the containment and incarceration of politically affiliated prisoners shaped the contemporary penal process. Illustrating the state's changing response

[1] The term 'politically affiliated' is used throughout this chapter to indicate those prisoners whose offences for which they were convicted were self-attributed to political motives, usually committed in accordance with their membership of paramilitary groups (see also chapter by Dwyer in this volume).

[2] The Civil Authorities (Special Powers) Act (NI) was emergency legislation first introduced in April 1922, renewed annually and made permanent in 1933. It extended to discretionary prohibition of public meetings, named organisations and seditious literature, curfews and internment without trial. Following the imposition of direct rule from Westminster it was replaced by the Northern Ireland (Emergency Provisions) Act 1973.

to the imprisonment of politically affiliated prisoners, McEvoy (2001: 204) notes that between 1969 and the 1980s regimes progressed through three distinct stages: 'reactive containment', including internment without trial; 'criminalisation', which abandoned 'political' status for affiliated prisoners; and 'managerialism', emphasising organisational efficiency and regime effectiveness. To understand the contemporary prison system in Northern Ireland it is crucial to provide an overview of its recent historical context focusing on the period from 1969 through to the early release of politically affiliated prisoners in 2000.

The chapter then details the policy reviews and official inspections commissioned and published as the Northern Ireland Prison Service (NIPS) adjusted to accommodating a post-conflict prison population. It maps the slow progress of transition and the inhibitions on, and barriers to, institutional and organisational change. What follows is an account of the post-devolution (justice and policing) commitment to policy reform, including regimes, staffing and practices within Northern Ireland's prisons: Magilligan (low and medium risk/sex offenders/foreign nationals), Maghaberry (high security, complex mix of remand/convicted; short-term/long-term; politically affiliated), and the shared site that accommodates Hydebank Wood Prison (women only, all categories) and Hydebank Wood Young Offenders Centre (young men aged 18–21). Following devolution, a review of prisons was commissioned, presenting two reports in 2011. Focusing on the substance of the review team's call for fundamental change and its comprehensive recommendations, the chapter concludes by reviewing work-in-progress towards their realisation. To introduce the Northern Ireland context, however, it is necessary to reflect on the broader theoretical and political debates concerning punishment, incapacitation and rehabilitation.

Prison Regimes and Penal Policy: The Progressive-Regressive Spectrum

Through the incarceration of its citizens the state imposes a penultimate punishment exceeded only by execution, now abandoned in most advanced democratic societies. As an outcome of due process the prison sentence is a universally adopted sanction. In their introduction to the moral and political justifications for punishment, Cavadino and Dignan (2007: 37–50) prioritise two distinct, yet often interlocked, elements: retributivism (punishment administered proportionate to an offence committed) and reductivism (incorporating well-established principles of deterrence, incapacitation and rehabilitation). They also reflect on the significance of denunciation (public condemnation of certain acts), restoration (reparation to victims) and reintegration (of the contrite offender to the community). Whatever the particular historical foundations and contemporary manifestations of penal processes, tensions between and within these elements prevail in all jurisdictions.

Following prison reformer John Howard's late-eighteenth-century invocation to build 'new' prisons in which a 'just measure of pain' would be inflicted proportionate to the crime committed (see Ignatieff 1978), within Europe the contemporary prison system emerged. Its objective was not to punish 'less' but to punish 'better' (Foucault 1977: 82). Yet, the 'penal complex' that emerged and consolidated in twentieth-century Britain did not succeed in 'repairing' prisoners but 'propel[led] them into a deterred conformity or, more usually, into closely supervised spirals of failure and continued failure' (Garland 1985: 260). The enduring tension between the incapacitation and rehabilitation of prisoners has remained central to political and public discourses regarding the welfare and rights of prisoners, not least the debate concerning 'humane' containment.

Currently its most extreme manifestation is evident in the enthusiasm for long sentences served in harsh conditions within US prisons, accompanied by a sharp reduction in community-based alternatives and reduced welfare provision (Currie 1998; Parenti 1999). This retributive climate produced a 'stunning evisceration of prisoners' rights' with rehabilitation lost to 'aggressive incapacitation' and 'containment' (Fleury-Steiner and Longazel 2014: 8). Maximising security through inhibiting prisoners' physical movement and interaction creates 'a space of pure custody, a human warehouse … a kind of social waste management' (Simon 2007: 142). Political acceptance of, and public support for, harsh conditions in US prisons have permitted an 'overriding emphasis on efficiency and security' facilitated by 'intense surveillance', devoid of minimum 'sensory stimulation, social contact and privacy' (Rhodes 2006: 76).

In his comparative study of punishment in the United States and Europe, specifically France and Germany, Whitman (2005: 69) notes that with the exception of England and Wales Western European states have not caught the US carceral 'chill', yet warns that its impact 'has struck worldwide … purg[ing] individualization and resocialization from the practice of punishment, substituting retribution, incapacitation, and determinate sentencing'. As Pratt and Eriksson (2013: 10) show, 'in Anglophone countries', prisons have become 'progressively larger' to accommodate an ever-expanding prison population thereby, *per capita*, 'rationalizing and reducing prison costs'. The commitment to economies of scale has resulted in planning three 'Titan' prisons in England and Wales, each to accommodate 2500 prisoners. In marked contrast, the Nordic model of 'human prison design' views punishment through a lens that prioritises small accommodation blocks, reduced social distance, constant interaction, maintenance of family contact and a high proportion of open conditions. Thus, 'the usual indicators of prison existence are camouflaged, hidden or removed' (Pratt and Eriksson 2013: 2).

The moral and political justifications for punishment and, across jurisdictions, the spectrum of progressive (Nordic) to harsh (US) penal regimes to which they have given rise, provide the foundation on which the role, function and future of prisons in advanced democratic societies can be assessed. Angela Davis notes that the prison occupies a 'simultaneous presence and absence' in public consciousness, through which incarceration is 'taken for granted' as necessary and inevitable while masking 'the realities they produce' (Davis 2003: 15).[3] Ambivalence and indifference to prison regimes, to the removal of citizenship rights, has personal and social consequences for prisoners deprived of all movement and interaction other than that permitted by the prison regime. In a classic essay Erving Goffman considers that the 'barrier that total institutions place between the inmate [sic] and the wider world' renders invisible the routine 'series of abasements, degradations, humiliations and profanations of self' (1968: 24). More recently, Leder (2004) discusses the infantilising and disempowering impact of imprisonment, affecting every aspect of prisoners' lives as they are contained, controlled and determined by institutionalised processes. Such impacts are identified by Carrabine (2005: 910) as 'normative commitments and ritual compulsions' which together establish and maintain 'routine sources of order'. While Western democratic states operate distinctive penal systems, they share to varying degrees a commitment to prisons as places of punishment, correction and rehabilitation reflecting the punitive legacy of the nineteenth-century 'modern' prison—the prisoner as 'disciplined subject' expected to reform through, 'habits, rules, orders, an authority that is exercised around him [sic] and upon him which he must allow to function automatically in him' (Foucault 1977: 128).

Davis (1990: 52) considers that prisons function internally at two levels. The first reflects the 'routines and behavior prescribed by the governing penal hierarchy': the operational and administrative daily routine. The second, the 'prisoner culture itself', is less routinised and potentially more volatile, yet it generates a 'resistance of desperation … based on an assumption that the prison system will survive'. However expressive or oppositional the 'prisoner culture', eloquently portrayed by (Quinney 2006: 270) as the 'dance of the … inmate and captor, prisoner and non-prisoner', the capacity to negotiate even the slightest modification in regimes is circumscribed by the discretionary power and authority institutionalised in the roles of prison guard and prison manager. In that sense, the metaphor of the prison as an island—and prisons within a jurisdiction as an archipelago—is apposite.

Acknowledging these tensions, particularly the progressive-regressive spectrum, it is important to address the political and institutional developments that contextualise imprisonment in contemporary Northern Ireland. In most jurisdictions the penal estate is a complex mix of institutions reflecting a diverse prison population: long-term; short-term; remand; open; men; women; young offenders; sex offenders; mentally ill. The assumption being that in each, often specialised, establishment the identified needs of its population are addressed. Such diversity is well illustrated in briefly considering the penal estate in England and Wales. Divided into 11 regions, in early November 2014 the jurisdiction held 85,903 prisoners including 3921 women and approximately one-fifth were young offenders.[4]

[3] Angela Davis is Professor Emerita at the University of California Santa Cruz and a former US political prisoner.

[4] These figures, which fluctuate weekly and reflect a gradual upward trend, are from the 'prison list', available at www.justice.gov.uk, and from the International Centre for Prison Studies, available at www.prisonstudies.org. The prison estate is a mix of local and dispersal prisons and includes eight prisons designated 'high security'.

While most of the hundred plus prisons are managed by the Prison Service, 13 are contracted out to private companies. There are 36 young male offenders' institutions, 14 women's prisons, 13 young women offenders' institutions and several holding 'foreign nationals' or facilitating 'immigration removal'. Prisoners serving sentences for 'politically-related' offences are a small minority. In contrast, prisons in Northern Ireland—in size, purpose and function—are significantly different. Since the early release of politically affiliated prisoners, four prisons remain operational on three sites serving a population of approximately 1.8 million. Proportionately the prison population is considerably lower than in England and Wales or Scotland.[5] The legacy of the conflict, however, remains significant.

In the Shadow of the Conflict

As established in the introduction to this collection, since 1922 the history of devolved powers from the UK Parliament to the Northern Ireland Parliament has been difficult and ambiguous. The constitution of a partitioned Ulster, losing three of its nine counties, led inevitably to persistent conflict as nationalists and republicans continued to pursue their commitment to a united Ireland in the face of institutionalised political and economic discrimination.[6] As Boyle et al (1975: 7) note, the 'basic aspiration' of the majority of Roman Catholics in the six counties 'was and remains unification' and they 'regarded the use of a legal system to support the Unionist state as wholly unjustifiable'.

Post-partition Northern Ireland did not experience gradual transition from war to peace, a shift from conflict to normalisation. 'Special' or 'emergency' powers were embedded in legislation, internment without trial recurred across generations and policing was exceptional—not least in the vast part-time reserve, pre-eminently Protestant 'B Specials' (see O'Dowd et al 1980). The emergence and consolidation of the civil rights movement during the late-1960s, and the violent opposition to which it was subjected, led in August 1969 to the deployment of the British Army, reflective of a broader strategy 'to pressurize the government [in Northern Ireland] to establish a series of institutions to guarantee equality of treatment and freedom from discrimination for the Catholic community' (Hillyard 1987: 282). Yet the Unionist Government introduced the Criminal Justice (Temporary Provisions) Act 1970—a tough political response to the demands from within Catholic/nationalist/republican communities for civil, political and economic rights. In August 1971 the conflict hardened when, supported by the UK

[5] While imprisonment per 100,000 of the population has risen to 149 in England and Wales, 144 in Scotland, the most recent figure for Northern Ireland is 98. This is closer to Ireland (81), Germany (81) and France (102)—see www.prisonstudies.org.

[6] The Government of Ireland Act 1920 partitioned Ireland, establishing six of the nine northern counties of Ulster as Northern Ireland within the United Kingdom (May 1921). The Irish Free State was established as a British Commonwealth Dominion and in 1937 the creation of Ireland as a sovereign state replaced the 1922 constitution. In 1949 it secured full independence as the Republic of Ireland.

Government, the Unionist administration reverted to internment without trial (see McEvoy 2001).

Within six months '2,357 persons had been arrested and 1,600 released after interrogation', as internment became 'an example of unfettered ministerial discretion' confirming the state's 'clear and unequivocal … involvement in suppressing political opposition' (Hillyard 1987: 283–84).[7] Internees were accommodated in compounds at Long Kesh, a former military base, and the imprisoned population expanded exponentially with many proclaiming political affiliation. At various periods during the conflict 'politically motivated' prisoners constituted between a half and two-thirds of the overall prison population (McEvoy 2001). Their presence became, and has remained, a distinctive and defining feature of imprisonment in Northern Ireland.

In 1972, following the killing of 13 civilians by soldiers of the Parachute Regiment in Derry, the semi-autonomous Northern Ireland Parliament constituted under the Government of Ireland Act 1920 was suspended and the UK Government imposed direct rule. According to Boyle et al (1975: 32), following the collapse of negotiations led by the UK Conservative Government, 'it was decided to turn the full force of the British Army against the IRA' alongside a 'new system of arrest and detention'. The impact on imprisonment is well illustrated by Rolston and Tomlinson (1986: 164–65), who demonstrate that while the percentage of male long-term prisoners (sentences of four years to life) committed to prison in 1972 was 0.9 per cent of the prison population, within two years it had risen to 23.8 per cent. Yet the wider prison population remained relatively consistent and short-term prison sentences (under four years) actually declined by 25 per cent. This was a major shift in the prison population and in the status of those imprisoned—'ordinary' or 'politically affiliated'. The dispute about how prisoners were categorised became central and significance in terms of prison policy and practice has been defining.

Initially, 'politically affiliated' prisoners were granted 'special category status', challenged by the 1975 Gardiner Committee. Five years later it was removed. Politically affiliated male prisoners, previously held at the nineteenth-century HMP Belfast (Crumlin Road Gaol) alongside ordinary prisoners, were transferred to HMP Maze, a new 800 cell prison adjacent to the Long Kesh internment camp. Cellular accommodation was in a series of self-contained blocks, each in the shape of an 'H', providing four wings served by a central spine. They mounted a strong campaign to have their political status recognised.

The 'blanket' protest (refusal to wear prison clothes) and the 'no-wash' protest culminated in hunger strikes, initially in 1980 and again in 1981. Determined not to accede to the republican prisoners' demands, the Conservative Government,

[7] Internment without trial was the detention by the state of individuals considered a 'threat' yet against whom there was insufficient or no evidence to charge them with a criminal offence. Given that it amounted to a violation of human rights, particularly those relating to Art 5 (right to liberty) and Art 6 (right to a fair trial) it was justified as a temporary, emergency power during a period of 'war' or civil unrest.

refused to negotiate (see McKeown 2001) and 10 hunger strikers died. While concessions were gained as a consequence of the hunger strikes, special category status was not reintroduced and the strategy of criminalisation of politically motivated offences remained central to the politics and conditions of incarceration in Northern Ireland.[8] Refusal to accept special category status exposed contradictions in the government's position. Prisoners 'were arrested under emergency powers and convicted in radically modified [political] courts' and their 'motivations' were distinct 'from those of "ordinary" criminals'—arrested, tried and imprisoned as 'terrorists' (Hillyard 1987: 298). Rolston and Tomlinson (1986: 163) note that within a decade those ascribed special category status fell from 1476 to 'less than 175'.

During the conflict, therefore, the politics, priorities and policies governing imprisonment in Northern Ireland were locked into, if not determined by, the containment of politically affiliated prisoners. Crumlin Road Gaol (HMP Belfast) remained the primary male prison for 'ordinary' prisoners. All women prisoners were held in Armagh Gaol, built between 1780 and 1852. Republican women had been interned in Armagh during the Second World War and again during the 1956–62 'Border Campaign' (McGuffin 1973).[9] Demanding political status, in February 1980 women prisoners instigated 'no-wash' protests followed by a brief hunger strike in December 1980 (Corcoran 2006: 37–41). Their treatment by prison officers, particularly the punitive use of strip-searching, resulted in international condemnation (Amnesty International 1991; see also the chapter by Moore and Wahidin in this volume).

Armagh was closed in 1986 and all women prisoners were transferred to Mourne House, designated a self-contained high-security unit within the walls of the newly constructed high-security Maghaberry Prison. Its security status reflected its primary function—the incarceration of women politically motivated prisoners. By default all women prisoners were held in high-security conditions regardless of their offence. The male prison opened a year later primarily to accommodate longer-term sentenced prisoners. Although on the same site, Mourne House retained relative autonomy in accommodation, management, staffing and other facilities. Its capacity was 59 cells within four wings.

Two years after the 1998 Good Friday/Belfast Agreement, the Northern Ireland (Sentences) Act 1998 enabled the early licensed release, regardless of the length of sentence served, of prisoners affiliated to republican and loyalist paramilitary organisations[10] that had declared ceasefire (McEvoy 2001). Between 1998 and 2007, 449 politically affiliated prisoners were released, the majority in the first two years (Dwyer 2007). This significantly reduced the 'high-risk' maximum security prison population; yet, as will be discussed, it had minimal impact on prison regimes.

[8] In 1972 'special category status' had been granted to politically affiliated prisoners who were convicted of criminal offences that they claimed to be politically motivated. It was rescinded following the Gardiner Committee Report (1975). Thus, prisoners sentenced for offences committed after 1 March 1976 were considered criminals leading to protests and hunger strikes.

[9] Between 1956 and 1962 the IRA mounted cross-border incursions from the Irish Republic into Northern Ireland as part of its strategy to secure a united Ireland.

[10] See n 5 in ch 10 by Dwyer in this volume.

In 2000 HMP Maze/Long Kesh was closed and the remaining small cohort of politically affiliated prisoners, either not entitled to early release or recently convicted, was transferred to HMP Maghaberry to be 'integrated' into the general prison population.

The Chief Inspector of Prisons concluded that Maghaberry had become 'the most complex and diverse prison establishment in the UK' (HMCIP 2003). The Northern Ireland Association for the Care and Resettlement of Offenders (NIACRO), echoed this concern, specifically regarding the diversity of 'pressures' within one prison (NIAC 2004: 5). The complex mix of distinct groups of prisoners was identified by the Select Committee as follows:

> [M]ales and females; ordinary remand prisoners; sex offenders; asylum seekers; members of different Loyalist organisations, both on remand and on sentence; members of different Republican organisations on remand and on sentence; short-term sentenced ordinary prisoners, long-term sentenced ordinary prisoners, and so on (NIAC 2004: 5).

Within months, and without additional training, many prison managers and staff had changed daily routines from an environment in which they had minimal contact with politically affiliated prisoners who conducted their own affairs, to one where interaction between prison officers and 'ordinary' prisoners was a priority.[11]

The remaining politically affiliated prisoners protested against the policy of integration raising concerns about the safety of prisoners and officers (NIAC 2004: 6). On 7 August 2003, the then Secretary of State for Northern Ireland commissioned a policy review, chaired by John Steele, former Director of NIPS. His review recommended that the relatively low number of politically affiliated prisoners should be held separately from ordinary prisoners according to their affiliation (Steele Report 2004). Despite opposition from the Prison Officers' Association and the Chief Inspector of Prisons, a policy of separation, that did not 'concede control of the wings to prisoners as happened at the Maze' (NIAC 2007: 31), was implemented. Because of their low numbers, the separation policy initially did not extend to politically affiliated women prisoners in Mourne House (Scraton and Moore 2005; see also Moore and Wahidin in this volume).

2000–10: A Decade of Stagnation

At the time of the early release of politically affiliated prisoners, the Northern Ireland Prison Service (NIPS) was administered via the Northern Ireland Office under UK Government direct rule. Following the closure of HMP Maze/Long

[11] Following the 'no-wash' protests and hunger strikes many politically affiliated prisoners shifted their emphasis to resistance through education, cultural reclamation and revival of the Irish language (McKeown 2001; Mac Ionnrachtaigh 2013). Running their own affairs, there was minimal contact with prison staff. Following the mass early release, the role of and expectations on prison staff and management changed to dealing with the routine demands of 'ordinary' prisoners.

Kesh three prisons remained: HMP Maghaberry near Lisburn, within which women were held in the discrete Mourne House unit; HMP Magilligan on the north coast of Northern Ireland; and Hydebank Wood Young Offenders Centre (young male adults and boys), Belfast. In contravention of international children's rights standards,[12] young women under 18 were held in Mourne House and boys as young as 15 years were held in the young offenders' centre.[13] Located in a rural setting 20 miles south-west of Belfast, 73 miles south-east of Derry and 30 miles north of Newry, HMP Maghaberry was opened as a male prison in 1987; the women's unit was opened a year earlier. It is not easily accessed by public transport.

HMP Magilligan was opened in 1972 at picturesque Magilligan Point, designated a site of outstanding natural beauty. Consistent with so many prisons throughout the world, its fences and walls of total confinement are incongruous in a place of spectacular openness and freedom. Located 90 miles north of Newry, 67 miles north-west of Belfast and 25 miles north-east of Derry, it is desolate, remote and inaccessible and poorly served by public transport. Despite some modernisation, the prison retains the appearance and atmosphere of a temporary prison. Across the site there is limited in-cell sanitation and the facilities for their families, many of whose visits are expensive, day-long excursions, are unacceptable. Most male prisoners held in Magilligan are categorised as low or medium risk.

Hydebank Wood Young Offenders Centre (YOC) was opened in 1979 as a low-security prison. The only prison for young offenders in Northern Ireland, it was built in a wooded area close to the ring road five miles south of Belfast, 76 miles west of Derry and 38 miles north of Newry. Those visiting the YOC on public transport from across the region travel via Belfast. It consists of an arc of five, self-contained, discrete houses without in-cell sanitation, accommodating young adults (18–21) and also male children aged 17 and under, categorised as 'juveniles'.

As previously discussed, the early-2000s were dominated by persistent controversies and protests concerning the status, accommodation and conditions under which politically affiliated prisoners were held. The regimes, routines and provision experienced by 'ordinary' prisoners, by far the majority, received little political, academic or policy attention. In 2003 the Prisons Inspectorate presented a detailed report on Maghaberry, noting its extraordinary diversity and complexity (HMCIP 2003). It was highly critical of Mourne House as a seriously deficient regime, stating there was no recognition of the distinctive needs of women in the context of a large male prison (Moore and Scraton 2014; see also Moore and Wahidin in this volume).

Following independent, in-depth research within Mourne House, the Human Rights Commission recorded its 'profound concern' that the regime 'neglected even

[12] UN Standard Minimum Rules for the Administration of Juvenile Justice 1985 (Beijing Rules); the UN Guidelines for the Prevention of Juvenile Delinquency 1990 (Riyadh Guidelines); the UN Convention on the Rights of the Child 1989.

[13] Administered by the Department of Health, Social Services and Public Safety, Woodlands Juvenile Justice Centre held remand and sentenced children aged under 17.

the identified needs of women and girl prisoners', failing to meet even minimal 'duty of care' expectations (Scraton and Moore 2005: 169). Rather than develop Mourne House as a low-security, self-contained, gender-specific and independent facility, women prisoners were transferred to Ash House, a unit within Hydebank Wood male YOC. The Criminal Justice Inspection Northern Ireland (CJINI) and HMCIP[14] conducted an unannounced inspection of Ash House, concluding that its previous recommendations had not been met and the regime was seriously deficient in policies, strategies and procedures (HMCIP/CJINI 2005). These findings were endorsed by Alvaro Gil-Robles, Commissioner for Human Rights for the Council of Europe who reported that it was not possible for women prisoners 'to receive appropriate treatment' and 'conditions were likely to aggravate their fragile condition still further' (Gil-Robles 2005: paragraph 126). The Committee for the Prevention of Torture and Inhuman or Degrading Treatment or Punishment (CPT) described conditions as unacceptable, criticising the lack of gender-specific policies and the disproportionate number of male guards (CPT 2004).

The second phase of the Human Rights Commission research found that while some progress had been achieved from the 'worst excesses and deprivations of the Mourne House regime', core recommendations for a gender-informed strategy and facility had not been addressed and 'urgent progress regarding self-harm, substance use, mental ill-health, therapeutic provision, counselling, occupational therapy and constructive work and educational opportunities is still required' (Scraton and Moore 2007: 127). As this research was published, the Hydebank Wood Young Offenders Centre was inspected. The Inspectorates described 'overuse of handcuffs' in transport vans, lack of implementation of the induction policy and routine strip-searching, 'excessive' adjudication punishments, bullying, 'little purposeful activity', 'unpredictable cancellations of association', minimal access to outdoor activity and inadequate development of effective resettlement policies. The YOC was considered deficient in the 'four tests of a healthy prison establishment: safety, respect, purposeful activity and resettlement' (HMCIP/CJINI 2008: 6).

Three years later, a follow-up inspection recorded that many of the 'safety' and 'respect' recommendations had not been addressed and there was 'excessive use of cellular confinement as a punishment' (CJINI/HMCIP 2011: 5). Prison officers were criticised for their 'negative and punitive approach' and the absence of personal officer provision (CJINI/HMCIP 2011: 5). Despite the transfer of responsibility for health care to the Health and Social Care Trust, 'there was little evidence that services had improved and progressed' with mental health care 'under-resourced' (CJINI/HMCIP 2011: 6). None of the recommendations for 'purposeful activity' and only five of the 19 regarding 'resettlement' had been achieved (see also Moore and Scraton 2014).

[14] Prison inspections in Northern Ireland are conducted jointly by the Inspectorates of Prisons, England and Wales and of Criminal Justice, Northern Ireland.

Maghaberry was inspected again in 2009. As stated above, it was built as a high-security prison, but accommodated all categories of prisoner including remand, short sentences and long sentences including life, with loyalist and republican prisoners accommodated in two separate houses. While recognising Maghaberry's diverse population, the Inspectorates were concerned that 'someone serving five days for fine default receives the same security regime as someone serving a 10-year sentence for serious assault' (HMCIP/CJINI 2009: v). They concluded that when assessed against the four elements of a 'healthy prison' Maghaberry was seriously under-performing. Only 44 of the 155 recommendations made in 2006 had been realised and given it operated as 'one of the most expensive prisons in the United Kingdom' it was a 'situation ... that cannot be permitted to continue' (HMCIP/CJINI 2009: vii).

The Review of Prisons 2010–11

While the 1998 Good Friday/Belfast Agreement established the foundation for the devolution of powers to the Northern Ireland Assembly, devolution of policing and justice was delayed until the 2006 St Andrews Agreement. In 2010 the Hillsborough Agreement committed the Assembly to penal reform including: 'alternatives to custody'; a 'review of the conditions of detention, management and oversight of all prisons'; a 'comprehensive strategy for the management of offenders'; a 'fit for purpose' women's prison in line with 'international obligations'; and a comprehensive review of children and young people 'at all stages of the criminal justice system, including detention' (Hillsborough Agreement 2010: paragraph 7). Consequently, the Minister of Justice, David Ford, announced a 'rolling review' of prisons and appointed a Prison Review Team (PRT). While focusing initially on Maghaberry, it prioritised the replacement of Magilligan, recognising that 'much of the accommodation and infrastructure is not fit for purpose' together with the 'development of a strategy for women offenders including ... a discrete facility' and appropriate 'developments for juvenile offenders at Hydebank Wood' (PRT 2011a: 76).

On 28 February 2011, the PRT published an interim report stating it was not possible 'to deal with the problems facing Maghaberry without tackling the underlying issues—management, leadership, vision, objectives, culture—in the prison system of which it is a part' (PRT 2011a: 2). It noted that the 'components of the problems facing NIPS' together with appropriate 'solutions' had to be addressed before moving to the 'shape and detail of the new service' including identifying the needs of 'specialist groups' of prisoners (PRT 2011a: 2). The PRT confirmed previous criticisms: over-emphasis on security; absence of rehabilitative initiatives; inadequate health care, education and purposeful activities; unacceptable physical environment and conditions; lack of engagement by staff with prisoners; hostile and destructive industrial relations; and weak leadership in dealing with endemic, systemic problems (PRT 2011a). Reflecting concerns raised by the Inspectorate Reports, the Independent Monitoring Boards and prison researchers, the PRT recognised the complexity of the problems within a 'demoralised and dysfunctional service, resigned to bad press and routine criticism … defensive [and] with little confidence that anything could or, in some cases should, change' (PRT 2011a: 4).

The PRT challenged the 'defeatism' it found, demanding 'transformative change' and 'sustainable improvement' that tackled the existing ingrained 'approach, culture and ways of working'. Necessary reform required 'political will' at 'all levels', discarding 'processes or attitudes that are familiar and comfortable' and significantly improving 'communication skills, within and outside the prison service' with 'more visible leadership, and support and professional development for those undergoing and implementing change' (PRT 2011a: 6). NIPS managers and the Prisoner Officers' Association (POA) were left in no doubt about the 'scale of change required' with 'privatisation' of the Service preferred as a possible alternative (PRT 2011a: 8). The interim recommendations revisited familiar ground: a discrete women's prison; the abandonment of Magilligan as an appropriate location; the inappropriate imprisonment of fine defaulters and excessive use of pre-trial remand. It proposed 'real and measurable reductions' in imprisonment (PRT, 2011a: 10), prioritising 'justice reinvestment' from custodial disposals to community initiatives (PRT 2011a: 22).

The PRT recommended that the 'absence of visible leadership and oversight' and the 'culture of denial and compromise' should be resolved by a 'properly resourced change programme' (PRT 2011a: 12–13) led by the Director General and assisted by a manager with extensive experience of change management (PRT 2011a: 45). A 'staff development package' would combine 'personal development [training] packages for leaders and managers' alongside 'an early retirement scheme for those wishing to leave' and a 'recruitment and progression programme to refresh and diversify the workforce' (PRT 2011a: 14). The PRT was concerned that the workforce remained 'unrepresentative of the community'; of managers and staff only 10 per cent were Roman Catholic and 22 per cent were women (PRT 2011a: 52).

The imprisonment of politically affiliated prisoners had left a legacy of 'high staffing levels' and 'a general approach to security and control which is not consistent with assessed risk' reinforcing 'an apprehensive and security-dominated mind-set' (PRT 2011a: 38). Thus, Maghaberry's operational priorities were 'configured' to a 'level of risk' disproportionate to that posed by most prisoners. In the two 'separated houses' holding politically affiliated prisoners, the PRT considered staffing excessive, well beyond maximum security levels in England. It recommended a 'reconfiguration of existing prison space for lower risk prisoners' together with 'settlement of the continuing issues around separated prisoners' through a 'less restrictive regime with appropriate levels of supervision and security' (PRT 2011a: 14).

The PRT proposed that a reinvigorated Prison Service, monitored by an external, independent oversight body, could contribute positively to 'the creation of a safer society' (PRT 2011a: 26). It identified 'three pillars' necessary to achieve that objective: punishment delivered in prisons 'justly and fairly'; security and safety; and conditions protecting and promoting 'respect for human dignity' in line with 'human rights'. In such an environment, prisoners could be challenged 'to change their behaviour and their lives, repair the harm or address the conflicts linked to their offending, and improve their prospects for successful resettlement' (PRT 2011a: 27). The three pillars were presented as 'preconditions for a modern, progressive and effective prison system' consistent with the World Health Organization's commitment to four tests of a 'healthy prison': prisoners should be held in *safety*, treated with *respect and dignity* as human beings, engaged in *purposeful activity* and prepared for *resettlement* delivered within a custodial ethos characterised by 'care', 'positive expectations' and 'respect' (World Health Organization 1999). The developmental priorities were:

— Central and local strategies, targets and standards that support and reflect the aim of creating a safer society by encouraging desistance from crime.
— Profiling the prison population to assess risks, needs and resources for change as an evidence base for rehabilitation.
— Individual sentence and custody plans for each prisoner actively supporting change rather than simply assessing risk or need.
— Effective partnerships with outside agencies and groups interlinking crime prevention, rehabilitation and reintegration.
— A revision of education and skills provision, offending behaviour programmes and information systems to support the core safer custody strategy (PRT 2011a: 66).

In June 2011, following publication of the PRT's Interim Report the recently appointed Director General of NIPS, Colin McConnell, launched the Northern Ireland Prison Service Strategic Efficiency and Effectiveness Programme (SEE).

Claimed as heralding 'a new and challenging era', SEE would offer a 'four year change programme the scale of which is not dissimilar to the changes [in policing] proposed by the Patten Commission' delivering 'end-to-end reform of the Prison Service' (Director General 2011: 1). Accepting the 'overwhelming need' for reform, he acknowledged that NIPS had failed in its duty of care for the 'most vulnerable'. It had been 'found wanting in management, organisational structures and work practices', in 'leadership and oversight' and in 'organisational culture'. The workforce was 'disaffected, demoralised and demotivated'. NIPS, therefore, would focus on becoming a 'cutting edge' public organisation making 'an invaluable contribution' to a 'new' and 'emerging' post-conflict society (Director General 2011: 2).

The Director General accepted that NIPS was 'rooted in the past', perpetuating 'wrong behaviours, attitudes and values'—yet he justified that prevailing ethos as both 'appropriate' and 'required' at the time (Director General 2011: 4). This was a thinly veiled reference to the incarceration of politically affiliated prisoners. He did not comment, however, on the extent to which the negative ethos had permeated throughout the prison system in which 'ordinary' prisoners were the majority population living in deficient accommodation and experiencing punitive, disengaged regimes. He proposed a 'back to basics' approach to provide 'safe and secure custody'. Reform would prioritise: a 'new deal for prison staff and managers'; 'more dynamic security', 'rehabilitative capability'; goal-setting and 'performance monitoring'; 'external partnerships'; 'training, support and development opportunities' for officers; and a 'Prison Estate Strategy'. This reform would be delivered under the banner of a new 'statement of purpose' to ensure 'public safety by reducing the risk of offending through the management and rehabilitation of offenders in custody' (Director General 2011: 5–6).

In an implicit admission that NIPS systemically had failed to address the World Health Organization's fundamental principles for 'healthy prisons', the Director General committed 'from this day' to 'safe, decent and secure custody' (Director General 2011: 6). To that end he guaranteed 'structural change', including a redundancy scheme to reduce significantly the size of the workforce. For retained staff, 'prisoner engagement' would be an operational priority enabling rehabilitation. New officers would be recruited at a cheaper support grade mentored by qualified Prison Officer Offender Supervisors. The new training and development process laid bare the deeply institutionalised malaise within the management and staffing of the prisons: resistance to cultural change; operational inflexibility; ineffective engagement with outside professionals and prisoners; and endemic failure in the duty of care. The programme would be delivered through a 'change management' strategy, implemented by 'a dedicated—and experienced—change team' with identified targets met by 2015 (Director General 2011: 14).

Four months after the Director General's speech the PRT presented its final report (PRT 2011b). While welcoming the launch of the SEE Programme it criticised the lack of progress towards resolving the 'endemic and systemic problems' identified in its interim report with 'little or no buy-in' from the Prison Officers Association (PRT 2011b: 5–6). The sense of frustration was palpable as it criticised the lack of progress in cultural transformation and working practices, making it clear that 'those not prepared to make the journey' should be confronted (PRT 2011b: 6). Asserting that the Review offered a 'once in a generation' opportunity to reform a 'service whose ethos was shaped' by the conflict, the PRT considered eight months had been lost. The 'public sector', it stated, could not 'continue to operate or defend a system which is both wasteful and ineffective' (PRT 2011b: 7).

The scope of the final report was unprecedented, culminating in 40 detailed recommendations for immediate attention (PRT 2011b: 81–84). A progressive and effective prison system 'must support and reflect human rights standards and ethical values … based on the premise that prisoners within it can develop and change … provid[ing] the opportunities for them to do so' (PRT 2011b: 9). Thus it embedded NIPS reform within moral and human rights obligations restricted not only to humane containment, but extending to rehabilitation as the 'core function' of incarceration thus generating: personal development; purposeful activity;

education; vocational training; social skills; independent living; reintegration; and desistance from offending. Based on internationally agreed standards and rules, the PRT established priorities for appointing and training prison staff.

The PRT identified three significant alternatives to prison custody: supervised activity orders for fine defaulters; statutory time limits for remands; and community-based sanctions for those sentenced to three months or less (PRT 2011b: 28). It proposed that Maghaberry should operate as three smaller, discrete units: remands and short sentences; long sentences and life; and 'high risk', operating within 'appropriate levels of security, activity and care'. Stepping back from much of the evidence gathered, the PRT recommended *either* re-siting Magilligan *or* reconfiguration for long or life-sentenced prisoners *or* refurbishment. Given the PRT's unambiguous call for Magilligan's closure this left the door open to its retention, albeit with a potentially redefined role and improved conditions.

Recognising that Hydebank Wood remained an 'unsuitable environment' shared by women and young male adults, the PRT recommended a new, small, discrete prison for women 'within an actual or virtual community network, to prevent isolation and ensure a range of service provision … a complex of buildings that contained a secure custodial pod, with other services … attached and within a secure perimeter' for 'all women in custody, under supervision or subject to other court orders' (PRT 2011b: 69). Noting the success of initiatives for women prisoners offered via discrete funding for those most in need of support, the PRT recommended further partnerships between statutory, voluntary and community organisations alongside appropriate mental health care support integrated with community-based services.

The PRT identified young offenders, also held in Hydebank Wood, as 'the forgotten group in the Northern Ireland prison system', denied the level of resources available to under-18s held at the juvenile justice centre (PRT 2011b: 70). It considered provision for young adults to be 'woefully short', inadequate as 'an environment which supports, stretches and challenges young adults' to change their behaviour. Reflecting previous inspection and independent monitoring board findings it specified: 'insufficient activity, some of dubious quality'; 'no coherent strategy'; 'an outdated curriculum'; 'insufficient collaboration with external partners'; 'serious problems of teaching and under-achievement'; 'wasted' resources; and 'wholly unsuitable' accommodation (PRT 2011b: 71–72). It recommended a community-based multi-agency partnership to offer an alternative to the prevailing culture, a rebuilding programme to establish accommodation and facilities conducive to proactive and 'safe' staff–young people relationships and the redesignation of the institution as a secure college with a comprehensive skill-based programme delivered by a 'multi-disciplinary trained staff group … in partnership with a range of external providers and agencies' (PRT 2011b: 72). Repeating the severe critique in its first report, the PRT was unequivocal in stating that 'gradual or incremental improvements' could not 'achieve the scale of change required'; this would be advanced only through a 'high level and well-resourced change programme' (PRT 2011b: 5).

'Change Management'; 'Fundamental Reform'?

Accepting without reservation the PRT's findings and recommendations, the Justice Minister, David Ford, stated that he and the Prisons Director, Colin McConnell, were committed to fundamental reform. Within a month, 650 prison officers aged over 50, approximately a third of all serving officers, were offered voluntary redundancy and 99 per cent registered interest.[15] In December 2011, the Prisons Review Oversight Group was appointed to oversee and guarantee implementation of the PRT's recommendations. In late May 2012, Sue McAllister was appointed as the new Director General, identifying the NIPS 'reform programme' as 'one of the most challenging undertaken by the public sector anywhere in the United Kingdom'.[16]

In the 2012–13 NIPS Annual Report she heralded the progress of the 'extensive programme of reform' (NIPS 2013: 6). Regarding staffing, she noted that 544 applications for early retirement had been received and 360 granted. A further 157 would be allowed to leave when 'operationally possible'; eight governors and 20 senior officers had applications under consideration. Of the £173,660,000 NIPS net operating costs for 2012–13, £84,531,000 were staffing costs. Early retirement packages within the Voluntary Early Retirement scheme (VER) alongside the Strategic Efficiency and Effectiveness programme (SEE), amounted to £43,873,000 (NIPS 2013: 34). The first recruitment of prison officers since the early 1990s followed. Redefining the previously ring-fenced officer's role and responsibilities, 241 custody officers were recruited and 166 operational support grades and night officers were upgraded. The Director General's intention was the integration of newly appointed staff with experienced officers, 'transform[ing] the Service to provide regimes that support prisoners through custody and back into the community' (NIPS 2013: 6). Reflecting the PRT expectations, prisoner support and rehabilitation would be central to the change programme.

Alongside reduced staffing levels a 'Target Operating Model' was introduced to challenge 'outdated and ineffective' working practices. It revealed that key targets previously agreed to meet the strategic aim of safe, secure and decent custody had not been met. These included: reduction in self-harm; reduction in prisoner complaints to the Prison Ombudsman; out-of-cell time; and adequate staff training. By July 2013, of the 40 PRT recommendations only four had been achieved: 'maintaining and publishing detailed routine data; setting up a change management team; setting up a Ministerial oversight group; [and] under 18s moved from Hydebank Wood' (NIPS 2013: 20).

A new inspection of Maghaberry, however, was critical. In three of the four tests of a 'healthy prison'—safety, respect, and purposeful activity—the outcomes for

[15] V Kearney, 'Huge response to prison officers' redundancy plan' *BBC News*, 9 December 2011.

[16] Department of Justice (DoJ), 'New Director General for Northern Ireland Prison Service appointed' press release, 31 May 2012.

prisoners were assessed 'insufficient' (CJINI/HMCIP 2012). The fourth, resettlement, was considered 'reasonable'. Some progress had been made but 'significant weaknesses' remained, not least being the prison's failure to 'provide a sufficiently safe environment' for prisoners (CJINI/HMCIP 2012: v). Over half the prison's population (538) shared small cells designed for one prisoner, and minimal activities were available with prisoners locked for long periods in their cells; 50 per cent of prisoners had no work and were locked down, many sharing cramped cells, for 20 hours a day. Despite such a critical report NIPS remained confident that its recommendations were being progressed (NIPS 2013: 27).

A year later Hydebank Wood Young Offenders Centre was inspected. Given the severe criticisms raised by inspectors in 2008 and 2011 and the concerns of the PRT in 2013 there had been little progress. Of the four healthy prison tests 'only in resettlement work were outcomes for prisoners reasonably good' (CJINI/HMCIP 2013: v). The tests for 'safety' and 'respect' were found to be 'not sufficiently good', and 'purposeful activity' was rated 'poor'. Summarising its detailed report the Chief Inspectors were concerned about: the 'overall safety of the institution'; 'inertia in developing a robust approach to violence reduction'; the failure to fully learn 'lessons from recent deaths in custody'; 'complacent' staff attitudes to self-harm; 'care' for the 'most vulnerable'; 'reactive' security that 'lacked proportionality'; a 'poor' segregation regime; and 'disengagement and indifference on the part of some staff'. The majority of prisoners 'spent too long locked in their cells and lacked opportunity to spend time in the open air.' They experienced 'regime slippage, frequent and unpredictable lock-downs, and activities were often cancelled at short notice, all of which was fundamentally disrespectful'. Finally, 'only a small number of prisoners accessed work or education regularly' and were offered a 'narrow' curriculum with little relevance to 'the needs of prisoners, employers or the local labour market' (CJINI/HMCIP 2013: v). The inspectors made 95 recommendations.

Persistent negative inspections clearly raised problems for the independent Prison Review Oversight Group whose principal task was to oversee the realisation of the PRT reforms. It recognised the parlous state of industrial relations in the prisons, exemplified in managers' and officers' profound resistance to change. Meeting with the Northern Ireland Assembly's Committee for Justice, it reported that both the Prison Officers Association and the Prison Governors Association considered reform was being imposed without consultation.[17] Stating its commitment to 'positive' initiatives to transform the Prison Service and benefit prisoners, the Prison Review Oversight Group (PROG) noted a 'disturbing breakdown between the staff, the governors, the managers and the director'. The POA considered this was an inevitable consequence of rushing reform without full consultation administered by senior managers unfamiliar with the jurisdiction

[17] Northern Ireland Assembly, Committee for Justice, Session 2012/2013, Prison Review Oversight Group *Annual Report: Briefing from Independent Members*, 13 June 2013, Official Report (Hansard).

and its recent history. It claimed that the new Director General and her 'change management' team had imported an inappropriate 'English model' without contextualising proposed reforms within the Northern Ireland situation and its recent past.[18] PROG also identified the failure to progress health care, particularly mental ill-health, to lessen the hours of lock-up, or to provide education and work opportunities for prisoners.

In March 2014, PROG reported that eight PRT recommendations had been met, with a further seven referred for independent assessment (PROG 2014). Those signed off focused on the role of Magilligan, health care governance, transfer of health care staff, integration of the SEE programme, delivery of the awards scheme, appointment of a Director of Rehabilitation, new NIPS discipline and performance management systems, and the development of a cross-departmental safer society strategy. Having appointed an 'Organisational Change Director', to bring to fruition the 40 PRT recommendations, NIPS sub-divided its reform programme into nine projects: Programme Management; NIPS Headquarters; Offender Management; Operating Leadership and Development; Learning and Skills; Processes; Estate Management; Strategy; and Health Care (PROG 2014: 6).

PROG provided a detailed account of each project's progress and an anticipated time frame for the realisation of planned objectives noting that 12 of the PRT's 40 recommendations had been signed off. A further seven had been referred for assessment to Criminal Justice Inspection Northern Ireland and two to the Regulation and Quality Improvement Authority (PROG 2014: 6). Thus, it had taken three years to accomplish less than half of the PRT's urgent objectives. Closer examination also reveals the delays in delivering fundamental reform. Given the strong critiques of the penal estate levelled by successive inspections and critical research reports, it was no surprise that the PRT established four major capital priorities: reconfiguration of Maghaberry; redevelopment of Magilligan; a new facility for women; and improvements to Hydebank Wood.

Regarding Maghaberry, 'progress has seen draft strategic outline cases for a high-security facility and a new visits facility' and further planning would 'produce a series of high level, costed options' for approval (PROG 2014: 18). While there had been a convincing case for the expected replacement of Magilligan with a new prison in a more accessible location for prisoners' families, the PRT's initial recommendation, this was rejected. Despite its difficult location Magilligan would be redeveloped. 'High level costed options' had been completed for a new women's prison with 'detailed designs and a planning application … proceeding through NIPS Integrated Design Team' (PROG 2014: 18). Finally, the refurbishment of

[18] At the meeting it was reported that the Prison Officers Association had claimed to the Committee that 'outsiders', meaning the Director General and senior members of the NIPS 'change management' team, were 'coming in from other jurisdictions' and imposing reforms that failed to take account of Northern Ireland's 'unique circumstances'. It was a position described as a managerial approach adopting an 'English solution to an Irish problem' without understanding fully the 'local' situation thereby causing 'resentment' among officers.

three houses at Hydebank Wood was under way. Noting the 'current financial climate' the report states that the 'financial pressures are very real and ultimately could influence the ability of the programme to deliver' (PROG 2014: 19). Within three years, realisation of the PRT's demand for a 'root and branch' reconfiguration of the Prison Service and the implementation of fundamental reform was in doubt.[19]

Conclusion

This chapter opened by emphasising the significance of contextualising the theoretical foundations and moral and philosophical justifications for punishments administered by the state on behalf of its citizens. It identified the enduring tension between the incapacitation and the rehabilitation of those who breach the criminal code noting a spectrum of incarceration from harsh regimes of deprivation to progressive regimes of resettlement. As discussed, that spectrum incorporates distinct but related objectives: to deter; to incapacitate; to rehabilitate. Whatever alternatives to prison exist, removing a citizen's freedom and status through incapacitation, underpins the politics, ideologies and policies of punishment. Calculating the time taken from the offender to the harm done to the victim—proportionality—remains a central defence of imprisonment. It is shared not only by those who 'make' laws and those who administer sentences, but also throughout a broad popular constituency under the apprehension that as long as sentences are proportionate to a crime's severity, they will deter others thereby reducing offending.

In all advanced democratic states there is, in principle, a commitment to incarceration that incapacitates but also rehabilitates and reintegrates prisoners into their communities. The defining tension is between incapacitation through inhumane containment (the most regressive being solitary confinement) and rehabilitation through enhanced regimes (the most progressive being open conditions). Where jurisdictions are located on this punishment spectrum reflects their historical, political, ideological and cultural contexts. Each differs, for example, in its minimum age of criminal responsibility, rate of incarceration, lengths of sentence, prisoner welfare and rights, prison conditions, family access and so on. The earlier discussion also noted the differential impact of prison on the lives of

[19] At an event, 'Delivering Prison Reform', held in November 2014 in Belfast, the Prison Reform Programme Team announced that NIPS would 'sign off' on all 40 PRT recommendations by April 2015 and reforms would be delivered despite severe budgetary cuts. Over 500 staff had left the Service and 300 custody officers had been appointed 'refreshing the prison officer group' and by 2024 NIPS staffing would be reduced from 3075 to 1250. While the team was confident that the 'fundamental transformation' required by the PRT would be realised, it recognised that 'much of what we do is still dictated by custom and practice'. In terms of 'embedding a culture of [staff] wanting to work differently' there remained a 'long, long way to go to see tangible changes'.

individuals and their communities. Societies transitioning from long-term political conflict face not only its out-workings in managing a declining population of politically affiliated prisoners, but also in the resettlement of those released early (see chapter 10 by Dwyer in this volume). Simultaneously they are faced with managing an 'ordinary' prison population previously marginalised and living with the conflict's legacy—in staffing, facilities, regimes, culture, and relations.

To understand and analyse current shifts in penal policy and practice in Northern Ireland's prisons, therefore, it is imperative to reflect on the impact of the conflict on the prison estate and the operational policies and practices embedded within a punitive, high-security culture of containment that continued beyond the mass early release of politically affiliated prisoners. Transitioning from prisons as primary sites of political conflict to places that house primarily ordinary prisoners inevitably has been a significant challenge for NIPS. Negotiations between the Prison Service and politically affiliated prisoners, held on restricted high-security regimes in Maghaberry, remain volatile. While significant, that has not been the sole issue of concern. As this chapter demonstrates, throughout the 2000s, inspection reports and primary research have revealed the parlous state of Northern Ireland's prisons. While the PRT was given neither the scope nor resources available to the Patten Commission on policing (see the chapter by Topping in this volume), its consultation, analysis and recommendations offered a template for 'root and branch' reform.

Central to the PRT's report, and reflected in the sparse independent research conducted during this period, remains the abdication of responsibility for the welfare of prisoners. Specifically, this includes mental ill-health, suicide and self-harm, restrictive regimes, lack of opportunity for creative and productive endeavour, disproportionate time spent locked in cells, inadequate prison visiting and the impact on prisoners' families, and persistent tensions in staff–prisoner relations. The PRT's profound concern regarding the operational strategies and practices across the penal estate, alongside the multiple failings identified in highly critical inspectorate reports, cannot be resolved by policy statements of intent. While many of these failings, particularly mental ill-health, suicide and self-harm and lock-downs are present in prisons in England and Wales, Northern Ireland has a relatively low prison population and therefore the potential to develop alternatives *to* custody alongside alternatives *in* custody. Yet, as Sim (2009: 4–5) concludes from his extensive work in English prisons, given the 'deeply punitive array of policies and practices carried out in the name of rehabilitation' there remains an inherent disjuncture between the 'rhetoric and reality' of penal reformism. In most prisons what was proclaimed as rehabilitation was '*never* put into practice' (Sim 2009: 6, emphasis in original).

The NIPS stated intention to progress the PRT's 40 recommendations to fulfilment in principle suggests a commitment to reforming a demonstrably dysfunctional service. Yet, as stated, it will take considerable time and independent research to assess the impact of such reforms, if realised in practice, on the daily lives and experiences of prisoners especially in a climate of economic stringency.

While the severe punitive regimes of US prisons are not present for the majority of prisoners in Northern Ireland, its regimes fall significantly short of the progressive end of the spectrum exemplified by the Nordic states. The prison estate as a whole, for all the reasons discussed, remains unfit for purpose, with out-of-cell-time seriously limited and engaging programmes absent for most prisoners. In contrast to other European states, provision for families of prisoners remains inadequate (see Scharff-Smith and Gampell 2011). These contextual pressures have consequences for prisoners' agency, their potential as 'independent actors whose actions help to determine the meanings and effects of punishment' and their 'ability to negotiate power' (Bosworth 1999: 3). On the landings, behind the doors, prisoners are clearly at a disadvantage in this negotiation, bereft of 'choice, autonomy and responsibility'—the components of agency. In this closed environment each prisoner's personal history and unique present is objectified and 'mortified' (Goffman 1968), their identity reduced to a name, a number and a sentence to be served.

The introduction to this chapter establishes that prisons function as total institutions administered through hidden circuits of governance. Thus, penal management in Northern Ireland (NIPS) operates within the responsible state department (Justice). Yet, as also discussed, prisons are sites of confinement in which discretionary uses and abuses of power by those in authority often is arbitrary and, despite formal processes of inspections, monitoring and oversight, are rarely visible. As the preceding discussion shows, the uniqueness of Northern Ireland's prisons is derived in the conflict's legacy and their location within a relatively small jurisdiction. Despite the apparent political commitment to reform, all four prisons have continued to fail when assessed against international minimum standards expected of an advanced democratic society. As the projected period for implementation of the PRT's 40 recommendations draws to a close (mid-2015), the delay and disruption to their realisation threatens to derail the process. Successful implementation of intended reforms cannot be achieved simply by voicing the managerialist language of 'change management' and 'target operating models', but in the personal, social and opportunity contexts of incarceration in all its complex forms and manifestations. Alongside rigorous inspections, independent research into the operational regimes is necessary, prioritising the experiences of prisoners and staff, within a framework of internationally agreed rights, standards and compliance.

References

Amnesty International (1991) *Women in the Front Line* (London, Amnesty International).

Bosworth, M (1999) *Engendering Resistance: Agency and Power in Women's Prisons* (Dartmouth, Ashgate).

Boyle, K, Hadden, T and Hillyard, P (1975) *Law and State: The Case of Northern Ireland* (London, Martin Robertson).

Carrabine, E (2005) 'Prison Riots, Social Order and the Problem of Legitimacy' 45 *British Journal of Criminology* 896.
Cavadino, M and Dignan, J (2007) *The Penal System: An Introduction*, 4th edn (London, Sage).
Criminal Justice Inspection Northern Ireland (CJINI)/Her Majesty's Chief Inspector of Prisons (HMCIP) (2011) *Report on an unannounced short follow-up inspection of Hydebank Wood Young Offenders Centre, 21–25 March 2011* (Belfast, CJINI).
—— (2012) *Report on an announced inspection of Maghaberry Prison, 19–23 March 2012* (Belfast, CJINI).
—— (2013) *Report on an announced inspection of Hydebank Wood Young Offenders Centre, 18–22 February 2013* (Belfast, CJINI).
Corcoran, M (2006) *Out of Order: The Political Imprisonment of Women in Northern Ireland 1972–1998* (Cullompton, Willan Publishing).
CPT (2004) *Conclusions and Recommendations of the Committee against Torture* Committee Against Torture (CAT/C/CR/33/3) Recommendation (m).
Currie, E (1998) *Crime and Punishment in America* (New York, Holt).
Davis, A (1990) *Angela Davis: An Autobiography* (London, The Women's Press).
—— (2003) *Are Prisons Obsolete?* (New York, Seven Stories Press).
Director General (2011) *Director General's Speech: NIPS SEE Launch, 28 June* (Belfast, Northern Ireland Prison Service).
Dwyer, C (2007) 'Risk, Politics and the "Scientification" of Political Judgement: Prisoner Release and Conflict Transformation in Northern Ireland' 47 *British Journal of Criminology* 779.
Fleury-Steiner, B and Longazel, J (2014) *The Pains of Mass Imprisonment* (New York, Routledge).
Foucault, M (1977) *Discipline and Punish: The Birth of the Prison* (London, Allen Lane).
Gardiner Committee (1975) *Report of a Committee to Consider, in the Context of Civil Liberties and Human Rights Measures to Deal with Terrorism in Northern Ireland* (Cmnd 5847) (London, HMSO).
Garland, D (1985) *Punishment and Welfare: A History of Penal Strategies* (Aldershot, Gower).
Gil-Robles, A (2005) *Report on Visit to the UK 4–12 November 2004* (Strasbourg, Office of the Commissioner for Human Rights).
Goffman, E (1968) *Asylums* (Harmondsworth, Penguin).
Hillsborough Agreement (2010) *Agreement at Hillsborough Castle* (Belfast, Northern Ireland Office).
Hillyard, P (1987) 'The Normalization of Special Powers: from Northern Ireland to Britain' in P Scraton (ed), *Law, Order and the Authoritarian State: Readings in Critical Criminology* (Milton Keynes, Open University Press).
Her Majesty's Chief Inspector of Prisons (HMCIP) (2003) *Report on a full announced inspection of HM Prison Maghaberry, 13–17 May 2002* (London, HM Inspectorate of Prisons).
Her Majesty's Chief Inspector of Prisons (HMCIP)/Criminal Justice Inspection Northern Ireland (CJINI) (2005) *Report on an unannounced inspection of the imprisonment of women in Northern Ireland, Ash House, Hydebank Wood Prison, 28–30 November 2004* (Belfast, HM Inspectorate of Prisons).
—— (2008) *Report on an announced inspection of Hydebank Wood Young Offenders Centre, 5–9 November 2007* (Belfast, HM Inspectorate of Prisons).
—— (2009) *Report on an unannounced full follow-up inspection of Maghaberry Prison, 19–23 January 2009* (Belfast, CJINI).

Ignatieff, M (1978) *A Just Measure of Pain* (London, MacMillan).
Leder, D (2004) 'Imprisoned Bodies: The Life-World of the Incarcerated' 31 *Social Justice* 51.
Mac Ionnrachtaigh, F (2013) *Language, Resistance and Revival* (London, Pluto Press).
McEvoy, K (2001) *Paramilitary Imprisonment in Northern Ireland: Resistance, Management, and Release* (Oxford, Oxford University Press).
McGuffin, J (1973) *Internment* (Dublin, Anvil Books).
McKeown, L (2001) *Out of Time: Irish Republican Prisoners Long Kesh 1972–2000* (Belfast, Beyond the Pale).
Moore, L and Scraton, P (2014) *The Incarceration of Women: Punishing Bodies, Breaking Spirits* (Basingstoke, Palgrave Macmillan).
Northern Ireland Affairs Committee (NIAC) (2004) *The Separation of Paramilitary Prisoners at HMP Maghaberry, Second Report of the Session 2003–04* (HC 302-1) (London, The Stationery Office).
—— (2007) *The Northern Ireland Prison Service, First Report of the Session 2007–08* (HC 118-1) (London, The Stationery Office).
Northern Ireland Prison Service (NIPS) (2013) *Delivering Structural Change, Beginning Cultural Change: Annual Report and Accounts 2012–2013* (Belfast, Northern Ireland Prison Service).
O'Dowd, L, Rolston, B and Tomlinson, M (1980) *Northern Ireland: Between Civil Rights and Civil War* (London, CSE Books).
Parenti, C (1999) *Lockdown America: Police and Prisons in the Age of Crisis* (New York, Verso).
Pratt, J and Eriksson, A (2013) *Contrasts in Punishment: An Exploration of Anglophone Excess and Nordic Exceptionalism* (London, Routledge).
Prison Review Oversight Group (PROG) (2014) *Second Annual Report* (Belfast, Prison Oversight Group).
Prison Review Team (PRT) (2011a) *Review of the Northern Ireland Prison Service: Conditions, Management and Oversight of all Prisons. Interim Report, February 2011* (Belfast, Prison Review Team/Department of Justice NI).
—— (2011b) *Review of the Northern Ireland Prison Service: Conditions, Management and Oversight of all Prisons. Final Report, October 2011* (Belfast, Prison Review Team/ Department of Justice NI).
Quinney, R (2006) 'The Life Inside: Abolishing the Prison' 9 *Contemporary Justice Review* 269.
Rhodes, L (2006) 'Can there be Best Practice in Supermax?' in D Jones (ed), *Humane Prisons* (Oxford, Radcliffe Publishing).
Rolston, B (2010) '"Trying to Reach the Future through the Past": Murals and Memory in Northern Ireland' *Crime, Media, Culture* 285.
Rolston, B and Tomlinson, M (1986) 'Long-Term Imprisonment in Northern Ireland: Psychological or Political Survival?' in B Rolston and M Tomlinson (eds), *The Expansion of European Prison Systems* (Belfast, The European Group for the Study of Deviance and Social Control).
Scraton, P and Moore, L (2005) *The Hurt Inside: The Imprisonment of Women and Girls in Northern Ireland* (Belfast, NIHRC).
—— (2007) *The Prison Within: The Imprisonment of Women at Hydebank Wood 2004–2006* (Belfast, NIHRC).
Scharff-Smith, P and Gampell, P (2011) *Children of Imprisoned Parents* (Copenhagen, Danish Institute for Human Rights).

Shirlow, P and Murtagh, B (2006) *Belfast: Segregation, Violence and the City* (London, Pluto Press).

Sim, J (2009) *Punishment and Prisons: Power and the Carceral State* (London, Sage).

Simon, J (2007) *Governing Through Crime: How the War on Crime Transformed American Democracy and Created a Culture of Fear* (Oxford, Oxford University Press).

St Andrews Agreement (2006) *The St Andrews Agreement, October 2006* (Belfast, Northern Ireland Office).

Steele, J (2004) *Review of Safety at HMO Maghaberry* (Belfast, Safety Review Team to Secretary of State for Northern Ireland) (Steele Report).

Whitman, JQ (2005) *Harsh Justice: Criminal Punishment and the Widening Divide between America and Europe* (Oxford, Oxford University Press).

World Health Organization (1999) *Mental Health Provision in Prisons: A Consensus Statement* (Copenhagen, WHO Regional Office).

10

Prisoner Reintegration in a Transitional Society: The Northern Ireland Experience

CLARE DWYER

Introduction

The criminal justice system in Northern Ireland is experiencing a period of transition from dealing with intense political violence to a situation of relative peace. Although this period has witnessed seismic changes to the justice system it is evident that many challenges still lie ahead. The Belfast (Good Friday) Agreement (hereafter the Agreement), reached at multi-party talks on Northern Ireland on 10 April 1998, had as its political objective to bring an end to the conflict, which had lasted 30 years. Emerging from this three-decades-long conflict between groups loyal to the British state and republican groups seeking a unified Irish state, Northern Ireland has become a 'model' for transitional justice practices internationally (see Campbell et al 2004; McEvoy 2007; McEvoy and Shirlow 2009). The Agreement dealt with, inter alia, key process issues such as decommissioning, security, policing and justice, and the release of prisoners.

The central requirement of dealing with prisoner issues for both the British and Irish governments was to put in place a programme for the early release of prisoners convicted of 'conflict-related' offences. It is estimated that as many as 30,000 were interned or imprisoned throughout the 'Troubles' (see Shirlow and McEvoy 2008; Jamieson et al 2010), most notably in Long Kesh and the H-Blocks of the Maze Prison made infamous by the hunger strikes of 1981 (see McEvoy 2001). Although there is limited exploration in the literature on conflict transformation, the concept of releasing prisoners has had a prominent role in the international experience of political conflict (see Gormally and McEvoy 1995; Bell 2000; McEvoy 2001). International examples including Israel/Palestine, South Africa and Northern Ireland would confirm that prisoner release was an essential part of any negotiated peace agreement, not only as a confidence building measure, but as a major factor in securing peace. There are, however, key distinctions between the various international examples, particularly in regard to the actual modalities of release. Where some international experiences demonstrate the use of amnesties and/or release by executive order (Gormally and McEvoy 1995; Mallinder 2008), the system implemented in Northern Ireland, despite being part of a political process, introduced a 'normal' structured legalistic process for release. This legalistic mechanism was utilised successfully to circumnavigate ideologically charged discussions on political motivation, by setting out a process which included conditions for release of prisoners on licence and mechanisms for prisoner recall (Dwyer 2007). Whilst prisoner release under the Agreement was achieved by a politically informed but nonetheless pragmatic, instrumental and technical approach to peacemaking, the failure to formally recognise the political character of those imprisoned and released has continued to bedevil the process of reintegration.

Although the prisoner provisions under the Agreement[1] (and again in the St Andrews Agreement 2006)[2] emphasised the importance of the reintegration of 'politically motivated'[3] former prisoners (hereafter PMFPs) in this transitional process, 20 years after the ceasefires, reintegrative issues remain. In response to reintegration challenges, numerous Irish republican and British loyalist PMFP organisations emerged during and after the conflict to support ex-prisoners and prisoners' families in achieving full civic, social and economic participation, despite the considerable stigma of their criminal records and imprisonment experiences. Emerging from a history of political conflict, self-help values were developed and practised by 'politically motivated' prisoners in jail, which then continued outside the prison. This informed the work of many of the PMFP organisations whose objectives remained to ensure that PMFPs fully integrate into society, that all discrimination barriers are removed, to change the attitudes of wider society, to reconstruct the ex-prisoner identity in a positive direction and to contribute to broader social issues including the promotion of conflict transformation and peace building (see Shirlow and McEvoy 2008; Dwyer 2012, 2013b).

[1] 'The British and Irish Governments continue to recognise the importance of measures to facilitate the reintegration of prisoners into the community by providing support both prior to and after release, including assistance directed towards availing of employment opportunities, re-training and/or re-skilling, and further education' (The Belfast (Good Friday) Agreement 1998: annex b, para 5).

[2] 'The Government will work with business, trade unions and ex-prisoner groups to produce guidance for employers which will reduce barriers to employment and enhance re-integration of former prisoners' (St Andrews Agreement 2006: annex b).

[3] Prisoners were deemed as 'politically motivated' if they were serving a 'conflict-related' sentence and were convicted of scheduled offences during the conflict in Northern Ireland. Scheduled offences are those offences listed as an appendix to the emergency legislation in Northern Ireland (including sch 1 of the Northern Ireland (Emergency Provisions) Acts 1973, 1978, 1996). Scheduled offences are those normally associated with the commission of terrorist acts (eg, murder, manslaughter, explosions, serious offences against the person, rioting, collecting information likely to be of use to terrorists etc). Those convicted of scheduled offences were members of or had connections to various paramilitary organisations including (but not limited to): the Provisional Irish Republican Army (PIRA), Official Irish Republican Army (OIRA), Irish National Liberation Army (INLA) from the republican community; and the Ulster Volunteer Force (UVF) and Ulster Defence Association (UDA) from the loyalist community.

This chapter will explore the ways in which the organisations that work with, and for, the 'politically motivated' ex-prisoner community were developed through an ethos of 'self-help'. In presenting a critical analysis of the concept of 'self-help' and its application to the experience of the reintegrative process, this chapter will underscore the views of the PMFP community and will illustrate the fundamental importance that the 'self-help' approach has been to prisoners released following a political conflict. PMFPs understand that they are best placed to empathise and understand the effect imprisonment has had on their colleagues, to ensure that they control their own destiny and to resist any attempts made to 'criminalise' their prison or post-prison experience (see McEvoy 2001). Set within Northern Ireland's unique circumstances as a society transitioning out of conflict, this experience of prisoner reintegration provides a platform for wider discussions of ex-prisoner self-help groups, and contains important lessons for those seeking to promote desistance from crime and violence, politically motivated and otherwise. In the widespread discussion of how to combat terrorism, few are discussing the issue of politically motivated ex-prisoners and the question of reintegration (for exceptions see McEvoy et al 2007; LaFree and Miller 2008; Bjorgo and Horgan 2009; Horgan 2009). The chapter concludes with discussions on the wider implications of the Northern Irish experience for the reintegration of prisoners, including the role of reintegration in peace building and conflict transformation more generally.

Prisoner Reintegration: Contested Terminology and Challenges in a Transitional Society

Northern Ireland is a society emerging from years of violent political conflict (referred to locally as the Troubles) in which more than 3600 people have been killed and over 40,000 injured. The main participants in this ethno-national conflict included republican and loyalist groups and state agencies, including the local police and the British Army. The non-state actors (primarily members of republican and loyalist paramilitary groups), claiming to 'fight' on behalf of their constituent communities, were responsible for almost 90 per cent of these deaths, and a majority of their victims were civilians (see McEvoy et al 2006). Research has shown that the motivations for involvement in the conflict could be understood as a fusion of 'experiential' factors (driven by the onset of violence and brutality, and community violations), 'ideological frameworks' (strengthened by a strong sense of collective identity) and 'structural' factors (political leadership, social injustice and socio-economic positions) (see McAuley et el 2009: 24).

As noted, it is estimated that during the course of the conflict, over 30,000 people were imprisoned (or interned) as a result of their participation in the conflict (Jamieson et al 2010). These individuals draw a clear distinction between themselves and those prisoners convicted of crimes that were not 'political'. Of course, few would dispute that all crimes are in fact inherently political (Quinney 1970; Tunnell 1993), and that the entire criminal justice process is politicised because of the broader social ordering of the state which defines what crime is. However, whilst this notion of the politicised nature of crime is unquestionable, for many the notion of 'political crime', in the context of the Northern Irish conflict, is further distinguished. It is not the crimes themselves that distinguish them as 'political crimes' but rather a higher ideological goal, the particular motivation behind the act and finally the systems used for 'processing' those convicted of such crimes (see McEvoy 2001; Dwyer 2010).

Throughout the conflict the criminal justice system in Northern Ireland found itself dealing with two distinct prisoner types. First, 'traditional', 'ordinaries' or 'ordinary decent criminals', who once convicted were processed through the courts, sentenced and served their sentence in a 'traditional' prison setting. Second, there were those charged with a suspected terrorist offence (a 'scheduled offence'),[4] who had their case heard before a single judge in a special juryless (Diplock) court and subsequently served their sentence in a very distinct prison regime. The 'politically motivated' prisoner population therefore understood that their political ideology and experience with the criminal justice system set their experience apart from the experience of 'ordinary' prisoners (see McEvoy 2001).

The Agreement provided for the release and reintegration of the remaining 'qualifying'[5] 'politically motivated' prisoners (see Dwyer 2007). The government gave effect to its commitment through the provisions of the Northern Ireland (Sentences) Act 1998 which provided for a collective early release scheme and set out both the conditions for release of prisoners on licence and the mechanisms for prisoner recall. This framework was therefore distinct from a 'blanket amnesty', insofar as those released could have their licences revoked if they re-engaged in criminal/terrorist activities and they also continued to hold a criminal record (Dwyer 2007). It is widely acknowledged that holding a criminal record can be a serious obstacle for prisoners post-release, and as with 'ordinary' ex-prisoners, PMFPs have encountered various barriers in their attempt to reintegrate in post-conflict Northern Ireland. Before moving to explore the reintegration experience of PMFP in Northern Ireland, it is important to note the various similarities and differences that exist between 'ordinary' and 'politically motivated' former prisoners,

[4] See n 3 above.

[5] Qualifying prisoners are defined in the Northern Ireland (Sentences) Act 1998 (s 3(7)) as prisoners convicted of a 'scheduled' or 'terrorist' offence before the signing of the Agreement (10 April 1998) and who were not subject to an Attorney General certificate indicating that the offence has been de-scheduled. In order to qualify for release, prisoners must be serving a sentence passed in Northern Ireland which was for a qualifying offence and is one of imprisonment for life or for a term of at least five years. The prisoner must not be a supporter of a 'specified' organisation (a 'specified' organisation is one specified by the Secretary of State in legislation as not being committed to exclusively peaceful and democratic means); and that if released immediately, she or he would not be likely to become a supporter of a 'specified' organisation or involved in acts of terrorism connected with Northern Ireland. Finally, prisoners serving life sentences, if released immediately, must not be considered a danger to the public.

their understanding of the reintegration process and the challenges faced. This next section of the chapter aims to briefly contextualise the notion of 'reintegration' and the various barriers encountered by former prisoners in their attempt to 'resettle' post-release.

One key area of contention across the broader discussions within the reintegrative literature is the actual use of the term 'reintegration' itself, which remains highly controversial for numerous reasons. The traditional notion of 'reintegration' draws from generic criminological discourses on prisoner reintegration and is often linked to a series of 'R's including resettlement, re-entry, recovery, rehabilitation and reforming. There is a broad philosophical understanding that reintegration is a process to create opportunity for individuals to voluntarily change the way they act and think about themselves and their relationships. It is then through this process that former prisoners address their offending behaviour and subsequently deal with criminal motivations. However, scholars across the criminological discipline, whose focus is on 'ordinary' former prisoners argue that this notion of reintegration remains highly contested (Braithwaite 1989; Sampson and Laub 1993; Maruna 2001; Maruna and LeBel 2003; Petersilia 2003; Raynor and Maguire 2006), 'operating in a theoretical vacuum with no clear explanation for how the process is supposed to work' (Maruna et al 2004: 8).

Literature on PMFPs in Northern Ireland goes further and draws out key distinctions between the identity of PMFPs and 'ordinaries' and explores the challenges linked to the understanding of the reintegration process (see Shirlow and McEvoy 2008; Dwyer 2013b). Many PMFPs considered their incarceration to be part of a wider political struggle and viewed their incarceration as a continuation of their struggle for 'the cause' (see McEvoy et al 2004). Therefore, any connection to concepts like rehabilitation and reformation, where the ex-prisoner must somehow change their 'unacceptable ways' in order to rejoin society is quickly rejected by the PMFP community. It has been often claimed that such a notion of reformation and identity change does not consider the very particular relationship PMFPs have within their local communities (see McEvoy et al 2004; Shirlow et al 2005; Gormally et al 2007; Shirlow and McEvoy 2008; McEvoy and Shirlow 2009; Dwyer 2013b). Counter to criminological understandings of reintegration, PMFPs would strongly contend that they do not need to be 'reintegrated' back into their communities; on the contrary, they argue that they would have full community acceptance and support 'on return' (see Shirlow et al 2005). Many PMFPs maintain that they are an organic element of their communities and indeed that the respect in which they were held locally was evidenced by the fact that they often assumed leadership positions in civil and community life (Dwyer 2012), not to mention as political representatives as in the case of the republican political party, Sinn Féin.[6] In earlier research, Dwyer (2010) notes that PMFPs claim that they do not

[6] At least 17 members of the Legislative Assembly in Northern Ireland have 'conflict-related' convictions, including the deputy First Minister Martin McGuiness and Junior Ministers Gerry Kelly and Jennifer McCann. PMFPs also act as special advisers to members of the Executive and serve as local councillors throughout Northern Ireland (see Dwyer 2013a).

need to address 'individualistic' motivation and reject any linkage with 'criminal' motivation. One former republican prisoner stated:

> Everybody and their granny knows that it doesn't matter who you are, what political position you come from … [they] know that the people held in Long Kesh [Maze prison] would not have been there if it wasn't for the political conflict (cited in Dwyer 2010: 134).

Notwithstanding these contested debates on the terminology and understandings of the reintegrative process, it is evident that as a consequence of holding a criminal record, all former prisoners inevitably face numerous obstacles throughout the resettlement process, regardless of whether they are 'political' or 'ordinary'. The role of full social, political and economic inclusion in the reintegration process is well established among 'ordinary', 'non-political' ex-prisoners (Uggen 2000; Laub and Sampson 2001; Visher and Travis 2003; Gadd and Farrall 2004; Ward and Maruna 2007). Uggen et al (2004) claim that it is often the case that possession of a criminal record effectively strips the most basic rights of citizenship, and in turn impacts on the wider reintegration process (see also Metcalf et al 2001; Travis and Petersilia 2001; Farrall 2004; Farrall and Sparks 2006; Behan and O'Donnell 2008). Research on the consequences of holding a criminal record and the reintegration process has highlighted the numerous difficulties former prisoners face, including psychological and emotional trauma, re-establishing family life and community relations, political participation, education and training and gaining employment (see Uggen 2000; Laub and Sampson 2001; Padfield 2011; Naylor 2011).

Similar to 'ordinary' ex-prisoners, 'politically motivated' former prisoners also experience numerous barriers in their attempt to reintegrate into post-conflict Northern Ireland and although it is 17 years since the signing of the Agreement, discussions on such challenges remain (see Dwyer 2013a). It is widely reported that PMFPs continue to encounter various social, psychological and emotional needs (see Gormally et al 2007; Shirlow and McEvoy 2008; Dwyer 2010; Jamieson et al 2010), but they also experience many legislative barriers which lead to limitations on obtaining employment, insurance, ability to travel and many other areas of civil participation (see Dwyer 2013a). A recent report published by the Office of First Minister and deputy First Minister (OFMdFM) highlights these issues and sets out that, despite the commitment to the reintegration and inclusion of former prisoners within the Agreement, PMFPs continue to, 'experience labour market exclusion and legislative barriers regarding their inclusion into economic life. Resulting low income may also predict psychological morbidity, the extension of social exclusion, poor life chances and negative impacts upon their families' (OFMdFM 2012: 15).

The distinct feature of the reintegrative process for 'politically motivated' ex-prisoners in Northern Ireland, however, has been how former prisoners have responded to reintegrative challenges and how numerous ex-prisoner groups have been developed to manage the reintegration process for PMFPs. Given the view of 'politically motivated' former prisoners of themselves as 'political' and their subsequent refusal to utilise the services of traditional reintegration agencies, a large number of community-based self-help groups (largely based on paramilitary factions, ie, loyalist or republican) were established, wherein former prisoners and staff, manage and deliver services to their colleagues (see Dwyer 2012). These organisations have been engaged in exploring both the individual and collective consequences of imprisonment for former prisoners and focus on areas such as family breakdown, psychological and emotional support, including risks to physical and mental health, trauma, addiction, education, job training and securing employment, welfare and legal representation and legislative lobbying (see Grounds and Jamieson 2003; Shirlow et al 2005; Shirlow and McEvoy 2008; Jamieson and Grounds 2008; Jamieson et al 2010; Dwyer 2010; Rolston 2011), as well as working on keys issues related to peace building and conflict transformation. Gormally et al (2007: 10) suggest that the 'reintegration' of PMFPs should be understood as a process that 'both seeks to address specific problems generated by the conflict and also to encourage active steps to build a peaceful and stable society'.

What is most apparent from the research in this area and what is most relevant for discussions in this chapter, is the importance of the ethos of 'self-help'. The various PMFP self-help reintegration organisations in Northern Ireland were developed and are managed by the former prisoner constituency, they are premised on a vision of 'community-based' reintegration and are grounded in the idea of mutual aid, whereby members look after or deal with the needs of both PMFPs and their wider local communities. In order to understand and contextualise this notion of 'self-help', this next section will examine the traditional understandings of self-help and mutual aid, before moving to examine how this has influenced the work of scholars working in the area of the reintegration of former prisoners more generally.

'Unpacking' the Notion of 'Self-Help'

There can be a general understanding that the term 'self-help' implies that individuals get involved in efforts to benefit themselves. However, contrary to this, one of the key features of self-help groups is that people come together to help one another (see Humphreys and Rappaport 1994; Humphreys 1997). The 'self-help' concept stems from the belief that people *facing a similar challenge* can help each other simply by coming together. When functioning as a helper, the individual experiences an extremely valuable and unique opportunity to enhance his or her self-worth and to feel empowered in a very therapeutic manner (King 2004). So, in effect, helping others validates the helper as an important member of his or her community. Indeed, Riessman (1965) proposed in his 'helper therapy principle' that those who help others, help themselves, by increasing their commitment to recovery, perception of importance to others, social status and sense of independence (see Zemore et al 2004). Riessman (1997) further notes that this notion of the 'helper therapy principle' is an age-old therapeutic approach. This is evident in the writings of Kropotkin which state that the notion of mutual aid 'is so remote an origin and is so deeply interwoven with all the past evolution of the human race that it has been maintained by mankind up to the present time notwithstanding all vicissitudes of history' (1907: 223).

This innate nature of 'mutual aid' has been confirmed in the numerous studies that indicate that common interest groups, which transcend kinship ties, appear very early and were more widespread among ancient societies (see Lowie 1947; Anderson 1971; Katz 1981). An important element that produces the healing effect of self-help is that the helper has experienced a common problem and it is this shared experience that makes help therapy possible. Scholars would argue that 'woundedness', therefore, has a significant sensitising effect for some healers, and that a significant experience of suffering is highly conducive to becoming an effective healer (Laskowski and Pellicore 2002). Jackson (2001: 36) notes that as a 'wounded' healer, the healer 'may turn those sufferings to account as sources of knowledge, as a basis for understanding, appreciating, and empathising with the wounds and sufferings of others'.

This notion of 'wounded healer' has been referred to as both a metaphor and an archetype and this theme can be found in mythology, religion, traditional stories and Western psychology (see Miller and Baldwin 1987; Sedgwick 1994; Laskowski and Pellicore 2002). Heavily influenced by the notion of the 'wounded healer', psychotherapists such as Carl Jung discuss the idea of the 'wounded physician' wherein psychotherapists should undergo training analysis which would prepare therapists to take into account their own personal psychological problems. It is this acknowledgement of 'own hurt' that allows 'the measure of his power to heal' (Jung cited in Jackson 2001: 21). Interestingly, the writings of Carl Jung had significant bearing on the development of one of the oldest and most widely known self-help organisations, Alcoholics Anonymous (AA). AA's very essence is the notion of ill or 'wounded' people playing a crucial role in the healing of other ill or a 'wounded' people (Kurtz 1997).

This self-help 'wounded healer' approach has at its core, the principle of members sharing their experience in attempt to solve their common problem together, which often results in members feeling a general de-stigmatisation and acceptance of their concerns. Referred to as the 'homogeneity of concern' (see Jacobs and Goodman 1989), identifying with others who share a 'problem' enables the therapeutic aspect of the self-help group. Humphreys (1997: 15) argues that this 'experience of learning that we need not suffer life's burdens alone … that we have something both to offer and to receive from other beings is too profound to be captured by such terms as … "better coping"'. As such, the development of self-help/mutual aid groups has not been confined to sharing coping strategies. In her work on self-help groups, Katz has categorised groups under two main umbrellas: first those that are 'natural and informal social networks of family, workmates, schoolmates, neighbours, friends and peers'; and second, those which are 'largely self-organised and self-directing, educational, healing, economic and socially supporting groups' (Katz 1981: 131). Katz has highlighted the array of groups which include anything from self-care in physical, mental and emotional help, including 'physical disabilities, bereavement, eating disorders, child abuse, ex-service men/women', to groups which have been set up to 'help so-called "deviants" (for example, ex-convicts, ex-prostitutes and former mental patients) reclaim or redefine their position among humanity' (Katz 1981: 131).

There are profound differences in the basic make-up of varying types of self-help group. Some groups focus on a condition members have which is permanent. Some focus on behaviour which can be changed, and others are focused on trying to effect changes in the larger political arena, and the participation varies greatly from group to group. But participants gain a sense of confidence and of being a worthwhile member by sharing with others who also identify with the problem. The evident grassroots nature of the self-help phenomenon (Gartner and Riessman 1984) is therefore reliant on the collective 'experiential knowledge' possessed by the membership. Broadly defined as information and wisdom gained from one's own life experiences or from the experiences of others (see Borkman 1976; Schiff and Bargal 2000), the exchange and communication of experiential knowledge is one of the fundamental aspects of all self-help groups (Powell 1990; Hasenfeld and Gidron 1993; Schubert and Borkman 1994). As is discussed below, this notion of 'experiential knowledge' was particularly important for members of the various PMFP organisations established since the end of the conflict in Northern Ireland. Self-help organisations provide the space for group members to have a sense that they are experts on their own 'problem' and are therefore best placed to provide the necessary support to fellow group participants. Most relevant for discussions on PMFP organisations, studies on self-help demonstrate that the development and motivation of self-help organisations plays a large role in the 'de-stigmatisation' and empowerment of its members by allowing a sense of autonomy and control, with an emphasis that 'those who help are helped most' (Gartner and Riessman 1984: 19). Interestingly, there have been a number of criminological studies which demonstrate a positive link between self-help and the reintegration process for 'ordinary' former prisoners. This next section, illustrates that whilst scholars have clearly highlighted the benefits of a self-help approach to prisoner reintegration, they also present arguments for the need to rethink the 'process' of reintegration, focusing on the wider role and impact a self-help approach can have on a prisoner's post-release experience.

The Role of 'Self-Help' Groups for Former Prisoners

Recent criminological research has identified the important role the self-help/mutual aid model can play in the reintegration of 'ordinary' former prisoners who work for the benefit of other former prisoners (see Maruna 2001; Maruna and Lebel 2003; Lebel 2008). This 'New Careers Movement' was premised on the idea that the skills, experience and knowledge of former prisoners would be utilised to help persons who have also been incarcerated.

Influenced by the 'New Careers Movement' (NCM) of the 1960s, various scholars have rejuvenated discussions of the 'helper principle' under the umbrella of the 'strengths-based' paradigm, wherein the skills, experience and knowledge of former prisoners would be utilised to help persons who have also been incarcerated (Maruna 2001; Maruna and LeBel 2003). One of the main contributors to the NCM, Cressey (1978) argues that both prisoners and former prisoners could make a positive contribution to the rehabilitation and reintegration of offenders. In his discussions on 'reflective reformation', Cressey contends that 'in attempting to reform others, the offender almost automatically accepts the relevant common purpose of the group, identifies himself closely with the other persons engaging in reformation and assigns status on the basis of anti-criminal behaviour' (Cressey 1955: 119). In their discussions on the 'helper principle', Pearl and Riessman (1965) also argue that the goal would be to 'devise ways of creating more helpers! Or to be more exact: how to transform receivers of help into dispensers of help; how to structure the situation so that receivers of help will be placed in roles requiring the giving of assistance' (Pearl and Riessman 1965: 88–89). The theoretical arguments found in Cressey's 'reflective reformation' and Riessman's 'helper principle' were subsequently implemented in a number of 'new careers development' programmes throughout the 1960s and 1970s (see Pearl and Riessman 1965; Grant 1968; Grant and Grant 1975). Grant (1968: 226–34) noted the impact of utilising ex-prisoners as a 'manpower resource in correctional rehabilitation and re-entry programs, building the benefits for training prisoners for "change agent roles"'.

Maruna and LeBel highlight the limited academic research on the area of ex-prisoner self-help/mutual aid groups even though many reintegrative measures exist which incorporate the 'helper principle'. In their recent work, Maruna and LeBel referred to a number of key examples of self-help prisoner organisations. LeBel (2008) observed the increased role which the 'self-help' and the 'helper principle' played in programmes developed in the 1970s, reflecting on the work of McAnany et al on former prisoners which found that, 'a self-help orientation comes very close to being the identifying mark of [the] groups, and appears to be based on a realisation that their identity as prisonised persons requires self-help' (McAnany et al 1974: 26 cited in LeBel 2008). Although there is a limited amount of academic research on the benefits of help given to and by former prisoners, that which does exist is both rich and significant (see Bazemore 1998; Maruna 2001; Maruna and LeBel 2003; Maruna et al 2004). Maruna's research in 2001 offers clear support to the link between offender reformation and helping others. In his work on desistance, Maruna demonstrates that many former prisoners assumed the role of 'wounded healer or professional ex' and argued that, 'the desisting self-narrative frequently involves reworking a delinquent history into a source of wisdom to be drawn from while acting as a drug counsellor, youth worker, community volunteer, or a mutual help group member' (Maruna 2001: 117). Therefore, by sharing one's experiences and acting as either a role model or mentor, former prisoners can 'reach back' and help other similarly stigmatised people 'make it' after incarceration (see White 2000; Maruna 2001).

As noted, the concept of 'self-help' was paramount to groups formed to facilitate the reintegration of PMFPs in Northern Ireland. Coming from a history of political conflict, values were developed and practised by prisoners in jail which then continued outside the prison. As discussed below, this informed the work of many of the self-help organisations which saw themselves as trying to aid the reintegration of their colleagues, but also to achieve a broader social impact which still maintained their collective post-imprisonment identity.

The Reintegration of 'Politically Motivated' Former Prisoners: A Case Study of 'Self-Help'

Although a small number of reintegration self-help groups were developed in the early 1990s to assist the return of PMFPs (see Shirlow and McEvoy 2008), it was not until the signing of the Agreement that the number of self-help groups multiplied.[7] The fundamental component of these various organisations has been that they have remained driven by the ethos of 'self-help'. Members of the former prisoner community have an understanding that only those who have been through the experience are best placed to empathise and acknowledge the effect imprisonment has had on their colleagues (Shirlow and McEvoy 2008; Dwyer 2013b). Providing services within a framework of trust, confidentiality and mutual support has been important, not least because those working with self-help groups generally struggle with the same issues and can connect and build trust with those who use their services. Members of the self-help organisations claim that the 'politically motivated' former prisoner constituency needs to be in control of any mechanisms or structure put in place to aid reintegration, arguing that, 'it's not a matter of power, it's a matter of trust and a matter of common sense' (republican ex-prisoner, cited in Dwyer 2012: 291).

Studies have highlighted the importance of self-help not only in regard to the management of these projects, but also in the role and development of its members. Dwyer and Maruna (2011) found that many ex-prisoners embraced the notion of 'self-help' and the 'helper principle', demonstrating their desire to 'give something back' and contribute to the community and society more broadly. A project coordinator/former prisoner from a loyalist self-help organisation stated that,

> a lot of them [ex-prisoners] find themselves in community work … and there would be a number of them who would be working with other people. *It's about giving back to the*

[7] Although a number of projects existed prior to the end of the conflict (including republican group, Tar Anal and loyalist group, the Ex-Prisoners Interpretive Centre (EPIC)), the Agreement provided the conditions for the development of many more. A large network of organisations associated with the PIRA were developed and worked within the umbrella network of Coiste na nIarchimi. On the loyalist side, EPIC continued and developed a number of regional groups. Other loyalist groups included REACT (Reconciliation Education and Community Training), Charter, Prisoner Aid and Post Conflict Resettlement Group and LINC (Local Initiatives for Needy Communities). Smaller organisations have included An Eochair and EXPAC (Ex-Prisoners Assistance Committee) (see Dwyer 2010).

> *community and using their experiences in a positive way in the community* ... there are a lot of things that ex-prisoners have to offer (cited in Dwyer and Maruna 2011: 300).

Another former loyalist prisoner noted,

> the objective is not so much what can society do for ex-prisoners but what ex-prisoners can do for society and how can groups facilitate ex-prisoners like myself getting back into society (cited in Dwyer and Maruna 2011: 302).

These points strongly resonate with much of the desistence literature and in particular the 'strengths-based approach' to corrections outlined by Maruna et al (2004). They refer to this idea as 'generative activity' which allows 'convicts and ex-convicts to make amends, demonstrate their value and potential, and experience success in support and leadership roles' (Maruna et al 2004: 140). Maruna argues that 'ex-offenders need to develop a coherent, prosocial identity for themselves' (2001: 1). He found that desisters had changed or repaired their ideas of self and argued that desisters must not only be able to explain their reform in terms of their experiences to others, but also 'perhaps more importantly, ex-offenders need to have a believable story of why they are going straight to convince *themselves* that this is a real change' (Maruna 2001: 86). Maruna notes that 'newly empowered, he or she [the former prisoner] now also seeks to "give something back" to society as a display of gratitude' (Maruna, 2001: 87). Through this process the former prisoner may then go on to adopt 'a new identity and a new self and a new set of goals' (Toch 2000: 276).

Whilst the PMFP community would refute the idea that they are seeking redemption or wanting to desist from 'crime', many have argued that they view their reintegration process as an opportunity to fully participate by emphasising the role former prisoners can take in both their local community and wider society (Shirlow and McEvoy 2008; Dwyer 2013a). Dwyer and Maruna (2011) found that whilst many PMFP self-help organisations were motivated by the need for reintegrative support for former prisoners, there are examples of organisations running educational and training courses, working with young people at risk, working with other community services and cross-community work, and also implementing services which reach out to wider society (see also Shirlow and McEvoy 2008; Rolston, 2011). Dwyer and Maruna report that many members of self-help organisations emphasised the broader work of former prisoners and their attempts to contribute to society more widely:

> [T]he objective is ... how can groups facilitate ex-prisoners like myself getting back into society and above all developing some form of conflict transformation programme which would help prevent young people getting involved in the paramilitaries? (loyalist ex-prisoner, cited in Dwyer and Maruna 2011: 302).

Dwyer notes that for some PMFPs, it is through this self-identity as someone who can contribute and give something back that they have found a sense of purpose. One worker for a republican ex-prisoner group stated:

> I think that ex-prisoners as a community have a massive role to play in the ongoing social and political development within our community. I think that they are playing a daily

> role in all aspects of community life (project coordinator of a republican ex-prisoner group (cited in Dwyer 2010: 156).

Therefore, for many former prisoners, the self-help setting of the reintegration projects help to create an environment where former prisoners can express 'who they really are' and 'what they really feel', without a fear of betrayal (see Dwyer 2013b). So rather than feel ashamed of their 'ex-prisoner' identity, some have argued that it is the difficulties and challenges *associated* with the label that makes them move to reposition their former prisoner identity. As noted, one of the key areas of focus for the PMFP self-help groups has been the achievement of full reintegration for their members and working to ensure that barriers to full reintegration are removed. PMFPs encounter very particular barriers as a result of their 'conflict-related' conviction, which include but are not limited to obstacles related to accessing finance, accessing consumer credit licences, securing service contracts, applications for taxi and bus operator licences, difficulty accessing insurance and mortgage facilities, inability to adopt children, inability to get compensation for tort claims against their person or property, restrictions on travel to the United States, Canada and Australia, and bars on employment in the civil service sector. As a consequence of these very particular barriers to reintegration, many organisations have mobilised to engage with legislative reform and policy development, with examples of former prisoner groups challenging legal barriers through both the courts and lobbying policymakers (see Dwyer 2013a; OFMdFM 2012).

Where there have been slow protracted moves towards legislative and policy change to aid reintegration for PMFPs, particularly in regard to accessing employment, Dwyer (2013a) highlights that throughout this process, the ethos of 'self-help' has remained paramount. Much of this effort has been driven by the ex-prisoner community itself, where PMFP organisations have mobilised and coordinated their efforts to challenge these key legislative barriers through the wider political arena. As a consequence of these collective efforts, in more recent years the PMFP constituency has now largely transcended the typical mutual aid and support functions associated with self-help. Although groups are still involved in providing assistance to members, many groups that began as mutual aid support groups have metamorphosised into agents for both political and social change (see Dwyer 2013b).

The Role of Former Prisoners: Moving Beyond 'Self-Help'

Although motivated initially by the need for reintegrative support for former prisoners, many PMFP self-help organisations also reach out to the wider community with the aim of increasing further involvement of the PMFP in wider society. In particular they have become engaged in various conflict transformation projects which have focused on various aspects of transitional justice, interface violence, anti-sectarianism, the truth recovery process, outreach to victims groups, working with young people at risk, and community restorative justice projects (see Shirlow and McEvoy 2008; Rolston 2011; Dwyer 2012). It is argued that it is not only their imprisonment experience which provides a level of legitimacy for their involvement in such community-led strategies of conflict transformation (McEvoy and Shirlow 2009), but it is also because they were indigenous, organic and rooted in their respective local communities (Rolston 2007). McEvoy and colleagues note,

> having fought on behalf of those communities … they have the credibility to engage in … real reconciliation work in the working-class areas in which it is most needed. It is also they who have arguably taken the greatest risks in the peacemaking process, many of them explicitly on the basis that they do not want the next generation to go through what they experienced (McEvoy et al 2006: 99).

Various studies have demonstrated that members of the PMFP community have a key role in grassroots conflict transformation and have, when given the opportunity, made a positive contribution to the overall peace process (Shirlow and McEvoy 2008; McEvoy and Shirlow 2009; Dwyer 2010). Therefore, an argument can be advanced that when considering the reintegration process of the PMFP, it should not be a process narrowly defined, but should include a dynamic programme of reconstruction that recognises the skills former prisoners have to enable them to take a lead role in reconstruction and community development in a post-conflict society (Dwyer 2012).

It would, of course, be remiss to suggest that the process of self-help reintegration in Northern Ireland is without its limitations. For example, not all former prisoners in Northern Ireland have engaged in either community-based self-help organisations or peace building activities. Paramilitary organisations continue to operate in various forms throughout Northern Ireland (Dwyer 2012). The Agreement resulted in a splintering in the republican movement, and new groups, which opposed the peace agreement, continue to be involved in an armed campaign (see Cochrane 2011). It is further claimed that armed groups have taken advantage of the new physical and social spaces which have opened up following the peace agreement (Moore 1997). It is argued that some paramilitaries have continued to be involved in various illegal activities including extortion, counterfeiting, fraud, drug dealing as well as weapons and petrol trafficking. Since 1998, some loyalist communities have been witness to periods of intra-communal violence which resulted in a number of deaths and expulsions of many families from their homes. It is also interesting to note that one of the main loyalist PMFP reintegration projects EPIC (Ex-Prisoners Interpretive Centre) faced criticism when one of its regional headquarters in Ballymoney, North Antrim had £30,000 worth of funding suspended after a substantial amount of weaponry was found on the premises.[8]

[8] *BBC News*, 'Funding Frozen after Arms Find', 19 May 2000, available at www.news.bbc.co.uk/1/hi/northern_ireland/754532.stm.

Nevertheless, it is evident that there are differences between 'unreconstructive paramilitaries' who are driven by individual gain and continue their involvement in illegal activities and those who have abandoned violence in order to pursue community development and conflict transformation (Edwards 2009). Some PMFPs have been instrumental in keeping communities 'on board' during the peace process, particularly in areas where there has been little change in the socio-economic conditions of the communities that provided the bulk of the people who fought in the conflict (Dwyer 2012). Some international literature suggests that former participants in armed conflict have remarkable social and personal resources which can be drawn upon in promoting peace building initiatives. For example, van der Merwe and Smith (2006) argue that many former activists have been found to be passionate about contributing to their communities, and the qualities that drove them to take up militant action make them well suited for developmental and peace building activities. They also suggest that they

> are far more than simply fighters, they are often social activists with a strong understanding of the nature and cause of social injustice. They are often the carriers of the social memory of struggle taking on the role of preserving the history of the struggle against injustice (van der Merwe and Smith 2006: 15).

It is therefore this commitment to social justice that could motivate former activists, including PMFPs to promote peace and social change. A key lesson of the Northern Ireland experience is that community-based reintegrative programmes underline the leadership and agentic capacity of members of the PMFP community. The dialectical nature of the relationship between PMFPs and their communities in Northern Ireland demonstrates the ways in which PMFP-led, community-based reintegrative programmes not only aid in reintegrating former prisoners, but also in the broader process of post-conflict regeneration, social development and the 'embedding' of the peace process in communities which were most affected by the conflict (see Dwyer 2012).

Conclusion

With individuals once branded (and convicted) as 'terrorists' routinely elected as members of the devolved Parliament in Northern Ireland, the place is truly exceptional in many ways. However, this sort of transformation from self-help work to political advocacy is hardly unknown outside the context of the Troubles (see Dwyer and Maruna 2011). For example in their Chicago research, McAnany and colleagues found that the ex-prisoner groups were 'formed to confront the stigma, which these prisonized persons were running away from' (McAnany et al 1974: 27). These groups argue that there is a 'common bond' between all persons who are formerly incarcerated and that 'helping "the brothers" was essential for continued group identity' (McAnany et al 1974: 28). LeBel's (2008) research emphasises the benefits of involvement in advocacy as a coping orientation for ex-prisoners. His survey research found that an activist or advocacy orientation is positively correlated with one's psychological well-being, and in particular satisfaction with life as a whole. Moreover, he found a strong negative correlation between one's advocacy/activism orientation and criminal attitudes and behaviour. This indicates that advocating on behalf of others in the criminal justice system may help to maintain a person's prosocial identity and facilitate ongoing desistance from crime.

As noted, in the widespread discussion of how to combat terrorism, few are discussing the issue of 'politically motivated' ex-prisoners and the question of reintegration (for exceptions see McEvoy et al 2007; LaFree and Miller 2008; Bjorgo and Horgan 2009; Horgan 2009). When the subject is raised, as in the concept of DDR (Disarmament, Demobilisation, and Reintegration), the focus is typically on reducing the risks posed by PMFPs in society (Dwyer 2012). Likewise, the wider conversation about the re-entry of large numbers of 'ordinary' prisoners back into society tends to focus on the risks this process entails and the plethora of needs that people in that situation have to minimally satisfy to ensure safe and successful reintegration. It is less common to think of re-entry in terms of the contributions that people returning from prison can make to their communities and to wider society. However, reintegration is 'a two-way street' (Mosley 1997; Maruna 2001; Johnson 2002) involving changes on the part of the returning prisoner as well as in society. The strengths-based approach of the self-help/activist model recognises this and therefore has considerable appeal for stigmatised and marginalised groups (see Dwyer and Maruna 2011). Finally, the Northern Ireland experience speaks to the dynamic potential of PMFPs as agents of change and conflict transformation in transitional societies. It is both the shared experiences and development of particular skills which have made certain PMFPs more likely to play a conflict transformation role. This example of community-based reintegration, implemented and delivered by former prisoners, broadly demonstrates the merits and value of self-help led reintegration. Whilst it is not contended that such an approach could be easily transferable to other post-conflict peace building measures, it could help to inform debate on the notion of the role of self-help in the process of former prisoner reintegration more generally.

References

Anderson, R (1971) 'Voluntary Association in History' 73 *American Anthropology* 209.

Bazemore, G (1998) 'Restorative Justice and Earned Redemption: Communities, Victims and Offender Reintegration' 41 *American Behavioral Scientist* 768.

Behan, C and O'Donnell, I (2008) 'Prisoners, Politics and the Polls: Enfranchisement and the Burden of Responsibility' 48 *British Journal of Criminology* 319.

Belfast/Good Friday Agreement (1998) *The Agreement Reached in the Multi-Party Negotiations* (Belfast, Northern Ireland Office).

Bell, C (2000) *Peace Agreements and Human Rights* (Oxford, Oxford University Press).
Bjorgo, T and Horgan, J (2009) *Leaving Terrorism Behind* (London, Routledge).
Borkman, T (1976) 'Experiential Knowledge: A New Concept for the Analysis of Self-help Groups' 50 *Social Service Review* 445.
Braithwaite, J (1989) *Crime, Shame and Reintegration* (Cambridge, Cambridge University Press).
Campbell, C, Bell, C and Ní Aoláin, F (2004) 'Justice Discourses in Transition' 13 *Social & Legal Studies* 305.
Cochrane, F (2011) 'From Transition to Transformation in Ethnonational Conflict: Some Lessons from Northern Ireland' *Ethnopolitics* 22.
Cressey, DR (1955) 'Changing Criminals: The Application of the Theory of Differential Association' 61 *American Journal of Sociology* 116.
—— (1978) 'Criminological Theory, Social Science, and the Repression of Crime' 16 *Criminology* 171.
Dwyer, CD (2007) 'Risk, Politics and the "Scientification" of Political Judgement: Prisoner Release and Conflict Transformation in Northern Ireland' 47 *British Journal of Criminology* 779.
—— (2010) '"*Sometimes I wish I was an 'ex' ex-prisoner…*" Release and Reintegration: The Experience of "Politically Motivated" Former Prisoners in Northern Ireland' (unpublished PhD thesis, Queen's University Belfast).
—— (2012) 'Expanding DDR: The Transformative Role of Former Prisoners in Community-Based Reintegration' 6 *International Journal of Transitional Justice* 274.
—— (2013a) '"They might as well be walking around the inside of a biscuit tin": Barriers to Employment and Reintegration for "Politically Motivated" Former Prisoners in Northern Ireland' 5 *European Journal of Probation* 3.
—— (2013b) '"*Sometimes I wish I was an 'ex' ex-prisoner*": Identity Processes in the Collective Action Participation of Former Prisoners' 16 *Contemporary Justice Review* 425.
Dwyer, CD and Maruna, S (2011) 'The Role of Self-help Efforts in the Reintegration of "Politically Motivated" Former Prisoners: Implications from the Northern Irish Experience' 55 *Crime, Law and Social Change* 293.
Edwards, A (2009) 'Abandoning Armed Resistance? The Ulster Volunteer Force as a Case Study of Strategic Terrorism in Northern Ireland' 32 *Studies in Conflict & Terrorism* 100.
Farrall, S (2004) 'Social Capital and Offender Reintegration: Making Probation Desistance Focused' in S Maruna and R Immarigeon (eds), *After Crime and Punishment: Pathways to Offender Reintegration* (Cullompton, Willan Publishing).
Farrall, S and Sparks, R (2006) 'Introduction' 6 *Criminology & Criminal Justice* 7.
Gadd, D and Farrall, S (2004) 'Criminal Careers, Desistance and Subjectivity: Interpreting Men's Narratives of Change' 8 *Theoretical Criminology* 123.
Gartner, A and Riessman, F (1984) *The Self-help Revolution* (New York, Human Sciences Press).
Gormally, B, Maruna, S and McEvoy, K (2007) *Thematic Evaluation of Funded Projects: Politically motivated Former Prisoners and their Families* (Monaghan, Border Action).
Gormally, B and McEvoy, K (eds) (1995) *Release and Reintegration of Politically Motivated Prisoners in Northern Ireland, A Comparative Study of South Africa, Israel/Palestine, Italy, Spain, the Republic of Ireland and Northern Ireland* (Belfast, NIACRO).
Grant, JD (1968) 'The Offender as a Correctional Manpower Resource' in F Riessman and HL Popper (eds), *Up from Poverty: New Career Ladders for Nonprofessionals* (New York, Harper and Row).
Grant, J and Grant, JD (1975) 'Evaluation of New Careers Programs' in EL Struening and M Guttentag (eds), *Handbook of Evaluation Research* (Beverly Hills, CA, Sage).

Grounds, A and Jamieson, R (2003) 'No Sense of an Ending: Researching the Experience of Imprisonment and Release upon Republican Ex-Prisoners' 7 *Theoretical Criminology* 347.
Hasenfeld, Y and Gidron, B (1993) 'Self-Help Groups and Human Service Organizations: An Inter-organizational Perspective' 67 *Social Service Review* 217.
Horgan, J (2009) *Walking Away from Terrorism* (New York, Routledge).
Humphreys, K (1997) 'Individual and Social Benefits of Mutual Aid/Self-help Groups' 27 *Social Policy* 12.
Humphreys, K and Rappaport, J (1994) 'Researching Self-help/Mutual Aid Groups and Organizations: Many Roads, One Journey' 3 *Applied and Preventive Psychology* 217.
Jackson, SW (2001) 'Presidential Address: The Wounded Healer' 75 *Bulletin of the History of Medicine* 1.
Jacobs, K and Goodman, G (1989) 'Psychology and Self-help Groups: Predictions on a Partnership' 44 *American Psychologist* 536.
Jamieson, R and Grounds, A (2008) *Facing the Future: Ageing and Politically-motivated Former Prisoners in Northern Ireland and the Border Region* (Monaghan, Ireland, EXPAC/Border Action).
Jamieson, R, Shirlow, P and Grounds, A (2010) *Ageing and Social Exclusion among Former Politically Motivated Prisoners in Northern Ireland* (Belfast, Changing Ageing Partnership).
Johnson, R (2002) *Hard Time* (Belmont, CA, Wadsworth).
Katz, AH (1981) 'Self-help and Mutual Aid: An Emerging Social Movement?' 7 *Annual Review of Sociology* 129.
King, SA (2004) 'The Therapeutic Value of Virtual Self Help Groups' (unpublished thesis, Faculty of Pacific Graduate School of Psychology, Palo Alto, California).
Kropotkin, P (1907) *Mutual Aid: A Factor of Evolution* (Dover, Value Editions).
Kurtz, LF (1997) *Self-help and Support Groups: A Handbook for Practitioners* (Thousand Oaks, CA, Sage).
LaFree, G and Miller, E (2008) 'Desistance from Terrorism: What Can We Learn from Criminology?' 1 *Dynamics of Asymmetric Conflict* 203.
Laskowski, C and Pellicore, K (2002) 'The Wounded Healer Archetype: Applications to Palliative Care Practice' 19 *American Journal of Hospice & Palliative Care* 403.
Laub, J and Sampson, R (2001) 'Understanding Desistance from Crime' 28 *Crime and Justice: A Review of Research* 1.
LeBel, TP (2008) 'An Examination of the Impact of Formerly Incarcerated Persons Helping Others' 46 *Journal of Offender Rehabilitation* 1.
Lowie, RH (1947) *Primitive Society* (Harper Torchbooks/Academy Library).
Mallinder, L (2008) *Amnesty, Human Rights and Political Transitions: Bridging the Peace and Justice Divide* (Oxford, Hart Publishing).
Maruna, S (2001) *Making Good: How Ex-Convicts Reform and Rebuild Their Lives* (Washington DC, APA Books).
Maruna, S, Immarigeon, R and LeBel, T (2004) 'Ex-Offender Re-Integration: Theory and Practice' in S Maruna and R Immarigeon (eds), *After Crime and Punishment: Pathways to Offender Reintegration* (Cullompton, Willan Publishing).
Maruna, S and LeBel, TP (2003) 'Welcome Home? Examining the "Reentry Court" Concept from a Strengths-Based Perspective' 4 *Western Criminology Review* 91.
Maruna, S, LeBel, T and Lanier, C (2004) 'Generativity Behind Bars: Some "Redemptive Truth" about Prison Society' in E de St Aubin, D McAdams and T Kim (eds), *The Generative Society* (Washington DC, American Psychological Association).

McAnany, PD, Tromanhauser, E and Sullivan, D (1974) *The Identification and Description of Ex-offender Groups in the Chicago Area* (Chicago, IL, University of Illinois Press).
McAuley, JW, Tonge, J and Shirlow, P (2009) 'Conflict, Transformation, and Former Loyalist Paramilitary Prisoners in Northern Ireland' 22 *Terrorism and Political Violence* 22.
McEvoy, K (2001) *Paramilitary Imprisonment in Northern Ireland: Resistance, Management, and Release* (Oxford, Oxford University Press).
—— (2007) 'Beyond Legalism: Towards a Thicker Understanding of Transitional Justice' 34 *Journal of Law and Society* 411.
McEvoy, K, McConnachie, K and Jamieson, R (2007) 'Political Imprisonment and the "War on Terror"' in Y Jewkes (ed), *Handbook on Prisons* (Cullompton, Willan Publishing).
McEvoy, L, McEvoy, K and McConnachie, K (2006) 'Reconciliation as a Dirty Word: Conflict, Community Relations and Education in Northern Ireland' 60 *Journal of International Affairs* 81.
McEvoy, K and Shirlow, P (2009) 'Re-Imagining DDR: Ex-combatants, Leadership and Moral Agency in Conflict Transformation' 13 *Theoretical Criminology* 31.
McEvoy K, Shirlow, P and McElrath, K (2004) 'Resistance, Transition and Exclusion: Politically Motivated Ex-prisoners and Conflict Transformation in Northern Ireland' 16 *Terrorism and Political Violence* 646.
Metcalf, H, Anderson, T and Rolfe, H (2001) *Barriers to Employment for Offenders and Ex-offenders* (London, Department for Work and Pensions Research).
Miller, GD and Baldwin, DC (1987) 'Implications of the Wounded-healer Paradigm for the Use of the Self in Therapy' 3 *Journal of Psychotherapy and the Family* 139.
Moore, J (1997) 'Paramilitary Prisoners and the Peace Process in Northern Ireland' in A O'Day (ed), *Political Violence in Northern Ireland: Conflict and Conflict Resolution* (Connecticut, Westport).
Mosley, W (1997) *Always Outnumbered, Always Outgunned* (London, Serpent's Tail).
Naylor, B (2011) 'Criminal Records and Rehabilitation in Australia' 3 *European Journal of Probation* 79.
Office of First Minister and deputy First Minister (OFMdFM) (2012) *Report of the Review Panel, Employers Guidance on Recruiting People with Conflict Related Convictions* (Belfast, OFMdFM).
Padfield, N (2011) 'Judicial Rehabilitation? A View from England' 3 *European Journal of Probation* 36.
Pearl, A and Riessman, F (1965) *New Careers for the Poor: The Non-professional in Human Service* (New York, The Free Press).
Petersilia, J (2003) *When Prisoners Come Home: Parole and Prisoner Re-entry* (Oxford, Oxford University Press).
Powell, TJ (1990) 'Self-help, Professional Help, and Informal Help: Competing or Complementary Systems?' in TJ Powell (ed), *Working with Self-help* (Silver Spring, MD, NASW).
Quinney, R (1970) *The Social Reality of Crime* (Boston, MA, Little Brown and Co).
Raynor, P and Maguire, M (2006) 'End-to-End or End in Tears? Prospects for the Effectiveness of the National Offender Management Model' in M Hough, R Allen and U Padel (eds), *Reshaping Probation and Prisons: The Implications of NOMS* (Bristol, Policy Press).
Riessman, F (1965) 'The "Helper" Therapy Principle' 10 *Social Work* 27.
—— (1997) 'Ten Self-help Principles' 27 *Social Policy* 6.
Rolston, B (2007) 'Demobilisation and Reintegration of Ex-Combatants: The Irish Case in International Perspective' 16 *Social & Legal Studies* 259.

—— (2011) *Review of Literature on Republican and Loyalist Ex-prisoners* (Belfast, OFMdFM).

Sampson, RJ and Laub, J (1993) *Crime in the Making: Pathways and Turning Points through Life* (Cambridge, MA, Harvard University Press).

Schiff, M and Bargal, D (2000) 'Helping Characteristics of Self-help and Support Groups: Their Contribution to Participants' Subjective Well-being' 31 Small Group Research 275.

Schubert, MA and Borkman, T (1994) 'Identifying the Experiential Knowledge Developed within a Self-help Group' in TJ Powell (ed), *Understanding the Self-help Organization: Frameworks and Findings* (Thousand Oaks, CA, Sage).

Sedgwick, D (1994) *The Wounded Healer: Countertransference from a Jungian Perspective* (London, Routledge).

Shirlow P, Graham B, McEvoy K, Ó hAdhmaill, F and Purvis, D (2005) *Politically Motivated Former Prisoner Groups: Community Activism and Conflict Transformation* (Belfast, Northern Ireland Community Relations Council).

Shirlow, P and McEvoy, K (2008) *Beyond the Wire: Former Prisoners and Conflict Transformation in Northern Ireland* (London, Pluto Press).

St Andrews Agreement (2006) *The St Andrews Agreement, October 2006* (Belfast, Northern Ireland Office).

Toch, H (2000) 'Altruistic Activity as Correctional Treatment' 44 *International Journal of Offender Therapy and Comparative Criminology* 270.

Travis, J and Petersilia, J (2001) 'Reentry Reconsidered: A New Look at an Old Question' 47 *Crime & Delinquency* 291.

Tunnell, K (ed) (1993) *Political Crime in Contemporary America: A Critical Approach* (New York, Garland Publishing).

Uggen, C (2000) 'Work as a Turning Point in the Life Course of Criminals: A Duration Model of Age' 65 *American Sociological Review* 529.

Uggen, C, Manza, J and Behrens, A (2004) 'Less than the Average Citizen: Stigma, Role Transition, and the Civic Reintegration of Convicted Felons' in S Maruna and R Immarigeon (eds), *After Crime and Punishment: Pathways to Offender Reintegration* (Cullompton, Willan Publishing).

van der Merwe, H and Smith, R (2006) *Ex-Combatants as Peacebuilders: Opportunities and Challenges in Struggles in Peacetime, Working with Ex-Combatants in Mozambique: Their Work, Their Frustrations and Successes* (Netherlands Institute for Southern Africa).

Visher, CA and Travis, J (2003) 'Transitions from Prison to Community: Understanding Individual Pathways' 29 *Annual Review of Sociology* 89.

Ward, T and Maruna, S (2007) *Rehabilitation: Beyond the Risk-Paradigm. Key Ideas in Criminology Series* (London, Routledge).

White, W (2000) 'Toward a New Recovery Movement: Historical Reflections on Recovery, Treatment and Advocacy', available at www.fead.org.uk/docs/toward_new_recovery.pdf.

Zemore, SE, Kaskutas, LA and Ammon, LN (2004) 'In 12-step Groups, Helping Helps the Helper' 99 *Addiction* 1015.

11

Probation and Community Sanctions in Northern Ireland: Historical and Contemporary Contexts

NICOLA CARR

Introduction

This chapter focuses on probation and community sanctions and measures in Northern Ireland. It situates this aspect of the criminal justice system within the wider penal landscape and notes in particular the changing dynamics of the interrelationship between probation and prisons. Exploring some of the trends in the expansion of probation and community sanctions in Northern Ireland in recent decades, the chapter begins with an overview of the current configuration of probation in Northern Ireland, and proceeds to locate this within the historical context. The particular 'neutrality' stance adopted by probation in the course of the 'Troubles' is explored and the changing context of probation practice including a shift towards a more risk-oriented public protection role in the post-conflict era is set out. The parallels of recent developments with broader international trends are noted.

The chapter draws on primary research, which was conducted by Carr and Maruna (2012) exploring the context of probation practice during the Troubles. This oral history of probation included interviews with eight retired and serving probation officers who had worked in the service between 1969 and 2012 and with two senior managers who had strong links with the service during this period. This research was reported in Carr and Maruna (2012). This data is further supplemented with ongoing research being conducted by the author and Maruna focusing on the context of probation practice within the Maze/Long Kesh Prison. To date this includes in-depth interviews with nine probation officers whose collective period of service spanned from 1971 until the prison's closure in 2000.[1]

[1] Throughout the chapter this full set of interviews (n=19) are denoted Probation History Interviews (PHI) with a relevant interview number.

The Current Configuration of Probation in Northern Ireland

The Probation Board for Northern Ireland (PBNI) is a non-departmental public body that has legislative responsibility for the supervision of people sentenced by the courts to community sanctions and/or released from prison on licence. Its other core function is the provision of assessments on the request of the court prior to sentencing (pre-sentence reports). The Probation Board employs Probation Officers, Probation Service Officers and Community Service Officers to carry out these various tasks. In Northern Ireland (as in Scotland) social work remains the recognised professional qualification for probation officers (Doran and Cooper 2008; McCulloch and McNeill 2011).

This contrasts with England and Wales where fundamental changes were made to probation officer training and qualification requirements in the early 1990s, which dispensed with the requirement for probation officers to be qualified social workers (Deering 2010). These changes were viewed in the context of the increased emphasis placed on risk and public protection and the marginalisation of the 'social' or 'welfare' dimension of practice (Mawby and Worrall 2013). While there was some debate as to whether probation in Northern Ireland would follow suit, a decision was made to retain social work as the core qualification for probation officers. This was viewed as important with proponents arguing that a social work perspective was critical to understanding offenders' lives in context and for promoting positive change (Doran and Cooper 2008: 34).

The governance structures of probation services also differ markedly within the United Kingdom. In England and Wales recent reforms have led to the disestablishment of existing Probation Trusts under the Coalition Government's 'Transforming Rehabilitation' agenda (MoJ 2013a). Here a newly formed National Probation Service (NPS) will work with the most 'high-risk' offenders (estimated to be 30 per cent of the current case load), while the remainder of probation's work will be outsourced to private contractors via 'Community Rehabilitation Companies' (CRCs). These changes, effected in June 2014, represent the most significant restructuring of probation England and Wales and they have been the subject of widespread critique (for example, Burke 2013; Annison et al 2014).[2] The parallels with the part privatisation of the prisons in England and Wales and the difficulties that have ensued have been observed (Fitzgibbon and Lea 2014). Concerns have also been voiced regarding the issues raised for legitimacy when a public service so fundamentally involved in the administration of justice is outsourced to private companies whose raison d'etre is the pursuit of profit (Burke 2013; Annison et al 2014).

[2] See also R Allen, 'A Sad Day for Probation and for Policy-Making' available at reformingprisons.blogspot.ie/2013/09/a-sad-day-for-probation-and-for-policy.html.

In Scotland the responsibility for the assessment and supervision of offenders lies with local authority social work departments (McCulloch and McNeill 2011). Here criminal justice social workers are employed by local authorities in collaboration with criminal justice authorities, which were established under the Management of Offenders Act (Scotland) 2005. The purpose of the criminal justice authorities is to coordinate strategy and service delivery with a central objective of reducing reoffending. There are over 1000 criminal justice social workers employed in Scotland, which has a population of over five million people (Carr and Robinson (2012). This contrasts with Northern Ireland, with a population of approximately 1.8 million, where the PBNI employs just over 400 staff, of which approximately 160 are probation officers working directly with clients (Fulton and Carr 2013).[3] As a Non-Departmental Public Body (NDPB), the Probation Board operates at arm's length from government. The organisation is governed by a board, whose members are appointed by the Minister of Justice and whose functions are set out under the Probation Board (NI) Order 1982.[4] While the merits of NDPB status, ostensibly affording a greater level of independence have been noted (Blair 2000; Fulton and Carr 2013), in practice the extent of any such independence is significantly curtailed. The Probation Board is resourced through government funding and it is ultimately accountable to the Minister of Justice with the legislation prescribing that '[t]he Department of Justice may, after consultation with the Board, give the Board directions of a general character as to the exercise and performance of its functions, and the Board shall give effect to any such directions' (Probation Board (NI) Order 1982, part 6).

Currently the numbers of people under supervision of probation in Northern Ireland is more than double the prison population. On 30 September 2014, 4387 people were subject to probation supervision (PBNI 2014)[5] compared with a prison population of 1803 on the same date (NIPS 2014). This follows trends in many countries where the use of probation and community sanctions has expanded—a phenomenon that has tended to be overshadowed by the understandable attention directed towards prison populations (McNeill and Beyens 2014; McNeill and Dawson 2014). The expansion in the use of community sanctions does not necessarily lead to a reduction in the use of custody as the interrelationship between these forms of penality is invariably more complex (Phelps 2013). In Northern Ireland while the numbers of people under community supervision has grown, prison numbers have also risen in recent years (DoJ 2014).

[3] PBNI also employs approximately 40 Probation Service Officers (PSOs) who work directly with clients. PSOs are not qualified social workers, but undertake National Vocational Qualification training in Offending Behaviour (Fulton and Carr 2013).

[4] As amended by the Northern Ireland Act 1998 (Devolution of Policing and Justice Functions) Order 2010.

[5] This figure includes a proportion of people who are subject to orders, which include a period of imprisonment followed by probation supervision.

A Brief History of Probation in Northern Ireland

Although the origins of probation date back to court-based missionaries of the mid-nineteenth century, it was not until the beginning of the twentieth century that probation was placed on a statutory footing by the Probation of Offenders Act 1907. This enabled courts to sentence a person to a Probation Order as an alternative to custody under the supervision of a Probation Officer, whose role was to 'advise, assist and befriend' (Fulton and Parkhill 2009). This legislation provided the founding basis for the development of probation in Britain and Ireland, and it continues to provide the main legislative underpinning for probation in the Republic of Ireland (Healy 2009; Carr et al 2013). Following the establishment of a separate administration of Northern Ireland under the Government of Ireland Act 1920 and during the first half of the twentieth century probation in Northern Ireland was sporadic, poorly funded and concentrated in Belfast. In 1950, the Ministry for Home Affairs took on the responsibility for probation services and in the following years the numbers of people subject to probation supervision expanded but remained at relatively low levels (Fulton and Carr 2013).

In the 1970s the role of the probation officer became more professionalised with the establishment of a trainee scheme linked to a social work qualification. In this period also, probation officers were placed in prisons in Northern Ireland for the first time (Fulton and Carr 2013). Although as this probation officer who was seconded to work in prison in the late 1970s notes, there was some debate about the role of probation within this setting:

> I think one of the big questions was—what is the role of probation at that time? That has changed hugely over the years, but at that time there was a big question, should probation be in prison or should they not? Should we be based in prison? Should we be based outside and go into prison to work? There were all sorts of models. And should we be there at all? Was it a probation role, and if so what was that role? And at that time the role was very largely around, it was, we were the welfare department, not the probation department as it would be now. We were the welfare department (PHI 13).

This account regarding probation's place within the prisons in Northern Ireland in the 1970s also points to a clear view that the probation role at this time was clearly seen as a welfare-focused enterprise. Indeed this 'penal-welfarist' perspective, broadly understood as recognition of the importance of social context and an emphasis placed in the prospect of reform and rehabilitation of the individual (Garland 1985), had been a defining feature of probation's role since its inception in the late-nineteenth century (Mair and Burke 2012; Robinson et al 2013). However, analyses of broader penal trends in Western democracies in this period (for example, Young 1999; Garland 2001; Simon 2007) note that the 1970s also marked a fundamental shift in approaches to criminal justice. This was manifest in the so-called 'collapse of the rehabilitative ideal' (Allen 1981), meaning that faith in a rehabilitative criminal justice purpose and in the role of experts to facilitate this had entered into decline. Various analyses note the influences of economic, social, political and cultural contexts in tandem with rising crime rates on such developments (see, for example, Downes 1988; Young 1999; Garland 2001; Lacey 2008).

Garland (2001) for example characterises the emergence of a 'culture of control' marked by several indices including an increased politicisation of crime and justice and the re-emergence of punitive sanctions. His analysis, however, draws largely on examples from the United States and England and has been subject to some critique (Zedner 2002); further its utility as an explanatory framework in other countries has been questioned (see, for example, Kilcommins et al 2004 for a discussion on the Republic of Ireland). The extent to which any such analysis would apply to Northern Ireland also has to be considered in light of the critical impact of civil and political conflict on all aspects of the criminal justice system. A considerable body of literature (much of it considered in this volume) has explored the impact of the Troubles and the transition towards post-conflict for the criminal justice system and its constituent agencies. However, apart from a small range of work (for example, O'Mahony and Chapman 2007; Carr and Maruna 2012) to date the role of probation in the Troubles has been subject to limited critical attention. This relative neglect of probation's role is significant given that it was unique among agencies within the criminal justice system for the 'neutrality' stance it adopted during the course of the conflict (Carr and Maruna 2012).

Probation and Neutrality

For probation the political conflict raised key ethical issues about the role of the service in the rehabilitation of people whose actions were politically motivated and who disavowed the label of 'criminal' or 'offender'. The enactment of 'Emergency Provisions' legislation which outlawed membership of 'prohibited' organisations, and provided for summary conviction with imprisonment for a range of associated offences, led to a decision by probation officers in 1975 to cease statutory work with 'politically motivated' offenders.[6] As a probation officer working during this period explains:

> [W]e sort of started to debate it within the union and realised … that we were being asked to treat people who were breaking the law out of political motivation and we were asked to sort of pathologise in some way this sort of behaviour, to see it as a sort of personal problem … And that led us on to think that there was something unethical about assessing and supervising people on statutory orders who were committing offences out of political reasons (PHI 01).

[6] Northern Ireland (Emergency Provisions) Act 1973; Northern Ireland (Various Emergency Provisions) (Continuance) Order 1974.

On a more pragmatic level, this decision meant that, unlike other staff within the criminal justice system (for example, prison officers and police), probation officers were not considered 'legitimate targets' and no probation officer was killed in the course of the conflict. As the respondent below describes, remarkably probation staff maintained a presence and legitimacy in communities that were considered 'no-go' areas by other criminal justice agencies:

> [W]e were right in the middle of the community, here's a probation office in the flats, in the area where we have high crime … it was quite a dangerous area … we had this unspoken rule with both the IRA and the police for that matter, you don't, obviously our office is known for offenders, but if you're looking for an offender, you can't because we are not going to get any people coming to see us if they think that if we come here, either the IRA or the police … so that was an unwritten agreement … you would get into a situation where it was a bit scary, but you never felt that they were actually targeting us. There was a certain agreement that you know, you don't target probation (PHI 09).

The distancing of probation from central government and the Northern Ireland Office during the period of the Troubles, in the highly politicised arena of criminal justice was part of probation's conscious efforts to maintain neutrality in the political conflict. This also informed the rationale for its establishment as a NDPB in legislation (Probation Board (NI) Order 1982). The merits of this organisational structure were noted in a research paper prepared as part of the Criminal Justice Review (CJR) (2000). Arguments put forward in favour of the maintenance of probation's NDPB status noted the benefits of the perceived 'distance' of probation from government and the need for community representation in the board structure (Blair 2000).

However, following the Good Friday Agreement (1998) and the requirement to comprehensively review the entire criminal justice system, the continuing status of probation as a separate body was considered. In particular the interface between probation and prisons was explored. Such thinking was influenced by developments elsewhere, notably in England and Wales, where a more closer alignment between prisons and probation under the rationale of 'offender management' and the imposition of 'seamless sentences' eventually led to the integration of the management structures of prisons and probation under a National Offender Management Service (NOMS) (Worrall 2008; Mair and Burke 2012). However, in Northern Ireland, the Criminal Justice Review (2000) concluded that amalgamation of prison and probation services was not feasible or realistic at that time:

> We considered whether to recommend unifying the two organizations … However unification is not a panacea. Even in unified correctional services there remain organisational tensions between community and custodial staff. In the Northern Ireland context there is a very real danger that the Prison Service with its larger staff, larger budget and higher profile would tend to dominate the unified organisation to the detriment of community working. We would be concerned that the community ethos and credibility achieved by the Probation Service might be put at risk if such an amalgamation took place at this stage or within the foreseeable future (CJRG 2000: 304).

The decision to maintain a clear dividing line between the Probation Board and the Prison Service at this time was clearly influenced by the differences in the size, composition and budgets of the respective organisations.[7] As the above excerpt indicates another critical factor was the perceived differences in the 'ethos and crediblity' of the two organisations. The credibility of the Probation Board was understood to be grounded in its community-based role, which alongside its neutrality stance afforded it a greater degree of legitimacy. In essence the difficulties facing the Prison Service, including the necessity to restructure, which continue in their outworkings today (PRT 2011), would be large enough challenges without considering an amalgamation of both services under an integrated offender management service similar to the England and Wales model (Robinson and Burnett 2007).

Public Protection

While the decision to maintain the organisational structure of probation was clearly influenced by the challenges facing the Prison Service, the question of how to deal with so-called 'ordinary crime' (ie, non-conflict related offending), in the post-conflict era gained increased attention (see chapter five by Dwyer in this volume for further discussion). In the 1990s the traditional emphasis on probation's welfarist role began to shift more towards 'public protection'. This shift paralleled developments elsewhere, notably in England and Wales, which saw the emergence of what Lacey (2008: 23) has characterised as 'a strangely bifurcated criminal justice policy', ie, a distinction made between different categories of offender. Here we see the development of a panoply of interventions and punishments targeted towards 'high-risk' or 'dangerous' individuals and more managerial approaches to 'everyday' or less serious crime (see also Feeley and Simon 1992; Cavadino and Dignan 2006).

In Northern Ireland this was evident in legislation enacted and a range of measures targeted specifically at sexual and violent offenders including the development of multi-agency risk management arrangements (McAlinden 2012; see also the chapter by McAlinden in this volume). The Criminal Justice (NI) Order 1996, inter alia, expanded the range of community orders available to the Court. Part 10 of the Order states that a Probation Order (which can be for a minimum term of six months and a maximum term of three years) is suitable in:

a. Securing the rehabilitation of the offender.
b. Protecting the public from further harm by him or preventing the commission by him of further offences.

[7] The Criminal Justice Review (2000) noted that for 1999/2000 the Northern Ireland Prison Service had a budget of £160.7 million (£20 million of which was earmarked for a staff reduction programme). This contrasted with Probation's annual budget of £11.8 million in the same period, a more than tenfold difference (CJRG 2000).

The dual emphasis on rehabilitation and public protection set out in legislation marks a shift in the orientation of probation in Northern Ireland in the mid-1990s. It parallels developments in England and Wales, where the traditional focus aimed at the rehabilitation of the individual had come under sustained criticism for a variety of reasons, including whether such endeavours were proportionate or effective (Mair and Burke 2012; Robinson et al 2013). The hardening of criminal justice discourse in this period is linked to the politicisation of crime and justice issues and, as Garland (1996) would argue, to attempts of governments to bolster their legitimacy as the role and influence of 'sovereign states' shrank in other areas of public policy in the context of economic decline and globalisation. Again, these analyses find widest currency when applied to the United States and England and Wales and the question of 'state sovereignty' is clearly problematised in the context of Northern Ireland. Nonetheless, the move away from welfarism and the increased emphasis on public protection is clearly evident in Northern Ireland at this time (Fulton and Carr 2013).

This promise to 'protect the public' is, however, problematic (Robinson and McNeill 2004; Nash 2000; McNeill 2011). While such a commitment is rooted in a quest for legitimacy (ie, to appear credible, necessary and relevant), particularly in the context of changing attitudes towards crime and justice, as McNeill (2011: 10) notes, it points also towards a fundamental paradox, paving the way towards inevitable failure:

> Whenever the promise to protect is made, the existence of a threat is confirmed and fear is legitimized and reinforced ... Similarly, when probation commits itself to the assessment and management of risks, it exposes itself not to the likelihood of failure, but to its inevitability.

In the early 2000s, the issue of public protection was brought very firmly to the fore by the murder of Attracta Harron by Trevor Hamilton, a convicted rapist four months after his release from prison. Hamilton had been sentenced to a Custody Probation Order comprising seven years' custody, followed by one year on probation.[8] Under customary practice he was released from prison having served half of his custodial term. He was considered a high-risk sexual offender and was subject to probation supervision and Multi-Agency Sex Offender Risk Assessment and Management (MASRAM) scrutiny.[9] The Serious Case Review (MASRAM 2006) conducted in respect of Hamilton, identified a number of shortcomings in the management of his case by various agencies. Amongst the most significant was the fact that Hamilton did not undertake a Sex Offender Treatment Programme when in prison, the principle reason being that he continued to deny the original offences.

[8] *R v Trevor Hamilton* [2008] NICA 27.

[9] The MASRAM arrangements have since been superseded by Public Protection Arrangements Northern Ireland (PPANI). PPANI involves interagency cooperation in the assessment and management of high-risk offenders. These arrangements were placed on a statutory footing in the Criminal Justice (Northern Ireland) Order 2008.

All of the agencies working with Hamilton considered him to pose a high risk of further serious offending (MASRAM 2006); however, he was automatically released at the halfway point of his sentence. Each agency involved in the case (police, prison and probation) prepared a report on their involvement for the Serious Case Review and here the Prison Service noted the following:

> It is suggested that the legislative position relating to discharge at half sentence needs to be reviewed if the public are to be adequately protected by the criminal justice system. Had there been a parole board in this jurisdiction for considering such cases it is extremely unlikely the board would have agreed to Hamilton's release at the stage he was released given all the indications of his dangerousness ... In my view automatic release at the half sentence stage for offenders who are assessed as dangerous and likely to cause serious harm in the community fails to give adequate protection to the public (MASRAM 2006: paragraph 6.2).

Following the Hamilton case and a review of the arrangements for the management of sex offenders in the community (CJINI 2006), legislation modelled on the Criminal Justice Act 2003 in England and Wales was introduced which ended the practice of automatic 50 per cent remission in prison sentences. The Criminal Justice (Northern Ireland) Order 2008 introduced Determinate Custodial Sentences (DCS), where the length of custody and period of post-custodial supervision is specified on sentence and Extended Custodial Sentences (ECS) and Indeterminate Custodial Sentences (ICS) for offenders deemed by the court to be 'dangerous'. These so-called 'public protection' sentences, which came into force in April 2009, allow courts to sentence offenders convicted of serious offences of a violent and sexual nature to lengthier periods of imprisonment (Bailie 2008). Decisions on release are made by Parole Commissioners.[10]

The Criminal Justice (Northern Ireland) Order 2008 also provided that the Life Sentence Review Commissioners (LSRC) established as an independent body following a recommendation of the Criminal Justice Review (2000), be renamed the Parole Commissioners for Northern Ireland.[11] This also extended the responsibilities of the Commissioners to include decisions on the release and recall of prisoners subject to the new range of custodial sentences introduced in the 2008 legislation (formerly, as their title suggested, this role had been confined to decisions regarding life-sentenced prisoners). The Criminal Justice (Northern Ireland) Order 2008 requires that all prisoners subject to 'public protection' sentences, ie,

[10] A recent analysis of the Northern Ireland prison population in the period between 2009 and 2013 explores the growth in prison numbers. The prison population in September 2009 was 1437; in September 2013 it was 1858; and in September 2014 it was 1803. Some of the factors relating to this include more custodial sentences being given by the courts, driven in part by greater numbers coming before the courts, an increase in sentence lengths and higher numbers of recalls to prison (DoJ 2014).

[11] Prior to the establishment of the Life Sentence Review Commissioners under the Life Sentences (Northern Ireland) Order 2001, a non-statutory body comprising of officials within the Northern Ireland Office had fulfilled aspects of this function. However, the advent of the Human Rights Act 1998 and compliance with the European Convention on Human Rights entailed that each prisoner should be entitled to have his or her case reviewed periodically by an independent body.

extended or indeterminate custodial sentences, must be referred to the Parole Commissioners to assess suitability for release.[12]

Evidence-Based Practice

In tandem with this emphasis placed on 'public protection', the work of probation has become more focused on risk—namely risk of reoffending and risk of harm. Again this follows trends elsewhere, where the ascendancy of the 'risk-need-responsivity' (RNR) model of 'offender supervision' bolstered the legitimacy of probation agencies, whose rehabilitative claims had been undermined (Andrews et al 1990; Chapman and Hough 1998; Robinson et al 2013). The RNR model emphasises that effective interventions aimed at reducing recidivism should be targeted at levels of risk, criminogenic need (those factors that are associated with offending) and responsivity (the learning style of the offender). Fundamentally, this marks a further shift from a welfarist perspective towards working only with those needs associated with offending and linking any intervention proportionately with the level of risk posed. Interventions drawing on aspects of cognitive behavioural therapy have also been dominant within this paradigm and throughout the late 1990s and early 2000s the PBNI developed a range of 'offending behaviour programmes' based on these principles. These include programmes targeted at specific aspects of offending and specific types of offenders, for example, medium to high risk repeat offenders, offences involving domestic violence, anger management and sexual offending.

Typically at the pre-sentence stage, the probation officer will make an assessment as to a person's suitability to take part in an offending behaviour programme. The assessment will be based on risk of reoffending and risk of harm and where a person is required to take part in an offending behaviour programme this requirement will be made a condition of a community order in the sentence imposed by the court. For people subject to custodial sentences, there may be a requirement to undertake an offending behaviour programme in prison, although this is usually determined as part of a sentence plan (PBNI 2012; CJINI 2012). Participation in an offending behaviour programme may also be one of the factors taken into account by the Parole Commissioners in determining a prisoner's release and a requirement to participate in a programme can also be stipulated as a licence condition post-release (PBNI 2012).

Critiques of the risk-focused, public protection orthodoxy have argued that the reduction of offenders to 'risk subjects' who require management through a range

[12] The powers and remit of the Parole Commissioners in Northern Ireland are governed by the following: the Criminal Justice (Northern Ireland) Order 2008; the Life Sentences (Northern Ireland) Order 2001 and the Parole Commissioners' Rules (Northern Ireland) 2009.

of techniques is inherently problematic. Ward and Maruna (2007) for example, contend that it fails to adequately account for individual motivation towards change. More recently the findings from desistance research, which has explored the processes and mechanisms through which people cease offending, have been integrated into practice (Burnett 2004; Farrall 2002; McNeill and Weaver 2010). For example, the PBNI's Best Practice Framework Incorporating Northern Ireland Standards (2012), which sets out key elements of practice and decision-making for probation officers and managers, directs attention towards supporting desistance-based practice. Here the importance of fostering a positive working relationship, ensuring the necessary practical supports, providing the opportunities for change and promoting self-efficacy are articulated in practice guidance. Whether this is in fact 'old wine in new bottles' in the sense that these elements represent a return to some of the earlier features of probation practice is one that this probation officer who has worked in the service for over 30 years considers:

> I think we [Probation Board] are doing a pretty good reverse turn on ourselves at the minute, we're doing like a reverse motion. I think that we need to believe, we need to remember our basic principles which were that we are social work trained and that I still am of the belief that the relationship is the biggest vehicle of change. And that's how we help people make their lives better and I still believe that and it has driven me the whole way through my career and that I think that we need to remember that those interpersonal skills that we all went and social work trained to develop and cultivate and use for other people's you know improvement (PHI 07).

The question of where probation in Northern Ireland sits along a spectrum of risk or relationship-based practice is one that is open to debate, and indeed these dual orientations are not mutually exclusive (McNeill and Weaver 2010). The type of interventions that a person is subject to in the course of their sentence will be determined by the level of risk they are assessed to pose, but effecting change in people's lives requires attention towards what motivates them and necessitates moving beyond viewing individuals as 'risk subjects'. Indeed, research (largely focusing on England, Scotland and Wales), which has explored the practice of offender supervision in different contexts suggests that these tensions have been consistent features of probation practice over time even in the context of larger organisational and penal changes which have seen greater numbers of people become subject to supervision in the community (Cheliotis 2006; McNeill et al 2009; Mawby and Worrall 2013).

Current Trends in Community Sanctions in Northern Ireland

The prison population in Northern Ireland has been rising in recent years and has understandably been the subject of policy attention (PRT 2011). Less remarked upon is the fact that the numbers of people subject to supervision in the community has also been growing. The relationship between both populations is not necessarily straightforward. For instance greater numbers of people sentenced in the community does not necessarily entail a reduction in the prison population. In fact in some contexts, community sentences and the strictures of post-custodial supervision can have the opposite effect, providing an alternative entry route into prison. In an analysis of this phenomenon in the United States, Phelps (2013) has described this as the 'paradox of probation'. Legislative frameworks including sentencing options will clearly have an impact in this area and in Northern Ireland the effect of the changes implemented in the Criminal Justice (Northern Ireland) Order 2008, as outlined above, are beginning to be evident.

Data on probation in Northern Ireland shows that the numbers of people subject to community sanctions and measures has risen markedly in the past number of years. Information on the numbers of people subject to supervision by the Probation Board on an annual date showed that this population rose from 2969 at year end 2000/01 to 4468 in 2012/13, an increase of approximately one-third.[13] The breakdown in the numbers of people under the supervision of the PBNI on 30 September 2014, included more than half who were subject to a community sentence (2450) and over a third who were the subject of a combined custodial/community sanction (1647), such as a Custody Probation Order (CPO), or a DCS (PBNI 2014).[14]

Custody Probation Orders (CPOs) requiring that a person serves a period of imprisonment followed by a period of supervision in the community following release (1–3 years) remain on the statute books but are being phased out.[15] They are only an applicable disposal for offences committed prior to 1 April 2009. For offences committed after that date they have since been replaced by the aforementioned DCS. A DCS allows the court to sentence a person to a period of imprisonment followed by a period of supervision in the community. The court specifies the length of both elements at the point of sentencing, thus making them a more flexible, and potentially more attractive, sentencing option.

This seems to be borne out by recent statistics. Since their introduction the use of these more flexible sentences, combining elements of prison and probation have increased in popularity, rising from 316 such sentences imposed in 2010/2011 to 530 in 2012/2013 (PBNI 2013).[16] In the same period there has been a decline in

[13] Data provided by PBNI, including caseload statistics (the number of people on caseload at year end) and number of pre-sentence reports written for years 2000/01 until 20 December 2013 inclusive (27 June 2013), on file with author.

[14] There were 4387 people subject to probation supervision on 30 September 2014 in addition to those cited above, the remaining numbers constituted those on licences (including Life Licences and Sex Offender Licences) and those subject to 'Public Protection Sentences' ie, Extended or Indeterminate Custodial Sentences. Of the Probation caseload, 26 per cent were in custody, and probation's involvement pertained largely to pre-release work (PBNI 2014).

[15] Criminal Justice (NI) Order 1996, art 24(1).

[16] Data shows that in 2012/13 the average length of a DCS was 14–15 months in prison and 18–19 months on probation (PBNI 2013: 12).

the number of Probation Orders and Community Service Orders made by the courts. Figures provided by PBNI (2013) show a 12 per cent reduction in Probation Orders and a 6 per cent reduction in Community Service Orders, while there was a 21 per cent increase in Determinate Custodial Sentences between 2011/2012 and 2012/2013. This trend is further borne out by statistics for the second quarter of 2014, which show that the number of DCSs under probation supervision is 18 per cent higher and the number of Community Service Orders were 15 per cent lower than in the previous year (PBNI 2014).

There are of course numerous factors that impact on sentences, including the seriousness of offence, previous convictions, mitigating factors and the proposals made to the court in pre-sentence reports. Information is not available on whether this rise in blended sentences and the potential displacement of community-only options is attributable to, for example, an increase in serious offences coming before the courts (data on crime rates, while not directly comparable would suggest not). Nor do we know if DCSs have become more popular because of recommendations made in pre-sentence reports, because data on the congruence between sentences and sentence recommendations made by probation officers is not publicly available.[17]

However, a recent analysis of the factors contributing to the rise in the Northern Ireland prison population points to some concerning trends (DoJ, 2014). It shows that there has been an increase in the number of short custodial sentences dispensed by magistrates' courts and states:

> There is no single explanation for this increase, which may reflect a changing public and judicial attitude to sentencing, a reaction to some earlier sentences being reviewed by a higher court as being too lenient and/or a change in offending patterns (DoJ 2014: 6)

In addition to a higher number of custodial sentences being dispensed by magistrates' courts there has also been an increase in numbers of cases before the Crown Court, and this compounded by increased custodial lengths have been significant population drivers within the prison system (DoJ 2014).[18] Significantly, one of the recommendations made in this report is for further explorations to be undertaken with the judiciary to explore confidence in the use of community sentences as alternatives to short prison sentences.[19]

If we view sentences of the court as the 'front door' point of entry into prison, 'back door' entry routes are also of concern. The latest data on the work of the Parole Commissioners published in their Annual Report (Parole Commissioners

[17] There has been no published research in Northern Ireland on the role of pre-sentence reports in the sentencing process. A CJINI inspection on this area commented positively on the overall quality of reports, but noted the increase in volume of reports requested by the courts and the 'widening net of PSR users' (CJINI 2011a: 9).

[18] The average length of a Crown Court DCS is 1 year and 8 months, and the average ECS is 5 years and 2 months (DoJ 2014: 7).

[19] A recommendation is made that the Department of Justice should 'consider initiating a conversation with the judiciary about their confidence in using community sentencing as an alternative to short prison sentences' (DoJ 2014: 25).

NI 2014) and in inspections conducted by the Criminal Justice Inspection Northern Ireland (CJINI 2011b) illustrates increases in the overall workload of this body. In 2012–13, 173 people subject to release on licence under a DCS were referred to the Parole Commissioners for recall and 143 were subsequently recalled to prison for breach of their licence conditions. A further 11 individuals released on licence under an Extended or Indeterminate Custodial sentence were recalled to prison in this period (Parole Commissioners NI 2014). An analysis of the prison population in Northern Ireland notes that 42 per cent of recalls occurred because an individual's 'risk factors' were deemed to have increased represented by licence breaches (DoJ 2014: 9). The work of the Parole Commissioners and the evidence of the expansion in the number of cases that they are dealing with are significant for a number of reasons.

The practice of 'recalling' people to prison has an impact on the prison population. In England and Wales, for example, recalls account for a significant proportion of the large (and rising) prison population (Padfield 2012).[20] As Padfield (2012) has noted, the introduction of the Criminal Justice Act 2003 in England and Wales (the legislation on which the Criminal Justice (Northern Ireland) Order 2008 is modelled), extended the periods that people were subject to licence and has therefore had an effect on the number of people being recalled to prison.[21] Similar trends are evident in the Northern Ireland context. The Prison Review Team (2011) identifies the recalls of prisoners sentenced under the Criminal Justice (Northern Ireland) Order 2008 as one of the drivers contributing to the increase in the prison population (PRT 2011). This is supported by a recent analysis of factors attributing to the growth in the Northern Ireland prison population where it is noted that a significant proportion of recalls (42 per cent) under the new regime (ie, post-2010 when the first sentences under the Criminal Justice (Northern Ireland) Order 2008 came into effect), were for breaches of licence conditions rather than commission of new offences. Here the report notes that '[o]nly a small number of such individuals would have been committed to custody before the Criminal Justice Order and, consequently, they are taken as being an addition to the prison population' (DoJ 2014: 9).

By September 2013, the recall population accounted for 9 per cent of the Northern Ireland prison population and this proportion is estimated to grow further (DoJ 2014). However, despite occupying an expanding role as 'back door sentencers', the work of parole bodies has been subject to limited research attention (Padfield and Maruna 2006). The processes and practices of recall, including the

[20] The prison population in England and Wales was 85,406 in December 2014. The population has more than doubled over 20 years (it was 41,800 in 1993). See 'Prison Population Statistics, Ministry of Justice', available at www.gov.uk/government/publications/prison-population-figures-2014; See also MoJ (2013b, 2013c).

[21] Padfield (2012: 39) notes a rise from 2457 determinate sentenced prisoners recalled in 2000–01 to 13,919 in 2009–10. Figures from the MoJ (2013c) also show that in England and Wales recalls accounted for 13 per cent of the increase in the prison population between 1993 and 2012.

evidential requirements and experiences of these processes are important areas to consider. Digard's (2010) study of sex offenders who had been subject to recall in England and Wales for breaching the terms of their licences highlights concerns regarding 'procedural fairness'. Here issues were raised regarding the standard of evidence used to justify recalls, the inadequacy of representation in the process and the sense in which licence conditions were so all-encompassing they were perceived as ambiguous.[22] The significance of this is that this sense of 'procedural justice' (Tyler 2004), has important links with compliance (Ugwidike and Raynor 2013). Some recent work has explored the link between compliance (both formal and substantive) and legitimacy and postulates that a greater sense of legitimacy, significantly involving the actions or 'moral performance' of the practitioner, may lead to more significant engagement and better longer-term outcomes (McNeill and Robinson 2013).[23]

While having people subject to licence conditions with an associated muscle of recall may be attractive in terms of public perception, the actual effect of the recall process beyond temporally limited incapacitation is not known. The expansion of 'conditionality' in these terms widens the sphere of penality and further blurs the boundary between prison and the community. Such practices are legitimised under a promise to 'protect the public' and they are underscored by a managerial orthodoxy, one where the offender is *managed* throughout their sentence and in particular in their transition from prison to the contingent community. The more porous boundaries between prison and community have some potentially important implications. While it may be grounded in a (re)-integrative premise (ie, that licence conditions and other interventions are intended to support reintegration), it is possible—as the examples above indicate—that it has precisely the opposite effect, further increasing the level of system contact and resulting in re-entry into prison for short periods of time, only to begin the process of return to the community again.

[22] Digard (2010: 49) provides the specific example of this licence condition relating to 'good behaviour' which was routinely included as part of range of conditions in England and Wales. It stipulates that the released prisoner must 'be of good behaviour, and not behave in a way which undermines the purposes of the release on licence, which are to protect the public, prevent re-offending and promote successful re-integration into the community' (Criminal Justice (Sentencing) (Licence Conditions) Order 2003, para 2(2)(f)). Digard (2010) argues that the concept of 'good behaviour' is not well defined, a point of contention raised by his interview participants. It is worth noting that this condition is slightly modified in Northern Ireland under the Standard Conditions of the Criminal Justice (Sentencing) (Licence Conditions) (Northern Ireland) Rules 2009. S 3(a) states that the 'prisoner must not—behave in a way which undermines the purposes of the release on licence, which are the protection of the public, the prevention of re-offending and the rehabilitation of the offender'.

[23] McNeill and Robinson (2013) make a distinction between *formal compliance*, ie, adherence to the rules, and *substantive compliance*, ie, engaging productively in supervision to make positive changes. Drawing on Liebling's (2004) work on moral performance in prisons, they argue that a probation practitioner's 'moral performance' will affect the 'meaning, nature and experience' of community sanctions (McNeill and Robinson 2013: 133).

Electronic Monitoring

Another important recent development in Northern Ireland that emphasises the contingent links between prison and the community has been the introduction of Electronic Monitoring (EM). Northern Ireland was the last UK jurisdiction to introduce this measure and some of the concerns regarding implementation are highlighted by this manager within the PBNI:[24]

> Some of the main concerns about the increasing use of technology to monitor offenders are the fear that EM is the thin end of the wedge, that more and more resources will be diverted into surveillance and that technology will displace rehabilitative approaches rather than augment them (Best 2009: 95).

In international terms the use of EM has grown exponentially with increased numbers of people subject to this form of surveillance and regulation (Nellis et al 2013). Mair and Nellis (2013: 73) note, for example, that between 1999 and 2011 more than three-quarters of a million people had been monitored in England and Wales. There have also been developments in the technology used for EM with increasingly sophisticated equipment being used in some countries (for example, GPS—global positioning systems, which can track an individual's specific movements) (Nellis et al 2013).

The provisions of the Criminal Justice (Northern Ireland) Order 2008 allow for EM to be imposed as a condition of bail, a community sentence or as part of a post-custodial licence. In Northern Ireland, EM, as is customary in many jurisdictions, is provided and maintained by a private contractor which is required to send any reports of non-compliance to the relevant agencies (for example, PSNI or Probation). There are no current publicly available figures on the use of EM in Northern Ireland. However, some evidence of the scale of use is available. In response to an Assembly question in 2010, Minister of Justice, David Ford, provided information that there had been 550 electronic monitoring orders imposed as part of bail conditions between 1 April 2009 and 31 March 2010.[25] In the financial year 2012/2013 £1.24 million was spent on the contract with the private provider (G4S).[26]

Part of the rationale for the use of EM is to allow people to remain in the community who may otherwise be in custody. In Northern Ireland EM is used most (in 88 per cent of cases) at the pre-sentence stage, ie, as part of a bail condition

[24] Electronic Monitoring (EM) was implemented in England and Wales in 1989 (the first European jurisdiction to do so) and in Scotland in 1998 (Mair and Nellis 2013).

[25] This information was provided in response to a query from Carál Ní Chuilín, Sinn Féin MLA, on the extent of the use of electronic monitoring for people on bail, 25 May 2010 (Northern Ireland Assembly, AQO 1303/10).

[26] This information came from a written parliamentary question tabled by Lord Morrow, a MLA for the Democratic Unionist Party (DUP) to the Minister of Justice, enquiring how much the security company G4S had been paid for the provision of electronic monitoring services in 2011/12 and 2012/13, 7 March 2013 (Northern Ireland Assembly, AQW 20692/11–15).

(DoJ 2014). However, the available information suggests that the expansion in the use of EM has not led to any significant reduction in the prison population (specifically in relation to remands) (DoJ 2014). Given this, the recent review of the factors contributing to the growth in the Northern Ireland prison population, identifies that the use of EM is an area that requires further scrutiny (DoJ 2014). It may be that EM is being used for people who would have been considered for bail without this additional condition paradoxically suggesting a possible net widening rather than a penal reduction effect.

Conclusion

Aspects of the history and trajectory of probation in Northern Ireland share common characteristics with other countries. The origins of probation and shifts in focus in the context of changing economic, social and political climates, including the move from penal welfarism towards public protection are similar to other countries including England and Wales where probation has been forced to adapt in response (Robinson et al 2013). The Troubles have also had a shaping influence on probation in Northern Ireland. The 'neutrality' stance adopted by probation in the mid-1970s allowed the service to function at a community level at the height of the conflict. The out-workings in the years following the ceasefires have seen scrutiny and reform of the criminal justice system with recent attention addressed towards the prison system (PRT 2011).

The process of 'normalisation' of criminal justice policy has seen the implementation of legislation aimed towards 'public protection' and some blurring of the boundaries between the community and prisons. However, to date there has not been a sustained push towards an integrated 'offender management' service along the lines of NOMS in England and Wales focusing on the end-to-end management of offenders from prison to community. However, the question of the interface between community and custodial sanctions and the 'management' of offenders as they transition from prison to the community is an area that continues as the subject of policy attention. The PRT (2011: 58) recommended that the prison and probation partnership 'should develop much further without threatening the operational independence and different traditions of the two services'. Community probation staff should do more work inside prisons, particularly regarding offending work and prison staff could do more work in the community, for example by linking in with post-release supervision of released prisoners.

The interrelationship between probation and prisons is further underscored by the movement of people between these spheres. In recent years Northern Ireland has seen a move towards penal expansionism, both in terms of rises in prison numbers *and* in those subject to forms of community supervision. This follows trends seen elsewhere (McNeill and Beyens 2014). In England and Wales, for example, the ratio between people under some form of community supervision and those in prison is approximately 3:1 (McNeill 2013).[27] In the United States in 2012, almost 4.8 million adults were under some form of community supervision, accounting for about 1 in 50 adults in the population (Maruschak and Bonczar 2013). Similarly in many European countries, some with recently developed probation services, the numbers of people subject to supervision in the community has grown (van Kalmhout and Durnescu 2008; Durnescu and McNeill 2014).

It is argued that the neglect of this area, particularly when community sanctions are viewed as a more benign form of penality when compared with imprisonment, fails to adequately pay attention to the widening and intensifying forms of social control that are occurring in this area (McNeill and Beyens 2014). Alongside increased numbers under supervision in the community, there has also been an expansion in the repertoire of sanctions and surveillance techniques available. The widening use of EM is one example (Nellis et al 2013), as are the expanding panoply of 'public protection' measures including longer periods of post-custodial supervision and multi-agency fora (Kemshall and Maguire 2001; Padfield and Maruna 2006).

Some of the areas of evident 'policy transfer' have been drawn out throughout this chapter (Newburn and Jones 2007). The influence of trends occurring in England and Wales has been noted, in particular the recent disestablishment of Probation Trusts as a precursor to privatisation (Burke 2013).[28] Various analyses have pointed to some of the precursors to this move, including the influence of managerialism (McCulloch and McNeill 2007). A desire to 'toughen up' the criminal justice system and to more effectively manage those who were processed through it formed part of the rationale for the changes to probation services in England and Wales that occurred in the late-1990s and early-2000s. These changes were as much political imperative as evidence-led (Mair and Burke 2012) and the notion of 'seamless sentencing' was part of the illusory notion that supported the rationale of amalgamating prisons and probation (Worrall 2008).

The public protection emphasis in the criminal justice system in Northern Ireland is illustrative of a wider 'normalisation' process where attention has moved from political conflict towards more 'ordinary' criminality. Here the temperature of public debate and policy discourse in the context of devolved policing and justice responsibilities is more likely to have an influence of the shape and future direction of the Probation Service in Northern Ireland. Indeed some commentators (for example, O'Mahony and Chapman 2007) have argued that the Probation Service in Northern Ireland escaped some of the more profound changes experienced by other probation services in the UK precisely because the political context meant that attention was focused elsewhere. The paradox both of probation and the wider criminal justice system is that in a post-conflict dispensation, the numbers coming under the gaze of the penal system have risen exponentially in recent years.

[27] This ratio should also be viewed in light of the fact that the prison population more than doubled in England and Wales over the past 20 years (MoJ 2013c): see n 20 above.

[28] See P Senior, 'Privatizing Probation: The Death Knell of a Much Cherished Public Service?' available at www.youtube.com/watch?v=O26l_ZT0qyc; see also Allen (2013), n 2 above.

References

Allen, F (1981) *The Decline of the Rehabilitative Ideal* (New Haven, CT, Yale University Press).

Andrews, DA, Bonta, J and Hoge, RD (1990) 'Classification for Effective Rehabilitation. Rediscovering Psychology' 17 *Criminal Justice and Behavior* 19.

Annison, J, Burke, L and Senior, P (2014) 'Transforming Rehabilitation: Another Example of English "Exceptionalism" or a Blueprint for the Rest of Europe?' 6 *European Journal of Probation* 23.

Bailie, R (2008) 'Criminal Justice (Northern Ireland) Order 2008' 5 *Irish Probation Journal* 20.

Best, P (2009) 'Curfew/Electronic Monitoring: The Northern Ireland Experience' 6 *Irish Probation Journal* 91.

Blair, C (2000) *Prisons and Probation. Research Report 6. Review of the Criminal Justice System in Northern Ireland* (Belfast, Criminal Justice Review Group).

Burke, L (2013) 'Grayling's Hubris' 60 *Probation Journal* 377.

Burnett, R (2004) 'One-to-one Ways of Promoting Desistance: In Search of an Evidence-base' in R Burnett and C Roberts (eds), *What Works in Probation and Youth Justice* (Cullompton, Willan Publishing).

Carr, N, Healey, D, Kennefick, L and Maguire, N (2013) 'A Review of the Research on Offender Supervision in the Republic of Ireland and Northern Ireland' 10 *Irish Probation Journal* 50.

Carr, N and Maruna, S (2012) 'Legitimacy through Neutrality. Probation and the Conflict in Northern Ireland' 51 *Howard Journal* 474.

Carr, N and Robinson, G (2012) 'Practising Offending Supervision, UK Report' *COST Offender Supervision in Europe*, available at www.offendersupervision.eu/wp-content/uploads/2013/05/Practising-OS-in-the-UK-December-2012.pdf.

Cavadino, M and Dignan, J (2006) *Penal Systems: A Comparative Approach* (London, Sage).

Chapman, T and Hough, M (1998) *Evidence Based Practice. A Guide to Effective Practice* (London, Her Majesty's Inspectorate of Probation).

Cheliotis, L (2006) 'How Iron is the Iron Cage of New Penology? The Role of Human Agency in the Implementation of Criminal Justice Policy' 8 *Punishment & Society* 313.

Criminal Justice Inspection Northern Ireland (CJINI) (2006) *The Management of Sex Offenders in Light of the Murder of Mrs Attracta Harron, Interim Report* (Belfast, CJINI).

—— (2011a) *Pre-Sentence Reports* (Belfast, CJINI).

—— (2011b) *Governance Inspection of the Parole Commissioners for Northern Ireland* (Belfast, CJINI).

—— (2012) *The Management of Life and Indeterminate Sentence Prisoners in Northern Ireland* (Belfast, CJINI).

Criminal Justice Review Group (CJRG) (2000) *Review of the Criminal Justice System in Northern Ireland:* The Report of the Criminal Justice Review (Belfast, HMSO).

Deering, J (2010) 'Attitudes and Beliefs of Trainee Probation Officers: A "New Breed"?' 57 *Probation Journal* 9.

Department of Justice (DoJ) (2014) *Prison Population Review. A Review of the Factors Leading to the Growth in Prisoner Numbers between 2009 and 2013* (Belfast, Department of Justice).

Digard, L (2010) 'When Legitimacy is Denied: Offender Perceptions of the Prison Recall System' 57 *Probation Journal* 43.

Doran, P and Cooper, L (2008) 'Social Work: The Core Qualification of Probation Officers in Northern Ireland' 5 *Irish Probation Journal* 35.
Downes, D (1988) *Contrasts in Tolerance: Post-War Penal Policy in the Netherlands and England and Wales* (Oxford, Oxford University Press).
Durnescu, I and McNeill, F (eds) (2014) *Understanding Penal Practice* (Oxford, Routledge).
Farrall, S (2002) *Rethinking What Works with Offenders: Probation, Social Context and Desistance from Crime* (Cullompton, Willan Publishing).
Feeley, M and Simon, J (1992) 'The New Penology: Notes on the Emerging Strategy of Corrections and its Implications' 30 *Criminology* 449.
Fitzgibbon, W and Lea, J (2014) 'Defending Probation: Beyond Privatisation and Security' 6 *European Journal of Probation* 24.
Fulton, B and Carr, N (2013) 'Probation in Europe: Northern Ireland' in *Probation in Europe* (CEP, Probation in Europe).
Fulton, B and Parkhill, T (2009) *Making the Difference. An Oral History of Probation in Northern Ireland* (Belfast, PBNI).
Garland, D (1985) *Punishment and Welfare: A History of Penal Strategies* (Aldershot, Gower).
—— (1996) 'The Limits of the Sovereign State. Strategies of Crime Control in Contemporary Society' 36 *British Journal of Criminology* 445.
—— (2001) *The Culture of Control: Crime and Social Order in Contemporary Society* (Oxford, Oxford University Press).
Healy, D (2009) 'Probation Matters' *Irish Jurist* XLIV 239.
Kemshall, H and Maguire, M (2001) 'Public Protection, Partnership and Risk Penalty: The Multi-agency Risk Management of Sexual and Violent Offenders' 3 *Punishment & Society* 237.
Kilcommins, S, O'Donnell, I, O'Sullivan, E and Vaughan, B (2004) *Crime, Punishment and the Search for Order in Ireland* (Dublin, Institute of Public Administration).
Lacey, N (2008) *The Prisoners' Dilemma: Political Economy and Punishment in Contemporary Democracies* The Hamlyn Lectures 2007 (Cambridge, Cambridge University Press).
Liebling, A (2004) *Prisons and their Moral Performance* (Oxford, Clarendon Press).
Mair, G and Burke, L (2012) *Redemption, Rehabilitation and Risk Management. A History of Probation* (London, Routledge).
Mair, G and Nellis, M, (2013) '"Parallel Tracks": Probation and Electronic Monitoring in England, Wales and Scotland' in M Nellis, K Beyens and D Kaminski (eds), *Electronically Monitored Punishment. International and Critical Perspectives* (Abingdon, Routledge).
Maruschak, LM and Bonczar, TP (2013) *Probation and Parole in the United States, 2012, Bureau of Justice Statistics Bulletin*, December 2013 (NCJ 243826 US Department of Justice Statistics).
Mawby, RC and Worrall, A (2013) *Doing Probation Work: Identity in a Criminal Justice Occupation* (London, Routledge).
McAlinden, A (2012) 'The Governance of Sexual Offending Across Europe: Penal Policies, Political Economies and the Institutionalization of Risk' 14 *Punishment & Society* 166.
McCulloch, T and McNeill, F (2007) 'Consumer Society, Commodification and Offender Management' 7 *Criminology & Criminal Justice* 223.
—— (2011) 'Adult Criminal Justice' in R Davis and J Gordon (eds), *Social Work and the Law in Scotland*, 2nd edn (Basingstoke, Palgrave Macmillan).
McNeill, F (2011) 'Probation, Credibility and Justice' 58 *Probation Journal* 9.
—— (2013) 'Community Sanctions and European Penology' in T Daems, S Snacken and D Van Zyl Smit (eds), *European Penology* (Oxford, Hart Publishing).

McNeill, F and Beyens, K (eds) (2014) *Offender Supervision in Europe* (Basingstoke, Palgrave MacMillan).
McNeill, F, Burns, N, Halliday, S, Hutton, N and Tata, C (2009) 'Risk, Responsibility and Reconfiguration. Penal Adaptation and Misadaptation' 11 *Punishment & Society* 419.
McNeill, F and Dawson, M (2014) 'Social Solidarity, Penal Evolution and Probation' 54 *British Journal of Criminology* 892.
McNeill, F and Robinson, G (2013) 'Liquid Legitimacy and Community Sanctions' in A Crawford and A Hucklesby (eds), *Legitimacy and Compliance in Criminal Justice* (Abingdon, Routledge).
McNeill, F and Weaver, B (2010) *Changing Lives? Desistance Research and Offender Management* (Glasgow, The Scottish Centre for Crime and Justice Research).
Ministry of Justice (MoJ) (2013a) *Transforming Rehabilitation. A Strategy for Reform* (London, The Stationery Office).
—— (2013b) *Offender Management Statistics Quarterly Bulletin January to March 2013, England and Wales* (London, The Stationery Office).
—— (2013c) *Story of the Prison Population 1993–2012 England and Wales* (London, The Stationery Office).
Multi-Agency Sex Offender Risk Assessment and Management (MASRAM) (2006) *Serious Case Review—Trevor Hamilton* (Belfast, Northern Ireland Sex Offender Strategic Management Committee).
Nash, M (2000) 'Deconstructing the Probation Service—The Trojan Horse of Public Protection' 28 *International Journal of the Sociology of Law* 201.
Nellis, M, Beyens, K and Kaminski, D (2013) (eds), *Electronically Monitored Punishment: International and Critical Perspectives* (Abingdon, Routledge).
Newburn, T and Jones, T (2007) *Policy Transfer and Criminal Justice. Exploring US Influence over British Crime Policy* (Maidenhead, Open University Press).
Northern Ireland Prison Service (NIPS) (2014) *Analysis of NIPS Prison Population from 01/07/2013 to 30/09/2014* (Belfast, Department of Justice).
O'Mahony, D and Chapman, T (2007) 'Probation, the State and Community—Delivering Probation Services in Northern Ireland' in L Gelsthorpe and R Morgan (eds), *Handbook of Probation* (Cullompton, Willan Publishing).
Padfield, N (2012) 'Recalling Conditionally Released Prisoners in England and Wales' 4 *European Journal of Probation* 34.
Padfield, N and Maruna, S (2006) 'The Revolving Door at the Prison Gate: Exploring the Dramatic Increase in Recalls to Prison' 6 *Criminology & Criminal Justice* 329.
Parole Commissioners for Northern Ireland (2014) *Annual Report 2013–2014* (Belfast, Parole Commissioners for Northern Ireland).
Phelps, MS (2013) 'The Paradox of Probation: Community Supervision in the Age of Mass Incarceration' 35 *Law & Policy* 51.
Prison Review Team (PRT) (2011) *Review of the Northern Ireland Prison Service: Conditions, Management and Oversight of all Prisons* (Belfast, Prison Review Team).
Probation Board Northern Ireland (PBNI) (2012) *Best Practice Framework Incorporating Northern Ireland Standards* (Belfast, PBNI).
—— (2013) *PBNI Caseload Statistics (2012/2013)* (Belfast, PBNI).
—— (2014) *PBNI Caseload Statistics (Quarter 2 2014–2015)* (Belfast, PBNI).
Robinson, G and Burnett, R (2007) 'Experiencing Modernization: Frontline Probation Perspectives on the Transition to a National Offender Management Service' 54 *Probation Journal* 318.

Robinson, G and McNeill, F (2004) 'Purposes Matters: The Ends of Probation' in G Mair (ed), *What Matters in Probation Work* (Cullompton, Willan Publishing).
Robinson, G, McNeill, F and Maruna, S (2013) 'Punishment *in* Society: The Improbable Persistence of Probation and Other Community Sanctions and Measures' in J Simon and R Sparks (eds), *The Sage Handbook of Punishment and Society* (London, Sage).
Simon, J (2007) *Governing Through Crime: How the War on Crime Transformed American Democracy and Created a Culture of Fear* (Oxford, Oxford University Press).
Tyler, TR (2004) 'Procedural Justice' in A Sarat (ed), *The Blackwell Companion to Law and Society* (Oxford, Blackwell Publishing).
Ugwidike, P and Raynor, P (eds) (2013) *What Works in Offender Compliance. International Perspectives and Evidence-Based Practice* (Basingstoke, Palgrave Macmillan).
van. Kalmhout, A and Durnescu, I (eds) (2008) *Probation in Europe* (Nijmegen, Wolf Legal Publishers).
Ward, T and Maruna, S (2007) *Rehabilitation* (London, Routledge).
Worrall, A (2008) '"The 'Seemingness' of the "Seamless Management" of Offenders' in P Carlen (ed), *Imaginary Penalties* (Cullompton, Willan Publishing).
Young, J (1999) *The Exclusive Society* (London, Sage).
Zedner, L (2002) 'Dangers of Dystopia in Penal Theory' 22 *Oxford Journal of Legal Studies* 341.

12

Revisiting the Past: Miscarriages of Justice, the Courts and Transition

MARNY REQUA[1]

Introduction

This chapter considers official acknowledgment of miscarriages of justice in Northern Ireland, in the years since the peace process, through the quashing of convictions and compensation. Conflict-related cases continue to dominate proceedings in this area. The establishment of the Criminal Cases Review Commission (CCRC) in 1997 created new powers for reviewing potential miscarriages of justice and referring them to the Northern Ireland Court of Appeal (NICA). The appellate system in Northern Ireland echoes that in England and Wales,[2] and the CCRC referral process is quite similar to the approach in Scotland.[3] But 89 per cent of the cases referred to the NICA from the CCRC involved convictions under counterterrorism legislation from the period of conflict (1968–98). As a consequence, the jurisprudence on miscarriages of justice is distinct from elsewhere in the United Kingdom and has strong political resonance in post-conflict Northern Ireland. The high percentage of conflict-related referrals from the CCRC reflects the applicant pool—about 75 per cent of applications to the CCRC involved convictions under counterterrorism legislation[4] (CCRC 2013: 11)—and is indicative of a continued political focus on the past. This perspective overshadows the development of contemporary criminal standards in more routine cases.

Miscarriages of justice in Northern Ireland also provide a cautionary tale about 'emergency' legislation that lowers the threshold for admitting evidence within a regular criminal justice system. The term 'miscarriage of justice' is used here as it is in UK legislation, to refer to convictions overturned by the NICA after a referral

[1] I would like to thank Hannah Quirk and the editors of this collection for thoughtful comments on a previous draft of the chapter. Any errors or omissions are my own.

[2] Criminal Appeal Act 1995, c 35.

[3] Criminal Procedure (Scotland) Act 1995, c 46, pt XA (see Griffin 2013).

[4] Email correspondence with CCRC Head of Communication, Justin Hawkins, on file with author (December 2012).

from the CCRC or an out-of-time appeal.[5] As discussed below, cases identified as miscarriages of justice in Northern Ireland do not include all convictions made on the basis of fabricated or altered confessions, or where detainees were abused, and they omit scores of cases in which the Judges' Rules, governing detention and interview of suspects prior to the Police and Criminal Evidence (NI) Order (PACE) 1989, were violated. Moreover, it is difficult to believe that the CCRC referrals, identifying abuses and misinformation in terrorism trials, are not indicative of additional wrongful convictions that are unable to meet current evidential demands of the NICA. Recent case law restricts future referrals in conflict-related cases, adding to what is characterised in this chapter as an 'acknowledgement gap' regarding miscarriages of justice in Northern Ireland.

The Northern Irish experience is instructive in identifying limitations of certain post-conflict mechanisms and reform projects. Societies undergoing political transition are called on to strengthen criminal justice institutions and address past human rights violations, but the two processes are often disconnected. In Northern Ireland policing reform and the early release of prisoners were among the most crucial features of the negotiated peace. Even so, many parties to the Agreement would not consider that the reform agenda recognised the political nature of policing and crime during the conflict (McGarry 2004: 377–79, 388–89). There has not been a post-conflict process to document police abuses or potential wrongful convictions, although individual cases of police mistreatment can be raised as complaints to the Police Ombudsman for Northern Ireland. While criminal justice agencies in Northern Ireland continue to expend resources on the past, processes of reform prompted by the Good Friday Agreement looked back at the conflict only as the impetus for change. For example, the Report of the Independent Commission on Policing for Northern Ireland (ICP 1999: the 'Patten Report') acknowledged conflict-era criminal justice failings vaguely. It mentioned 'all that has gone wrong' and '[w]here the powers available to the police have been particularly extensive, because of terrorist violence, the opportunity for abuse has been extensive too' (1999: paragraphs 1.13–1.15). The Patten Commission was targeted at addressing systemic issues in policing practice (ICP 1999: 2–4) but was not charged with investigating individual cases or evaluating past practices. The Review of the Criminal Justice System in Northern Ireland (CJRG 2000) had a comparable remit in relation to other criminal justice agencies. Similarly, prisoner release[6] did not address errors in prosecuting individuals, and ex-prisoners maintain a criminal record. In the absence of a comprehensive review of human rights abuses, potential miscarriages of justice—as a result of police mistreatment or the application of counterterrorism legislation for example—have been reviewed individually through the appeals system and the CCRC.

[5] Definitions of miscarriage of justice and related terms vary significantly in literature and public discourse (Grounds 2005). For useful consideration of miscarriages of justice in a wider sense, see eg Brian Forst (2013), whose definition includes wrongful police intrusions against the public and failure to bring offenders to justice.

[6] Northern Ireland (Sentences) Act 1998, c 35.

Cases have been referred from the CCRC to the NICA at a significantly higher rate than to the Court of Appeal in England and Wales (EWCA).[7] In total, 38 potential miscarriages of justice have been sent to the NICA; 34 of those were conflict related[8] and 91 per cent have been overturned, compared with a 70 per cent quash rate in all referrals by the CCRC. Despite the high 'success' rate in Northern Ireland cases, the number of officially recognised miscarriages of justice is miniscule relative to conflict-related convictions,[9] and the jurisprudence of the NICA in this area limits future referrals from the CCRC. The results are striking when considered alongside credible allegations of widespread police abuses (Taylor 1980: 334; Weschler 1990: 4; Amnesty International 1978; Cobain 2012: chapter 6) and modification of criminal procedure under counterterrorism laws during the conflict.

In the past 15 years the criminal justice system has undergone significant reform and, in many respects, fair trial rights have been strengthened. It might be assumed that an appellate court, considering convictions in what is now an ordinary regime, would be receptive to arguments regarding errors and misconduct that occurred during the period of conflict (Mureinik 1994; see also Dyzenhaus 2010: 263). Instead, individuals face similar barriers in challenging convictions as those identified in settled societies such as England and Wales and the United States, where researchers have extensively studied the incidence, causes and consequences of wrongful convictions (Gould and Leo 2010; Zalman 2012). Wrongful conviction detection rates are notoriously low in non-transitioning societies (Gross 2008; Walker and McCartney 2008; Zalman 2012; Gross 2013). In Northern Ireland, appellants must meet a high evidential threshold to succeed, discussed further below. The NICA generally does not take into consideration political circumstances surrounding conflict-era convictions, such as reasons why appellants may not have challenged their convictions (Requa 2014: 44–45, 49, 61). Neither has there been a targeted approach by political leaders to address state abuses related to the detention and interrogation of terrorism suspects during the conflict, and exonerated individuals suffer long delays before receiving compensation. (Many, in fact, are not compensated.)[10] Observers have noted, in the aftermath of

[7] The CCRC has power to refer cases to the NICA and the EWCA. Criminal Appeal Act 1995, c 35, ss 8–12. (The Scottish CCRC handles cases in that jurisdiction.) The first Northern Irish case was referred during the 1998–99 term (CCRC 1999: 13).

[8] 'Conflict-related' convictions include those processed under counterterrorism legislation, which designated certain offences as 'scheduled' and required special procedures including non-jury trials. In addition, at least one case discussed here involved ordinary crime but was processed under counterterrorism legislation, *R v Adams* [2006] NICA 6 and, in *R v Holden* [2012] NICA 26, the defendant was convicted by a jury for the murder of a soldier in 1973.

[9] Jackson and Doran considered that there had been 'well over 10,000 defendants' processed in non-jury courts from 1973 through the early 1990s (1995: 19). (Trial without jury for scheduled offences was introduced in 1973.) Shirlow and McEvoy have estimated that 15,000 Republican and between 5,000 and 10,000 Loyalist members of paramilitary groups were imprisoned, although not necessarily convicted, during the conflict (2008: 2).

[10] See discussion in 'Compensation in Northern Ireland' section below.

wrongful convictions, 'the persistent refusal of state actors to take responsibility for injustices they helped to create' (Westervelt and Cook 2011: 1225; see also Westervelt and Cook 2010: 261). Resistance to accountability is apparent in Northern Ireland as well, despite political change and reforms within many of the relevant criminal justice agencies.

The next part of this chapter, Section I, discusses what is meant by official acknowledgment and why it is significant to victims of human rights abuses. In that regard the chapter identifies commonalities in academic literature covering circumstances of conflict and 'peace', between the interests of victims of widespread atrocities and those who have been wrongfully convicted. In the latter cases, rights violations often occur incidental to normal functioning of state bodies or as the result of embedded biases in criminal justice systems. Miscarriages of justice in Northern Ireland are distinctive, but by no means unique in the world or indeed in the United Kingdom (see, for example, Huff 2013), because they occurred during a conflict and relate to the use of extraordinary measures. In both settled and transitioning societies, judicial decisions that overturn convictions are viewed by victims of miscarriages of justice as a mode of acknowledgement—despite their limited scope—with practical outcomes for individuals. Section II of the chapter outlines the process for identifying miscarriages of justice in Northern Ireland.

Section III covers the cases referred from the CCRC to the NICA. The section assesses NICA jurisprudence, arguing that it limits future referrals from the CCRC and creates two tiers of review, in which conflict-era convictions are not afforded the benefits of contemporary standards of fairness. As was the case during the conflict (Walker 1999a: 166), only egregious and blatant abuse is recognised by the courts. Section IV provides data on compensation for miscarriages of justice in Northern Ireland. In conclusion the chapter discusses the acknowledgement gap in Northern Ireland. The courts have not adequately explored the consequences of irregular practices and procedures in individual cases, and processes of reform have not considered the issue of wrongful convictions.

Acknowledgement and Abuses of the Past

In Stan Cohen's influential work on the tendency of individuals and governments to deny atrocities, he regarded public acknowledgment—when 'knowledge ... becomes officially sanctioned and enters the public discourse'—as exceptional (2001: 225, chapter 4). Acknowledgement may be uncommon and incomplete (Weschler 1990: 4; Ignatieff 1996: 113) but, without a form of public recognition, certain effects of abuses continue. Denial of rights violations perpetuates victims' suffering and prevents informed political decision-making in society (Cohen 2001: 295). After wrongdoing perpetrated by state actors, official acknowledgement is sought as a moral imperative as well as an obligation predicated on deceptions and denials of the past (Popkin and Roht-Arriaza 1995: 81–82, 93; Haynor 2002: 25).

The confirmation and publicity of knowledge about an injustice may settle a dispute, vindicate victims, and temper anger.[11] Acknowledgement entails the dissemination of relevant information about rights violations and the identification of that conduct as wrong by an official source, whether government representative, a judge, or an independent (or quasi-independent) body appointed by government to investigate such claims. While the information must be sufficient to demonstrate that abuses took place, inevitably facts will remain unknown and, as with criminal trials (Osiel 2002: 159), analysis into the circumstances behind the facts will be lacking. The struggle, therefore, is often over the nature and degree of acknowledgement. Campaigners inevitably face strong state resistance. Denial is entrenched and supports the status quo or the 'status quo ante' (Requa 2014: 59–60), with revelations often unappealing even to successor governments tasked with responding to state wrongdoing. Partial acknowledgement can be seen as obfuscation, for example where torture is disclosed but suspicions about the criminal conduct of victims are not dispelled. Officials also may have alternative motives for acknowledgements. Recognition of abuses might be interpreted as ineffectual, biased, or an attempted means of placating those who challenge the government.[12]

In societies undergoing political transition, acknowledgement is among the goals of truth recovery and an integral aspect of formal truth-telling processes (Haynor 2002: 24–27; Bassiouni 2006: 275–76; see also the chapter by Lawther in this volume). Arguments supporting a right to truth are built upon a battle against denial (Méndez 1997: 261–62; Groome 2011: 198). The South African Truth and Reconciliation Commission identified 'healing and restorative truth' as one category of truth, which aspires to facts being 'fully and publicly acknowledged' including the acceptance of accountability (TRC 1998: 114, paragraph 45; see also Boraine 2001). While informal truth-telling processes have particular benefits, formal recognition of abuses requires a political response and lends an air of veracity to facts, even those that were widely known.[13] Yet there are multiple truths about incidents and series of events—and many facts will remain unconfirmed. The 'truth' is socially dependent (Naqvi 2006: 249–53), often controversial and always incomplete.

[11] Joanna Quinn considers acknowledgment critical (albeit insufficient) to rebuilding community trust and strengthening social cohesion (2010: 33).

[12] eg, Claire Moon has argued that offers of reparations to the Madres de Plaza de Mayo in Argentina, an association of women whose relatives disappeared during the military dictatorship, rather than simply serving as an acknowledgement of wrongful acts, were viewed as attempts to control protest demands and to avoid processes of retributive justice (2012).

[13] Erin Daly, however, questions the efficacy of truth commissions in establishing an authoritative record (2008: 28–30). Scholars have also questioned the validity of assumptions about the consequences and benefits of truth recovery in transitioning societies (see Daly 2008: 36–39).

Similar themes arise in individual miscarriage of justice cases, even in politically stable societies: state denial, arduous efforts by victims to uncover information and demand that suffering be recognised, and frustration when truth recovery is limited and information remains contested. Prisoner release is generally the most urgent concern. But exoneration regardless of sentencing status is important due to the emotional, social and practical burdens of criminal records. In addition, apologies and acknowledgement of state wrongdoing can be crucial to a victim's well-being. Westervelt and Cook have likened experiences of exonerees to the suffering of serious trauma (2008: 35) and refer to Judith Herman's work on the aftermath of trauma: 'the community must take action to assign responsibility for the harm and to repair the injury. These two responses—recognition and restitution—are necessary to rebuild the survivor's sense of order and justice' (1997: 70 cited in Westervelt and Cook 2011: 1227). In a longitudinal clinical study in the United Kingdom, Adrian Grounds identified prevalent and serious mental health and adjustment problems among those who had been wrongfully imprisoned. In many cases '[t]he extent of the suffering was profound' (2005: 15, 21–37). Among other needs, participants sought apologies and public exposure of their innocence and the failings of the criminal justice system (Grounds 2005: 20; 2011: 14–15). Narrative accounts similarly suggest a connection between official recognition and the psychological welfare of victims (Vollen and Eggers 2008: 12, 137). A victim's understanding of justice is shattered by a wrongful conviction, and acknowledgement can go some way towards restoring confidence in public authorities.

An overturned conviction provides only partial acknowledgement of the harm suffered by a miscarriage of justice victim. Appellate courts do not necessarily explore errors in depth, designate criminal justice actors as potentially culpable, or recognise suffering and hardships experienced by appellants. Yet a successful appeal is essential to the state's acknowledgment of a wrongful conviction, which might also include an apology, prosecutions or disciplinary action, compensation and social services. Exonerations are extremely difficult to obtain. The barriers to challenging a conviction are numerous, necessitating sustained effort—usually over years or decades—by the convicted person and his or her supporters. After an unsuccessful appeal, procedural rules limit opportunities for individuals to challenge convictions and generally require new or extraordinary information to review cases. The principle of finality guards against reopening cases, and courts consider (and rules are based on the assumption) that each accused person has been afforded advantages and safeguards and offences have been proven beyond a reasonable doubt. Those involved in a conviction often have professional, political or personal interests in it being upheld and, at the institutional level there can be resistance to reviewing a 'closed' case.

There is now an extensive literature covering the parameters and frequency of miscarriages of justice in a variety of settings (for example, Naughton 2007; Gould and Leo 2010; Zalman 2012; Naughton 2012; Huff and Killias 2013). Although it is not possible here to compare data across jurisdictions, two points emerge that resonate with the Northern Ireland experience. First, recent studies into routine use of particular types of evidence have identified high error rates, with police-generated evidence as a problematic type (Cole 2005; Gould and Leo 2010: 841–54; Guerra Thompson 2012). Second, after conviction and an initial appeal, it can be extremely difficult for a case to be reviewed, with many errors discovered only by 'extraordinary circumstances' (for example, Cole 2005: 1021–22). When investigations reveal many cases in which a certain form of evidence was misused, it belies the argument that the particular system works to uncover errors at the appeal stage. Michael Naughton argues that rates of successful appeals in England and Wales are evidence of the prevalence of errors (2007: 42–43), but in those cases the system *has* successfully exposed flaws. More dangerous, of course, are assumptions that a low number of post-appeal exonerations reflect the rarity of errors in a criminal justice system. These themes will be returned to in the conclusion. The following sections discuss the formal recognition of miscarriages of justice in Northern Ireland.

Identifying Miscarriages of Justice in Northern Ireland

In 1993 the Royal Commission on Criminal Justice recommended the establishment of a new body to investigate and consider potential miscarriages of justice, in part a response to high profile wrongful convictions for Provisional Irish Republican Army bombings in England in the 1970s (Runciman 1993: 1, 180, chapter 11). The 'Guildford Four' were released after 15 years in prison; the 'Birmingham Six', convicted of murder and other crimes in 1975, each spent 16 years in prison prior to having their convictions quashed in 1991; and the 'Maguire Seven' served sentences of between four and 10 years.[14] In these cases the defendants, all of whom were tried in England, had been subjected to threats and violence by police and confessed. After jury convictions, appeals were dismissed which seemed to reflect pressure surrounding terrorism convictions (Walker and McCartney 2008: 191) and 'a deep-seated reluctance of the Court to disturb the verdicts of juries', particularly verdicts that depended on police evidence (Kennedy 1991: 311).

The CCRC was established in 1997, in response to a 'crisis of confidence' in the criminal justice system (Quirk 2013: 949), and covers England and Wales and Northern Ireland. It is independent of government and can investigate and review cases in which appeals have been exhausted or the time to appeal has expired. In most cases investigations are instigated through applications brought by a convicted person or his or her relatives.[15] Before its establishment, applications were

[14] *R v Richardson Conlon, Armstrong and Hill* [1989] *The Times* 20 October 1989 (EWCA); *R v McIlkenny and others* [1992] 2 All ER 417 (EWCA); *R v Maguire and others* [1992] 2 WLR 767.

[15] Criminal Appeal Act 1995, c 35, s 14.

made on an ad hoc basis to the Secretary of State for Northern Ireland (or, in England and Wales, the Home Office) for an out-of-time referral to the appellate court. The process in England and Wales was described by Clive Walker as a 'ramshackle and secretive review by Home Office officials' (1999b: 55); in Northern Ireland, scheduled offence cases were only rarely referred by the Northern Ireland Office (NIO) to the NICA.

Currently the CCRC has the power to refer cases in limited circumstances—when it considers there is a 'real possibility' that the Court of Appeal will quash the conviction.[16] The CCRC must defer to previous decision-making by the appellate courts and declines to refer cases that it believes are unlikely to succeed. Schehr has described the CCRC as a 'state strategic selection mechanism', dependent on Parliament and the courts and serving to diffuse public dissatisfaction (2005: 1296–98). According to Walker and McCartney, CCRC procedures have transferred the test into one of 'a real possibility of a real possibility' (2008: 198). The test entrenches appellate jurisprudence and can lead to the CCRC excluding cases that a subsequent panel of the NICA might find meritorious. The case law, discussed further in the next section, sets a high evidential bar for appellants and, by inference, applicants before the CCRC. Although the referral rate to the NICA is higher than it is to the EWCA, many Northern Irish applications fail in decades old convictions because of insufficient evidence, even when the applicant had confessed without being afforded protections considered central to fair trials today, including access to counsel during detention.

Determinations by the CCRC must be made on the basis of a new argument or evidence not raised at trial or on an original appeal, and the convicted person must usually have attempted an appeal.[17] In exceptional circumstances the CCRC can refer a case outside these parameters.[18] The CCRC has used the former power (to refer without a new argument or evidence) in Northern Irish cases only rarely,[19] but it has referred several conflict-era cases which had not been appealed.[20] Given the low appeal rate in scheduled offence cases, for strategic, practical and personal

[16] ibid, ss 10, 13.

[17] ibid, s 13(1)(b), (c).

[18] ibid, s 13(2).

[19] Of cases referred to the NICA, only one was based on an issue which had been raised at trial and on an original appeal without significant new evidence. The appellant, who was 16 when interrogated and was found at trial to suffer from a mental handicap, had challenged the admissibility and reliability of statements he made to police: *R v Brown and others* [2012] NICA 14, [15], [54] (McCaul). See *R v McCaul* [1980] 9 NIJB (dismissing appeal).

[20] See, eg, *R v Gorman and McKinney* (NICA, 29 October 1999) (appeals abandoned), in which police interview notes had been rewritten; at trial defendants had alleged police ill-treatment; *R v Hindes and Hannah* [2005] NICA 36, [2], youth confession cases in which rules of detention and interrogation were violated; *R v Mulholland* [2006] NICA 32, [13] (two notices of appeal abandoned), involving the admissibility of confession evidence alongside allegations of police abuse; *R v McMenamin* [2007] NICA 22, [3], a youth confession case in which defendant's admissions were made without adequate safeguards, and he pleaded guilty to offences he could not have committed; and *R v Brown and others* [2012] NICA 14, [39] (Brown), another youth confession case.

reasons (Quirk 2013: 958–60), this might be viewed as a necessary accommodation to the conditions of conflict. Once a case is referred, the NICA determines whether it believes the conviction to be unsafe[21] (also referred to as the 'safety test'). Generally appellate courts focus on doubt about an appellant's guilt (as a result of error or procedural irregularity at or before trial), but a conviction can be unsafe even where there is certainty of the appellant's guilt[22] or suspicion of it.[23] In most of the CCRC-referred cases, the NICA indicated that it had a 'significant sense of unease' about the original verdicts without addressing guilt or innocence.

The 38 cases referred from the CCRC to the NICA represent about 11 per cent of applications received from Northern Ireland. This rate is significantly higher than that to the EWCA; the CCRC's overall referral rate is 3.5 per cent of total applications (CCRC 2013: 11). Most Northern Irish applications involve scheduled offences (about 250 out of 335 through November 2012, or 75 per cent) (Hawkins 2012;[24] see also CCRC 2013: 11), and 34 of the 38 referred cases were conflict related, all but one processed in non-jury courts. The four non-conflict referrals have been overturned by the NICA, 28 of the conflict-related convictions have been quashed, and three cases are still pending. The quash rate of 91 per cent can be compared with that of 70 per cent for all cases referred by the CCRC, to the NICA and EWCA combined. Thus, the CCRC's predominant function to date in relation to Northern Ireland has been to assess convictions under the counter-terrorism regime, spanning the 1970s (17 cases), 1980s (seven cases) and early-1990s (10 cases). The rates of referrals and convictions overturned are high but consist of a small number of cases, which arguably reflects the many barriers that prevent recognition of miscarriages of justice.[25] Nonetheless, the cases highlight significant errors and abuses in the prosecution of suspects during the conflict. In 1999 Brice Dickson (1999: 287) noted that a 'myth has ... been constructed that Northern Ireland has had very few, if any' miscarriages of justice. There is now a sufficient number of acknowledged miscarriages of justice to dispel that perception. Moreover, it cannot be assumed the courts were able to ensure just outcomes despite the circumstances of interrogation and low threshold for the admissibility of confessions. Although in most CCRC-referred cases the NICA reviews information not available to trial courts, the cases include several in which original courts failed to identify discrepancies or weaknesses in critical prosecution evidence.

[21] Criminal Appeal Act (NI) 1980, c 47, ss 1–2 (as amended).

[22] *R v Mullen* [2000] QB 520, 535–36, 540 (prosecution was an abuse of process and should not have taken place).

[23] *R v Davis and others* [2001] 1 Cr App R 8 (EWCA), [50]–[56], [95] (errors at trial were relevant to a determination of safety irrespective of guilt. The quashing of the conviction was 'not a finding of innocence, far from it').

[24] See n 4 above.

[25] On factors that have limited applications to the CCRC from Northern Ireland, see Requa (2014: 42–45).

Past Convictions and the Post-Conflict Court of Appeal

In most of the conflict-era convictions overturned (25 of 28), the NICA had doubts about the reliability of the person's confession because of potential police misconduct, violations of procedural rules, or the suspect's vulnerability. Police misconduct included the alteration or rewriting of police notes[26] and claims of assault in custody.[27] Applicants alleged physical mistreatment in at least 12 of the cases referred by the CCRC, but these claims were the basis for overturning convictions in only three cases.[28] In each of these, there was evidence that other former detainees had lodged formal complaints against the same police officers, suggesting that the NICA requires independent evidence impugning an officer to support an appellant's claims. In *Livingstone*, the NICA found that evidence of physical mistreatment and untruthfulness by the key Royal Ulster Constabulary (RUC) witnesses in separate cases, if they had been introduced in the appellant's trial, may have affected the trial judge's evaluation of the officers' testimony.[29] Eight convictions were overturned in *Morrison* for reasons not disclosed, but which included the failure of security forces to provide to prosecutors directly relevant material in the case. The Court considered that, if the undisclosed evidence had been given at trial, it would have led to acquittals, if the appellants had been prosecuted at all.[30] The case seems to indicate criminality on the part of security force informants.

Several convictions were quashed in which teenage suspects had confessed having had no access to a solicitor and without being accompanied by an adult, in violation of the Judges' Rules[31] governing detention and interrogation.[32] In terrorism cases, it was RUC policy to delay access to counsel and, for young people, accompaniment by an appropriate adult (Bennett 1979: paragraphs 123, 129, 272). In cases such as *McCaul*, in which a mentally handicapped teenager was subjected to hours of questioning on consecutive days, the confessor's physical or mental vulnerability was the decisive factor in the appellate decision.[33] In others, the Court considered vulnerability in addition to the conditions of detention and interview.[34] In two cases teenage suspects confessed to crimes they could not have committed.[35]

[26] *R v Gorman and McKinney* (NICA, 29 October 1999); *R v Boyle* (NICA, 29 April 2003). See also *R v Magee* [2001] NICA 217 (conviction quashed on other grounds).

[27] *R v Mulholland* [2006] NICA 32; *R v McCartney, R v MacDermott* [2007] NICA 10.

[28] ibid.

[29] *R v Livingstone* [2013] NICA 33.

[30] *R v Morrison and others* [2009] NICA 1.

[31] Practice Note (Judges' Rules), [1964] 1 WLR 152 (Eng) (introduced in Northern Ireland in 1976).

[32] *R v Fitzpatrick and Shiels* [2009] NICA 60.

[33] *R v Brown and others* [2012] NICA 14. See also *R v Green* [2002] NICA 14.

[34] *R v Magee* [2001] NICA 217; *R v Hindes and Hanna* [2005] NICA 36 (both teenagers); *R v Adams* [2006] NICA 6 (teenager).

[35] *R v McMenamin* [2007] NICA 22; *R v Brown and others* [2012] NICA 14 (McDonald).

Only one case was quashed on the basis of errors by the court—in *R v McCourt*, [2010] NICA 6, the trial judge seemingly had not issued a written judgment, required in non-jury cases under successive Northern Ireland (Emergency Provisions) Acts (EPAs).[36] No case focused on the performance of counsel or prosecutors. The 1992 conviction of Christy Walsh was overturned after several legal applications, based on new forensic evidence and a discrepancy in an investigating soldier's evidence.[37]

In the final case, soldiers who detained Liam Holden in 1972 had violated Ministry of Defence (MOD) orders prohibiting military interrogation of detainees.[38] (At age 19 Holden was convicted for the murder of Private Frank Bell, sentenced to death—a sentence commuted to life in prison after four weeks—and imprisoned for 17 years.) Holden alleges, and argued at trial, that he confessed after having been subjected to water-boarding for hours, hooded, taken to a field and threatened with a gun to his head.[39] These claims were not interrogated by the appellate court. The conviction was overturned on the grounds that, if newly uncovered MOD documents and a witness statement had been disclosed at trial, the judge may have doubted the credibility of the soldiers' version of events and found Holden's confession inadmissible (paragraphs 14–19, 20–22). Even if the confession had been admitted, the MOD documents could have been explored at trial and affected the jury's decision to convict (paragraph 23).

Holden highlights a limitation of appeals as an acknowledgement of state wrongdoing: the NICA shed little light on the conduct of the soldiers or the extent of state harm in the case. Ultimately the central issue in the judgment was not torture; neither was it based on unlawful detention and questioning by the army. Rather the new evidence indicated the soldiers knew they were acting contrary to instructions, implicating their credibility as witnesses. Holden's plausible allegations of abuses and brutality (Cobain 2012: 166–70)[40] were relevant to the decision—doubting the soldiers' credibility implies Holden's version of events may have been accurate—but not directly addressed. This limitation reflects efficiency concerns and the breadth of the test used by appellate courts to determine the safety of convictions. Considering obstacles to determining 'truth' through

[36] See, eg, EPA 1973, c 5, s 2(5).

[37] *R v Walsh* [2010] NICA 7. Walsh was convicted of possessing a coffee jar bomb and sentenced to 14 years' imprisonment. From the time of his original trial, Walsh maintained that he had been walking through an alleyway in Belfast and was stopped by a soldier, who accused him of having removed the device from his pocket. According to Walsh, another man was in the alleyway as well, and the device was on a wall when Walsh was stopped. In this appeal, the NICA considered that fresh evidence, if given at trial, might have affected the trial judge's evaluation of the case. That evidence included the admission of a soldier who allegedly observed the arrest that his original evidence was inaccurate, and testimony of an expert witness regarding the likelihood that Walsh's fingerprints would have been on the jar if he had handled it.

[38] *R v Holden* [2012] NICA 26.

[39] V Kearney, 'Death Sentence Man Liam Holden: "I Was Tortured into a False Confession"' *BBC News*, 21 June 2012, available at www.bbc.co.uk/news/uk-northern-ireland-18525630.

[40] See also H McDonald, 'Man granted soldier murder appeal following waterboarding evidence' *The Guardian*, 4 May 2012.

court processes, the scope of the test, under which judges can quash convictions if they have a significant sense of unease about a verdict without determining innocence, can assist appellants.[41] But when courts decline to explore claims of wrongdoing, it can be a bittersweet outcome for an appellant and affect other legal actions related to the case, such as compensation claims and proceedings against perpetrators. The NICA expressed regret in narrow terms in only the most egregious of CCRC-referred cases involving vulnerable defendants, and in no case was an apology made.

During the conflict commentators debated whether the courts too readily admitted confessions and discounted claims of abuse. Judicial review prior to the Human Rights Act 1998 (HRA) was 'unlikely to pick up anything other than the isolated and fairly blatant abuse' (Walker 1999a: 166). In terrorism cases,

> the Northern Ireland Court of Appeal solemnly sat through case after case in 1976 and thereafter in which confessions were disputed but without any wider inquiry into what was happening at the Castlereagh Holding Centre, the eventual investigation into which was far more attributable to investigative journalism than inquisitorial judicialism (Walker 1999a: 165–68).

Confessions were the main form of evidence in these cases and subjected to a lower standard of admissibility than in ordinary trials. Counterterrorism legislation stipulated that confessions were inadmissible if the accused provided prima facie evidence that he was subjected to torture or inhuman or degrading treatment and the prosecution was not able to prove that the confession was not obtained in that manner.[42] But courts did retain discretion to exclude statements induced by violence or impropriety.[43] Studies have demonstrated RUC tunnel vision—interrogators convinced that terrorism suspects were guilty—and documented evidence that detainees were mistreated to garner confessions (Taylor 1980: 80–81, 155–56, 193; Cobain 2012: 178, 183).

As detailed above, the NICA has now reviewed several of these cases outside the pressures of conflict and benefiting from factual investigations undertaken by the CCRC. Despite the high quash rate, the jurisprudence limits the potential for subsequent referrals by the CCRC and only captures cases involving clear errors or discrepancies. In the main, successful cases depended on new evidence which led the NICA to reassess facts considered at trial. The Court was otherwise reticent to disturb factual determinations made by trial courts, and in the most recent cases has rejected arguments dependent on general conditions of detention. The judgments place pressure on potential applicants to the CCRC to identify new lines of enquiry, a challenge in decades old cases. The jurisprudence does not account for difficulties of proof related to the conditions of conflict and the passage of time, or systemic patterns stemming from counterterrorism convictions. An applicant's assertion of abuse, without independent evidence, will not succeed.

[41] See text accompanying nn 21–23 above for further discussion of the safety test.

[42] eg, EPA 1973, s 6.

[43] *R v O'Halloran* [1979] NI 45.

The Court's overall approach, deferring to factual determinations made by trial courts, which is routine in normal appeals, is difficult to justify alongside NICA findings in numerous cases that police officers were untruthful or their evidence was potentially unreliable.[44]

The case law upholds the conflict-era courts' interpretations of emergency legislation and admissibility rules. In *Brown and others*, the leading decision on juvenile confession cases, the NICA found that violations of the Judges' Rules did not necessarily render (and will not now render) a conviction unsafe. The four appellants, aged 15 and 16 at the time of conviction, were interviewed without access to counsel or in the presence of an appropriate adult. Such breaches were not a sufficient ground to exclude confessions under the EPA, and the NICA found that two of the convictions were not unsafe.[45] The convictions of Stephen McCaul and Peter McDonald were overturned because of additional circumstances: in the former case, the defendant's vulnerability at the time of interview; and in the latter, an inaccuracy in the confession.[46]

Previously the NICA was sympathetic to arguments related to the wider conditions of detention and the pressures faced by young detainees, finding routine violations of the Rules a sufficient basis to overturn convictions in some historic cases.[47] Contemporary standards of fairness require that defendants whose confessions are admitted at trial had access to counsel during interview.[48] In historic cases, it is relevant to consider 'whether and to what extent [the suspect] may have lacked protections which it was later thought right that he should enjoy'.[49] The NICA is able to do so within the parameters of statutory law applicable at the time of the convictions. Under the EPA, judges were not obliged to exclude confessions that might be involuntary because of abuse or impropriety, but held a discretionary power to do so.[50] Thus, the Court in *Brown* could have remained

[44] See, eg, regarding the alteration or rewriting of police notes: *R v Gorman and McKinney* (NICA, 29 October 1999); *R v Magee* [2001] NICA 217; *R v Boyle* (NICA, 29 April 2003) and *R v Latimer* [2004] NICA (Crim) 3. Regarding allegations of physical mistreatment see, eg, *R v McCartney*, *R v MacDermott* [2007] NICA 10; *R v Mulholland* [2006] NICA 32; and *R v Livingstone* [2013] NICA 33.

[45] *R v Brown and others* [2012] NICA 14 [18], [23], [34], [39], [46], [54] (Brown, Wright).

[46] In *McCaul*, the trial judge had acknowledged that the 16-year-old defendant had a mental handicap and attended a special school but relied on police evidence that McCaul had dictated five statements to police investigators in a four-and-a-half hour interview at night. This was his fifth interview totalling 13 hours of questioning in a 36-hour period. See *R v Brown and others* [2012] NICA 14, [51]–[53]. In *McDonald*, the applicant had allegedly admitted luring army personnel into a trap which it seems did not actually occur and affected the reliability of additional admissions. *R v Brown and others* [2012] NICA 14, [2], [30].

[47] See *R v Mulholland* [2006] NICA 32 [44]–[46] (violations of rules existing at the time of conviction would constitute prima facie grounds for concluding that a conviction was unsafe); *R v Fitzpatrick and Shiels* [2009] NICA 60 (two juvenile confessions had been 'obtained by objectionable means' because of breaches of the Judges' Rules). Also see *Magee* [2001] NICA 217, 229–32, but note in that case the NICA applied the HRA retrospectively, an interpretation since rejected, and an ECtHR judgment had found in favour of the appellant (*Magee v UK* (2001) 31 EHRR 35).

[48] *Cadder v HM Advocate* [2010] UKSC 43 [63], [93].

[49] *R v King* [2000] 2 Cr App Rep 391 [402]. See Requa 2014: section IVC.

[50] *R v O'Halloran* [1979] NI 45.

faithful to the legislative regime while doubting the reliability of all four juvenile confessions in light of contemporary standards. Instead, although it considered that changed standards of fairness might be relevant in determining admissibility, the Court declined to engage in such an analysis and provided no guidance on how such rules might affect terrorism convictions. *Brown* now serves to preclude CCRC referrals based mainly on violations of rules of detention and interrogation. The approach aligns with that of the appellate system during the conflict, in which egregious abuses and those with substantial evidence are acknowledged but 'inquisitorial judicialism' (Walker 1999a) is not apparent.

Compensation: Eligibility and Awards in Northern Ireland

Not all of those whose convictions are quashed will be compensated. Eligibility for compensation is governed by section 133 of the Criminal Justice Act 1988, limiting compensation to out-of-time appeals or CCRC-referred cases in which 'a new or newly discovered fact shows beyond reasonable doubt that there has been a miscarriage of justice'.[51] Thus, someone wrongfully convicted will not be compensated if his or her case was overturned on the basis of an argument not presented at trial (as opposed to fresh evidence). A person will not be compensated if the evidence in his or her favour is ambiguous or an ordinary appeal led to the quashing of the conviction. In conflict-related youth confession cases in Northern Ireland, changes in legal standards and procedural safeguards—leading to the quashing of some convictions—are not 'newly discovered facts' according to the courts, and pleading guilty generally precludes compensation.[52] Secretaries of state determine eligibility (in Northern Ireland, the Minister of Justice, and in national security-related cases the Secretary of State for Northern Ireland).

Until recently, section 133 established no clear definition of 'miscarriage of justice', and governments have sought to limit compensation to cases in which innocence has been demonstrated. A string of legal challenges followed denial of section 133 applications. The UK Supreme Court brought some clarity to the topic in 2011 in *R (Adams) v Secretary of State, Re MacDermott's Application and Re McCartney's Application* (*Adams*).[53] The Court found that section 133 includes cases in which: (1) fresh evidence shows clearly that the defendant is innocent of the crime of which he was convicted; and (2) new evidence so undermines the

[51] The test reflects the UK's international duty under Art 46 of the International Covenant on Civil and Political Rights 1966.

[52] *In re Fitzpatrick and Shiels* [2013] NICA 66 [23], [27].

[53] *R (Adams) v Secretary of State, Re MacDermott's Application and Re McCartney's Application* (*Adams*) [2011] UKSC 18; [2011] 2 WLR 1180.

evidence against the defendant that no conviction could possibly be based on it.[54] *Adams* can be criticised for providing secretaries of state with a complicated test prone to varying interpretations, one that is difficult for rejected applicants to challenge (Quirk and Requa 2012: 395–97). Additionally it excludes many cases of serious abuse by the state, if the applicant was nonetheless possibly guilty of an offence (Quirk and Requa: 397–400), or where applicants are not privy to all the information in their cases.[55]

Adams was overshadowed in early 2014 by the enactment of section 175 of the Anti-social Behaviour, Crime and Policing Act 2014 (s 185(2)(a)), which applies to cases arising in England and Wales as well as national security-related cases in Northern Ireland. Under the 2014 Act, a miscarriage of justice occurs when new evidence shows beyond reasonable doubt that the person '*did not commit*' the offence (italics added). (Section 175, inserting section 133(1ZA) into the 1988 Act, applies to decisions by the Secretary of State for Northern Ireland but not those made by the Minister of Justice.) The amendment to section 133 received the support of the House of Commons with little media attention. In the House of Lords, peers challenged the test as equivalent to an innocence requirement and had sought to codify the *Adams* test. Home Office minister Damian Green asserted that a fact should 'entirely exonerat[e]' the accused but nonetheless the new standard 'does not require anyone to prove they are innocent'.[56] This distinction remains nebulous despite repeated challenges on the point.[57]

Under both *Adams* and the new test, applicants are in a bind: secretaries of state look to the applicant's appellate court judgment in determining whether a miscarriage of justice has occurred. But appellate courts simply determine whether an original conviction is unsafe.[58] (When reviewing decisions *not* to compensate, courts similarly take into account the decision overturning the applicant's conviction.)[59] In criminal appeals, courts generally avoid enquiries into innocence; a person is, after all, presumed innocent if not convicted. Moreover, the decision to quash might be based on a technical legal argument rather than new facts, might not be disclosed, or might be agreed by the prosecution precluding extensive argument. The onus remains on applicants to convince secretaries of state that they satisfy the definition of miscarriage of justice in the 1988 Act, and often it is impossible to prove one did not commit an offence or that no conviction could be based on the available facts.

Prior to 2006, exonerated persons who had spent time in custody could apply to the Secretary of State for *ex gratia* payments, authorised in 'exceptional circumstances' but not restricted to out-of-time appeals or cases involving fresh

[54] See also *R (Ali) v Secretary of State* [2014] EWCA Civ 194, [21]–[26].

[55] eg, in *R v Morrison and others* [2009] NICA 1, the Court did not disclose all of the reasons for quashing the convictions of eight appellants.

[56] HC Deb 4 February 2014, vol 575, cols 163–65.

[57] HC Deb 4 February 2014, vol 575, cols 163–83.

[58] This point was discussed above. See text accompanying nn 21–23 and 41 above.

[59] eg, *In re Fitzpatrick and Shiels* [2013] NICA 66 [33].

evidence.[60] Use of the *ex gratia* scheme was criticised for lack of consistency and transparency, but it provided secretaries of state with flexibility in determining eligibility for compensation. In principle it was particularly aimed at wrongful convictions resulting from 'serious default' by a member of the police force or another public authority.[61] The practice was halted in 2006 after Home Secretary Charles Clarke vowed to 'modernise and simplify the system' and to bring about a 'better balance' with treatment of victims of crime.[62] Of course '[i]t is difficult to see why those subject[ed] to wrongful imprisonment might not have seen themselves as victims' (Taylor 2013: 591) and unclear how reform of compensation policy would aid in 'rebalancing'. The government's stated concerns were the cost of the scheme (£2 million per year), the low number of beneficiaries (five to ten applicants annually), and that compensation could be awarded beyond the UK's international obligations.

Changes were also made to the assessment of payments under section 133[63] and linked to assertions that victims of crime received 'less than one fiftieth of what is paid to those eligible under the miscarriages of justice scheme' (Taylor 2013: 591). Assessors were to take greater account of the criminal convictions of applicants and conduct that may have contributed to the conviction, and caps on payments were introduced. In sum the reforms sought to reduce compensation to wrongfully convicted individuals, even when the government acknowledged miscarriages of justice had occurred. By positioning the wrongfully convicted in opposition to victims of crimes, the government suggests the taint of a criminal conviction endures beyond exoneration. The perspective affirms a familiar dichotomy in popular discourse between deserving and undeserving victims (McEvoy and McConnachie 2012: 531–32).

Compensation in Northern Ireland

Compensation trends can be discerned from anonymised NIO and Department of Justice (DoJ) data from 1993 through December 2014.[64] The vast majority of compensation payments have been in cases brought under emergency legislation. Most applicants currently receiving payments were convicted two to four decades ago and will not receive a final payment until a decade after their convictions were quashed, based on patterns to date. The NIO paid more than £4.7 million in total to 12 individuals under the statutory and *ex gratia* schemes between 1993 and

[60] D Hurd, *Compensation*, HC Deb 29 November 1985, vol 87, cols 689–90W.

[61] ibid.

[62] C Clarke, *Miscarriages of Justice (Compensation)* HC Deb 19 April 2006, vol 445, cols 15–17WS.

[63] These were subsequently codified in ss 133A and 133B Criminal Justice Act 1988, c 33, inserted by ss 61(7) and 153 of the Criminal Justice and Immigration Act 2008, c 4.

[64] Data on compensation payments were provided by the departments in response to freedom of information (FOI) requests in 2011, 2013 and 2014 (NIO 2011; DoJ 2013; NIO 2013b; DoJ 2015) on file with author.

12 April 2010, averaging £393,454 for each case.[65] Successful applicants have tended to receive interim payments for years before a final award is made, even though guidance states that interim payments are exceptional (DoJ 2012; NIO 2013a). The DoJ paid close to £3.2 million in compensation payments to 11 individuals between April 2010 and December 2013, an average of £288,342 per person, which again does not reflect total payments to individuals (DoJ 2013). Whereas the annual average of spending on miscarriage of justice compensation was under £300,000 prior to devolution, the DoJ annual average is over £900,000 (DoJ 2013; NIO 2013b). All but one of the DoJ payments were in terrorism-related cases, and payments continue in some cases under the *ex gratia* scheme.

Payments ranged from £550 to £732,806 by the NIO and between £6,009 and £485,000 by the DoJ (again, this is no indication of full payments to individuals). Of the first five cases in which a final award had been paid by the DoJ, in two of the cases the DoJ contribution had been between £20,000 and £25,000; the three others ranged from approximately £347,000 to £456,000 (DoJ 2013). Current guidance in Northern Ireland requires assessors to consider non-pecuniary losses such as mental suffering and pecuniary losses, including loss of earnings and future earning capacity. The assessor must take into account the seriousness of the offence and the severity of punishment suffered by the applicant, as well as the conduct of the investigation and the prosecution of the offence (section 133A(2)). She may deduct an 'appropriate' amount for conduct by the appellant that caused or contributed to the conviction or other convictions (section 133A(3)). Deductions can also be made for 'saved living expenses'—a major fount of resentment for those wrongfully convicted which the government insists is not a 'board and lodging' charge (DoJ 2012; NIO 2013a). Compensation is capped at £500,000 except in certain cases where a person was detained for at least 10 years (sections 133A(5), 133B). The onus is on successful applicants to quantify losses resulting from the miscarriages of justice and to provide supporting documentation (DoJ 2012: paragraph 3; NIO 2013a: paragraph 5). Such a task can be onerous for individuals convicted as teenagers or young adults, in a society with high unemployment levels.

The small number of cases is notable: the NIO completed payments in three cases between 1993 and 2010; is currently processing eight approved cases; and transferred 15 cases to the DoJ in 2010 (three of those were subsequently rejected). In addition to those transferred from the NIO, the DoJ received nine additional applications. Five are pending a decision and four were rejected. Therefore the DoJ has had 12 live cases, with payments ongoing or completed (DoJ 2015). In sum, this represents just 23 successful compensation claims from 1993 through 2014, with 12 applicants still receiving payments, and five applications pending.

[65] These are incomplete sums given that most of the cases were transferred to the DoJ upon devolution and at least five received further payments (these numbers also include legal costs): DoJ 2011; NIO 2011; DoJ 2013; NIO 2013b.

(As compared with the 32 CCRC-referred cases overturned by the NIO, compensation in 23 cases is significant. Not all compensation cases were CCRC referrals.) An unknown number of applications was refused by the NIO from the early 1990s—the Department did not retain these records—and the DoJ's rejection rate is around 30 per cent (NIO 2011; DoJ 2013; NIO 2013b; DoJ 2015).

The following table, identifying cases in which final payments have been made by the DoJ, provides an indication of delays endured by wrongfully convicted individuals.

Table 1: Cases where assessment is complete as at December 2014 (DoJ 2015)

Case no	Time between original conviction and first payment	Time between quashing conviction and first payment	Time between quashing of conviction and last payment
1	19 years, 5 months	7 months	11 years, 6 months
2	33 years, 3 months	4 years	7 years, 2 months
3	19 years, 5 months	7 months	11 years, 6 months
4	5 years	6 months	9 years, 2 months
5	28 years, 11 months	1 year, 6 months	4 years, 2 months
6	32 years, 10 months	3 years, 6 months	8 years, 5 months
7	33 years, 1 month	7 years, 7 months	11 years, 8 months
8	30 years, 8 months	2 years, 4 months	8 years, 6 months

In cases completed by the NIO, the shortest time between reversal and a final payment was three-and-a-half years and the longest was 16 years. In ongoing cases in the DoJ, most convictions occurred in the late 1970s, first payments were made over a year after applicants' convictions were quashed, and assessments are still incomplete up to eight years later. Even considering exchange of information among the applicant, the department, and the assessor, these delays are excessive.

Conclusion

> Post-exoneration, the harm produced by a wrongful conviction is amplified when the state appears unwilling to 'own' its role in creating the injustice or provid[e] adequate redress (Westervelt and Cook 2011: 1225).

Studies of criminal justice systems around the world routinely reveal what can be termed acknowledgment gaps, in which wrongful convictions are only exceptionally and partially recognised, generally after arduous efforts by victims. In Northern

Ireland, the vast majority of CCRC-referred cases have been overturned by the NICA, but those cases are few in number. The process used to identify miscarriages of justice, through referrals from the CCRC, cannot uncover the volume of abuses and wrongful convictions that occurred during the conflict. Northern Ireland thus provides another example of the dangers of police-generated evidence, as most terrorism convictions were based on confession evidence. Reticence to acknowledge past errors, by judges and other state actors is complicated by the political context of counterterrorism convictions. Certainly the appellate system is not the appropriate forum for a wide-scale investigation. But it is within the NICA's mandate to consider whether individual miscarriages of justice resulted from police misconduct or the modification of procedures for investigating and prosecuting terrorism offences. The Court has declined to consider systemic problems, instead focusing on errors in isolation. In addition, recent jurisprudence serves to limit cases that will be referred from the CCRC and reviewed by the NICA.

James Williams argues that criminal justice actors generally 'are dedicated to the presentation of an image of efficacy in the face of contradiction and uncertainty' (1999: 154). Judicial decision-making can serve to legitimise law enforcement interventions into individuals' lives (Williams 1999). In Northern Ireland, the presentation of efficiency by police, prosecutors, and the courts in the form of convictions during the conflict is durable, even surviving a negotiated peace process and root and branch police reform, paradoxically prompted in part by police abuses in terrorism cases. Those convicted of terrorism offences, most of whom finished prison sentences prior to the Agreement and others released as part of that process, continue to face high hurdles in challenging their convictions. As discussed in this chapter, the NICA retains faith in prosecution evidence and the administration of justice during the conflict. To succeed, appellants generally must present fresh and independent evidence of police misconduct or irregularities, which is difficult to amass in very old cases. Human rights principles accepted today regarding conditions of detention and interrogation will not necessarily apply, not only because the HRA is not retroactive. More significantly, the NICA recently declined to employ contemporary standards of fairness in evaluating conditions surrounding convictions. Even when convictions are overturned, compensation is not guaranteed and can take years to secure, requiring further wrangling with the state.

These circumstances—difficulties in overturning convictions, partial acknowledgment of wrongdoing and obstacles to collecting compensation—are not inevitable in a post-conflict setting but echo those identified in wrongful conviction literature covering quite different criminal justice systems, in settled societies such as the United States (Gould and Leo 2010). While it could be assumed that miscarriages of justice stemming from a conflict would be more robustly acknowledged in a transitioning society, experience in Northern Ireland underscores the durability of convictions, particularly terrorism convictions, even after threats to the political system have subsided. Northern Ireland is unique within the United Kingdom in that terrorism cases have dominated the first 15 years of the CCRC mechanism, which has dramatically improved and streamlined the process for challenging convictions. This area is just one in which criminal justice agencies in Northern Ireland continue to deal with past cases, arguably at the expense of strengthening contemporary practice within the system.

It was argued above that acknowledgment of miscarriages of justice by the NICA has been insufficient, and appellate review that consistently identifies human rights violations lacking. Yet individual court cases are not the most appropriate way to deal with systemic problems from the past. Indeed many potential victims of miscarriage of justice do not apply to the CCRC for referral to the NICA, perhaps in recognition that the 'ordinary' criminal justice system cannot sufficiently address issues arising from recent political conflict. A quashed conviction and compensation is difficult to attain, and it can be particularly unsatisfactory when state wrongdoing is not recognised or punished. Wrongful convictions, and convictions under legislation and policies that are at odds with contemporary standards of fairness, have not otherwise been formally acknowledged. Individuals continue to suffer psychological, social and economic consequences as a result of imprisonment and the retention of criminal records. Northern Irish society suffers as well. In the absence of a mechanism to review police abuses and other misconduct related to counterterrorism convictions—issues outside reform projects stemming from the Good Friday Agreement—the CCRC referral process remains the most viable pathway for acknowledgement of miscarriages of justice.

References

Amnesty International (1978) *Report of an Amnesty International Mission to Northern Ireland (28 November–6 December 1977)* (London, Amnesty International).

Bassiouni, MC (2006) 'International Recognition of Victims' Rights' 6 *Human Rights Law Review* 203.

Bennett, HG (1979) *Report of the Committee of Inquiry into Police Interrogation Procedures in Northern Ireland* (Cmnd 7497) (London, HMSO).

Boraine, A (2001) *A Country Unmasked: Inside South Africa's Truth and Reconciliation Commission* (Oxford, Oxford University Press).

Cobain, I (2012) *Cruel Britannia: A Secret History of Torture* (London, Portobello Books).

Cohen, S (2001) *States of Denial: Knowing About Atrocities and Suffering* (Cambridge, Polity Press).

Cole, SA (2005) 'More than Zero: Accounting for Error in Latent Fingerprint Identification' 95 *Journal of Criminal Law and Criminology* 985.

Criminal Cases Review Commission (CCRC) (1999) *Annual Report 1998–99* (Birmingham, CCRC).

—— (2013) *Annual Report and Accounts 2012/13* (HC 482) (London, The Stationery Office).

Criminal Justice Review Group (CJRG) (2000) Review of the Criminal Justice System in Northern Ireland: *The Report of the Criminal Justice Review* (Belfast, HMSO).

Daly, E (2008) 'Truth Scepticism: An Inquiry into the Value of Truth in Times of Transition' 2 *International Journal of Transitional Justice* 23.

Department of Justice (DoJ) (2011) FOI reference 11/66, documentation in response to request by the author and Hannah Quirk, on file with author.

—— (2012) *Compensation for Wrongful Conviction: Note for Successful Applicants*, on file with author.

—— (2013) FOI reference 13/176, documentation in response to request by the author, on file with author.

—— (2014) *Northern Ireland Conviction and Sentencing Statistics 2010–2012* (Belfast, NISRA).

—— (2015) FOI reference 14/190, documentation in response to request by the author, on file with author.

Dickson, B (1999) 'Miscarriages of Justice in Northern Ireland' in C Walker and K Starmer (eds), *Miscarriages of Justice: A Review of Justice in Error* (Oxford, Oxford University Press).

Dyzenhaus, D (2010) *Hard Cases in Wicked Legal Systems: Pathologies of Legality* (Oxford, Oxford University Press).

Forst, B (2013) 'Wrongful Convictions in a World of Miscarriages of Justice' in CR Huff and M Killias (eds), *Wrongful Convictions and Miscarriages of Justice: Causes and Remedies in North American and European Criminal Justice Systems* (New York, Routledge).

Gould, J and Leo, R (2010) 'One Hundred Years Later: Wrongful Convictions after a Century of Research' 100 *Journal of Criminal Law and Criminology* 825.

Griffin, L (2013) 'International Perspectives on Correcting Wrongful Convictions: the Scottish Criminal Cases Review Commission' 21 *William & Mary Bill of Rights Journal* 1153.

Groome, D (2011) 'The Right to Truth in the Fight Against Impunity' 29 *Berkeley Journal of International Law* 175.

Gross, S (2008) 'Convicting the Innocent' 4 *Annual Review of Law and Social Science* 173.

—— (2013) 'How Many False Convictions Are There? How Many Exonerations are There?' in CR Huff and M Killias (eds), *Wrongful Convictions and Miscarriages of Justice: Causes and Remedies in North American and European Criminal Justice Systems* (New York, Routledge).

Grounds, A (2005) 'Understanding the Effects of Wrongful Imprisonment' 32 *Crime and Justice* 1.

—— (2011) 'The Effects of Wrongful Conviction and Imprisonment', paper presented to the School of Law, Queen's University Belfast, 23 November 2011 (on file with author).

Guerra Thompson, S (2012) 'Judicial Gatekeeping of Police-Generated Witness Testimony' 102 *Journal of Criminal Law and Criminology* 329.

Haynor, PB (2002) *Unspeakable Truths: Facing the Challenge of Truth Commissions* (New York, Routledge).

Herman, J (1997) *Trauma and Recovery: The Aftermath of Violence—From Domestic Abuse to Political Terror* (New York, BasicBooks).

Huff, CR (2013) 'Wrongful Convictions, Miscarriages of Justice, and Political Repression: Challenges for Transitional Justice' in CR Huff and M Killias (eds), *Wrongful Convictions and Miscarriages of Justice: Causes and Remedies in North American and European Criminal Justice Systems* (New York, Routledge).

Huff, CR and Killias, M (eds) (2008) *Wrongful Conviction: International Perspectives on Miscarriages of Justice* (Philadelphia, Temple University Press).

—— (eds) (2013) *Wrongful Convictions and Miscarriages of Justice: Causes and Remedies in North American and European Criminal Justice Systems* (New York, Routledge).

Ignatieff, M (1996) 'Articles of Faith' 25 *Index on Censorship* 110.
Independent Commission on Policing for Northern Ireland (ICP) (1999) *A New Beginning: Policing in Northern Ireland*—The Report of the Independent Commission on Policing in Northern Ireland (Belfast, HMSO) (Patten Report).
Jackson, J and Doran, S (1995) *Judge Without Jury: Diplock Trials in the Adversary System* (Oxford, Clarendon Press).
Kennedy, L (1991) *Truth to Tell: The Collected Writings of Ludovic Kennedy* (London, Bantam Press).
McEvoy, K and McConnachie, K (2012) 'Victimology in Transitional Justice: Victimhood, Innocence and Hierarchy' 9 *European Journal of Criminology* 527.
McGarry, J (2004) 'The Politics of Policing Reform in Northern Ireland' in J McGarry and B O'Leary (eds), *The Northern Ireland Conflict: Consociational Engagements* (Oxford, Oxford University Press).
Méndez, J (1997) 'Accountability for Past Abuses' 19 *Human Rights Quarterly* 255.
Moon, C (2012) '"Who'll Pay Reparations on My Soul?": Compensation, Social Suffering and Social Control in Argentina' 22 *Social & Legal Studies* 149.
Mureinik, E (1994) 'A Bridge to Where? Introducing the Interim Bill of Rights' 10 *South African Journal on Human Rights* 32.
Naqvi, Y (2006) 'The Right to the Truth in International Law: Fact or Fiction?' 88 *International Review of the Red Cross* 245.
Naughton, M (2007) *Rethinking Miscarriages of Justice: Beyond the Tip of the Iceberg* (Basingstoke, Palgrave Macmillan).
—— (2012) *Rethinking Miscarriages of Justice: Beyond the Tip of the Iceberg* (Basingstoke, Palgrave Macmillan).
Northern Ireland Office (NIO) (2011), FOI reference 11/112, documentation in response to request by the author and Hannah Quirk, on file with author.
—— (2013a) *Compensation for Wrongful Conviction: Note for Successful Applicants*, on file with author.
—— (2013b) FOI reference 13/202, documentation in response to request by the author, on file with author.
Osiel, M (2002) *Mass Atrocity, Ordinary Evil, and Hannah Arendt: Criminal Consciousness in Argentina's Dirty War* (New Haven, NJ, Yale University Press).
Popkin, M and Roht-Arriaza, N (1995) 'Truth as Justice: Investigatory Commissions in Latin America' 20 *Law & Social Inquiry* 79.
Quinn, JR (2010) *The Politics of Acknowledgement: Truth Commissions in Uganda and Haiti* (Vancouver, UBC Press).
Quirk, H (2013) 'Don't Mention the War: The Court of Appeal, the Criminal Cases Review Commission and Dealing with the Past in Northern Ireland' 76 *Modern Law Review* 949.
Quirk, H and Requa, M (2012) 'The Supreme Court on Compensation for Miscarriages of Justice: Is it Better that Ten Innocents are Denied Compensation than One Guilty Person Receives it?' 75 *Modern Law Review* 387.
Requa, M (2014) 'Considering Just-World Thinking in Counter-Terrorism Cases: Miscarriages of Justice in Northern Ireland' 27 *Harvard Human Rights Journal* 7.
Runciman, Viscount (1993) *Report of the Royal Commission on Criminal Justice* (Cm 2263) (London, HMSO).
Schehr, RC (2005) 'The Criminal Cases Review Commission as a State Strategic Selection Mechanism' 42 *American Criminal Law Review* 1289.

Shirlow, P and McEvoy, K (2008) *Beyond the Wire: Former Prisoners and Conflict Transformation in Northern Ireland* (London, Pluto Press).
Taylor, N (2013) 'R (on the application of Ali) v Secretary of State for Justice: Compensation–Guidance on the Application of the Supreme Court decision in R (on the application of Adams) v Secretary of State for Justice' *Criminal Law Review* 587.
Taylor, P (1980) *Beating the Terrorists? Interrogation in Omagh, Gough and Castlereagh* (Harmondsworth, Penguin Books).
Truth and Reconciliation Commission of South Africa (TRC) (1998) *Report of the Truth and Reconciliation Commission of South Africa; Volume 1, Chapter 5* (Cape Town, Juta).
Vollen, L and Eggers, D (eds) (2008) *Surviving Justice: America's Wrongfully Convicted and Exonerated* (San Francisco, CA, McSweeney's Books).
Walker, C (1999a) 'The Commodity of Justice in States of Emergency' 50 *Northern Ireland Legal Quarterly* 164.
Walker, C (1999b) 'Miscarriages of Justice in Principle and Practice' in C Walker and K Starmer (eds), *Miscarriages of Justice: A Review of Justice in Error* (Oxford, Oxford University Press).
Walker, C and McCartney, C (2008) 'Criminal Justice and Miscarriages of Justice in England and Wales' in CR Huff and M Killias (eds), *Wrongful Conviction: International Perspectives on Miscarriages of Justice* (Philadelphia, PA, Temple University Press).
Weschler, L (1990) *A Miracle, A Universe: Settling Accounts with Torturers* (New York, Pantheon).
Westervelt, S and Cook, K (2008) 'Coping with Innocence after Death Row' 7 *Contexts* 32.
—— (2010) 'Framing Innocents: The Wrongly Convicted as Victims of State Harm' 53 *Crime, Law and Social Change* 259.
—— (2011) 'Foreward: Miscarriages of Justice' 75 *Albany Law Review* 1223.
Williams, JW (1999) 'Taking it to the Streets: Policing and the Practice of Constitutive Criminology' in S Henry and D Milovanovic (eds), *Constitutive Criminology at Work: Applications to Crime and Justice* (Albany, State University of New York Press).
Zalman, M (2012) 'Qualitatively Estimating the Incidence of Wrongful Conviction' 48 *Criminal Law Bulletin* 1.

Part III

Contemporary Issues in Criminal Justice

13

Transition, Women and Criminal Justice in Northern Ireland

LINDA MOORE AND AZRINI WAHIDIN

Introduction

With emphasis on imprisonment in a society in transition, this chapter focuses on women's experiences of the criminal justice system, from the most violent years of conflict through to developments which followed the Belfast/Good Friday Agreement (1998), notably the devolution of criminal justice to the locally elected Northern Ireland Executive. Proposals for a new women's prison are also examined along with recent community-based initiatives aimed at reducing reliance on custodial sentencing. Our analysis draws on primary research conducted by both authors with women prisoners and former prisoners, including Wahidin's research on female republican former prisoners' experiences of Armagh and Maghaberry (Wahidin 2015) and Moore's research (with Phil Scraton) on women's imprisonment in Maghaberry and Hydebank Wood (Moore and Scraton 2014).

Penological research demonstrates the gendered nature of criminal justice processes and acknowledges the damaging effects for women of incarceration within institutions and regimes designed with male prisoners in mind (Carlen 1983). In Northern Ireland the positioning of female units within predominantly male prison environments has given rise to serious and persistent rights abuses and marginalisation of women's needs, as documented by a series of inspections, monitoring and research reports. Throughout the conflict the inherent difficulties associated with women's imprisonment have been compounded by the prioritisation of security demands over care and rehabilitation (Moore and Scraton 2014). This chapter analyses how violence and sectarian divisions have shaped penal regimes, both for politically motivated and so-called 'ordinary' women prisoners and discusses women's responses to gendered control and punishment.

In analysing gendered experiences of criminal justice, we draw on international scholarship on women's imprisonment, with the aim of understanding how the situation in Northern Ireland is consistent with other jurisdictions and identifying ways in which the experience of conflict has uniquely shaped the Northern Ireland system. The chapter opens with reference to research on the global expansion of the female prison population, the particular characteristics and needs of women prisoners and gendered experiences of incarceration. In recent years, gender-specific community sanctions have been introduced in many jurisdictions with the aim of reducing the numbers of women in prison, yet evidence indicates that these have tended to supplement, rather than replace, the prison (Pollack 2008; Malloch and McIvor 2013).

Having examined these core issues, the chapter turns to the recent history of women's imprisonment in Northern Ireland, from Armagh, the transfer of women to Mourne House in Maghaberry high-security prison and then the move to Hydebank Wood (Ash House) where all women prisoners are currently detained within the confines of a male Young Offender Centre. Despite long-standing and consistent recommendations from local and international bodies, the prison system has been stubbornly resistant to change, and over a decade after the Belfast/Good Friday Agreement 'remained relatively untouched by the reforms of the criminal justice system' (CJINI 2010: v) raising questions about the effectiveness and reach of transitional processes. Following concerns expressed in the media regarding serious breaches of women's rights in prison, the multi-party Hillsborough Agreement (2010) provided for a review of women's imprisonment in light of international human rights standards. The independent Prison Review Team's (PRT 2011) recommendations, including for a new women's prison unit and greater use of community-based alternatives to custody, are analysed here.

The concluding section sets the experiences of women prisoners in Northern Ireland against a backdrop of United Kingdom and international developments, noting shared issues as well as divergent practice. In the context of recent transitional justice scholarship, which highlights conflict-related violence against women and the marginalisation of women's rights both during conflicts and in their aftermath (Bell and O'Rourke 2007; McMinn and O'Rourke 2012), the limitations of the transitional process in relation to women prisoners in Northern Ireland are acknowledged and alternative strategies explored.

Women's Gendered Experiences of Imprisonment and 'Resettlement'

Since the eighteen and nineteenth-century development of the modern penal-industrial complex, women have remained a small minority of the total prison population globally and nationally, their minority status contributing to the marginalisation and neglect of their needs (Moore and Scraton 2014). Women prisoners are deemed 'doubly deviant' by society, failures as wives and mothers as well as being offenders, routinely pathologised and subjected to infantilising regimes (Carlen 1983). Despite their small numbers relative to men, increased female imprisonment has been a 'defining feature of western jurisdictions in recent years', especially in the United States, Australia, New Zealand and many European countries including the United Kingdom (McIvor and Burman 2011: 6). This increase is not primarily an indication of more serious or persistent offending, but is attributable to factors including greater use of custodial remand (Scott and Codd 2010) and more women receiving custodial sentences for non-serious property offences and minor drug offences (Gelsthorpe and Morris 2002), the criminalisation of migration (Sudbury 2005) and greater severity in sentencing (Medlicott 2007). The majority of women entering prison are there 'primarily because of the poverty of their circumstances' rather than the seriousness of their offending (Carlen, cited in Carlton and Segrave 2013: preface). Women typically have experienced high levels of mental health needs, addictions, bereavement and trauma; sexual abuse and violence; and social and economic marginalisation prior to entering prison (HMCIP 1997; Singleton et al 1998; Medlicott 2007). Most are mothers and separation from children weighs heavily (Scott and Codd 2010).

Women's experiences of penal regimes are highly gendered, with access to a more restricted range of services and opportunities than male prisoners (Carlen 1983; Scraton and Moore 2005, 2007). Specific groups, such as older women (Wahidin 2004), young women, pregnant women or nursing mothers suffer particular neglect. Basic needs such as access to sanitary protection are regulated by penal regimes (Smith 2009). Security practices are experienced as aspects of a continuum of violence (McCulloch and George 2009; Scraton and Moore 2005, 2007), for example strip-searching as 'sexual coercion, which reinforces women's sense of powerlessness and undermines self-esteem and self-worth' (McCulloch and George 2009: 121–22). Women with mental health difficulties, including those with addictions and distressed, self-harming or suicidal women, may bottle up feelings for fear of being placed in isolation under oppressive surveillance, nominally for their own protection (Moore and Scraton 2014). Despite the introduction of initiatives aimed at reducing self-harm and suicide, these issues form a 'permanent and enduring feature of prison life' (INQUEST 2013: paragraph 10).

Feminist scholars have highlighted women's resistance to penal regimes, stressing that 'even under the most violent and oppressive conditions women can resist their violent oppressors' and 'contest and evade the rules that grind them down' (Carlen and Worrall 2004: 88) This is particularly the case for politically motivated prisoners[1] for whom 'there is a well-documented history of carefully constructed and thought-through strategies' aimed at creating 'alternative frames of action in opposing the administration of the prison' (Moore and Scraton 2014: 36). Women typically adopt a 'range of strategies, ploys and disruptions—formal and informal, individual and collective—to negotiate and challenge the authority to which they are subjected' (Moore and Scraton 2014: 37) yet the prison is a

[1] For the purpose of this chapter we have adopted Shirlow et al's description of 'politically motivated' prisoners defined as those 'convicted through the Emergency Law system and subsequently imprisoned for their role in acts related to the conflict' (2005: 22).

powerful institution and 'the forces deployed against resisting women are significant' (Moore and Scraton 2014: 41).

Institutionalised into prison 'routine and discipline', women may find it 'difficult to take responsibility for the most mundane of tasks' (Eaton 1993: 18–19). Up to one-third will lose their previous accommodation during their imprisonment (Corston 2007) some being placed in unsuitable and unsafe hostels, sometimes shared with men. As Carlen observes, women prisoners are 'repeatedly released back into those same circumstances of poverty and malign neglect which catapulted them into jail in the first place', they are 'put back into their class and cultural milieus ... put back in their place' (Carlton and Segrave 2013: preface). Carlton and Segrave (2011: 560) also found that the trauma of the prison experience makes it more difficult for women to cope after release leading to 'loneliness, boredom, coping with disappointment', some former prisoners ending their own lives in despair.

Feminist scholarship, coupled with work by campaigning groups, has encouraged the development of gender-specific strategies and initiatives. In her review of the needs of vulnerable women within the justice system, Baroness Corston (2007: 5) stated, 'we must find better ways to keep out of prison those women who pose no threat to society and to improve the prison experience for those who do'. Concluding that prison is 'not the right place' for women who require a therapeutic environment she recommended the 'dismantling' of the women's penal system and its replacement by 'smaller secure units for the minority of women from whom the public requires protection' (2007: 5). In 2010, the United Nations Rules for the Treatment of Women Prisoners and Non-custodial Measures for Women Offenders (the Bangkok Rules) established the right to gender-sensitive treatment for women in prison, and for alternatives to imprisonment so far as possible. Regarding 'women centred' approaches, however, Pollack (2008: 7) found a persistent emphasis on discipline and punishment. Critics warn that, even if well-intentioned, gender-specific initiatives are often aimed at the reinvention of the prison, an ultimately flawed project (Hannah-Moffatt 2001).

Northern Ireland's penal system demonstrates many of the characteristics witnessed in other jurisdictions as described above. However, there are some distinct features arising from the specific contexts of sectarianism, violence and conflict. The following section therefore turns to the experience of politically motivated prisoners in Armagh in such a framework.

Gendered Punishment and Resistance: Women's Imprisonment in Armagh

Armagh was Northern Ireland's only prison for women, until its closure in 1986. Built in 1780, in its early days Armagh held three groups of prisoners: women, and male 'debtors' and 'felons'. From 1920, Armagh became a women-only facility. However, male internees were also held there in the 1950s and a Borstal for boys operated in Armagh from the 1960s through to 1975. Staffed by both male and female officers, generally speaking male officers were in charge of the Borstal boys and female officers supervised the women (Murray 1998). Prior to 1970, Armagh rarely housed more than a dozen or so women at a time: prisoners mainly on charges such as drunkenness, assault, theft, fraud, forgery, prostitution and occasionally murder (Murray 1998). The resurgence of political conflict and violence led to a dramatic rise in the prison population, including for women. The number of politically motivated women imprisoned in Armagh increased from two in 1971 to more than 100 during the 1972–76 period, including more than 30 internees (Brady et al 2011: 10). The majority of politically motivated female prisoners were republican with much smaller numbers of loyalists (Aretxaga 1997). Conditions in Armagh were austere. Cells were eight by ten foot in dimension with an arched window high above as the only source of natural light. Women had to 'slop out' using a chamber pot (known as a 'po') (Wahidin 2015). In August 1972, 132 men were moved from Belfast (Crumlin Road) Gaol to Armagh (Brady et al 2011; Corcoran 2006) before being transferred to Long Kesh (later renamed as the Maze Prison). This exacerbated overcrowding, and resulted in women's confinement to limited areas. In the allocation of resources, the 'needs of male prisoners prevailed over the women': the 'poor quality of prison food, and inadequate recreation, washing and cooking facilities', providing the 'first focal point for a collectively organized campaign by women prisoners' (Corcoran 2006: 21). Women prisoners were expected to perform traditionally female tasks such as laundering and cleaning and education provision was also gendered (Corcoran 2006). In an interview with Wahidin (2015: 100) Che-Mah,[2] one of the first women to go to Armagh in the late 1960s, describes hating the compulsory uniform: 'I went into Armagh and I had to wear this prison uniform which was horrendous. The women had to wear a uniform and it had been in place circa since 1840. That's how old the style was'. On 15 May 1972, four women at Armagh and republican men at Crumlin Road went on hunger strike for political status. Che-Mah participated in the protest explaining that 'I didn't want to wear this prison uniform. We were on it for political status. We were fighting for political status'. In June 1972 'special category status' was introduced and prisoners were permitted to wear their own clothes (See the chapter by Scraton in this volume for further discussion.) Che-Mah stated:

> At the end of 17 days, I remember the Governor sending for us, to tell us that we had political status. They brought me in my guitar and they brought me in my jeans and my sneakers and it was like, 'oh it was worth it, it was worth it!' We got the uniform and fired it out onto the wing, 'we don't have to wear that no more!'

[2] Names have been anonymised to protect the identities of the women unless otherwise stated.

The gains achieved by the politically motivated prisoners also benefited other prisoners as recalled by former prisoner Maud:

> He [Secretary of State, William Whitelaw] gave us our demands, so we didn't have to wear the uniform after that and we were allowed a visit every week where before it was one a month. We were allowed free association, and we were allowed the right to education. Everything before that was a privilege which could be taken away from you, and what I was particularly pleased about was that it was also extended to the ordinary prisoner (cited in Wahidin 2015: 250).

From 1974, republican women were designated as 'A' company of the Provisional Irish Republican Army (IRA), organising along disciplined military lines and conducting communication with the prison authorities through their 'commanding officer' (Corcoran 2006). Prisoners' victory regarding political recognition was short-lived, however, and on 1 March 1976 special category status was removed for those convicted from that date, as part of the state's strategy of criminalisation (and was removed from all prisoners in March 1980). Republican women participated in the campaign to restore political status, refusing to do prison work and thus enduring long periods of lock-down. Unlike male prisoners, women in Armagh were permitted to wear their own clothes so long as these did not resemble paramilitary uniforms. In February 1980, however, a search was carried out for clothing worn by republican women during a parade to honour a fellow IRA volunteer 'killed in action'. Maureen Gibson described officers in 'full riot gear with shields and batons', one of whom was 'actually kneeling on Anne-Marie Quinn's stomach—a huge big man—pushing her on to the bed' (cited in Fairweather et al 1984: 219–20). Following this incident, women were locked up and refused appropriate access to sanitation. When chamber pots were full women poured the contents through cell 'spy holes', marking the start of the 'no-wash' or 'dirty' protest (Brady et al 2011). Throughout the protest, women remained locked in cells for 23 hours a day smearing faeces and menstrual blood on the walls. Fairweather et al (1984: 222) argue that by denying access to sanitation the authorities were trying to 'break the prisoners in an exclusively female way.'

In 1980 the campaign for political status escalated into a hunger strike in which republican women participated. This ended without resolution, and a further hunger strike involving only male prisoners commenced in March 1981, the 'no-wash' or 'dirty protest' ending to provide a focus for this action. The hunger strike culminated in the deaths through starvation of 10 men. When the strike ended most of the prisoners' demands were conceded, including the right to wear their own clothes and to associate together. Corcoran (2006: 182) argues that whereas the conclusion of the hunger strike in the Maze represented a 'critical turning point' for male prisoners, in Armagh the introduction of routine strip-searches from November 1982 led to 'intensified conflict' there and 'brought to the fore a renewed focus on controlling the bodies of unruly women prisoners'. For women, being stripped—sometimes forcibly—was harrowing, as evidenced in the testimonies below:

> A hostile screw will order me to remove all my clothes. She stands watching me while I undress. Each item of clothing has to be passed out to the screws. When I have passed the last item out the screws will then inspect my naked body. I stand there naked, trying to control my breathing, my anger and other confused feelings (Marie Wright, cited in Brady et al 2011: 243).

> Despite my medical condition [having recently given birth] I was strip searched. Once naked I attempted to cover my breasts with my arms as I was embarrassed with my breasts leaking with milk. I was ordered to remove my arms to facilitate the warders' inspection of my naked body (Jacqueline Moore, cited in Stop the Strip-Searches undated: 10).

Strip-searching brought international attention to the Armagh situation and 'came to epitomise, for many, the resolve of the security services to have women submit to the process of criminalisation and surveillance by taking control of women's nakedness' (Pickering 2002: 181).

Armagh closed in 1986, as part of the Prison Service's strategy of modernisation and 'normalisation' (Gormally et al 1993; McEvoy 2001), all women prisoners being transferred to Mourne House, a unit in the newly built, high-security Maghaberry Prison complex. In Armagh, women's lives had, at times, been particularly restricted, and conditions worsened, due to pressures created by the accommodation of boys and men on the same site. The level of female imprisonment related to 'ordinary' offences was consistently low, but the situation differed from other UK jurisdictions due to the larger numbers of politically motivated women being interned or imprisoned. These women were routinely subject to harsh punishment expressed in gendered forms, collectively resisting such treatment. The analysis below of women's imprisonment in Mourne House, Maghaberry, examines the continued marginalisation of women's needs within a highly controlled and punitive environment, even after the numbers of politically motivated prisoners were reduced as Northern Ireland entered into political transition.

The Failure of Normalisation: Women in Mourne House, Maghaberry

In building Maghaberry, the authorities' intention was to provide a modern, high-security prison based on integrated regimes where politically motivated prisoners would be held on normal landings along with other prisoners. The female unit, Mourne House, held up to 59 women remanded and sentenced for both politically motivated and 'ordinary' offences, over four wings. In March 1992, a mass strip-search of republican and other women belied the claims of normality and was an indication of the continuation of gendered punishment and institutionalised sectarianism within the prison system. A woman in Wahidin's (2015:120) study recalls her 'waking nightmare' of that day:

> [M]y cell-door was flung open and the riot squad surged forward. Three or four of them wore visors and wielded shields and batons, the other two, clad in overalls. A shield was rammed straight into my face, forcing me back against the bars on my window, while another two attacked me from either side. I was seized, flung face down on the floor and sat upon, while my arms were twisted and locked up my back … Having satisfied themselves that I'd been immobilised, my assailants proceeded to pull my clothes off from the waist down. They then proceeded to pull all the clothes from my upper body before getting up and leaving me. As I raised myself onto my elbows, feeling shocked and disorientated, I looked at my clothes strewn all around my cell and saw the backs of my attackers passing out through the door.

Following the early release of prisoners affiliated to organisations on ceasefire, as a result of the Belfast/Good Friday Agreement (1998), politically motivated women represented only a small minority of the female prison population. The Agreement established a Criminal Justice Review (2000) which made recommendations aimed at encouraging the development of a modern, professional justice system. Noting the difficulties in detaining the small number of women (on average 20) in Maghaberry within a larger, male institution the Review recommended the sharing of some facilities with the men, expressed hope that the issue of girl children being detained in the adult prison would be resolved by changes in the youth justice process, and proposed that women's imprisonment be kept 'under review' (CJRG 2000: paragraph 12.18).

With the closure of Belfast Prison (Crumlin Road) in 1996 and the Maze in 2000, male prisoners affiliated to paramilitary organisations not on ceasefire were transferred to Maghaberry. Prison officers had also been transferred from the Maze to Maghaberry, bringing with them a culture of 'containment' (HMCIP 2003: 3). An inspection (HMCIP 2003: 4) found that Mourne House required 'some development to fulfil its role as Northern Ireland's only women's facility', including retraining of management and staff and a change in ethos in order to meet the needs of women rather than being just a 'small adjunct to the male prison'. Despite the inspectors' optimism that the overall situation in Maghaberry was progressing, in summer 2003 the prison was seized by a series of protests by both loyalist and republican prisoners demanding separation. The Steele Review (2004) established to inquire into safety in the prison, recommended a 'degree of separation' to 'protect paramilitaries of opposing factions from each other, and to protect the "ordinary" prisoners from the paramilitaries as a group' (NIAC 2004: 3). Subsequently, politically motivated male prisoners who agreed to a 'Compact' with the authorities were imprisoned separately, loyalists in Bush House and republicans in Roe House. The small number of politically affiliated women remained within an integrated regime, continuing to protest against what they saw as a policy of criminalisation (Scraton and Moore 2005; see also the chapter by Scraton in this volume for further discussion).

In 2004, the Northern Ireland Human Rights Commission (the Commission) initiated an investigation into women's imprisonment focusing on the rights to life (European Convention on Human Rights (ECHR), Article 2) and freedom from torture, inhuman and degrading treatment (ECHR, Article 3).[3] This investigation revealed a regime in Mourne House in which women were routinely locked up for a minimum of 15 hours out of 24 (Scraton and Moore 2005: 53) and without a structured induction programme, formal sentence management or appropriate resettlement programmes. Family contact was curtailed by limited access to expensive telephones and inadequacies in the visits system. The majority of officers were men and often the night shift was entirely male. A small minority of staff engaged constructively with prisoners but the predominant attitude was 'disinterest' with some officers openly abusive. There were inappropriately high levels of staffing and women were not permitted to move about the site unless escorted by prison officers, a legacy of the high-security regime established to deal with politically motivated prisoners. The Prison Officers Association strenuously resisted any attempts to reduce numbers or alter conditions of employment. For officers who had lost colleagues through paramilitary violence, or who had feared for their own or their family's safety, to be asked to work constructively with prisoners was a difficult cultural shift, which most had not yet made (Scraton and Moore 2005).

Health care was provided in the male prison hospital and despite the extent of depression and trauma, there was minimal counselling or therapeutic provision and no treatment for women classified as 'personality disordered'. Distressed and self-harming women were routinely locked in isolation in the 'special supervision unit', where typical cells had no mattress, no pillow, a potty for a toilet and no sink for washing. Women deemed 'at risk' were forced to wear anti-suicide gowns and forbidden underwear even during menstruation (Scraton and Moore 2005). Two women had died in Mourne House since its inception, Janet Holmes in 1996 and Annie Kelly in 2002. Early in the Commission's research fieldwork, Roseanne Irvine took her own life through hanging. Roseanne suffered persistent mental health problems and alcohol addiction, self-harmed and feared she would lose access to her young daughter, yet she did not receive appropriate medical care either in the community or in prison. At the inquest into her death at Belfast coroners' court the jury stated that 'the prison system failed Roseanne' (Moore and Scraton 2014: 166).

Republican women continued to resist what they saw as the criminalising impact of association with 'ordinary' prisoners, and during the Commission's investigation the only two republicans in Mourne House were protesting, including going

[3] One of the authors of this chapter, Linda Moore, was investigations worker at the NIHRC and co-researched and co-authored the Commission's two investigations into women's imprisonment along with Phil Scraton, Professor of Criminology at Queen's University Belfast.

on hunger strike in pursuance of separation. Their campaign was successful and a separate landing was granted; however, the space to provide this was achieved by moving girls as young as 16 years of age from the designated 'young offender' landing on to an adult landing, in clear breach of Article 37 of the United Nations Convention on the Rights of the Child which requires the separation of detained children from adults (Scraton and Moore 2005). The difficulties of providing for the complex needs of different groups of women prisoners in a confined site, and within a mainly male environment, were all too apparent. The Commission's report recommended the prioritisation of alternatives to custody, development of a gender-specific strategy, policy and programmes, and establishment of a 'distinct, gender-specific identity' for the women's custody unit. It also called for an independent public inquiry into the deterioration of conditions for women prisoners, and the deaths of women in custody (Scraton and Moore 2005).

The history of women's imprisonment in Mourne House demonstrates the prison authorities' ineffectiveness in pursuing the normalisation project, exacerbated by a lack of understanding of the needs of women prisoners. The legacy of the conflict contributed to prison officer disengagement and an inappropriately security-focused regime. Moreover, as a small minority in a larger male establishment, women's needs were neglected and highly punitive practices persisted especially in relation to self-harming and suicidal women. With few politically motivated prisoners there was little collective resistance to the regime. Mourne House closed in June 2004 and women were transferred to Ash House, a unit within Hydebank Wood, a medium security male young offenders' centre on the outskirts of Belfast. The prison authorities anticipated that the transfer would result in a reduction in staffing levels and make better use of spare capacity in Hydebank Wood, while providing a less oppressive environment for women (Scraton and Moore 2005). Although highly critical of the Mourne House regime, the Human Rights Commission opposed women's transfer from one male environment to another, arguing that this would lead to continued rights abuses. Its views were disregarded (Scraton and Moore 2005).

Women in a Young Male Environment: Ash House, Hydebank Wood

Ash House can accommodate up to 71 women and is one of five units in Hydebank Wood, a male young offender centre (CJINI 2013: v). Within months of women being transferred to Ash House, an unannounced inspection (HMCIP/CJINI 2005) raised serious concerns about the safety of 'vulnerable' and 'damaged' women and girls. Officers without appropriate training and 'anxious, by any means available, to prevent another self-inflicted death' relied on disciplinary procedures to place vulnerable women in cellular confinement as punishment for self-harming. With little activity for women, boredom was 'likely to compound feelings of depression and anxiety' (HMCIP/CJINI 2005: 6). There was 'no Northern Ireland Prison Service strategy, policies or procedures to deal with the specific needs of women and girls; and no separate, properly trained, management of the women's prison' (HMCIP/CJINI 2005: 6). In 2004 Alvaro Gil-Robles (2005: paragraph 126), Commissioner for Human Rights for the Council of Europe, visited Ash House and concluded there was 'no possibility for the women to receive appropriate treatment, indeed, the conditions could only be considered likely to aggravate their fragile condition still further'. Likewise, the Committee Against Torture described 'unacceptable conditions' including: 'a lack of gender-sensitive facilities, policies, guarding and medical aid, with male guards alleged to constitute 80 per cent of guarding staff and incidents of inappropriate threats and incidents affecting female detainees' (CAT 2004: 5). Research conducted for the Prison Service in Ash House provided evidence of female prisoners' vulnerabilities, finding that: 88 per cent had suffered depression and 76 per cent recent bereavement; 60 per cent were on medication and 68 per cent had been referred for psychiatric assessment; and 44 per cent had not felt safe in their communities prior to entering prison and women were very fearful about being released (NIPS 2005).

Initially barred from carrying out an investigation in Hydebank Wood, the Human Rights Commission was granted access later in 2004, conducting extensive fieldwork in Ash House until 2006. The Commission (Scraton and Moore 2007) noted that only a small number of the women had been convicted of serious offences and around 40 per cent were imprisoned for fine default, including for non-payment of television licences. Women reported experiencing highly sexualised verbal abuse from the young men, especially during shared transport. Frequent strip-searching (called 'Full Searching' by the prison service) was experienced as humiliating and even traumatic:

> When you're on your menstrual cycle you still have to strip. It's very degrading. You have to show them the pants and pad with the blood on it. It's disgusting, you're embarrassed. Their attitude is indifferent. It's their job, but it's not a nice thing to do (sentenced prisoner, cited in Scraton and Moore 2007: 52).

At best women were unlocked for eight hours out of 24 but often were locked up for 23 hours a day due to 'staff shortages' and industrial relations breakdowns. A long-term prisoner described the monotony:

> Education is rarely available to us and, at that, it's very basic. It's hard to cope, especially when you were used to a busy life, for it to become the opposite and you end up doing nothing all day long (Scraton and Moore 2007: 56).

Discipline was strict and women feared being 'zeroed' for minor breaches of rules:

> They change the rules handsomely. It depends on the person [staff] and what mood the person's in. There's no structure and no consistent rules. A woman officer said to me, 'You shouldn't query. You shouldn't ask questions. That's a rule' (Scraton and Moore 2007: 55).

In comparison with Mourne House, there was increased access to mental health services in Hydebank Wood but nonetheless these were limited and the health care centre was shared with young men. Women were often locked in isolation for 'their own safety', with the result that many were afraid to reveal their problems:

> They put me in the observation cell from Friday to the Monday. I'd gone through a great loss. I was just out [of her cell] for the shower, no interaction, nobody asking to speak with me. I'm shit scared of going back to the hospital. There's nothing. So I say I'm fine. There's no therapeutic help, nothing (remand prisoner, cited in Scraton and Moore 2007: 78).

Part of the stated rationale for the transfer to Hydebank Wood was that this lower-security environment would provide a more relaxed regime. Yet, in practice, women's movements were strictly 'choreographed' to avoid contact with young men and they were at all times escorted by prison officers:

> The whole point of this place was that it would be lower security with a see through fence rather than a wall, that we'd be able to have more outdoor freedom in a nice environment. The reverse is true. We have less access to the grounds. We can see the environment but we can't experience it (woman prisoner, cited in Scraton and Moore 2007: 55).

The Commission recommended the development of a discrete women's prison unit, staffed by a minimum of 80 per cent female staff, with its own management structure; an end to strip-searching except where risk assessment demonstrated this as necessary to protect the women or others from serious harm; the ending of extended periods of cellular confinement; and a review of health care. A core recommendation was for the enactment of legislation to ensure that custody for women was a last resort and the development of community-based alternatives (Scraton and Moore 2007).

The Commission's findings were later mirrored by those of the Independent Monitoring Board (IMB), a body of volunteers with statutory powers to visit prisons and report on conditions (IMB 2010). The IMB recorded an increase in the use of cellular confinement as a punishment and no move towards establishing a therapeutic regime. There had been 'no manifestations of the [promised] culture change' and only 'marginal improvement in the level of staff engagement with prisoners' (IMB 2010: 5). Positive engagement with prisoners had been sacrificed in favour of a 'strong emphasis on security and control' (IMB 2010: 6). No progress had been made towards the construction of a separate female prison and only minimal advances towards the development of gender-specific policies.

In 2010, the Northern Ireland Prison Service introduced Gender Specific Standards for working with women prisoners (NIPS 2010) and an inspection the following year (CJINI 2011) described Ash House as performing 'reasonably well' in terms of prisoner safety. Sadly, this was contradicted by the death by hanging that same year of Frances McKeown, a young mother with long-standing mental health difficulties, on the very same day as a young male prisoner also took his own life (Prisoner Ombudsman for Northern Ireland 2012). Despite her vulnerability, Frances experienced a six-month wait before accessing a prison psychiatrist.

A diary entry made shortly before she died, reflected the painful impact of confinement:

> Because I suffer from mental health my time for thinking is my biggest problem, when I have too much time to think on my hands that is when my mood lowers severely and I become suicidal. My thoughts make my mind snap and I just can't cope with it anymore so I self-harm to try and stop it and block out the thinking and sometimes I even go far enough to plan a new way to end it all just to stop my pain from my thoughts. Once I lose the head and cut I end up on a SPAR [Supporting Prisoner At Risk] and have to put up with being watched which makes my paranoia worse and the voices I hear go mad because of it and I stress out. It is the worst combination of emotions you could possibly imagine (cited in Prisoner Ombudsman 2012: 15).

The Prisoner Ombudsman's investigation (2012: 29) into the death of Frances McKeown confirmed inadequacies in communication, poor record-keeping, limited access to mental health care, long periods of lock-up and lack of 'purposeful activity'.

The most recent inspection of Ash House in 2013 (CJINI 2013: v) stated that although women were 'reasonably well cared for', they were still subject to verbal abuse from young men and were 'inevitably marginalized and restricted in their access to facilities and services'. Staff–prisoner relationships were judged to have improved, but security remained overly restrictive. The inspection survey found that 42 per cent of women self-defined as having mental health problems and 45 per cent had felt depressed or suicidal on reception into the prison (CJINI 2013: 26). Excessive amounts of lock-up continued to be damaging to women's mental health (2013: 27). At the time of the inspection around three-quarters of women prisoners were sentenced and one-quarter detained on remand. Eight women were on life sentences and one on an indeterminate sentence. Over one-third of convicted women were on sentences of less than two years (CJINI 2013: 55). Once again the inspectorates concluded that it was 'wrong to run a female prison at the margins of an overwhelmingly male environment' and the overall impact was 'fundamentally disrespectful' (CJINI 2013: vi).

The continued imprisonment of a small number of politically motivated women continues to raise human rights concerns. The imprisonment of prominent Irish republican prisoner Marian Price from 2011 until 2013 illustrates these concerns. During the 1970s, Marian had been imprisoned in England along with her sister Dolours, for their part in an IRA bombing campaign. During this imprisonment, both sisters were on hunger strike and were force fed on more than 400 occasions, which led to serious and persistent health problems (Moore and Scraton 2014). The sisters were transferred to Armagh Prison in 1974, and in 1980 Marian was released under a Royal Prerogative of Mercy due to life-threatening ill health (Moore and Scraton 2014). In 2011, Marian was returned to prison on licence (the legality of which was challenged by her lawyers) following her involvement in a republican commemoration. Demanding separation from 'ordinary' prisoners, Marian was initially held as the sole woman prisoner in Maghaberry, the isolated conditions of detention impacting severely on her mental and physical health.

In 2012, she was transferred to Hydebank Wood and again held in solitary conditions. Marian's health continued to deteriorate significantly, resulting in her transfer to a community-based mental health facility (Moore and Scraton 2014). Solitary confinement beyond 15 days has been declared to be cruel, inhuman or degrading treatment or punishment by UN Special Rapporteur on Torture, Mr Juan Mendez (United Nations General Assembly 2011) yet Marian had spent more than a year in isolation (Moore and Scraton 2014). Since her release, at least one other republican woman has been imprisoned in Hydebank Wood, yet there has been little official recognition of the issue of the imprisonment of politically motivated women.

The experiences of women in Ash House demonstrate their continued marginalisation within a male penal environment, and the persistence of gendered punishment. Numbers of female life-sentenced prisoners have grown, and the women's prison population has more than doubled since women were transferred from Mourne House. With around one-quarter of women on remand, and over one-third on short sentences, there is a clear need for alternatives to custody. The imprisonment of women with serious mental health problems also draws attention to the need for more appropriate responses to women's offending. The section below focuses on the government Strategy for dealing with women's offending (DoJ 2010) inspired Baroness Corston's (2007) review of vulnerable women within the criminal justice system in England and Wales.

Government Strategy and Community-Based Initiatives

Following Corston's report (2007), the Department of Justice (2010) in Northern Ireland developed a strategy to 'manage women offenders and those vulnerable to offending behaviour' [the Strategy]. This Strategy identified women's 'pathways' to offending as including homelessness, poverty, mental illness, addictions and experiences of violence and abuse and prostitution. Despite the acknowledgement of these structural issues, they were to be tackled largely on an individual basis, for example by encouraging women to be more 'motivated' about seeking employment (DoJ 2010: 29). Reflecting an individualistic and risk-focused framework, 'attitudes, thinking and behaviours' was also named as a 'pathway' with a commitment to develop gender-specific 'offending behaviour programmes' including anger management (DoJ 2010: 39). When identifying 'pathways', the Strategy did not consider the context of communal violence, sectarianism or conflict and nor did it adequately address 'how appropriate, accessible and effective resources, services and support for women', would be provided in a context of scare resources, including very limited mental health provision (Convery 2013: 169).

Core to the Strategy was the development of the Inspire Women's Project, for women under probation supervision, those awaiting pre-sentence reports and a small number on day release from prison. In October 2008, Inspire opened with a caseload averaging 150 women, of whom 16 had served prison sentences. Programmes on alcohol and drugs, victim awareness, individual counselling, offence-focused work, restorative practice, creative arts, and support with employment were provided in cooperation between Probation and external community agencies. Unlike comparative initiatives, for example the 218 Service in Scotland (Beglan 2013), Inspire did not facilitate self-referral by women who had not been processed through the criminal justice system. The first evaluation of Inspire (Easton and Matthews 2011) identified much good practice, with the benefits of this women-only environment praised by clients and practitioners alike. Few criticisms were made, but the evaluation did raise questions about the capacity of some community-based groups to respond appropriately to 'criminogenic' issues and noted that some key agencies, including housing and mental health authorities and the police, had yet to engage effectively with the project. Moreover, women were aware that failure to engage effectively could result in being returned to court and some felt stigmatised by the connection to Probation. Participation was sometimes difficult for women with mental health problems and addictions. Engagement with women's centres built useful connections with local communities, but a few women felt uneasy as to whether their privacy would be respected in this context (Easton and Matthews 2011).

The Strategy (DoJ 2010) promoted alternatives to prosecution and custody including police issued penalty notices, conditional cautions and electronic monitoring. However, as Convery (2013) states these were introduced in the absence of appropriate research on decision-making by criminal justice agencies regarding women's offending in Northern Ireland. A further initiative has been the introduction through the Criminal Justice (Northern Ireland) Order 2008 of Supervised Activity Orders piloted as a community-based alternative to imprisonment for fine default. Despite the introduction of such alternatives, as noted below, the female prison population remains significantly higher than a decade ago.

Social and political concerns led to the inclusion of a review of prison conditions within the multi-party Hillsborough Agreement (2010) which established the devolution of criminal justice and policing. This Agreement stipulated that there should be consideration of a women's prison, 'which is fit for purpose and meets international obligations' (Hillsborough Agreement 2010: 7). Headed by Dame Anne Owers, former Chief Inspector of Prisons for England and Wales, the independent Prison Review Team (PRT 2011) recognised the distortion of the prison system by the experience of conflict to the extent that it had become highly dysfunctional, with an over-emphasis on security and control and limited focus on prisoner rehabilitation or resettlement. The PRT recommended an early retirement scheme for long-serving staff, to facilitate the recruitment of more Catholic and female officers. It also recommended the establishment of a women's prison based on therapeutic principles for the small number of women convicted of serious and violent offences as well as the development of strategies aimed at decarceration with an emphasis on community-based punishments (PRT 2011). A Prison Review Oversight Group was established by the Minister of Justice to monitor progress on the implementation of the PRT recommendations.[4] At the time of writing, women remain imprisoned in the young male environment of Hydebank Wood, and levels of female imprisonment remain persistently high despite the introduction of alternatives. The conclusions which follow, include analysis of the imprisonment of women in Northern Ireland, as discussed in the preceding sections, in comparison with penal practices for women in other UK regions and globally. Having identified issues shared across jurisdictions, the discussion turns to the specific context of transition from conflict, citing relevant literature and identifying the key challenges raised by the failure to transform women's experiences of imprisonment during the transition process.

Women's Imprisonment and Alternatives to Custody within a Transitional Context

From Armagh, to Maghaberry and then Hydebank Wood, women's imprisonment in Northern Ireland has shared some fundamental characteristics with penal practice in other jurisdictions. Although the female prison population has remained small in comparison to men, levels have risen by approximately threefold within recent years: at the end of September 2014 there were 62 women in Hydebank Wood[5] in comparison to an average of 20 in Mourne House at the turn of the twenty-first century when the Criminal Justice Review (2000) reported. Explanations for the increase include high levels of custodial remand and the use of short sentences; however, the number of life-sentenced and long-term women prisoners has also risen. As acknowledged by research within the Great Britain and international contexts, women prisoners typically have vulnerabilities and histories of abuse, trauma and disadvantage, a high proportion having mental health difficulties (Mills et al 2013). Such problems are often inadequately addressed within the penal context, and the isolation inherent in imprisonment may exacerbate mental health problems, leaving women re-traumatised and vulnerable to self-harm and suicide (Coles 2013). Successive inspection, monitoring and independent research reports, as cited above, have commented on the significant health and mental health needs of women in prison in Northern Ireland: needs not appropriately met either within the community or penal contexts. Carlen's (1983) study of social control within the Scottish female prison context is mirrored by the findings of the

[4] Department of Justice, 'Ford Appoints Members to Prisons Reform Oversight Group', 14 November 2014, available at www.dojni.gov.uk/ford-appoints-members-to-prisons-reform-oversight-group. See also the Prison Review Oversight Group Reports, available at www.dojni.gov.uk/index/ni-prison-service/nips-prison-review-oversight-group-reports.htm.

[5] See Department of Justice, *Population Statistics 01 July 2013 to 30 September 2014*, available at www.dojni.gov.uk/index/ni-prison-service/nips-population-statistics-2/population-statistics-01-july-2013-30-sept-2014.htm.

Human Rights Commission's reports on Mourne House, Maghaberry (Scraton and Moore 2005) and Ash House, Hydebank Wood (Scraton and Moore 2007) which exposed regimes where women experienced discipline for petty offences and where being placed in isolation was the routine response to self-harm. As is the case in other jurisdictions, their small numbers left women prisoners in Northern Ireland marginalised and with restricted facilities and activities in comparison to male prisoners. The siting of women's prison units within male penal establishments, in breach of international human rights principles (CPT 2013) exacerbated the neglect of women's needs and exposed women to sexualised verbal abuse from male prisoners (Scraton and Moore 2007).

That women's imprisonment in Northern Ireland shares much in common with other jurisdictions is clear; however, the conflict also shaped the penal system, with prisons becoming 'ideological battlegrounds' (McEvoy 1998). Research has exposed the distinctly gendered characteristics of penal regimes within this context of violence, conflict and sectarianism, and resistance to regimes also took gendered forms (see Scraton and Moore 2005; Corcoran 2006). The development of rights-compliant criminal justice agencies was a key transitional demand within the Belfast/Good Friday Agreement (1998); however, the Criminal Justice Review (2000) erroneously assumed that the prison system would return to 'normal' following the early release of politically motivated prisoners and consequently failed to adequately address the urgency of penal reform. The failure to prioritise penal reform as a transitional project has contributed to the continuation of a system, which is 'over-focused on physical security, with excessive staffing levels, and where concessions to separated prisoners merely serve to highlight the deficiencies and inconsistencies in the regime for others' (PRT 2011: 6). Women prisoners—politically motivated and others—have been significantly impacted on by the dysfunctional nature of Northern Ireland's penal regimes. Whereas politically motivated women actively resisted criminalisation and punitive practices, women remanded or convicted of ordinary offences, especially those experiencing mental ill health, were more isolated and their agency seriously constricted (Moore and Scraton 2014).

Transitional justice discourse and practice has been criticised for the routine absence of gender awareness leading to a failure to understand the needs of women and children who are among the most affected by conflict and with least resources (Ní Aoláin 2006). In discussing the deep 'conceptual exclusion' of women, Bell and O'Rourke (2007: 23) note a 'growing feminist unease with the "from" (male-defined political violence) and "to" (liberal democratic frameworks) of transitional justice discourse' (2007: 24). Some developments have been made regarding truth recovery processes with the potential to have a positive impact for women (Orford 2006; Ní Aoláin 2006; Bell and O'Rourke 2007). However, as Bell and O'Rourke (2007: 24) argue, it remains a priority to reform transitional justice mechanisms so as to address women's needs. The marginalised position of women prisoners has been discussed in some detail above, and the Criminal Justice Review (2000) neglected to seriously address the issue. The Hillsborough

Agreement (2010) was unusual among transitional agreements in acknowledging the issue of women's imprisonment. Timely implementation of the Prison Review Team's recommendations is needed to ensure that the commitment to respect for women's rights becomes more than a promise on paper. Despite the Justice Minister's announcement of a new women's prison,[6] at the time of writing women remain incarcerated within a primarily male environment at Hydebank Wood in breach of their rights.

Transitional justice includes both backward and forward facing aspects, and processes aimed at achieving truth recovery and justice for victims and survivors are necessary in order that society may come to terms with the legacy of conflict (Hayner 2010). While acknowledging differences in approach, Sandoval Villalba (2011) identifies four core features of transitional processes which are: bringing perpetrators to justice for past wrongdoing; reparation and redress for victims; truth recovery; and reform of key institutions to protect against future rights abuse. The violation of women's rights in prison raises the questions of what constitutes victimhood and whether 'offenders' can simultaneously be 'victims', including of the prison system. Knox (2001) found routine denial of the status of victimhood for young people subjected to paramilitary 'punishment' attacks for alleged anti-social behaviour. McEvoy and McConnachie (2013: 493) also concluded that 'drug addicts, prisoners (or indeed former prisoners), prostitutes and other social groupings who themselves may have been involved in criminality are troublesome victims in terms of public discourse'. Given their extensive social, economic and health needs (Bloom and Covington 1998) women in prison may be simultaneously 'offender' and 'victim', requiring us to acknowledge the complexity of these labels. Despite the requirement within transitional justice discourse to deal with past breaches of rights and provide justice and redress for victims, and an increasing emphasis on the importance of acknowledging the issue of gender-based violence in transitional processes, there has been a lack of accountability regarding the violations of women's rights in Armagh, Maghaberry or Hydebank Wood and the Northern Ireland Human Rights Commission's demand for an inquiry (Scraton and Moore 2005) has not been met.

In response to legalistic interpretations, focused mainly on civil and political rights (for example, rights to fair trial and to freedom from abuse within the criminal justice system), critical theorists have argued for a 'deeper', 'thicker' transitional justice with a strong emphasis on social and economic rights and local and community participation (McEvoy 2007; Pasipanodya 2008). As noted within the recent Haass proposals, 'the first requirement of any comprehensive treatment of the legacy of the past must be to provide for the social and health needs of victims and survivors' (Haas 2013). Hamber (2003) observes that if transitional processes fail to address social and economic inequality, this may lead to an experience

[6] *BBC News*, 'Ford Announces New Jail to be Built on Magilligan Site', 19 March 2013, available at www.bbc.co.uk/democracylive/northern-ireland-21843521.

similar to that in South Africa where 'despite constitutional commitments to equality, social stability has involved the reassertion of power and advantage by those elites who benefited most from the apartheid regime' (cited in Ní Aoláin and Rooney 2007: 348). As articulated by Laplante (2008: 332) 'post-conflict recovery entails a holistic approach that should include economic, political and social structural reform'. Yet as former United Nations High Commissioner for Human Rights, Louise Arbour (2006) notes, social and economic rights are often viewed as aspirations rather than as entitlements.

Underpinning transitional justice studies is the defining feature of transition as a movement between a previously oppressive, dictatorial or illegitimate regime towards a democratic and just society (Teitel 2000). As Lundy and McGovern (2008: 273) observe, the notion of transition 'tends to involve a particular and limited conception of democratization and democracy based on liberal and essentially Western formulations of democracy', thus ignoring the problem that 'human rights abuses may continue to take place in circumstances where in theory at least, the norms of liberal democratic accountability prevail'. Much transitional justice discourse uncritically accepts the end goal of a liberal democratic 'rule of law' including the creation of modern, professional, and rights-compliant institutions—including police and prisons. Yet as Sharp (2013: 151) argues, without the reconfiguring of power relationships and steps to tackle inequality and injustice, transitional justice may be a 'paradigm closely associated with transitions to liberal market democracy'. Devolved governance in Northern Ireland has been developed within a neo-liberal model that perpetuates social exclusion and sectarian division (Murtagh and Shirlow 2012). Within this context the various 'pathways' to women's offending are predominantly viewed as individual failings or misfortune. Gender-sensitive programmes are important in providing support for individual women, but do not challenge the structural inequality and disadvantage endemic in neo-liberal democracies.

The 'once in a generation' opportunity for change offered by the transition process (PRT 2011: 7) gives the opportunity for Northern Ireland to 'lead the way among jurisdictions in pursuing a decarceration strategy' (Wahidin et al 2012: 470) and rights-based legislation and policy. For the Prison Review Team (PRT 2011: 9) reform of the prison system is 'an essential part of the move to a normalised society', yet as Scraton and McCulloch (2009) remind us even 'normal' prisons are built on a continuum of violence that ranges from routine procedures such as strip-searching and lock-up, through to actual physical violence and attacks on prisoners. Rather than pursuing 'normalised' prisons, therefore, we argue that the transition process provides an opportunity to reimagine ways of responding to social harms, advocating a decarceration strategy underpinned by the principles of social justice. Such a challenge requires a vision based on social justice which addresses the structural basis of the 'pathways to offending' through provision of adequate public housing and employment, effective education and training, and appropriate health and mental health and trauma services. It involves also tackling the culture of masculinity within which much violence against women occurs.

References

Arbour, L (2006) 'Economic and Social Justice for Societies in Transition' (Second Annual Transitional Justice Lecture hosted by the Center for Human Rights and Global Justice at New York University School of Law and by the International Center for Transitional Justice, October 2006).

Aretxaga, B (1997) *Shattering Silence: Women, Nationalism, and Political Subjectivity in Northern Ireland* (Princeton, NJ, Princeton University Press).

Beglan, M (2013) 'The 218 Experience' in M Malloch and G McIvor (eds), *Women, Punishment and Social Justice: Human Rights and Penal Practices* (London, Routledge).

Belfast/Good Friday Agreement (1998) *The Agreement Reached in the Multi-Party Negotiations* (Belfast, Northern Ireland Office).

Bell, C and O'Rourke, C (2007) 'Does Feminism Need a Theory of Transitional Justice? An Introductory Essay' 1 *International Journal of Transitional Justice* 23.

Bloom, B and Covington, S (1998) 'Gender-specific Programming for Female Offenders: What is it and Why is it Important?' (50th Annual Meeting of the American Society of Criminology, Washington DC, November 1998).

Brady, E, Patterson, E, McKinney, K, Hamill, R, and Jackson, P (2011) *In the Footsteps of Anne Devlin: Stories of Republican Women Ex-prisoners* (Belfast, Shanaway Press).

Carlen, P (1983) *Women's Imprisonment: A Study in Social Control* (London, Routledge & Kegan Paul).

Carlton, B and Segrave, M (2011) 'Women's Survival Post-imprisonment: Connecting Imprisonment with Pains Past and Present' 13 *Punishment & Society* 551.

——(eds) (2013) *Women Exiting Prison: Critical Essays on Gender, Post-Release Support and Survival* (London, Routledge).

Carlen, P and Worrall, A (2004) *Analysing Women's Imprisonment* (Cullompton, Willan Publishing).

Coles, D (2013) 'Deaths of Women in Prison: The Human Rights Arising' in M Malloch and G McIvor (eds), *Women, Punishment and Social Justice: Human Rights and Penal Practices* (London, Routledge).

Committee Against Torture (CAT) (2004) *Conclusions and Recommendations of the Committee against Torture* (CAT/C/CR/33/3).

Committee for the Prevention of Torture and Inhuman or Degrading Treatment or Punishment (CPT) (2013) *CPT Standards CPY/Inf/E (2002) I-Rev.2013* (Strasbourg, Council of Europe).

Convery, U (2013) 'An Offending Strategy: The State's Response to Women within the Criminal Justice System in Northern Ireland' in M Malloch and G McIvor (eds), *Women, Punishment and Social Justice: Human Rights and Penal Practices* (London, Routledge).

Corcoran, M (2006) *Out of Order: The Political Imprisonment of Women in Northern Ireland 1972–1998* (Cullompton, Willan Publishing).

Corston, J (2007) *The Corston Report: A Review of Women with Particular Vulnerabilities in the Criminal Justice System* (London, Home Office).

Criminal Justice Inspection Northern Ireland (CJINI) (2010) *Northern Ireland Prison Service Corporate Governance Arrangements* (Belfast, CJINI).

—— (2011) *Report on an unannounced short follow-up inspection of Hydebank Wood Women's Prison, 21–25 March 2011* (Belfast, CJINI).

—— (2013) *Report on an announced inspection of Hydebank Wood Women's Prison, 18–22 February 2013* (Belfast, CJINI).

Criminal Justice Review Group (CJRG) (2000) *Review of the Criminal Justice System in Northern Ireland: The Report of the Criminal Justice Review* (Belfast, HMSO).

Department of Justice (DoJ) (2010) *A Strategy to Manage Women Offenders and those Vulnerable to Offending Behaviour 2010–2013* (Belfast, DoJ).

Easton, H and Matthews, R (2011) *Evaluation of the Inspire Women's Project* (London, South Bank University).

Eaton, M (1993) *Women after Prison* (Milton Keynes, Open University Books).

Fairweather, E, McDonagh, R and McFadyean, M (1984) *Only the Rivers Run Free: Northern Ireland—The Women's War* (London, Pluto Press).

Gelsthorpe, L and Morris, A (2002) 'Women's Imprisonment in England and Wales' 2 *Criminal Justice* 277.

Gil-Robles, A (2005) *Report on Visit to the UK 4–12 November 2004* (Strasbourg, Office of the Commissioner for Human Rights).

Gormally, B, McEvoy, K and Wall, D (1993) 'Criminal Justice in a Divided Society: Northern Ireland Prisons' 17 *Crime and Justice* 51.

Haas, R (2013) *Proposed Agreement 31 December 2013: An Agreement among the Parties of the Northern Ireland Executive on Parades, Select Commemorations and Related Protests; Flags and Emblems; and Contending with the Past*, available at www.northernireland.gov.uk/haass.pdf.

Hamber, B (2003) 'Rights and Reasons: Challenges for Truth Recovery in South Africa and Northern Ireland' 26 *Fordham International Law Journal* 1074.

Hannah-Moffatt, K (2001) *Punishment in Disguise: Penal Governance and Canadian Women's Imprisonment* (Toronto, Toronto University Press).

Hayner, P (2010) *Unspeakable Truths: Transitional Justice and the Challenge of Truth Commissions*, 2nd edn (London, Routledge).

Her Majesty's Chief Inspector of Prisons (HMCIP) (1997) *Women in Prison: A Thematic Review* (London, Home Office).

—— (2003) *Report on a full announced inspection of HM Prison Maghaberry, 13–17 May 2002* (London, HM Inspectorate of Prisons).

Her Majesty's Chief Inspector of Prisons (HMCIP)/Criminal Justice Inspection Northern Ireland (CJINI) (2005) *Report on an unannounced inspection of the imprisonment of women in Northern Ireland, Ash House, Hydebank Wood Prison, 28–30 November 2004* (Belfast, HM Inspectorate of Prisons).

Hillsborough Agreement (2010) *Agreement at Hillsborough Castle* (Belfast, Northern Ireland Office).

Independent Monitoring Board (IMB) (2010) *Hydebank Wood Prison and Young Offenders Centre: Independent Monitoring Board's Annual Report for 2009/2010* (Belfast, IMB).

INQUEST (2013) *Preventing the Deaths of Women in Prison: The Need for an Alternative Approach* (London, INQUEST).

Knox, C (2001) 'The "Deserving" Victims of Political Violence: Punishment Attacks in Northern Ireland' 1 *Criminology & Criminal Justice* 181.

Laplante, LJ (2008) 'Transitional Justice and Peace Building: Diagnosing and Addressing the Socioeconomic Roots of Violence through a Human Rights Framework' 2 *International Journal of Transitional Justice* 331.

Lundy, P and McGovern, M (2008) 'Whose Justice? Rethinking Transitional Justice from the Bottom Up' 35 *Journal of Law and Society* 265.

Malloch, M and McIvor, G (eds) (2013) *Women, Punishment and Social Justice: Human Rights and Penal Practices* (London, Routledge).
Medlicott, D (2007) 'Women in Prison' in Y Jewkes (ed), *Handbook on Prisons* (Cullompton, Willan Publishing).
McCulloch, J and George, A (2009) 'Naked Power: Strip Searching Women in Prison' in P Scraton and J McCulloch (eds), *The Violence of Incarceration* (London, Routledge).
McEvoy, K (1998) 'Prisoner Release and Conflict Resolution: International lessons for Northern Ireland' 8 *International Criminal Justice Review* 33.
—— (2001) *Paramilitary Imprisonment in Northern Ireland: Resistance, Management, and Release* (Oxford, Oxford University Press).
—— (2007) 'Beyond Legalism: Towards a Thicker Understanding of Transitional Justice' 34 *Journal of Law and Society* 411.
McEvoy, K and McConnachie, K (2013) 'Victims and Transitional Justice: Voice, Agency and Blame' 22 *Social & Legal Studies* 489.
McIvor, G and Burman, M (2011) *Understanding the Drivers of Female Imprisonment in Scotland* (Stirling, Scottish Centre for Crime and Justice Research).
McMinn, K and O'Rourke, C (2012) *Baseline Study on UNSCR 1325: Women and Peacebuilding Toolkit—Sharing the Learning: Women and Peacebuilding Project* (EU, PEACE 111).
Mills, A, Kendall, K, Lathlean, J and Steel, J (2013) 'Researching the Mental Health Needs of Women in Prison: Problems and Pitfalls' in M Malloch and G McIvor (eds), *Women, Punishment and Social Justice: Human Rights and Penal Practices* (London, Routledge).
Moore, L and Scraton, P (2014) *The Incarceration of Women: Punishing Bodies, Breaking Spirits* (Basingstoke, Palgrave Macmillan).
Murray, R (1998) *Hard Time: Armagh Gaol, 1971–1986* (Dublin, Mercier Press).
Murtagh, B and Shirlow, P (2012) 'Devolution and the Politics of Development in Northern Ireland' 30 *Environment and Planning C: Government and Policy* 46.
Ní Aoláain, F (2006) 'Political Violence and Gender During Times of Transition' 15 *Columbia Journal of Gender and Law* 829.
Ní Aoláain, F and Rooney, E (2007) 'Under-enforcement and Intersectionality: Gendered Aspects of Transition for Women' 1 *International Journal of Transitional Justice* 338.
Northern Ireland Affairs Committee (NIAC) (2004) *The Separation of Paramilitary Prisoners at HMP Maghaberry, Second Report of Session 2003–2004* (London, The Stationery Office).
Northern Ireland Prison Service (NIPS) (2005) *The Reintegration Needs of Women Prisoners in Northern Ireland* (Belfast, NIPS).
—— (2010) *Gender-specific Standards for Working with Women Prisoners* (Belfast, NIPS).
Orford, A (2006) 'Commissioning the Truth' 15 *Columbia Journal of Gender and Law* 851.
Pasipanodya, T (2008) 'A Deeper Justice: Economic and Social Justice as Transitional Justice in Nepal' 2 *International Journal of Transitional Justice* 378.
Pickering, S (2002) *Women, Policing and Resistance in Northern Ireland* (Belfast, Beyond the Pale Publications).
Pollack, S (2008) *Locked In, Locked Out: Imprisoning Women in the Shrinking and Punitive Welfare State* (Ontario, Wilfred Laurier University).
Prison Review Team (PRT) (2011) *Review of the Northern Ireland Prison Service: Conditions, Management and Oversight of all Prisons. Final Report, October 2011* (Owers Report) (Belfast, Prison Review Team).

Prisoner Ombudsman for Northern Ireland (2012) *Report by the Prisoner Ombudsman into the circumstances surrounding the death of Frances McKeown who died whilst in the custody of Hydebank Wood Women's Prison on 4 May 2011 aged 23* (Belfast, Prisoner Ombudsman for Northern Ireland).

Sandoval Villalba, C (2011) *Briefing Paper—Transitional Justice: Key Concepts, Processes and Challenges* (Institute for Democracy and Conflict Resolution, University of Essex).

Scott, D and Codd, H (2010) *Controversial Issues in Prison* (Maidenhead, Open University Press/McGraw Hill).

Scraton, P and McCulloch, J (eds) (2009) *The Violence of Incarceration* (London, Routledge).

Scraton, P and Moore, L (2005) *The Hurt Inside: The Imprisonment of Women and Girls in Northern Ireland* (Belfast, NIHRC).

—— (2007) *The Prison Within: The Imprisonment of Women at Hydebank Wood 2004–2006* (Belfast, NIHRC).

Sharp, D (2013) 'Interrogating the Peripheries: The Preoccupations of Fourth General Transitional Justice' 26 *Harvard Human Rights Journal* 149.

Singleton, N, Meltzer, H and Gatward, R (1998) *Psychiatric Morbidity among Prisoners* (London, Office for National Statistics).

Shirlow, P, Graham, B, McEvoy, K, Ó hAdhmaill, F and Purvis, D (2005) *Politically Motivated Former Prisoner Groups: Community Activism and Conflict Transformation* (Belfast, Northern Ireland Community Relations Council).

Smith, C (2009) 'A Period in Custody: Menstruation and the Imprisoned Body' in *Internet Journal of Criminology.*

Steele, J (2004) *Review of Safety at HMO Maghaberry* (Belfast, Safety Review Team to Secretary of State for Northern Ireland) (Steele Review).

Stop the Strip-Searches Campaign (undated circa 1987) *Stop Strip Searching* (Dublin, Stop the Strip-Searches Campaign).

Sudbury, J (2005) *Global Lockdown: Race, Gender and the Prison-Industrial Complex* (New York, Routledge).

Teitel, R (2000) *Transitional Justice* (Oxford, Oxford University Press).

United Nations General Assembly (2011) *Interim Report of the Special Rapporteur of the Human Rights Council on Torture and other Cruel, Inhuman or Degrading Treatment or Punishment* A/66/268.

Wahidin, A (2004) *Older Women in the Criminal Justice System: Running Out of Time* (London, Jessica Kingsley).

—— (2015) *Ex-combatants, Gender and Peace in Northern Ireland: Women Political Protest and the Prison Experience* (London, Palgrave).

Wahidin, A, Moore, L and Convery, U (2012) 'Prisons and the Legacy of Conflict in Northern Ireland' in A Wahidin (ed), The Legacy of Conflict and the Impact on the Northern Irish Criminal Justice System' 51 *Howard Journal* 442.

14

Young People, Crime and Justice in Northern Ireland

DEENA HAYDON AND SIOBHÁN McALISTER

Introduction

Mirroring broader developments in criminology, within the field of youth justice there has been increased interest in the extent and impact of policy transfer in UK jurisdictions and the influence of devolution. Common themes underpinning approaches to those in conflict with the law or deemed 'at risk' of offending include a 'culture of crime control' (Garland 2001), the criminalisation of social policy (Rodger 2008) and the expansion of 'risk focused prevention' (Farrington 2007). Goldson and Muncie (2006: x) argue that, while there is some distinction, Scotland and Northern Ireland have adopted comparable priorities to England and Wales in that:

> Politically derived anxieties and the steadily developing conflation of 'crime', 'disorder' and 'anti-social behaviour' is similarly serving to legitimise expanding and diversifying modes of intervention, regulation and governance targeted especially at troublesome, or potentially troublesome, children and young people.

Regardless of declining crime rates in England and Wales (ONS 2013), Scotland (Scottish Government 2014) and Northern Ireland (Campbell and Cardogan 2013), there has been a persistent 'obsession with the crimes of the young and a growing number of programmes aimed at identifying and targeting potential offenders' (Armstrong 2006: 269). Media and political discourses reinforce unfounded concerns about youth crime and negative stereotyping has resulted in the vulnerabilities of young people being overridden by their representation as 'threats' or 'problems' requiring greater control (see Hendrick 2006). Kemshall (2008: 22) notes that the problematisation of youth has produced a 'blurring of social policy and crime policy in which *social* problems are reframed as *crime* problems and crime control strategies are increasingly deployed to manage intractable social ills'.

The ideology and politics of risk upon which these trends are based have been traced across the penal and welfare systems of many Western societies, demonstrating the regulation of marginalised populations (Pollack 2010). Grounded in the process of 'responsibilisation', UK welfare and justice practices have promoted self-regulation to 'correct' behaviours defined as 'risky', 'harmful', 'anti-social' or 'offending' (see Kemshall 2010). For those in conflict with the law, interventions have focused on provision of additional support to help the individual 'self-regulate' or more coercive disciplinary techniques aimed at the child, young person or their parents (Sharland 2006: 255).

Despite some commonalities, the policies and practices of individual countries or jurisdictions are affected by their political economies (Downes 2012) and historical, social and cultural contexts (Muncie 2011). A focus on specific youth justice systems reveals the basis upon which broader trends have been 'challenged, rebranded, versioned, adapted or resisted' (Muncie 2011: 41). Criminal justice reform can be 'a key element of the nation-building narrative' (Muncie 2011: 41). This is particularly pertinent for Northern Ireland, a society in transition from conflict and in the process of re-imaging itself on the world stage. While policy transfer from Westminster has undoubtedly had an impact on youth justice in Northern Ireland, key reforms demonstrate the uniqueness of a system informed by the legacy of conflict and experience of conflict transformation.

This chapter outlines the evolution of youth justice policy as Northern Ireland emerged from the imposition of 'direct rule' to devolution, examining three specific forms of state intervention—early intervention targeting those 'at risk' of offending, restorative justice, and imprisonment—while also noting the non-state interventions experienced by many children and young people. Drawing out comparisons with England and Wales where relevant, the chapter considers what is unique about policy and practice in Northern Ireland and assesses whether claims made about implementation of human rights standards match the reality of young people's experiences.

Young People, Crime and Justice in Northern Ireland: 1990s–2014

Prior to devolution, welfare and criminal justice policy in Northern Ireland generally mirrored developments in England. Although the youth justice system was 'protected' from the counterterrorist and security-focused nature of the broader criminal justice system during Northern Ireland's conflict (O'Mahony and Campbell 2006), poor relationships between communities and state agencies, including the police, meant that these lacked legitimacy and thus (potentially) effectiveness (Doak and O'Mahony 2011).

Lack of trust in the police within some communities led to a 'crime prevention vacuum' (O'Mahony and Campbell 2006: 100), prompting the emergence of community-based forms of regulation and control in which paramilitary organisations provided 'protection' from external threats and ensured 'appropriate' behaviour through warnings, exiling, public humiliation, beatings and shootings targeted at those accused of criminal, 'anti-social' or 'anti-community' behaviour (Smyth et al 2004). Young people under the age of 25 accounted for the largest proportion of those experiencing such punishments (Knox 2002). At the same time, suspicion towards statutory agencies and state institutions led to a strong community and voluntary sector, which offered community-based alternatives to these forms of 'rough justice' (see the chapter by Eriksson in this volume). Primarily diversionary in nature, evaluation has highlighted the perceived value of these schemes (Mika 2006). However, they have only operated in a few communities and promotion of their success masks the 'informal' justice which continues in some neighbourhoods.

Recognising need for change as part of the conflict transformation process, the 1998 Good Friday/Belfast Agreement included commitment to a wide-ranging review of policing and criminal justice intended to embed human rights, accountability and transparency into all institutions and practices (see the chapter by Harvey in this volume). While children and young people were not a major focus of the Agreement, emphasis on 'human rights for all' equally applied to them. The subsequent Criminal Justice Review (2000) detailed the international human rights instruments bearing on youth justice arrangements. Proposing that the youth justice system 'pay particular regard to the provisions of the United Nations Guidelines for the Prevention of Juvenile Delinquency, and the duty to regard the best interests of the child as a primary consideration under Article 3 of the United Nations Convention on the Rights of the Child' (UNCRC), it noted the merit of enshrining this principle in future juvenile justice legislation (CJRG 2000: 237).

Many of the Criminal Justice Review Group's recommendations were legislated within the Justice Act (Northern Ireland) 2002 which, consistent with the Crime and Disorder Act 1998 in England and Wales, established that the 'principal aim of the youth justice system is to protect the public by preventing offending by children'.[1] Those exercising functions in relation to the youth justice system are expected to encourage children to 'recognise the effects of crime and to take responsibility for their actions'[2] while also considering the welfare of children with a view to 'furthering their personal, social and educational development'.[3] Although an important counter to the responsibilising agenda, this welfare orientation does not establish the best interests of the child as the *primary* consideration.

After many years of policy development within the context of direct rule, the Hillsborough Castle Agreement led to the devolution of policing and criminal justice powers and the establishment of Northern Ireland's Department of Justice in 2010. Included among this Agreement's priorities was a review of how children and young people are processed at all stages of the criminal justice system to ensure compliance with international obligations and best practice (Hillsborough Agreement 2010: section 1, paragraph 7). Incorporation of the best interests

[1] Justice Act (Northern Ireland) 2002, pt 4, s 53(1).
[2] ibid, s 53(2).
[3] ibid, s 53(3).

principle into the aims of the youth justice system was again advised, alongside a further 30 substantive recommendations (YJRT 2011: 10–14 and 113–18).

The Youth Justice Agency (YJA) was established by the Justice Act (Northern Ireland) 2002. In addition to custodial provision for 10- to 17-year-olds, the YJA provides a range of services to implement the disposals incorporated into the 2002 Act. Youth justice initiatives in Northern Ireland now encompass responses including: early intervention programmes to prevent offending; civil Anti-Social Behaviour Orders; diversionary measures;[4] community-based restorative justice schemes; various non-custodial disposals;[5] and custody. The following sections outline how the local context has informed developments in Northern Ireland, exploring key tensions between policy principles and practice concerning early intervention, restorative justice, custody and 'informal' justice.

Early Intervention

As in Britain, prevention and early intervention have been prioritised in Northern Ireland social policy since the late 1990s. 'Prevention' services available through universal provision are intended to stop problems arising in the first place, while 'early intervention' is expected to limit the development of evident problems by targeting assistance at those considered 'vulnerable' or 'at risk' of 'negative' outcomes (see Statham and Smith 2010). Significantly, in Northern Ireland emphasis has been placed on a 'whole child', 'family support' based approach to addressing children's needs *and rights* (see McTernan and Godfrey 2006). In contrast with the emphasis in England on reducing 'negative' outcomes and managing 'risk' (see Turnbull and Spence 2011), promotion of positive outcomes is prioritised (see, for example, OFMdFM 2006). Reference in policy and practice to children 'at risk' generally relates to 'child protection' concerns, with those requiring additional support more often defined 'vulnerable' (Haydon 2014).

Attempts to instigate punitive, mandatory 'support' targeting young people deemed 'at risk of offending' and 'the most troublesome families' (Northern Ireland

[4] All decisions regarding diversion are within the remit of the Public Prosecution Service which, following advice from the Police Service of Northern Ireland (PSNI), YJA and others can impose one of three disposals (which are incremental): informal warning, restorative caution, and diversionary youth conference. Before a diversionary measure can be considered there has to be a clear admission of guilt, the offence must not be considered serious, and the young person must not be deemed a persistent offender. Although not a conviction, a record is kept on the young person's criminal record for 12 months for an informal warning and 2.5 years for a restorative caution or diversionary youth conference.

[5] The range of non-custodial disposals available for 10- to 17-year-olds includes: Probation Order, Community Service Order (16+), Combination Order (16+). Community-based measures (implemented by the YJA) include: an Attendance Centre Order, a Community Responsibility Order, a Reparation Order and a Youth Conference Order.

Office 2008: 30) have been resisted by the devolved Department of Justice (DoJ). It has defined interventions during the early years and key transition periods as 'positive child-focused support services rather than "crime prevention" strategies', in which the justice system is intended to play 'a supportive role' (DoJ 2012: 16). Among those consulted during an inspection of early youth interventions there was consensus that criminal justice agencies should jointly fund early intervention programmes and be able to refer young people, although it was agreed that the justice sector 'should engage in a non-direct way' to avoid stigmatisation or bringing young people further into the criminal justice system and that the family support model was more appropriate (CJINI 2012a: viii).

The Youth Justice Review Team (YJRT) (2011: 35) recommended delivery of early intervention services 'on the ground by trusted voluntary agencies working in partnership with universal service providers such as health and education'. In 2013, the Department of Justice produced a *Strategic Framework for the Prevention of Offending*. Highlighting need for government commitment to address the root causes of offending, it stated that this extended beyond the criminal justice system. This Framework includes the core principles of 'respect for human rights', 'prevention and early intervention' (DoJ 2013).

In practice, similar to pre-crime interventions targeting children in England and Wales (see Armstrong 2004: 103–04), an 'Early Intervention for the Prevention of Offending Programme' (the Programme) was introduced in Northern Ireland in 2008. Research conducted during 2010 with those delivering the Programme highlighted implicit tensions between welfare and justice priorities. Contrasting with policy emphasis on addressing 'vulnerability' or 'need', this Programme targeted 8- to 13-year-olds deemed '*at risk of offending*' and their families. Despite intended outcomes emphasising the personal and social development, well-being and educational progress of referred children, plus increased access to support for their parents, *prevention of offending* was prioritised in the Programme title and longer-term objectives (SHSSB 2007).

Demonstrating the influence of the 'risk factor prevention paradigm', linking antecedent risk factors with potential involvement in offending (see Farrington 1996), 'risk and protective factors' grouped under specific domains (individual, family, school, community) formed the criteria for referral in four of the five projects established by the NGOs commissioned to deliver the Programme (Haydon 2014). However, practitioners highlighted the difficulty of separating children 'in need' from those 'at risk of offending'. The majority of those referred to the Programme were *not* known to the police but experiencing a range of significant issues in their family, school and community. Project staff suggested that the capacity of their parents to provide appropriate care and socialisation was 'compromised' by previous experience of abuse, domestic violence, bereavement, depression and poor mental health, substance use, poverty and social isolation, illustrating how extensive welfare 'needs' have been redefined as 'criminogenic risk factors'. Although they described their work as non-stigmatising, strengths-based support to children and their parents, practitioners acknowledged that use of offending-related risk factors as referral criteria was 'almost criminalising, in a way, a *helping* process' (Haydon 2014: 6).

The risk factor domains in intervention referral and screening tools include the child's social and economic circumstances, yet assessments focus on the individual's attitudes and behaviour. For practitioners delivering Northern Ireland's 'Early Intervention for the Prevention of Offending Programme', the behaviours triggering a referral were perceived as symptomatic of unmet need. Poverty, 'informal' regulation in communities, unnecessary police monitoring of children in public spaces, 'normalisation' of interpersonal and inter-community violence were recognised as significant issues. Practitioners raised concern about the child's behaviour becoming the focus of attention, but programmes of work with individuals mainly concentrated on helping them develop strategies to change their behaviour and 'get on better' with family members or friends—reinforcing self-regulation by the child rather than addressing the broader social, cultural and economic factors affecting their circumstances and opportunities (Haydon 2014).

Case (2006: 173) argues that the 'welfare-oriented and rights-based provision of universal and needs-based' services has been 'undermined by the retrenchment of the welfare state and the burgeoning popularity of deficit models, which target interventions on the most "at risk", failing, and, by implication, most likely to offend, young people'. However, involvement in 'anti-social' or 'offending' behaviour is just one *potential* outcome for those identified as requiring early intervention. Classification of children and young people as either 'vulnerable', 'troubled' *non-offenders* who require 'care and protection' or 'troublesome' (potential) *offenders* who require greater regulation and support to change their behaviour leads to a loss of focus on the individual child and the common needs of both groups (Goldson 2000a; McGhee and Waterhouse 2007).

At a legislative level, the Children (NI) Order 1995 actually incorporates those 'at risk of offending' within the remit of children 'in need' as authorities are expected to take steps to reduce proceedings, including criminal proceedings, and encourage children not to commit criminal offences.[6] In Northern Ireland, and England and Wales, removal of 'prevention of offending' from the remit of the youth justice system, together with raising the age of criminal responsibility from 10 to 16 in line with other social responsibilities, would commit early intervention and diversion to welfare priorities. Thus, children's 'problematic' behaviour would be viewed 'as a symptom of disadvantage and need, rather than indicative of criminality; as a failure of society and responsible adults rather than of the individual child' (Bateman 2012). In this, more onus would be placed on parents, community members, teachers, health professionals, youth and community workers identifying the child or young person's personal, social, educational and material needs and/or the causes of 'problematic' behaviour with the aim of providing appropriate support to meet their developmental needs and well-being. This may include helping individuals understand the impacts of and take responsibility for

[6] Children (NI) Order 1995, sch 2, art 8(a)(ii) and (b).

their behaviours and actions, but within the context of recognising their evolving capacities, ensuring their entitlements to ongoing care and protection, promoting their participation and social inclusion.

Restorative Justice

Linked to preventative early intervention is the promotion of diversion from the criminal justice system for children and young people involved in the early stages of 'anti-social' or 'criminal' behaviour. While restorative justice approaches exist elsewhere, they are at the centre of the youth justice system and its philosophy in Northern Ireland, largely informed by community models in existence prior to devolution. Grounded in and reflective of a society emerging from conflict, methods of conflict resolution (such as mediation and dialogue) have been adapted for use in the criminal justice setting (McVie 2011; Muncie 2011). Doak and O'Mahony (2011: 311) note, for example, the paradigmatic overlap between the principles of transitional justice and restorative justice: 'truth, accountability, reparation, reconciliation, conflict resolution and democratic participation'.

The Justice Act (Northern Ireland) 2002 formalised restorative justice approaches by integrating youth conferences into the youth justice system. As the main non-custodial disposal, referrals to the Youth Conference Service (YCS) can take two forms—diversionary (ie, diverted from court on the recommendation of the Public Prosecution Service) or court ordered.[7] Intended to be victim and community-orientated, and restorative in ethos, a youth conference typically entails one or a series of meetings between the young person, their parent or an appropriate adult, the victim or a representative, a police officer and a youth conference coordinator (who will have met the victim and young person separately in advance to prepare for the meeting).[8] The expectation is that the young person is confronted with the impact of their behaviour and acknowledges any harm done. A Conference Plan is drawn up for the young person and agreed by all present. This comprises of actions intended to meet the needs of the victim and prevent further offending. A Diversionary Youth Conference Plan is presented for approval to the prosecutor while a plan resulting from a court ordered conference is subsequently agreed by the court and forms the basis of a Youth Conference Order.[9] Between 2007/08 and 2011/12, the number of young people each year receiving YCS referrals ranged from 1636 to 2012 (McAvoy 2012: 16).

Youth conferencing in Northern Ireland has been promoted as an example of international best practice. The Youth Justice Agency (2010: 12) define it as 'a world leader' in addressing youth crime, the concerns of victims and the safety of

[7] Justice Act (Northern Ireland) 2002, ss 58 and 59 respectively.
[8] ibid, pt 3A, s 57(2).
[9] ibid, ss 58 and 60 respectively.

communities 'in a balanced way', while the Youth Justice Review Team (2011: 12) describe it as offering 'an inclusive, problem-solving and forward-looking response to offending in which the victim plays an important role'. Reviewing the English youth justice system, the Independent Commission on Youth Crime and Antisocial Behaviour (2010) recommended consideration of Northern Ireland's restorative model to see what lessons could be learned. While Northern Ireland has often been subject to policy transfer 'in' from England, the restorative approach is an example of policy transferred 'out'.

In terms of critique, evaluation has noted the satisfaction of victims (Campbell et al 2005) and lower rates of reoffending in comparison with other disposals (YJRT 2011: 15). However, questions have been raised about the philosophical approach and its impact. Reporting mixed experiences of the process and long-term outcomes, some young people have found the youth conference to be positive and associated it with desistance from offending while others have described the experience as oppressive, punitive and shaming (Maruna et al 2007). Despite inclusionary aims, some report having limited input during meetings, finding the tone 'lecturing' and 'berating' (Maruna et al 2007: 3). Emphasis on acceptance of responsibility also led some to feel that the process was unfair because behaviour is often more complicated than implied by a focus on individual responsibility. Maruna et al (2007) note that such experiences may elicit feelings of frustration, resentment and defiance, resulting in the conference having no, or a negative, impact. Young people feeling that they have little choice but to accept rather than 'negotiate' the conference plan has also been highlighted as a concern (O'Mahony and Campbell 2006), raising questions about the extent to which restorative practices are truly inclusive. A consistent finding is that those who have experienced multiple youth conferences report limited impact (Maruna et al 2007; CJINI, 2008a).

While such disposals may be viewed as less punitive given their focus on diversion, restoration and alternatives to custody, Muncie (2008) cautions against assessing 'punitiveness' too narrowly. Eliaerts and Dumortier (2001) note that restorative justice can mask what are essentially punitive practices. The youth conference procedure and outcomes (ie, the duration of the conference plan and the requirements it places on an individual) can be experienced as punitive. Further, Snacken and Dumortier (2012: 4) argue that 'non-custodial sanctions, restorative justice or treatment programmes can also be "punitive" measures by their interference in the fundamental rights and freedoms of offenders'. Diversion from the criminal justice system is often assumed to be in the best interests of the child and more effective than processing individuals through the formal system. However, diversionary conferences are a diversion from court proceedings only. The young person has to admit guilt, agree to meet the victim and agree a plan. While a Diversionary Youth Conference is not classed as a criminal conviction, details of a recent conference will be disclosed under standard or enhanced criminal record checks (AccessNI 2014). A court ordered Plan is recorded on the young person's criminal record in the same way as any other court disposal.

Questions have also been raised about whether participation of the young person is really 'consensual', with anecdotal evidence from NGOs in Northern Ireland suggesting that children were not always aware their agreement to a Youth Conference Plan involved admission of guilt and a criminal record (Haydon 2008: 46). Commenting on experiences of the process in England and Wales, Hudson (2003) suggests that some young people, even if not guilty, may admit guilt and agree to a diversionary conference rather than face attending court—a situation confirmed by many who participated in an evaluation of the scheme in Northern Ireland during the mid-2000s (Doak and O'Mahony 2011: 318).

Alongside issues concerning procedural safeguards are deeper questions about whether restorative justice can fulfil its intended aims. Gray (2005) notes that in England, emphasis on responsibilisation detracts from the restorative potential. In Northern Ireland, the requirement to admit guilt and accept responsibility also demonstrates a strong responsibilising ethos. Thus, while restorative justice is grounded in multiple rationales (diversion, restoration, responsibilisation, reintegration), responsibilisation is most prominent (McAlister and Carr 2014; Gray 2005). As restorative justice measures do little to alter structural disadvantage or young people's experiences of social and economic marginalisation their reintegrative potential can be limited, hampering the long-term potential of diversion. These critical issues receive limited attention in policy accounts of restorative justice and youth conferencing in Northern Ireland.

In theory, early intervention programmes and youth conferencing represent efforts to divert young people from the criminal justice system, with custody reserved for the most serious and prolific offenders. The juvenile custodial population in Northern Ireland appears relatively low in comparison with other UK jurisdictions. However, as with early intervention and restorative justice, a deeper analysis reveals long-standing problems and the continued over-representation of disadvantaged and vulnerable young people in this population.

Custody

Hagell (2005: 157) notes that levels of custody 'do not necessarily reflect levels of juvenile crime nor do they particularly reflect evidence of its effectiveness'. Custody rates can be affected by political or financial priorities and policing practices, and reoffending is higher among those receiving custodial sentences than for those receiving pre-court disposals (Bateman 2013). Levels of custody have been identified as an area of divergence in UK youth justice policy. The 'rush to custody' and penal expansion that occurred in England and Wales (Goldson 2006) was not replicated in Northern Ireland where, following changes initiated by the introduction of the Criminal Justice (Children) (Northern Ireland) Order 1998 and the Criminal Justice Review in 2000, the number of young people held in custody has progressively fallen. While under-18s have been detained in Hydebank

Wood Young Offenders Centre, the focus of this chapter is detention in the Juvenile Justice Centre (JJC) for those who are sentenced, on remand, or held under Article 39 of the Police and Criminal Evidence (NI) Order 1989 (PACE), which was amended in 1998 to include a JJC as a 'place of safety' after arrest.

Northern Ireland's three JJCs[10] were reduced to one in 2003, comprising updated accommodation on the Rathgael site. This resulted in a decrease in the capacity of the system from 110 to 40 places for girls and boys, aged 10–17, of any religion (Kilkelly et al 2002: 4). The Rathgael Centre was superseded in 2007 by a newly built 'state-of-the-art' secure facility operated by the Youth Justice Agency. Woodlands JJC can hold up to 48 young people but is rarely full. In 2011/12 the average population was 28, the maximum was 36 (McAvoy 2012: 11). During that year the number of initial (new) admissions to the JJC was 400, of whom 347 (87 per cent) were male. Illustrating the continued over-representation of looked after children, 67 (17 per cent) of those initially admitted to the JJC were subject to a Care Order with a further 59 (15 per cent) from Voluntary Accommodation. The majority were aged 16–17 (33 per cent were 16, 34 per cent were 17) with 26 per cent aged 14–15 and 8 per cent aged 10–13 (McAvoy 2012: 11).[11]

As in England and Wales (see Bandalli 2000; Fortin 2009: 690–93), the rebuttable presumption of *doli incapax* for 10- to 13-year-olds was abolished in Northern Ireland under Article 3 of the Criminal Justice (Northern Ireland) Order 1998. The Justice Act (Northern Ireland) 2002 made provision for children aged 10–13 to serve a custodial sentence in secure accommodation but this provision has never been enacted. Although only one young person in this age group was sentenced to custody between 2007/08 and 2011/12, initial admissions to the JJC during 2011/12 included eighteen 10- to 13-year-olds under PACE and thirteen on remand (McAvoy 2012: 13).

The Criminal Justice (Children) (Northern Ireland) Order 1998 stipulates that a child or young person should be remanded in custody for public protection or if the alleged offence is serious. In 2011/12, remand to the JJC comprised 36 per cent of initial (new) admissions and 47 per cent of total admissions (ie, new admissions plus internal change of status such as movement from PACE to Remand or from Remand to Sentence) (McAvoy 2012: 11–12). Inappropriate use of remand has consistently been noted as a more pronounced problem in Northern Ireland

[10] The three Juvenile Justice Centres were all former Training Schools. St Patricks in West Belfast mainly held Catholic boys before being closed in November 2000. Rathgael in Bangor, Co Down, accommodated 'non Roman Catholic children' until the introduction of the Criminal Justice (Children) (Northern Ireland) Order in 1998 and then accommodated girls plus a small number of younger or vulnerable boys. St Patricks and Rathgael were open institutions, although both had some secure facilities. Lisnevin in Millisle, Co Down, was a secure centre built on the model of a Grade C prison and accommodated 25–30 boys of any religion. It closed in October 2003 (Kilkelly et al 2002: 4).

[11] Reflecting similar characteristics, during the same year in England and Wales 94 per cent of young people in custody were male and 96 per cent were aged 15–17 (MoJ/HO/YJB 2013: 38). Of the 15- to 18-year-olds detained in Young Offenders' Institutions in England and Wales during 2011/12 who responded to a survey by the Inspectorate of Prisons, 30 per cent had been looked after at some point (Murray 2013: 8).

than elsewhere in the UK (CJINI 2008b: vii; CJINI 2011: 4).[12] Criminal Justice Inspectors have highlighted that many remanded children are neither serious nor persistent offenders but 'troubled children' (CJINI 2008b: vii), most of whom are subsequently bailed and do not go on to serve a custodial sentence. According to the Youth Justice Review Team (2011: 55), 'the courts are using custodial remands wrongly—as a kind of "short, sharp, shock" or more benignly to secure the young person's safety'.

In 2011/12, 59 per cent of initial admissions to the JJC were via PACE (McAvoy 2012: 11). Given that these children generally stay for less than 24 hours, the Criminal Justice Inspectorate commented that this 'begs the value of admitting them to custody in the first place' (CJINI 2011: 4). The justification presented to inspectors was that JJC placements were used for some children 'in the absence of alternative accommodation when they presented chronic social problems' (CJINI 2011: 4). Use of PACE to remove disruptive children from care homes has been identified as a particular problem (CJINI 2008b). The Youth Justice Review Team (2011: 54) recommended development of an appropriate range of supported (if necessary) secure, accommodation which is accessible at short notice.

The number actually sentenced to custody is relatively low, representing a small proportion of those in the JJC.[13] The 'constant churn' (YJRT 2011: 76) of children passing through Woodlands is expensive, at around £4,000 per week for each child, and also causes significant disruption. Staff capacity to meet individual needs and address behaviour related to offending is affected by the accommodation of convicted and non-convicted children, aged from 10 to 17, detained for varying lengths of time, in the same facility. Unlike previous JJCs, the physical environment and facilities at Woodlands are modern and well designed. Those detained have access to high standards of education and health care (CJINI 2011), including programmes to address offending behaviour, specialist mental health services and health promotion. Young people value the safety and support provided by staff in the Centre (YJRT 2011: 75). However, while the JJC is a 'model of good practice' with a 'strong childcare ethos', it is 'fundamentally a custodial facility' (CJINI 2011: v). That some children consider themselves to be 'better off in the JJC than living at risk in the community or in residential care' (CJINI 2008b: 5) is an indictment of care and provision in their communities, and indicative of the difficulties they face before and after release.

As Goldson and Muncie (2008: 63) state, young offenders—particularly those in custody—are 'routinely drawn from some of the most disadvantaged, damaged and distressed families, neighbourhoods and communities'. Many have experienced an accumulation of deprivation and unmet needs (see Jacobson et al 2010). Young

[12] Young people on remand accounted for 24 per cent of the total population of young people in custody in England and Wales during 2011/12 (MoJ/HO/YJB 2013: 35).

[13] In 2011/12 the number of initial admissions sentenced to custody was 24 (6 per cent) while the number of total admissions who were sentenced was 53 (10 per cent) (McAvoy 2012: 11–12). The court is obliged to provide justification for each Juvenile Justice Order (a custodial sentence, half of which is served under supervision in the community).

people who have been in conflict with the law in Northern Ireland describe the impacts of exclusion or truancy from school, undiagnosed special educational needs, poor mental health, drug/alcohol/solvent use, lack of routine, few leisure opportunities, difficult family relationships, negative experiences of care, homelessness, and feeling marginalised and unsafe in their communities (Haydon 2009; Include Youth 2011a). The legacy of the conflict is an added dimension, leading to young people being both the victims and perpetrators of sectarian-related offences and experiencing actual or threatened regulation through 'informal' justice (CJINI 2012a: 10–11).

Given their vulnerabilities, the complex circumstances of their lives, and limited access to appropriate support in their communities, it is not surprising that some appreciate the routine, safety and individualised provision they receive while in custody, describing it as providing an opportunity to 'detox' and 'get fit' (McAlister and Carr 2014). Rather than indicating beneficial aspects of detention, this reveals the significant shortcomings of community-based welfare, health and education services. Since these are the communities to which young people return on release from custody, it also highlights the importance of holistic resettlement support which should be coordinated across the statutory, voluntary, community and private sectors to include: suitable accommodation in a community where the young person feels safe and comfortable; education, training and employment opportunities which are accredited and reasonably paid; access to counselling, substance misuse services and health care; constructive activities; personal development and preparation for independent living; ongoing support and guidance to help them achieve positive changes in their lives and deal with the difficulties they face (see Bateman et al 2013; Include Youth 2011b).

Informal Justice

The previous sections outline key issues concerning 'formal' interventions by, or on behalf of, state agencies. Yet some of the most marginalised young people continue to experience 'informal' regulation and punishment within their communities. Despite decommissioning of arms and the negotiated withdrawal of paramilitary activity, 'paramilitary-style' intimidation and violence are endemic in some communities. Of the 272 recorded casualties from 'paramilitary-style' shootings and attacks between January 2008 and December 2010, 47 per cent were young people under the age of 25 (PSNI 2011). This figure is likely to be an under-representation due to under-reporting. In 2008, the Northern Ireland Commissioner for Children and Young People expressed concern to the UN Committee on the Rights of the Child that punishment beatings against children and young people 'have not been traditionally dealt with as child abuse by relevant authorities' (UK Children's Commissioners 2008: 16).

The issue of informal regulation and punishment has consistently emerged in research with children and young people in Northern Ireland (see Roche 2008;

McAlister et al 2009; Harland 2011) yet is rarely the focus of literature on paramilitarism. Young people struggle with the morality of this form of control, perceiving it to be a particularly harsh and violent form of 'justice' applied disproportionately to them. However, in the absence of 'normal policing', some feel there is a need for internal regulation within communities (McAlister et al, 2009; Harland 2011). The impacts of 'double punishment' are most harshly felt by young offenders—punished formally within the youth justice system and also informally in their community (Haydon 2009; McAlister and Carr 2014).

Formal policing has also been experienced arbitrarily with young people reporting discrimination, antagonism and harassment (CJINI/NICCY 2007: 12) and being treated disrespectfully by police officers (McAlister et al 2009). The Youth Justice Review Team (2011: 39) commented that its discussions with young people suggested 'too many officers are still adopting a judgemental and prejudicial, even antagonistic attitude towards some of the young people they encounter'. While relations between young people and the police undoubtedly continue to be affected by family and community experiences during the conflict, negative representations of young people in media and political discourse also impact on their interactions.

The Northern Ireland Policing Board (NIPB 2011: 13–15) acknowledges that negative stereotyping 'feeds perceptions of anti-social behaviour', reinforcing the 'demonisation' of young people. Noting that perceptions rarely match the actual level of such behaviour in a community, it argues that negative stereotyping and inaccurate perception 'almost certainly results in increased numbers of reports and therefore an increased focus by the police in response' (NIPB 2011: 15). Since the introduction of civil Anti-Social Behaviour Orders to Northern Ireland in 2004, on average 41 per cent have been granted against young people aged under 18 (CJINI 2012b: 58), raising concerns about discriminatory use against young people and the potential for them to enter the criminal justice system via this route (CJINI 2012b: vii).

While young people's accounts often reveal high levels of monitoring and control—from parents, community members, the police and paramilitaries—the populist view is of a 'post-conflict generation' lacking guidance and regulation (McAlister et al, 2009). Their demonisation, however, underplays their status as victims of intolerance, harm and crime. Further, the rights agenda has not been extended to children and young people considered 'anti-social' by virtue of how and where they spend their free time, or those experiencing 'informal' justice within their communities.

Conclusion

Within the UK, 'distinctive approaches to youth justice' have been identified (Goldson and Hughes 2010: 215). Areas of divergence include differing outcomes (for example, in relation to rates of custody, use of diversionary and restorative methods, the minimum age of criminal responsibility) and dominant agendas broadly defined as 'risk' in England, 'welfare' in Scotland, 'restoration' in Northern Ireland and 'rights' in Wales. Points of convergence include policy discourses of 'youth crime prevention', 'early intervention', 'better integrated and co-ordinated provision', a shared 'commitment to target anti-social, as well as criminal, behaviour' and promotion of 'restorative justice' (Muncie 2011: 4). Significantly, all UK jurisdictions also 'ostensibly seek to comply with the benchmarks for practice' established by the UNCRC and European Convention on Human Rights (Muncie 2011: 43). However, these common priorities have been emphasised to different degrees in each jurisdiction, informed by the social, political, historical and cultural context at national and local levels.

Northern Ireland's commitment to criminal justice reform as part of the conflict transformation process has impacted significantly on the structure and philosophy of its youth justice system. Restorative justice, reflecting and potentially propelling 'the values of political transition' (O'Mahony et al 2012: 271), is now a central element of responses to young people in conflict with the law. Informed by the commitments of the Good Friday/Belfast Agreement, the rights discourse has been firmly embedded in reviews examining the criminal and youth justice systems. The language of rights and a *stated* commitment to achieving positive outcomes for all children and young people is evident in key policies (OFMdFM 2006; DHSSPS 2009; DoJ 2012, 2013). Yet effective implementation of rights-based policy has been minimal.

Given that the system of government in Northern Ireland involves a mandatory coalition of the five main political parties, securing and progressing shared priorities is difficult.[14] As there is 'no principle of collective responsibility', the result is often 'policy impasses' or a 'lowest common denominator approach' (Birrell 2011) with 'individual ministers presid[ing] over personal fiefdoms in which they can act with virtual impunity' (Carmichael and Osborne 2003: 213). Significantly, the Criminal Justice Inspectorate's first report monitoring progress in implementation of the 2011 Youth Justice Review recommendations found that 50 per cent of the 45 sub-recommendations showed limited or no progress (CJINI 2013: 7). Demonstrating the disjuncture between discourse and implementation, 14 years after the initial recommendation that the aims of the youth justice system should

[14] The 12 government departments in the Northern Ireland Executive are allocated using the D'Hondt system of proportional representation. Using a mathematical formula, departments are assigned one at a time beginning with the party gaining the highest total number of seats in the election. In June 2014, the First Minister was from the Democratic Unionist Party and the deputy First Minister was from the Republican Party Sinn Féin. The ministers for Health, Social Services and Public Safety; Finance and Personnel; Enterprise, Trade and Investment; and Social Development were from the Democratic Unionist Party. The ministers for Education; Agriculture and Rural Development; Culture, Arts and Leisure were from Sinn Féin. The ministers for Employment & Learning and Justice were from the Alliance Party; Environment was from the Social Democratic Labour Party; and Regional Development was from the Ulster Unionist Party.

include the 'best interests' principle, the Executive has drafted legislation with this objective.[15]

International standards explicitly define the rights to which all children, including those in conflict with the law, are entitled. General Comment No 10: Children's Rights in Juvenile Justice (UN Committee on the Rights of the Child 2007), provides a detailed statement of the relevant principles and provisions of the UNCRC and guidance about the measures required for a rights-based approach to the administration of youth justice. According to Kilkelly (2008: 191) standards concerning youth justice are 'too vague on detention as a last resort', 'too weak on the age of criminal responsibility', 'incomplete on the trial process, sentencing and serious crime', 'give states too many options—such as whether to divert children away from the criminal justice system to social services—without requiring them to do so' and, in the absence of effective enforcement mechanisms, states can ignore them. Despite these limitations, the standards 'are consistent with regard to a commitment to age-appropriate treatment, the importance of diversion and the imperative of rehabilitation' (Kilkelly 2008: 188).

Yet rights have an offensive as well as a defensive role (Tulkens 2012), acting 'as a bulwark against, but also a motor for, criminalisation' (Snacken and Dumortier 2012: 14). Under the remit of 'preventing offending', pre-emptive early intervention programmes can potentially label children at a young age and net widen: bringing to the attention of state agencies, including the police, those experiencing difficulties at home, in school and in their communities. This may actually be damaging in the longer term (McAra and McVie 2013). In Northern Ireland, policing interventions targeting children thought to be involved in 'anti-social' behaviour or 'sectarian rioting' on the basis of identifying those requiring support may in fact breach their rights (Haydon et al 2012). Packaged 'as a courtesy to the child', such interventions may 'criminalise the most structurally vulnerable children' (Goldson 2000b: 52) but also increase their susceptibility to 'informal' regulation and punishment. While negative representation of young people has been identified as an issue throughout the UK, the existence of quasi-paramilitaries who continue to regulate behaviour carries additional consequences in Northern Ireland. Focus on the risks or 'nuisance' posed by young people shifts emphasis away from the risks experienced by them and adult responsibility for ensuring their care, protection, development and well-being.

Ironically, promotion of human rights can lead to implementation of policies and practices which are actually experienced punitively and may contain fewer procedural safeguards than formal criminal justice processes (Eliaerts and Dumortier 2001). While restorative justice 'has become prominent in an era of rights' (Hudson 2003: 91), the potential for denial of rights to voluntary participation, legal assistance, due process protections and proportionality is concerning (Eliaerts and Dumortier 2001). These issues are particularly pertinent in Northern Ireland, where restorative approaches are a central element of the youth justice

[15] Justice Bill 2014, Pt 8, para 84.

system. Further, despite relatively low rates of youth imprisonment, custody is not being used as a last resort for those presenting a risk to themselves or others. Use of remand and PACE as a punishment, or because there is a gap in suitable alternative provision, is inappropriate and breaches international standards.

While it might be argued that Northern Ireland's youth justice system has 'benefited' from conflict transformation in ways that the systems of other conflict affected societies such as South Africa have not (see O'Mahony et al 2012), rights discourses have not always been translated into practice. Key Northern Ireland policies refer to respecting children's rights but, as in other UK jurisdictions, the UNCRC has not been incorporated into domestic legislation so its standards are not enforceable in courts. However, legal defence of rights implementation offers only one safeguard against current breaches. More significant is changing perceptions about children and young people—challenging negative stereotypes, separating rights from responsibilities, recognising and addressing individuals' needs and vulnerabilities. Fundamentally, this means responding to all under-18s as 'children', entitled to non-stigmatising support in which the primary consideration is the best interests of the child and the objective is their personal, social and educational development.

References

AccessNI (2014) *Filtering of Old and Minor Convictions and Routine Disclosures of Cautions and Other Disposals.* ANI Circular: 1/2014 (Belfast, DoJ).

Armstrong, D (2004) 'A Risky Business? Research, Policy, Governmentality and Youth Offending' 4 *Youth Justice* 100.

—— (2006) 'Becoming Criminal: The Cultural Politics of Risk' 10 *International Journal of Inclusive Education* 265.

Bandalli, S (2000) 'Children, Responsibility and the New Youth Justice' in B Goldson (ed), *The New Youth Justice* (Lyme Regis, Russell House Publishing).

Bateman, T (2012) *Criminalising Children for No Good Purpose: The Age of Criminal Responsibility in England and Wales*, available at www.thenayj.org.uk/wp-content/files_mf/criminalisingchildrennov12.pdf, 15.

—— (2013) *Children in Conflict with the Law. An Overview of Trends and Developments—2012*, available at www.thenayj.org.uk/wp-content/files_mf/nayjbriefingchildreninconflictwiththelaw1.pdf.

Bateman T, Hazel, N and Wright, S (2013) *Resettlement of Young People Leaving Custody: Lessons from the Literature* (London, Beyond Youth Custody).

Birrell, D (2011) 'Qualitative Research and Policy Making in Northern Ireland: Barriers Arising from Lack of Capacity, Conceptualisation and Consensus' Powerpoint, available at www.slideshare.net.

Campbell, P and Cardogan, G (2013) *Experiences of Crime: Findings from the 2012/13 Northern Ireland Crime Survey*, Research and Statistical Bulletin 8/2013 (Belfast, DoJ).

Campbell, C, Devlin, R, O'Mahony, D, Doak, J, Jackson, J, Corrigan, T and McEvoy, K (2005) *Evaluation of the Northern Ireland Youth Conference Service* (Belfast, Northern Ireland Office, Statistics and Research Branch).

Carmichael, P and Osborne, R (2003) 'The Northern Ireland Civil Service under Direct Rule and Devolution' 69 *International Review of Administrative Sciences* 205.
Case, S (2006) 'Young People "At Risk" of What? Challenging Risk-focused Early Intervention as Crime Prevention' 6 *Youth Justice* 171.
Criminal Justice Inspection Northern Ireland (CJINI) (2008a) *Inspection of the Youth Conference Service in Northern Ireland* (Belfast, CJINI).
—— (2008b) *Inspection of Woodlands Juvenile Justice Centre* (Belfast, CJINI).
—— (2011) *Announced inspection of Woodlands Juvenile Justice Centre* (Belfast, CJINI).
—— (2012a) *Early Youth Interventions. An Inspection of the Contribution the Criminal Justice Agencies in Northern Ireland Make to Preventing Children and Young People from Entering the Criminal Justice System* (Belfast, CJINI).
—— (2012b) *Anti-Social Behaviour. An Inspection of the Criminal Justice System's Approach to Addressing Anti-social Behaviour in Northern Ireland* (Belfast, CJINI).
—— (2013) *Monitoring of Progress on Implementation of the Youth Justice Review Recommendations* (Belfast, CJINI).
Criminal Justice Inspection Northern Ireland (CJINI) and Northern Ireland Commissioner for Children and Young People (NICCY) (2007) *The Handling of Complaints in the Criminal Justice System. A review of how the main Criminal Justice Organisations deal with complaints* (Belfast, CJINI/NICCY).
Criminal Justice Review Group (CJRG) (2000) *Review of the Criminal Justice System in Northern Ireland:* The Report of the Criminal Justice Review (Belfast, HMSO).
Department of Health, Social Services and Public Safety (DHSSPS) (2009) *Families Matter: Supporting Families in Northern Ireland. Regional Family and Parenting Strategy* (Belfast, DHSSPS).
Department of Justice (DoJ) (2012) *Building Safer, Shared and Confident Communities. A Community Safety Strategy for Northern Ireland 2012–2017* (Belfast, DoJ).
—— (2013) *Strategic Framework for Reducing Offending. Towards a Safer Society 2013* (Belfast, DoJ).
Doak, J and O'Mahony, D (2011) 'In Search of Legitimacy: Restorative Youth Conferencing in Northern Ireland' 31 *Legal Studies* 305.
Downes, D (2012) 'Political Economy, Welfare and Punishment in Comparative Perspective' in S Snacken and E Dumortier (eds), *Resisting Punitiveness in Europe? Welfare, Human Rights and Democracy* (London, Routledge).
Eliaerts, C and Dumortier, E (2001) 'Restorative Justice for Children: In Need of Procedural Safeguards and Standards' in E Weitekamp and HJ Kerner (eds), *Restorative Justice: Theoretical Foundations* (Cullompton, Willan Publishing).
Farrington, DP (1996) *Understanding and Preventing Youth Crime.* Social Policy Research 93 (York, Joseph Rowntree Foundation).
—— (2007) 'Childhood Risk Factors and Risk-Focused Prevention' in M Maguire, R Morgan and R Reiner (eds), *The Oxford Handbook of Criminology*, 4th edn (Oxford, Oxford University Press).
Fortin J (2009) *Children's Rights and the Developing Law*, 3rd edn (Cambridge, Cambridge University Press).
Garland, D (2001) *The Culture of Control: Crime and Social Order in Contemporary Society* (Oxford, Oxford University Press).
Goldson, B (2000a) '"Children in Need" or "Young Offenders"? Hardening Ideology, Organisational Change and New Challenges for Social Work with Children in Trouble' 5 *Child and Family Social Work* 255.

—— (2000b) 'Wither Diversion? Interventionism and the New Youth Justice' in B Goldson (ed), *The New Youth Justice* (Lyme Regis, Russell House Publishing).
—— (2006) 'Penal Custody: Intolerance, Irrationality and Indifference' in B Goldson and J Muncie (eds), *Youth Crime and Justice* (London, Sage).
Goldson, B and Hughes, G (2010) 'Sociological Criminology and Youth Justice: Comparative Policy Analysis and Academic Intervention' 10 *Criminology & Criminal Justice* 211.
Goldson, B and Muncie, J (2006) 'Editors' Introduction' in B Goldson and J Muncie (eds), *Youth Crime and Justice* (London, Sage).
—— (2008) 'Children in Custody' in B Goldson (ed), *Dictionary of Youth Justice* (Cullompton, Willan Publishing).
Gray, P (2005) 'The Politics of Risk and Young Offenders' Experiences of Social Exclusion and Restorative Justice' 45 *British Journal of Criminology* 938.
Hagell, A (2005) 'The Use of Custody for Children and Young People' in T Bateman and J Pitts (eds), *The RHP Companion to Youth Justice* (Lyme Regis, Russell House Publishing).
Harland, K (2011) 'Violent Youth Culture in Northern Ireland: Young Men, Violence, and the Challenges of Peacebuilding' 43 *Youth & Society* 414.
Haydon, D (2008) *Northern Ireland NGO Alternative Report* (Belfast, Save the Children and Children's Law Centre).
—— (2009) *Developing a Manifesto for Youth Justice in Northern Ireland. Background Paper* (Belfast, Include Youth).
—— (2014) 'Early Intervention for the Prevention of Offending in Northern Ireland' 14 *Youth Justice* 226.
Haydon, D, McAlister, S and Scraton, P (2012) 'Young People, Conflict and Regulation' 51 *Howard Journal of Criminal Justice* 503.
Hendrick, H (2006) 'Histories of Youth Crime and Justice' in B Goldson and J Muncie (eds), *Youth Crime and Justice* (London, Sage).
Hillsborough Agreement (2010) *Agreement at Hillsborough Castle* 5 February (Belfast, Northern Ireland Office).
Hudson, B (2003) *Understanding Justice: An Introduction to Ideas, Perspectives and Controversies in Modern Penal Theory*, 2nd edn (Buckingham, Open University Press).
Include Youth (2011a) *Getting the 'Right' Youth Justice … Engaging with the Findings of the Review of the Youth Justice System in Northern Ireland, Conference Report*, Ch 3: 'Changes Needed to the Youth Justice System', available at www.includeyouth.org/i/3_Conference_report_young_people.pdf.
—— (2011b) *Include Youth Submission to the Youth Justice Review Team's Review of the Youth Justice System in Northern Ireland*, available at www.includeyouth.org/i/Include_Youth_Submission_to_the_Youth_Justice_Review_Team_FINAL_19_April_2011.pdf, 93–100.
Independent Commission on Youth Crime and Antisocial Behaviour (2010) *Time for a Fresh Start* (London, The Police Federation).
Jacobson, J, Bhardwa, B, Gyateng, T, Hunter, G and Hough, M (2010) *Punishing Disadvantage: A Profile of Children in Custody* (London, Prison Reform Trust).
Kemshall, H (2008) 'Risk, Rights and Justice: Understanding and Responding to Youth Risk' 8 *Youth Justice* 21.
—— (2010) 'Risk Rationalities in Contemporary Social Work Policy and Practice' 40 *British Journal of Social Work* 1247.
Kilkelly, U (2008) 'Youth Justice and Children's Rights: Measuring Compliance with International Standards' 8 *Youth Justice* 187.

Kilkelly, U, Moore, L and Convery, U (2002) *In Our Care: Promoting the Rights of Children in Custody* (Belfast, Northern Ireland Human Rights Commission).
Knox, C (2002) '"See No Evil, Hear No Evil": Insidious Paramilitary Violence in Northern Ireland' 42 *British Journal of Criminology* 164.
Maruna, S, Wright, S, Brown, J, van Marle, F, Devlin, R and Liddle, M (2007) *Youth Conferencing as Shame Management: Results of a Long-term Follow-up Study* (Belfast, Youth Justice Agency/Youth Conferencing Service, ARCS).
McAlister, S and Carr, N (2014) 'Experiences of Youth Justice: Youth Justice Discourses and their Multiple Effects' 14 *Youth Justice* 241.
McAlister, S, Scraton, P and Haydon, D (2009) *Childhood in Transition: Experiencing Marginalisation and Conflict in Northern Ireland* (Belfast, Queen's University Belfast/Save the Children/Princes Trust).
McAra, L and McVie, S (2013) 'Delivering Justice for Children and Young People: Key Messages from the Edinburgh Study of Youth Transitions and Crime' in *Justice for Young People* (London, The Howard League for Penal Reform).
McAvoy, A (2012) *Youth Justice Agency Annual Workload Statistics 2011/12* Statistical Bulletin1/2012 (Belfast, DoJ, Statistics and Research Branch).
McGhee, J and Waterhouse, L (2007) 'Classification in Youth Justice and Child Welfare: In Search of "the Child"' 7 *Youth Justice* 107.
McTernan, E and Godfrey, A (2006) 'Children's Services Planning in Northern Ireland: Developing a Planning Model to Address Rights and Needs' 12 *Child Care in Practice* 219.
McVie, S (2011) 'Alterative Models of Youth Justice: Lessons from Scotland and Northern Ireland' 6 *Journal of Children's Services* 106.
Mika, H (2006) *Community-based Restorative Justice Initiatives in Northern Ireland* (Belfast, Queen's University).
Ministry of Justice (MoJ)/Home Office (HO)/Youth Justice Board (YJB) (2013) *Youth Justice Statistics 2011/12 England and Wales,* 31 January 2013 (London, YJB/MoJ).
Muncie, J (2008) 'The Punitive Turn in Juvenile Justice: Cultures of Control and Rights Compliance in Western Europe and the USA' 8 *Youth Justice* 107.
—— (2011) 'Illusions of Difference: Comparative Youth Justice in the Devolved United Kingdom' 51 *British Journal of Criminology* 40.
Murray, R (2013) *Children and Young People in Custody 2011–12. An Analysis of the Experiences of 15–18 year olds in Prison* (London, HM Inspectorate of Prisons/Youth Justice Board).
Northern Ireland Office (NIO) (2008) *Together. Stronger. Safer. Community Safety in Northern Ireland: A Consultation Paper* (Belfast, NIO).
Northern Ireland Policing Board (NIPB) (2011) *Thematic Review on Children and Young People* (Belfast, NI Policing Board Human Rights and Professional Standards Committee).
Office of First Minister and deputy First Minister (OFMdFM) (2006) *Our Children and Young People—Our Pledge. A Ten Year Strategy for Children and Young People in Northern Ireland 2006–2016* (Belfast, OFMdFM).
Office for National Statistics (ONS) (2013) *Crime in England and Wales. Year Ending June 2013*, Statistical Bulletin, available at www.ons.gov.uk/ons/dcp171778_331209.pdf.
O'Mahony, D and Campbell, C (2006) 'Mainstreaming Restorative Justice for Young Offenders through Youth Conferencing: The Experience of Northern Ireland' in J Junger-Tas and SH Decker (eds), *International Handbook of Juvenile Justice* (New York, Springer).
O'Mahony, D, Doak, J and Clamp, K (2012) 'The Politics of Youth Justice Reform in Post-Conflict Societies: Mainstreaming Restorative Justice in Northern Ireland and South Africa' 63 *Northern Ireland Legal Quarterly* 269.

Police Service of Northern Ireland (PSNI) (2011) *Paramilitary Style Incidents*. Freedom of Information Request F-2011-00341, available at www.psni.police.uk/para_style_incidents.pdf, 4.
Pollack, S (2010) 'Labelling Clients "Risky": Social Work and the Neo-liberal Welfare State' 40 *British Journal of Social Work* 1263.
Roche, R (2008) *Sectarianism and Segregation in Urban Northern Ireland: Northern Irish Youth Post-Agreement. A Report on the Facts, Fears and Feelings Project* (Belfast, Queen's University).
Rodger, JJ (2008) *Criminalising Social Policy: Anti-social Behaviour and Welfare in a Decivilised Society* (Cullompton, Willan Publishing).
Scottish Government (2014) *Scottish Crime and Justice Survey 2011/13: Main Findings* (Edinburgh, The Scottish Government).
Sharland, E (2006) 'Young People, Risk Taking and Risk Making: Some Thoughts for Social Work' 36 *British Journal of Social Work* 247.
Smyth, M, Fay, MT, Brough, E and Hamilton, J (2004) *The Impact of Political Conflict on Children in Northern Ireland* (Belfast, Institute for Conflict Research).
Snacken, S and Dumortier, E (2012) 'Resisting Punitiveness in Europe? An Introduction' in S Snacken and E Dumortier (eds), *Resisting Punitiveness in Europe? Welfare, Human Rights and Democracy* (London, Routledge).
Southern Health and Social Services Board (SHSSB) (2007) *Early Intervention Programme for the Prevention of Offending 'Terms of Reference'* (Armagh, SHSSB).
Statham, J and Smith, M (2010) *Issues in Earlier Intervention: Identifying and Supporting Children with Additional Needs* Research Report 205 (Nottingham, Department for Children, Schools and Families).
Tulkens, F (2012) 'Human Rights as the Good and Bad Conscience of Criminal Law' in S Snacken and E Dumortier (eds), *Resisting Punitiveness in Europe? Welfare, Human Rights and Democracy* (London, Routledge).
Turnbull, G and Spence, J (2011) 'What's at Risk? The Proliferation of Risk across Child and Youth Policy in England' 14 *Journal of Youth Studies* 939.
UK Children's Commissioners (2008) *UK Children's Commissioners' Report to the UN Committee on the Rights of the Child* (Belfast, Northern Ireland Commission for Children and Young People).
UN Committee on the Rights of the Child (2007) *General Comment No 10 (2007) Children's Rights in Juvenile Justice*, 2 February 2007, CRC/C/GC/10.
Youth Justice Agency (YJA) (2010) *Annual Report and Accounts 2009–2010* (London, The Stationery Office).
Youth Justice Review Team (YJRT) (2011) *A Review of the Youth Justice System in Northern Ireland*, (Belfast, DoJ, Youth Justice Unit).

15

Public and Official Responses to Sexual and Violent Crime in Northern Ireland

ANNE-MARIE McALINDEN

Introduction

This chapter examines contemporary criminal justice policies on sexual and violent crime in Northern Ireland within the broader context of national and international debates on crime and justice and concerns related to the risk, security and governance of dangerous offenders. Drawing on the theme of 'policy transfer' and picking up on the legal and political relationship with England and Wales in particular as outlined in the introductory chapter, it will be demonstrated that both pre- and post-devolution, Northern Ireland has to a large extent emulated penal policies on sexual and violent crime which have been put in place in England and Wales. Some of these policies have in themselves derived from similar developments in the area of crime control in the United States. The chapter also examines public attitudes and responses to sex offenders in the community in Northern Ireland. Sexual and violent crimes, especially those against children, are in general highly contentious by nature, often eliciting a deeply emotive or outwardly retributive response on the part of society. Drawing on original empirical data collected by the author, it will be argued that Northern Ireland also has a number of distinct dimensions pertaining to public responses to sexual and violent crime which can be related directly to the legacy of the 'conflict.' These relate to the presence of paramilitaries, the parochial nature of society, and the geographical land border with the Republic of Ireland. These factors create additional challenges for offender reintegration, as well as for policing and the criminal justice management of risk in a society transitioning from political conflict.

Risk, Security and Governance

For more than two decades, debates on crime and justice within contemporary neo-liberal societies such as the United States and the United Kingdom have been dominated by concerns with 'risk' and public protection. Such concerns have been manifested in relation to the regulation of crime and anti-social behaviour as well as terrorism and policing and security in general (Shearing 2000; Crawford 2006; Loader and Walker 2007). Consistent with broader academic discourses on state regulation, the notions of risk management (Parton et al 1997; Kemshall and Maguire 2001) and, more recently, preventative governance (Ashenden 2004) have become the watchwords for legislative and policy discourses on child protection and the treatment and management of sexual offenders.

Sexual and violent offenders have been singled out as a special category of 'risky' offender for whom exceptional forms of punishment and control are thought necessary (Simon 1998; McAlinden 2010). Central to this form of 'differential justice' for sex offenders (Weaver and McNeill 2010: 274) is a policy of 'radical prevention' (Hebenton and Seddon 2009: 2). This pre-emptive approach to penal policy is characterised by 'precautionary logic' (Ericson 2007) and the imposition of risk-averse policies which seek to govern 'worst case scenarios' and prevent all possible manifestations of future harms—both known and unknown risks—before they occur (Zedner 2009).

Within the United Kingdom, regulatory, risk-based approaches to sexual crime have developed alongside the overt politicisation of deviant sexual behaviour. The state's prioritisation of the dangers posed by potential sex offenders over other forms of deviant behaviour is driven in large part by media fuelled popular concerns. High profile cases such as those relating to 'Sarah Payne' or the 'Soham murders' become 'signal crimes' (Innes 2004) in shaping legislative and policy agendas.[1] As a result of a populist approach to criminal justice policymaking (Bottoms 1995; Johnstone 2000), a zero-tolerance approach to risk has developed and a plethora of legislation pertaining to sexual offending has been enacted within a relatively short period. Recent initiatives range from preventative detention and restrictions placed on dangerous offenders on release from custody (Rose 2000). As discussed below, a specific focus of this recent 'hyper innovation' (Moran 2003; Crawford 2006) has been the compilation of 'knowledge' about sex offenders and their whereabouts in order to control risk and increase security (Ericson and Haggerty 1997).

Across the United Kingdom, risk assessment and management have become the watchwords of the 'new penology' (Feeley and Simon 1992) and 'actuarial justice' (Feeley and Simon 1994). Many continental jurisdictions have configured the sex offender conundrum very differently via what has been termed the 'medicalization of deviance' (Conrad and Schneider 1980). This takes the form of a range

[1] See nn 17 and 13 below respectively.

of inclusionary therapeutic options which recognise the transformative potential of sex offenders. In contrast, Western neo-liberal jurisdictions such as the United States and the United Kingdom have opted for broadly exclusionary regulatory measures based on incapacitation and targeted surveillance (McAlinden 2012a) which have lost sight of the humaneness and reintegrative potential of such offenders. As discussed further in the next two sections, within the broader legislative landscape of the United Kingdom, Northern Ireland has, for a range of reasons, closely emulated the criminal justice policies of England and Wales.

Policies relating to childcare and protection and the regulation of sex offending in Northern Ireland have not emerged in isolation from developments in the United Kingdom as a whole and indeed internationally. The presence of a strong voluntary sector in Northern Ireland, however, has prevented the jurisdiction from adopting some of the more extreme forms of risk regulation that have been enacted in England and Wales, such as chemical castration and community notification. The voluntary sector in Northern Ireland, for example, has provided a professional, pragmatic and considered approach to questions relating to the management and reintegration of sex offenders in the community and has played the role of liaison between statutory agencies and the community on contentious sex offender issues (McAlinden 2007a: 30). At the same time, however, as will be outlined further below, the post-conflict transitional dimension of civil society in Northern Ireland has produced an additional set of practical considerations for policy and professional discourses concerning sex offender risk management.

Comparing Policy and Legislative Frameworks for Managing Risk

The legal systems of the various jurisdictions which comprise the United Kingdom and the Republic of Ireland, although now quite separate, have shared legal histories and traditions. In brief, Northern Ireland has a criminal justice system which broadly replicates that of England and Wales and is governed by many of the same legislative measures on sex offending or has later ratified reciprocal measures. The Republic of Ireland has had a completely different legal system and legislative framework since at least the late-1940s. Scotland has had a unique but related momentum on sex offending particularly following devolution of justice in 1999.[2] Before undertaking an examination of the recent key legislative and policy developments relating to the management of violent and sexual offenders within Northern Ireland it is perhaps useful, therefore, to place Northern Ireland within the context of its political relationship with England and Wales in particular. Local legislative policies in Northern Ireland have had a 'consistent' and

[2] For a detailed comparative overview see McAlinden (2012b: 55–60).

'shared' relationship with those adopted in England and Wales but have also been modified to meet Northern Ireland's 'own strategic political needs' (Pinkerton 1994: 29).

The legislative relationship between Northern Ireland and England and Wales is a rather intricate one (McLaughlin 2005). As noted in the introductory chapter, the full devolution of criminal justice and policing powers from Westminster to Stormont did not take place until March 2010. In the interim, there have been periods of direct rule under which 'the process of assimilation between the content of the law in Northern Ireland and that in England was, if anything, fortified' (Dickson 2001: 8). As a result, criminal justice policy in Northern Ireland has been heavily influenced by and tended to track developments in England and Wales (Birrell and Murie 1980: 65; Dickson 2001: 5), particularly in relation to safeguarding children (Northern Ireland Assembly Research and Library Service 2010: 1), where the step by step or 'parity principle' has generally held sway (Pinkerton 1994: 28).

By way of example, several pieces of legislation pertaining to the post-release control of sexual offenders enacted in Westminster—such as Part I of the Sex Offenders Act 1997 and subsequently Part 2 of the Sexual Offences Act 2003 (discussed further below), extend also to Northern Ireland. Alternatively, reciprocal legislation first enacted in Westminster was later adopted in Northern Ireland in the ensuing months or years. An example of this latter approach is the legislative provision for sex offender orders, first enacted in England and Wales by the Crime and Disorder Act 1998[3] and later adopted in Northern Ireland by the Criminal Justice (Northern Ireland) Order 1998.[4] This process has been termed one of 'delay and quasi-imitation' (Pinkerton 1994: 28).

There have been a number of key legislative and policy developments relating to sex offender management in the United Kingdom as a whole as well as Northern Ireland specifically over the last few years. From the 1990s onwards contemporary therapeutic strategies for sex offenders became embedded and subsumed within a broader penal rhetoric of risk management and public protection (Kemshall 2002). A policy of 'punishment plus' (Weaver and McNeill 2010: 274) for sex offenders has been manifested in two main ways—via extended 'public protection' sentences and in particular through enhanced post-release management which effectively extend the sphere of control from prison into the community (Kleinhans 2002: 244–46).

Following the enactment of the Criminal Justice Act (CJA) 1991 in England and Wales, the enactment of the similarly constituted Criminal Justice (NI) Order 1996 was highly significant in transforming the ethos of both therapeutic and penal interventions with sex offenders. It marked a shift from voluntary to mandatory court ordered treatment for sex offenders and a distinct emphasis on retributive

[3] See s 2 of the 1998 Act. Sex offender orders, together with restraining orders (the Criminal Justice and Courts Services Act 2000, s 66 and sch 5, s 6) were replaced with a new and extended measure—sexual offences prevention orders (SOPOs) (see the Sexual Offences Act 2003, ss 104–13).

[4] See s 6; see n 9 below.

penal policies for such offenders (McAlinden 2012a: 172). A 1996 Home Office consultation document (Home Office 1996) outlined a range of proposals to control sex offenders in the community more effectively based on the twin aims of specific deterrence and community protection. These eventually became embodied in a comprehensive body of legislation in England and Wales as well as across the United Kingdom as a whole. In Northern Ireland, two key areas have been subject to significant legislative and policy focus—sex offender notification and related orders and pre-employment vetting.

Notification was originally enacted by Part I of the Sex Offenders Act 1997 and later replaced by enhanced arrangements under Part 2 of the Sexual Offences Act (SOA) 2003 (Thomas 2003). The scheme, which applies to the whole of the United Kingdom, requires certain categories of sex offender to notify the police in person of their name and address and any changes to these details. The conditions attached to notification and the degree of public disclosure vary depending on the assessed level of risk.[5] The scope of notification has also been widened through two further measures—notification orders[6] and foreign travel orders.[7] The former require offenders who have received convictions for sexual offences abroad to comply with the legislation. The latter prevent offenders with convictions involving children from travelling abroad and targeting children in other countries. Part 2 of the SOA 2003 also introduced risk of sexual harm orders (RSHOs)[8] and sexual offences prevention orders (SOPOs)[9] (Shute 2004). SOPOs can be used to prohibit the offender from frequenting places where there are children, such as parks and school playgrounds. RSHOs are more controversial because they seek to criminalise the preparatory acts involved in abuse, including pre-abuse 'grooming', and can be used whether or not the individual has a prior record of offending.

In relation to vetting, a number of high profile cases of institutional child abuse in Northern Ireland and elsewhere in the United Kingdom, such as the Kincora[10] (DHSS 1982; Hughes 1985), Martin Huston (SSI 1993),[11] and Father Brendan Smyth[12] (Ferguson 1995), highlighted the vulnerability of children in places traditionally considered secure such as homes, clubs and schools. In response, a further

[5] The Supreme Court has ruled that lifetime notification without periodic review breaches privacy rights under art 8 of the ECHR (*R (on the application of F and Thompson) v Secretary of State for the Home Department*) [2010] UKSC 17.

[6] ss 97–103.

[7] ss 114–22, as amended by the Policing and Crime Act 2009, ss 23–25.

[8] ss 123–29.

[9] ss 104–13, both orders are now amended by the Anti-social Behaviour, Crime and Policing Act 2014.

[10] This case involved the abuse of boys through vice rings and prostitution in Kincora hostel in East Belfast which came to light in the early 1980s but which could be traced back at least two decades.

[11] Care worker Martin Huston was convicted in 1992 on 25 counts of sexual offences against children. He had been on probation for two years between 1987 and 1989 for committing sexual offences, yet was able to find employment with a voluntary agency involving work with children.

[12] Smyth was sentenced to 12 years in prison after pleading guilty to the sexual abuse of 20 young people over a period of 36 years. He previously served four years in a Northern Ireland prison for similar offences. The extradition crisis surrounding the case also triggered a political crisis in Dublin and the resignation of the government.

range of legislation has been enacted to prevent offenders from making contact with children or the vulnerable through organisations. These have included the Sexual Offences (Amendment) Act 2000, which made it an offence for an adult to engage in sexual activity with a child if they are in a position of trust and Part V of the Police Act 1997, which established the Criminal Records Bureau in England and Wales (and later AccessNI in Northern Ireland) to provide a more effective means of carrying out criminal record checks. More recently, the Safeguarding Vulnerable Groups (Northern Ireland) Order 2007 introduced a new regulatory framework which gives legislative effect to many of the recommendations of the Bichard (2004) Inquiry.[13] The Act combines previously disparate disqualification lists and establishes a centralised online register and continuous criminal records monitoring of every person who works or volunteers with children or vulnerable adults.[14]

Throughout the United Kingdom, the legislative and policy framework on sex offender risk management has been enhanced by the development of a cohesive inter-agency infrastructure which emphasises the exchange of relevant information about offenders who pose a risk to public safety (Kemshall and Maguire 2001). Since at least the late-1990s, previously informal initiatives by various agencies have been reinforced by the adoption of 'joined up' working (Crawford 1997). Multi-agency arrangements on sex offender risk assessment and management were in part formalised as a result of Part I of the Sex Offenders Act 1997, which came into force on 1 September 1997 (Home Office 1997). These arrangements were further formalised with the introduction of Multi-Agency Public Protection Arrangements (MAPPA), first in England and Wales, and later elsewhere.

In Northern Ireland, the Multi-Agency Sex Offender Risk Assessment and Management (MASRAM) arrangements were formally launched in in May 2002. Following the enactment of Part 3 of the Criminal Justice (Northern Ireland) Order 2008, the MASRAM arrangements were replaced with a broader statutory framework under the auspices of the Public Protection Arrangements Northern Ireland (PPANI).[15] The central task of PPANI/MAPPA is to facilitate the exchange of information between core agencies (principally police, probation, prisons, and social services) and other statutory and voluntary agencies and to classify sex offenders into appropriate risk categories based on likelihood of reoffending (Kemshall and Maguire 2001; Maguire et al 2001).[16] While low-risk/category 1 offenders are managed on a single agency basis, usually by police or probation, high-risk/category 3 offenders

[13] The Bichard Inquiry was established in the aftermath of the murders of Soham school girls Holly Wells and Jessica Chapman by school caretaker Ian Huntley to examine vetting procedures in two police constabularies in England and Wales including the effectiveness of information sharing.

[14] The scope of the SGVG framework has been scaled back under the Protection of Freedoms Act 2012, Pt V.

[15] See arts 49–51.

[16] The categories of offender to whom public protection arrangements apply are broadly consistent across the UK. England and Wales, however, has a further 'very high risk' category in addition to high, medium and low risk. For a detailed overview of key similarities and differences between the constituent schemes, see Stafford et al (2011).

are managed on a multi-agency basis. In Northern Ireland, the framework has now been extended to non-sexual violent offenders and includes lay advisers who work on a voluntary basis, as happens in England and Wales but not Scotland. The introduction of the ViSOR (Violent and Sexual Offender Register) computer database across the United Kingdom from August 2005 has further enhanced cooperative working and information sharing between agencies and jurisdictions. The UK paradigm has been endorsed as an exemplar of best practice (Bryan and Doyle 2003; Lieb 2003) to the extent that the Republic of Ireland has recently introduced the Sex Offender Risk Assessment Management (SORAM) model which has been rolled out nationally since May 2013 (Wilson et al 2013).

Explaining the Convergence of Penal Policies on Sex Offending

Within the wider international context, England and Wales has developed one of the most stringent penal policies for protecting the public from the risk posed by sex offenders within Western Europe (McAlinden 2012a) with the other jurisdictions within the United Kingdom generally following suit (McAlinden 2012b: chapter 3). In addition to shared legal histories and traditions which predate the transition from conflict in Northern Ireland, this section of the chapter considers other possible explanations for recent policy convergence on sex offending both within and across the United Kingdom.

The first of these is the recurring theme of the 'policy transfer' (Jones and Newburn 2006) of punitive crime control policies on sex offending derived from the United States (Hebenton and Seddon 2009; McAlinden 2012a; Jones and Newburn 2013). Particular reasons for the parity in approaches to the regulation of sexual crime between the United States and the United Kingdom include high profile cases of sexual abuse or murder of young children, which have acted as 'precipitating events' (Lieb 2000: 423), related campaigns involving 'co-victims' or the immediate family, and the pivotal role played by the media in garnering public support for policy campaigns (Jones and Newburn 2013).

One of the best examples of policy transfer in this area is sex offender notification. The United States, the United Kingdom and the Republic of Ireland are among only a handful of countries which have a system requiring sex offenders to notify their details to the police. In the United States, a body of state and federal laws, known collectively as 'Megan's Law', require certain classes of sex offender to register their personal details with law enforcement agencies and permit various forms of notification of this information to the community. Despite the initial reluctance of the British Government to legislate in this area (Thomas 2003), 'Sarah's Law' has established a community disclosure scheme allowing parents to check the backgrounds of those with unsupervised access to their children

(Kemshall and Weaver 2012).[17] The scheme was implemented in all 43 police forces in England and Wales from April 2011, and across Scotland from October 2010, bringing policies on notification even more closely in line with those in the United States. As Croall et al (2010: 13) have argued, devolution 'throw[s] up the possibilities of policy transfer across the different constituent countries of the UK' as well as on a global level.

At the time of writing, Northern Ireland, however, has yet to implement a public disclosure scheme. The tentative progress of implementing 'Sarah's Law' throughout the whole of the United Kingdom, therefore, is indicative of the limitations of policy transfer. As Muncie notes, the process is not 'one-dimensional' (2005: 37) but is instead subject to important socio-cultural differences in the way in which policies are negotiated and reconfigured within national and localised cultures (Muncie 2005: 44; Crawford, 2006). Indeed, as discussed further below, there are important reasons underlying political and professional reluctance to extend a disclosure scheme to Northern Ireland.

A second explanation for convergence in both the mode and severity of punishment relates to similarities in the political economies of 'neo-liberal' states (Cavadino and Dignan 2006). In the United States and throughout the United Kingdom, the neo-liberal turn of recent penal policy in both jurisdictions also helps to account for the alignment of regulatory policies on sex offending. While there has been a global trend towards punitiveness and increasing rates of imprisonment, this tendency has perhaps been most marked in the United States and the United Kingdom (McAlinden 2012a).[18]

According to this view, in 'neo-liberal' societies, such as the United States and England and Wales, the demise of the 'welfare state' (Garland 1985, 1996) has resulted in an ethos of individualism, and penal and social policies which are fixated upon forms of segregation and stigmatisation of those on the margins of society (Petrunik and Deutschmann 2008). 'Law and order' or incapacitation is the dominant penal ideology which is shaped by the social exclusion of deviants and high rates of imprisonment (Wacquant 2001) and an emphasis on punishment rather than correction. Despite lower rates of imprisonment in general,[19] Northern Ireland, as noted above, shares many of the measures relating to the post-release control of sex offenders enacted either simultaneously or previously in England and Wales. The forces of neo-liberalism, therefore, have also spread to

[17] 'Sarah's Law' was named after eight-year-old Sarah Payne who was abducted and murdered by known sex offender, Roy Whiting, in Sussex in July 2000. The campaign, led by Sarah's mother and backed by the former *News of the World* newspaper's 'Name and Shame' campaign, called for the authorities to publicly identify all known sex offenders. The campaign was initially accompanied by public protest and vigilante activity in Paulsgrove (Ashenden 2002).

[18] Although the United States is the world leader in incarceration rates, with a figure of 756 per 100,000 (Walmsley 2009), England and Wales imprison more people per 100,000 (152) than most other Western European nations (apart from Scotland (156) and Spain, including Catalonia (173)), and approximately 50 per cent more than Belgium (101), France (103), Germany (89), Italy (106), the Netherlands (99) and Sweden (77) (Council of Europe 2011: 38–40).

[19] Northern Ireland and the Republic of Ireland have had corresponding lower rates of imprisonment—88 and 81 per 100,000 respectively (Council of Europe 2011: 38).

Northern Ireland and Scotland (Horgan 2006) as related jurisdictions which share 'broadly similar standards of living and constitutional arrangements' (Grimshaw 2004: 3). As outlined briefly above, prior to devolution Scotland and Northern Ireland had shared legal histories and traditions with England and Wales with either joint or reciprocal legislative provision. Moreover, as Garland (1999) has contended more generally, on a broader scale, the small size of these respective jurisdictions, which form part of the United Kingdom as a whole, means that they may be especially susceptible to global influences.

A third factor which may help to explain the convergence of penal policies on sex offending across the United Kingdom is the social construction of risk and its control. Consistent with the argument of criminologists that punishment and crime control are 'an index of culture' (Nelken 2007: 153; see also Sparks 2001), levels of punitivity may also have their roots in prevailing religious cultures. Melossi (2001) affirms that social, economic and political relationships and conditions which shape leniency or forgiveness on the one hand and punitivity on the other, have their roots in religious traditions. His comparison of Protestant societies such as the United States or England and Wales and Catholic societies such as Italy in relation to differential rates of imprisonment reveals a juxtaposition of 'a rhetoric of strong penal repression' and 'soft authoritarian paternalism' (Melossi 2001: 412).

According to these arguments, other predominantly Protestant societies such as Scotland and Northern Ireland would also have a tendency to adopt more punitive criminal justice responses. The Republic of Ireland, for example, as a state profoundly shaped by Catholic morality and ideology has not pursued a punitive regulatory agenda on sex offending with the same rigour as in Northern Ireland or England and Wales (McAlinden 2012b: 58, 67–68), and legislation enacting supervisory methods for sex offenders has often emerged some years later (Northern Ireland Assembly Research and Library Service 2010: 7).[20] In Northern Ireland and the rest of the United Kingdom, risk is grounded in a 'wider politics of fear and insecurity' (Seddon 2008: 312) concerning sex offenders where professional assessments are often subjected to emotive and sometimes misplaced populist assumptions about risk. This has ultimately resulted in harsher, less tolerant public attitudes and official policies towards sex offenders.

Public Attitudes and Responses to Sex Offenders in Northern Ireland

Despite the fact that sexual crime in Northern Ireland is low in comparison to other types of offences, representing only about 3 per cent of all crime recorded by the police, there are high levels of public concern about sex offending (McAlinden 2007b). A 2007 research study commissioned by the then Northern Ireland Office

[20] The reduced reliance on formal methods of social control has also been attributed, inter alia, to high levels of confidence in the police and other justice agencies (O'Donnell et al 2008).

on 'Public Attitudes towards Sex Offenders in Northern Ireland', revealed misinformed and stereotypical public understandings of risks posed by sex offenders and of treatment and management processes, and the general societal unwillingness to accept sex offenders in the local community, particularly where child sex offenders are concerned (McAlinden 2007b; see also Brown et al 2005; Wilson et al 2007: 1–2). In particular, communities in Northern Ireland appear to have a much more collective response to sexual offending than other social or political issues. Although attitudes were not uniform and, as might be expected, women, parents of children aged under 18, and those in the older age bracket appear to have stronger attitudes than others, there were a number of noteworthy findings.

Attitudes to child sex offenders were more punitive and emotive than for adult sex offenders: 23 per cent agreed that 'most people who commit sexual offences against adults can go on to live law abiding lives' whereas this figure was only 16 per cent for those who had committed sexual offences against children (McAlinden 2007b: 35, 49). Similarly, 70 per cent thought it was unacceptable for child sex offenders to live in their local community while 92 per cent thought that they should be informed if they were living near a child sex offender (McAlinden 2007b: 52, 49). There was significant overestimation of levels of sex offending, including recidivism rates, and homogeneity in levels and types of risk: only 29–35 per cent agreed that 'treatment programmes can help sex offenders to stop re-offending' (McAlinden 2007b: 66) and 66 per cent overestimated that recidivism rates for child sex offenders were over 40 per cent (McAlinden 2007b: 71).[21] Further, there were also low levels of awareness of risk management and treatment processes and prevention initiatives including MASRAM, as it then was, and community-based initiatives such as circles of support and accountability (McAlinden 2007b: 39, 54). Finally, there was evidence of absorption of media-generated stereotypes of offending (Berry et al 2012) including association of the commission of a sexual offence with 'stranger danger' (a predatory adult male and a young victim), with little or no cognisance of sexual offending by children or young people or females (McAlinden 2007b: 42–43, 56–59). Such findings broadly accord with the national and international literature which generally demonstrates significant levels of myth and misconceptions among the public concerning sex offenders (Katz-Schiavone et al 2008; Craun and Theriot 2009). Sex offenders tend to generate high levels of anxiety and fear in contemporary society (Levenson et al 2007; Brown et al 2008) where there is concern in particular about strategies to reintegrate and manage child sex offenders into the local community (Tewksbury and Mustaine 2007; Brown et al 2008).

This general trend in public attitudes to sex offenders in Northern Ireland has also been reflected more recently in community responses to the presence of sex offenders in their local community. In tandem with official discourses, as outlined

[21] Although official reoffending rates are likely to underestimate true offending rates, recidivism rates for sex offenders are generally low in comparison to other offenders, particularly for those who have only committed one offence (Harris and Hanson 2004).

above, which single sex offenders out as a special class of offender, public attitudes in Northern Ireland as elsewhere in the United Kingdom reflect the 'labelling' (Becker 1963) and 'Othering' (Garland 2001) of sex offenders or what has been termed the NIMBY syndrome for short hand ('not in my back yard'). For example, in October 2011, a pipe bomb was found at an offender's hostel in North Belfast by a builder during renovation work,[22] and in June 2011, protestors, most of whom were young mothers accompanied by their children, protested outside the premises of a voluntary sector agency involved in the provision of employment and reintegrative initiatives for sex offenders.[23] As outlined further below, the adverse consequences of such hostile community reactions to sex offenders can be termed 'disintegrative shaming' (Braithwaite 1989) which may impede offender rehabilitation and undermine risk management and desistance (McAlinden 2005, 2007a; Willis et al 2011). On one level engaging the public in measured discourse on emotive and contentious issues concerning sex offending against children may be no more problematic in Northern Ireland than elsewhere in the United Kingdom. There are augmented difficulties, however, in engaging the public and in particular overcoming levels of fear and mistrust concerning sex offending and those who 'police' it.

Extra-Legal Dimensions to Managing Sexual and Violent Crime in Northern Ireland: The Legacy of the Conflict

Despite the convergence within legislative and policy frameworks across the United Kingdom, there are a number of unique cultural, socio-political factors relating to the management of sexual offenders in the community in Northern Ireland stemming from the legacy of the conflict. This section of the chapter draws on original empirical work conducted by the author in the summer of 2011, just over one year after full devolution of policing and justice. This primary research entailed in-depth semi-structured interviews with professionals across the four jurisdictions which comprise the United Kingdom (England and Wales, Scotland and Northern Ireland) and the Republic of Ireland who work in the fields of sex offender assessment, treatment and management or child protection or victim support.[24]

[22] *BBC News*, 'Pipe Bomb at Offenders' Hostel in North Belfast', 18 October 2011, available at www.bbc.co.uk/news/uk-northern-ireland-15348235.

[23] *Belfast Telegraph*, 'South Belfast a Dumping Ground for Paedophiles, Claim Picketers', 23 June 2011.

[24] The interviews are cited below by a two letter abbreviation for the jurisdiction (NI, EW, RI), along with the interview number within that jurisdiction and the date the interview was conducted.

The Presence of Paramilitaries

In Northern Ireland, there are some local variations in relation to police legitimacy and paramilitary involvement in sexual offender issues which do not occur elsewhere in the United Kingdom. Historically, such problems have manifested themselves in the form of 'punishment beatings' of known or suspected sex offenders by paramilitary groups (Leggett 2000; Knox 2002: 174). These groups may play on the fears of the local community concerning the presence of sex offenders and consequently present themselves as protectors and alternative law enforcers in stark contrast to what they see as the failure of the local authorities to deal adequately with the problem (McAlinden 2007a: 91).

As a transitional society, this factor continues to have an adverse effect on sex offender management and reintegration in post-devolution Northern Ireland. This view was shared by several interviewees in the study. A police officer commented:

> We have that sort of paramilitary type activity still, whether we like to accept it or not ... there might be a hue and cry and he might be ousted from his community in England ... But he's more likely to suffer significant harm at the hands of a paramilitary attack ... that's still quite unique to us in Northern Ireland.[25]

A voluntary sector professional explained further:

> Here in Northern Ireland ... we have a different dimension as well because we have paramilitary involvement in things like that ... I think the closest thing you might get in England is gang culture ... but not for the same reasons ... I've dealt with at least four [cases] where they've actually been moved out of their houses because the threat has been so high and the whole community then, and the paramilitaries, have gone and stood in a group outside ... while the person was marched out and they were all shouting, sex offender, get out ... And the trauma of being responsible for your whole family being taken out is absolutely huge.[26]

This culture-specific aspect of Northern Ireland society may facilitate 'disintegrative shaming' (Braithwaite 1989) of sex offenders including threats or actual physical harm to offenders, causing some to go underground where risk is increased or at least displaced. Moreover, however, it may also have a number of knock-on effects for how the community perceive not only sex offenders, but also the authorities charged with public protection. That is, the presence of paramilitaries may result in public mistrust and fear of the police or social services and in consequence, ultimately in non-disclosure. This may take the form of individual and collective failures of children or young people as victims to make disclosures, of adult carers to report suspicions of abuse to the authorities, or of sex offenders themselves to self-disclose.

[25] Interview NI 8 (6 July 2011).
[26] Interview NI 11 (11 July 2011).

The Parochial Nature of Northern Irish Society

A further cultural aspect of sex offender management in Northern Ireland relates to the relatively small size of the jurisdiction and the provincial and tightly knit nature of society. While there are some positive aspects of this feature, the negative aspects also relate to the detrimental impact on sex offenders and the reintegrative process post-release. Another voluntary sector interviewee explained this facet as being particularly acute in more rural communities:

> It's probably slightly more difficult because we're such a smaller community here ... and we only have the three prisons. So a lot of offenders coming out know each other, so when you try to reintegrate back, there's always going to be someone there who knows you from somewhere ... Especially maybe more so out in rural areas. I live in a rural area and ... everybody in the community knows who they are, where they are, whereas say in Belfast you could slip about a bit. In rural communities, people soon get to know there's a stranger about and the word soon gets out no matter how well things are kept ... word gets out somebody's living in a caravan at the back of somebody's farmyard.[27]

For others, however, particularly those of 'outsiders looking in', the transitional justice context of Northern Ireland was regarded as a positive in terms of facilitating public discourse around the prevention of sexual offending. A voluntary sector interviewee in the Republic of Ireland stated:

> Northern Ireland, I mean it's a perfect size, it's small, so it's possible to do things relatively quickly. And again, perhaps because of the history in the North, that there is more of an openness or acceptance that change needs to happen.[28]

Similarly, another voluntary sector interviewee in England and Wales reflected on their experience of working in Northern Ireland: 'there seemed to be the ability to have a conversation about it that wouldn't happen in England in the same way'.[29] Indeed, the upside of the size of the jurisdiction relates to the more localised nature of criminal justice delivery which may ultimately be more facilitative of cohesive inter-agency structures and cooperation between agencies.[30] Nonetheless, the small size of the jurisdiction may be especially impactful for the release of information about offenders. It may be harder, for example, to keep controls on the release of information without undermining reintegration and management.

The Border with the Republic of Ireland

A final unique aspect of the governance of sex offending in Northern Ireland relates to its geographical proximity to the Republic of Ireland as a distinct yet

[27] Interview NI 5 (22 June 2011).
[28] Interview RI 2 (11 May 2011).
[29] Interview EW (1 September 2011).
[30] For example, there is only one police service in contrast to the 43 local police force areas in England and Wales.

adjacent legal jurisdiction on the same island. A specific issue concerns the possibility of sex offenders leaving one jurisdiction in which they reside and entering another in order to escape notice. As one police officer commented, 'Given the fact that we've a shared border there, there's a lot of guys just head south and disappear into the ether. And that makes it very difficult for us'.[31] There have been a number of such cases involving a cross-border dimension where released sex offenders have left Northern Ireland or the Republic of Ireland and travelled to England and Wales or Scotland and even continental Europe, or the other way around.[32] These cases and the overall danger of this occurring perhaps remain more acute, however, for Northern Ireland and the Republic of Ireland because of the relatively small size of the respective jurisdictions and the ease with which individuals may access and cross the land border.[33]

The Criminal Justice Review Group, set up as part of the 1998 Good Friday Agreement, recommended an element of 'structured co-operation' between Northern Ireland and the Republic of Ireland and 'mutual recognition and harmonisation' of criminal justice policies, including 'dangerous offender registers' (CJRG 2000: chapter 17). A number of initiatives have been set up to facilitate the sharing of information and best practice regarding sex offenders including the North–South Child Protection Network (NIARLS 2010) and the Public Protection Advisory Group (Wilson et al 2013). Such developments are also broadly in line with those within the European Union where there has been a growing emphasis on enhanced judicial and police cooperation (Ramage 2007; Constantin 2008), including exchanges of information between Member States about dangerous offenders. In practice, however, cross-border police cooperation between the Republic of Ireland and Northern Ireland may thrive 'at the micro-level of engagement' among officers on the ground based on 'personal relationships and hoc arrangements' (Walsh 2011: 302, 327) rather than formal mandates. Moreover, the potential differences concerning standardised criminal record information and vetting and policing arrangements concerning sex offenders within and across the United Kingdom and the Republic of Ireland (Fitch et al 2007; McAlinden 2010) many serve to problematise or undermine true and effective 'structured cooperation'.

Conclusion: Challenges for Offender Management and Reintegration

Future challenges for policymakers and professionals in Northern Ireland, as in other neo-liberal societies which are heavily influenced with concerns about 'risk'

[31] Interview NI 8 (6 July 2011).

[32] See, eg, *BBC News*, 'High Risk Sex Offender Paden "May Be in NI"', 26 June 2010, available at www.bbc.co.uk/news/10422284.

[33] See, eg, *Belfast Telegraph*, 'Sex Beast Paul Redpath Recaptured', 28 July 2009.

and governing the dangerous, are manifold. These relate to drawing back from 'the culture of control' (Garland 2001) and the 'Othering' of sex offenders to facilitate effective reintegration of sex offenders, as well as risk management; fostering positive engagement with the local community on contentious sex offender issues; and striking an appropriate balance between the needs and interests of the offender and the local community (Power 2003). Central to these processes are the need to address 'populist punitiveness' (Bottoms 1995) concerning sex offending against children and the high levels of myths, mistrust, fear and panic which surround this category of offender. Communities, however, can also be facilitative of sex offender desistance and reintegration (Wilson et al 2007; Willis et al 2011). Many of these challenges could be addressed through the adoption of a public health approach to sex offending (Laws 2000), alongside the current community protection model (Kemshall and Wood 2007), and in particular the development of a government sponsored public education and awareness campaign. This has been done effectively with respect to domestic violence in Northern Ireland via, for example, media campaigns in the form of television advertisements, and the distribution of household leaflets concerning key facts and statistics surrounding domestic violence.

Key messages of such a scheme would at a minimum confront the 'stranger danger' construct and underline the diversity in levels and types of risk posed by sex offenders. It would make clear that the majority of abuse is intra-familial in nature, that sexual abusers can be women as well as children and young people, and that legal and policy frameworks are but one plank of a broader collective and individual social response to risk in which child protection is everyone's responsibility (McAlinden 2012b: 259–64). A better informed public would help promote social inclusion and may ultimately help the community make a more positive contribution to sex offender reintegration (McAlinden 2007a). The extension and promotion of measures such as circles of support and accountability beyond the current ad hoc provision across the United Kingdom may also help to engage the wider community in sex offender reintegration and management in a 'partnership approach' with statutory and voluntary agencies (Crawford 1997; McAlinden 2007a).

Public disclosure of information about sex offenders beyond the 'need to know' basis in Northern Ireland remains a contentious issue and one of the main lines of departure from the rest of the United Kingdom. I would argue that disclosure has its place within an overall framework of public protection if it is implemented and used as a means of promoting broader community engagement and responsibility. The provision of information about the identities of sex offenders and their whereabouts, however, has to be balanced with current inflated levels of fear and concern. In this respect, punitive attitudes to sex offenders, particularly those who offend against children may be no more punitive than other similarly constituted political economies, such as England and Wales or the United States. The legacy of political conflict in Northern Ireland in terms of segregation, sectarianism, fear and mistrust of the authorities, however, may mean that issues around sex offending are not easily raised within public discourses. This, therefore, also underlines the importance of framing public discourses and developing a coordinated social and political response to combat sexual abuse which are culturally and politically sensitive and tailored to localised contexts.

References

Ashenden, S (2002) 'Policing Perversion: The Contemporary Governance of Paedophilia' 6 *Cultural Values* 197.

—— (2004) *Governing Child Sexual Abuse: Negotiating the Boundaries of Public and Private, Law and Science* (London, Routledge).

Becker, H (1963) *Outsiders: Studies in the Sociology of Deviance* (New York, Free Press of Glencoe).

Berry, M, Philo, G, Tiripelli, G, Docherty, S and Macpherson, C (2012) 'Media Coverage and Public Understanding of Sentencing Policy in relation to Crimes against Children' 12 *Criminology & Criminal Justice* 567.

Bichard, M (2004) *The Bichard Inquiry Report* (London, Home Office).

Birrell, D and Murie, A (1980) *Policy and Government in Northern Ireland: Lessons of Devolution* (Dublin, Gill and Macmillan).

Bottoms, AE (1995) 'The Philosophy and Politics of Punishment and Sentencing' in C Clarkson and R Morgan (eds), *The Politics of Sentencing Reform* (Oxford, Oxford University Press).

Braithwaite, J (1989) *Crime, Shame and Reintegration* (Sydney, Cambridge University Press).

Brown, K, Deakin, J and Spencer, J (2005) 'A Pilot Study of Public Attitudes Towards Sex Offender Reintegration' (unpublished research report, IMPACT partnership).

Brown, K, Spencer, J and Deakin, J (2008) 'What People Think About the Management of Sex Offenders in the Community' 47 *Howard Journal of Criminal Justice* 259.

Bryan, T and Doyle, P (2003) 'Developing Multi-Agency Public Protection Arrangements' in A Matravers (ed), *Sex Offenders in the Community: Managing and Reducing the Risks* (Cullompton, Willan Publishing, Cambridge Criminal Justice Series).

Cavadino, M and Dignan, J (2006) 'Penal Policy and Political Economy' 6 *Criminology & Criminal Justice* 435.

Conrad, P and Schneider, JW (1980) *Deviance and Medicalization: From Badness to Sickness* (Philadelphia, PA, Temple University Press).

Constantin, S (2008) *Towards a European Criminal Record* (Cambridge, Cambridge University Press).

Council of Europe (2011) *Council of Europe Annual Penal Statistics—SPACE I—2009* (Strasbourg, COE).

Craun, SW and Theriot, MT (2009) 'Misperceptions of Sex Offender Perpetration: Considering the Impact of Sex Offender Registration' 24 *Journal of Interpersonal Violence* 2057.

Crawford, A (1997) *The Local Governance of Crime: Appeals to Community and Partnerships* (Oxford, Clarendon Press).

—— (2006) 'Networked Governance and the Post-Regulatory State? Steering, Rowing and Anchoring the Provision of Policing and Security' 10 *Theoretical Criminology* 449.

Criminal Justice Review Group (CJRG) (2000) *Review of the Criminal Justice System in Northern Ireland: The Report of the Criminal Justice Review* (Belfast, HMSO).
Croall, H, Mooney, G and Munro, M (2010) *Criminal Justice in Scotland* (Oxford, Willan Publishing).
Department of Health and Social Services (Northern Ireland) (DHSS (NI)) (1982) *Report on Homes and Hostels for Children and Young People in Northern Ireland* (Belfast, DHSS) (Sheridan Report).
Dickson, B (2001) *The Legal System of Northern Ireland*, 4th edn (Belfast, SLS Publications).
Ericson, R (2007) *Crime in an Insecure World* (Cambridge, Polity Press).
Ericson, RV and Haggerty, KD (1997) *Policing the Risk Society* (Oxford, Clarendon Press).
Feeley, M and Simon, J (1992) 'The New Penology: Notes on the Emerging Strategy of Corrections and its Implications' 30 *Criminology* 449.
—— (1994) 'Actuarial Justice: The Emerging New Criminal Law' in D Nelken (ed), *The Futures of Criminology* (London, Sage).
Ferguson, H (1995) 'The Paedophile Priest: A Deconstruction' 84 *Studies* 247.
Fitch, K, Spencer, K and Hilton, Z (2007) *Protecting Children from Sexual Abuse: Safer Recruitment of Workers in a Border-free Europe* (London, NSPCC).
Garland, D (1985) *Punishment and Welfare: A History of Penal Strategies* (Aldershot, Gower).
—— (1996) 'The Limits of the Sovereign State: Strategies of Crime Control in Contemporary Society' 36 *British Journal of Criminology* 445.
—— (1999) 'Preface' in P Duff and N Hutton (eds), *Criminal Justice in Scotland* (Aldershot, Ashgate).
—— (2001) *The Culture of Control: Crime and Social Order in Contemporary Society* (Oxford, Oxford University Press).
Grimshaw, R (2004) 'Whose Justice? Principal Drivers of Criminal Justice Policy, Their Implications for Stakeholders, and Some Foundations for Critical Policy Departures', vol 7 (British Society of Criminology conference, London, July 2004).
Harris, AR and Hanson, RK (2004) 'Sex Offender Recidivism—A Simple Question' (Ottawa, Public Safety and Emergency Preparedness Canada).
Hebenton, B and Seddon, T (2009) 'From Dangerousness to Precaution: Managing Sexual and Violent Offenders in an Insecure and Uncertain Age' 49 *British Journal of Criminology* 343.
Home Office (1996) 'Protecting the Public: The Government's Strategy on Crime in England and Wales' (Cm 3190) (London, HMSO).
—— (1997) *The Sex Offenders Act 1997* Home Office Circular 39/97 (London, Home Office).
Horgan, G (2006) 'Devolution, Direct Rule and Neo-liberal Reconstruction in Northern Ireland' 26 *Critical Social Policy* 656.
Hughes, WH (1985) *Report of the Committee of Inquiry into Children's Homes and Hostels* (London, HMSO) (Hughes Report).
Innes, M (2004) 'Signal Crimes and Signal Disorders: Notes on Deviance as Communicative Action' 55 *British Journal of Sociology* 335.
Johnstone, G (2000) 'Penal Policy Making: Elitist, Populist or Participatory?' 2 *Punishment & Society* 161.
Jones, T and Newburn, T (2006) 'Three Strikes and You're Out: Exploring Symbol and Substance in American and British Crime Control Politics' 46 *British Journal of Criminology* 781.
—— (2013) 'Policy Convergence, Politics and Comparative Penal Reform: Sex Offender Notification Schemes in the USA and UK' 15 *Punishment & Society* 439.

Katz-Schiavone, S, Levenson, JS and Ackerman, AR (2008) 'Myths and Facts About Sexual Violence: Public Perceptions and Implications for Prevention' 15 *Journal of Criminal Justice and Popular Culture* 291.

Kemshall, H (2002) 'Effective Probation Practice: An Example of "Advanced Liberal" Responsibilisation?' 41 *Howard Journal of Criminal Justice* 41.

Kemshall, H and Maguire, M (2001) 'Public Protection, Partnership and Risk Penalty: The Multi-agency Risk Management of Sexual and Violent Offenders' 3 *Punishment & Society* 237.

Kemshall, H and Weaver, B (2012) 'The Sex Offender Public Disclosure Pilots in England and Scotland: Lessons for "Marketing Strategies" and Risk Communication with the Public' 12 *Criminology & Criminal Justice* 549.

Kemshall, H and Wood, J (2007) 'Beyond Public Protection: An Examination of Community Protection and Public Health Approaches to High-Risk Offenders' 7 *Criminology & Criminal Justice* 203.

Kleinhans, MM (2002) 'Criminal Justice Approaches to Paedophilic Sex Offenders' 11 *Social & Legal Studies* 233.

Knox, C (2002) '"See No Evil, Hear No Evil": Insidious Paramilitary Violence in Northern Ireland' 42 *British Journal of Criminology* 164.

Laws, DR (2000) 'Sexual Offending as a Public Health Problem: A North American Perspective' 8 *Journal of Research and Treatment* 243.

Leggett, S (2000) 'Paedophiles and other Child Abusers' 5 *The Ulster Humanist* 7.

Levenson, JS, Brannon, YN, Fortney, T and Baker, J (2007) 'Public Perceptions about Sex Offenders and Community Protection Policies' 7 *Analyses of Social Issues and Public Policy* 1.

Lieb, R (2000) 'Social Policy and Sexual Offenders: Contrasting United States and European Policies' 8 *European Journal on Criminal Policy and Research* 423.

—— (2003) 'Joined-up Worrying: The Multi-Agency Public Protection Panels' in A Matravers (ed), *Sex Offenders in the Community: Managing and Reducing the Risks* (Cullompton, Willan Publishing, Cambridge Criminal Justice Series).

Loader, I and Walker, N (2007) *Civilizing Security* (Cambridge, Cambridge University Press).

Maguire, M, Kemshall, H, Noakes, L, Wincup, E and Sharpe, K (2001) 'Risk Management of Sexual and Violent Offenders: The Work of Public Protection Panels' Police Research Series Paper no 13 (London, Home Office).

McAlinden, A (2005) 'The Use of "Shame" with Sexual Offenders' 45 *British Journal of Criminology* 373.

—— (2007a) *The Shaming of Sexual Offenders: Risk, Retribution and Reintegration* (Oxford, Hart Publishing).

—— (2007b) 'Public Attitudes Towards Sex Offenders in Northern Ireland' *Research and Statistical Bulletin 6/2007* (Belfast, Northern Ireland Office, Statistics and Research Branch).

—— (2010) 'Vetting Sexual Offenders: State Over-extension, the Punishment Deficit and the Failure to Manage Risk' 19 *Social & Legal Studies* 25.

—— (2012a) 'The Governance of Sexual Offending Across Europe: Penal Policies, Political Economies and the Institutionalization of Risk' 14 *Punishment & Society* 166.

—— (2012b) *'Grooming' and the Sexual Abuse of Children: Institutional, Internet and Familial Dimensions.* Clarendon Studies in Criminology (Oxford, Oxford University Press).

McLaughlin, E (2005) 'Governance and Social Policy in Northern Ireland (1999–2004): The Devolution Years and Postscript' in M Powell, L Bauld and K Clarke (eds), *Social Policy Review 17* (Bristol, Policy Press/Social Policy Association).

Melossi, D (2001) 'The Cultural Embeddedness of Social Control: Reflections on the Comparison of Italian and North-American Cultures Concerning Punishment' 5 *Punishment & Society* 403.

Moran, M (2003) *The British Regulatory State: High Modernism and Hyper Innovation* (Oxford, Oxford University Press).

Muncie, J (2005) 'The Globalization of Crime Control—The Case of Youth and Juvenile Justice: Neo-liberalism, Policy Convergence and International Conventions' 9 *Theoretical Criminology* 35.

Nelken, D (2007) 'Comparing Criminal Justice' in M Maguire, R Morgan and R Reiner (eds), *The Oxford Handbook of Criminology*, 4th edn (Oxford, Oxford University Press).

Northern Ireland Assembly Research and Library Service (NIARLS) (2010) *Safeguarding Children Between the Jurisdictions of Northern Ireland, Great Britain and the Republic of Ireland* Assembly Briefing Note 73/10 (Belfast, NIARLS).

O'Donnell, I, Baumer, EP and Hughes, N (2008) 'Recidivism in the Republic of Ireland' 8 *Criminology & Criminal Justice* 123.

Parton, N, Thorpe, D and Wattam, C (1997) *Child Protection: Risk and the Moral Order* (Basingstoke, Macmillan).

Petrunik, M and Deutschmann, L (2008) 'The Exclusion–Inclusion Spectrum in State and Community Response to Sex Offenders in Anglo-American and European Jurisdictions' 52 *International Journal of Offender Therapy and Comparative Criminology* 499.

Pinkerton, J (1994) *In Care At Home: Parenting, The State and Civil Society* (Aldershot, Avebury).

Power, H (2003) 'Disclosing Information on Sex Offenders: The Human Rights Implications' in A Matravers (ed), *Sex Offenders in the Community: Managing and Reducing the Risks* (Cullompton, Willan Publishing, Cambridge Criminal Justice Series).

Ramage, S (2007) 'Data Protection and Criminal Justice: Some Recent Developments in EU and Domestic Law' 169 *Criminal Lawyer* 7.

Rose, N (2000) 'Government and Control' 40 *British Journal of Criminology* 321.

Seddon, T (2008) 'Dangerous Liaisons: Personality Disorder and the Politics of Risk' 10 *Punishment & Society* 301.

Shearing, C (2000) 'Punishment and the Changing Face of Governance' 3 *Punishment & Society* 203.

Shute, S (2004) 'The Sexual Offences Act 2003: (4) New Civil Preventative Orders—Sexual Offences Prevention Orders; Foreign Travel Orders; Risk of Sexual Harm Orders' *Criminal Law Review* 417.

Simon, J (1998) 'Managing the Monstrous: Sex Offenders and the New Penology' 4 *Psychology, Public Policy, and Law* 452.

Social Services Inspectorate (SSI) (1993) *An Abuse of Trust: The Report of the Social Services Inspectorate into the Case of Martin Huston* (Belfast, DHSS (SSI)).

Sparks, R (2001) 'Degrees of Estrangement: The Cultural Theory of Risk and Comparative Penology' 5 *Theoretical Criminology* 159.

Stafford, A, Parton, N, Vincent, S and Smith, C (2011) *Child Protection Systems in the United Kingdom: A Comparative Analysis* (London, Jessica Kingsley Publishers).

Tewksbury, R and Mustaine, EE (2007) 'Collateral Consequences and Community Re-Entry for Registered Sex Offenders with Child Victims: Are the Challenges Even Greater? 46 *Journal of Offender Rehabilitation* 113.

Thomas, T (2003) 'Sex Offender Community Notification: Experiences from America' 42 *Howard Journal of Criminal Justice* 217.
Wacquant, L (2001) 'The Penalisation of Poverty and Neo-liberalism' 9 *European Journal on Criminal Policy and Research* 401.
Walmsley, R (2009) *World Prison Population List*, 8th edn (London, International Centre for Prison Studies, King's College London).
Walsh, D (2011) 'Police Cooperation Across the Irish Border: Familiarity Breeding Contempt for Transparency and Accountability' 38 *Journal of Law and Society* 301.
Weaver, B and McNeill, F (2010) 'Public Protection in Scotland: A Way Forward?' in A Williams and M Nash (eds), *Handbook of Public Protection* (Cullompton, Willan Publishing).
Willis, GM, Levenson, JS and Ward, T (2011) 'Desistance and Attitudes Towards Sex Offenders: Facilitation or Hindrance' 25 *Journal of Family Violence* 545.
Wilson, M, McCann, J and Templeton, R (2013) 'SORAM: Towards a Multi-agency Model of Sex Offender Risk Assessment and Management' 10 *Irish Probation Journal* 177.
Wilson, RJ, McWhinnie, A, Picheca, JE, Prinzo, M and Cortoni, F (2007) 'Circles of Support and Accountability: Engaging Community Volunteers in the Management of High-Risk Sexual Offenders' 46 *Howard Journal* 1.
Zedner, L (2009) 'Fixing the Future? The Pre-emptive Turn in Criminal Justice' in B McSherry, A Norrie and S Bronitt (eds), *Regulating Deviance: The Redirection of Criminalisation and the Futures of Criminal Law* (Oxford, Hart Publishing).

16

Restorative Justice in the Northern Ireland Transition

ANNA ERIKSSON

Introduction

A society moving through a transition faces considerable challenges: establishing a strong, peaceful and democratic social order, and ensuring all groups in society have equal access to social, economic and political power structures. After 30 years of protracted violent conflict, this was the task facing Northern Ireland after the signing of the Peace Agreement in 1998. No easy undertaking during the best of circumstances, but Northern Ireland at this point was still a deeply divided society where grievances stemming from historical and political injustice remained significant contributors to violent action in local communities. It was necessary for communities to heal, to move closer to each other, and for community and state to form a less antagonistic relationship. This chapter will discuss these challenges and explore how restorative justice, within both state and community spheres, has provided tools to aid this difficult journey. The core strength of restorative justice in relation to conflict resolution at all levels—individual, community, society—is that it removes the focus from the *outcome* and places it where the important interactions take place, the *process* (Eriksson 2008, 2009a). By employing such a procedural justice lens, the principles and practices of restorative justice have the potential to facilitate the overall transition and transform previously antagonistic relationships by addressing the underlying needs of participants instead of focusing on sanitised outcome measures. The chapter will discuss restorative justice practices initiated both within and outside the formal criminal justice system in Northern Ireland and attempt to draw out the key context-specific lessons and those that might be generalised to other jurisdictions.

The chapter will discuss the role of restorative justice in Northern Ireland from 1998 to the present day. Restorative justice initiatives, at both state and community levels, have continued to flourish after the first crucial 10 years of the transition, but they have moved into a more mainstream and less controversial position compared with the earlier years of their practice (Knox 2013). Restorative justice is an inherently flexible practice, adapting to the needs of the participants and the type of conflict addressed. Hence, the shape and form of these practices have changed since their inception, both due to the shifting needs of participants and the political landscape of Northern Ireland. This latter factor has been a major influence on the practice of restorative justice in the jurisdiction, particularly at the community level. Politics always plays a role in the construction of and response to crime and conflict, but in a society going through a transition, it permeates all aspects of initiatives aimed at addressing crime, conflict and disorder. Importantly, in this context the values of restorative justice reflect the aims of transitional justice more broadly, such as seeking accountability and truth, achieving reparation and restitution, and allowing for healing and reconciliation. By providing a process whereby people can meet face to face and openly talk about all the circumstances of their conflict, not just what would have been allowed as evidence in court, it allows for democratic participation and conflict resolution (Clamp and Doak 2012). As a consequence, this paradigm overlap between restorative and transitional justice (O'Mahony 2012) means that restorative justice can be viewed as a micro-process that encourages transformation and a forward-looking focus at the macro-level in a society.

Since restorative justice emerged as an alternative to the dominant adversarial practices in the early 1990s, it has been utilised in relation to offences within the criminal justice system ranging from juvenile crime (Sherman and Strang 2007) to sexual offences (McAlinden 2011a, 2011b; Daly et al 2013; CIJ 2014). Its application has also spread to many different locations, such as schools, prisons and wider community resolution (Hopkins 2002; Barabás et al 2012; Vanfraechem and Zinsstag 2012). Importantly, the principles of restorative justice also resonate strongly with the needs of a society in the midst of political transition, whereby values such as justice reconstruction, peace-building, and reintegration often needs to be pursued concurrently (Minow 1998; Teitel 2000; Leebaw 2001; McEvoy and Eriksson 2006). The inclusion of restorative justice processes during periods of political transitions has increased dramatically since the first well-known example of South Africa's Truth and Reconciliation Commission (Hayner 2001; Skelton 2002; Llewellyn 2007; Froestad and Shearing 2007). It has also been utilised in Rwanda, in the aftermath of genocide (Drumbl 2002; Waldorf 2006), in Timor Leste (Stanley 2009) and Serbia (Nikolic-Ristanovic 2006), essentially building a bridge between needs and activities of state and community actors. In this chapter, I will discuss these unique bridging capabilities of restorative justice within the particular context of Northern Ireland. I will explore how it has been used to reduce distance between individuals, communities, and community and state. It has arguably been successful in this by utilising face to face meetings, essentially functioning as a tool that can increase the recognition of the 'Other', and encouraging feelings of responsibility towards the other person or group, moving towards a creation of moral relationships and moral behaviour towards the previously excluded.

Restorative Justice Practice in Northern Ireland

Restorative justice is a response to crime and conflict that promotes inclusive dialogue; direct participation in the resolution of one's own conflicts; acceptance of responsibility; reparation of harm and rebuilding of relationships among victims, offenders and communities; reintegration; and empowerment (Braithwaite 1989; Braithwaite and Mugford 1994; Roche 2002). A fundamental tenet of this approach is a shift in accountability, from offenders owing a debt to the loosely defined 'society', to being accountable directly to the victims of their actions, and taking personal responsibility for the wider consequences of those actions (Christie 1977; Braithwaite 1989; Roche 2003; Eriksson 2009a). At its core, restorative justice personalises, whereas the more traditional criminal justice process tends to depersonalise. Or, put another way, restorative justice includes, and criminal justice excludes. This personalisation, of putting a face to the victim, offender and other persons affected, in combination with a process that is inclusive instead of exclusive, is one of the key reasons why restorative justice practices can be a facilitator of transformation and previously unimaginable change during a period of transition and beyond.

Restorative practice around the world takes several forms, including victim–offender mediation, group conferences, and shuttle mediation (McCold 2006). All the forms of practice are utilised in Northern Ireland, both within community-based initiatives and within the juvenile justice system, the latter of which has been completely remodelled and now has restorative justice conferencing at its core (O'Mahony 2012). The community-based initiatives, freed from the constraints of operating within a formal and traditional system, have further extended the principles and philosophy of restorative justice to engage in larger community education work, crime prevention, victim support, and engagement with disaffected youth in local communities, an indication of the flexibility of restorative justice to meet the needs of participants in whatever circumstances they might be found (Eriksson 2009a). Both practices will be briefly described below, before a more detailed exploration of their contributions during the transition.

Community-Based Restorative Justice in Northern Ireland

Community-based restorative justice in Northern Ireland was initially designed to supplant systems of violent informal 'justice' practices by paramilitary organisations in both republican and loyalist communities. But since their inception in 1998, their practice has broadened considerably and now encompasses a wide range of community mediation work, crime prevention with young people, victim support, and reintegration post-release in cooperation with the Probation Service

(Eriksson 2009a; 2009b). There are two distinct projects, one in republican areas called Community Restorative Justice Ireland (CRJI), the other in loyalist areas called Northern Ireland Alternatives (NIA). Both were established and are led by former political ex-prisoners and former combatants of the Provisional Irish Republican Army (PIRA) and the Ulster Volunteer Force (UVF) respectively, and the presence of these individuals has caused much controversy within Northern Ireland and elsewhere (Eriksson 2009a). CRJI now exists in eight different nationalist areas of Northern Ireland, and NIA in five unionist areas. During the first 10 years of practice, there was very limited cooperation between the two projects, reflecting the entrenched and deep division between the two. However, over time, this cooperation has strengthened and there is now a recognised partnership between the two organisations, forming a stronger platform and working together to draw attention to the serious issues facing working class communities throughout Northern Ireland.

The projects were established with the explicit intention of providing a non-violent alternative to punishment violence, as practised by paramilitary groups in both communities at the time. Punishment violence formed part of an informal system of 'justice', and could involve shootings (in the arms, legs or a combination of both), and/or beatings (using baseball bats, iron bars, cudgels, hurley sticks[1] and so on) for the purpose of punishing those who committed crimes or engaged in anti-social behaviour, or as a means of internal discipline within the paramilitary organisations. Measures such as warnings, curfews and exclusions from the community were also common (Bell 1996; Hamill 2002; Monaghan 2002). These 'policing' activities were undertaken by republican and loyalist paramilitary groups in the working class communities in which they lived and operated. These practices had their origins in the 'Troubles', beginning in the early 1970s, when the police were engaged in fighting insurgents and consequently paid less attention to 'ordinary' crime. Additionally, the police were seen as an illegitimate force in republican communities and as such were largely denied access to these areas. The existence of this informal system of 'justice' was not a problem confined to local communities, but signified a direct challenge to the legitimacy of the Northern Irish state, resulting in a high profile contest between state and community over the ownership of justice and in debates around the management and prevention of crime and anti-social behaviour within the period of transition (McEvoy and Eriksson 2006).

The paramilitary ceasefires and the signing of the Good Friday Agreement in 1998 did not lead to an end to the violence in Northern Ireland. The punishment violence, vigilante attacks and rioting proved difficult to eradicate, arguably existing as part of an ingrained culture of violence in Northern Ireland (MacGinty and

[1] A wooden stick, up to a metre long, used in the Irish sport of hurling, with a flattened, curved end used for striking the leather ball. Because of its strong connections with Irish identity and culture, it was rarely used by loyalist paramilitaries for the purpose of punishment beatings, who seemed to prefer cricket bats (author's fieldwork notes).

Darby 2002; Knox and Monaghan 2002; Jarman 2004). Post the Peace Agreement, sectarian attacks between the communities led to a new cycle of degeneration in community relations and the number of 'peace walls'—physical and starkly visible divisions between the two communities throughout Belfast—increased during the transitional period (Shirlow and Murtagh 2006). This pattern is common to many other transitional societies, where a decrease in political violence occurs simultaneously with an increase in ordinary violence and crime, which is what Steenkamp (2005) has referred to as 'a culture of violence', characterised by an environment where it is socially permissive to use violence as a response to both interpersonal conflict and to communal problems of crime and disorder following a period of protracted violent conflict. Such a culture arguably exists in many other communities around the world, many of which have not experienced conflict on the scale of Northern Ireland, but where large distances between state and community has left room for an informal system of 'justice' to operate, where the community 'other' is often constructed around race and class (Hope and Foster 1992). In the transitional society, such an ingrained culture does not end overnight after the signing of a peace agreement, but can continue for years or indeed decades if the underlying drivers of such a culture are not addressed. During such a transitional period, and beyond, violence thus 'loses its political meaning and becomes a way of dealing with everyday issues … a socially accepted mechanism to achieve power and status in society' (Steenkamp 2005: 254). And it was this situation that community-based restorative justice in Northern Ireland aimed to address.

The practice of these projects has been covered extensively elsewhere (McEvoy and Mika 2001, 2002; Eriksson 2009a; Clamp 2013), and I will not spend time rehearsing that literature here. Instead I will summarise their key features, and then spend more time in exploring how they have contributed to reducing violence during the period of transition and beyond, drawing on scholarship that focuses on the sociological processes underlying the initiation and maintenance of conflict, which will hopefully contribute some new thinking to the area of restorative justice overall, and the use of restorative practices within the transitional context in particular. So to summarise, community-based restorative justice in Northern Ireland is characterised by three key features. First, the presence of former combatants and political ex-prisoners which was crucial in providing moral, political and military leadership during this period of transition (McEvoy and Eriksson 2006). Second, in combination with the first point, the strong grassroots ethos and the emphasis on local community members as volunteers provided the moral authority and legitimacy at the local level to challenge and educate both paramilitary organisations and the wider community in non-violent approaches to conflict resolution. This is especially important in the context where the legitimacy of the state and the criminal justice system has been severely questioned (McEvoy and Newburn 2003; Shearing et al 2006). And third, the firm adherence to certain key restorative justice *values* in combination with a strong focus on a flexible *process*, have resulted in the projects in both communities being able to respond to a wide range of communal and interpersonal conflicts.

The caseloads in both projects have been high since their inception, and in 2012, CRJI dealt with 1722 cases, involving almost 7000 people across their locations.[2] For NIA, it is somewhat less, due to their different model of practice, but their reach and impact in local communities is no less extensive. Importantly, both projects utilised a large number of volunteers to undertake much of the mediation and support work. This also means that the 'ripple effect' of restorative justice processes and values travels far beyond individual cases. And from being seen as a threat to the legitimacy of the criminal justice system, as unruly community projects led by people who the state wish would just go away, both projects have now received official accreditation and work in partnership with police and other criminal justice agencies, including the Youth Justice Agency, which delivers restorative justice practice within the formal criminal justice system. This is no small feat, and the road towards closer cooperation between the Northern Irish state and formerly disaffected communities has not only been rocky, but also slippery, ill lit and without road signs; their continued success by adapting to the constantly changing landscape of a political transition is nothing short of remarkable.

Youth Conferencing in the Criminal Justice System

Restorative justice does not only take place in local communities however, but has also been introduced in the criminal justice system and now exists at the centre of the juvenile justice system through the Youth Justice Agency.[3] Restorative youth conferencing and Youth Conference Orders were introduced in the Belfast area in 2002, by the Justice Act (Northern Ireland) 2002, and after a gradual expansion, became available across Northern Ireland from 2006. Part of its aim was to increase participation and confidence in the criminal justice system, a particularly important task in a transitional period where the legitimacy of the formal system has been severely eroded. Moreover, the fact that almost all personnel of the criminal justice system was drawn from only one community in this divided society further diminished its legitimacy in the eyes of the other community (O'Mahony 2012).

The legislation empowers the Public Prosecution Service to arrange a conference for most young people charged with a criminal offence in Northern Ireland. The young person can be diverted to a youth conference that covers all types of offences, apart from those that attract a mandatory sentence such as murder, which will be heard in the formal court instead. Also, persistent offenders and those who do not comply with the outcome agreement, will be referred back to court and not offered a youth conference (Zinsstag and Chapman 2012). A referral to a conference requires that the offender admits guilt and that there is an agreement about

[2] The author has assisted CRJI with their annual reports from 2007 to 2012, and has had first-hand access to the relevant statistics.

[3] See chapter by Haydon and McAlister in this volume for further discussion of youth justice in Northern Ireland and the wider UK.

the basic facts of a case. For those who plead 'not guilty' the restorative process is closed. Outcomes of a conference may include,

> a verbal or written apology, reparation directly to the victim or indirectly to the community in form of unpaid work, financial compensation, supervision by an adult, participation in activities or programmes to address offending, restrictions on actions (may include curfews, prohibitions from entering certain places, eg a shop, electronic monitoring, and custody), and treatment for a mental health condition or for alcohol and drugs (Zinsstag and Chapman 2012: 176).

However, the agreed upon outcome is not final and will be referred back to the Prosecution Service or youth court, whichever made the referral. Here, the outcome can be modified based on the principles of proportionality or the more loosely defined 'public interest' (Zinsstag and Chapman 2012). Such amendments may be necessary to prevent excessive or too lenient outcomes, which can arguably serve to undermine the legitimacy of the conference and the views of the people in that room. This however is an inevitable compromise for a restorative initiative that operates at the heart of the criminal justice system.

The Youth Justice Agency has engaged in continued evaluation of its practice since its inception. The evaluations indicate that these restorative justice practices have largely been successful in relation to participant satisfaction with both process and outcome (Campbell at al 2005; Maruna et al 2007). But importantly, what restorative practices within the criminal justice system can achieve, beyond the more traditional 'outcome' measures, is to bring members of disaffected communities and representatives of the criminal justice system closer, providing legitimacy and understanding to both, which in a transitional and divided society ought to be seen as more important than simple recidivism statistics.

The Social Production of Immorality and the Northern Irish Conflict

The expression 'a culture of violence' (Steenkamp 2005) was mentioned above in relation to the existence of punishment violence, high levels of youth offending, large-scale rioting, and cross-community attacks. It contains the assertion that there is a direct link between exposure to violence over a long period of time and an acceptance of violence as a means of resolving conflict and responding to frustrations in everyday life (Hayes and McAllister 2001; Laplante 2008; Lambourne 2009). Hence, the experience of prolonged violent conflict in Northern Ireland arguably resulted in the use of violence as a means of conflict resolution becoming embedded in the norms which guide behaviour in interpersonal interactions, as well as interactions between the two communities, and between community and state. Importantly, a culture of violence can exist on several levels simultaneously—-individual, communal, and state (Steenkamp 2005). These levels are interconnected, and individual actions take place within and are affected by the violence supporting values at community and state levels. The task within a period of transition, then, becomes to address these violence supporting norms at *all* levels. This is where restorative justice can play an important part, by offering non-violent solutions to conflict. But I would argue that the impact of restorative justice goes beyond this, that it addresses, sometimes unconsciously, the drivers that have maintained Northern Ireland as a divided society. To fully explore this argument, I first need to locate those drivers, and then explain how restorative justice fits into the picture.

The key to understanding a culture of violence is that culture is not something one is born with but rather it is learned through socialisation, using the symbols and behavioural codes available to members of any one group or society (Groff and Smoker 1996). In the Northern Irish context, such a transfer of knowledge formed part of a 'socialisation which is restricted almost exclusively to a reproduction of the values in one's own respective political community' (McAuley 2004: 545). The distance between the communities—in terms of identity and history—seemed unbridgeable in the years following the Peace Agreement, and to a certain extent today, still is. The two communities were comprehensively 'Othered' in the eyes of one another, but so was the state in the eyes of the republican community, and the republican community in the eyes of the state. These distances maintained the conflict, and continue to maintain violence as a response to various grievances. A culture of violence may be the catch-all term for this, but the analysis would benefit from some more nuance, by more clearly identifying the variables that create and maintain division and that move a group from 'us' to 'them'. Once identified, restorative justice, as I hope to show, can play a central part in reducing the distance and, as a consequence, the violence.

The concept of a 'culture of violence' has been addressed from a psychological perspective, focusing on the frustrations of basic human needs, such as the need for security, a positive identity, and how the frustration or blocking of such needs can create an inclination towards aggression and violence (Staub 1989, 1996, 1999, 2003). The communal level of such a culture has also been addressed, but mainly in relation to the American South (Gastil 1971; Cohen and Nesbitt 1994), and the Sicilian Mafia (Cottino 1999). This literature is, however, largely exploratory and descriptive, and is not particularly useful in providing guidance for how such embedded cultural norms are maintained, nor how they can be challenged. The avoidance of a more in-depth analysis is a missed opportunity, in that such an omission prevents an exploration of the variables and processes that not only maintain such cultures, but which can challenge them as part of broader peace-building and crime prevention efforts in the transitional context. Arguably, such an analysis can also be an important component of crime prevention efforts in high-crime communities in more 'settled' societies.

As I have argued elsewhere (Eriksson 2009a), restorative justice can be an important facilitator for challenging such embedded cultural norms at all levels. But to further understand how this takes place in practice, and what it is restorative justice actually *does*, I would like to introduce a new area of literature into this discussion, which can significantly contribute to exploring the social drivers of conflict, and which can add nuance and explanatory power to the 'culture of violence' concept. It can also challenge narrow notions of 'success' when it comes to restorative justice outcomes within a transition. This is an area of scholarship that I have not discussed in my previous writings on this topic and one that I think can significantly add to our understanding of the potential effectiveness of restorative justice, both within and outside Northern Ireland. The scholarship I am referring to is that by Zygmunt Bauman, and in particular his seminal work *Modernity and the Holocaust* (1989). In this book, he discussed the *social production of immorality* and this sociological model not only allows for theorisation and operationalisation of the drivers of conflict, but when extended, can also explain why, and through what processes, restorative justice can be an effective tool by which ingrained cultures of violence can be addressed during a transitional period. So for the remainder of the chapter I will first, explain the model of the social production of immorality; second, I will apply it to the Northern Irish context, aiming to identify at least some of the relevant variables; and third, I will explain how I see the role of restorative justice fitting into the equation.

The social production of immorality is essentially a process of 'social othering' through the use of techniques that dehumanise and devalue other individuals or groups. Importantly, it removes the focus on individual actors and locates the emergence and maintenance of conflict in its wider social, historical and political context. The process can be summarised as: social **proximity**—the sense that we all belong to the same group, the same community, the same society, where we share commonly held norms and values—leads to feelings of **responsibility** towards the other, towards the people who are also part of the group of 'us' (Bauman 1989). This sense of responsibility, in turn, leads to moral behaviour towards the other person. The more we identify with another person, the more we can see that person within the full circumstances of his or her life, and understand and empathise with those circumstances, the less likely we are to treat that person badly. But when this sense of **responsibility is diffused**, due to an **erosion of proximity**, immoral behaviour becomes possible, without accompanying feelings of guilt. When such an erosion of proximity takes place in relation to a whole group, or community, which is then effectively labelled as the 'Other', immoral behaviour can escalate from tit for tat attacks to genocide (Bauman 1989; Jamieson 1999). Morality, in this instance, is an *object* of social processes, not simply its *product* as many individual level theories argue. Importantly, there are so-called **techniques** that **erode proximity,** and in the context of Northern Ireland these take the form of physical barriers between communities (so-called 'peace walls'); flags that mark territory and ownership for a particular group; a political rhetoric that marks a community as 'the terrorist Other'; uniforms and clothes that mark group belonging; certain terminology that is used about people in the 'Other' community; the Protestant annual marches that remind everyone about the historical 'justifications' for the division, and so on.

Hence, the mechanisms that produce distance, a distance that can then lead to 'immoral behaviour towards the other' (Bauman 1989) are mechanisms that divide people and groups into 'us' and 'them'. Through social processes, increasingly negative characteristics are attached to the Other, marking them as a threat to 'our' world order, to 'our' society, to 'our' way of life, and social and cultural proximity becomes eroded, leading to a diffusion of responsibility and, ultimately, to immoral behaviour towards the constructed Other (Bauman 1989). This social process has largely been applied to explain the drivers of genocide, but I think it can be very useful in describing not only conflict and violence on a smaller scale, but also in helping to identify the variables that fuel and sustain the conflict in the first place. The point of this is of course to be able to address those very variables in an effort to reduce conflict as part of larger peace-building efforts during the transition.

Importantly however, even though the variables that fuel and maintain conflict can be found in social processes, the consequences of conflict and violence are always intensely personal. Hence, the resolution of conflict ought to be personal too, and include those directly affected by it, and not be imposed as a 'one size fits all' solution from the top; participatory community practices, which actively involve individuals in the resolution of their own conflicts, and where the techniques of erosion can be challenged and distance reduced, would arguably be the most effective. And this is obviously where I see restorative justice fitting into the equation.

Restorative Justice and the Building of Proximity

The key aim in a transitional period, following this model then, is to reduce distance—between people, communities, and community and state. So what does restorative justice have to do with the social production of immorality? I would argue that it could act as a central tool or facilitator by which distance—social, cultural, historical and political distance—can be reduced. The potential lies in the personal meeting, the opportunity to see the other party in his or her life context, when a conflict can become personalised, individualised and humanised. The process of restorative justice provides the opportunity to critically question many of the techniques that erode proximity, many of which have deep roots in the Troubles. The rather extensive literature on restorative justice and emotions talks about shame, guilt, forgiveness and empathy, all of which can surface in a restorative meeting (Braithwaite 1989; Ahmed et al 2001; Maxwell and Morris 2004). But to simplify matters somewhat, one could argue that the feelings of shame and guilt stem from encouraging the proximity between the two parties, allowing them to experience a 'sameness' which, if successful, can lead to feelings of responsibility towards the other, for example, empathy. So what the restorative justice process is capable of achieving is a humanisation of the Other, by challenging techniques of erosion, encouraging proximity and responsibility, and by extension, moral behaviour towards the Other. It moves the Other from the outside to the inside, into one's own personal universe of obligation (Fein 1979) where moral bonds connect in a web of responsible actions.

Social rewards for violence, limited sanctioning for attacks on the Other community, a communal glorification of violence, an overall punitive community, and a not fully legitimate police force have all been important factors in maintaining a culture of violence in Northern Ireland. These factors are expressions of the diffusion of responsibility that has taken place due to the erosion of proximity—between people, groups, communities and the state. Arguably, restorative justice, with its focus on (re)integration, of addressing underlying reasons for offending with its future-looking philosophy and emphasis on participation, inclusiveness and responsibilisation, can be well placed to address such complex issues within the transitional society. This potential of restorative justice also means that the process is capable of addressing conflict at all sustaining levels of a culture of violence—individual, community and society. This is because the inherent flexibility of the restorative processes makes it capable of being highly sensitive to the political, social and cultural context in which it is applied. Restorative justice in Northern Ireland, both state-based and community-based models have arguably had some success in all three areas, but particularly the first and third, but have had limited success addressing the entrenched division between the two communities.

Reducing Distance within Communities

It has been argued that if 'restorative justice projects can foster greater involvement in and ownership over crime management … then they may become a tool for greater community tolerance, cohesion and non-violence' (McEvoy and Mika 2001: 375). It is this involvement, this move back to ownership of one's own conflicts (Christie 1977) that is the very feature of restorative justice which is aimed at reducing distance, by encouraging proximity and by extension, feelings of responsibility. The two community-based restorative justice projects—CRJI and NIA—have done this by aiming their practice beyond the narrow focus of dealing with individuals under threat by paramilitary groups, by also including the perpetrators of punishment violence as well as victims' families.

In earlier empirical research carried out by the author, one practitioner in CRJI mentioned in an interview that,

> the work we do, it gives us the opportunity to create awareness among the armed group in the area about community needs. Like when you talk to the armed groups about a particular person, then there is a better understanding by the armed groups about where that person is coming from (interview, 2 December 2004).

This, following Bauman's model, reduces distance by encouraging us to recognise the inherent humanity of the Other, and by extension, facilitates feelings of moral responsibility towards that person. Also during fieldwork in 2005, the manager of NIA said, in relation to punishment violence and community attitudes:

> We had it for 30 years and it did not solve anything. We don't say that we have a magic wand but we feel that in the long term it is far more valid for our community to address these issues by having residents taking responsibility, to have young people address and own up to the damage they have done within their communities, and to do so in a restorative way, as opposed to beating them … I think that slowly but surely it is a trickle towards that. There is still an appetite among people towards a punitive way, but there is a shift, there is a change (interview, 19 May 2005).

This change, this shift, was referred to by restorative justice practitioners in both communities as aiming towards 'a new mindset'. The expression reflects the point made previously, that although the causes of a conflict might be found in the historical and social processes of a place, its resolution and the potential to move forward are deeply personal. It is a new way of thinking, a new way of viewing oneself, one's place in society and that of those around us. Needless to say, this is no easy task and one reason why societal transformation, which is what a period of transition is, is a slow and arduous task.

Hence, the aim of community restorative justice praxis in relation to punishment violence, and the means by which the projects have encouraged proximity and responsibility, can be said to be fourfold: mediating directly with people who come under threat by paramilitaries; addressing underlying causes of why people came to the attention of the paramilitaries in the first place; engaging paramilitary groups themselves in terms of modes of conflict resolution; and involving the wider community in education forums. Viewed in such a way, the practice of restorative justice at the micro-level, working directly with individuals and their families, can have an impact on the macro-level which, particularly in the beginning, included both paramilitaries' organisations and the wider community, a dynamic referred to by many practitioners and volunteers of restorative justice as 'the ripple effect'. Like rings on water, the distance between people and groups is reduced, when the moral universe of responsibility (Fein, 1979) gradually includes more and more people.

Reducing the Distance Between Community and State

Restorative justice in transitional societies faces a number of additional difficulties compared with those in more stable jurisdictions. State-based initiatives are most likely regarded with some cynicism by affected communities where the criminal justice system was contorted during the conflict (for example, through emergency legislation) or where the police or state security forces have been guilty of human rights abuses in their war against the non-state forces (Roche 2002; Nowrojee 2005). Indeed, as has been the case in Northern Ireland, restorative justice programmes that are led by police or other criminal justice agencies may struggle to develop partnerships with precisely those local communities most directly affected by the conflict, thus severely limiting the transformative potential of restorative justice in areas where it is most needed. Not only did the community-based projects display some suspicion and mistrust towards state-based restorative justice, the Northern Irish state was not welcoming of community-based efforts during the first 10 years of their practice (Eriksson 2009a). In Northern Ireland, 'the community' has long been a highly contested, divided and politicised concept. For decades, it was constructed as the 'sea in which the paramilitary fish swims' (Sluka 1989), a rhetoric that essentially served to 'other', not just the paramilitaries, but the entire community in which they lived.

The communities themselves, in particular working class Catholic communities, were also characterised by norms and values which contained strong opposition to the state (Shirlow and Murtagh 2006), which would come as no surprise for those who have read the preceding chapters in this book. At the front line of the state's defence was the police force, which as a consequence, was actively constructed as the enemy (Ellison and Smyth 2000), existing in a totally different moral universe (Fein 1979) from that of many working class communities. This can be attributed to the moral bonds between state and community being comprehensively ruptured due to the Troubles, where the police were on the front line of violent confrontations with local communities, backed up by the British Army (Ellison and Smyth 2000). In such circumstances, a top-down approach to dealing with community conflict may not only fail, but further alienate the community in question, being a counterproductive strategy due to the almost total erosion of proximity and the dual abdication of moral responsibility for the Other. The ongoing effect of such ruptured bonds can be seen in the attitudes and behaviours of groups of disaffected young people in the post-conflict society (Shirlow and Murtagh 2006). And as noted by Jarman (2004: 434):

> These types of activities, whether it's rioting, antisocial behaviour, low-level crime, or just hanging around on street corners, also bring many young people into contact with the police *and here too is a relationship based on mutual suspicion and hostility and lack of mutual respect, which serves to increase the marginalisation of many young people* (emphasis added).

One would think that challenging and ending practices of paramilitary punishment violence would have been the biggest challenge during the transitional period. But I would argue that it is the relationship between state and community that has presented the largest obstacles and is perhaps also where the most significant changes have taken place, and where they are continuing to take place. A reduction of the distance between state and community requires changing of mindsets, not just amongst former paramilitaries and disaffected communities, but amongst all the individuals who work in the criminal justice system and other statutory agencies. A successful transition requires former enemies to become friends, or at least to exist in a relationship of mutual respect, if not full understanding. The fraught relationship between the republican communities and the Northern Irish state is well rehearsed (McGarry and O'Leary 1995; Ruane and Todd 1996; Hayes and McAllister 2001), but the relationship between loyalist communities and the state is not unambiguous either, particularly when every gesture of reconciliation towards the republican community is perceived as an automatic loss for the loyalist counterpart. It is a zero-sum game which often stands in the way of real change. Hence, the police, who have been regarded as legitimate by the loyalists, were subject to serious criticism throughout the transition due to their efforts of engaging in community policing in the 'other' community, and for this reason were seen as 'selling out', as was commented on by a restorative justice volunteer in the loyalist area of the Shankill:

> The RUC could much better deal with what was happening here, they had much more manpower. Now, with the way the whole situation has changed here [to the PSNI and operating under new Human Rights directives], the police, to me, seem to be perfectly useless. I am pro the police and totally believe that we have to have a police force ... but at the moment the police force seem to have been destroyed ... And this community has completely lost faith in the police. They don't look up to the police, they don't trust the police (interview, 19 May 2005).

NIA managed to develop a working partnership with some local police officers soon after its establishment, but this cooperation was largely unofficial and based on personal contacts, and by no means without its problems. As mentioned by the manager of NIA:

> [A]ll relationships are built on trust and it takes a long time for that to happen. At the beginning there was a lot of suspicion on us from the police, and I can understand that. But there was a lot of suspicion from *us* regarding the police, and I think it took them a wee bit longer to understand that (interview, 27 May 2005).

That the relationship between police and local communities in republican areas was significantly more fraught is an understatement. In an interview with the author in 2008, the coordinator of CRJI said:

> If you had said eight years ago that there is a legitimate reason for dealing with the police, you would have been laughed out of existence. Just a silly idea, as to be completely nonsensical. But the political argument has moved, so the rationale for having a relationship with the PSNI has changed. But people are still using the old arguments and rationales. So, you know, they can't fit the two of them together.

This quote clearly illustrates that even though Northern Ireland had come a long way in the 10 years since the Peace Agreement, people on the ground had not come to terms with this new reality. And this is where the two community-based restorative justice projects have done some of their most important work. The effect of the leadership provided by these projects in working with the police, which in the last few years have been guided by official protocols of cooperation, should not be underestimated. Indeed, in a transitional context, some of the most effective leadership at the community level can be provided by the very people who were at the front lines of the armed struggle (McEvoy and Eriksson 2006) and that is arguably what we have seen through the praxis of restorative justice projects in both communities.

It is not only communities, however, which need to change their mindset in a transition; state actors are also responsible for this. One of the many difficulties with first the informal, and then the formal partnerships between community restorative justice and the police as highlighted by a senior police officer, was the building of relationships that had never been there in the first place. In this regard, the manager of CRJI commented:

> What seems to have happened is that individuals in both organisations have contact at a human level and have started to build trust [and] their experiences as human beings is then reflected back into both organisations. Because relationships in those organisations are like relationships anywhere else; those things will rub off and there is a ripple effect within the organisations (interview, 18 January 2008).

This quote reflects the efforts of promoting proximity, through personal face to face interaction, which in turn encourages responsibility and moral relationships; personal transformation that then trickles down into the organisations on the respective sides of the divide. The erosion of proximity between the two has also led to neither having any significant direct knowledge about the Other; what they know is built on the constructions of the Other as the enemy, entrenched over decades of violent conflict. The partnerships between community and state organisations facilitate such knowledge transfer, slowly building trust and understanding on a case-by-case basis. The restorative conferencing taking place in the Youth Justice Agency also has an important role to play here.

As argued by O'Mahony (2012: 571):

> The successful adoption of restorative justice within criminal justice can help to foster confidence in criminal justice and allows for the devolution and ownership of aspects of justice back into civil society. Such measures are likely to contribute to increased levels of social justice and civic agency, necessary for the effective function of civil society moving forward in a transitional environment.

In the restorative conferences run by the Youth Justice Agency, victims and offenders are sometimes from different communities, but importantly, the young people and their support persons are participants in an inclusive process that involves police and other criminal justice actors. This is an excellent opportunity for techniques of erosion to be challenged, to increase the understanding and knowledge of the Other and hopefully, over time and with the same ripple effect that emanates from the community, similar rings on the water that is contemporary Northern Ireland will continue to spread, including more and more people within the same moral universe.

Reducing the Distance Between Communities

This is probably the area where restorative justice in Northern Ireland has been least successful. As mentioned previously, early attempts by the community-based projects to work together failed due to the deep division and long-standing construction of the 'Other' community as 'the enemy'. Some progress has been made here, but there is still a long way to go. When talking to practitioners of restorative justice in Northern Ireland about the factors that could ease the tension between the communities, the most common answer is 'time'. The Youth Justice Agency, whose conference practice includes young people from both communities as victims and offenders, might have had more of an impact here by allowing for techniques of erosion, such as prejudice and hatred that have their roots firmly planted in the history of Northern Ireland, to be challenged through face to face meetings. But even this is only making a small dent, and other solutions will be needed to heal this division. Current work on truth recovery and other tools to deal with the past in Northern Ireland hold considerable promise in this area (see McEvoy 2006; McEvoy and Gormally 2009).

Conclusion

The development and affirmation of new social norms through participatory practice such as restorative justice is an especially important feature in a transitional society, where systems of informal and formal justice, and the relationship between them, are in a process of renegotiation. And because injustice is incurred, not just as a result of interpersonal violence, but as a result of 'societal structural violence, that is violence done to people through the exercise of power, and hierarchical social arrangements that support the maintenance of this power' (Sullivan and Tifft 1998: 43), it is of central importance to address the societal processes and conditions that reproduce harm, inequality and violence by actively working with the underlying and fuelling conditions of conflict. The principles and practices of restorative justice, for example, non-violence, inclusiveness, respect, reparation, integration, and empowerment, can provide a useful organising framework through which communities and the state can themselves take the lead in the transformation required. Importantly, it is the opportunity to actually *experience* the use of such values in interpersonal interaction that is of central value. It is a case-by-case journey, offering alternatives to the traditional, violent ways of dealing with crime and anti-social behaviour in post-conflict Northern Ireland.

Bauman's concept of the social production of immorality (1989) provides a tool through which these variables and processes can be identified, understood, and placed in their maintaining historical, social and political context. Restorative justice, with its focus on the face to face meeting, breaking down the barriers between us and them, with its forward-looking and inclusionary philosophy, can serve as a vehicle through which such transformation can take place; one meeting, one case at a time. Restorative justice builds proximity, whereas many 'formal' criminal justice processes erode it. In contrast to the formal criminal justice system, restorative justice personalises and humanises, allowing for social and cultural distances to be overcome. By encouraging proximity and facilitating feelings of responsibility, restorative justice at all levels can challenge punitive attitudes, increasing understanding and legitimacy of community and state alike. Considering that the consequences of conflict are often deeply personal, a process that allows for recognition of the Other and feelings of responsibility to emerge, can be a powerful vehicle by which social division is reduced—between individuals and community, and community and state. By bringing in the Other into one's own universe of obligation—one person, one meeting at a time—restorative justice in Northern Ireland is arguably contributing to transforming the discourse of 'us' and 'them' in Northern Ireland which, I would argue, is peace-building in practice.

With regard to restorative justice in transitional societies, Northern Ireland is arguably unique in that the community-based projects developed independently from the state survived despite considerable opposition, and have managed to build tangible bridges between communities and the state. It has become part of an embedded approach to conflict resolution in Northern Ireland, instead of fading away once the most urgent part of the transition is over, where such 'unruly' initiatives often become absorbed by the state or finish serving their purpose altogether. This is also evident by the continued success of restorative justice as a guiding principle and praxis for the youth justice system in the jurisdiction. The community-based projects are also unique when compared with more mainstream practices, in that they have dealt with a level of violence and conflict usually shied away from by the latter, such as punishment violence and large-scale rioting. Hence, restorative justice in Northern Ireland is a clear example of the breadth and depth of praxis that is possible when the needs of individuals and communities are placed at the centre of peace-building, rather than forcing participants to fit within rigid structures of 'justice' delivery.

References

Ahmed E, Harris, N, Braithwaite, J and Braithwaite, V (2001) *Shame Management Through Reintegration* (Cambridge, Cambridge University Press).

Barabás, T, Fellegi, B and Windt, Sz (eds), (2012) *Responsibility-taking, Relationship-building and Restoration in Prisons* (Budapest, OKRI).

Bauman, Z (1989) *Modernity and the Holocaust* (Ithaca, NY, Cornell University Press).

Bell, C (1996) 'Alternative Justice in Ireland' in N Dawson, D Greer and P Ingram (eds), *One Hundred and Fifty Years of Irish Law* (Legal Publications (NI), Sweet & Maxwell).

Braithwaite, J (1989) *Crime, Shame and Reintegration* (Cambridge, Cambridge University Press).

Braithwaite, J and Mugford, S (1994) 'Conditions of Successful Reintegration Ceremonies' 34 *British Journal of Criminology* 139.
Campbell, C, Devlin, R, O'Mahony, D, Doak, J, Jackson, J, Corrigan, T and McEvoy, K (2005) *Evaluation of the Northern Ireland Youth Conference Service* (Belfast, Northern Ireland Office, Statistics and Research Branch).
Centre for Innovative Justice (CIJ) (2014) *Innovative justice responses to sexual offending: Pathways to better outcomes for victims, offenders and the community* (Melbourne, CIJ).
Christie, N (1977) 'Conflict as Property' 17 *British Journal of Criminology* 15.
Clamp, K (2013) *Restorative Justice in Transition* (London, Routledge).
Clamp, K and Doak, J (2012) 'More than Words: Restorative Justice Concepts in Transitional Justice Settings' 12 *International Criminal Law Review* 339.
Cohen, D and Nesbitt, R (1994) 'Self-protection and the Culture of Honor: Explaining Southern Violence' *20 Personality and Social Psychology Bulletin* 551.
Cottino, A (1999) 'Sicilian Cultures of Violence: The Interconnections between Organized Crime and Local Society' 32 *Crime, Law and Social Change* 103.
Daly, K, Bouhours, B and Broadhurst, K (2013) 'Youth Sex Offending, Recidivism and Restorative Justice: Comparing Court and Conference Cases' 46 *Australian & New Zealand Journal of Criminology* 241.
Drumbl, MA (2002) 'Restorative Justice and Collective Responsibility: Lessons for and from the Rwandan Genocide' 5 *Contemporary Justice Review* 5.
Ellison, G and Smyth, J (2000) *The Crowned Harp: Policing Northern Ireland* (London, Pluto Press).
Eriksson, A (2008) 'Challenging Cultures of Violence through Community Restorative Justice' in H Ventura Miller (ed), *Sociology of Crime, Law and Deviance: Restorative Justice: From Theory to Practice* (Bingley, Emerald/JAI Press).
—— (2009a) *Justice in Transition: Community Restorative Justice in Northern Ireland* (London, Routledge).
—— (2009b) 'A Bottom-up Approach to Transformative Justice in Northern Ireland' 3 *International Journal for Transitional Justice* 1.
Fein, H (1979) *Accounting for Genocide: National Responses and Jewish Victimization during the Holocaust* (Chicago, University of Chicago Press).
Froestad, J and Shearing, C (2007) 'Conflict Resolution in South Africa: A Case Study' in G Johnstone and D van Ness (eds), *Handbook of Restorative Justice* (Collumpton, Willan Publishing).
Gastil, RD (1971) 'Homicide and a Regional Culture of Violence' 36 *American Sociological Review* 412.
Groff, L and Smoker, P (1996) 'Creating Global/Local Cultures of Peace' in UNESCO (ed), *From a Culture of Violence to a Culture of Peace* (Paris, UNESCO Publishing).
Hamill, H (2002) 'Victims of Paramilitary Punishments Attacks in Belfast' in C Hoyle, R Young and RP Young (eds), *New Visions of Crime Victims* (Oxford, Hart Publishing).
Hayes, BC and McAllister, I (2001) 'Sowing Dragon's Teeth: Public Support for Political Violence and Paramilitarism in Northern Ireland' 49 *Political Studies* 901.
Hayner, PB (2001) *Unspeakable Truths: Facing the Challenge of Truth Commissions* (London, Routledge).
Hope, T and Foster, J (1992) 'Conflicting Forces Changing the Dynamics of Crime and Community on "Problem" Estates' 32 *British Journal of Criminology* 488.
Hopkins, B (2002) 'Restorative Justice in Schools' 17 *Support for Learning* 144.

Jamieson, R (1999) 'Genocide and the Social Production of Immorality' 3 *Theoretical Criminology* 131.

Jarman, N (2004) 'From War to Peace? Changing Patterns of Violence in Northern Ireland, 1990–2003' 16 *Terrorism and Political Violence* 420.

Knox, C (2013) 'From the Margins to the Mainstream: Community Restorative Justice in Northern Ireland' 8 *Journal of Peacebuilding and Development* 57.

Knox, C and Monaghan, R (2002) *Informal Justice in Divided Societies: Northern Ireland and South Africa* (Basingstoke, Palgrave Macmillian).

Lambourne, W (2009) 'Transitional Justice and Peacebuilding after Mass Violence' 3 *International Journal of Transitional Justice* 28.

Laplante, LJ (2008) 'Transitional Justice and Peace Building: Diagnosing and Addressing the Socioeconomic Roots of Violence through a Human Rights Framework' 2 *International Journal of Transitional Justice* 331.

Leebaw, B (2001) 'Restorative justice for Political Transitions: Lessons from the South African Truth and Reconciliation Commission' 4 *Contemporary Justice Review* 267.

Llewellyn, J (2007) 'Truth Commissions and Restorative Justice' in G Johnstone and D van Ness (eds), *Handbook of Restorative Justice* (Collumpton, Willan Publishing).

MacGinty, R and Darby, J (2002) *Guns and Government: The Management of the Northern Ireland Peace Process* (Basingstoke, Palgrave Macmillan).

Maruna, S, Wright, S, Brown, J, van Marle, F, Devlin, R and Liddle, M (2007) *Youth Conferencing as Shame Management: Results of a Long-term Follow-up Study* (Belfast, Youth Justice Agency/Youth Conferencing Service, ARCS).

Maxwell, G and Morris, A (2004) 'What is the Place of Shame in Restorative Justice?' in H Zehr and B Towes (eds), *Critical Issues in Restorative Justice* (Collumpton, Willan Publishing).

McAlinden, A (2011a) 'Transforming Justice': Challenges for Restorative Justice in an Era of Punishment-based Corrections' 14 *Contemporary Justice Review* 383.

—— (2011b) 'The Reintegration of Sexual Offenders: From a "Risks" to a "Strengths-based" Model of Offender Resettlement' in S Farrall, R Sparks, S Maruna and M Hough (eds), *Escape Routes: Contemporary Perspectives on Life After Punishment* (London, Routledge).

McAuley, JW (2004) 'Peace and Progress? Political and Social Change among Young Loyalists in Northern Ireland' 60 *Journal of Social Issues* 541.

McCold, P (2006) 'The Recent History of Restorative Justice: Mediation, Circles, and Conferencing' in D Sullivan and L Tifft (eds), *The Handbook of Restorative Justice: Global Perspectives* (London, Routledge).

McEvoy, K (2006) *Making Peace with the Past: Options for Truth Recovery Regarding the Conflict in and about Northern Ireland* (Belfast, Healing Through Remembering).

McEvoy, K and Eriksson, A (2006) 'Restorative Justice in Transition: Ownership, Leadership and "Bottom-up" Human Rights' in D Sullivan and L Tifft (eds), *The Handbook of Restorative Justice: Global Perspectives* (London, Routledge).

—— (2008) 'Who Owns Justice? Community, State and the Northern Ireland Transition' in J Shapland (ed), *Justice, Community and Civil Society: A Contested Terrain* (Collumpton, Willan Publishing).

McEvoy, K and Gormally, B (2009) *Dealing with the Past in Northern Ireland 'From Below'* (Belfast, Community Foundation for Northern Ireland).

McEvoy, K and Mika, H (2001) 'Punishment, Politics and Praxis: Restorative Justice and Non-violent Alternatives to Paramilitary Punishment' 11 *Policing and Society* 359.

—— (2002) 'Restorative Justice and the Critique of Informalism in Northern Ireland' 43 *British Journal of Criminology* 534.
McEvoy, K and Newburn, T (eds) (2003) *Criminology, Conflict Resolution and Restorative Justice* (London, Palgrave).
McGarry, J and O'Leary, B (1995) *Explaining Northern Ireland: Broken Images* (Oxford, Blackwell).
Minow, M (1998) *Between Vengeance and Forgiveness: Facing History after Genocide and Mass Violence* (Boston, MA, Beacon Press).
Monaghan, R (2002) 'The Return of "Captain Moonlight": Informal Justice in Northern Ireland' 25 *Studies in Conflict & Terrorism* 41.
Nikolic-Ristanovic, V (2006) 'Truth and Reconciliation in Serbia' in D Sullivan and L Tifft (eds), *The Handbook of Restorative Justice: Global Perspectives* (London, Routledge).
Nowrojee, B (2005) *'Your Justice is Too Slow': Will the ICTR Fail Rwanda's Rape Victims?* (Geneva, United Nations Research Institute for Social Development).
O'Mahony, D (2012) 'Criminal Justice Reform in a Transitional Context: Restorative Youth Conferencing in Northern Ireland' 12 *International Criminal Law Review* 549.
Roche, D (2002) 'Restorative Justice and the Regulatory State in South African Townships' 42 *British Journal of Criminology* 514.
—— (2003) *Accountability in Restorative Justice* (Oxford, Oxford University Press).
Ruane, J and Todd, J (1996) *The Dynamics of Conflict in Northern Ireland: Power, Conflict and Emancipation* (Cambridge, Cambridge University Press).
Shearing, C, Cartwright, J and Jenneker, M (2006) 'A Grass Root Governance Model: South African Peace Committees' in V Luker, S Dinnen and A Patience (eds), *Law, Order and HIV/AIDS in Papua New Guinea* (Canberra, Pandanus).
Sherman, L and Strang, H (2007) *Restorative Justice: The Evidence* (London, The Smith Institute).
Shirlow, P and Murtagh, B (2006) *Belfast: Segregation, Violence and the City* (London, Pluto Press).
Skelton, A (2002) 'Restorative Justice as a Framework for Juvenile Justice Reform: A South African Perspective' 42 *British Journal of Criminology* 496.
Sluka, J (1989) *Hearts and Minds, Water and Fish: Support for the IRA and the INLA in a Northern Irish Ghetto* (Greenwich, CT, Jai Press).
Stanley, E (2009) *Torture, Truth and Justice: The Case of Timor Leste* (Oxford, Routledge).
Staub, E (1989) *The Roots of Evil: The Origins of Genocide and Other Group Violence* (New York, Cambridge University Press).
—— (1996) 'The Cultural-societal Roots of Violence: The Examples of Genocidal Violence and of Contemporary Youth Violence in the United States' 5 *American Psychologist* 117.
—— (1999) 'The Origins and Prevention of Genocide, Mass Killing and other Collective Violence' 5 *Peace and Conflict: Journal of Peace Psychology* 303.
—— (2003) 'Notes on Cultures of Violence, Cultures of Caring and Peace, and the Fulfillment of Basic Human Needs' 24 *Political Psychology* 1.
Steenkamp, C (2005) 'The Legacy of War: Conceptualising a "Culture of Violence" to Explain Violence After Peace Accords' 94 *The Round Table* 253.
Sullivan, D and Tifft, L (1998) 'Criminology and Peacemaking: A Peace-orientated Perspective on Crime, Punishment and Justice that Takes into Account the Needs of All' 11 *The Justice Professional* 5.
Teitel, R (2000) *Transitional Justice* (Oxford, Oxford University Press).

Waldorf, L (2006) 'Rwanda's Failing Experiment in Restorative Justice' in D Sullivan and L Tifft (eds), *The Handbook of Restorative Justice: Global Perspectives* (London, Routledge).
Vanfraechem, I and Zinsstag, E (eds) (2012) *Restorative Conferencing in Europe* (Oxford, Oxford University Press).
Zinsstag, E and Chapman, T (2012) 'Conferencing in Northern Ireland: Implementing Restorative Justice at the Core of the Criminal Justice System' in E Zinsstag and I Vanfraechem (eds), *Conferencing and Restorative Justice: International Practices and Perspectives* (Oxford, Oxford University Press).

Part IV

Overview and Prospects

17

'Doing' Criminal Justice in Northern Ireland: 'Policy Transfer', Transitional Justice and Governing Through the Past

ANNE-MARIE McALINDEN AND CLARE DWYER

Introduction

One of the core tasks of this volume was to extend the 'criminological gaze' (see, for example, Muncie et al 2009, cited in Croall et al 2010: 5) to Northern Ireland as a jurisdiction which has either traditionally been neglected specifically in many United Kingdom based texts on criminal justice, or been subsumed within the broader hegemony of England and Wales. Indeed, similar to that which has occurred with Scotland, in synonymising England and Wales with the United Kingdom as a whole, Northern Ireland has been 'othered' within criminological and criminal justice discourses and given scant mention in the criminological endeavour. The most controversial aspects of criminal justice provision in Northern Ireland (including internment without trial; non-jury trials or 'Diplock courts'; 'shoot-to-kill' policies; 'special category status' of paramilitary prisoners and their early release; state collusion; extrajudicial killings; and inquiries into controversial deaths), have been subject to international attention and have become woven into a dominant populist narrative on crime and justice in Northern Ireland that may be regarded by outsiders as being representative of the criminal justice system as a whole. This book has sought to counter such tendencies by drawing out and differentiating that which is unique to the fabric of the criminal justice system in Northern Ireland as a society transitioning from political and sectarian conflict, as well as the aspects which are shared with the rest of the United Kingdom. The book has therefore sought to provide a more nuanced account of criminal justice provision within and across the United Kingdom. As Croall and colleagues have argued in relation to the Scottish context, 'a wider consciousness of what is both shared and diverse' helps 'contribute to a richer, more complex and more challenging British criminology' (2010: 6).

In this vein, the book has attempted to go beyond the surface and populist views of criminal justice in Northern Ireland to explore key trends in criminal justice provision over the last few decades, examining the core ideologies and working practices which have shaped it. In relation to the former, key conceptual frameworks, primarily related to transitional justice and human rights discourses, have emerged as central to the process of moving on from the legacy of an abusive past. Human rights questions in particular remain central to policing, the trial process, and the use and impact of imprisonment. These discourses have in turn helped to shape the new structures of criminal justice in Northern Ireland as well as institutional praxis in terms of what is actually happening on the ground. In addition, the book has also offered a critical understanding of the key aspects of the criminal justice process in Northern Ireland and the related working practices of legal actors (for example, policing, judicial decision-making, correctional services, and mechanisms for correcting error), particularly since political settlement and the subsequent devolution of policing and justice. In examining a number of specific 'crime problems' as contemporary issues in criminal justice (for example, youth offenders, female offenders, sexual and violent offenders, and restorative justice), it also set out to consider the extent to which criminal justice in Northern Ireland was becoming more or less divergent from broader global policy developments in the rest of the United Kingdom and elsewhere.

At this juncture, it may be useful to reflect on any possible shortcomings or omissions of the book. As noted at the outset, this project was not envisaged as a core criminal justice text on aspects of the criminal justice system which could be used as a frame of reference against which to contrast other parts of the United Kingdom. In this respect, it is acknowledged that some issues or topics may have been omitted (for example, victims, or social or racial equality), or others given more explicit or detailed treatment. We hope, however, that for the reader the book will have met what we envisaged to be among its core purposes as set out above—to broaden and deepen our understanding of crime and criminal justice in Northern Ireland and to provide a detailed critical examination of the cutting edge of critical thinking in criminal justice practice in transitional justice contexts. In particular, it sought to go well beyond conventional criminal justice texts in locating accounts of criminal justice within broader social and cultural, and primarily, political and historical contexts. With these caveats in mind, this final chapter will address a number of summative and residual themes which underlie the broad contribution of this book. These relate to the significance of the 'policy transfer' thesis within neo-liberal societies, the impact of the past in the contemporary governance of criminal justice, and the broader relevance of this volume for criminal justice in transitional contexts.

Policy Transfer and the Influence of the Neo-Liberal Thesis

Criminal justice policy in Northern Ireland has been strongly influenced by and tended to mirror developments in England and Wales (Birrell and Murie 1980: 65;

Pinkerton 1994: 28; Dickson 2001: 5). As noted at the outset of the book, the legal systems of the various constituencies within the United Kingdom and the Republic of Ireland, although now quite separate, have shared legal histories and traditions which have impacted on social and penal policymaking. In this respect, social and penal policies in Northern Ireland have not emerged in isolation from developments in the United Kingdom as a whole and indeed internationally. Even post-devolution, criminal justice policymaking in Northern Ireland has tended to track developments in England and Wales in a number of key areas such as youth offending and sexual and violent offending (see chapters by Haydon and McAlister; and McAlinden). As discussed further below, however, there are also a number of important distinctions including those related to segregation, sectarianism, fear and mistrust of the authorities as a direct legacy of the conflict which continue to impact on public discourses on criminal justice.

The 'policy transfer' thesis (Jones and Newburn 2006, 2013) has generally been viewed as the spread of penal policies derived from the United States' 'culture of control' (Garland 2001) to other jurisdictions within Europe, including the United Kingdom (see, for example, McAlinden 2012). Policy convergence between the United States and the United Kingdom is thought to derive, inter alia, from the shared political ideologies and rhetorical politics of neo-liberal societies. In 'neo-liberal' societies, 'penal welfarism' (Garland 1985, 1996) has been replaced by 'law and order' or incapacitation as the dominant penal ideology which is shaped by the social exclusion and stigmatisation of those on the margins of society and high rates of imprisonment (Wacquant 2001). The forces of neo-liberalism have also spread to Northern Ireland and Scotland (Horgan 2006) as related jurisdictions which share 'broadly similar standards of living and constitutional arrangements' (Grimshaw 2004: 3). As Garland (1999) argues, small jurisdictions it seems may be especially susceptible to global influences. Indeed, devolution also opens up the possibility of 'policy transfer' within the different component jurisdictions of the United Kingdom as well as globally. As Croall et al (2010: 13) put it, '[t]ransnationalism, ... works within the UK as it does on a global level'.

The book in this respect has provided examples of policy convergence and exposure to populist penal policymaking (Bottoms 1995; Johnstone 2000) across a number of key sites of criminal justice where there is growing evidence of the institutionalisation of the risk-based paradigm of criminal justice and managerialist concerns (Ericson and Haggerty 1997; Brownlee 1998; O'Malley 2004). Carr's chapter, for example, on the historical and contemporary context of probation, evidences a particular 'neutrality' stance adopted by the Probation Service in the course of the 'Troubles' and the changing context of probation practice in the post-conflict era which is marked by a shift towards a more risk-oriented public protection ethos and evidence-based practice. McAlinden's chapter on public and political responses to sexual and violent crimes provides a further example of 'policy transfer'. Northern Ireland has to a large extent emulated penal policies on sexual and violent crime, such as sex offender notification and related orders, which have been put in place in England and Wales, in themselves derived from laws governing 'sexual predators' in the United States. Similarly, Haydon and McAlister note how Northern Ireland and Scotland have adopted comparable policies on youth crime to England and Wales which are based on concerns with 'problem' or 'troublesome' youth and the need for increased intervention and regulation.

There is an extensive contemporary literature on comparative criminal justice and criminology (for example, Downes 1988; Ruggiero et al 1993; van Swaaningen 1998; Reichel 2008). Indeed, as McEvoy and Ellison (2003: 45) have argued on the generalisability of the Northern Ireland context, criminology is, inter alia, 'an international and comparative project'. Comparative criminology has as much to do with 'understanding one's own country better as it has to understanding anyone else's' (Nelken 1994: 221). In drawing out examples of convergence and divergence in criminal justice policies between Northern Ireland and the other constituencies within the United Kingdom and internationally the book has also made a contribution to comparative criminology and criminal justice. It has thus provided at least a partial antidote to 'ethnocentrism' (Beirne and Nelken 1997: xiii) and in particular to the hegemony of England and Wales based discourses within British criminology.

The effects of 'policy transfer', however, are not mechanistic and 'one dimensional' but are rather subject to important differences in terms of how the substance as well as the scope of global policies are mediated and implemented on the ground (Muncie 2005). McNeill et al (2009) refer to 'the governmentality gap' to denote the distinction between global policy discourses and the localised practices and culture that modify these. Criminologists have long contended that punishment and crime control are 'an index of culture' (Nelken 2007: 153) or socially and culturally conditioned (for example, Garland 1990; Nelken 2000; Sparks 2001). In Northern Ireland as elsewhere, criminal justice policies are in themselves shaped by a complex interplay of social, political and cultural factors. A range of specific values and practices and organisational culture characterise criminal justice in Northern Ireland that do not have a bearing elsewhere. The key question which arises is whether these features reflect surface or more systemic differences—are they due simply to differing infrastructures or operational paradigms, or more to intrinsic differences in values and approaches?

It is our contention, as this volume has highlighted, that criminal justice provision in Northern Ireland is a complex hybridisation of newer policy narratives transferred or 'borrowed' from elsewhere in tandem with older differing infrastructures and intrinsic values stemming from the legacy of the conflict. Dwyer in chapter five of this volume notes how the complex geopolitics of Northern Ireland has not only presented various barriers to the policy transfer of 'traditional' risk-based criminal justice policy, but has also facilitated the development of its own unique risk paradigm over the last few decades, chiefly via a 'preventative' response to 'political' crime risks. It is this intersection of 'old' and 'new' which has contributed to the distinctiveness of the criminal justice climate in Northern Ireland. Within this broader context, as discussed further below, the nuances and dynamics of law-making in the sphere of criminal justice in Northern Ireland have been shaped by three distinct historical aspects—the role of criminal justice during the conflict in responding to political violence, during the process of transition and conflict resolution, and in the aftermath of political settlement and devolution.

Governing Justice Through the Past

While the previous section has highlighted the newer more contemporary aspects of criminal justice policy in Northern Ireland which have been transposed from elsewhere, this section explores the influence of the historical context in shaping the criminal justice landscape in Northern Ireland. Lacey (2008) has contended that differences in contemporary criminal justice policies between relatively similar societies are best understood in terms of differing historical contexts. According to this view, it is this historical milieu which best explains any divergence in the style if not the substance of local penal policies and governance structures. We are also persuaded by Osiel's (1997) argument that the criminal law and the criminal justice process have important backward and forward-looking functions beyond the intrinsic value of punishment (for example, retribution or deterrence)—backward-looking in the sense of cementing 'a particular interpretation of the country's history' (1997: 6) or collective 'imagined' identity, and forward looking in terms of 'the cultivation of collective memory' (1997: 18) towards enhanced solidarity. This tension between past and present is perhaps even more acute in a society such as that in Northern Ireland which has sought to move on from the legacy of over 30 years of violent and political conflict and establish a new political and legal order. More particularly, 'buy-in' from all sections of society to a shared future is fundamental to the process of peacemaking and the lasting stability of that peace.

The distinctiveness of criminal justice discourses in Northern Ireland, therefore, also stems in large part from tradition and the history of the past which have an important influence on contemporary criminal justice and the current legal order. As Croall et al (2010: 263, citing Farmer 1997) have argued in relation to the Scottish context, 'the practices and institutions of law have in important ways come to represent and carry the burden of … culture, identity and privilege'. Unlike in Scotland, however, what these authors refer to as 'historical criminology'—comprised of both 'the history of the past and a detailed critical "history of the present"'—(Croall et al 2010: 262) is already well developed in Northern Ireland. This book is testament to that tradition providing as it does a range of original accounts of pivotal moments in Northern Ireland's recent legal and juridical past, the central role played by key individuals and leading institutions in lobbying for change (see in particular the chapter by Dickson), together with the voices of leading protagonists such as judges and lawyers, a range of other criminal justice practitioners who administered justice during the conflict, and prisoners themselves (see the chapters by Morison; McEvoy and Schwartz; McAlinden; and Moore and Wahidin).

A further unique element to criminal justice discourses in Northern Ireland relates to its unique position on the island of Ireland as part of the United Kingdom but geographically proximate and historically linked to the neighbouring Republic of Ireland. As McEvoy and Ellison (2003: 54) argue, 'any discussion of crime and the role of repressive state apparatus (the police, the law, the criminal justice system) could not be considered independently of the broader structural issues and in Northern Ireland, the constitutional question'. The shared legal relationship with England and Wales and the impact this had on policymaking in the sphere of criminal justice has been outlined in the opening chapter. In a similar vein, the relationship between Northern Ireland and the Republic of Ireland also merits further consideration as two distinct yet adjacent legal jurisdictions on the same island which are separated by a land border. The Criminal Justice Review Group (CJRG 2000: chapter 17) recommended an element of 'structured co-operation' between Northern Ireland and the Republic of Ireland and 'mutual recognition and harmonisation' of a range of criminal justice policies, including 'dangerous offender registers'. As McAlinden's chapter notes, in addition to informal cooperation between key criminal justice agencies on both sides of the border regarding high-risk sex offenders, a number of formal initiatives have been set up to facilitate the exchange of information about dangerous offenders. This also opens up the possibility for policy transfer at the operational, as well as at the managerial or policymaking level within as well as across jurisdictions. Indeed, the land border with the Republic of Ireland and the relatively small size of the respective jurisdictions has also historically provided opportunities for paramilitary activists as well as sex offenders to access and cross the border in order to avoid notice or carry out further criminal activities elsewhere.

Following on from the previous point, there are also 'extrajudicial' dimensions to 'doing' criminal justice in Northern Ireland which can be directly related to the legacy of the conflict. In essence, the presence of paramilitary factions which may operate as an alternative form of policing or as an adjunct of state justice has also proliferated through a number of justice arenas. Historically, such problems have manifested themselves in the form of 'punishment beatings' of known or suspected sex offenders by paramilitary groups (see chapter by McAlinden; see also Knox 2002). This particular legacy of the conflict is one of the reasons why Northern Ireland is unique across the United Kingdom in not formally implementing 'Sarah's Law' or public disclosure of criminal record information about known sex offenders. More broadly, however, the presence of paramilitaries has impacted in a number of ways including on the perceived legitimacy of state policing, especially so in republican areas (see chapter by Topping); via the evolution of a dual-tier system of justice and cases coming before the courts involving 'ordinary decent criminals' and terrorist offenders (see variously chapters by McEvoy and Schwartz; Dwyer; and Requa); via the introduction of an array of emergency legislation comprised of extraordinary measures as a form of 'justice plus' or 'punishment plus' for 'politically motivated' offenders as a special category of offender; and on the structuralist provision of correctional services, in particular prisons, where the politics of imprisonment in Northern Ireland have been shaped by the containment of politically affiliated prisoners (see chapter by Scraton; see also chapter by Moore and Wahidin).

Although paramilitary assaults or shootings seem to have occurred less frequently or at least less overtly over the last number of years as Topping notes, the legacy of sectarianism and fear and mistrust of the authorities, in large part stemming from the operational elements of the conflict, has had a lasting impact. As Eriksson eloquently outlines in this volume, the formulation and delivery of legitimate forms of 'justice', including alternative forms of justice such as restorative justice, must now take account of three discrete elements in order to 'build proximity' and reduce social, cultural, historical and political distance between key stakeholders. This includes efforts to reduce the distance within communities, between the community and the state, and between communities. Doing criminal justice in contemporary Northern Ireland, therefore, is as much about local communities as it is the state. 'Networked' or 'nodal' governance' (Shearing and Wood, 2003) entails a move away from old modes of governance based on hierarchal and bureaucratic control towards the local governance of crime (Crawford 1997) comprised of decentred regulation involving state and non-state actors in shared networks and alliances (Crawford 2006: 450; see also McEvoy and Eriksson 2008).

Finally, and following on from the previous point, criminal justice provision by state agencies in Northern Ireland such as the police, the courts, prisons, and probation, has historically been tempered by the presence of a strong voluntary sector. Dickson's chapter, for example, outlines the influential role played by small pressure groups such as the Committee on the Administration of Justice in commenting critically on aspects of the criminal justice system which fell short of accepted human rights standards and in building the momentum for change. Similarly, McAlinden notes how the voluntary sector in Northern Ireland has provided a professional, pragmatic and considered approach to questions relating to the management and reintegration of sex offenders in the community often playing the role of liaison between statutory agencies and the community on contentious sex offender issues. Indeed, the influence of such groups on polity has been sustained during the conflict and throughout the transitional justice process in ensuring in particular compliance with human rights standards as the building blocks of transitional and devolved criminal justice frameworks. While one of these factors on their own may not be enough to support the uniqueness hypothesis of criminal justice in Northern Ireland, it is this particular combination of factors which makes Northern Ireland distinctive in both UK and wider international criminal justice contexts. As the next section will demonstrate, however, there are also broader lessons and themes to be drawn as part of a meta-narrative for other societies transitioning from violent and political conflict.

Criminal Justice in Transitional Justice Contexts

While one of the key aims of this book was to address the need for a specifically focused critical text on criminal justice in Northern Ireland, the chapters have underlined a range of issues which have relevance and resonance beyond this jurisdiction. In this respect, there are a number of issues which have emerged as fundamental for societies transitioning from serious social and political conflict. These include police legitimacy, reform of judicial decision-making and corrections, including the prison and probation services, in a society which has predominantly been focused on anti-terrorism and paramilitary activity as opposed to ordinary crime (see chapters by Dickson; and Dwyer). Within this broader context, as noted above, in Northern Ireland as elsewhere, the complex interplay between human rights and transitional justice frameworks are pivotal to the process of moving on from the legacy of an abusive past (Cohen, 1995; Huyse 1995; Arthur 2009). 'Truth recovery', accountability, and healing in relation to previous human rights violations emerge as a vital part of dealing with the past and transitioning to a new social order (see chapters by Lawther; Ericson; and McEvoy and Schwartz). Equally, human rights are the guiding principles promoting the legality and authenticity, and ultimately measuring the transformative impact of such new regimes (see chapter by Harvey).

More broadly, however, this book and the constituent chapters have also highlighted the significance of criminal justice discourses in transitional contexts. In this vein, the chapters have collectively underlined the axiomatic role of criminal justice as a locus for the conflict and conflict resolution along three primary contours: during the conflict in responding to atrocities and 'terrorist' offences and in its response to ordinary crime, which was also fashioned around responses to the conflict; during the process of transition and conflict resolution; and in the aftermath of political settlement and devolution. In relation to the second and third of these elements, criminological discourses have been central to the process of peacemaking in Northern Ireland (McEvoy and Ellison, 2003). The criminal justice system, and key figures and institutions within it, were key to the process of transitioning from political conflict (see chapter by Dickson). As outlined in the introductory chapter and throughout the second part of this volume, in addition to broader constitutional questions, much of the Belfast (Good Friday) Agreement was focused on the criminal justice system. The Criminal Justice Review Group (CJRG 2000), commissioned as part of the Agreement, instigated a root and branch reform of the criminal justice system as one of the key cornerstones of the 'New Northern Ireland'. Reform of judicial appointments, the prison and probation services (see chapters seven to eleven) and policing in particular as constitutive of 'a new legal space' in post-agreement Northern Ireland (see chapter by Morison), remain central to the political and transitional landscape (see chapter six by Topping). Furthermore, in the aftermath of political settlement and formal devolution of policing and justice, some elements of these reforms remain outstanding in their implementation not least in relation to the Prison Service (see chapter by Scraton). Even post-transition and post-devolution, therefore, the contested terrain of criminal justice and the conceptual battle lines within this are constantly being replayed and renegotiated.

It is the first aspect, however, which is arguably the most interesting and which perhaps proves the most insightful in terms of examining the role of criminal justice in conflicted societies. In the response of the state to violent political conflict, the criminal justice system occupies a front and centre role in the formulation and performance of that response. In this respect, the picture of policy transfer which emerges in relation to Northern Ireland is perhaps rather more complex than that traditionally conceived as outlined above. In essence, Northern Ireland was not only the 'end game' of the transfer of penal policies from England and Wales, but also in itself acted as a catalyst for what could be termed 'experiments in criminal justice' which were later rolled out elsewhere. In effect, as Hillyard (1987) and others have argued, Northern Ireland operated as a litmus test for the introduction of a range of 'special powers' or emergency measures which were subsequently 'normalised' within the authoritarian British state. Counter-insurgency measures became standardised within the administration of criminal justice more generally as the veneer of criminal justice was transposed over political violence in the struggle for both risk and conflict management (see chapter five by Dwyer). Moore and Wahadin in this volume, for example, illustrate how violence and sectarian divisions helped shape penal regimes, both for politically motivated and so-called 'ordinary' female offenders, resulting in a 'gendered' response to the control and punishment of women prisoners.

At the same time, a 'dual track' system of justice evolved, one for terrorist and another for non-terrorist offences, which also facilitated abuse of state power by the police in particular in relation to terrorist cases (see generally chapter by Requa). As Topping argues in this volume in relation to policing, this helped to justify 'normal policing' in an 'exceptional environment'. McEvoy and Schwartz's insightful chapter on judicial performance during the conflict to a range of audiences further highlights judicial deference to wider security imperatives as well as examples of judicial resistance to such imperatives. The law governing inferences from silence provides a useful illustration of the conflation of these factors. Legislation allowing the drawing of inferences from a suspect's silence was first introduced in Northern Ireland[1] to combat 'the wall of silence' in terrorist cases and 'ambush defences' and later extended to England and Wales,[2] although the framework applies to both scheduled and non-scheduled offences.[3] This legislation has been subject to a number of challenges and judicial pronouncements on human rights (particularly relating to the right to a fair trial under article 6) and

[1] See the Criminal Evidence (NI) Order 1988, arts 3–6.

[2] See the Criminal Justice and Public Order Act 1994, ss 34–37.

[3] The broad distinction between scheduled and non-scheduled offences relates to those terrorist offences usually subject to 'emergency powers' and those offences tried under the ordinary criminal law.

due process grounds (Jackson 2009; Quirk 2013). However, despite the fact that we are now more than 25 years on from the first enactment of the silence provisions, and in a period of 'peace time' post-conflict, the legislation remains in force and has not been repealed.

Concluding Comments: Future Directions of Criminal Justice in Northern Ireland

Taken as a whole, this volume has demonstrated that the devolution of policing and justice has made little if any significant difference to the shape and direction of criminal justice policy and practice in Northern Ireland. It may be that at the time of writing, some four to five years post-full devolution, it is simply too early to make any discerning judgements. For the most part, however, criminal justice provision in Northern Ireland continues to be shaped contemporaneously by policy trends elsewhere as well as the legacy of the conflict. It thus may face many of the same justice and system challenges as other jurisdictions elsewhere (for example, the reconciliation of justice and welfare imperatives or the tension between the 'risk' paradigm and wider resource implications), but these are often mediated within the distinct social, political and cultural context of 'doing' criminal justice in Northern Ireland. As noted in the introductory chapter, concerns about ordinary crime are generally low. Comparatively, stories about ordinary crime do not feature as much in news headlines and rates of imprisonment are also low in comparison to England and Wales and other European neighbours. Indeed, traditionally, concerns about ordinary crime have been subjugated by accounts of 'conflict-related' crime. By way of example, even as late as November 2014, stories still feature in the print and broadcast media about 'the disappeared'[4] and other deaths directly related to the legacy of the conflict. More generally, in academic accounts, concerns about victims have been deemed synonymous with victims of the conflict (see, for example, Brewer and Hayes 2011, 2014). While such high-profile conflict-related cases will remain an indelible part of 'truth' recovery and dealing with the past, especially for those directly affected by them, with the passage of time, post-devolution it is likely that we will see this balance shift at least slightly within public discourses. Moreover, there may also be new avenues of research and scholarship emerging on victims of crime per se as opposed to the narrow category of those victimised as a result of the conflict.

[4] See, eg, *BBC News*, 'The Disappeared: Meath Remains were those of Brendan Megraw', 2 November 2014. 'The disappeared' is the term generally used to refer to 'missing' individuals thought to have been abducted and murdered mainly by the republican movement and secretly buried in unmarked graves some of whose bodies have yet to be recovered. One of the most infamous and high profile of these was Jean McConville, a 37-year-old widow and mother of 10 who 'disappeared' in 1972, whose body was found buried on a beach in County Louth in 2003. A number of arrests were made in 2014 including that following the four-day detention of Sinn Féin president, Gerry Adams.

In this vein, at the time of writing, there are a number of key pieces of legislation going through the Assembly which are unrelated to the legacy of the conflict. For example, the Human Trafficking and Exploitation (Criminal Justice and Support for Victims) Act (Northern Ireland) 2015, introduced as a Private Member's Bill by Lord Morrow, received Royal Assent in January 2015. This Act makes provision for offences related to human trafficking and exploitation, measures to prevent and combat human trafficking and for the support of victims. Concerns about human trafficking are emerging as an issue of global significance within international law (Gallagher 2010; Shelley 2010). The fact that Northern Ireland is legislating against such measures is indicative of not only the lateral effects of 'policy transfer', but of the concern with other narratives of victimhood unrelated to the legacy of the conflict.

In a similar vein, the ongoing Historic Institutional Abuse Inquiry, which is being led by retired High Court judge Sir Anthony Hart, is due to report in 2017 at the earliest. The terms of reference of the inquiry, which includes but is not limited to religious institutions are, inter alia, to examine if there were systemic failings by institutions or the state in their duties towards children in their care between 1922 and 1995; and to provide a report to the Executive, making recommendations as to 'apology', the findings and nature of institutional or state failings in their duties of care towards children, an appropriate memorial or tribute to victims, and the requirement or desirability for redress.[5] Thus, beneath the macro-level politics relating to the history of sectarian and violent political conflict, there are also emerging micro-level polities surrounding particular versions of victimhood related to historic institutional child abuse. In this respect, going forward, inquiry 'narratives' are also likely to feature strongly in how we remember and come to terms with the past in Northern Ireland (McAlinden and Naylor 2014). One recent example of this, as also highlighted in the opening chapter, is the allegations of sexual abuse by Maíria Cahill at the hands of former IRA members and in particular 'the cover-up' of this by the relevant paramilitary 'authorities'.[6] Calls for an all-Ireland inquiry into paramilitary responses to sexual abuse demonstrate that even seemingly 'ordinary crime' such as sexual abuse is caught up in fierce political contests about the past conflict.[7]

Writing in 2003, McEvoy and Ellison predicted that 'human rights considerations will become an epistemological given, a key feature of the criminological landscape' (McEvoy and Ellison 2003: 65). Post-devolution, however, further pragmatic challenges remain relating to the mainstreaming of human rights concerns and the resources and tools which are necessary to do this. In particular, there is an axiomatic tension between the aspiration of building 'a transformational

[5] As set out by the First Minister and deputy First Minister in a written statement to the Assembly on 18 October 2012. See also the Inquiry into Historical Institutional Abuse Act (Northern Ireland) 2013.

[6] *Irish News*, 'Maíria Cahill Case Forms Backdrop to Debate about Abuse in North', 19 November 2014.

[7] *New York Times*, 'Sinn Féin Leader is Accused of Covering Up Rape', 20 October 2014.

human rights culture for Northern Ireland' (see chapter by Harvey) and the proposed scaling back of the human rights legislation. The embedding of the human rights legislation into the legal and criminal justice process within the United Kingdom as a whole has facilitated legal and policy challenge in Northern Ireland in relation, for example, to prison conditions and practices, and has underpinned the creation of an accountable and human rights compliant police service (see chapters by Scraton; Moore and Wahidin; and Topping respectively). To repeal the Human Rights Act 1998, as has been proposed by some Westminster politicians, and replace it with a 'Bill of Rights' would have profound implications for all devolved administrations, including Scotland (Croall et al 2010: 274), and not least Northern Ireland where the legacy of the conflicts continues to impact. At the same time, the proposed ongoing cuts to the budget which Northern Ireland gets from Westminister will inevitably impact on the delivery of a broad range of public services and not just on criminal justice provision. In relation to the criminal justice sphere, this will likely undermine in particular the delivery of local policing and further ongoing reforms to the Prison Service. More broadly, this tension underlines that ultimately the capacity for seismic change to the criminal justice system in societies transitioning from conflict is also subject to more systemic structuralist concerns and, moreover, that 'justice' rights cannot be viewed in isolation from a broader range of socio-economic rights.

References

Arthur, P (2009) 'How "Transitions" Reshaped Human Rights: A Conceptual History of Transitional Justice' 31 *Human Rights Quarterly* 321.

Beirne, P and Nelken, D (1997) *Issues in Comparative Criminology* (Aldershot, Ashgate).

Birrell, D and Murie, A (1980) *Policy and Government in Northern Ireland: Lessons of Devolution* (Dublin, Gill and Macmillan).

Bottoms, AE (1995) 'The Philosophy and Politics of Punishment and Sentencing' in C Clarkson and R Morgan (eds), *The Politics of Sentencing Reform* (Oxford, Oxford University Press).

Brewer, J and Hayes, B (2011) 'Victims as Moral Beacons: Victims and Perpetrators in Northern Ireland' 6 *Contemporary Social Science* 73.

—— (2014) 'Victimhood and Attitudes towards Dealing with the Legacy of a Violent Past: Northern Ireland as a Case Study' *British Journal of Politics & International Relations*, article first published online: 20 May 2014, DOI: 10.1111/1467-856X.12050.

Brownlee, I (1998) 'New Labour—New Penology? Punitive Rhetoric and the Limits of Managerialism in Criminal Justice Policy' 25 *Journal of Law and Society* 313.

Cohen, S (1995) 'State Crimes of Previous Regimes: Knowledge, Accountability and the Policing of the Past' 20 *Law & Social Inquiry* 7.

Crawford, A (1997) *The Local Governance of Crime: Appeals to Community and Partnerships* (Oxford, Clarendon Press).

—— (2006) 'Networked Governance and the Post-Regulatory State? Steering, Rowing and Anchoring the Provision of Policing and Security' 10 *Theoretical Criminology* 449.

Criminal Justice Review Group (CJRG) (2000) *Review of the Criminal Justice System in Northern Ireland:* The Report of the Criminal Justice Review (Belfast, HMSO).
Croall, H, Mooney, G and Munro, M (2010) *Criminal Justice in Scotland* (Oxford, Willan Publishing).
Dickson, B (2001) *The Legal System of Northern Ireland*, 4th edn (Belfast, SLS Publications).
Downes, D (1988) *Contrasts in Tolerance: Post-War Penal Policy in the Netherlands and England and Wales* (Oxford, Oxford University Press).
Ericson, RV and Haggerty, KD (1997) *Policing the Risk Society* (Oxford, Clarendon Press).
Farmer, L (1997) *Criminal Law, Tradition and Legal Order* (Cambridge, Cambridge University Press).
Gallagher, AT (2010), *The International Law of Human Trafficking* (Cambridge, Cambridge University Press).
Garland, D (1985) *Punishment and Welfare: A History of Penal Strategies* (Aldershot, Gower).
—— (1990) *Punishment and Modern Society* (Oxford, Clarendon Press).
—— (1996) 'The Limits of the Sovereign State: Strategies of Crime Control in Contemporary Society' 36 *British Journal of Criminology* 445.
—— (1999) 'Preface' in P Duff and N Hutton (eds), *Criminal Justice in Scotland* (Aldershot, Ashgate).
—— (2001) *The Culture of Control: Crime and Social Order in Contemporary Society* (Oxford, Oxford University Press).
Grimshaw, R (2004) 'Whose Justice? Principal Drivers of Criminal Justice Policy, Their Implications for Stakeholders, and Some Foundations for Critical Policy Departures', vol 7 (British Society of Criminology Conference, London, July 2004).
Hillyard, P (1987) 'The Normalization of Special Powers: From Northern Ireland to Britain' in P Scraton (ed) *Law, Order and the Authoritarian State: Readings in Critical Criminology* (Milton Keynes, Open University Press).
Horgan, G (2006) 'Devolution, Direct Rule and Neo-liberal Reconstruction in Northern Ireland' 26 *Critical Social Policy* 656.
Huyse, L (1995) 'Justice after Transition: On the Choices Successor Elites Make in Dealing with the Past' 20 *Law & Social Inquiry* 51.
Jackson, J (2009) 'Reconceptualising the Right of Silence as an Effective Fair Trial Standard' 58 *International and Comparative Law Quarterly* 835.
Johnstone, G (2000) 'Penal Policy Making: Elitist, Populist or Participatory?' 2 *Punishment & Society* 161.
Jones, T and Newburn, T (2006) 'Three Strikes and You're Out: Exploring Symbol and Substance in American and British Crime Control Politics' 46 *British Journal of Criminology* 781.
—— (2013) 'Policy Convergence, Politics and Comparative Penal Reform: Sex Offender Notification Schemes in the USA and UK' 15 *Punishment & Society* 439.
Knox, C (2002) '"See No Evil, Hear No Evil": Insidious Paramilitary Violence in Northern Ireland' 42 *British Journal of Criminology* 164.
Lacey, N (2008) *The Prisoner's Dilemma: Political Economy and Punishment in Contemporary Democracies* The Hamlyn Lectures 2007 (Cambridge, Cambridge University Press).
McAlinden, A (2012) 'The Governance of Sexual Offending Across Europe: Penal Policies, Political Economies and the Institutionalization of Risk' 14 *Punishment & Society* 166.
McAlinden, A and Naylor, B (2014), 'Official Response Mechanisms: A Critique of the Public Inquiry Model in Ireland, the UK and Australia' (workshop on Sexual Abuse in the Church and Other Institutional Settings, Clerical Sexual Abuse, International Institute for the Sociology of Law, Oñati, Spain, April 10–11 2014).

McEvoy, K and Ellison, G (2003) 'Criminological Discourses in Northern Ireland: Conflict and Conflict Resolution' in K McEvoy and T Newburn (eds), *Criminology, Conflict Resolution and Restorative Justice* (London, Palgrave).

McEvoy, K and Eriksson, A (2008) 'Who Owns Justice? Community, State and the Northern Ireland Transition' in J Shapland (ed), *Justice, Community and Civil Society: A Contested Terrain* (Cullompton, Willan Publishing).

McNeill, F, Burns, N, Halliday, S, Hutton, N and Tata, C (2009) 'Risk, Responsibility and Reconfiguration: Penal Adaptation and Misadaptation' 11 *Punishment & Society* 419.

Muncie, J (2005) 'The Globalization of Crime Control—The Case of Youth and Juvenile Justice: Neo-liberalism, Policy Convergence and International Conventions' 9 *Theoretical Criminology* 35.

Muncie, J, Talbot, D and Walters, R (eds) (2009), *Crime: Local and Global* (Collumpton, Willan Publishing).

Nelken, D (1994) 'Whom Can You Trust?: The Future of Comparative Criminology' in D Nelken (ed), *The Futures of Criminology* (London, Sage).

—— (2000) *Contrasting Criminal Justice: Getting From Here to There* (Aldershot, Dartmouth).

—— (2007) 'Comparing Criminal Justice' in M Maguire, R Morgan and R Reiner (eds), *The Oxford Handbook of Criminology*, 4th edn (Oxford, Oxford University Press).

O'Malley, P (2004) *Risk, Uncertainty and Government* (London, Glasshouse Press).

Osiel, M (1997) *Mass Atrocity, Collective Memory and the Law* (New Brunswick, NJ, Transaction Publishers).

Pinkerton, J (1994) *In Care At Home: Parenting, The State and Civil Society* (Aldershot, Avebury).

Quirk, H (2013) 'Twenty Years On, the Right of Silence and Legal Advice: The Spiralling Costs of an Unfair Exchange' 64 *Northern Ireland Legal Quarterly* 465.

Reichel, P (2008) *Comparative Criminal Justice Systems: A Topical Approach*, 4th edn (Englewood Cliffs, NJ, Prentice Hall).

Ruggiero, V, Ryan, M and Sim, J (eds) (1993) *Western European Penal Systems* (London, Sage).

Shearing, C and Wood, J (2003) 'Nodal Governance, Democracy, and the New "Denizens"' 30 *Journal of Law and Society* 400.

Shelley, L (2010) *Human Trafficking: A Global Perspective* (Cambridge, Cambridge University Press).

Sparks, R (2001) 'Degrees of Estrangement: The Cultural Theory of Risk and Comparative Penology' 5 *Theoretical Criminology* 159.

van Swaaningen, R (1998) *Critical Criminology in Europe* (London, Sage).

Wacquant, L (2001) 'The Penalisation of Poverty and Neo-liberalism' 9 *European Journal on Criminal Policy and Research* 401.

INDEX

www.ingramcontent.com/pod-product-compliance
Ingram Content Group UK Ltd.
Pitfield, Milton Keynes, MK11 3LW, UK
UKHW020131290926
15471UKWH00003B/425

9 781509 918331